CW01496263

Electronic Lexicography

Electronic Lexicography

Edited by

SYLVIANE GRANGER AND MAGALI PAQUOT

OXFORD
UNIVERSITY PRESS

OXFORD
UNIVERSITY PRESS

Great Clarendon Street, Oxford, OX2 6DP,
United Kingdom

Oxford University Press is a department of the University of Oxford.
It furthers the University's objective of excellence in research, scholarship,
and education by publishing worldwide. Oxford is a registered trade mark of
Oxford University Press in the UK and in certain other countries

First Edition published in 2012

Published in the United States of America by Oxford University Press
198 Madison Avenue, New York, NY 10016, United States of America

British Library Cataloguing in Publication Data

Data available

Library of Congress Cataloging in Publication Data

Data available

ISBN 978-0-19-965486-4

Contents

Notes on Contributors

ANDREA ABEL is coordinator of the Institute for Specialized Communication and Multilingualism at EURAC (Italy); lecturer at the Free University of Bolzano and at the University of Trento; freelance second language teacher; and trainer in several seminars for students and teachers. She has published extensively in the fields of lexicography (e.g. pedagogical lexicography, e-lexicography), first and second language learning and teaching (e.g. language competences, CEFR, languages and migration, language contact), and corpus linguistics (e.g. language variants, learner corpora).

LYNNE BOWKER is Associate Professor at the School of Translation and Interpretation at the University of Ottawa in Canada. Her research interests include language for special purposes, specialized lexicography, and translation technologies. She holds a PhD in Language Engineering from the University of Manchester Institute of Science and Technology (UMIST) and is the author of *Computer-Aided Translation Technology: A Practical Introduction* (Ottawa) and co-author of *Working with Specialized Language: A Practical Guide to Using Corpora* (London).

ANNA DZIEMIANKO is an assistant professor at Adam Mickiewicz University in Poznań, Poland. Her main research interests include English pedagogical lexicography, user studies, syntax in dictionaries, lexicographic coding systems, and metalexicography. Her publications include the monograph *User-friendliness of Verb Syntax in Pedagogical Dictionaries of English* (Tübingen, 2006). Her other main area of research is e-lexicography, especially issues connected with actual benefits of the electronic medium to dictionary users.

PEDRO A. FUERTES-OLIVERA is Associate Professor at the University of Valladolid, where he teaches specialized discourse, and Velux Visiting Professor 2011–2012 (Aarhus Business and Social Sciences). He has obtained his accreditation for Full Professor in 2011, and has published around 100 academic contributions, and several printed and Internet dictionaries. He is co-author of *Pedagogical Specialized Lexicography* (Amsterdam), editor of *Specialized Dictionaries for Learners* (Berlin), and co-editor of *E-Lexicography: The Internet, Digital Initiatives and Lexicography* (London).

SYLVIANE GRANGER is Professor of English Language and Linguistics and Director of the Centre for English Corpus Linguistics at the University of Louvain (Belgium). Her current research interests focus on the integration of corpus data into a range of user-oriented tools, in particular electronic dictionaries and writing aids. Her latest publications include *Phraseology: An Interdisciplinary Perspective* (with Fanny Meunier, Amsterdam, 2008), *International Corpus of Learner English* (Granger *et al.* Louvain-la-Neuve, 2009) and *eLexicography in the 21st Century* (with Magali Paquot, Barcelona, 2010).

IRYNA GUREVYCH is a Full Professor in the Computer Science Department of the Technische Universität (TU) Darmstadt in Germany. She holds an endowed Lichtenberg-Chair 'Ubiquitous Knowledge Processing' of the Volkswagen Foundation with a focus in Natural Language Processing (NLP) and analysing unstructured text data on the Web. Her research primarily concerns approaches that utilize the collective intelligence on the Web, such as collaboratively constructed semantic resources, to enhance the performance of NLP techniques.

PATRICK HANKS is a lexicographer and corpus linguist. He is a visiting professor at the Universities of Wolverhampton and the West of England. He was managing editor of the first edition of Cobuild (1987) and chief editor of current English dictionaries at Oxford University Press (1990–2000). His research interests are corpus pattern analysis of lexical collocations; the relationship between word meaning and word use; metaphor and figurative language; and the origin and history of personal names.

ADAM KILGARRIFF is Director of Lexical Computing Ltd., which has developed the Sketch Engine, a leading tool for corpus research used for dictionary-making at Oxford University Press, Cambridge University Press, HarperCollins, Le Robert, and elsewhere. His scientific interests lie at the intersection of computational linguistics, corpus linguistics, and dictionary-making. Following a PhD on 'Polysemy' from Sussex University, he has worked at Longman Dictionaries, Oxford University Press, and the University of Brighton. He is a Visiting Research Fellow at the University of Leeds. He is active in moves to make the Web available as a linguists' corpus and was the founding chair of the Association for Computational Linguistics Special Interest Group on Web as Corpus.

ALEXANDER KOPLENIG works as a research assistant at the Institute for German Language in Mannheim, Germany. He has an academic background in Social Science and Economics. His primary research interests include lexical change, the application of empirical methods, and the statistical analysis of linguistic data.

IZTOK KOSEM is Director of Trojina, Institute for Applied Slovene Studies, which has collaborated in the creation of new corpora and language resources for Slovene, developed as part of the 'Communication in Slovene' project. Following an MA in Language and Lexicography from the University of Birmingham, he completed a PhD in Corpus Linguistics at Aston University with a thesis titled 'Devising a Model for a Corpus-driven Dictionary of Academic English'. His lexicographic experience includes working as a lexicographer on the Oxford—DZS Comprehensive English—Slovene Dictionary. His scientific interests include dictionary-making, corpus linguistics, (corpus) pedagogy, English for academic purposes, translation, and, more recently, the design of user-friendly dictionaries and corpus tools.

JETTE HEDEGAARD KRISTOFFERSEN was trained as a sign language interpreter at Copenhagen Business School and subsequently received a BA in Linguistics from the University of Copenhagen and has since been teaching linguistics and ethics as part of the sign language interpreter training at the Centre For Sign Language (now a department of University College Capital, Copenhagen: UCC) and been working in the field of lexicography. She is the leader of the Danish Sign Language Dictionary at UCC.

NATALIE KÜBLER is a Full Professor at the University Paris Diderot. She runs the LSCT research team and is head of the Language Resource Center at the University. Her research focuses on corpus linguistics, languages for specific purposes, specialized translation, phraseology, and teaching with language corpora. She is currently working on the specific aspects of semantic prosody in languages for specific purposes for translation and on the issue of integrating this collocational phenomenon in the ARTES online database.

PATRICK LEROYER, PhD, is Associate Professor of French and Danish LSP and Business Communication at the University of Aarhus, Business and Social Sciences, Department of Business Communication, and is attached to the Centre for Lexicography. His current research is on theoretical lexicography in a broad, functional perspective, and includes the development of specific theories for data-access, -selection, and -presentation in connection with communicative and cognitive functions in lexicographic information tools (specialized dictionaries, tourist dictionaries, corporate dictionaries). He has published widely in the fields of LSP and Business Communication, Terminography, and Lexicography.

ROBERT LEW is Professor of Linguistics at Adam Mickiewicz University, Poznań, Poland. His current interests centre around dictionary use, and he is involved in a number of research projects including topics such as access-facilitating devices, definition formats, dictionaries for production, space in dictionaries, and training in dictionary skills. He has also worked as a practical lexicographer for various publishers, including Harper-Collins, Pearson-Longman, and Cambridge University Press. He is Associate Editor and Reviews Editor for the *International Journal of Lexicography* (Oxford University Press).

MARIE-CLAUDE L'HOMME is Full Professor at the Department of Linguistics and Translation of the University of Montreal where she teaches terminology and translation technology. She is also the director of the Observatoire de linguistique Sens-Texte (OLST), a research group interested in various aspects of the lexicon (general and specialized). Her main research interests are lexical semantics applied to terminology and corpus-based terminology. Along with a team of researchers in linguistics, terminology, and computer science, she develops specialized databases in the fields of computer, the Internet, and the Environment.

CHRISTIAN M. MEYER is a research associate at the Ubiquitous Knowledge Processing (UKP) Lab at the Technische Universität Darmstadt in Germany. His research primarily concerns studying collaboratively constructed resources such as Wiktionary and Wikipedia, utilizing their knowledge in natural language processing applications, and aligning sense inventories at the level of word senses. He is the main author of numerous papers accepted at peer-reviewed conferences and a book chapter on Wiktionary-based ontology construction.

CAROLIN MÜLLER-SPITZER, PhD, works as a linguist at the Institute for German Language in Mannheim, Germany. She is the project leader of the dictionary portal OWID and BZVelexiko, a research project on online dictionary use. Her research interests include dictionary use, and accessing and modelling lexicographic data. Before she joined the IDS, she worked as an information architect in the field of publishing consultancy.

HILARY NESI is a Professor in English language at Coventry University, UK. Her research interests include academic corpora, and the design and use of lexical reference tools. She was principal investigator for the project to create the BASE corpus of British Academic Spoken English, for the BAWE corpus project 'An Investigation of Genres of Assessed Writing in British Higher Education', and for the project to develop the Word Tree, an adaptable and learnable corpus interface.

MAGALI PAQUOT is a postdoctoral researcher at the Centre for English Corpus Linguistics, University of Louvain (Belgium). Her current research interests include academic vocabulary, phraseology, English as a Foreign Language writing, and pedagogical lexicography. Her latest publications include *Academic Vocabulary in Learner Writing: From Extraction to Analysis* (London, 2010), *eLexicography in the 21st century* (with Sylviane Granger, Louvain-la-Neuve, 2010), and *A Taste for Corpora: In Honour of Sylviane Granger* (Amsterdam, 2011).

MOJCA PECMAN is in charge of courses on terminology and lexical resources creation in the department of Applied Languages at Paris Diderot University. Her research focuses on terminology, phraseology, discourse analysis, LSP, specialized translation, and corpus linguistics. She is currently running a research project on the creation of terminological and phraseological resources within ARTES (Aide à la Rédaction de TExtes Scientifiques), an online multilingual and multidomain database for improving translation-related research and studies.

GEERT PEETERS is a programmer at the Leuven Language Institute. He has programmed a number of online applications for language teaching and testing as well as several online dictionaries and corpus query tools (e.g. for the Dutch Parallel Corpus: www.inl.nl/en/corpora/dpc-corpus).

D. J. PRINSLOO is a professor in African languages at the University of Pretoria, South Africa. His research interests are corpus-based African-language lexicography and Human Language Technology. His research outputs include numerous peer-reviewed articles, dictionaries, books, and chapters in books and conference papers. His current and future research projects include new designs for paper dictionaries and intelligent and dynamic electronic dictionaries.

BENOÎT ROBICHAUD holds an MA in Linguistics from the Université de Montréal and a DEA in computational linguistics from the Université Paris-7. He has worked for private companies developing software such as grammar checkers and controlled language checkers, machine translation, and vertical web search engines. Since 2009, he has also given courses on computer tools for translators at the Université de Montreal and Concordia University. He started to work as a researcher at the Observatoire de linguistique Sens-Texte (OLST) in 2009. His main research interests are natural language processing and ergonomics in the human–computer interaction.

MICHAEL RUNDELL has been a lexicographer since 1980 and has managed numerous dictionary projects. He is currently Editor-in-Chief of Macmillan Dictionaries, and is co-author (with Sue Atkins) of the *Oxford Guide to Practical Lexicography* (2008). He has been at the forefront of applying computational techniques to the creation of corpus-based dictionaries. He is now deeply involved in another lexicographic revolution, as reference resources move from print to digital media.

SVEN TARP is Professor at the University of Aarhus, Centre for Lexicography, Business, and Social Sciences, Extraordinary Professor at the University of Stellenbosh, South Africa, and Visiting Professor at the University of Pretoria. He has written more than 140 academic contributions in well-known journals and academic series. With Henning Bergenholtz, he has developed most of the tenets of the *Function Theory of Lexicography*, e.g. *Lexicography in the Borderland between Knowledge and Non-knowledge: General Lexicographical Theory with Particular Focus on Learner's Lexicography* (Tübingen, 2008). He has also co-edited several printed and electronic dictionaries.

TOMA TASOVAC is the director of the Centre for Digital Humanities in Belgrade, Serbia. He has degrees in Slavic Language and Literatures from Harvard and Comparative Literature from Princeton. He works on complex lexical architectures in eLexicography, retrodigitization of historic dictionaries, and the integration of digital libraries and language resources. He is equally active in the field of new media education, regularly teaching seminars and workshops in Germany, Eastern Europe, the Caucasus, and Central Asia.

Antje Töpel, PhD, works as a linguist at the Institute for German Language in Mannheim, Germany. Her primary research interests include lexicography, especially learner's lexicography, dictionary use, and word formation.

Thomas Troelsgård received an MA in Russian language and computational linguistics from the University of Copenhagen, and has since worked in the field of lexicography. He participated in the development of the Danish Sign Language Dictionary at the Centre for Sign Language (now a department of UCC, University College Capital, Copenhagen). At present he is working partly at the Centre for Sign Language, and partly at the Society for Danish Language and Literature.

Serge Verlinde is Professor of French for Specific Purposes (Business French, Legal French) and Director of the Leuven Language Institute at the University of Leuven, Belgium. His main research interests are corpus linguistics, pedagogical lexicography, and CALL (computer-assisted language learning). He is currently working on online reading, translating, and writing assistants for Dutch and French.

Acknowledgements

We are indebted to the Fonds de la Recherche Scientifique (FNRS) for funding the project on 'Lexicography and Phraseology: Onomasiological and Semasiological Approach to English for Academic Purposes' (FRFC 2.4501.08) within the framework of which this volume has been produced. We would also like to thank all the contributors to this volume for their diligence in keeping to deadlines and patience in complying with our editorial demands. Special thanks are due to John Davey for his much appreciated trust and support.

1

Introduction: Electronic lexicography—from challenge to opportunity

SYLVIANE GRANGER

The roots of electronic lexicography, which is only now beginning to be recognized as a field in its own right, date right back to the late 1950s/early 1960s, when it went under the names of computer or computational lexicography and the dictionaries themselves were referred to as machine-readable rather than electronic. At that point, the scope of the field was restricted to "the use of computers in making dictionaries" (Logan 1991: 353). The role of computers at the time appears clearly from Urdang's (1966) report on one of the earliest dictionaries to have relied on computer technology, the first edition of the *Random House Dictionary of the English Language*: "We had been alert to the development of computer technology in the years preceding and we hoped to use computers to do the sorting, codifying, re-arranging, and checking the data at hand, and the text to be written" (p. 31). Those expectations were amply fulfilled. However, the computer technology of the time did not extend to the actual production of the dictionary, which was still published by conventional means: "Originally, we had intended preparing a tape for input to some automatic typesetting device. Unfortunately, there were no firms large enough or versatile enough or confident enough of their equipment to convince our manufacturing department that such an undertaking would be feasible" (p. 33). In those days, neither lexicographers nor dictionary users had any contact with the computer. Lexicographers "continued to write dictionary entries on paper (increasingly, using structured forms), and it was left to computer specialists to input the data" (Atkins and Rundell 2008: 112). The first dictionary to move from the machine-readable dictionary to the lexical database, thereby greatly helping lexicographers design dictionary entries, was the *Longman Dictionary of Contemporary English* (1978). Quite a few years elapsed before the first dictionaries began to appear on CD-ROM and dictionary users could truly begin to experience for themselves the benefits of having a dictionary in electronic form. Things really began to accelerate in the 1990s with the rapid development of a range of new mediums, in particular handheld devices and (a little later) online dictionaries. Today lexicography is largely synonymous with electronic lexicography and many specialists predict the disappearance of paper dictionaries in the near future. Symptomatic of this trend is the announcement by Oxford University Press in 2010 to the effect that the next edition of the *Oxford English Dictionary,* the uncontested historical dictionary of the English language, will probably no longer be published in paper format because demand for the online version is so radically outstripping demand for the printed version.

This introductory chapter has three main objectives. First, it aims to define the scope of the field of electronic lexicography as profiled in the volume and give a general overview of the profound changes brought about by the electronic medium. Second, it describes the structure of the volume and briefly summarizes the contribution made by each chapter. And third, it pulls the threads together and sketches some priorities for the future of electronic lexicography.

In this volume 'electronic lexicography' is used as an umbrella term to refer to the design, use, and application of electronic dictionaries (EDs), which are in turn defined as primarily human-oriented collections of structured electronic data that give information about the form, meaning, and use of words in one or more languages and are stored in a range of devices (PC, Internet, mobile devices) (for typologies of EDs, see De Schryver 2003, Nesi 2009, and Lew 2011a). However, computer-oriented lexicons, i.e. lexical tools that are primarily designed for use in natural language processing (NLP) applications, are not totally absent from the volume, given that the line between these two types of lexical resources is progressively narrowing and NLP resources like *WordNet* are increasingly being integrated into human-oriented tools.

The growing integration of computer technology into dictionaries has led to changes of varying degrees of importance. Overall, these have tended to be rather trivial, often consisting of a mere conversion of the content of the paper dictionary to the electronic medium. Weschler and Pitts's (2000) observation that "electronic dictionaries are still fundamentally paper dictionaries on a microchip" is unfortunately still valid for a number of electronic dictionaries today. However, this has started to change and many recent dictionary projects are testimony that the innovations afforded by the electronic medium can radically transform every facet of dictionary design and use. In what follows, I discuss six of what I believe to be the most significant innovations: (1) corpus integration; (2) more and better data; (3) efficiency of access; (4) customization; (5) hybridization; and (6) user input. My analysis takes into account both the opportunities they open up and the difficulties they might pose to lexicographers and/or users.

Corpus Integration

Corpora, i.e. electronic collections of authentic language data, are playing an increasing role in today's lexicography, both upstream, as raw material which lexicographers mine and refine to produce rich lexical entries, and downstream, as an integral part of the electronic dictionary to which users have direct access and which they can mine for themselves. The role of corpora has become so essential that "no serious compiler would undertake a large dictionary project nowadays without one (and preferably several) at hand" (De Schryver 2003: 167). The abundance and diversity of data provided by corpora coupled with powerful tools designed to handle it quickly and efficiently enable lexicographers to produce much richer descriptions than was the case when the only source of language data came from their own intuition and/or 'citation slips'. However, the rapid growth of corpora, from collections counted in millions of words to today's gigantic corpora counted in billions, is leading lexicographers to abandon raw corpus data as primary resource and turn instead to semi-processed data, i.e. data that has already been analysed and sorted into a range of lexicographically meaningful patterns (subject + verb, verb + object, etc.).

More and Better Data

Space limitations have always been one of the main frustrations of dictionary professionals. The change-over to the CD-ROM medium and, much more drastically, to the Internet has lifted these limitations and led to some highly welcome changes like the adoption of a more natural dictionary style devoid of cryptic abbreviations and, more importantly, the integration of more and better data: richer collocational coverage, an exponential increase of example sentences, integration of multimedia content (images, graphs, videos, sound files), and extended notes (usage notes, cultural notes, error notes, etc.). However, the old adage 'too much of a good thing can be a bad thing' applies here too and great care must be taken not to "swamp the user" (Atkins 1996: 527). In addition, while space restrictions may not be an issue for Internet dictionaries, they pose a different but no less acute problem for small-screen devices (smart-phones, PDAs, mobile phones), especially in the case of long entries. Highly relevant in this connection is the distinction made by Lew (in press) between 'storage space' and 'presentation space', the latter referring to the amount of content that can be presented on screen to the user at a given time.

Efficiency of Access

As rightly observed by De Schryver (2003: 173), "[n]o matter how outstanding the contents of a dictionary, if the contents cannot be accessed in a quick and straightforward way, the dictionary de facto fails to be a good dictionary". Multiplicity of access is one of the main benefits of electronic dictionaries. Users have been "liberated from the straitjacket of the printed page and alphabetical order" (Atkins 1996: 516) and now have the choice between a wide range of search options beside the traditional ones (fuzzy search, incremental search, all text search, etc.). In addition, hyperlinks enable them to navigate easily both within and beyond the dictionary. Accessibility is not yet optimal, however, and users still often struggle to get to the right headword or phrase and/or to find the specific information they are looking for. As Lew quite rightly points out (2011a: 238), "it is perfectly possible to produce an online dictionary where access is more cumbersome than in a paper book". Improved accessibility therefore remains a key challenge.

Customization

The amount of data included in electronic dictionaries and the ease with which it can be accessed are worthless if the type of information the user is getting does not correspond to his/her needs. For Atkins (1996: 516), the real challenge of the computer age is "to look at the needs of dictionary users, of every language, and every walk of life, users as diverse as people themselves, and give them the kind of information they need for whatever they are using the dictionary for". The key word here is 'customization', a process which allows the dictionary to be adapted to users' needs. Gamper and Knapp (2002) distinguish between two types of customization: dictionaries can be 'adaptable', i.e. involve manual customization by the user, or 'adaptive', i.e. adapt automatically to the user thanks to the dictionary logs (for an investigation of Internet log files, see Bergenholtz and Johnsen 2005). In both cases, electronic dictionaries are no longer static but dynamic tools and in fact, as noted by De Schryver (2003: 163), they "needn't really be there anymore, meaning that they might only exist at the time of access", i.e. they are "virtual" (Atkins 1996: 516). Users' needs have become a central issue not only for practical lexicography but also for lexicographic theory. The function theory of lexicography, which underlies several chapters in this volume, "takes the users, the user needs and the user situations as the starting point for all lexicographic theory and practice" (Bergenholtz and Tarp 2003: 172).

Hybridization

One of the most striking results of the electronic revolution in lexicography is that barriers between the different types of language resources—dictionaries, encyclopedias, term banks, lexical databases, vocabulary learning tools, writing aids, translation tools—are breaking down. Hartmann (2005a) refers to this trend as 'hybridization', which he defines as the "combination of one or more types of reference work in a single product". Among the examples he provides are compromise genres like 'dictionary-cum-grammar', 'dictionary-cum-thesaurus', 'dictionary-cum-usage guide', and 'monolingual-cum-bilingual dictionary'. According to Varantola (2002: 35), the future electronic dictionary will be "an integrated tool or a number of tools in a professional user's toolbox where it coexists with other language technology products". One particularly promising development in this connection is the convergence of electronic lexicography and computer-assisted language learning (CALL) in hybrid tools that Abel (2010) refers to as either 'dictionary-cum-CALL' or 'CALL-cum-dictionary' according to which of the two functionalities plays the central role.

User Input

The invention of wiki technology has brought about one of the most spectacular changes in lexicography, i.e. the integration of collaborative or community-based input. Whereas in the past lexicography was a field accessible only to language experts, wiki technology now allows any user to create or amend dictionary entries. As rightly observed by Dutton (2011: 240), "[i]ncreasing numbers of people who would not describe themselves as lexicographers and may not even know the word now contribute to online dictionaries". One of the main assets of collaborative lexicography, in addition to its sheer manpower advantage, is its capacity to keep up with language change and lexical innovation: "their very functionality allows them to stay up-to-date, literally cataloguing the language as it is used every day" (Penta 2011). The downside, however, is that accuracy is no longer guaranteed and therefore, in the eyes of some, user-generated dictionaries are "of little scientific value" unless mechanisms for quality control are put in place (De Schryver 2003: 160). Not everybody agrees, however. Penta (2011) insists that we are only beginning to see the potential of collaborative lexicography and that dictionary-makers need to "plug into the collective" for fear of "being written out of the future of lexicography".

This volume explores these issues of corpus integration, more and better data, efficiency of access, customization, hybridization, and user input from a theoretical, methodological, and practical viewpoint, in a range of language use situations. The nineteen chapters are grouped into three parts: 'Lexicography at a watershed', 'Innovative dictionary projects', and 'Electronic dictionaries and their users'.

Part I sets the scene. It introduces some of the major changes that computer technology has brought to the theory and practice of lexicography: new theoretical paradigms; the profound reshaping of the role played by all the practitioners involved in the dictionary-making process; the ever-growing role of corpora and corpus-handling tools; enhanced ways of describing and integrating phraseology; the added value of dictionary writing systems. Taking the standpoint of the dictionary editor and publisher, **Michael Rundell** shows that the recent transfer of many lexicographic tasks from humans to computers is both a blessing and a curse for the dictionary-making business. For example, the relative ease with which gigantic corpora can now be compiled or purchased has reduced the cost of corpus creation but has led to a massive increase in editorial costs as lexicographers need a lot more time to analyse the data. This in turn has triggered the development of new technologies that are progressively changing the lexicographers' task from that of writing entries from scratch to editing provisional entries generated by the computer. The chapter provides rare insights into the daily running of ambitious lexicographic projects like the recent *DANTE* project. The corpus angle is pursued by **Adam Kilgarriff** and **Iztok Kosem**, who focus on the corpus tools used for lexicographic purposes. An overview of commonly-used tools and their basic features is presented, followed by a more detailed description of the features that are targeted mainly at lexicographers. Particular attention is paid to the main features of the *Sketch Engine*, currently the leading corpus tool for lexicographers. Some of the most innovative features include word sketches, i.e. automatic summaries of words' grammatical and collocational behaviour, automatic selection of good examples, facilities for exporting corpus information into the dictionary writing system, and a range of customization options. The chapter concludes with a discussion of possible improvements of current tools. **Patrick Hanks**'s contribution also examines the role of corpora, in particular the radical possibilities that corpus evidence opens up for the treatment of meaning and patterns of use. Such evidence was inaccessible to pre-corpus lexicographers who could only rely on their own intuitions and a bundle of citations. As a result, they tended to focus on words in isolation and failed to capture the phraseological patterns within which words are used. Hanks describes *Corpus Pattern Analysis*, the approach he has designed to capture these patterns and map meanings onto them, based on close analysis of corpus evidence in the light of prototype theory. The chapter concludes by considering the pros and cons of wiki-based dictionaries like *Wiktionary* as a possible model for electronic lexicography of the future. Adopting the lexicographer's viewpoint, **Andrea Abel** provides a survey of the software tools currently used in most dictionary projects to support a consistent and structured lexicographic process from the conception phase to the final product. These tools, called dictionary writing systems (DWSs), contain a range of innovative features which liberate lexicographers from the most routine tasks, thereby allowing them to concentrate more on their core business. Abel describes the three main components of DWSs—an editing tool, a database, and project management tools—and provides useful keys for choosing between off-the-shelf packages and in-house software. The last part of her chapter stresses the need for DWSs to serve as multifunctional databases from which a range of different dictionaries can be produced according to users' needs. This leads nicely to **Sven Tarp**'s chapter which is grounded in the *function theory of lexicography*, a theory in which user needs are key. Tarp argues that lexicography should be considered part and parcel of a broader consultation discipline integrated into information science. Within this framework dictionaries are seen as utility tools designed to be consulted to satisfy specific needs for information. The main advantage of electronic lexicography is its potential to satisfy the needs of the individual user, by providing new forms of access and presentation of the selected data. Tarp suggests three main methods for achieving this individualization and classifies electronic dictionaries accordingly. Part I ends with a chapter by **D. J. Prinsloo** which follows on neatly from Tarp with an investigation into the specific needs of dictionary users in a specific context, the South African context. Though focused on South African languages, the chapter raises the more general issue of electronic lexicography for lesser-resourced languages. Taking recent electronic dictionaries of English as a benchmark, Prinsloo provides a survey of electronic dictionaries for both Afrikaans and Bantu languages and finds very little evidence of the sophisticated features displayed by the English dictionaries. This situation is all the more regrettable as these features would in fact be extremely useful for dealing with the highly complex morphology that characterizes the Bantu languages. Prinsloo also argues for the design of dynamic, intelligent, and adaptive dictionaries to serve users' encoding needs and highlights the role that user-generated content can play to speed up the compilation of electronic dictionaries for lesser-resourced languages.

Part II focuses on a number of innovative dictionary projects which incorporate recent developments in metalexicography and/or take advantage of the technological advances described in Part I. The first chapter by **Serge Verlinde** and **Geert Peeters** introduces readers to the new types of search functions that can help develop dictionaries that are more responsive to the needs and profile of the user and thereby pave the way for a more user-oriented lexicography. They show how they have used insights from a usability study to customize data access and search facilities in the *Interactive Language Toolbox* (*ILT*), a combined dictionary and learning tool for French and Dutch. One distinctive feature of the *ILT* website is that the user can enter full sentences, paragraphs, and texts beside the traditional searches for words and word combinations. Another particularly innovative feature is that the interface is adapted according to the following three types of user needs: decoding, translating, and encoding. The primacy of user needs is also in evidence in **Magali Paquot**'s chapter, which describes the *Louvain English for Academic Purposes Dictionary* (*LEAD*), an integrated dictionary and corpus tool which can be customized according to the user's mother tongue and discipline. Corpora play a central role in the dictionary. Corpora of academic texts written by native speakers of English were used to select the academic words and identify their typical phraseological patterning, while learner corpus data allowed for the inclusion of tailor-made error warnings.

Users can also query corpora directly within the dictionary interface, and here the *LEAD* innovates by giving access to discipline-specific corpora rather than generic corpora, thus allowing users to visualize academic words in contexts close to their specific situations. The chapter by **Natalie Kübler** and **Mojca Pecman** also tackles language for specific purposes (LSP) but this time in a bilingual perspective. They focus more particularly on innovative ways of introducing collocations in a scientific terminological and phraseological database. They describe the *ARTES dictionary*, an online bilingual LSP dictionary that can be adapted to the needs of three categories of users—translators, learners, and professionals—and put forward solutions for including higher-order phraseology (semantic preference and semantic prosody). The chapter also highlights the advantages of including student-generated content validated by experts in an LSP dictionary. In a similar vein, **Marie-Claude L'Homme**, **Benoît Robichaud**, and **Patrick Leroyer** present *DiCoInfo,* an online trilingual database which provides a complete lexico-semantic picture of computing and Internet-related terms in English, French, and Spanish. They provide a detailed description of the structure of dictionary entries and of the system used for encoding collocations based on Mel'čuk's theory of lexical functions. They also demonstrate the strength of the system for retrieval and translation and describe the mechanisms they have designed to translate Mel'čuk's formalisms into user-friendly natural language explanations. **Toma Tasovac** explores the potential and challenges of basing pedagogical, bilingual electronic dictionaries on *WordNet*, a comprehensive machine-readable lexical database of the English language which is mainly used in natural language processing. After introducing the specifics of *WordNet*'s complex lexical architecture and the few pedagogical and bilingual lexicography projects that have used it, Tasovac presents the *Transpoetika Dictionary*, a collaborative, open-access bilingualized Serbian-English learners' dictionary aligned with *WordNet*. The author also discusses strategies for expanding the scope of *WordNet*-based dictionaries through Web services and social media platforms such as Flickr and Twitter. The following chapter by **Christian M. Meyer** and **Iryna Gurevych** investigates the status and implications of collaborative dictionaries through a comprehensive description of *Wiktionary*, a freely available, collaborative online lexicon. They study the variety of encoded lexical, semantic, and cross-lingual knowledge of three different language editions of *Wiktionary*—English, German, and Russian— and compare the coverage of terms, lexemes, word senses, domains, and registers to a number of expert-built lexicons in the three languages. In their conclusion the authors suggest a number of categories of users who might benefit most from *Wiktionary*. The last chapter in Part II, by **Jette H. Kristoffersen** and **Thomas Troelsgård**, demonstrates the potential of the electronic medium for sign language dictionaries. The main problem posed by sign languages for lexicographers is that they use visual modality and have no written representation that is commonly used among native signers. The authors start by describing some of the essential differences between dictionaries of sign language and dictionaries of spoken/written language, and describe some of the features that exploit the potential of the electronic medium, in particular the inclusion of video recordings and the possibility of searching on the basis of handshape and place of articulation. They focus on the *Danish Sign Language Dictionary* and describe some of the functionalities that have been implemented to accommodate the needs of different categories of users.

Part III adopts the users' perspective and investigates the effectiveness of electronic dictionaries for different categories of users, in particular students and translators. The first chapter, by **Anna Dziemianko,** compares the respective use and usefulness of paper and electronic dictionaries as evidenced by several recent empirical studies. Various formats of electronic dictionaries are taken into consideration and the following functionalities are investigated: decoding, encoding, speed, look-up frequency, learning, and appreciation. The wide variety of studies reviewed raises issues of comparability. However, some interesting trends emerge. For example, while electronic dictionaries prove to greatly reduce search-related lexicographic costs, paper dictionaries appear to be better language learning tools. The chapter ends with possible directions for further investigations into paper vs. electronic dictionary use. **Robert Lew** examines two areas in which current electronic dictionaries can be further improved so as to serve human users better: access to lexicographic data and inclusion of novel types of data. In terms of access, the author considers how electronic dictionaries can help in situations where users are unsure about the spelling of the word they want to look up; efficient entry navigation and access to multi-word expressions are also discussed. As regards types of data, Lew discusses the potential benefit of including different categories of multimedia data—audio (recorded or synthesized), static pictorials, animations, and videos—and concludes that not all of them may be equally useful for dictionary users. **Hilary Nesi** explores some popular types of electronic dictionary that are less prestigious than those produced by established research centres or publishing houses. These dictionaries, which she calls 'alternative e-dictionaries' (AEDs), have been largely ignored in the academic literature. Nesi reviews previous surveys of teacher and student attitudes to AEDs in their various formats: online, on disc, and in pocket electronic dictionaries. She examines the wide range of information found in AEDs. Sometimes they include dictionaries from reputable publishing houses (though the AEDs tend to be vague about their exact provenance), but they typically also include much more dubious lexicographical material of uncertain origin, as well as raw data taken directly from the Web. The chapter encourages teachers and metalexicographers to critique AEDs so that users' choices can be better informed. **Lynne Bowker** considers translators' lexicographic needs, exploring how these might be better met in the age of electronic lexicography. A variety of possibilities, covering both content-related and presentation-related aspects, are considered. These include combining general and specialized content, adding frequency and terminometric data, explicitly identifying relations, providing additional usage information (including cautions against inappropriate usage), integrating more multimedia content, standardizing the design of search techniques, introducing customization options, and creating integrated collections of resources. The chapter ends with a plea for increased communication between lexicographers and translation experts. **Pedro A. Fuertes-Olivera** takes a look at free Internet dictionaries and examines their usability for the teaching and learning of Business English in the light of the function theory of lexicography. The analysis of a range of features of free Internet dictionaries (links to Internet texts and videos, integration in a language portal, updated data, monolingual/bilingual hybridization) coupled with a comparison of the information displayed in free Internet dictionaries and some widely-used printed dictionaries leads Fuertes-Olivera to conclude that, as long as users are trained to use them critically, free Internet dictionaries can be reliable teaching and learning tools. The last chapter, by **Carolin Müller-Spitzer, Alex Koplenig**, and **Antje Töpel**, summarizes some key findings of a research project on the use of online dictionaries, using established methods of empirical social research. Through an analysis of the results of two extensive online surveys conducted in 2010 with more than 1,000 participants, they present four different aspects of practical relevance for electronic lexicography: (1) which electronic devices are used for online dictionaries; (2) which type of screen layout is best suited; (3) how users rate different characteristics of online dictionaries; and (4) how users form evaluative judgements about innovative features of online dictionaries such as multimedia elements or user-adaptive access. The study shows that when combined with other methods, in particular the analysis of log files, questionnaire surveys can provide highly valuable insights into online dictionary use.

Lexicography is clearly at a turning point in its history. In the words of Bergenholtz *et al.* (2009: 8), it "has reached a crossroads where it is difficult to develop further without a thorough rethink". Developments have never been as quick and diverse, and language needs are growing exponentially. And yet the field of dictionary-making is in danger. Scientific articles, blogs, and newspapers resonate with bleak forebodings about the future of lexicography. For Wallraff (2009) "now that [...] all of us Internet users can find out for ourselves much of what we do want to know, dictionaries' days may be numbered". It is paradoxical that dictionaries should be under threat precisely at a time when, as rightly observed by Rundell in this volume, "dictionaries have at last found their ideal platform in the online medium". This volume is a direct reflection of the current state of electronic lexicography. It shows that all the facets of the field are undergoing a transformation so profound that the resulting tools bear little resemblance to the good old paper dictionary. The developments are clearly promising but many challenges remain, especially for dictionary publishers who have to compete with purveyors of free online dictionaries. In this climate it is essential that users go for the good tools rather than using anything that happens to be out there on the Web. But this will only happen if, (a) all the people involved in the dictionary-making process have the user perspective as their top priority, and (b) users are properly trained. The user perspective runs as a unifying thread throughout the volume. Significant efforts are being made to identify user needs and bring to bear all the available technology to try and meet them. However, as pointed out by experts and non-experts alike, there is still ample scope for improvement. Wallraff (2009), for example, deplores the fact that lexicographers "invest a lot of hard work in things users don't need or want" and De Schryver (2003: 163) regrets that "methods to avoid swamping the user are still very much underdeveloped". The abundance of language-oriented websites and the wealth of language descriptions they contain lead to an 'embarras de richesse' which may well be counterproductive. This is especially true of online dictionaries where "without proper guidance users run the risk of getting lost in the riches" (Lew 2011a: 248). While dictionary publishers are certainly wise to invest time and energy in Search Engine Optimization to enhance their online visibility (cf. Lannoy 2010a), it is important that they continue to allocate a large portion of their resources to another equally important type of optimization, which, to parallel Search Engine Optimization, one could label 'Dictionary Use Optimization', entirely focused on tailor-making the dictionary to users' needs. At the same time, we need to bear in mind that dictionaries have become quite complex tools which require specialized training. Even if increased attention is being paid to users' specific needs, one cannot take it for granted that dictionaries will be used appropriately. Weschler and Pitts (2000) remind us that "[i]t takes time to learn to use the functions of an ED". As the electronic medium is gradually moving lexicography into the more general field of 'information science' (Tarp 2011, and this volume), training could take the form of a lexical reference module integrated into a much-needed electronic literacy programme spanning the whole curriculum. This would ensure that users are equipped with the necessary knowledge to tell the difference between a good tool and a bad one. The new challenges that the field of lexicography is currently facing are so diverse that they call for multi-disciplinary teams involving, besides experts in lexicography, specialists in information technology, corpus linguistics, translation, and, for the many learner-oriented tools, second language acquisition and computer-aided language pedagogy. With the right priorities and the right teams, I have no doubt that it will be possible to turn the challenges that we face into as many opportunities for success to the benefit of all involved.

Part I

Lexicography at a watershed

2

The road to automated lexicography: An editor's viewpoint

MICHAEL RUNDELL

2.1 Introduction

In 2010, it was announced that the next edition of the *Oxford English Dictionary* (*OED*) would probably not exist as a printed book. This provoked a good deal of anguished comment in the media, but it came as no surprise to anyone involved in lexicography, still less to those of us working in the field of pedagogical dictionaries. Here, the trend away from books to electronic media is already well under way, and has accelerated in the last few years. The English 'advanced learner's dictionary' (ALD)—a publishing success story in the twentieth century—now faces an uncertain future. Its main user group is in the 17–24 age range, and most of this cohort are now 'digital natives': people who routinely go to the Web for information of any kind, and generally expect to get it for nothing. If the fate of printed encyclopedias is any guide, the transformation, once started, will be rapid. For the time being, there remains a residual market for ALDs in print form, mainly in places with poor connectivity. On the digital front, the same may be true for hand-held devices (or pocket electronic dictionaries [PEDs], cf. Nesi, this volume) in places where these represent a well-established consumer preference. But in the longer term, the Web-based dictionary (whether accessed from a computer, smartphone, or tablet—or from devices yet unknown) looks like the only serious contender.

For dictionary publishers, these developments are not altogether welcome: a reliable revenue stream is drying up, and an alternative business model has not yet emerged. But there are many positives too—above all the sense that dictionaries have at last found their ideal platform in the online medium. The printed book has many limitations and is far from adequate as a medium for dictionaries. For some time, lexicographers have been struggling with the constraints of print: with access to powerful corpus-querying software applied to billion-word corpora, we have the tools (and the data) to provide a fuller and more systematic account of how language works. A printed book cannot accommodate all the information we want to convey. It is only through digital media that we can make the fruits of our language analysis available to users at a level of detail that was never previously possible, and in ways that meet their needs more effectively. There is a third piece to this jigsaw. Along with unlimited linguistic data at the 'back end' (where lexicographers analyse language) and unlimited space at the 'front end' (where information is published), there is a developing body of computational techniques which have enabled us to transfer many lexicographic tasks from humans to machines. In other words, some of the jobs involved in making a dictionary from raw language data are now partially or completely done by computers. Plans for automating more of the lexicographic work are under discussion, and the prospects are encouraging (Rundell and Kilgarriff 2011). As well as delivering cost savings for publishers (editorial salaries are a major overhead in any dictionary project), this approach has positive implications for the quality of the product because computers tend to be more thorough and systematic than people.

The subtitle of Dr Johnson's *Dictionary of the English Language* (1755) reads: "In which words are deduced from their originals, and illustrated in their different significations by examples from the best writers." This neatly encapsulates what are still the key tasks in lexicography. First, deducing words "from their originals" implies the extraction of salient linguistic facts from language in its raw state. This in turn presupposes a body of language data to analyse: thus, the collection of authentic instances of communicative acts (in Johnson's time, citations, nowadays, a corpus) represents another essential stage in the project of making a dictionary. Describing the "different significations" of words brings us into the area of creating lexical entries, and specifically of disambiguating word senses and providing either definitions (for monolingual dictionaries) or translation equivalents (for bilingual dictionaries). Finally, Johnson talks of illustrating usage by examples. We no longer restrict ourselves to quoting from "the best writers" (Johnson had didactic ambitions, contemporary lexicographers tend to be less judgemental), but the provision of good illustrative examples is the last major component in the lexicographic process. To a degree, corpus linguistics and the insights it has provided have broadened the scope of what lexicographers do: the currency of dictionaries is no longer just 'words' in isolation, but the larger units of language in which they typically participate. But in essence, Johnson's subtitle covers most of the areas we will discuss in this chapter: corpus creation; corpus analysis; and dictionary entry writing.

In this chapter, I will chart the progress of this enterprise, from the time when computers first entered the picture, to the current state of the art in computer-assisted lexicography. I will do this from the point of view not of the working lexicographer or of the computer specialist, but of those responsible for running dictionary projects: the project manager, chief editor, and publisher. The chief editor's job is to produce the best possible reference resource within an agreed schedule and a finite budget. This remains the objective, but the nature of the task has changed in two key respects. First, the role of technology has become so central that editors need to be aware of the possibilities it offers (even as these are constantly developing) and able to engage with people from the computational community in order to take advantage of these opportunities. Second, the nature of the end product is also undergoing major changes, as it makes the transition from printed book (a finished product of finite size, which can only realistically be updated every few years) to dynamic Web-based resource of potentially infinite size. This challenges many of the traditional 'rules' of lexicography, and here too the editor needs to be ready to adapt to the new reality.

Against this background, automating lexicography has an obvious appeal. How far this threatens the livelihood of lexicographers is an important issue—one which was first mooted in a paper by Gregory Grefenstette in 1998. Grefenstette posed the question: "Will there be lexicographers in the year 3000?", and considered what sort of help "the field of computational linguistics will bring to this task of describing the fundamental meaning of a word". In an influential paper, Grefenstette showed how a series of computational procedures—some already in place, some on the horizon, and each 'bootstrapping' from the previous one in the sequence—had the potential to progressively reduce the need for human intervention in lexicographic processes. Grefenstette's time horizon (still almost 1,000 years away) turns out to be far too distant: many of the advances he predicted at the end of the twentieth century are already in place barely a decade later, and many others which he never even imagined are already under development (or at least being discussed).

It is worth adding that John Sinclair, with characteristic prescience, was thinking along these lines as far back as 1991. He foresaw the development of "a modularised kit of software tools" (Sinclair 1991a: 395) which, collectively, would make possible a fully automated analysis of the language in a corpus. This toolkit would include components he described as a "collocator" (to identify regularly co-occurring items), a "compounder" (for identifying complex lexical items), a "disambiguator" (for automatic sense disambiguation), and a "typologiser" (which would classify source texts on the basis of internal linguistic evidence). Sinclair's position was in a sense 'ideological': his interest in automation was driven, one suspects, by an instinctive distrust for human intervention in the lexicographic process. I take a more pragmatic view. From the standpoint of the editor and publisher, the shift to automation offers the prospect of producing a more diverse range of lexical resources without the enormous costs associated with conventional dictionary-making. It seems likely that, for the time being, there will be a central role for skilled lexicographers and editors. But their role is changing, from selecting and synthesizing information, to 'editing' and validating choices already made by the software. So the provisional answer to

Grefenstette's question is: yes, there will still be lexicographers, but they won't be doing quite the same job.

The main focus of this chapter is on the lexicography of English, and there are two reasons for this. First, this is the area in which I have spent most of my working life. Second, the privileged position of English (as a lingua franca in academia, science, business, and the online world) means that most of the relevant technologies (especially in natural language processing) have been developed initially for English, where they are already quite mature, before being applied to other languages. But, as we shall see, all the key components of the automation project discussed here are now being developed for many other languages too. Despite the lead which English-language lexicography currently enjoys, it would be a mistake to imagine that the innovations discussed here are beyond the reach of lexicographers working outside the English-speaking world.

We are still in the middle of all these changes, and there is much more to do and much more to learn. The chapter will conclude with some predictions of how things may develop during the next few years.

2.2 Corpus creation and corpus size

Collecting data for a corpus was initially almost as labour-intensive as the citation-reading programmes it replaced (on citations, see Atkins and Rundell 2008: 48-53). Few printed texts existed in digital form (and even when they did, there was no standardization in the way they were encoded), so millions of words had to be scanned or keyboarded. The computer technology of the 1980s was stretched to its limits by the requirement to sort and store a corpus of even ten million words. So although the arrival of the first lexicographic corpora opened a major new chapter, the corpus revolution was slow to take off. Corpus-building was expensive, so it is no accident that two of the first lexicographic corpora—the 'Birmingham Collection of English Texts' (BCET, Renouf 1987) and the Longman-Lancaster Corpus (Summers 1993)—were developed to support publishing programmes in the profitable area of English pedagogical dictionaries. The high 'entry cost' to corpus lexicography ensured that—despite its demonstrable benefits—it remained a minority enterprise for well over ten years.

The other big constraint was size. The original COBUILD corpus—almost ten times larger than Brown and LOB and, from the beginning, a source of stunning revelations—was nevertheless too small to support reliable generalizations about anything but the main meanings and uses of the core vocabulary of English. The 100-million-word British National Corpus, collected at great expense over a three-year period in the early 1990s (e.g. Leech 1992), raised the bar by an order of magnitude. But it was not until the start of the twenty-first century that the constraints of cost and size began to be relaxed. Quite suddenly, a number of factors combined to make it possible, at relatively low cost, to collect, annotate, and store corpora measured in billions of words rather than millions. What happened was that, almost simultaneously, the cost of data storage became negligible; the processing power of ordinary computers reached levels capable of analysing massive databases on the fly; the software for automatically encoding the corpus data (e.g. lemmatizers and taggers) became fast and reliable; and text in digital form became available through the Internet in almost infinite quantities. This changed everything. From the publisher's point of view, the benefits were significant: in the 1980s, building a corpus was almost as big a budget item as lexicographers' salaries, but by 2010 large, diverse corpora could be acquired, processed, and loaded into a corpus-query system with fairly minimal costs in time or money.

In the English-speaking world, lexicographers now routinely work with corpora of two billion words or more, and a twenty-billion-word corpus of English is already in the pipeline. Other languages are not far behind: the Sketch Engine, for example, hosts two-billion-word corpora of Italian and German and a 750-million-word corpus of Slovene, while the Czech National Corpus Centre's 'SYN' (synchronic) corpus stands at 1.3 billion words of contemporary Czech.[1] These are huge language resources.

One is tempted to ask: Surely this is large enough, and don't we now risk drowning in too much data? In fact, this is not the case, for two reasons. First, the well-known Zipfian distribution of words in a language means that only a large corpus can provide adequate data for a dictionary (e.g. Atkins and Rundell 2008: 59-61). This applies not only to rarer words but also to the less central meanings of common words and, above all, to specific word combinations (e.g. collocations, multi-word expressions, and grammatical patterns). Consider a medium-frequency word like *seal*. As a verb it is around the 4,300th most common word in the British National Corpus (BNC), while its noun use has a rank of around 4,400. In the 7.3-million-word corpus which underpinned the first COBUILD dictionary, there are a total of 23 instances for all forms of this word: *seal, seals, sealed, sealing*. (The original corpus was not part-of-speech [POS] tagged, so occurrences of *seal* and *seals* covered both noun and verb uses.) In the 1.7-billion-word corpus used from 2008-2010 for the DANTE project,[2] there are 42,138 hits for *seal* (of which slightly over half are nouns).

This may seem a lot—until we notice the numerous patterns of usage in which *seal* is regularly found. A quick scan of the data for the verb, for example, shows that *seal* frequently combines with the particles *off, up,* and *in* to form phrasal verbs; that its typical objects include a semantically-diverse range of nouns such as *envelope, fate, border, victory, meat,* and *leak*; that common adverb collocates include *tightly, permanently, hermetically, securely,* and *environmentally*; and that it regularly

---

[1] http://ucnk.ff.cuni.cz/english/syn.php.   [2] http://www.webdante.com.

participates in prepositional phrases (simple or complex) with (among others) *into*, *against*, and *with*. Most, if not all, of these different features activate different meaning potentials.

The DANTE database mentioned above is the product of a major lexicographic project, in which the core vocabulary of English was analysed in great depth. The resulting lexical database is the most fine-grained analysis of English currently available. DANTE's entry for *seal* includes seventeen separate word senses, six idiomatic phrases, and three phrasal verbs (each having at least two senses). Since Zipfian distribution applies to word *uses* as well as to the lexicon as a whole, we may find ourselves—when studying patterns of usage for the less central meanings of *seal*–working with just ten or fifteen corpus instances. And from these, we may have to find a good example sentence for the dictionary, one which is natural, typical, and accessible. Suddenly, a corpus of 1.7 billion words does not seem excessive.

The second, related, benefit of very large volumes of language data is that the regularities drown out the oddities. Many texts include eccentric or creative uses of language, and therefore every corpus has its share of atypical, one-off instances of usage. It is important not to be misled by these (cf. Hanks, this volume). But experience of working with small datasets suggests that lexicographers may some-times mistake noise for signal, and see a rogue corpus line as evidence of something lexicographically relevant. (There is an analogy here with what happens in citation-reading programmes, and the well-known tendency of human readers to focus on the remarkable rather than the typical; see e.g. Atkins and Rundell 2008: 52.) But, as Sinclair pointed out, a single instance in a corpus is "not necessarily typical of anything but itself" (Sinclair 1991a: 392). What matters, and what lexicographers need to focus on, is whatever is recurrent: the 'regularities' of the language. And with the corpus-querying tools available now, the more data we have, the better the software performs (see Section 2.3, and Kilgarriff and Kosem, this volume). Anything atypical simply fails to make the cut, so the lexicographer does not even see it and cannot be distracted by it. Conversely, any accumulation of instances which share some common feature will be identified by the software, and presented to the lexicographer as a potentially significant linguistic fact.

2.3 Corpus analysis

From the outset, working with corpora produced a better description of language than could be achieved by more traditional means. But from the point of view of the publisher and chief editor, improvements to the end product entailed a significant increase in editorial costs. Early corpus output was, to put it mildly, clunky. Typically in the form of static, non-lemmatized and non-part-of-speech-tagged concordances (usually produced in advance in batch mode), the data was raw, and it left lexico-graphers with a great deal of work to do. Every line had to be scanned to identify anything of possible relevance, and even in a small (by today's standards) corpus, a high-frequency word might require many hours of concentrated analysis. Initially, therefore, the benefits of corpora were less obvious to budget-holders than they were to linguists and lexicographers. Corpus-driven lexicography took longer, and was therefore more expensive. In the field of English pedagogical lexicography, the last pre-corpus dictionary to be created from scratch—the first edition of the *Longman Dictionary of Contemporary English* (*LDOCE1*), published in 1978—was produced by a fairly small team in a little over three years. By contrast, the first corpus-based dictionary project began in 1980, involved a larger team, and was not completed until the COBUILD dictionary was published in 1987.

As corpora grew larger in the late 1980s and early 1990s, manual interaction with concordance lines became correspondingly more time-consuming. Publishers had to calculate whether higher origination costs would be recouped through increased sales. The outcomes were uneven. In many European countries (most obviously the UK, but also in Germany, the Netherlands, and Denmark, for example), corpus lexicography took root firmly. But in other areas (notably in the US and France), dictionary developers found it surprisingly easy to resist the lure of using corpora. The interests of linguists and lexicographers were out of sync with those of publishers and project managers. For the former, access to higher volumes of language data was an unqualified good. For the latter, the potential benefits (in terms of better dictionaries and perhaps higher sales) had to be weighed against the additional costs—which continued to rise in direct proportion to the growth in corpora.

How could this conundrum be resolved? The key was more intelligent corpus-analysis software. To a degree, general improvements in processing speeds made the job of analysing concordances more efficient. But a bigger breakthrough came with the development of the 'lexical profile', the best-known example of which is the 'word sketch' (Kilgarriff and Rundell 2002). As far back as 1989, a seminal paper by Church and Hanks had demonstrated the potential of applying statistical measures to the task of automatically finding frequent patterns of co-occurrence of words in a corpus. Ten years later, the potential of this approach was realized when the first word sketches were used in the creation of the *Macmillan English Dictionary* (*MEDAL1*, 2001). From the point of view of the dictionary's chief editor (the present writer), the initial requirement was quite specific: to find a systematic and cost-effective way of automatically identifying the common collocations of the 7,500 most frequent English words. Preliminary versions of the software looked promising, so the next challenge was to persuade the publisher (who held the purse strings) to invest in it. The argument was that licensing the software and contributing to its development would enable the dictionary to provide a comprehensive account of collocation, and this would give it a valuable advantage in a competitive market.

The new software delivered on its promise, but it brought significant additional benefits too. As discussed elsewhere (Kilgarriff and Rundell 2002, Rundell and

Kilgarriff 2011), an unintended consequence of the word sketches was that they largely resolved the problem of data overload. For any given dictionary headword, the word sketch provided the lexicographer with a convenient one-page summary of the significant patterns of co-occurrence. So, instead of being used as an adjunct to 'traditional' concordances, word sketches became the main mechanism for corpus analysis. Not only did this bring welcome efficiencies in the dictionary-making process, the continued growth in corpora became an advantage instead of a problem: higher volumes of data helped to make the sketches an ever-more reliable reflection of real usage, but without adding to the lexicographer's workload.

2.4 From corpus to dictionary

In the years that followed, further efficiencies were generated by customizing word sketches to specific dictionary projects. Any dictionary will have its own particular way of describing syntactic patterns or classifying types of collocation. It follows that the more closely the word sketch conforms—in its layout, content, and nomenclature—to the systems used in a specific dictionary, the easier it will be for lexicographers to home in on the precise information they need in order to populate their dictionary's database. Different 'Sketch Grammars' have been applied in a number of lexicographic projects, including the ongoing *Algemeen Nederlands Woordenboek* (ANW; cf. Tiberius and Kilgarriff 2009) and the projects which produced the DANTE database and the *Macmillan Collocations Dictionary* (*MCD*), both completed in 2010. In all cases the resulting word sketches have helped to optimize the compilation process. Further refinements include the 'GDEX' software, which streamlines the task of finding suitable illustrative examples in the corpus, and 'one-click copying', which enables lexicographers to quickly copy complete sentences from the corpus into the dictionary-writing software: again, these functions are being quite widely applied, not only in the UK (DANTE and *MCD*, for example), but also in the ANW and in the soon-to-be-completed Slovene Lexical Database (Rundell and Kilgarriff 2011, Tiberius and Kilgarriff 2009, Kilgarriff and Kosem, this volume). In the case of one-click-copying, it might seem a trivial benefit to replace the usual method of grabbing an example from the corpus (a standard copy-and-paste routine) with a procedure which saves perhaps three or four seconds. But from a publisher's point of view this has big advantages. Learner's dictionaries include tens of thousands of example sentences, while the DANTE database has well over half a million. Consequently, where refinements to the software can reduce by a few seconds the time needed for each individual operation, the time savings over the lifetime of a project may be really significant. The DANTE database—which covers at least a third more headwords than the first COBUILD dictionary, and with far greater granularity—was completed in a little under three years, and this demonstrates the potential of automation to achieve major time (and cost) savings in the origination of complex reference resources.

Building on these developments, initial experiments in TickBox Lexicography (TBL) have already delivered encouraging results. A TBL approach was used, for example, in the creation of the *MCD*, with reasonable success, and a more complex version of the same technology is in place for the ANW (Kilgarriff and Kosem, this volume). In this model, the corpus software presents the lexicographer with a range of possible choices, the lexicographer ticks any that look relevant, and all the related corpus data is transferred in a single move to the relevant fields in the dictionary-writing system (DWS). In the *MCD* project, the word sketches were first customized to match the set of grammatical relations which the dictionary would cover for each word class. Next, lexicographers were offered a number of collocates (the most frequent or salient) for each relation, and ticked a box next to the ones they wanted to cover in the dictionary. On a new page, a small set of 'good' examples (selected by the software) was offered for each collocational pair. Lexicographers again ticked boxes beside the ones they would include in the dictionary, and finally copied all this information across to the DWS in one go. On its first outing, the system was not without problems, and there was always an expectation that lexicographers would need to do some post-editing on the data thus transferred to the DWS. But the potential is obvious. Once all the components are optimized—with customized word sketches, a further improved GDEX tool, and a TBL interface—we can envisage a stage where the software makes most of the initial 'decisions', and automatically populates the dictionary database with a preliminary version of the dictionary entry (or at least, for now, significant sections of the entry). The lexicographer's job then consists not of identifying and selecting relevant data in the corpus but of reviewing and editing the selections made by the computer.

2.5 Using proformas

Proforma entries (discussed in detail in Atkins and Rundell 2008: 123–8, where they are referred to as 'template' entries) have been used for some time as a way of streamlining the compilation of words which belong to the same semantic category, and of ensuring that all the words in a given set are handled consistently in the dictionary. The principle is that members of the same semantic set will tend to share certain features, so it makes sense to identify these once, in advance, rather than leaving lexicographers to identify them on an ad hoc basis at each relevant entry.

Good dictionaries have always done this for 'obvious' finite sets. If you look up *Tuesday, Sagittarius, R, dinar*, or *magnesium*, you should find that the entry is similar, in content and structure, to other entries for (respectively) days of week, signs of the zodiac, letters of the alphabet, currencies, or chemical elements. But in the course of two fairly recent projects—the *Oxford–Hachette English–French Dictionary* and the *Macmillan English Dictionary for Advanced Learners*—it has been discovered that this approach can be applied to a much wider range of categories. In the DANTE project, sixty-eight proformas were developed, for sets such as academic qualifications, parts of the body, colours, illnesses, sports, fruits and vegetables, trees and flowers, and government departments. The DANTE proforma for 'drinks', for example, includes (among much else) two main senses: one a mass noun describing the drink itself (*coffee, whisky, mineral water*, etc.), the other— reflecting a well-known type of regular polysemy—a countable use referring to a glass, cup, etc. of the drink (*Two beers and three cokes, please*). In earlier implementations, lexicographers had access to these skeleton entries, and invoked them (if they remembered) whenever relevant. The DANTE project went a step further. Before the compilation phase began, every member of each of the sixty-eight proforma categories was identified, and the relevant proforma was pre-loaded into the dictionary database. This meant that a lexicographer tasked with writing the entry for *whisky* would find that an outline of the entry was already in place. The two 'drinks' senses would already be there in the database, and each was populated with information. Each sense, for example, had a ready-selected part-of-speech label (noun) and a grammatical type (mass for the first, countable for the second). Fields for recurring syntactic structures were pre-recorded too, providing a framework in which to record uses such as *a glass/shot of whisky* (itemizers) and *a whisky glass/bottle* (where the headword modifies another noun).

  In this model, the lexicographer's task is not to build up the entry from scratch, but to edit the provisional version supplied by the computer. In some cases, this might involve quite serious editing (adding new material, deleting anything irrelevant, and so on), but in many cases—where the behaviour of the word in the corpus conforms closely to the pre-selected features—the process could be quite straightforward. Somewhere between a quarter and a third of all the lemmas covered in the DANTE database included one or more proformas. It is a recurrent theme of this discussion that these moves towards automation bring multiple gains. In streamlining the compilation process, the use of proformas makes life easier for lexicographers, but it also helps to improve productivity. Yet these benefits are achieved without compromising editorial quality; on the contrary, proformas ensure that entries for words belonging to the same category are both complete, with no relevant features overlooked, and consistent with other entries in the same set.

2.6 Controlling extent and text-quality: new approaches

From the late 1990s, dedicated dictionary-writing systems began to replace the home-grown programs developed by individual publishers for their own projects (Atkins and Rundell 2008: 113ff.). Widely used packages such as IDM's DPS,[3] TshwaneDJe's TLex Suite,[4] and ABBYY's Lingvo Content,[5] not only provide an efficient and user-friendly editing environment for lexicographers to work in, but also include a range of tools which support the management of complex projects (cf. Abel, this volume). In the English-speaking world, it is increasingly rare for dictionaries to be compiled and edited by permanent in-house teams (the *OED* being an important exception). A far more common model is for lexicographers to work remotely, typically from home, accessing both corpus and DWS through a fast Web connection. With continuing improvements in the relevant technologies, this modus operandi is likely to become the norm in most parts of the world. For budget-holders this has obvious appeal because it reduces overheads. But for project managers there may be concerns about keeping track of a complex operation while working with a scattered out-of-house team. On the DANTE project, for example, the twenty or so editorial staff worked from locations in the UK, France, Ireland, Spain, Greece, and the US. With such a dispersed team, effective control of the whole operation was only possible thanks to the workflow management tools that formed part of IDM's DPS, the DWS chosen for this project.

Another enduring problem for project managers is controlling the level of detail in a dictionary, and hence the length of the completed product. At the planning stages of a dictionary, the overall extent of the text is (or should be) agreed. This has implications both for the schedule and budget, and for the size and scope of any individual entry. (Space constraints are less critical now that dictionaries are mainly published online, but this does not give editors carte blanche to include whatever data they want: notions of relevance and efficient information transfer still apply.) In this writer's experience, it is common for the first editorial pass of a dictionary to produce a text which is longer than it should be (sometimes alarmingly so). Editors then need to devise coherent strategies for cutting the text with minimum loss of relevant information, and although this is a perennial feature of the lexicographic process, it is a wasteful use of time and resources. This problem has been, if not solved, at least mitigated by the use of tools in the DWS which monitor the length of entries and batches in real time. At the start of a project, the uncompiled headwords are typically classified according to their complexity and hence their likely extent. The headwords that made up the DANTE database, for example, were assigned to one of twelve categories, ranging from single-sense referential items to highly polysemous 'light verbs' and complex grammatical words (Atkins and Grundy 2006: 1097ff., Convery *et al.* 2010). According to how it has been categorized, an individual entry will have an optimal extent, and the software provides lexicographers with the resources to monitor the entry as it develops and so avoid the problem of serious overruns.

---

[3] http://www.idm.fr.   [4] http://tshwanedje.com/.
[5] http://www.abbyy.com/lingvo_content/.

If the length of the dictionary is sometimes a cause for concern, the quality of the text is always critical. Central to the job of the chief editor are the imperatives of producing text of the highest quality within agreed constraints of time, money, and extent. Traditionally, text quality control has involved a labour-intensive process of senior editors scanning compiled text in order to identify and rectify any problems. While any entry may contain minor errors or infelicities, the editor's focus will be on anything that looks like a *systematic* issue. This may be something that an individual lexicographer is consistently getting wrong, or there may be an aspect of editorial policy which has been poorly explained and is therefore causing problems for everyone on the team. Remedial strategies include re-editing problematic entries, giving feedback to individuals, and issuing new policy guidelines to all the lexicographers. The process of bringing compiled text to final, ready-to-publish quality can involve several iterations, and there are limits to how far these important tasks can be automated. But recent developments in dictionary-writing software offer the prospect of streamlining quality-control processes and making them more systematic.

Most DWSs now provide mechanisms for constructing complex search strings which use the XML structure of the entries to identify every instance of a specific, user-defined phenomenon. On the DANTE project, almost 200 search scripts of this kind were devised, and a few examples will give an idea of what a useful new resource this is for editorial management (see Convery *et al.* 2010, for more detail). For instance, DANTE recognizes several classes of noun, and these include 'mass' and 'uncount' nouns. The boundaries between the two types are not always easy to draw, and—following established practice—the project's Style Guide includes detailed explanations of which types of noun fall into which category. Traditionally, this was as far as we could go, and editors would have to read lexicographers' text to spot cases where nouns were wrongly coded. But we can now use search strings to produce instant lists of every lexical unit coded as mass or uncount (see Figure 2.1): a quick scan of the lists will usually identify any obvious problems, and these can be fixed on the spot.

A second example shows how this approach can help editors to spot cases where important data has been *omitted*—always a harder thing to notice than instances of a policy being wrongly applied. In DANTE, every verb entry was required to include a 'structure statement'—a code indicating any syntactic construction which corpus data showed to be characteristic of the verb's behaviour. Lexicographers had no problem applying codes for clausal complements, but we noticed a tendency for structure statements to be omitted in the case of simple transitive or intransitive verbs. A search string was therefore devised (see Figure 2.2) which identified every lexical unit which had the part-of-speech label 'verb' but which did *not* include a structure statement. Every item thrown up by this search was a prima facie error, and editors could then go to the exact part of the entry that needed attention, and deal with the problem.

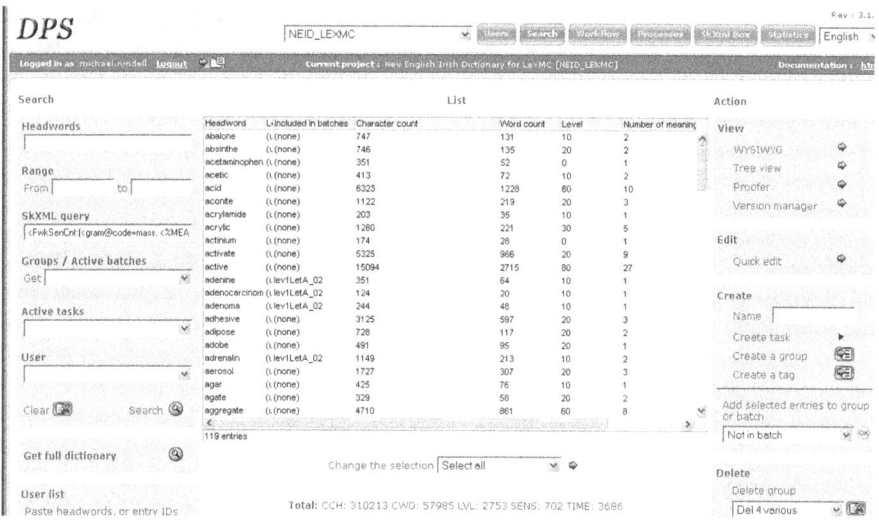

FIGURE 2.1 Partial output of search string finding nouns in letter A coded as 'mass'.

%<FwkSenCnt:(<pos@code:v,!<FwkStrCnt),<hwd:(^[a-m].*)

FIGURE 2.2 Search string for finding verbs, in the range A–M, where a 'structure statement' is missing.

A final example of this approach relates to what Levin and others refer to as the 'spray/load' verbs (Levin 1993: 117): verbs such as *dab*, *splash*, or *spray*, where you can say *I sprayed the wall with paint* or *I sprayed paint on(to) the wall*. Our objective was to ensure that every item in this category was consistently handled in the database, with codes and examples for both structures. A candidate list of spray/load verbs was assembled from various sources, and each item was checked. We then ran a search string over the whole text to find verbs where one or other of the two structures was recorded, and this enabled us to add to the list of spray/load verbs and to ensure that their entries were complete and consistently coded. This is a good example of linguistic theory being applied to practical lexicography—with benefits accruing, in return, to the theory, as new verbs belonging to this category are uncovered.

For project-management purposes, the text of DANTE was created in nine major alphabetic sections and, as each section was completed by the lexicographic team, a suite of search strings was run on the newly-compiled text. This gave the editorial management a powerful new tool to complement traditional quality-control mechanisms. Conventional editing might bring to light problems with particular aspects of the text, and these could then be targeted using specially-devised searches, and systematically addressed. Looking ahead, we can envisage a further development in which the DWS software is programmed to run certain types of search automatically and to correct any errors which these revealed, with little or no human intervention.

Editing dictionary text is an intuitive rather than 'scientific' process, and its effectiveness depends a great deal on the accumulated experience of the editor. But with XML search strings we have a useful new weapon in our armoury, which adds a degree of structure and system to the task while at the same time improving its efficiency. Our experience on the DANTE project has convinced us that this technique has much to offer, and, going forward, we can foresee further exploitations of this approach.

2.7 Conclusion

This is a good moment to return to a question posed at the beginning of this chapter: given that computers have gradually taken over many lexicographic tasks previously performed by humans, is it plausible to foresee this process continuing to a point where lexicographers are, ultimately, replaced by machines? This was roughly the question discussed by Grefenstette at the end of the twentieth century (Grefenstette 1998). Even earlier, Sinclair (1991a) was predicting the development of software tools which would make possible the automatic analysis of corpora—though he did not speculate on the automation of dictionary entry-writing itself. As discussed above, much progress has been made towards this goal. Lexical profiling software reliably identifies the salient syntactic constructions and lexical combinations characteristic of a particular word. Meanwhile, progress is being made towards answering Sinclair's call for a "typologiser": the goal here is extract the information which the DWS needs in order to automatically assign 'labels' to words or senses. This is discussed in greater detail elsewhere (Rundell and Kilgarriff 2011), but essentially it involves comparing a word's profile in a carefully-defined sub-corpus with its behaviour in the lexicographic corpus as a whole, in order to retrieve information about its stylistic, regional, or domain preferences. Finally, the task of selecting corpus example sentences appropriate for a particular dictionary can, to a significant degree, be delegated to programs such as GDEX (see above, and Kilgarriff *et al.* 2008, Kilgarriff and Kosem, this volume). Current versions of the software are far from perfect, and some functions (though well understood in principle) have yet to be applied in real projects. Further improvements are needed, but that is in the nature of the enterprise. What is clear is that in the new models now emerging, the role of the lexicographer and editor is moving away from the origination of dictionary text to the validation of decisions and selections made by the software.

For the time being, the hardest parts of lexicography—word sense disambiguation, definition-writing (for monolinguals), and providing translation equivalents (for bilinguals)—still require expert intervention by skilled lexicographers. But none of these operations is inherently intractable. Computationalists are rapidly closing in on the word sense disambiguation task, even if aspects of it (such as mapping the evanescent senses of highly polysemous verbs) remain challenging. Alternative approaches to defining are being investigated. For technical terms, for example, we may be able to exploit the frequent use in specialist texts of 'lexical familiarization' strategies, where a writer effectively defines a term as it is introduced (see e.g. Pearson 1996). A program which extracts such instances from a specialist corpus could in many cases pre-empt the need for dictionary definitions, or at the very least provide useful materials to supplement conventional definitions. For everyday, non-technical meanings, users could be given access to typical corpus sentences (selected by program) of varying degrees of complexity, and this too could—for some users, at least—make conventional definitions redundant.

It may be more productive to rephrase Grefenstette's question and ask, not, "Will there be lexicographers in the year 3000?", but "Will there be dictionaries?" As Tarp (2008: 40) has observed, "Dictionaries are basically an answer to specific types of need [...] Historically speaking, these needs arose before dictionaries existed, and are in principle not dependent on the existence of dictionaries"—or at least, not dependent on dictionaries in the form we are used to. It is already clear that the dictionary is morphing from its current incarnation as autonomous 'product' to something more like a 'service', often embedded in other resources.

From the point of view of editor and publisher—the focus of this chapter—most of these developments are positive. Twenty-five years ago, the infrastructure required for a serious, corpus-based dictionary project was so expensive that only a few large publishers or well-funded state institutions could embark on one. Now, the cost of acquiring corpora (in time and money) has fallen dramatically, while general computing power has increased by orders of magnitude yet costs a fraction of what it once did. Meanwhile, corpus-querying software and dictionary-writing systems have made it possible (and increasingly common) for lexicographers to work remotely—thus further reducing publishers' overheads. All of this tends to 'democratize' access to corpus lexicography. And as we have seen, the various software tools devised in recent years to streamline the corpus-analysis and dictionary-creation process have had the effect, first, of releasing lexicographers from the more banal tasks (the 'drudgery' famously referred to by Dr Johnson), and then enabling them, and the editorial management, to produce more systematic, more internally-consistent, and simply better descriptions of language in a shorter time than was previously possible. It will be fascinating to see how this process develops in the years to come. We live in interesting times.

Dictionaries

Correard, Marie-Hélène and Valérie Grundy (eds.) (1995). *Oxford-Hachette French Dictionary*, First Edition. Oxford: Oxford University Press.

Procter, Paul (ed.) (1978). *Longman Dictionary of Contemporary English*, First Edition. Harlow: Longman.

Rundell, Michael (ed.) (2001). *Macmillan English Dictionary for Advanced Learners*, First Edition. Oxford: Macmillan Education.

Rundell, Michael (ed.) (2010). *Macmillan Collocations Dictionary*. Oxford: Macmillan Education.

Sinclair, John and Patrick Hanks (eds.) (1987). *Collins COBUILD English Language Dictionary*, First Edition. London: Collins.

3

Corpus tools for lexicographers

ADAM KILGARRIFF AND IZTOK KOSEM

3.1 Introduction

To analyse corpus data, lexicographers need software that allows them to search, manipulate, and save data, a 'corpus tool'. A good corpus tool is the key to a comprehensive lexicographic analysis—a corpus without a good tool to access it is of little use.

Both corpus compilation and corpus tools have been swept along by general technological advances over the last three decades. Compiling and storing corpora has become far faster and easier, so corpora tend to be much larger than previous ones. Most of the first COBUILD dictionary was produced from a corpus of eight million words. Several of the leading English dictionaries of the 1990s were produced using the British National Corpus (BNC), of 100 million words. Current lexicographic projects we are involved in use corpora of around a billion words—though this is still less than one hundredth of one percent of the English language text available on the Web (see Rundell, this volume).

The amount of data to analyse has thus increased significantly, and corpus tools have had to be improved to assist lexicographers in adapting to this change. Corpus tools have become faster, more multifunctional, and customizable. In the COBUILD project, getting concordance output took a long time and then the concordances were printed on paper and handed out to lexicographers (Clear 1987). Today, with Google as a point of comparison, concordancing needs to be instantaneous, with the analysis taking place on the computer screen. Moreover, larger corpora offer much higher numbers of concordance lines per word (especially for high-frequency words), and, considering the time constraints of the lexicographers (see Rundell, this volume), new features of data summarization are required to ease and speed the analysis.

In this chapter, we review the functionality of corpus tools used by lexicographers. In Section 3.2, we discuss the procedures in corpus preparation that are required for some of these features to work. In Section 3.3, we briefly describe some leading tools and provide some elements of comparison. The Sketch Engine is introduced in Section 3.4. This innovative corpus tool was developed by the first author's company and used in the second author's projects; it has become a leading tool for lexicography and other corpus work since its launch in 2004. The Sketch Engine uses the formalisms and approach of the Stuttgart tools; it is available as a Web service, and corpora from forty different languages are already loaded within it. We focus first on basic features, which are used also by non-lexicographers, and then move on to the features that are targeted mainly at lexicographers. Section 3.5 is dedicated to the user-friendliness of corpus tools, a topic that, although rarely discussed in the literature, is becoming more relevant as corpus tools become more complex. Finally, we conclude by considering how corpus tools of the future might be designed to further assist lexicographers.

3.2 Preparing the corpus for automatic analysis

Many features of corpus tools work only if the corpus data is properly prepared. The preparation of a corpus has two parts: preparing the metadata, or 'headers', and preparing the text.

A corpus is a collection of documents, and instances of words come from a variety of documents representing different types of text. The lexicographer examining the instances of a word may want to know from what kind of text a particular instance has been extracted (i.e. the details and characteristics of the document, such as its date of publication, author, mode [spoken, written], and domain). For this to work, each document must come with metadata, usually located in a 'header', which lists the features of the document, in a way that the corpus tool can interpret. Using headers, corpus tools can not only provide information on the texts, but also use them to limit the searches to particular text types, build word lists and find keywords for a text type, etc.

Preparing the text starts with identifying and managing the character encoding and then typically involves marking up the text with (1) sections, paragraphs, and sentences, (2) tokens, (3) lemmas, (4) part-of-speech tags, and (5) grammatical structure. Each text comes with its character encoding. This is the way in which each particular character is encoded in a series of ones and zeros. Widely used character encodings include ASCII, ISO 8859-1 (also called Latin-1), Big-5 (for Chinese), and UTF-8. There are many different character encodings, most of which are language-specific or writing-system specific, and this can create a wide range of problems of misinterpretation where the system assumes that one encoding has been used, but in fact a different one was involved. In Latin-script languages, problems most often arise with accented and other non-standard characters since standard characters (a–z, A–Z, 0–9, etc.) are generally encoded in the same way. Over time, a growing proportion of documents are being encoded in UTF-8, which is based on the Unicode standard; however, most documents do not yet use Unicode or UTF-8, and the character encoding typically has to be guessed, with each text then converted to the same, standard, encoding.

Sentence, paragraph, and section mark-up (using structural tags) supports functionality such as the display of sentences, or not seeking patterns spanning sentence ends. Tokenization is the process of identifying the tokens, usually the words, which the user typically searches for. For some languages, such as Chinese and Arabic, this is a major challenge, since in Chinese there is no white space between words, and in Arabic many grammatical words are written as clitics, without white space between them and the core word. This is not a great problem in English since, most of the time, white space reliably indicates a word break: there are just a few difficult cases, mostly relating to apostrophes (e.g. whether *don't* is counted as one token or two—*do* and *n't*) and hyphens (*co-operate, first-hand*). How a text has been tokenized has an effect on searching, filtering, sorting, and many other features.

Lemmatization (also known as morphological analysis) is (at its simplest) the process of identifying the base form of the word (or the dictionary headword), called a lemma. In a language such as English, many corpus words may be instances of more than one lemma. Thus *tricks* may be the plural of the noun, or the present tense, third person singular form of the verb. The process of identifying, by computer, which part of speech applies in a particular context is called part-of-speech (POS) tagging. Finally, parsing is used to annotate the syntactic structure of each sentence in the corpus.

Once all the words in a corpus have been lemmatized and part-of-speech tagged, and this information made available to the corpus tool, each word in the corpus can be thought of as a <word form, lemma, POS-tag> triple, and searches can be specified in terms of any of these three parts. In addition to simple searches for single words, lexicographers often want to search for a phrase or some other more complex structure. A good corpus tool will support complex searches (such as those by surrounding context), while keeping the interface simple and user-friendly for the simple searches that users most often want to do. Another form of search uses a corpus query language (CQL), such as that developed at the University of Stuttgart (Christ 1995). This allows sophisticated structured searches, matching all- or part-strings, to be built for as many fields of information as are provided (such as the word form, lemma, and POS-tag).

3.3 An overview of corpus tools

The number of corpus tools available has grown over the past thirty years, as not only lexicographers, but also researchers from other linguistics sub-disciplines have become aware of the potential of corpora. These researchers have been interested in many different aspects of language, and so corpus tools have become more diverse.

Some leading corpus tools have been designed around the needs of a particular institution, project, and/or corpus or corpora, and are tailored for working well in that environment.

Corpus tools can be categorized using the following typology:

a) *Computer-based (stand-alone) tools vs. online tools:* Some tools work as stand-alone software that requires that the tool and the corpus are stored on the user's computer. Leading players here are WordSmith Tools and MonoConc Pro, both of which have been widely and successfully used in teaching. WordSmith and MonoConc Pro are both commercial projects: a free alternative that works in a similar way is AntConc. On the other hand, online corpus tools allow the users to access the corpus, or corpora, from any computer. Examples of online tools include the Sketch Engine (Kilgarriff *et al.* 2004), KorpusDK (developed by the Department for Digital Dictionaries and Text Corpora at the Society for Danish Language and Literature), and Mark Davies's tools at http://corpus.byu.edu.

b) *Corpus-related tools vs. corpus-independent tools:* Some corpus tools can be used only with a particular corpus, most often because they were designed as a part of a specific corpus project or for a specific institution. Examples include SARA[1] (and its newer XML version, XAIRA[2]) and BNCWeb, two high-specification interfaces designed to access the British National Corpus (BNC), a tool offered by Real Academia Española to access their Spanish reference corpus, Corpus de Referencia del Español Actual (CREA),[3] and special groups of corpus-related tools that use the same interface to access several different preloaded corpora (e.g. the tool KorpusDK that is used to access several Danish corpora). A set of corpus tools and software developed by Mark Davies at Brigham Young University are used to access leading corpora for Spanish, Portuguese, and American English. His websites are among the most widely-used corpus resources, particularly his Corpus of Contemporary American (COCA) (Davies 2009). Other tools are corpus-independent, which means that they can be used to upload and analyse any corpus. Examples include the Sketch Engine, Corpus WorkBench, WordSmith Tools, MonoConc Pro, and AntConc.

c) *Prepared corpus vs. Web as corpus:* The majority of corpus tools are used to access a corpus that has been compiled with linguistic research in mind. But the web can be viewed as a vast corpus, with very large quantities of texts for many languages, and lexicographers frequently use it in this way (Kilgarriff and Grefenstette 2003). Google and other Web search engines can be viewed as

---

[1] http://www.natcorp.ox.ac.uk/tools/chapter4.xml.
[2] http://xaira.sourceforge.net/.
[3] An online version of the tool is freely accessible, with limitations on searches (e.g. the maximum number of hits displayed is 1,000).

corpus tools: in response to a query, they find and show a number of instances of the query term in use. They are not designed specifically for linguists' purposes, but are often very useful, having access, as they do, to such an enormous source of language data. Some tools have been developed which sit between the search engine and the user, reformatting search results as a concordance and offering options likely to be useful to the linguist. They have been called Web concordancers. One leading system is WebCorp (Kehoe and Renouf 2002).

d) *Simple tools vs. advanced tools:* Due to the increasing size of corpora, and the increasing number of (different) users, corpus tools have become more and more multifunctional, i.e. they have started offering many different features to assist their users with analysis. The features of corpus tools range from basic features such as concordance, collocation, and keywords, to advanced features, such as word sketches and CQL searches. Most of these features are discussed in more detail in Section 3.4; for more on keywords, see Scott (1997) and Scott and Tribble (2006). Examples of simple corpus tools are AntConc and Mono-Conc Easy. Advanced corpus tools are designed for users who need access to more advanced functionality, e.g. lexicographers. Examples of advanced corpus tools are the Sketch Engine, XAIRA, and KorpusDK.

e) *Typical users:* The three main types of users of corpus tools are lexicographers, linguistics researchers and students, and language teachers and learners. Different tools have been designed with different target users in mind.

There are numerous corpus tools, but few with the full range of functionality that a lexicographer wants. Of these, most have been in-house developments for particular dictionary or corpus projects. The tools developed within the COBUILD project were used for lexicography at Collins and Oxford University Press throughout the 1980s and 1990s as well as with the 'Bank of English' corpus and WordBanks Online web service (Clear 1987). They set a high standard, and have only recently been decommissioned despite using a 1980s pre-Windows, pre-mouse interface.

The University of Stuttgart's Corpus WorkBench, sometimes also called 'the Stuttgart tools', was another influential early player, establishing in the early 1990s a very fast tool suitable for the largest corpora then available, which could work with sophisticated linguistic mark-up and queries. It is available free for academic use. Both the format it used for preparing a corpus, and the query language it used for querying corpora, have become de facto standards in the field. The group that prepared the corpus worked closely with several German dictionary publishers, so the tools were tested and used in commercial lexicographic settings.

As corpora have grown and Web speeds and connectivity have become more dependable, computer-based corpus tools have become less desirable for large lexicography projects since the corpus and software maintenance must be managed for each user's computer, rather than just once, centrally. Consequently, most lexicographic projects nowadays use online corpus tools that use http protocols (so users do not have to install any software on their computer) and work with corpora of billions of words.[4]

3.4 Moving on from concordances: the Sketch Engine

The number of features offered by corpus tools is continually increasing, and the development of a new feature often results from an attempt to meet a certain user's need. Recently, many new features have been introduced in the Sketch Engine, a tool aimed particularly at lexicography, and which is available for use with corpora of all languages, types, and sizes. Since its inception, the Sketch Engine has had a steady programme of adding functionality according to lexicographers' and corpus linguists' needs.

This section focuses on various features of the Sketch Engine, with particular attention being paid to the features used extensively by lexicographers. Many features, especially those presented in Section 3.4.1, are found in most corpus tools and should not be considered Sketch Engine specific. It should also be pointed out that while in general each new feature is at first used predominantly by lexicographers, at a later stage they are frequently widely adopted by linguists, educators, and other researchers. The features presented here should therefore not be regarded as simply lexicographic, although some of the most innovative features described in Section 3.4.2, such as sketch differences and the Good Dictionary Examples (GDEX) option, have (so far) mainly been used in dictionary-making.

3.4.1 *Analysing concordance lines*

The concordance, "a collection of the occurrences of a word-form, each in its textual environment" (Sinclair 1991b: 32), is the basic feature of corpus use, and is at the heart of lexicographic analysis. Concordance lines can be shown in the sentence format or in the KWIC (Key Word in Context) format. The KWIC format, preferred in lexicography, shows a line of context for each occurrence of the word, with the word centred (see Figure 3.1). Using the concordance feature, lexicographers can scan the data and quickly get an idea of the patterns of usage of the word, spotting meanings, compounds, etc.

The problem with reading raw concordance data is that it can be very time-consuming for lexicographers to gather all the required information on the item

---

[4] Recently, lexicographers have become interested in the potential of the World Wide Web for their data analysis, and consequently also in web concordancers. However, web concordancers rely heavily on search engines. This is problematic in various ways, for example there is a limit (for Google, 1,000) on the number of hits the user can access for any search, the corpus lines are sorted according to the search engine's ranking criteria, etc. There are also those who question the lexicographic potential of the web due to its constantly changing size and content. The debate is still continuing, but considering that the web makes so many documents so easily available, it would be a shame not to utilize such a resource.

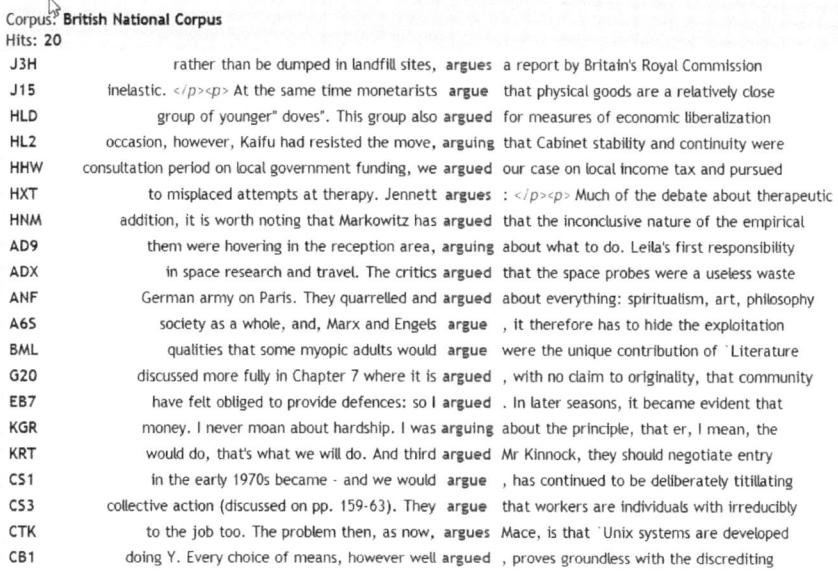

Corpus: **British National Corpus**
Hits: 20

J3H	rather than be dumped in landfill sites, argues	a report by Britain's Royal Commission
J15	inelastic. `</p><p>` At the same time monetarists argue	that physical goods are a relatively close
HLD	group of younger" doves". This group also argued	for measures of economic liberalization
HL2	occasion, however, Kaifu had resisted the move, arguing	that Cabinet stability and continuity were
HHW	consultation period on local government funding, we argued	our case on local income tax and pursued
HXT	to misplaced attempts at therapy. Jennett argues	: `</p><p>` Much of the debate about therapeutic
HNM	addition, it is worth noting that Markowitz has argued	that the inconclusive nature of the empirical
AD9	them were hovering in the reception area, arguing	about what to do. Leila's first responsibility
ADX	in space research and travel. The critics argued	that the space probes were a useless waste
ANF	German army on Paris. They quarrelled and argued	about everything: spiritualism, art, philosophy
A6S	society as a whole, and, Marx and Engels argue	, it therefore has to hide the exploitation
BML	qualities that some myopic adults would argue	were the unique contribution of `Literature
G20	discussed more fully in Chapter 7 where it is argued	, with no claim to originality, that community
EB7	have felt obliged to provide defences: so I argued	. In later seasons, it became evident that
KGR	money. I never moan about hardship. I was arguing	about the principle, that er, I mean, the
KRT	would do, that's what we will do. And third argued	Mr Kinnock, they should negotiate entry
CS1	in the early 1970s became - and we would argue	, has continued to be deliberately titillating
CS3	collective action (discussed on pp. 159-63). They argue	that workers are individuals with irreducibly
CTK	to the job too. The problem then, as now, argues	Mace, is that `Unix systems are developed
CB1	doing Y. Every choice of means, however well argued	, proves groundless with the discrediting

FIGURE 3.1 Concordance lines: the KWIC format.

being analysed. Lexicographers may also want to focus on a particular pattern found in the concordance, group similar concordances together, etc. It is therefore useful for lexicographers to have available additional features (such as 'sorting', 'sampling', and 'filtering') that help manipulate the concordance output and give some statistical information on it.

Sorting the concordance lines will often bring a number of instances of the same pattern together, making it easier for the lexicographer to spot the patterns. The most typical sorts are by the first word to the left, first word to the right, and by the node word. Sorting by the node word can be useful for lexicographers working with highly inflected languages where lemmas often have many different word forms. The type of sorting that yields the most useful results depends on the grammatical characteristics of the word. For English nouns, for example, sorting by the first word on the left will normally highlight the relevant patterns involving adjective modifiers and verbs of which the noun is object, whereas sorting on the right will show verbs of which the noun is subject. In Figure 3.2, where the concordance lines are sorted by the first word to the right, it is much easier to spot recurring patterns such as *argue about*, *argue for*, and *argue that*, compared to the sort in Figure 3.1. Other types of sorting include sorting according to the second, third, etc. word to the right or to the left of the node word, and more complex options such as sorting according to word endings.

There are two more types of sorting that differ from those mentioned so far, namely sorting according to the meaning of the node word, and sorting according to

Corpus: **British National Corpus**
Hits: **20**

CS1	in the early 1970s became - and we would **argue**	, has continued to be deliberately titillating
A6S	society as a whole, and, Marx and Engels **argue**	, it therefore has to hide the exploitation
CB1	doing Y. Every choice of means, however well **argued**	, proves groundless with the discrediting
G20	discussed more fully in Chapter 7 where it is **argued**	, with no claim to originality, that community
EB7	have felt obliged to provide defences: so I **argued**	. In later seasons, it became evident that
HXT	to misplaced attempts at therapy. Jennett **argues**	: </p><p> Much of the debate about therapeutic
J3H	rather than be dumped in landfill sites, **argues**	a report by Britain's Royal Commission
ANF	German army on Paris. They quarrelled and **argued**	about everything: spiritualism, art, philosophy
KGR	money. I never moan about hardship. I was **arguing**	about the principle, that er, I mean, the
AD9	them were hovering in the reception area, **arguing**	about what to do. Leila's first responsibility
HLD	group of younger" doves". This group also **argued**	for measures of economic liberalization
CTK	to the job too. The problem then, as now, **argues**	Mace, is that `Unix systems are developed
KRT	would do, that's what we will do. And third **argued**	Mr Kinnock, they should negotiate entry
HHW	consultation period on local government funding, we **argued**	our case on local income tax and pursued
HL2	occasion, however, Kaifu had resisted the move, **arguing**	that Cabinet stability and continuity were
J15	inelastic. </p><p> At the same time monetarists **argue**	that physical goods are a relatively close
HNM	addition, it is worth noting that Markowitz has **argued**	that the inconclusive nature of the empirical
ADX	in space research and travel. The critics **argued**	that the space probes were a useless waste
CS3	collective action (discussed on pp. 159-63). They **argue**	that workers are individuals with irreducibly
BML	qualities that some myopic adults would **argue**	were the unique contribution of `Literature

FIGURE 3.2 Sorting concordance lines.

how good a candidate for a dictionary example the concordance line is. Both types of sort require an additional preliminary stage: the former requires manual annotation of the concordance lines of the word (see Section 3.5.4), whereas the latter requires the computation of the good example score (see Section 3.4.3).

Sampling is useful as there will frequently be too many instances for the lexicographer to inspect them all. It is misleading just to look at the first instances as they will all come from the first part of the corpus: if the lexicographer is working on the entry for *language*, and there are a few texts about *language development* near the beginning of the corpus, then it is all too likely that the lexicographer who just works straight through the corpus will get an inflated view of the importance of the term, while missing others. The sampling feature in the corpus tool allows the lexicographer to take a manageable-sized sample of randomly selected concordance lines from the whole corpus.

Filtering allows the lexicographer to focus on a particular pattern of use (a positive filter), or to set aside the patterns that have been accounted for in order to focus on the residue (a negative filter). For example, if the lexicographer spots *local authority* as a recurrent pattern of the word *authority*, he or she can first focus on that pattern by using either the positive filter (searching for all the concordances where *local* occurs one word to the left of *authority*), or performing a search for the phrase *local authority*, and then continue the analysis by excluding the pattern *local authority* from the concordance output with the negative filter.

Search by sub-corpora can be considered as a type of filtering as it can be used to limit the analysis of the pattern to part of the corpus. Many words have different

doc.year	Freq	Rel [%]	
p/n 2000	111	15.8	——
p/n 2001	296	32.0	———
p/n 2002	899	69.0	■■■■■■■
p/n 2003	1580	102.5	■■■■■■■■■■
p/n 2004	2557	129.8	■■■■■■■■■■■
p/n 2005	2811	194.2	■■■■■■■■■■■■■■
p/n 2009	18	4.7	–

FIGURE 3.3 Frequency distribution of the lemma *random* in the OEC blog sub-corpus

meanings and patterns of use in different varieties of language, and the lexicographer needs to be able to explore this kind of variation. A vivid example is the English noun *bond*: in finance texts it means a kind of finance, as in *treasury bonds, Government bonds, junk bonds*; in chemistry, a connection between atoms and molecules as in *hydrogen bonds, chemical bonds, peptide bonds*; and in psychology, a link between people, as in *strengthening, developing, forging bonds*.

Frequency analyses are often useful to lexicographers. For example, analysing the word *random* shows the importance of combining analysis by text type and change over time using the Sketch Engine's frequency feature. The goal here was to explore the hypothesis that *random* has recently added an informal use to its traditional, formal, and scientific one, as in:

(1) Last was our drama but unfortunately our original drama went down the drain way down so Iffy came up with one very **random** drama involving me doing nothing but just sit down and say my one and only line "Wha?" and she just yell at me coz she was pissed off of something.

The Oxford English Corpus (OEC), containing over two billion words, includes a large component of blog material, so the blog sub-corpus could be used to explore the new pattern of use. Also, each text has the year in which it was written or spoken in its metadata. Figure 3.3 shows the frequency distribution of the word *random* in blogs over the period 2000–2009.

Sometimes the lexicographer cannot decipher the meaning of the word being analysed because the concordance line does not provide enough information. For example, for the concordance line for *random* offered in example (1), the default Sketch Engine context size of forty characters (excluding spaces) to the left and to the right of the searched word[5] does not provide enough information to get an idea of the meaning of *random*, as shown in example (2):

(2) drain way down so Iffy came up with one very random drama involving me doing nothing but just sit

---

[5] Only whole words within the context size are shown in the concordance.

It is thus useful to have quick access to more context, which in most corpus tools can be accessed by clicking on a concordance line.

3.4.2 *From collocation to word sketches*

Since COBUILD, lexicographers have been using KWIC concordances as their primary tool for finding out how words behave. But corpora continue to grow. This is good because the more data we have, the better placed we are to present a complete and accurate account of a word's behaviour. It does, however, present challenges. Given fifty corpus occurrences of a word, the lexicographer can simply read them. If there are five hundred, reading them all is still a possibility but might take longer than an editorial schedule permits. Where there are five thousand, it is no longer viable. Having more data is good—but the data then needs summarizing.

One way of summarizing the data is to list the words that are found in close proximity of the word that is the subject of analysis with a frequency far greater than chance, i.e. its collocations (Atkins and Rundell 2008). The sub-field of collocation statistics began with a paper by Church and Hanks (1989) who proposed a measure called 'mutual information' (MI), from information theory, as an automatic way of finding a word's collocations: their thesis was that pairs of words with high mutual information for each other would usually be collocations. The approach generated a good deal of interest among lexicographers, and many corpus tools now provide functionality for identifying salient collocates along these lines.[6]

One flaw in the original work is that MI emphasizes rare words (and an ad hoc frequency threshold has to be imposed or the list would be dominated by very rare items). This problem can be solved by changing the statistic, and a number of proposals have been made. Evert and Krenn (2001) evaluated a range of proposals (from a linguist's rather than a lexicographer's perspective). Statistics for measuring collocation, in addition to MI, include MI3, the log-likelihood ratio, and the Dice coefficient (for a full account see Manning and Schütze 1999, Chapter 5). Another, more recently proposed collocation statistic is logDice (Rychly 2008).

Tables 3.1 to 3.4 (each containing the top fifteen collocate candidates of the verb *save* in the OEC corpus, in the window of five tokens to the left and five tokens to the right, ordered according to MI, MI3, log-likelihood, and logDice scores respectively), offer a good demonstration of the differences between the various statistics. Collocate candidates offered by MI are very rare, and not at all useful to lexicographers. Better collocate candidates, many of them the same, are offered by MI3 and log-likelihood; however, in this case very frequent functional words dominate the list. Even more useful candidate collocates are provided by logDice, from which the lexicographer can already get an idea of a few meanings of the verb *save*, for example 'use less of or

---

[6] In our terminology, a *collocation* comprises *node word* + *collocate(s)*, in particular grammatical relations.

invest' (*money, million*), 'prevent from harm' (*life*), and 'store' (*file*). Collocation can thus be used not only to describe word meanings (Sinclair 2004), but also to distinguish between them (see also Hoey 2005). A list of collocates, representing an automatic summary of the corpus data, is therefore very useful for the lexicographer.

As shown in Tables 3.1 to 3.4, collocates are normally provided in the form of a list. Another way of displaying collocates, available in the COBUILD tools (called 'picture') and WordSmith Tools (the Patterns view), is to list collocates by frequency or by score of whichever statistical measure is used,[7] in each position between the selected span (see Figure 3.4). The information in this display needs to be read vertically and not horizontally. The drawbacks of this display are that it gives the user a lot of information to wade through, and fails to merge information about the same word occurring in different positions.

Word Sketches   Collocation finding as described above is grammatically blind. It considers only proximity. However, lexicographically interesting collocates are, in most cases, words occurring in a particular grammatical relation to the node word. For example, an examination of the concordance of the top collocates in Table 3.4 shows that a number of them occur as the object of the verb (e.g. *life, money, energy,*

TABLE 3.1. **Top fifteen collocates of the verb** *save* **(ordered by MI score)**

Lemma	freq	MI
BuyerZone.com	7	13.19
ac);	5	13.19
count-prescription	5	13.19
Christ-A-Thon	7	13.19
Teldar	6	12.61
Re:What	26	12.55
Redjeson	5	12.51
INFOPACKETS30	3	12.46
other-I	4	12.39
SetInfo	4	12.39
Ctrl-W	9	12.36
God	18	12.23
Walnuttree	3	12.19
Hausteen	5	12.19
MWhs	3	12.19

---

[7] WordSmith Tools lists collocates in the 'Patterns' view by frequency only.

TABLE 3.2. Top fifteen collocates of the verb *save* (ordered by MI3 score)

lemma	freq	MI3
to	99846	37.29
life	27606	36.98
.	102829	36.65
money	19901	36.51
the	106241	36.39
,	86327	35.69
be	70859	35.25
and	62030	35.22
from	28399	34.44
a	47129	34.14
of	41271	33.38
have	29869	33.21
you	20610	33.02
that	29260	33.01
for	25291	32.90

TABLE 3.3. Top fifteen collocates of the verb *save* (ordered by log-likelihood score)

lemma	freq	log-likelihood
to	99846	417952.13
.	102829	333836.91
the	106241	297431.94
life	27606	234592.45
,	86327	222779.39
and	62030	192235.46
be	70859	190628.16
money	19901	181861.45
from	28399	139301.25
a	47129	126211.75
have	29869	92837.93
of	41271	90602.61
you	20610	86952.62
that	29260	85631.78
for	25291	83634.16

TABLE 3.4. Top fifteen collocates of the verb *save* (ordered by logDice score)

lemma	freq	logDice
money	19901	9.34
Life	27606	9.05
save	2976	7.52
energy	2648	7.37
million	4742	7.17
dollar	1847	7.16
File	2147	7.14
Try	6380	7.11
£	6193	7.07
could	11904	7.05
effort	2844	7.05
◆	2583	7.01
retirement	1181	6.94
planet	1194	6.91
thousand	1894	6.89

N	L5	L4	L3	L2	L1	Centre	R1	R2	R3	R4	R5
1	THE	THE	THE	OF	THE	LOCAL	AND	AND	THE	THE	THE
2	OF	OF	OF	TO	OF		GOVERNMENT	OF	AND	AND	OF
3	AND	AND	TO	IN	A		AUTHORITIES	IN	IN	OF	AND
4	TO	TO	AND	AND	AND		LEVEL	THE	A	TO	TO
5	IN	IN	IN	THE	TO		AUTHORITY	TO	TO	IN	IN
6	A	A	A	AT	IN		COMMUNITY	IS	OF	A	A
7	THAT	IS	THAT	BY	FOR		GOVERNMENTS	FOR	IS	IS	IS
8	IS	THAT	IS	WITH	BY		COMMUNITIES	AS	AS	AS	THAT
9	FOR	AS	BE	ON	WITH		PEOPLE	ARE	ARE	THAT	AS
10	AS	FOR	BY	FOR	ON		MARKET	THAT	THAT	FOR	FOR
11	BY	BE	AS	THAT	THAT		OR	OR	FOR	WITH	WITH
12	WITH	WITH	FOR	FROM	FROM		CONDITIONS	WITH	THIS	BY	BY
13	ARE	BY	WITH	A	THEIR		RESIDENTS	WERE	WITH	ARE	BE
14	ON	ARE	ARE	IS	AS		CONTEXT	AT	BE	BE	THIS
15	BE	WAS	ON	AS	OR		POLITICAL	WAS	WHICH	ON	ARE
16	LOCAL	WERE	WERE	STATE	BETWEEN		POPULATION	REGIONAL	BY	THIS	LOCAL
17	WAS	ON	NOT	GLOBAL	ITS		KNOWLEDGE	BUT	NOT	LOCAL	ON
18	THIS	LOCAL	LOCAL	NATIONAL	OTHER		POWER	THIS	AT	HAVE	WAS
19	FROM	AN	GLOBAL	OR	AT		OFFICIALS	HAVE	ON	IT	FROM
20	IT	FROM	THIS	REGIONAL	THESE		AREA	ON	WERE	NOT	IT

FIGURE 3.4 WordSmith Tools' Patterns view for *local* in the Corpus of Academic Journal Articles (Kosem, 2010).

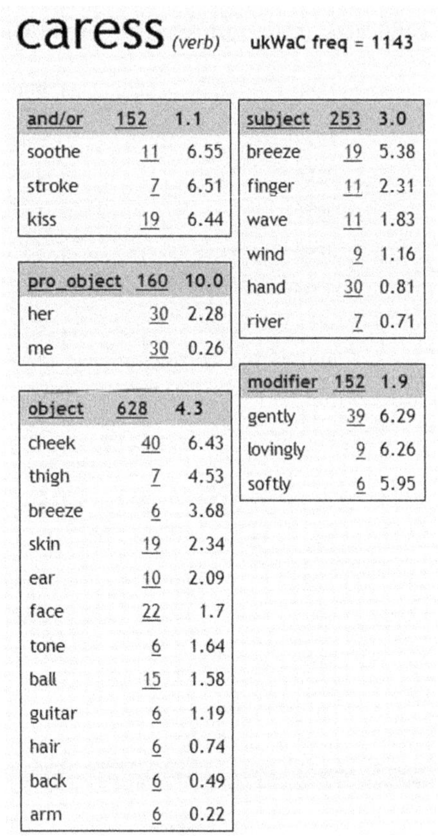

caress *(verb)*   ukWaC freq = 1143

and/or	152	1.1
soothe	11	6.55
stroke	7	6.51
kiss	19	6.44

pro_object	160	10.0
her	30	2.28
me	30	0.26

object	628	4.3
cheek	40	6.43
thigh	7	4.53
breeze	6	3.68
skin	19	2.34
ear	10	2.09
face	22	1.7
tone	6	1.64
ball	15	1.58
guitar	6	1.19
hair	6	0.74
back	6	0.49
arm	6	0.22

subject	253	3.0
breeze	19	5.38
finger	11	2.31
wave	11	1.83
wind	9	1.16
hand	30	0.81
river	7	0.71

modifier	152	1.9
gently	39	6.29
lovingly	9	6.26
softly	6	5.95

FIGURE 3.5 Word sketch of the verb *caress* in the ukWaC corpus.

file, planet). In order to identify grammatical relations between words, the corpus has to be parsed.

Corpus features combining collocation and grammar are Sketch Engine's 'word sketches'.[8] Word sketches are defined as "one-page automatic, corpus-based summaries of a word's grammatical and collocational behaviour" (Kilgarriff *et al.* 2004: 105). Figure 3.5 shows the word sketch for the verb *caress* in the ukWaC corpus (Ferraresi *et al.* 2008), which offers the lexicographer the most salient collocates that occur as the object, subject, modifier, or in the 'and/or' relation to *caress*.

Word sketches were first used for the *Macmillan English Dictionary* (Kilgarriff and Rundell 2002). Atkins and Rundell (2008: 107–11) saw word sketches as a type of lexical profiling, and they have become the preferred starting point for lexicographers analysing complex headwords.

---

[8] A similar feature is also provided by the DeepDict Lexifier tool (Bick 2009).

For word sketches to be built, the system must be told what the grammatical relations are for the language, and where in the corpus they are instantiated. There are two ways to do this. The input corpus may already be parsed, with grammatical relations given in the input corpus. However, such a corpus is only occasionally available. The other way is to define the grammatical relations, and parse the corpus, within the tool. To do this, the input corpus must be POS-tagged. Then each grammatical relation is defined as a regular expression over POS-tags, using corpus query language. The CQL expressions are used to parse the corpus, giving a database of -tuples such as *<subject, caress, breeze, 14566778>* where *subject* is a grammatical relation holding between the verb *caress* and the noun *breeze* at corpus reference point (for *caress*) 14566778. Word sketches are generated at run-time from the -tuples database. Parsing is done at compile time, and the results are stored, so users do not have to wait. The accuracy of the process is discussed and evaluated in Kilgarriff *et al.* (2010a).

A list of collocates is sometimes directly transferred, by the lexicographer, from the corpus tool to the dictionary entry, as shown in Figure 3.6. In the Macmillan English Dictionary Online, the box 'Collocations: result', for example, lists verbs that take *result,* in dictionary sense 3, as an object, as identified within the Sketch Engine.

Thesaurus   The thesaurus feature provides a list of "nearest neighbours" (Kilgarriff *et al.* 2004: 113) for the word. Nearest neighbours are those that 'share most collocates' with their node word: if we have encountered *<subject, caress, breeze>* and *<subject, caress, wind>* then *breeze* and *wind* share a collocate: the process of generating the thesaurus is one of finding, for each word, which other words it shares collocates with (and weighting the shared items; see Rychly and Kilgarriff 2007). The thesaurus provides a lexicographer with a list of potential (near)synonyms (and, in some cases, antonyms). For example, the thesaurus output of the ten nearest neighbours of the adjective *handsome* (1,578 occurrences in the BNC), as shown in Table 3.5, contains

---

3   [COUNTABLE] [OFTEN PLURAL] a piece of information that is obtained by examining, studying, or calculating something

Our results show that an effective vaccine is feasible.

result of: *The results of the survey will be published shortly.*

🔳 Thesaurus entry for this meaning of result

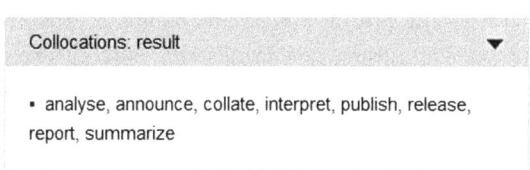

FIGURE 3.6 *Macmillan English Dictionary*'s online entry for the noun *result,* collocation box under sense 3.

TABLE 3.5. **Ten nearest neighbours for** *handsome* **offered by Thesaurus**

lemma	similarity score
good-looking	0.27
elegant	0.24
charming	0.24
beautiful	0.23
pretty	0.23
tall	0.22
lovely	0.20
attractive	0.20
clever	0.19
slim	0.19

several synonym candidates, such as *good-looking, beautiful, pretty, lovely,* and *attractive.*

Sketchdiffs   Sketch differences or 'sketchdiffs' compare word sketches for the two words, showing the collocations that they have in common and those they do not. Figure 3.7 shows the sketch difference for the adjectives *handsome* and *attractive* in ukWaC. The collocates *particularly, quite, extremely, so, very, really,* and *as* (highlighted in shades of red in the Sketch Engine) are more typical modifiers of *attractive*; *strikingly* and *devastatingly* (highlighted in green in the Sketch Engine), are more typical of *handsome*, while the remaining collocates in this relation show similar salience with both *handsome* and *attractive.*

The thesaurus and sketchdiff are linked. Clicking on a lemma in a thesaurus entry automatically opens the sketch difference comparing the original lemma with the one found in the thesaurus entry. Thesaurus and sketchdiffs were used extensively in compiling the *Oxford Learner's Thesaurus—a dictionary of synonyms* (Lea 2008).

3.4.3 *Good Dictionary EXamples (GDEX)*

Good dictionary examples are hard to find; lexicographers have often invented, rather than found, them but that runs the risk of accidentally failing to provide a natural context for the expression being illustrated (see Hanks, this volume). Sketch Engine's GDEX attempts to automatically sort the sentences in a concordance according to how likely they are to be good dictionary examples (Kilgarriff *et al.* 2008). GDEX operates as an option for sorting a concordance: when it is on, the 'best' examples will be the ones that the user sees first, at the top of the concordance. GDEX scores sentences using heuristics for readability and informativeness. Readability

handsome/attractive ukWaC freq = 10572/55372

Common patterns

| handsome | 6.0 | 4.0 | 2.0 | 0 | -2.0 | -4.0 | -6.0 | attractive |

and/or	3753	15021	3.2	2.1
comfortable	11	171	2.4	6.2
friendly	8	82	1.3	4.5
bright	11	105	2.2	5.3
healthy	11	74	2.0	4.6
convenient	11	85	3.3	5.9
Very	7	39	3.1	5.1
modern	52	204	3.0	4.9
wooden	15	52	3.4	4.9
slim	9	41	4.6	5.8
elegant	12	39	4.0	5.2
neat	11	37	4.2	5.3
Victorian	28	67	4.5	5.4
spacious	36	99	5.6	6.5
sexy	7	21	4.1	4.8
smart	12	23	3.7	4.2
intelligent	34	55	5.1	5.3
Georgian	23	39	5.9	5.8

modifier	1521	10048	2.2	2.4
particularly	23	983	2.3	7.6
quite	26	197	2.0	4.8
extremely	45	351	3.8	6.7
so	90	521	1.8	4.4
very	651	3524	4.2	6.6
really	24	119	0.7	3.0
as	73	322	1.6	3.7
too	17	65	0.6	2.5
rather	50	154	3.6	5.1
pretty	7	18	1.7	2.9
exceptionally	11	40	4.9	6.0
truly	9	18	2.1	2.9
incredibly	14	21	4.5	4.6
stunningly	11	41	6.8	6.8
remarkably	15	7	5.4	3.5
strikingly	31	20	8.1	5.7
devastatingly	12	8	7.7	4.7

pp_in-i	83	484	0.4	0.4
appearance	8	18	1.1	2.3
adj_comp_of	722	9349	3.8	8.2
look	94	636	2.5	5.3

FIGURE 3.7 Sketch difference for the adjectives *handsome* and *attractive*.

heuristics include sentence length and average word length, and penalize sentences with infrequent words, more than one or two non-a–z characters, or anaphora. Informativeness heuristics include favouring sentences containing words that are frequently found in the vicinity of the expression: it is likely that they are typical collocates of the expression. GDEX was first used in the preparation of an electronic version of the *Macmillan English Dictionary* (2nd edition, 2007).

GDEX was designed for English, so several heuristics are specific to the English language (e.g. a classifier that penalizes multi-sense words, based on the number of Wordnet synsets the word belongs to; see also Kosem *et al.* 2011) or were included with the needs of a specific group of dictionary users in mind (e.g. advanced learners of English). The usefulness of GDEX for other languages is more limited. This has been confirmed by experience when using it to produce a new lexical database of Slovene in the 'Communication in Slovene' project,[9] where the examples offered first by GDEX were rarely found to be useful to lexicographers. Infrastructure for customizing GDEX has recently been completed, and Slovene and other GDEXes are currently under development.

[9] www.slovenscina.eu.

3.4.4 *Why we still need lexicographers*

No matter how many features are used to summarize the data, the lexicographer still needs to critically review the summary to determine the meaning of each word. Concordances should always be available to check the validity of results: there are many stages in the process where anomalies and errors might arise, from the source data, or in its preparation, lemmatization, or parsing. It ought to be easy for the lexicographer to check the data underlying an analysis, to check for instances where the analysis does not immediately tally with their intuition.

One recurring area of difficulty, in all the languages for which we have been involved in lexicography—two recent examples being Polish and Estonian—is participles/gerunds. In English, most *-ed* forms can be verb past tenses or past participles, or adjectival, and *-ing* forms can be verbal, adjective, or gerunds; comparable distinctions apply to most European languages. In theory, it may be possible to distinguish the form (verbal participle) from the function (verbal, adjectival, or nominal) but the theory still leaves the lexicographer with a judgement to make: should the *-ing* form get a noun entry, or should the *-ed* form get an adjective entry? POS-taggers are stuck with the same quandary: Where they encounter an *-ing* form, should they treat it as part of the verb lemma, as an adjective, or as a noun?

The problem has two parts: some syntactic contexts unambiguously reveal the function (*the painting is beautiful; he was painting the wall*) but many do not (*I like painting; the painting school*). But this is only the first problem. The second problem is that some gerunds and participial adjectives are lexicalized, deserving their own entry in the dictionary, and others are not: thus we can have *the manoeuvring is beautiful* and there is no question that *manoeuvring* is functioning as a noun, but there is also no question that it is not lexicalized and does not need its own dictionary entry. The upshot is that many word sketches contain verb lemmas which would ideally not be there, because they are the result of lemmatization of adjectival participles and gerunds, which should have been treated as adjective and noun lemmas in their own right.

3.5 Developing corpus tools to meet lexicographers' needs

Lexicographers are demanding corpus users; they soon come to understand the potential of corpora, and expect a wide range of features. Initially, not a great deal of thought was given to the actual look and user-friendliness of the interface— functionality and speed were considered more important. But with the regular use of corpus tools, more time has to be spent on devising interfaces that are friendly to the lexicographers who use them on a daily basis. Training lexicographers in how to analyse data is already time-consuming, and a user-friendly interface helps them focus on the analysis.

3.5.1 *User-friendliness*

A comparison of older tools with modern ones testifies to progress in user-friendliness. Conducting searches no longer requires typing in complex commands. Corpus tools have become more Google-like, where the users write the search term in the box, specify the search (often using a drop-down menu) if they want to, and promptly get what they want (see Verlinde and Peeters, this volume).

Another difference is in the use of colour. Black and white are no longer the only options, and modern tools use colour highlighting to aid navigation in the output and/or to separate different types of information. For example, sketchdiff uses green for collocates more strongly associated with the first lemma, and red for those more strongly associated with the second, with the strength of colour indicating the strength of the tendency.

Some corpus tools also offer graphical representations of numerical data. Graphical representation often helps lexicographers quickly identify usage-related information, for example an increase or decrease in the use of a word or phrase over a period of time (see Figure 3.3), predominant use of the word in a certain domain, register, etc., typical use of the word in a specific form (e.g. when a noun occurs mainly in the plural form), and so forth.

Lexicographers have different preferences and use different equipment, such as computer screens of different sizes, so customizability is part of user-friendliness. An example of a basic customizable feature is adjustable font size. With online corpus tools, font size can also be changed in the settings of the Internet browser.

Many corpus tools also offer the option to change the concordance output, in terms of how much data is displayed (e.g. the number of concordance lines per page, the amount of context shown), and which type of data is displayed, e.g. attributes of the searched item (word form, lemma, POS-tag, etc.) and structure tags (document, paragraph, and sentence markers). A form of customization requiring deeper understanding is control of the word sketches by changing parameters such as the minimum frequency of the collocate in the corpus, or the maximum number of displayed items. The Sketch Engine also provides 'more data' and 'less data' buttons to make the word sketches bigger or smaller.

Recent developments relating to character sets have been a great boon for corpus developers and lexicographers. Not so long ago, the rendition of the character set for each new language, particularly non-Latin ones, would have been a large and time-consuming task. Now, with the Unicode standards and associated developments in character encoding methods, operating systems, and browsers, these problems have largely been solved, and well-engineered modern corpus tools can work with any of the world's writing systems with very little extra effort. The Sketch Engine, for example, correctly displays corpora for Arabic, Chinese, Greek, Hindi, Japanese, Korean, Russian, Thai, and Vietnamese, amongst others.

A related issue is the interface language. Chinese lexicographers working on Chinese, or Danes working on Danish, do not want an English-language interface. This has doubtless contributed to various institutions developing their own tools. The Sketch Engine is localizable, and the interface is currently available in Chinese, Czech, English, French, and Irish.

3.5.2 *Integration of features*

Because the number of features offered by corpus tools is increasing, it is useful and time-saving if the features are integrated. The lexicographer looking at a list of collocates is likely to want to check their concordance lines. If the collocation and the concordance features are integrated, the user can move between the two with a mouse-click.

Another time-saving technique that may help lexicographers in the future would be to combine two features into one. An example of this can be found in the online tool for Gigafida, a 1.18-billion-word corpus of Slovene (which targets lay users and not lexicographers), where the filters are offered in the menu to the left of the concordance output (see Figure 3.8) and enable the user to filter concordance lines by basic forms, text type, source, and other categories. They also provide frequency information for each available category in the filter (filter categories with zero concordance lines are not shown), ordering categories by frequency.

3.5.3 *Integration of tools*

A corpus tool is not the only piece of software a lexicographer needs to master. There is always at least one other tool, the dictionary writing system (see Abel, this volume). Lexicographic work often involves transferring corpus data to the dictionary data-base, and time and effort can be saved if the transfer is efficient. Copy-and-paste is possible in some cases, but the information often needs to be in a specific format (normally XML) for the dictionary writing system to read it. This issue is addressed by the Sketch Engine's 'TickBox Lexicography'.

TickBox Lexicography (TBL) allows lexicographers to select collocates from the word sketch, select examples of collocates from a list of (good) candidates, and export the selected examples into the dictionary writing system (see Figures 3.9 and 3.10). An XML template, customized to the requirements of the dictionary being prepared, is needed for the data to be exported in the format compatible with the dictionary writing system. Lexicographers do not need to think about XML: from their perspective, it is a simple matter of copy-and-paste.

Another option is to combine a corpus tool and a dictionary writing system in a single program, so that lexicographers use the same interface to search the corpus and write dictionary entries. Such software is already available, namely the TLex

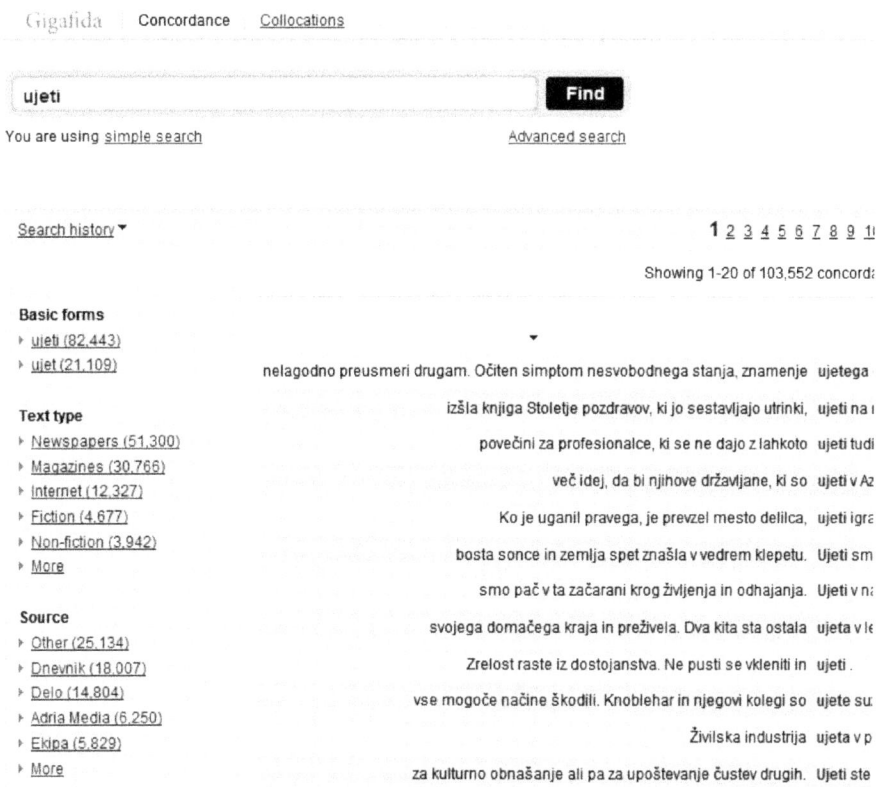

FIGURE 3.8 Available filters to query the Gigafida corpus.

Dictionary Production System (Joffe and De Schryver 2004a), as reviewed by Abel (this volume).

3.5.4 *Project customization*

A certain feature often needs to be customized to the requirements of a particular dictionary project. A critical concern at the Institute for Dutch Lexicology (INL) was bibliographical references: in the *ANW* (a Dictionary of Contemporary Dutch, in preparation), each example sentence was accompanied by its bibliographical details. These were available to the corpus system. However, the time it took to type, or copy-and-paste, all those details into the appropriate fields in the dictionary writing system was severely limiting the numbers of examples the lexicographers were using, and putting the whole schedule of the project at risk. The Sketch Engine team was able to customize the TBL machinery to provide a 'special copy-and-paste' option which automatically gathered together the bibliographic data for a sentence that the

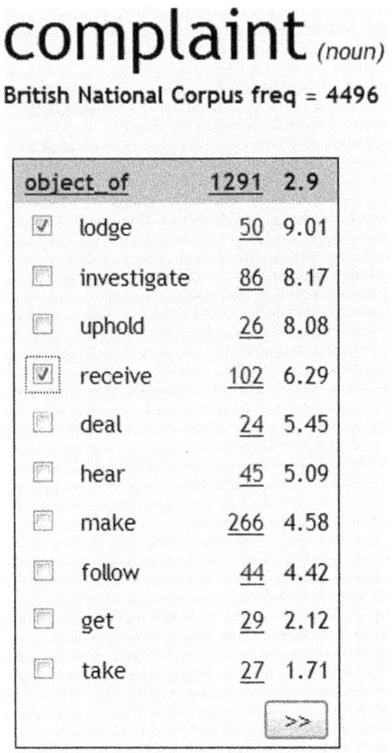

complaint *(noun)*

British National Corpus freq = 4496

object_of		1291	2.9
☑	lodge	<u>50</u>	9.01
☐	investigate	<u>86</u>	8.17
☐	uphold	<u>26</u>	8.08
☑	receive	<u>102</u>	6.29
☐	deal	<u>24</u>	5.45
☐	hear	<u>45</u>	5.09
☐	make	<u>266</u>	4.58
☐	follow	<u>44</u>	4.42
☐	get	<u>29</u>	2.12
☐	take	<u>27</u>	1.71
		>>	

FIGURE 3.9 TickBox Lexicography: selecting collocates.

lexicographer had selected, and, on pasting, inserted the 'example', 'author', 'title', 'year', and 'publisher' into the appropriate fields of the dictionary writing system.

Implementing a customized version of TBL does not require any changes to the corpus interface, but adding a new feature does. This is evident in the *Pattern Dictionary of English Verbs* (Hanks and Pustejovsky 2005, Hanks 2008, this volume) where lexicographers are using an enhanced version of the Sketch Engine, designed specifically for the project to annotate concordance lines of the verb with the number of the associated pattern in the database entry (Figure 3.11). In addition, the dictionary database is linked to the Sketch Engine, so that the users can view all the concordance lines associated with a pattern with a single click.

The relationship between the lexicographers working on a dictionary project, and the developers of the corpus tool used in the project is cyclical. Lexicographers benefit from the functionality of the corpus tools, and, since they are regular users of the tool and most of its features, provide feedback for the developers. This often results in further improvements to the tool, which again benefits lexicographers (as well as other users of the tool).

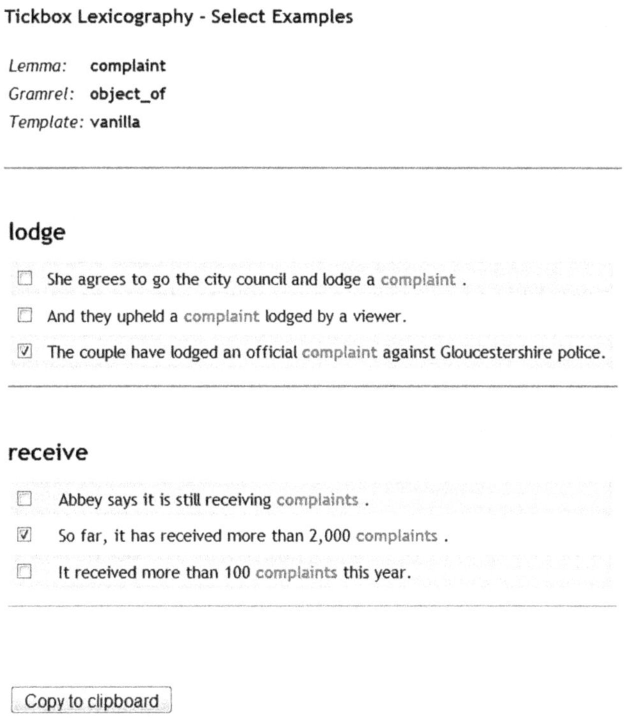

Tickbox Lexicography - Select Examples

Lemma: **complaint**
Gramrel: **object_of**
Template: **vanilla**

lodge

☐ She agrees to go the city council and lodge a complaint .

☐ And they upheld a complaint lodged by a viewer.

☑ The couple have lodged an official complaint against Gloucestershire police.

receive

☐ Abbey says it is still receiving complaints .

☑ So far, it has received more than 2,000 complaints .

☐ It received more than 100 complaints this year.

[Copy to clipboard]

FIGURE 3.10 TickBox Lexicography: selecting examples for export.

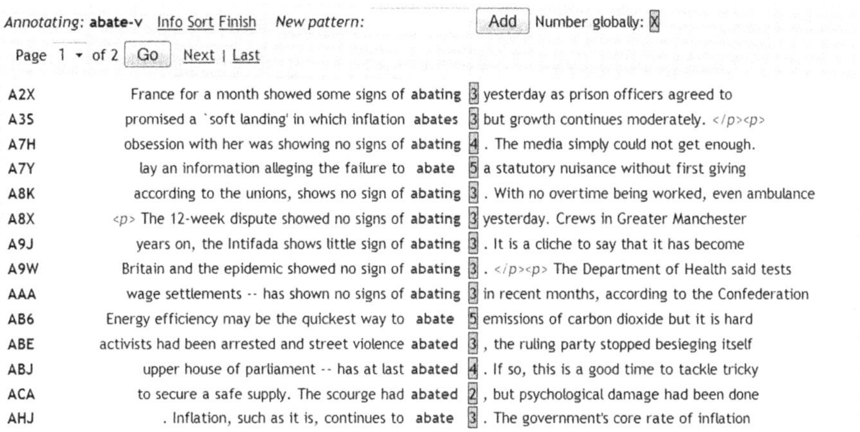

Annotating: **abate-v** Info Sort Finish   *New pattern:*   [Add] Number globally: ☒

Page 1 ▾ of 2 [Go] Next | Last

A2X	France for a month showed some signs of **abating**	3 yesterday as prison officers agreed to
A3S	promised a 'soft landing' in which inflation **abates**	3 but growth continues moderately. `</p><p>`
A7H	obsession with her was showing no signs of **abating**	4 . The media simply could not get enough.
A7Y	lay an information alleging the failure to **abate**	5 a statutory nuisance without first giving
A8K	according to the unions, shows no sign of **abating**	3 . With no overtime being worked, even ambulance
A8X	`<p>` The 12-week dispute showed no signs of **abating**	3 yesterday. Crews in Greater Manchester
A9J	years on, the Intifada shows little sign of **abating**	3 . It is a cliche to say that it has become
A9W	Britain and the epidemic showed no sign of **abating**	3 . `</p><p>` The Department of Health said tests
AAA	wage settlements -- has shown no signs of **abating**	3 in recent months, according to the Confederation
AB6	Energy efficiency may be the quickest way to **abate**	5 emissions of carbon dioxide but it is hard
ABE	activists had been arrested and street violence **abated**	3 , the ruling party stopped besieging itself
ABJ	upper house of parliament -- has at last **abated**	4 . If so, this is a good time to tackle tricky
ACA	to secure a safe supply. The scourge had **abated**	2 , but psychological damage had been done
AHJ	. Inflation, such as it is, continues to **abate**	3 . The government's core rate of inflation

FIGURE 3.11 Corpus Pattern Analysis version of the Sketch Engine: annotated concordance lines for the verb *abate*.

3.6 Conclusion

People writing dictionaries have a greater and more pressing need for a corpus than most other linguists, and have long been in the forefront of corpus development. From the Bank of English corpus (used in the COBUILD project), to the BNC, the largest corpora were built and used for lexicographic (as well as for natural language processing) purposes. Building large corpora is no longer problematic as many texts are readily available in electronic form on the Internet. But precisely because corpora have got larger and larger, it has become more important than ever that lexicographers have corpus tools with summarization features at their disposal.

This chapter has shown that the functionality and user-friendliness of corpus tools have improved considerably since they were first used in dictionary projects. Today's corpus tools are faster and more diverse on the one hand, but easier to use on the other. The needs of lexicographers have also prompted the creation of features such as TickBox Lexicography, which ease the exporting of corpus information into the dictionary writing system. Lexicographically-oriented features are also being used by linguists, teachers, and others, which indicates that the distinction between lexicographic corpus tools and linguistic corpus tools is blurred.

There is, however, still more work to be done in terms of making corpus tools as useful to lexicographers as possible. This includes coming up with more features that bridge the gap between raw corpus data and the dictionary. One strategy is to establish closer links between a corpus tool and a dictionary writing system, incorporating more features like TickBox Lexicography which support seamless data transfer. Currently, most of the focus is on examples; definitions are written in the dictionary writing system, which means that the lexicographer may need to switch between corpus tool and dictionary writing system quite often. Corpus tools of the future should perhaps offer a more complete solution, e.g. allowing the lexicographer to mark examples, devise a draft definition (in a pop-up window) and any other part of the meaning in the corpus tool, and only then export it into the dictionary entry.

Corpora and associated software do more and more by way of summarizing the information to be found about a word or phrase. A question worth asking then is: Will corpus tools reach a point where they act as dictionaries? The idea does not seem too far-fetched. There is already research showing that definitions of words can be extracted directly from corpora (Pearson 1996, 1998). In addition, GDEX incorporates a feature that helps identify good dictionary examples. Nonetheless, as Rundell and Kilgarriff (2011) point out, providing the users with automatically extracted corpus data, rather than data in a traditional dictionary format, may pose problems for some types of users, for example language learners. The position we take is this: lexicographers are better at preparing brief, user-friendly accounts of a word's meaning and behaviour than automatic tools—but they do not cover everything (just as no dictionary covers all new and obscure words, specialized uses, contextually appropriate collocations, etc.). Where a user wants to find something out, it is most convenient if the information can be found in a dictionary; but if the dictionary does not meet their needs, then, of course, yes, they should turn to the corpus.

Dictionaries

Rundell, Michael (ed.) (2002). *Macmillan English Dictionary for Advanced Learners*, First Edition. London: Macmillan.

Rundell, Michael (ed.) (2007). *Macmillan English Dictionary for Advanced Learners*, Second Edition. London: Macmillan.

4

Corpus evidence and electronic lexicography

PATRICK HANKS

4.1 Introduction

This chapter starts by identifying different traditions of lexicography and examining the impact that corpus evidence, i.e. electronic evidence of the way words are actually used, has had, is having, and will most probably continue to have. Electronic lexicography opens up all sorts of radical possibilities that were closed to traditional lexicography: new kinds of evidence, new modes of description, new ways of organizing evidence, new possibilities for exploiting database structure and hypertext links, and the need for new theoretical foundations. Most important among these new possibilities, from a practical lexicographical point of view, is the opportunity to build hypertext databases showing explicit links between word senses and patterns of actual word use. Allied to this are opportunities to study the situations or 'frames' in which words are actually used. These and other opportunities offered by electronic lexicography raise interesting issues at both a practical and a theoretical level.

The space constraint of the printed book has been removed by the Internet—but so has the commercial incentive to manufacture dictionaries as physical objects for sale to users. At present, lexicography is in transition: publishers, nervous about future commercial prospects, are wary of investing in large-scale innovations, just at a time when such innovations are most needed. At the same time, funding agencies and their advisers have not yet been convinced that major innovations such as FrameNet and Corpus Pattern Analysis would justify the large-scale research investments that would be needed to bring them to completion and yield practical benefits.

In this chapter at least, optimism must prevail. Let us assume that somehow, somewhen, the need for major lexicographical initiatives will be recognized and will be funded—even though, in the age of the Internet, the deliverables are unlikely to be in the form of traditional printed books. So the chapter continues by asking what needs to be done and concludes by suggesting a context in which it might be done.

4.2 Four traditions of lexicography

We may distinguish four different traditions in lexicography, each of which is affected in different ways by the advent of corpus linguistics and the Internet. In the first place, there are large historical dictionaries, whose purpose is to record and preserve the words of a culture, including words and meanings that are no longer used, and to record their origins and changes. Second, there are dictionaries that give enhanced access to the whole vocabulary and cultural assumptions of a language, including for example the meaning of scientific terminology, technical terms in fields as diverse as manufacturing, marketing, and sport, and even proper names that serve as shared reference points in a culture. Third, there are bilingual dictionaries, which are aimed at helping speakers of one language to access and use the words of another language; and finally, there are pedagogical dictionaries, designed to help people struggling to learn a new language. There is, of course, some overlap between categories.

4.2.1 *Scholarly dictionaries on historical principles*

Traditionally, the task of lexicography was seen, at least among scholars and literati, as being to compile an inventory of all the words in a given language and to trace their origins and their semantic development. Samuel Johnson (1755), in his famous definition of a lexicographer as "a harmless drudge", saw the task of the lexicographer as being not only "detailing the signification of words", but also "tracing the original [of words]" [my emphasis]. From Johnson's day up until very recently, it was assumed that origins determine meaning. That is to say, if a word changes its meaning over time, it was assumed that the older meaning was somehow more correct than any more recent development. This was an underlying assumption for three hundred years, and it influenced (among others) the Philological Society during their deliberations in the 1850s, which led to the foundation of "a New English Dictionary on Historical Principles" [my emphasis again], later to become better known as the *Oxford English Dictionary* (*OED*). The currently ongoing magnificent blend of scholarship and technology that is creating the third edition of *OED* (*OED3*), seeks to elaborate rather than challenge the basic historical principles and philosophical assumptions of the Philological Society and in particular of James Murray, first editor of the first edition of *OED*, during the nineteenth century. *OED3* is an exemplary online historical lexicographical product, with the results of lexical research being made available more or less immediately, rather than years later on completion of the whole book. It is no longer constrained by the requirement to work in alphabetical order. However, quite rightly, it does not seek to make radical alterations to the received nineteenth-century model of scholarly lexicography.

Dictionaries on historical principles play an important integrative social role in a culture, *sub specie aeternitatis*, not least in explaining the changes of meaning that so many words in all modern languages have undergone. Roots are culturally important and scholars and literati need to know about them. However, knowing about roots is not the same as knowing about meaning. Dictionaries in a single volume aimed at practical users among the general public are a different matter. Is it truly helpful to a general user to be told that sense 1 of *camera* is "a small vaulted room", and in particular "the treasury of the papal curia"? It is a matter for astonishment that throughout the twentieth century many one-volume monolingual English dictionaries arranged their senses in historical order, and this practice persists to this day in America's favourite dictionary (the Merriam-Webster Collegiate series). It would seem that, unless you already know what a word means in contemporary English, you cannot use such a dictionary with confidence to discover its meaning.

4.2.2 *Dictionaries of current usage for native speakers*

Recognition that people might want to use a dictionary to find out what words mean, rather than where they came from, was slow to establish itself in the face of blind reverence for erudition. Funk and Wagnall's *Standard Dictionary of the English Language* (1894–97) was the first large-scale dictionary to deliberately reject historical principles and instead record the current meaning of words, followed eventually by the *American College Dictionary* (1947), the *American Heritage Dictionary* (1968), and, in Britain, by the *Hamlyn Encyclopedic World Dictionary* (1971) and *Collins English Dictionary* (1979). However, the lexicographers working on these dictionaries, attempting to follow synchronic semantic principles, ran into a difficulty. For each entry for a polysemous word, the aim was to place the most common meaning first. But in the absence of large bodies of evidence, how were they to identify the most common meaning? This problem is particularly acute for light verbs such as *take* and *bear*, but it affects many less common words as well, such as *launch*, *spoil*, and *dope* (to mention just three of many hundreds of examples that could be given). And when very large bodies of evidence did eventually become available, for example the British National Corpus (BNC) and the Bank of English, there were some surprises in store. Our intuitions as native speakers about normal and most frequent senses of words turned out to be unreliable. Social salience (i.e. the most frequent sense or use of a word) and cognitive salience (memorability, or rather ease of recall) are independent variables (see Hanks 1990, 2010).

4.2.3 *Bilingual dictionaries*

At least since Colin Smith's *Collins Spanish–English Dictionary* of 1971 and the *Collins–Robert French–English Dictionary* by Beryl T. (Sue) Atkins and Alain Duval (1978), bilingual lexicographers have attempted to give practical implementation to the long-recognized fact that aiming at literal word-for-word translation between languages is a naive goal that leads to errors—often, ludicrous errors. Such lexicographers have paid increasing attention to phraseology. Their purpose in doing this was not to explore the relationship between word meaning and word use at a theoretical level, but rather to offer realizations in another language for phraseology that cannot be translated literally, word for word. To do this, Atkins, Duval, and their colleagues compiled large 'frameworks' consisting of typical phraseology for each word in each language. These frameworks were based on wide reading and introspection. Lexicographers then worked in pairs (each pair consisting of a native speaker of each language) to establish idiomatic and pragmatic equivalents in the target language for the phrases in the source-language framework. In this heroic endeavour, they were hampered by lack of evidence. What exactly are the typical phrases associated with each word in a particular language? Corpus evidence, as we shall see, was to provide at least a partial solution to this problem.

4.2.4 *Dictionaries for foreign learners*

A fourth, equally important lexicographic tradition began in 1942 with the publication in Japan of A. S. Hornby's pioneering *Idiomatic and Syntactic English Dictionary* (*ISED*, 1942, re-published without alteration in 1948 by Oxford University Press as the *Advanced Learner's Dictionary*). It was not until 1978 that a serious rival to this wonderful dictionary (by now greatly expanded and re-named *The Oxford Advanced Learners' Dictionary of Current English*, *OALDCE*) appeared: this was the *Longman Dictionary of Contemporary English* (*LDOCE*). Hornby's original aim had been to create a work that would help learners to use the syntactic patterns and idiomatic phraseology of English with reasonable accuracy when writing and speaking. In other words, *ISED* was intended as an aid for language production ('encoding' language) and would ignore words needed only for 'decoding' purposes (i.e. reading skills). Hornby also devised a system of verb patterns reflecting actual usage. These have been superseded now, but in their day they provided revolutionary insight into verb valency in English. Until the corpus revolution of the 1980s and 1990s, they stood the test of time remarkably well, and they must have helped literally millions of learners of English worldwide during the mid twentieth century. The evidence upon which they were based consisted largely of introspection by Hornby and his colleagues.

In the second and subsequent editions of *OALDCE*, this purely productive aim was watered down. Hornby and his successors found it impossible to resist the criticism that a dictionary ought to explain words that learners would be likely to encounter during their reading and listening activities in English, as well as words that they would actually use. Thus, many thousands of words were added to the second and subsequent editions—words presenting no serious difficulty in their idiomatic and syntagmatic behaviour: words that learners might be unfamiliar with (and for which they would therefore turn to a dictionary for an explanation) but would be unlikely ever to use in their spoken and written use of English. It was this dual aim—decoding as well as encoding—with which *LDOCE* and subsequent English learners' dictionaries set themselves the task of competing. Later dictionaries such as *COBUILD*, *CIDE* (*Cambridge International Dictionary of English*; subsequently re-titled *CALD* (*Cambridge Advanced Learners Dictionary*)), and *MEDAL* (*Macmillan English Dictionary for Advanced Learners*) were to enlist the assistance of corpus data in pursuance of this dual aim.

4.3 The impact of corpora on lexicography

The impact of corpus evidence on lexicography is described more fully in Hanks (2009) and explored in several chapters in this volume. Early electronic corpora (e.g. the Brown Corpus and its British counterpart, viz. the Lancaster–Oslo–Bergen Corpus) had little impact on lexicography, despite being consulted by major dictionaries (in particular, the *American Heritage Dictionary* (first edition 1968) and the *Longman Dictionary of Contemporary English* (*LDOCE*; first edition 1978) respectively). The reason was simple: these were each corpora of only one million words—corpora so small that it was impossible to distinguish statistically significant co-occurrences of words from chance co-occurrences. This implies that in order to discover and organize word meanings, it is necessary to study textual evidence in very large quantities and in particular patterns of collocations. This hypothesis is one that was first proposed by J. R. Firth (1957a, 1957b) and was developed by the late John Sinclair from his earliest, prophetic published work (Sinclair 1966) to his posthumously published essay entitled 'Defining the Definiendum' (Sinclair 2010). His life's work was largely devoted to the development of a theory of language and meaning based on the empirical investigation of the collocational preferences of words. In Sinclair (1987: 151–2), he asked:

How common are the phrasal verbs with *set*? *Set* is particularly rich in making combinations with words like *about, in, up, out, on, off*, and these words are themselves very common. How likely is *set off* to occur? Both are frequent words; [*set* occurs approximately 250 times in a million words and] *off* occurs approximately 556 times in a million words [...] The question we are asking can be roughly rephrased as follows: how likely is *off* to occur immediately after *set*? [...] This is 0.00025 × 0.00055, which gives us the tiny figure of 0.0000001375.

[...] The assumption behind this calculation is that the words are distributed at random in a text. It is obvious to a linguist that this is not so, and a rough measure of how much *set* and *off* attract each other is to compare the probability with what actually happens.

[...] *Set off* occurs nearly 70 times in the 7.3 million word corpus. That is enough to show its main patterning and it suggests that in currently-held corpora there will be found sufficient evidence for the description of a substantial collection of phrases.

The first fruits of the Sinclairian approach to corpus-driven lexicography emerged with the first edition of the *COBUILD* dictionary (1987), based on an initial corpus of approximately 7.3 million words, which by the time of publication had grown to eighteen million words—just large enough for the main patterns of collocation associated with each word to be perceived through what J. R. Firth (1950) had called "the mush of general goings-on":

We must separate from the mush of general goings-on those features of repeated events which appear to be part of a patterned process.

Sinclair devoted a substantial part of his life to developing the empirical study of collocations in corpora.[1]

Thus, the first major impact of corpora on lexicography was on a dictionary for foreign learners, namely *COBUILD*. Subsequent newly compiled learners' dictionaries (Cambridge, Macmillan) were also corpus-based, though none were corpus-driven in the way that *COBUILD* was. In due course complete recensions of the leading English dictionaries for foreign learners, *OALDCE* and *LDOCE*, were prepared on the basis of corpus evidence, though for marketing reasons the distinction between a dictionary as an encoding aid and as a decoding aid came to be fudged by the publishers and hence by the lexicographers. Comparing entries in pre-corpus editions of *OALDCE* and *LDOCE* with entries for the same words in post-corpus editions of the same dictionaries and in *COBUILD* and other corpus-driven dictionaries reveals that corpus-based dictionaries—even dictionaries based on different corpora—have tended to converge in what they say about the language, compared with pre-corpus dictionaries, as described for example in Atkins and Levin (1991).

Subsequently, the one-volume *New Oxford Dictionary of English* (1998; subsequently rechristened the *Oxford Dictionary of English*, *ODE*, 2001) made extensive use of corpus evidence to compile a brand-new account of contemporary English for use by native speakers. To date, *ODE* is the only monolingual dictionary of English for native speakers to be corpus-based. The *New Oxford American Dictionary* is an Americanization of it. For some languages, e.g. French, there is no major corpus-based dictionary at all. In other languages, the situation is rather different: for

---

[1] A special issue of the *International Journal of Lexicography* (21(3), September 2008) was devoted to the intellectual legacy of John Sinclair from a variety of lexical viewpoints.

example, major corpus-based dictionaries of languages as different as Danish, Modern Greek, and Malay have been published.

The impact of corpus data on synchronic lexicography since 1987 (the date of publication of *COBUILD*) has been overwhelming. At last lexicographers have sufficient evidence to make the generalizations that they need to make with reasonable confidence. We can now see that pre-corpus lexicography was little more than a collection of stabs in the dark, often driven by historical rather than synchronic motives. In word after word, pre-corpus lexicographers (consulting their intuitions and a bundle of more or less unusual citations collected by citation readers) failed to achieve the right level of generalization when describing the conventions of present-day word meaning in a language, as can be seen by attempting to map the old definitions onto the new evidence. Of all the many possible uses and meanings that a word might have, lexicographers now have better chances of selecting the ones that are actually used and of writing reasonably accurate descriptive definitions of commonly used words.

Large corpora provide monolingual lexicographers with sufficient evidence to decide what to include and (more importantly) what to leave out. Corpus evidence also contributes to the never-ending tasks of improving the accuracy of explanations and identifying the pragmatic uses of words and phrases, which had been largely neglected in traditional dictionaries. Large corpora can be used as a basis for constructing reliable accounts of 'local grammar' or 'valency'—the syntagmatic structures in which each word is normally used (as opposed to speculations about how it might possibly be used). Above all, they enable analysts to identify and measure collocations—the preferences that words have for the company of certain other words. This is a subject that could not be studied empirically before large corpora became available, together with statistical techniques for the analysis of word associations (see Church and Hanks 1989, Kilgarriff 2005a).

Turning back now to bilingual dictionaries, a careful comparison of the *Collins–Robert French–English Dictionary* with the later *Oxford–Hachette French Dictionary* (Corréard and Grundy 1994), in which Atkins played a major role as an adviser, will give an indication of how corpus evidence can be used to refine and extend the 'framework' approach to bilingual lexicography. It should be borne in mind that in the early 1990s, corpus evidence was extremely scarce. Nevertheless, the Oxford–Hachette shows a more focused (but not larger) selection of phraseology than its Collins–Robert predecessor. An entry for a commonplace English word such as *day* includes not only an indication of the French semantic distinction, not made in English, between *jour* and *journée*, but also over eighty model phraseological equivalents, including:

the day before = *la veille*
to come on the wrong day = *se tromper de jour*

before the day was out = *avant la fin de la journée*
at close of day = *à la tombée du jour* [notice that in French the day falls, whereas in English it is only nights that fall]
it was a hot day = *il faisait chaud*
in his/her younger days = *dans sa jeunesse*
in those days = *à cette époque*

In the first and the last three examples given here, there is no French word at all that can be literally translated as 'day'. The meaning is conveyed by other means. The earlier *Collins–Robert French–English Dictionary* has a larger but less well-selected collection of phraseology. What distinguishes the very different selection of phraseology in the *Oxford–Hachette French Dictionary* is improved selectivity—that is, corpus evidence has enabled the lexicographers to select phraseology that is more frequently used and therefore more likely to be useful to users, rather than merely relying on introspection and guesswork. The lexicographical emphasis has shifted from the hopeless aim of covering all phraseological possibilities to the more realistic (and empirically well-founded) one of covering the most salient probabilities.

In the context of scholarly lexicography on historical principles, the impact of corpus evidence has so far been less dramatic. Such an impact may be expected when large historical corpora of language become available, enabling lexicographers to distinguish phraseology that seems unusual to us today because the norms of the language have changed from phraseology that was idiosyncratic to a particular writer, text, or small group of texts.

4.4 How will electronic monolingual lexicography of the future be different from traditional models?

Analysing word meaning in context is a skill that is still in its infancy. Many roads will be tried. In current monolingual dictionaries other than (up to a point) *CO-BUILD*, context has been very largely neglected or at best regarded as a sort of optional extra. In dictionaries of the future, contextualization and phraseology will come to take centre stage. These dictionaries will be electronic products with hypertext structures and links, not printed books, nor the 'horseless carriages' that now pass for electronic dictionaries.

An underlying theme running through what has been said so far in this chapter is that word meaning can only be described accurately if the word is put into context. Part of the lexicographical task required of a lexicographer using a large corpus is to select contexts that are maximally general (and therefore offer maximum predictive power about the word's meaning in future, unseen contexts), while at the same time preserving a sharp semantic focus. 'Context' here can have two, interrelated meanings: context of utterance (the real-world situation in which a word is uttered) and textual context ('co-text'; syntagmatic preferences for use within a certain syntactic structure along with the company of other words, i.e. significant valency and collocations). Let us look at two theoretical and practical approaches that focus on each of these.

4.4.1 *Semantic analysis based on context of utterance: Frame Semantics and FrameNet*

Charles Fillmore has made at least three important contributions to linguistic theory with a semantic component: Case Grammar, Frame Semantics, and Construction Grammar, each of which represents a plank in a possible bridge between syntax and lexical semantics. He has always evinced an interest in meaning as well as syntax, and he was one of the first linguists to recognize the importance of prototype theory (see, for example, Fillmore 1975). His interest in semantics is associated with analysis of the lexicon, and for many years, during the development of the FrameNet project,[2] he worked closely with the lexicographer Sue Atkins. He is one of the few American linguists to show awareness of European schools of linguistics. His published works cite major European theorists such as Tesnière, Maurice Gross, Trier, and Helbig, among others, as well as contemporary American linguists.

In the following few paragraphs, I shall try to summarize and critique Fillmore's Frame Semantics, from its source in Case Grammar to its practical realization in FrameNet. Frame Semantics originated in Case Grammar (Fillmore 1968), in which every verb is identified as selecting a certain number of basic cases, which form its '**case frame**'. For example:

give selects three cases: *Agent* (the person doing the giving), *Benefit* (the thing given), and *Beneficiary* (the person or entity that receives the Object);
go selects two cases: *Agent* and *Path* (more specifically, subdivided into *Source, Path, Goal*);
break selects three cases: *Agent, Patient* (the thing that gets broken), and *Instrument* (the object used to do the breaking, for example a hammer).

These cases may appear in different syntactic positions. Levin's (1993) examples ((1)–(2) below) show that the 'Patient' may appear both as the direct object of a causative verb and as the subject of the same verb used intransitively (inchoatively).

(1)   *Janet broke the cup.*
(2)   *The cup broke.*

In Frame Semantics, frames are conceptual structures involving a potentially large number of lexical items, not just individual meanings of individual words. Fillmore

---

[2] http://framenet.icsi.berkeley.edu/.

(1982) says that Frame Semantics "offers a particular way of looking at word meanings", but then immediately goes on to say:

By the term 'frame', I have in mind any system of concepts related in such a way that to understand any one of them you have to understand the whole structure in which it fits. [my emphasis]

Thus, the claim in Frame Semantics is that to understand the meaning of a word, you need access to all the essential knowledge that relates to it. For example, to understand *sell,* you need to know about the 'frame' of commercial transactions, with *Seller, Buyer, Goods* [alternatively, *Service*], and *Money*. You also have to know about relations between *Money* and *Goods*; between *Seller, Goods*, and *Money*; between *Buyer, Goods*, and *Money*; and so on. According to Fillmore and Atkins (1992):

A word's meaning can be understood only with reference to a structured background of experience, beliefs, or practices, constituting a kind of conceptual prerequisite for understanding the meaning. Speakers can be said to know the meaning of a word only by first understanding the background frames that motivate the concept that the word encodes. Within such an approach, words or word senses are not related to each other directly, word to word, but only by way of their links to common background frames and indications of the manner in which their meanings highlight particular elements of such frames.

This is rather different from the goal of understanding how a word is normally and idiomatically used in a language to make meanings, as we shall see in the next section.

FrameNet, the practical implementation of the theory of Frame Semantics, is work in progress. An interesting question is whether, in principle, it can ever be fulfilled and regarded as complete. The answer is probably no, since there does not seem to be any very good reason to believe that the number of possible frames is finite.

Each **Frame** is populated by several **Lexical Units** and is supported by annotated corpus lines. A lexical unit is a pairing of a word with a meaning. **Frame Elements** are entities that participate in the frame. Different senses of polysemous words belong to different frames. A group of lexical units (words and multiword expressions (MWEs)) is chosen as representative of a particular frame. For each selected lexical unit, a concordance is created from a corpus, and sample concordance lines are selected and annotated. Labels (i.e. names) are created for each of the Frame Elements.

Fillmore (2006) discusses the example of the 'Revenge frame'. The following lexical items are identified as participating in this frame:

verbs: *avenge, revenge, retaliate; get even, get back at; take revenge, exact retribution*
nouns: *vengeance, revenge, retaliation, retribution*
adjectives: *retaliatory, retributive, vindictive*

The Frame Elements are:

Offender (O), *Injured Party (IP)*, *Avenger (A)* [may or may not be identical to the Injured Party], *Injury (I)* [the offence], *Punishment (P)*

The relationships are summarized as follows:

O has done I to IP; A (who may be identical to IP), in response to I, undertakes to harm O by P.

Despite the many examples in FrameNet taken from BNC, with extensive tagging of the thematic roles of lexical items, it would be a mistake to imagine that FrameNet is corpus-driven. The frame, its elements, and its lexical units are all dreamed up by introspection; examples are imported after the event. No attempt is made to analyse systematically the meanings or uses of any given lexical item. FrameNet proceeds frame by frame, not word by word. As a result, there are many gaps, which will remain unfilled unless some member of the FrameNet team invents a relevant frame for each one. Two examples will suffice, out of literally hundreds that could be mentioned.

- Most uses of the verb **spoil** denote destroying the pleasure of a special event, such as an outing or a party. Another large group of uses denote habitual pampering of a child. However, the only frame in FrameNet for this word is the rather rare Rotting frame (e.g. *I've got a piece of ham that'll spoil if we don't eat it tonight*), accounting for only about 3 per cent of uses in BNC.
- There are two main uses of the verb **admit**: one of them denotes saying something reluctantly; the other involves a pattern in which someone is taken into a hospital or a residential home for treatment or for care. A third pattern involves being allowed to join an institution or club. At present only the first of these is covered by a FrameNet frame.

FrameNet is work in progress, so maybe, if FrameNet goes on long enough and if someone invents an appropriate frame in each case, gaps like these will be plugged eventually. However, it seems unlikely that all of them will be plugged, for FrameNet does not have a target inventory of frames to create, does not have any criteria for distinction between frames, and does not have criteria for completion of the whole task. In other words, it is not based on systematic analysis of a target lexicon. Despite these somewhat negative comments, it must be emphasized that FrameNet has been an inspiration for recent approaches to lexical semantics and contains insights that repay careful study by anyone interested in meaning in language.[3]

---

[3] More information can be found in a special issue of the *International Journal of Lexicography* (16(3), September 2003), which was devoted to FrameNet and Frame Semantics.

4.4.2 *Semantic analysis based on textual context*

FrameNet places word meaning in context of utterance (so-called 'real-world context') and uses corpus evidence as a source of examples to support preconceived theories about a word's meaning, utterer's motivations, and so on. An alternative, somewhat complementary approach is to focus on the phraseological patterns within which each word is used and to find out to what extent phraseology affects word meaning and develop hypotheses and even a theory accordingly. This is the approach examined in this section. It has only become possible to analyse phraseology with any degree of objectivity and accuracy since the development of very large corpora in the past twenty years.

4.4.2.1 *The Corpus Pattern Analysis project*   Hanks (1994) proposed a new approach to lexicography, i.e. Corpus Pattern Analysis (CPA), based on close analysis of corpus evidence in the light of prototype theory. He argued that words in themselves have 'meaning potential' rather than meaning as such, and that, at least in the case of verbs, words need to be put into context before any attempt is made to define their meaning. Different contextual patterns activate different components of a word's 'meaning potential'. Context is, of course, highly variable, but it is not infinitely variable. One of the most important discoveries of corpus linguistics has been that the contexts surrounding any word are highly patterned. Alongside the almost infinite number of <u>possible</u> phrases in which a word may be used, there is a comparatively small number of patterns in which it is <u>regularly or normally</u> used. Each normal, regular pattern is associated with a meaning. Thus, meanings can be associated with phraseological patterns as well as or instead of words in isolation.

This work was eventually followed up by Hanks in a pilot investigation at Brandeis University (see Hanks and Pustejovsky 2005) and implemented in a large database at the Faculty of Informatics, Masaryk University, Brno, Czech Republic. Masaryk gave technological support to the project and set up useful hypertext links with other research projects, in particular the Sketch Engine (see Kilgarriff *et al.* 2004). The first fruits (an analysis of the phraseological patterns of 700 English verbs and their meanings) are publicly available at http://nlp.fi.muni.cz/projects/cpa/. No doubt the work would be further advanced if it had been properly funded in a stable location. On the other hand, it has benefited greatly in terms of theoretical robustness from collaboration with some of the best minds in the world studying language empirically.

4.4.2.2 *Authenticity and regularity*   It is not the case that any bundle of authentic citations is acceptable by way of lexicographic evidence. Authenticity alone is not enough. In addition to authenticity, citations must be chosen to illustrate usage that is normal and idiomatic. This is particularly important now that so many texts available via the Internet are written by non-native speakers, whose work obviously cannot be trusted as a source of information about idiomatic phraseology.

Another, equally important point is that normal phraseology is constantly exploited in abnormal ways to create new meanings or for rhetorical and other effects. Lexicographers must be trained to recognize such exploitations for what they are, and not treat them as a reason for broadening the scope of definitions to the point where the focus is lost or adding senses to a dictionary. Evidence of regularity must also be found.

Lexicographers of the future will develop different approaches to different words, depending on the function of each word in the language. Some words, especially nouns denoting concrete objects, will need definitions of a fairly traditional kind that show how the word has concrete reference to a set of objects in the world. Many other words, on the other hand, including most verbs and adjectives and many nouns, especially abstract nouns, need to be explained in the context of their normal phraseology. The set of phraseological norms for any word may be regarded as a linguistic gestalt, which is associated with a complex of meanings and beliefs and may be used normally or exploited creatively, according to the speaker's or writer's needs. We are now brought face to face with a problem that has confronted lexicographers from time immemorial, since dictionaries began. This is that the range of phraseology and meanings of certain words is of almost incredible complexity. How can any ordinary human language users carry lexical items of such enormous complexity in his or her head? I will hazard an answer to this question in a moment, but let me first give an example, which, I am sorry to say, will be rather space consuming. A corpus-based study of the verb *throw* yields the following observations, at a level of generalization suitable to account for the normal patterns of use of this verb found in the BNC (which claims to be a balanced and representative sample of English):

*People throw hard physical objects like stones, bricks, and bottles **at** other people and things, typically but not necessarily with the intention of causing damage* [the preposition 'at' in this context intensifies the notion of intention to cause damage]—*people throw tomatoes and eggs (and even shoes) at politicians to express contempt for them—terrorists throw bombs—soldiers throw grenades at the enemy—ball players throw balls **to** each other* [the preposition 'to' in this context intensifies the notion of cooperative behaviour; there is a whole complex of domain-specific secondary norms here]—*you can throw your hands or arms in the air (but they remain attached to your body)—you can throw your hat in the air (and you may fail to catch it as it comes down)—suicidal people throw themselves under trains, out of windows, into rivers or ponds—committed people throw themselves into an activity—you **throw away** (or **throw out**) things that you no longer want—if you are on a boat, you **throw** unwanted things **overboard**—if a proposition or argument (e.g. in a lawsuit) is unconvincing, the whole lawsuit or proposal may be **thrown out** by the judge or decision-maker—a person may be thrown out of a place where they are not wanted—'throwing out the baby with the bathwater' implies accidentally* *rejecting something of central importance at the same time as rejecting unwanted things associated with it.*

A person may **throw off** things like clothes and blankets—*you can also throw off abstract things like moral restraints—a moving object may throw a person or object off—a person trying to find out something may be thrown off the scent—a person may be thrown off course, or off balance—you can* **throw in your lot with** *someone else—you can* **throw** *something extra* **in** *(for good measure) with a set of things—a person may be* **thrown in at the deep end**, *in a new job for example—a person or physical object may literally be* **thrown into** *the air, for example by the force of an explosion—a person may be thrown into jail—a situation may be thrown into chaos, confusion, or turmoil—an idea may be thrown into doubt or into question—a concept can be thrown into relief by some contrasting event or concept—a defeated person* **throws in the towel**— *a troublemaker* **throws a monkey wrench** *(British:* **spanner**) **in the works**.

Less frequent but nevertheless conventional phrases, with highly idiomatic meanings, are the following (with cognitively salient collocates in bold): *bullies* **throw their weight around**— *powerful people throw their* **weight behind** *politicians or proposals—an event may* **throw light on** *a mystery—bad things* **throw a shadow over** *good things—evidence may* **throw doubt on** *a belief or hypothesis—boxers* **throw punches** *in a boxing match, while an aggressive person may* **throw a punch** *and start a fight—a group of people may* **throw a party**—*you might* **throw down the gauntlet** *or* **throw out a challenge** *to a rival—gamblers* **throw dice**—*an unstable or excitable person may* **throw a tantrum**, *a* **fit**, *or a* **wobbly**—*a reckless person* **throws caution to the wind**— *a situation may* **throw up** *new concepts or abstract entities—a person who has drunk too much or who has eaten something bad (or one who is exposed to extreme emotional distress) may* **throw up**.

Notice that, in this phraseological account of the verb *throw*, there are almost no explicit meaning statements—and yet the meaning of most of the phraseological prototypes listed here is probably clear enough to most people. Context clarifies meaning.

The answer to the question, 'How can we store all this in our heads?' may be that we don't. Probably, each member of a speech community has in his or her head only a subset of this whole gestalt (for purposes of vaguely recognizing meaning) and an even smaller subset for active use. If this is right, it is evidently a mistake to believe that native speakers know the whole of their native language. Probably, they don't. They know only a part of it—the part that they have internalized and use for communicative purposes. It is perfectly possible to go through life without ever encountering, let alone using, a rare phrase such as 'throw down the gauntlet'. Your subset of the phraseology and meanings of *throw* and all other words is probably rather different from mine and those of other people that you know, but nevertheless there must be enough overlap for communication among us to be possible.

On the other hand, the enormous capacity of the human brain for storing experiences and the words associated with these experiences must not be under-estimated. Maybe the various phrases embodying the verb *throw* that you use are stored separately in different places in the brain in the context of different communicative needs and associations, rather than as a homogeneous whole.

If this is right, at least one thing is wrong with this presentation here, namely that all the major syntagmatic components of this linguistic gestalt—*lexical gestalt* might be a better term—are listed en masse, in a quasi-rational sequence. This gives a misleading implication that all aspects of a lexical gestalt are or can be psychologically active at the same time in the mind of any one language user, or readily recalled to the conscious mind for purposes of exemplification and discussion. This is incorrect. In reality, the gestalts for such complex words are buried (and distributed, in ways that we do not yet fully understand) deep in the subconscious; different components are activated according to the context of utterance. In particular, the preceding text of any discourse—document or conversation—leading up to the choice of the word *throw* sets preconditions such that only a tiny subset, consisting of particular, relevant aspects of the gestalt, are activated in any context. It is highly implausible that (as some psycholinguists have argued) in writing, reading, or conversation all the possible norms for a word are activated first and then the relevant one is selected by a speaker, writer, listener, or reader. Thus, a corpus can show us a fairly full set of <u>what</u> may be stored mentally, but it does not tell us how it is stored.

Whatever the psycholinguistic reality may be, the duty of the lexicographer is generally seen as being to report all the conventions of a language, not just some of them. Having said that, we must also acknowledge the impossibility of reporting all the conventions of a living language, which is constantly changing and developing and which may have many sub-domains. The best we can hope for is to report all the common conventions of meaning and use, and to discover the general principles that relate one meaningful phrase to another and that govern the way in which conventional phraseology and meaning may be exploited.

Different aspects of this complex gestalt are open to exploitation in various ways. A few examples of uses of *throw* may now be given to illustrate how phraseology is exploited and the kind of exploitation rules that are needed. The implicatures range from semi-literal to highly idiomatic or metaphorical.

Throwing a physical object *at* something denotes a volitional human action with the intention (not necessarily successful) of causing harm or damage. This notion is exploited in (3), a metaphor where the brick in question is not a physical object at all, though the intention to cause damage is clearly present. Why would central bankers want to damage the world economy? Because, according to the writer of (3), in October 1989 the world economy was 'running too fast' and 'liable to overheat' (two fairly conventional metaphors used in the domain of economics).

(3)   Worldwide, the economy has continued to come on stronger than almost anyone forecast, which is why European central bankers agreed to **throw** another brick **at** it yesterday. (BNC: *Independent*, electronic edition of 6 October 1989: Business section)

Throwing bricks, *throwing stones*, and *throwing punches* are expressions that have approximately equal salience in the BNC. However, *throwing punches* is more often used metaphorically (and may be regarded as always somewhat metaphorical, for reasons explained in the next paragraph).

(4)   Punches **were thrown** outside the Queen's Head Hotel in Bishop Auckland. (BNC: *Northern Echo* [Date not given])

In order to understand the meaning in (4), the reader needs to take account of the semantic types of the collocates. A stone is a physical object; throwing a stone is a physical event. A punch, however, is itself an event, not a physical object. In (4), therefore, in the phrase 'throw a punch' the verb *throw* is semantically light: what is thrown is not a physical object but an event. The meaning of (4) is that various people literally and physically punched each other, not that some physical object was impelled through the air. However, this light-verb use may itself be exploited metaphorically, as in (5).

(5)   With the mass media now part of everyday life and with arguments about bias and balance commonplace, the modern British subject is not likely to succumb to some **Saddam sucker punch thrown** by the third party from the corner of the living room. (BNC: *Marxism Today* [Date not given])

The reference in (5) is to a possible aggressive remark, rather than to physical violence. In boxing, a *sucker punch* is a deceptive punch thrown in a way that deceives an inexperienced fighter, but here the domain is politics, not boxing. Instead, the expression denotes a deceptive and aggressive, potentially destructive remark. As readers, we deduce this interpretation from other collocates in the context: "arguments about [something]" and "the corner of the living room" are not compatible with a literal fight or boxing match, but they are compatible with aggressive remarks. The passing reference to Saddam [Hussein] reinforces the notion of a deceptive remark. This semantically dense sentence is therefore highly metaphorical. The collocates and their semantic types determine the interpretation of the target word.

To take another example, *throwing a shadow* likewise has a cline of metaphoricity, from light-verb uses to highly metaphorical references. In (6), the street light is a physical object, and shadows are visible objects (even though they have no physical substance). This is, then, an almost literal expression; the only thing about it that is idiomatic is the choice of *throw* as a light verb to denote what is in effect a visual perception. In (7), on the other hand, the collocates *hindsight* and *retrospective* (among other collocates in this fragment) invite a metaphorical interpretation of the *shadow* that is thrown over past people and events.

(6) The street light **threw strange shadows** among the hoardings. (BNC: W. B. Herbert, 1992, *Railway ghosts and phantoms*)

(7) There are dangers involved in the writing of contemporary history quite apart from the standard objection that distance and hard evidence are required if a true perspective is to be gained. Hindsight **throws a retrospective shadow** over people and events which distort light and shade as they were actually perceived at the time. The period of the Attlee governments of 1945–51 was particularly prone to retrospective retouching by the ideologically driven. (BNC: Peter Hennessy, 1990, *Cabinet*)

Let us now turn to some graphic metaphorical uses of some of the phrasal verbs formed with *throw*, starting with *throw something overboard*. This nautical expression is stronger and more expressive even than *throw something away* and *throw something out*. If you throw something away or out, in the short term you still have the option of going to the bin and retrieving it. But if someone on a ship throws something overboard, it is probably lost irrevocably, for ever. This fact, coupled with the salience of nautical expressions in general in figurative English—a by-product of the important role that the sea has played in English history—and in the spread of the English language, means that it is not surprising that this expression is often used metaphorically. Fifteen out of the thirty-five uses in the BNC of the expression *throw [something] overboard* are metaphorical.

(8) Emanuel Shinwell, who has never changed his mind on this issue, was clear in 1918 about the wrong-headedness of destroying the people's grammar schools while leaving unscathed the privileged Public Schools: 'We were afraid to tackle the public schools to which the wealthy people send their sons, but at the same time are ready to **throw overboard** the grammar schools which are for many working-class boys the stepping-stone to the universities and a useful career.' (BNC: Harry Judge, 1984, *A Generation of Schooling*)

Example (8) is a conventional metaphor. Less conventional is the metaphor in (9). The reader may feel that 'throw out' is a somewhat forced metaphor to describe what a bird does when it sings. From the point of view of analysing the semantic gestalt, we may note that there is dissonance with the notion of throwing out unwanted stuff.

(9) We all know, though, how a singing bird makes us feel and we can imagine how the bird feels as it **throws its song out** into the air. (BNC: Julia Casterton, 1992, *Creative writing: A practical guide*)

Finally, (10) exemplifies an exploitation embedded within an exploitation. The scene is set with a conventional metaphor ('metamorphosis'), but then a new metaphor is introduced—resonating with but not actually realizing the conventional metaphors *thrown in at the deep end* (and perhaps also the conventional expressions *thrown into doubt* and *thrown into confusion*). Not only is the writer here comparing his younger self to an insect ('metamorphosis'), but also the deep end of the conventional swimming pool into which beginners are thrown has been metamorphosed into a jungle—a jungle of jargon (note the alliteration). This plethora of mixed metaphors and stylistic devices may offend stylistic purists and pedants, but that is a matter of taste. It is hard to sustain the argument that the intended meaning of the text is obscured or diminished by them, and some readers may indeed feel that the meaning is enhanced by them.

(10)   It was to take me some time longer to undergo the metamorphosis from a 'teacher' to a 'lecturer'. I was **thrown into a jungle** of new jargon. The language of special education had long been tucked under my belt, but now I was faced with filling in timetables with terms such as 'DD' time—departmental duties, to the uninitiated—in other words, time when I was not actually in direct teaching contact with students. (BNC: Tony Booth *et al.*, 1992, *Policies for diversity in education*)

4.4.3 *Find the pattern: What is a pattern?*

It will be clear by now that, in my view, the sort of thing that needs to be said in order to report lexical meaning accurately, using corpus evidence, differs greatly from what is said in current dictionaries. In the first place, dictionaries must focus on reporting conventional patterns of phraseology. In the second place, lexical analysts also need an apparatus for recognizing and classifying different sorts of exploitations. In order to report patterns of conventional phraseology accurately, e-lexicographers must analyse corpora, find the patterns associated with each word, and map meanings onto them. To do this, they need access to at least the following kinds of tools for processing corpus data:

- a part-of-speech analyser;
- a sentence parser;
- an inventory of semantic types.

At the heart of each pattern lies a word. Patterns represent a combination of valency and collocational preferences of the target word. The collocations are organized into paradigm sets based on prototypical semantic types, as described in Pustejovsky *et al.* (2004).

4.4.4 *Are word senses mutually exclusive?*

Existing dictionaries postulate a comparatively small number of senses for each word, but say little about how each sense is realized in ordinary usage. As computational linguists have discovered belatedly and to their chagrin and cost (see, for example, Ide and Wilks 2006), not only is there very little indication in dictionaries of how one sense is to be distinguished from another, but also, to make matters worse, the senses in traditional dictionaries are not mutually exclusive. For example, two of the senses listed by *OALDCE* for the verb *pour* are:

1. [VN, usually + *adv/prep*] to make a liquid or other substance flow from a container in a continuous stream, especially by holding the container at an angle.

and:

3. ~ (**sth**) (**out**) to serve a drink by letting it flow from a container into a cup or glass.

There is almost total semantic overlap here. (What is a drink if it is not a liquid? What is the difference between "to serve [. . .] by letting it flow" and "to make a liquid or other substance flow"?) Also, there are a number of false implications lying in wait to ambush a naive user or computer program, especially one that is looking for disambiguation criteria. The grammatical information given with sense 3 might look as if its purpose is disambiguation, but it is not, because:

- The word **out** in sense 3 is a completive-intensive, not a disambiguator: it does not distinguish sense 3 from sense 1, as a naive reader or program might be tempted to believe. The round brackets indicate that it is optional.
- 'out' in sense 3 is nothing more than a realization of the adv/prep mentioned in 1. It does not have a semantically distinctive function.

This is not a criticism of the *OALDCE* entry or of similar treatments of such words in this and other dictionaries. Rather, it is partly a criticism of naive expectations among dictionary users and partly a criticism of the theoretical foundations and assumptions underlying pre-corpus dictionaries. The entry for *pour* in *OADLCE* is not an isolated example. Many other entries in many other dictionaries exhibit similar undisambiguated semantic overlap. For a human reader, such redundancy may have a reinforcing rather than a confusing effect. However, for hard-nosed linguistic theory and for applications in computer science and artificial intelligence, this sort of misinterpretation of the semantic redundancy in dictionaries has fatal consequences.

When we turn to corpus evidence and examine it carefully, we find that disambiguation is indeed possible, but not word by word. Rather, it has to be undertaken phrase by phrase. Moreover, it turns out to be necessary to abandon the comfortable expectation that all possible uses of each word can be covered. Words have innumerable rare and improbable but possible uses, for language is dynamic: a design feature of the lexicon is that it is made to be used creatively and innovatively as well as conventionally. The only realistic possibility for lexicographers is to aim to cover all probable uses of each word, that is, all normal, conventional uses. Each word in a language is associated with a small number of recurrent phraseological patterns. In most but not quite all cases, a unique sense can be associated with each pattern. A phraseological pattern consists of a mixture of valency and collocational preferences (see Hanks and Pustejovsky 2005).

Let us look now, by contrast, at the entry for *pour* in the very first dictionary of English that took phraseology and collocations seriously, namely *COBUILD* (1987). It, too, made a distinction between pouring liquid out of a container and pouring a drink, but with this difference: typically, pouring a drink takes a benefactive argument. You pour someone a drink, but you don't pour someone petrol. This can be regarded as a genuine semantic distinction. *COBUILD* says:

1. If you **pour** a liquid or other substance, you cause it to flow out of a container by holding the container at a particular angle.
2. If you **pour** *someone* a drink, you fill a cup or glass with the drink so that they can drink it. [my italics]

However, not even *COBUILD* rigidly adheres to a principle of mutually exclusive sense distinctions, and it is not immediately clear whether it should. Contrasts between word senses as presented in dictionaries and pattern senses as observed in corpora offer rich opportunities for future study. So far, neither dictionaries nor grammars have succeeded in defining or demonstrating systematically the associations between meaning and phraseological patterns at a sufficiently delicate level for reliable disambiguation of words in free text. This is a major goal for future e-lexicography.

Accurate description of lexical patterns requires analysis not only of the syntactic structures (valencies) in which each word participates, but also analysis of collocational preferences within such structures.

More fundamentally, lexicography is now in a position to spearhead (or, if you prefer a different metaphor, to provide the foundations for) radical new approaches to the theoretical understanding of meaning in language. It is not entirely clear why twentieth-century linguistics (in the English-speaking world) found it necessary to place so much emphasis on syntax, while having so little to say about lexis and meaning. What is clear now, in the age of electronic text processing, is that traditional assumptions about the nature of meaning and its relation to syntax are due for an overhaul and that lexicography and lexical studies are in a position to lead the way.

4.5 Is Wiktionary the right model for electronic dictionaries of the future?

What will major innovative dictionaries of the future be like? We don't know. Printed books are likely to remain extremely conservative and command little or no serious investment and hence little or no serious innovation. Future large-scale new dictionaries are likely to be electronic products, but a stable business model (or academic funding model) that would justify large-scale investment in such innovations has not yet emerged.

Some people argue that all information should be free, and point to the great success of Wikipedia as a free information source. The success of Wikipedia is undeniable. However, the success of its companion project, Wiktionary, "a collaborative project for creating a free lexical database in every language, complete with meanings, etymologies, and pronunciations", is less obvious. The contrast between Wikipedia and Wiktionary deserves a moment's consideration: it highlights the difference between a dictionary and an encyclopedia. If a reader wants expert information on some subject—let us say the reason why gold is valuable, or the characteristics of the Tocharian languages—he or she needs information from an expert. In the vast majority of Wikipedia articles, such expertise will be found, amply confirmed by other experts in the community, in accordance with what Putnam (1975a, 1975b) called "the division of linguistic labor": you and I may not be able to distinguish *gold* from iron pyrites (called 'fool's gold') or other metals, but we rely on there being someone in the English-speaking world who can.

Part of the genius of Jimmy Wales and Larry Sanger, co-founders of Wikipedia, was to recognize that there are: (a) enough people in the world ready and willing to write and publish well-informed, accurate, and reliable articles about almost every topic under the sun without pay; and (b) enough people in the world to spot poor or unreliable articles and be motivated to complain and even to provide something better. Wikipedia is a truly collective worldwide social endeavour. Part of their naivety was not to allow for the possibility that pranksters would try to slip in false, malicious, and/or damaging articles, as happened in the case of the Seigenthaler incident,[4] as a result of which Wikipedia introduced new control and vetting procedures. Such incidents and shortcomings are rare and immediately corrected when spotted.

So how does the Wiktionary enterprise match up to its encyclopedic brother? The avowed aim is "to include not only the definition of a word, but also enough information to really understand it".[5] This laudable aim is inspiring, but at present it is not achieved. In the English Wiktionary, the etymologies are taken from or based on those in older dictionaries, as are the definitions, which are extremely old-

---

[4] 2005: http://en.wikipedia.org/wiki/Seigenthaler_incident.
[5] http://en.wiktionary.org/wiki/ Wiktionary:Main_Page.

fashioned and derivative, taking no account of recent research in either cognitive linguistics or corpus linguistics.

Two topics here may be exemplified. If the aim is to give enough information for people to "really understand" the meanings of words, then some account must be given, among other things, (a) of the conventional phraseology that helps to determine the meaning of a word, and (b) of the fact that much meaning in everyday language is metaphorical or figurative in nature.

Let us look in a little more detail at each of these two points in turn, with examples. The Corpus Pattern Analysis research project has shown that the meaning of a verb is closely allied to the semantic types of its arguments. So, for example, the following (from the BNC) are among the most normal uses of the verb *admit*:

(11)   At least three people were admitted to hospital.
(12)   Julie Smith was admitted for an emergency appendicectomy.
(13)   John was admitted into a local residential home.
(14)   The children were eventually admitted into care as a result of neglect.
(15)   Namibia was formally admitted to the UN as the organization's 160th member on April 23, 1990.

The collocations and the passive voice in (11)–(15) distinguish this meaning of *admit* from the 'say reluctantly' meaning of the same verb. How does this work? First, note that we are talking here about normal, typical usage, not all possible uses. This is very important. The verb in this sense is normally passive, while in the 'say reluctantly' sense it is normally active—although the converse is also possible (e.g. it is possible, though less common, to say *the hospital admitted three people*; *negligence was admitted*). A painful lesson for linguistics of the past thirty years (though some people are reluctant to admit it) is that all linguistic analysis and especially lexical analysis must be conducted in terms of probabilities, not in terms of necessary and sufficient conditions. In (11)–(14) the combination of a human subject with the expressions 'to hospital', 'for an emergency appendicectomy', 'into a local residential home', and 'into care' select the sense (or, one might say, activate the meaning) 'be brought officially to a place where one can be looked after or treated medically, according to need'. Additionally, these collocations assign to the human subject of the passive verb the role of being a person who is suffering or judged to be in need.

In (15), the combination of 'Namibia' with 'to the UN' activates a related but slightly different sense, involving becoming a member of an organization, rather than being taken to a place in order to be looked after. Each of the words and phrases cited in the preceding paragraph forms part of a contextually relevant lexical set. Paradigmatic lexical sets of this kind may have a very large number—indeed, in some cases an open-ended number—of words and phrases as members, but they are united by certain shared semantic features. Part of the art of electronic lexicography in the future will consist of selecting from a corpus typical examples of such lexical sets and summarizing their semantic structure in different contexts. This is not a simple task: for example, in the above examples 'hospital' and 'residential home' can be classified easily enough as locations, with the added proviso that these are locations in which care is given. However, the word 'care' itself does not denote a location. Nevertheless, we can be certain that if a text says that a person is 'admitted into care', they are admitted to such a location. Thus, to borrow a term from Pustejovsky's Generative Lexicon theory (1995), *care* in this context is <u>coerced</u> into implying a location or, more specifically, a residential home—a care home—approved by the local authority. Notice, too, that conventional phraseology of this kind fills in all sorts of other gaps that are not explicitly stated but subliminally present: we know or can surmise that the people in (11) were injured or ill, that Julie in (12) went to a hospital, that John in (13) was a child or disabled person in need of care, and that in (14) the children were taken to a care home, although these facts are not explicitly stated. This kind of implicature is also one of the fundamental insights of Fillmore's Frame Semantics (1982, 2006).

Now compare how English Wiktionary (accessed 27 March 2011) defines and exemplifies this sense of the word:

To allow to enter; to grant entrance, whether into a place, or into the mind, or consideration; to receive; to take.
A ticket admits one into a playhouse.
They were admitted into his house.
to admit a serious thought into the mind
to admit evidence in the trial of a cause

The Wiktionary definition is not wrong, but it is stilted and archaic in wording (note, for example, the old-fashioned uses of 'grant' and 'whether' and the strange notion of 'granting entrance into the mind'). Moreover, it does not record that in this sense the verb is usually passive. It does not do a good job of explaining the meaning, which, in modern English, has more to do with activating an administrative procedure than with "allowing", "granting", "receiving", or "taking". The location to which admission is granted, as we have seen, is generally an institution of some kind, rather than "the mind, or consideration". (I could go on.) Wiktionary's examples do not illustrate the normal phraseology in which the verb is used: instead, they seem to be intended to illustrate extreme possibilities of usage. The examples, needless to say, are not corpus-based; they were invented by a lexicographer, either recently or (more probably) many decades ago. If they seem stilted and unnatural, it is because most human beings are, strangely, not very good at reporting or inventing examples of their own normal, everyday linguistic behaviour. The human mind, when pressed for an example, seems to reach unerringly for a boundary case, even at the expense of idiomaticity and naturalness, rather than for a central and typical, normal example.

If we turn now from verbs to Wiktionary's treatment of concrete nouns, we can illustrate our second point, namely how a traditional approach to definition fails to record essential components of lexical meaning that provide the foundations of everyday metaphorical exploitations of meaning. A very simple example is the conventional simile *treat someone like a dog*. This means 'to treat someone badly', despite the fact that in most English-speaking cultures dogs are typically pampered and well treated. It is necessary to distinguish between creative figurative language—genuine exploitations of conventional norms—and conventional figurative expressions. The latter types of figurative language deserve to be recorded in dictionaries, though at present this is not done systematically in any dictionary. A vast mass of research over the past thirty years has revealed that metaphor plays a central role in everyday linguistic meaning. See for example Lakoff and Johnson (1980), Glucksberg (2001), Giora (2003), Bowdle and Gentner (2005), and collections of papers such as those in Stefanowitsch and Gries (2006), Gibbs (2008), and Hanks and Giora (2011).

Conventional figurative exploitations of the meaning of *dog* are too many and complex to allow full discussion here. Let us instead take a simpler word: *elephant*. The Wiktionary definition of *elephant* (accessed 29 March 2011) reads as follows:

1. A mammal of the order *Proboscidea*, having a trunk, and two large ivory tusks jutting from the upper jaw.
2. (*figuratively*) Anything huge and ponderous.
3. (*paper, printing*) A printing-paper size measuring 30 inches x 22 inches.
4. (*UK, childish*) used when counting to add length. *Let's play hide and seek. I'll count. One elephant, two elephant, three elephant . . .*

Leaving aside senses 3 and 4, we may ask whether definitions 1 and 2 give a satisfactory account of the meaning. They do not. In the first place, sense 1 fails to say that elephants are large, a fact often exploited metaphorically. It is not the case that elephants are <u>necessarily</u> large, but they are <u>typically</u> large. This, too, is an important point. The discovery of dwarf elephants in Borneo and skeletons of extinct species of dwarf elephants in Crete must not be allowed to inhibit the lexicographer from saying that elephants are typically large. Only this will enable interpretation of examples such as (16) and (17) below. It also needs to be said that elephants have a proverbially good memory (18) and (19), that bull elephants are assertive (20), and that they make an extremely loud noise called trumpeting (21).

(16)   So what I'm actually saying is that I'm making my objective an elephant, it's too large. (BNC: spoken corpus; staff training session)
(17)   Och, I don't want a stranger to think that I'm built like an elephant. (BNC: spoken corpus; unscripted conversation)
(18)   "You've got the memory of an elephant, you're probably the cleverest girl in class and you can't read." (BNC: Celia Brayfield, 1990, *The Prince*)

(19)   But the odd rumour has gone round that Six has been operating someone big, someone quite high up in the KGB—someone with an elephant's memory who might be about to finger Mills once and for all. (BNC: Trevor Barnes, 1991, *A Midsummer Killing*)

(20)   He turned round to gaze at Cord Dillon, Deputy Director of the CIA. "A rough diamond," Paula called him. "The manners of a bull elephant," was Monica's elegant description. (BNC: Colin Forbes, 1991, *Whirlpool*)

(21)   Then someone asked me where the station was, and she was deaf, and I had to trumpet like an elephant for about ten minutes. (BNC: Mary Gervaise, 1983, *The Distance Enchanted*)

I have illustrated just two of the many kinds of improvements that could be made to a dictionary such as English Wiktionary using corpus evidence. The essential message here is that, as in many traditional dictionaries, the definitions may succeed in defining, but they do not do a very good job of explaining. Is it really of any help to anyone (except, perhaps, a taxonomic zoologist) to be told that an elephant is "a mammal of the order *Proboscidea*" or that an elephant seal is "a large marine mammal of the genus *Mirounga*, which is the largest of the pinnipeds"?

Does all this rule out Wiktionary as a model for electronic lexicography? No, absolutely not. There are many positive things to be said (cf. also Meyer and Gurevych, this volume). In the first place, Wiktionary shows how imaginative use can be made of multimedia hypertext links such as audio links to the pronunciation of the word in different standard accents of English (American and British), pictures of elephants, and text links to related terms such as *elephant seal, elephant shrew* (so called because of its long nose), *white elephant*, and *pink elephant*. Some links lead to the encyclopedic rather than the lexicographic components of the Wikimedia complex, which seems just right for a natural-kind term such as *elephant*. No doubt it would be technically straightforward enough to include film clips of typical elephant behaviour, including the sound of elephants trumpeting. Perhaps the technology is not far away by which we shall be able to sit at our computer and touch a simulation of an elephant's skin or smell a bull elephant in musth.

It is a cardinal point of principle for all Wikimedia that the information supplied should be freely available to everybody. This does not mean, however, that there is an absence of control. I noticed that there was no entry in Wikipedia for the term *rogue elephant*, so, as an experiment, I added a definition for this, in figurative sense, "someone or something that is large, dangerous, and unpredictable". Within minutes, my tiny contribution had been placed within a template for noun entries, and someone (presumably at Wiktionary central) had added the literal sense, "A solitary, old, male elephant that has become dangerously and unpredictably violent", together with a cross-reference to a term with similar meaning, *loose cannon*. This is very impressive.

Similar controls are evidently also in place to prevent use of Wiktionary for propaganda purposes, for example by religious groups such as Scientologists or lawyers representing commercial conglomerates such as the Edgar Rice Burroughs Foundation, both of whom have put pressure in the past on dictionary publishers to amend definitions to show their products ('Scientology' and 'Tarzan' theme parks respectively) in a favourable light.

The hypertext structure of Wikimedia, and in particular Wiktionary, is eminently suitable as a model for the electronic dictionary of the future. What is needed is some way of ensuring that definitions are properly supported by links to corpus evidence, including evidence for the ways in which word meanings are exploited in metaphors and other ways. This will entail that almost every definition of every content word must be radically re-examined in the light of corpus evidence, in the way suggested above. Such a re-examination needs to be conducted systematically and professionally. Our sympathies may be with an anarcho-syndicalist approach to lexicography, but it is hard to imagine how a radical new approach to defining verbs or natural-kind terms and thus enhancing our understanding of the nature of language and meaning could be carried out systematically by large, uncoordinated groups of enthusiasts and volunteers, some with more expertise than others. Nevertheless, the overall aim must remain "to include not only the definition of a word, but also enough information to really understand it"—and, we might add, to be able to use it correctly.

4.6 Conclusion

Lexicography is in a state of transition at the present time, between the technology of the printed word in a bound book that has served us so well for 500 years and the technology of the Internet and the electronic product; also between exploded Leibnizian assumptions about the relationship between words and concepts and newer theories of prototypes and stereotypes based on the work of philosophers such as Wittgenstein, Grice, and Putnam and cognitive scientists such as Rosch, Tomasello, Croft, Lakoff, Gentner, Glucksberg, and Giora.

It is too early to say what form innovative dictionaries of the future will take. Perhaps the Wiktionary model can be adapted, or perhaps an entirely new business model will be developed by an enterprising electronic publisher. One thing seems certain, however: all serious future lexicography will be corpus-driven, no longer based merely on collections of citations and certainly not merely a matter of guesswork based on speculation.

[Since this chapter was written, the Arts and Humanities Research Council of Great Britain has agreed to fund a three-year research project called 'Disambiguation of Verbs by Collocation', using the techniques of corpus pattern analysis, at the Research Institute of Information and Language Processing at the University of Wolverhampton. Work on this project started on October 1, 2012.]

5

Dictionary writing systems and beyond

ANDREA ABEL

5.1 Introduction

For many years, dictionary writing was a task accomplished with pen and paper. Nowadays, dictionaries are written on computers with the help of the increasingly targeted software tools which are being developed for this purpose. This allows lexicographers to concentrate better on their core business, that is, collecting data and compiling dictionary entries. Furthermore, the long-term storage and reusability of data can be guaranteed and, finally, a consistent and structured lexicographic process from the conception phase up to the final product, can be supported more efficiently. Depending on the context in which a specific project is being developed, a range of requirements and needs have to be considered (e.g. commercial vs. academic projects, financial issues and time constraints, print vs. electronic medium). Software that meets these needs and performs these tasks is generally referred to as a 'dictionary writing system'.

This chapter aims to give a general overview of dictionary writing systems, describing general trends rather than focusing more narrowly on single products. At the same time, the goal is to provide a holistic view of the additional tools and features that can be integrated into what we might call a 'pure' dictionary writing system. Section 5.2 provides a general overview of dictionary writing systems in an attempt to isolate the concept; it also includes some historical notes. The central functions and components of dictionary writing systems are presented in Section 5.3. Several recent issues are dealt with individually. Section 5.4 focuses on the advantages and disadvantages of off-the-shelf vis-à-vis in-house software, and combinations of the two. Possible further selection criteria for lexicographic tools are discussed, focusing on some emerging trends. In fact, the view beyond the pure dictionary writing system, and the additional features or tools now emerging, may be a decisive factor. There is significant convergence between the various systems, particularly when commercial software systems are compared. In Section 5.5, the integration of a range of tools is discussed, the most important being dictionary writing systems and corpus query software. Section 5.6 is devoted to the creation of multifunctional databases using a dictionary writing system. The chapter ends with a few concluding remarks.

5.2 Dictionary writing systems: a general overview

Both dictionaries as a whole and single dictionary entries are highly structured objects with many recurring elements. Several aspects of any specific dictionary must be defined: the principles of data collection and selection, the treatment of different types of information and parts of speech, the use of a specific metalanguage, the treatment of macro-, medio-, and microstructural elements, etc. Each entry in any dictionary contains a range of predetermined possible categories (e.g. headword, pronunciation, and collocations) that may differ depending on the entry type (e.g. different parts of speech or reference entries) and have one or more valid locations within any given entry. A noun entry in a monolingual dictionary may, for example, contain categories such as the headword, pronunciation, variant forms, inflected forms, register labels, definitions, lexicographic examples, collocations, idioms, and usage notes, while a conjunction entry does not require a category for inflected forms. Some categories have only one valid location within an entry (e.g. pronunciation usually follows the headword), while others may have several valid locations (e.g. lexicographic examples). Each entry type thus follows a specific configuration of components; in other words, each entry has its own 'syntax' (see also Atkins and Rundell 2008: 203).

Dictionary entries are also characterized by a series of navigational components and markers (e.g. font, font size, and symbols). A fixed and predictable structure with regard to both content and layout is essential to allow dictionary users to quickly and easily find the information they are looking for. In order to guarantee the necessary coherence and consistency for efficient dictionary use, it is important that a set of guidelines are clearly defined during the dictionary design phase. These guidelines, which lexicographers must follow carefully, are usually described in detail in a specific style guide (e.g. Atkins and Rundell 2008: 117ff., Svensèn 2009: 407ff.). In the past, style guides included detailed instructions on the correct order of various parts of an entry, the font (e.g. size, style, weight, etc.) to be used for each element, the precise wording of specific labels (e.g. geographical labels such as 'AmE' or 'American'), etc. Today, computerization has largely relieved lexicographers of the need to pay attention to such tasks (Atkins and Rundell 2008: 212). This is one of the respects in which targeted software comes into play, in particular the dictionary writing systems which are the subject of this chapter.

The first generation of dedicated dictionary writing systems was developed at the beginning of the 1990s, with the aim of making life easier on the entry-writing front (Rundell and Kilgarriff 2011). This still seems to be the main task of dictionary writing systems, whether the software is produced commercially or in-house. In addition to the requirement of supporting lexicographers in their work, sustainable data storage and—especially in larger projects—an efficient project management system (which may range from the conception phase to the final product) of the whole workflow are challenging demands that computerization should be able to meet (see Atkins and Rundell 2008). These three aspects should be taken into consideration when trying to outline the main features of a dictionary writing system.

If we compare some definitions of dictionary writing systems, we notice that, for the most part, they agree. According to Kilgarriff (2006: 7), a dictionary writing system is "a piece of software for writing and producing a dictionary. It might include an editor, a database, a Web interface and various management tools [...] It operates with a dictionary grammar, which specifies the structure of the dictionary." These key components are found in various definitions. For Atkins and Rundell (2008: 103), a dictionary writing system is "a program that enables lexicographers to compile and edit dictionary text, as well as facilitating project management and (later in the process) typesetting and output to printed or electronic media".

Several terms are used to refer to this type of application: here the focus will be on English ones. They usually designate somewhat complex software that includes several components in addition to the simple entry-writing editor, particularly in the case of commercial products, or a software program that is closely connected to a series of applications that together serve to assist dictionary production. Thus, besides 'dictionary writing system' (used, for example, by Atkins and Rundell 2008: 103), other terms include: 'dictionary editing system' (Svensén 2009: 422), 'dictionary compilation software', 'lexicography software', or 'dictionary production software' (De Schryver and Joffe 2006: 41, Joffe and De Schryver 2004b: 17), 'lexicographic workbench' (Ridings 2003: 204), 'dictionary management system' or 'lexicographer's workbench' (Langemets *et al.* 2010: 425), 'dictionary editing tool' (Krek 2010: 928), 'dictionary building software' (Mangeot 2006: 185), or simply 'editorial system' (Tittel 2010: 298).

In the past, a number of software packages have been developed, the best known being commercial products such as IDM DPS, TLex, ABBY Lingvo Content, and iLEX, offering off-the-shelf solutions suitable for the production of a great variety of dictionary products. In addition, a large number of in-house software programs exist that have been partly created for one dictionary publisher or one specific project (for example the DicSy for Norstedts, Sweden's leading dictionary publisher (Svensèn 2009: 423), based on the Compulexis system, the 'Wissensnetz deutsche Sprache' (German Language Knowledge Network) for the German publisher Duden (Alexa *et al.* 2002), the 'Duden Ontology' that is being developed in cooperation with the

TABLE 5.1 In-house dictionary writing systems

Dictionary writing system	Comments
EELex	Dictionary writing system developed at the Institute for Estonian Language (Langemets *et al.* 2010)
'Algemeen Nederlands Woordenboek' (ANW) Article Editor	Dictionary writing system developed at the Instituut voor Nederlandse Lexicologie, the Netherlands (Niestadt 2009)
Onoma	Dictionary writing system used in the compilation of the Woordeboek van die Afrikaanse Taal (Ridings 2003, Mongwe 2006: 20)
Jibiki platform	A generic online, open source environment suitable for different projects developed at the University of Savoy (Mangeot 2006)
'Dictionary Editor and Browser' (DEB)	An open source platform developed at Masaryk University (Horák and Rambousek 2007)
Termania	A free online dictionary portal with integrated dictionary browsing and editing tools (Krek 2010)

software company Intelligent Views using a special software for knowledge management, to mention only a few). Table 5.1 lists a number of specific dictionary writing systems created and used in academic and non-commercial contexts. In such environments, the in-house solution is the most common approach.

In addition to these projects, there are countless tailor-made solutions that do not have proper names. Examples includes the lexicographical–lexicological project elexiko at the Institut für Deutsche Sprache (Hahn *et al.* 2008, Müller-Spitzer 2011), the digital lexical system for the German language, 'Digitales Wörterbuch der deutschen Sprache' (DWDS) at the Berlin-Brandenburgische Akademie der Wissenschaften (Klein and Geyken 2010), and the etymological dictionary of Old French, *Dictionnaire étymologique de l'ancien français* (*DEAF*) at the University of Heidelberg (Tittel 2010). There are also smaller projects such as the electronic learner's dictionary for German and Italian *Elektronisches Lernerwörterbuch Deutsch–Italienisch* (*ELDIT*) at EURAC (Abel and Weber 2000) or dictionaries for minority languages like the German–Lower Sorbian Dictionary at the Sorbian Institute (Bartels 2010). Finally, special solutions exist where commercial dictionary writing systems are optimized for specific dictionary needs, as is the case with Pasadena, which has been specifically developed by IDM for the *Oxford English Dictionary* (*OED*) as a variant of the commercial software package DPS (Thompson 2005).

A dictionary writing system should never be viewed in isolation, but rather within the framework of a specific dictionary project and its whole environment, including related projects, long-term perspectives, etc. A dictionary project can be divided into three work phases: planning, implementation, and follow-up (see Svensén 2009: 398ff., Atkins and Rundell 2008: 18ff., 97ff.). A series of aspects have to be considered for each phase, with a clear distinction between commercial projects that concentrate primarily on the market and academic projects that focus on recent research trends.[1] During the planning phase, several aspects must be taken into account: the market-driven or research-oriented 'demand', users, contents, entry layout and design, distribution medium, dictionary layout, budget, time schedule, team, workflows, resources, software tools, etc. The implementation phase includes activities such as data selection, input, revisions, proofreading, (automated) typesetting, etc. Finally, issues such as maintenance and the reusability of data are crucial. Thus, the dictionary writing system can be seen as an aid or tool embedded in the entire dictionary writing process, while never losing its function for data synthesis, that is data input and editing.

While a dictionary writing system, being a dedicated system and more than a generic editor, basically supports dictionary compilation and dictionary entry editing, there is another type of software that supports lexicographers in dictionary-making, namely corpus-query systems. These are frequently used for data analysis and selection (see Kilgarriff and Kosem, this volume). In recent years, corpus-query systems have become a standard tool in lexicographic work (Atkins and Rundell 2008). A corpus-query system can be used in addition to a dictionary writing system or be an integral part of it (see below).[2]

5.3 Main characteristics of a dictionary writing system

The core function of a dictionary writing system is entry editing: nowadays dictionaries are written on computers and a dictionary writing system should first and foremost streamline entry writing. It should also be able to cope with the particular demands of complex dictionary writing projects (Atkins and Rundell 2008: 114).

As for dictionary writing, it is important to distinguish between three aspects, which we will briefly summarize here. The most crucial aspect is the content of the dictionary. Second, each dictionary has a specific configuration of its different components or a structured data model. We labelled this a specific 'syntax' earlier, but it might also be termed the 'dictionary grammar' or, using a more technical term,

---

[1] The huge field of well-known, sometimes even quite large and popular online dictionary products that are neither academic nor commercial is not discussed in this chapter, although they represent an important segment that would be worth analysing more in detail (see Nesi, this volume). Such dictionaries or lexical environments may include for example Leo, Linguee, yourdictionary, etc. Within this chapter we consider only products for which scientific literature or documentation on the dictionary writing system is available.

[2] A dictionary writing system should not be confused with desktop publishing (DTP) software (De Schryver and Joffe 2006: 41). These are WYSIWYG layout programs used on personal computers that produce print-ready documents (e.g. Adobe InDesign). A DTP program can be added to or supported by a dictionary writing system.

the document type definition (DTD).[3] Third, there is the data presentation aspect, the formatting and style (see e.g. De Schryver and Joffe 2006: 41). These three aspects should be considered individually, as specific programs are best suited to work on each of them.

Data inputting and editing in dictionaries can happen in many different ways, each of which has advantages and drawbacks. It is, in principle, possible to enter the entire dictionary text in one sequence into any word-processing system. In this way, text is processed and stored linearly, exactly in the way it should appear in the final product. Until recently, both institutions with smaller projects, and large publishing houses have used this method, and to some extent they still do so today in specific circumstances (e.g. the Sorbian Institute works with informants who may be elderly people lacking computer skills and lexicographic expertise).

When using a word-processing system, details such as font type and size can and must be selected directly. So, next to dictionary content, the form becomes an important aspect. The advantages of such a data input system lie in the high degree of flexibility, as the editors are completely free to add or change almost anything anywhere. Among possible disadvantages, different types of information are not always explicitly marked and thus the final product is not searchable; automatic checking of consistency and conformity can also only be done in a limited way. In addition, the reusability of data is not straightforward. For example, it is not possible to search for geographical labels if they are not explicitly tagged as such, or to quickly and easily check if these labels are used in a consistent way (e.g. always using non-abbreviated forms like 'American', etc.). Some drawbacks relating to form and content control or data reuse can be diminished, for example by consistently using uniform labels for single data categories (Svensén 2009: 421).

To spare editors the task of checking the order in which the data are stored, a lexical database can be used where the data are organized in records, each containing a specific series of different types of information (data categories such as definitions, examples, etc.). This allows easy filtering of the entire database according to any input field. As a consequence, users may detect connections in the data that would not be evident in a data set that was stored linearly. From the point of view of the dictionary producer, such a database has the advantage of generating a great variety of products based on one and the same material (Svensén 2009: 421). For example, it would be possible to easily filter out data regarding word spelling to produce a specific spelling dictionary starting from the database of a monolingual dictionary.

---

[3] In a DTD the tags, that is the standardized labels for text characteristics or linguistic phenomena, as well as the structure of a document, can be defined. However, there are more powerful means of defining an XML document. Nowadays an XML schema is frequently used, an advantage being, for example, that the type of information allowed in a document can also be defined and validated. As this chapter is not targeted at computer experts, we will not go into further detail here.

Another method of dictionary writing uses a mark-up language such as XML to input, organize, and edit the data. As in a database, the different types of information are kept separate. However, the data is organized in a hierarchical structure, which is not the case with the database. The hierarchy sees the entire dictionary as the first level, followed by the single dictionary entries, the senses, etc. XML allows data to be stored both as a file and as a database. This is, in fact, a fairly common procedure in dictionary production, since it ensures quicker and more direct access to the data than other storage systems (Svensén 2009: 421).

Mark-up languages, such as the popular XML, allow electronic documents to be structured in a machine-readable way by adding information to the text in the form of tags, that is, standardized labels. These tags may refer to the text and its features, or to the linguistic phenomena it contains. It is possible to define a basically unlimited number of tags for a document, and to define the relationships between the tags within the overall structure. Tagging covers document structure and content, but not appearance: its great advantage is that it is easy to change the appearance of a document without affecting its content (Svensén 2009: 49–50).

Different types of input software can be used when working with a mark-up language such as XML. Some dictionary projects use a generic XML editing tool such as Emacs, which can be adapted and used for lexicography. Figure 5.1 shows an extract from a possible template for a simple entry: the text is inserted by the lexicographer between an opening and a closing tag (in the example, an 'x' is used as a place-holder where the text can be entered).

Although they are efficient and popular programs, these generic tools do not necessarily meet the needs of complex dictionary projects, because they were not specifically designed for lexicographic work. For example, they are quite sensitive to errors made by the editors and often do not have very user-friendly interfaces. Another option is to develop a new system based on an XML editor and adapt it to dictionary production (this can be commercial, freeware, or open software, such as Oxygen or Xmetal). Several major publishers have followed this approach, refining their programs over the years and collecting input from lexicographers and different projects. However, as specific off-the-shelf dictionary writing system packages have been marketed in the last few years, publishers now tend to switch to these (see Atkins and Rundell 2008: 113–14).

Commercial dictionary writing systems are designed to manage the entire dictionary production workflow, from the first entry to the final product ready for publication in print or electronic format. They typically consist of three main components:

- a text editing interface, used by lexicographers to create and edit entries;
- a database, where data is stored; and
- a set of administrative tools for project management and publication (see Atkins and Rundell 2008: 113–14).

```
<word class="noun">
    <noun id="001">
        <lemma>x</lemma>
        <morphology>
            <rawData>x</rawData>
        </morphology>
        <sense>
            <nounSubsense>
                <definition>
                    <rawData>x</rawData>
                </definition>
                <comment>
                    <rawData>x</rawData>
                </comment>
                <translation>
                    <rawData>x</rawData>
                </translation>
                <example>
                    <rawData>x</rawData>
                </example>
            </nounSubsense>
            ...
        </sense>
    </noun>
</word>
```

FIGURE 5.1 An entry template using a generic XML editing tool.

From a conceptual point of view it is not always possible to separate these three components, as they are closely linked to each other in various phases of a dictionary project. Thus, it could be difficult to determine whether a certain feature is connected more to the administrative tools or the editing interface. In fact, the administrative tools can be configured so as to affect editing at the 'front-end' (for example, when entry templates are used). This affects entry operations and administration. Nevertheless, the distinction is a useful starting point to describe some general requirements that a dictionary writing system should be able to meet; in this section the focus will be, not on the dictionary project with its different phases, but on the dictionary writing system itself. The overview provided in Sections 5.3.1 to 5.3.3

summarizes the main characteristics of a dictionary writing system as described by Atkins and Rundell (2008: 113ff.) and Svensén (2009: 415ff.). Relevant Web pages and literature published by the best-known commercial providers of dictionary writing systems are also taken into account.

5.3.1 *The editing tool*

The editing tool allows lexicographers to enter their text into predefined slots or spaces. A dictionary writing system usually offers one editing interface but several different ways of viewing the data. A typical screen in an editing tool may show different panes, usually presenting administrative functions and editing possibilities. Visualizing the data may be as important as adding content (in order to proceed with corrections immediately).

Different views are provided for a 'what-you-see-is-what-you-get' (WYSIWYG) view (or 'preview mode'), and 'tree-diagram' view (Figure 5.2). Both views allow text

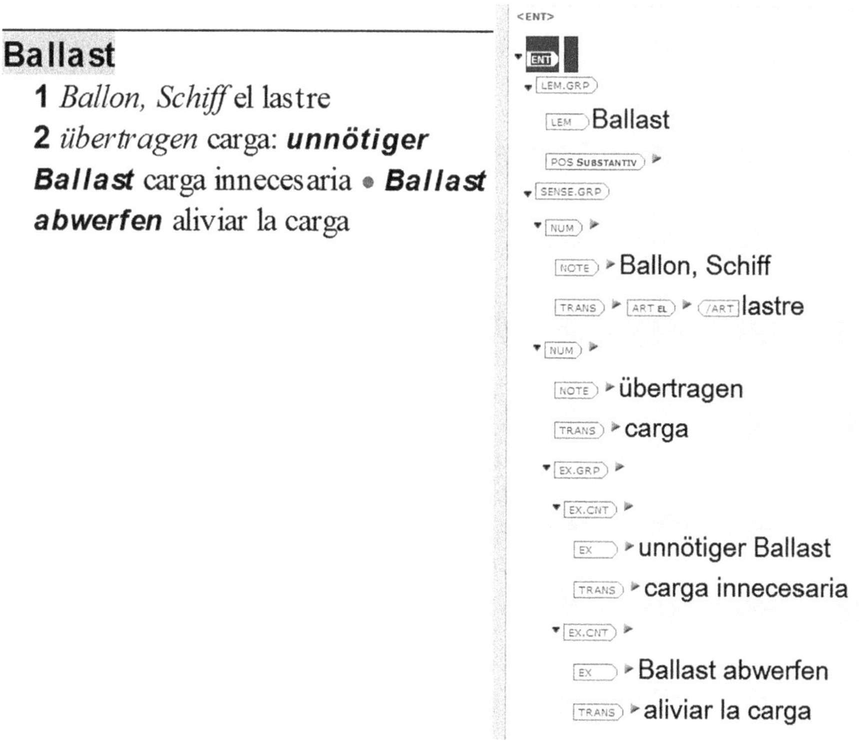

FIGURE 5.2 An extract from a typical screen of an editing interface in a dictionary writing system[4] (left pane: WYSIWYG view; right pane: tree-diagram view).

---

[4] In this example from the dictionary project 'Cornelsen Schulwörterbuch ¡Apúntate!', IDM's DPS is used as the dictionary writing system.

to be added or edited, and any change will automatically be stored centrally. However, the tree diagram is usually the most widely-used editing interface. The WYSIWYG view gives a good idea of the look and feel of the final dictionary entry, but the tree view shows the structural elements of the entry (headword, word class marker, definitions, derived forms, etc.), while at the same time providing the slots where data can be entered.

A good dictionary writing system relieves the lexicographer of routine tasks and automates many 'administrative' procedures that had to be taken care of manually before the introduction of dictionary writing systems. The dictionary writing system allows only a limited number of values and character strings for certain fields (labels and indications of part-of-speech, word-class markers, grammar codes, register labels, etc.), by using drop-down lists, for example. This helps to keep the entries consistent. Furthermore, some non-typographical structure indicators, for example commas that separate alternative meanings of a lemma, brackets around certain information types, a symbol introducing syntagmatic blocks, etc., are generated automatically. This further helps lexicographers who no longer have to worry about formal aspects (font, font style, etc.), which were previously defined in detail by the style guides. Now they can focus on entering text and content into the relevant slots while the final output is generated by style sheets.

The style guide can be integrated into the dictionary writing system to make context-sensitive help available and accessible with a simple click. This is useful, for example, when lexicographers are uncertain about the rules to be applied. Furthermore, style guides can easily be updated according to the changes made during the implementation of a dictionary project, and re-issued to the editorial team. Style guides used to contain many rules concerning presentation and layout; nowadays they offer detailed information on how to use the dictionary writing system and explain, for example, which types of data should be keyed into which fields.

A dictionary writing system also allows lexicographers to copy and paste text and to move fields or entire groups of fields, for example, to other parts of the dictionary. In some systems, lexicographers may create 'templates' for typical entry-types (e.g. a typical noun entry) or recurring parts of entries (e.g. collocation structures) that contain ready-made configurations of structural elements which can be used whenever needed.

While the lexicographer is entering data, the system checks that the syntax corresponds to the dictionary's document type definition, which defines the elements that are part of the dictionary and their required sequence. A dictionary writing system therefore also has a function that validates entry structure: if text elements are inserted in the wrong order, the system alerts the user. For example, if a definition is inserted before the lemma, which always needs to appear first, the dictionary writing system warns the lexicographer of the mistake. Nevertheless, exceptions must be possible, as there may be occasions where this is desirable or necessary.

Fortunately, some complex and highly error-prone procedures can be handled automatically, thus relieving dictionary editors of these tasks. For example, reordering the senses of a polysemous word or adding a new sense in the middle of an entry might call for changes in other parts of the dictionary. Nowadays, it is the dictionary writing system that takes care of re-numbering the whole entry, as well as making the appropriate changes to the sense numbers in any cross-reference. In addition, the dictionary writing system alerts the lexicographer when a lemma is already present in the dictionary. In case of homonymy it requires a homonym number.

Real-time spellcheckers reduce the presence of typos. In addition, if the dictionary requires a restricted defining vocabulary, that is a list of words to be used in the definitions (e.g. the Longman Defining Vocabulary), a dictionary writing system will usually check the words used in definitions against the list of possibilities.

5.3.2 *The database*

Text entered and edited in the 'front end' of the dictionary writing system is stored in the dictionary's database. Usually lexicographers do not work directly on the database to any great extent, but they can use it to run complex searches and filter the text with the help of the specific query language used by the dictionary writing system. It is possible, for example, to find all entries written or modified by an editor, example sentences containing specific patterns, entries including particular words, items having particular register labels, etc.

The database usually uses Unicode, an IT standard that assigns a unique and universal number to each character existing on any platform and in any program or language. In this way, all the characters of all written languages, including special characters such as those used in the International Phonetic Alphabet (IPA), can be universally recognized. This aspect is critical for the database and the editing system must support it.

Today's dictionary writing systems are typically based on a server–client architecture: lexicographers work on computers that are connected to a server where all changes are stored centrally. It thus becomes possible to work via the Internet from any location. This feature is a cornerstone in the recent development of dictionary writing systems. In the 1990s lexicographers began working directly on computers and it was in this period that the first generation of dictionary writing systems was created. At that time, staff usually still worked on the publisher's premises, but in the second half of the decade a variety of technical developments (falling hardware prices, rising hardware capacity, e-mail communication, etc.) enabled collective work to be conducted remotely. From 2000 onwards, fast 24/7 Internet connections have been available. This has supported the latest developments in computational lexicography, where both corpus and dictionary text in progress are stored on a server that editors can access online (from any location) through a corpus-query system and a dictionary writing system. Thus, distributed work is easy to manage via a dictionary writing system and other equivalent environments.

Another important issue is the import and export from and into different formats: the dictionary writing system should allow the export of entire dictionaries or parts of dictionaries in formats such as XML, RTF, PDF, or HTML. This is essential when selling dictionary material or producing electronic dictionaries. At the same time, it should also be possible to import other material into a dictionary in progress.[5]

5.3.3 *Administrative tools*

As well as providing an environment for dictionary writing, editing, and storage, dictionary writing systems also offer 'housekeeping' tools that help to manage large projects. A 'workflow manager' may allocate a batch of entries to be compiled or edited by a particular lexicographer. At any time the system keeps a record of who is working on which entries. Any delay in the planned work schedule will be automatically brought to the attention of the project manager by the dictionary writing system. Complete and exported batches of work can be imported back into the database, so that everyone working on the dictionary always has access to the latest version. The dictionary writing system allows project managers to keep track of progress against the working schedule and budget. Senior staff can also continually monitor the dictionary text as it develops and give feedback to the lexicographers.

The system should ensure that no more than one person at a time can edit an entry. Individual fields in the database should also be 'lockable'. This is useful, for example, when fields of the same type, such as all the pronunciation or etymology fields, are to be edited only by specialists, while other team members take care of the remaining parts of the entries. In addition, the program should have different levels of authorization so that, for example, freelance staff are allowed to edit only the dictionary project they have been hired for and not other products.

A useful feature is version control, that is a facility that makes it possible to track changes and, for example, to provide access to data that have been modified at a specific moment in time. A further aspect is scriptability, that is the possibility of automating processes through scripts. Mass data update allows, for instance, the same correction to be made to a whole set of documents with a single operation. Batch merges allow large amounts of data to be added to the database quickly and easily.

---

[5] A database usually uses XML and DTD, an XML schema or its own formats based on XML, and works on the basis of ORACLE, MSSQL, or Postgres databases.

A series of further issues should be taken into consideration when choosing a dictionary writing system. These are mainly technical aspects regarding service (e.g. hosting, maintenance, backup, setup, training), the operating system (e.g. Windows, Linux, Mac), prices and licences (e.g. commercial or academic licences).

5.4 Off-the-shelf versus in-house software

Every lexicographic project uses some kind of dictionary writing system. Sometimes these tools are written in-house, such as an XML-editor customized for one or more dictionary projects; in other cases, off-the-shelf dictionary writing system packages are preferred. The best-known ones have already been mentioned above. Some scholars (e.g. De Schryver 2011) argue that developing an in-house tool is a version of reinventing the wheel, in view of the fact that excellent, highly sophisticated dictionary writing systems already exist. Before good off-the-shelf dictionary writing system packages became available, it was normal or rather necessary for dictionary publishers to develop their own tools in-house and/or adapt generic XML editors. The same is true for corpus-query systems. In recent years, more and more dictionary publishers have 'walked the proprietary route' by switching to off-the-shelf products. All the main English language publishers have now done so, including well-established ones such as Merriam Webster in the US. This works well even for very complex projects, such as the *OED*, which opted for a special solution on the basis of a proprietary system (Pasadena). One argument in favour of proprietary solutions is that a range of different users will contribute their own suggestions and requests for improvements, many of which will eventually be incorporated into the standard packages. So a tool or a package used by many publishers means that they will collectively contribute to improving it, thus ensuring more rapid development. In this way, both dictionary compilers and developers may benefit from the new situation (De Schryver 2011).

While many publishers have shifted to the proprietary track, several commercial and academic institutions are still using, developing, and improving their own systems. In some cases such dictionary writing system tools are created within an open source and/or freely available development framework (e.g. DEB, Jibiki, EELex), although this is not always the case (e.g. Duden 'Wissensnetz deutsche Sprache').

The decision to develop an in-house tool may be due to the fact that, especially in long-term projects, publishers keep working with their home-grown systems and adapt them progressively to their own requirements. In addition, they may integrate them with a series of further tools tailored for a specific project or a growing number of projects. One difficulty is that, if in-house systems are used, the partly free, partly commercial additional tools must not only be specifically tailored but also need to be able to work together. If, however, commercial products composed of several components are used, the companies have to ensure that these components interoperate smoothly. We will mention only two examples of such home-grown systems being developed and constantly expanded within long-term projects: the elexiko and DWDS initiatives, both under development in a German-speaking academic context (the former at the Institut für Deutsche Sprache in Mannheim, the latter at the Berlin-Brandenburgische Akademie der Wissenschaften in Berlin).

elexiko (Müller-Spitzer 2011, Müller-Spitzer and Möhrs 2008) aims to create an electronic corpus-based dictionary of contemporary German. It is included in the Online Vocabulary System of German (OWID), with the intention of developing a network of interrelated but independent lexicographic products that share some of their data modelling features. A tailor-made, fine-grained XML-DTD containing a large number of elements was created for elexiko, and the structure was then implemented in an XML editor that is used for entering the data (XMLMetal, a commercial product). Dictionary entries are stored in an ORACLE database and lexicographers can perform queries throughout the entire database with the help of a specific interface. In addition, a corpus-query system is used to search within the in-house corpus COSMAS that allows lexicographers to analyse co-occurrences. Within the lexicographic working environment some workflows can be monitored, for example, those entries that are in progress. In order to support editorial work, a 'reference manager' was developed that allows in- and outgoing references in dictionary entries to be crosschecked. This system of coordinated products works well, even though some improvements have been suggested, such as an online preview and the use of templates for some entry parts (Müller-Spitzer and Möhrs 2008).

The DWDS is another example of a long-term lexicographic project that uses an in-house system for lexicographic work (Klein and Geyken 2010). It combines a series of tailor-made tools, such as an XML editor (Oxygen) for data input that has a direct interface to an administration tool for version control (currently used tool: Subversion) so that all lexicographers—including those based in remote locations—can access the central repository and check lexicographic entries in and out while the project manager keeps track of all changes. Corpus data is accessed via another in-house corpus-query system that is used together with other tools. A serious challenge posed by such large lexicographic projects with a substantial number of team members, some of whom work from different locations (as in the case of DWDS), is providing a tool to support good workflow management.

In some cases, an in-house system is developed due to the need to provide an environment for lexical database management as well as semantic networks and ontologies: that is, the system should be used not only for the production of dictionaries, but also for encyclopedias, Wordnets,[6] or similar products. Two examples

---

[6] Wordnets are large lexical databases in which nouns, verbs, adjectives, and adverbs are grouped into sets of synonyms called 'synsets', each expressing a distinct concept. By convention, 'WordNet' (capital W,

deserve particular mention. First, the Dictionary Editing and Browsing (DEB) platform is an open source and freely available development framework (Horák and Rambousek 2007, Horák *et al.* 2008, Vossen *et al.* 2007). Within this platform, which works on a client–server basis, a range of dictionary applications can be used. The tools include a dictionary browser (DEBDict), a dictionary writing system for the development of the Czech Lexical Database (PRALED) that will be linked to a corpus query system (Manatee/Bonito corpus manager and the Word Sketch Engine), a Wordnet editor and browser (DEBVisDic) including functionalities such as synset preview, remote teamwork capabilities, and an administration interface. On the basis of the Wordnet editor, a specific application has been developed for a project called Cornetto, designed to build a lexical semantic database for Dutch by combining and interconnecting two electronic dictionaries (the 'Referentie Bestand Nederlands' and the 'Dutch Wordnet') and thus containing, inter alia, semantic relations, combinatorial relations, and an ontology.

The German publisher Duden (Alexa *et al.* 2002) felt the need to replace the editorial system 'Reda' they had been using for more than twenty years, where each dictionary was compiled separately, by a new tool for the administration of language data that offers a new working environment for lexicographers. This innovation was based on a formal explicit representation of all Duden dictionary entries (integrating lexical and ontological information) and thus reduces the redundancy and increases the efficient maintenance of the dictionary data within a single data pool. It was also intended to support reusability for both print and electronic products, as well as the development of language technology applications. The current result is the 'Wissensnetz deutsche Sprache' (German Language Knowledge Network) which contains dictionary data that are semantically interlinked through a complex system of multiple and different underlying ontologies. Dictionary entries within the 'Wissensnetz' have a particular structure: an entry not only contains lemma- and sense-related data, but also a concept-related level. The sense level represents the bridge between lemma and concepts, as each sense can be linked to a concept through an explicit semantic relation (e.g. synonymy, hyperonymy, meronymy).

There are many good reasons for choosing one solution rather than another. The basic consideration when choosing a dictionary writing system is the need or needs that it is expected to meet, and whether the whole lexicographic environment can be managed by an off-the-shelf system or not. Obviously, the kind of financial investments that are possible or foreseen within a project are also an issue. It may be argued (cf. De Schryver 2011: 647–8) that sometimes the series of reasons given for the development of an in-house system is not in fact really decisive. Many of these

capital N) is used to refer to the original English-language lexical database developed at Princeton University. 'Wordnets' (without capital N) refers to the wide range of similar lexical databases that were subsequently created for other languages. See Chapter 12 for more information.

aspects, such as the need for a clear overview of complex articles, user-friendliness, or a system that can handle a very complex document type definition, are already standard features of any off-the-shelf tool.

There is a good deal of convergence between the various commercially available dictionary writing systems with respect to their main aspects and components (such as a text-editing interface with real-time preview, administrative tools, etc.), as it is inevitable that the positive innovations introduced by one supplier will soon be adopted by other providers as well. As a consequence, most commercial products are of good quality. Some have particular strengths. For example, ABBY (Rylova 2010, Kuzmina and Rylova 2010) has very good tools for search queries, offering a filter with tick boxes that can be easily used without knowing any special query language, while this may be necessary for other tools. TLex has an integrated corpus-query system and a ruler tool that helps ensure a balanced treatment of entries and space allocation (article length), a feature that is very useful for print dictionaries. IDM is particularly strong in its workflow and project management functions, although the system is not entirely intuitive. In order to take advantage of the large number of functions available, a certain amount of advanced knowledge is required of the user.

Differences between the systems may also relate to quite basic aspects, such as the price and availability of academic licences (e.g. TLex has quite affordable prices for its academic licences). Such aspects may be decisive when choosing one tool over the other.

The future will tell us whether new features will be offered or required by dictionary publishers and if so, which ones will be implemented. To name just one development, recent discussions focus on a supporting tool that could "activate 'layers of restricted defining vocabulary'" (De Schryver and Prinsloo 2011: 7). The underlying idea is that "one would be able to set a certain level or 'age range' for a particular dictionary under compilation and that the dictionary writing system would then, during the writing of the dictionary, automatically flag or colour-code those words not belonging to the approved defining vocabulary for that level" (pp. 7–8).[7]

5.5 Combination and integration of tools

Today, lexicographers can use a wide range of tools for different phases of dictionary production. Some may be part of a dictionary writing system package, while others are stand-alone products. In any case, they should ideally interoperate smoothly with

---

[7] Further research on specific user needs regarding (graded) dictionary definitions is needed. The findings of the study on dictionary definitions compiled for different age groups reported by De Schryver and Prinsloo (2011: 26) indicate that the definitions in the dictionaries examined are generally too difficult for the intended age groups.

dictionary writing systems. This is especially true for corpus-query systems, which are among the most important tools for lexicographers.

Dictionary writing systems share their main features. However, some dictionary writing system suppliers offer additional tools that may be of interest for commercial publishers in a competitive market, and thus be decisive when choosing one product or another. We will list some of these additional tools in a short excursus, before moving on to dictionary writing systems in a stricter sense.

Dictionary publishers are nowadays facing increasing competition from free online dictionaries (see Lannoy 2010a). While established dictionary publishers hire people to create content, other providers recycle and reuse this content, making it available for free. This obviously reduces the publishers' potential market share (Kilgarriff 2009). "Free" is therefore discussed as a "leading [business] model for online dictionaries" and IDM has "entered the online dictionary market to provide publishers with the means to compete with the most successful free websites that deliver well indexed content very quickly, have web pages optimised for search engines, multilingual interfaces and put extreme care in the data" (Lannoy 2010a: 174). Free dictionary websites, which undoubtedly have a strong attraction power, must be indexed and optimized for search engines. This can enhance the visibility of a product. The quality of the content helps in "building user loyalty and depth of visit on the websites" (p. 174). This may establish the brand of free dictionary websites and enhance the upsales potential for other products.

Dictionary writing system suppliers such as IDM have recently been discussing the issue of user-generated data. Accepting user-generated content means reverting to a democratic editorial process and an open critical review of the product. It represents, in fact, an essential source of improvement and is therefore well worth considering. From the point of view of commercial publishers, an online dictionary should be as comprehensive as possible, so that it is privileged in web searches (as it is subject to SEO (Search Engine Optimization) principles) (Lannoy 2010b).

In this context, it is interesting to note that in recent years several authors have considered aspects of collaborative dictionary writing and its methods, in which the boundaries between the lexicographer and the user have become blurred (Abel 2006). An example of this is "fuzzy simultaneous feedback", a concept that, in its electronic adaptation, refers to a type of intelligent and adaptive dictionary in which customization is performed online in real time (De Schryver, in print).

A variety of tools is usually provided as part of a dictionary writing system package, ranging from entry compilation to publication. Corpus-query systems (e.g. Sketch Engine, CQP, DWDS/DDC, COSMAS, etc.) are often presented as separate tools, being considered necessary to analyse future dictionary data. In an ideal world, in order to streamline the whole process, it would also be desirable to have the corpus-query system integrated. In this context, a historical note may be interesting:

the first true off-the-shelf tool was Gestorlex, developed by the software house Textware for the Danish publisher Gyldendal in the late 1980s, and later adopted by Longman. It was an integrated dictionary writing system and corpus-query system and, despite being a good system, it had the fatal flaw of running on an operating system (OS/2) that could not compete with Windows.[8] To the best of my knowledge, the only off-the-shelf dictionary writing system package which currently has an integrated corpus-query system is TLex, which offers basic functions such as the production of concordances based on corpus queries, that is lists of keywords in context. Word sketches, however, cannot be produced by TLex: these are lexical profiles, or rather corpus-based outputs of the grammatical and collocational behaviour of a word (Kilgarriff *et al.* 2004: 105 ff.), which "improve on standard collocation lists by using a grammar and a parser to find collocates in specific grammatical relations" (Atkins and Rundell 2008: 109). Rather than a single list built on grammar, they produce a list of subjects, one of objects, and so forth. The word sketches function is offered by the corpus-query system Sketch Engine that is used in many dictionary projects (e.g. in publishing houses such as Oxford University Press, Cambridge University Press, Collins, Macmillan, INL, Cornelsen) (Kilgarriff *et al.* 2010b: 412; see also Kilgarriff and Kosem, this volume).

Some may thus opt for maximum compatibility between the dictionary writing system and corpus-query system and not for integration of the two tools. An example where this works quite smoothly is the NEID/DANTE project, where the IDM-dictionary writing system and the Sketch Engine are closely connected. This obviously requires some collaboration between the suppliers. DANTE (Database of Analysed Texts in English) is a lexicographic project that aims at building a fine-grained lexical database on the basis of the analysis of corpus data (cf. Rundell, this volume). It is targeted at lexicographers as a basis for the compilation of a concrete dictionary, but it also has potential for other uses in language technology. In this case, the database is being developed as the basis for the elaboration of a New English–Irish Dictionary (NEID)[9] (Atkins *et al.* 2010, Rundell and Kilgarriff 2011). In the DANTE database, all word senses, constructions, and collocations are illustrated with one or more unedited corpus examples. Lexicographers were asked to extract example sentences from the corpus system and feed them into the dictionary editing system, using a fiddly standard copy-and-paste function. Later, a button for 'one-click copying' was added at the end of a concordance line to allow quick and smooth

---

[8] Further reading and background information can be found at http://www.lim.nl/monitor/textware. html, http://nlp.fi.muni.cz/projects/deb2/emasters/www/dps/03-04-03.html, and http://www.emp.dk/ilex-web/index.jsp?content=100000023,1&toc=100000025,1.

[9] The New English–Irish Dictionary is being developed for Foras na Gaeilge, Dublin, which is the official Irish government body responsible for the promotion of the Irish language (http://www.forasna-gaeilge.ie/).

selection of the sentences, at the same time pasting them directly into the correct field in the dictionary writing system (Rundell and Kilgarriff 2011).

The TickBox Lexicography (TBL) option is a further development towards making the lexicographer's life easier. TBL models and streamlines the process of extracting data from a corpus and inserting it into a dictionary writing system (Kilgarriff *et al.* 2010b: 413, Kilgarriff and Kosem, this volume). Thus, it is no longer necessary to mark single concordances: by clicking on tickboxes, entire chunks of data (e.g. a collocation type plus example) can be transferred into the correct fields of the dictionary writing system in one go. TickBox Lexicography includes another function, that is GDEX ('Good Dictionary Example eXtractor'; Kilgarriff *et al.* 2008), an algorithm targeted at identifying sentences that are likely to fulfil the criteria of being a 'good' example. With this function, lexicographers are not faced with long lists of concordances, as the system makes a choice of six corpus example sentences (by default, but this can be changed according to the project) (Rundell and Kilgarriff 2011, Kilgarriff *et al.* 2010b: 413). This function should spare the lexicographer from the demanding and time-consuming scanning of thousands of concordance lines, a task that has been called a "new form of drudgery for the lexicographer" (Rundell and Kilgarriff 2011: 260).

Other projects have also tried to make data transfer from the corpus to the dictionary writing system more efficient. To mention only one, elexiko has a function where example sentences from the COSMAS corpus can be inserted into the editing software with a drag-and-drop-function.

In conclusion, it is important to consider carefully which functions and features are really essential for the dictionary project that is to be started or further developed before choosing a dictionary writing system. It is in this phase that the choice between a known working environment and a new system has to be made. It is extremely important that project leaders make this decision only after intense discussion with lexicographers and IT experts, so as to make sure that all the advantages and disadvantages are well weighed against each other.

The questions to be asked include costs, time constraints, and issues of quality, quantity, and distribution; for commercial products, all these aspects are strongly market driven. In addition, the fierce competition from a growing number of resources that are freely available online must be faced. Finally, the functions and features of a dictionary writing system, as described earlier, must all be considered separately, including the modules that the dictionary writing system is expected to include or to be perfectly compatible with (e.g. workflow management, proofreading, data conversion for any electronic application, online publication, mobile devices, or CD-ROM/DVD, data searching in the whole repository, hosting). Practical issues such as in-house and/or external helpdesk support should also be considered.

5.6 Dictionary writing systems for multifunctional databases

A new challenge for today's dictionary writing systems is that they are increasingly used not just to write single dictionaries but to build databases that will serve as the basis for many dictionaries. Atkins and Rundell (2008: 98) describe "the ideal way to compile a corpus-based dictionary from scratch" as a two-fold process, as we can generally distinguish between analysis and synthesis. It could even be a three-fold process, if we include translation for bilingual dictionaries as well. Lexicographers compile a lexical database on the basis of corpus evidence; generally speaking database entries reflect dictionary entries, but they are much more detailed. For example, they contain a huge range of senses per headword, a rich selection of collocations, example sentences, etc. (pp. 97ff.), providing an excellent foundation for the next steps. For bilingual dictionaries, this means first and foremost translating the database; elsewhere, it means editing the entries and compiling a dictionary. This approach has been applied, for example in the NEID/DANTE project (Atkins and Rundell 2008), but also in other contexts where huge lexical databases are being developed. These include the lexical database of the Czech language in the twenty-first century ('Lexikon 21'; Rangelova and Králík 2007), the database for the Dutch language ('The Referentiebestand Nederlands' (RBN); Van der Vliet 2007), and the 'Online Vocabulary System of German' (OWID; Müller-Spitzer and Möhrs 2008),[10] to name just a few.

In these and other contexts, huge multifunctional lexicographic databases are being built as a basis that may meet the "different types of needs of different types of users in different types of situations" (Spohr 2011: 103)—in terms of the modern theory of lexicographic functions (cf. Bergenholtz and Tarp 2002)—and thus steer the creation of specific dictionaries.

This touches on another issue, which is currently quite relevant in the context of dictionary writing systems. It is an idea introduced or further developed in the context of function theory but also beyond: Spohr (2011) introduced the concept of a "pluri-monofunctional lexicographic tool", a tool "that is capable of deriving multiple monofunctional dictionaries". Gouws (2006: 53) describes the concept of a 'Mutterwörterbuch' ('mother dictionary') as a huge virtual dictionary that contains different dictionaries as subtexts (where the single items are marked so that it is possible to derive specific dictionaries). There are also some earlier, and to a certain extent related, ideas: the idea of multifunctional linguistic databases with multiple uses and multifunctional dictionaries was already of topical interest in the 1980s. Multifunctionality, as well as reusability, were discussed at two levels:

---

[10] OWID could be described as a lexical database "as it contains a huge amount of lexical data and it is not designed for a specific user type and specific situations" (Müller-Spitzer and Möhrs 2008: 43).

human users and natural language processing applications (see Kruyt, 2003, for an overview).[11] The issue of multifunctionality has also been raised in the context of specialized languages, in particular in the context of the creation of terminology databases. Martin and van der Vliet (2003: 338) describe a useful multi-purpose or multifunctional, and multi-user approach to a database from which specific dictionaries or front-end databases can be derived on the basis of different users and their needs (Martin 2000). Atkins (1996: 531) presented an early idea of a "virtual dictionary" to be derived from a "real" database within the frame of a "multilingual hypertextual lexical resource".

Lexical databases are not always compiled from scratch as in the DANTE case; they can be built on the basis of pre-existing dictionaries. For example, the Duden 'Wissensnetz' includes almost the entire lexicographic material owned by the publisher. In general, there is a trend towards change in the whole lexicographic process, as lexicographers become more and more engaged in adapting and enriching existing resources and targeting parts of resources at different user groups. In other words, lexicographic work is now largely becoming an activity that builds on existing material.

When creating lexicographic databases, it is preferable to work on the basis of models for the representation of different monofunctional dictionaries in order to assure quality (as proposed, for example, by Spohr 2011). Spohr presents a multilayer architecture that deals dynamically with user needs, thanks to the introduction of a layer that contains "function-specific information for each lexicographic indication in-between the user interface and the lexicographic database. This layer acts as a kind of filter that lets through only those indications which are believed to be relevant to certain types of users in particular types of situations (on the basis of Tarp 2008)". All indications are presented in a form that is appropriate for particular user types, for example by using labels in different languages and varying degrees of specialized terminology. As function-related specifications are separate from dictionary content, this additional layer can dynamically generate different monofunctional views of the lexical data in the database, on the basis of different combinations of situation and user types.

In a further step, not only user groups but individual users are considered. There is also a recognition of intelligent and adaptive media (De Schryver 2010, Trap-Jensen 2010a, Müller-Spitzer and Möhrs 2008, Gamper and Knapp 2000, 2002), although Trap-Jensen (2010a: 1134) stresses that "[t]he notion of dictionary customisation is still in its infancy". Thus, more research is needed into dictionary usability. It seems that dictionaries and dictionary entries will come to be considered more and more as dynamic entities (Spohr 2011) and that dictionary writing systems will have to be able

---

[11]   The idea of multifunctional linguistic databases is discussed with reference to Zampolli (1987), and that of multifunctional dictionaries with reference to Zimmermann (1984) (see Kruyt 2003: 194).

to deal with that. In many cases a 'dictionary writing system' is, strictly speaking, rather a 'database writing system'. In any case, it is a tool that allows lexicographers to create and manage comprehensive and increasingly dynamic resources.

5.7 Conclusion

Dictionary writing systems are quickly developing away from being pure editing systems and/or authoring tools towards becoming applications that include a huge range of components and modules with a great number of functions. The dictionary writing system in the sense of a mere editing aid is just a small part. This is certainly true for the big commercial products that support the workflow and routines of dictionary projects from the planning and design phase up to the publication of the final product. They have to be as flexible as possible to the different but recurring requirements of the various target groups. Commercial off-the-shelf tools mainly serve commercial publishers and try to respond to the market. This means that they have to focus their products more and more on other media alongside printed dictionaries: electronic media, online dictionaries, CD-ROM/DVDs, and mobile phones. Remaining competitive with non-commercial entities that publish freely accessible online dictionaries is another important issue for the dictionary market.

In-house products support lexicographers in the same way as off-the-shelf software, for example by following style guidelines in a coherent way. Essentially, they fulfil the same functions as their larger commercial siblings. Sometimes they are tailor-made applications to be used for single or smaller projects, sometimes for long-term projects and huge teams of workers. Close cooperation with a team of IT experts is always necessary, even when a commercial off-the-shelf tool has been chosen.

On the whole, when dealing with dictionary writing systems it is evident that recent developments indicate a fundamental change in lexicographic processes and the lexicographic workplace. Processes are characterized by growing automation and the work of the lexicographers is changing: for example, more often than not, lexicographers compile lexicographic databases and update existing material. User expectations are being discussed intensively, too. End user participation in the production of dictionaries, for example, represents a significant and ongoing debate (user-generated content and/or collaborative dictionary writing, user customization, and adaptive user views, etc.). Electronic media are increasingly becoming the centre of attention and will raise new questions about presentation and visualization in all phases of dictionary writing (for visualization of linguistic information, see Culy and Lyding 2010, Rohrdantz *et al.* 2010).

The dictionary writing system plays a central role in the whole process of dictionary production: it is developing towards an increasingly versatile, multifunctional 'all-in-one' tool that works as a dashboard from where a series of processes and tasks can be controlled, managed, and implemented.

Acknowledgements

I am grateful for many interesting and fruitful discussions and mail correspondence in the course of preparing this chapter. My particular thanks go to (in alphabetical order): Melina Alexa, Hauke Bartels, Model Benedikt, Henning Bergenholtz, Philippe Climent, Chris Culy, Gilles-Maurice De Schryver, Henrik Dittmann, Birgit Eickhoff, Angelika Haller-Wolf, Alexander Geyken, Holger Hvelplund, Adam Kilgarriff, Annette Klosa, Margit Langements, Verena Lyding, Christine Möhrs, Carolin Müller-Spitzer, Michael Rundell, Dennis Spohr, Antje Tölpel, and Ülle Viks. My special thanks, however, go to Elena Chiocchetti and Peter Farbridge for proofreading the text in English.

Dictionaries and websites

ABBY Lingvo Content. http://www.abbyy.com.

Cornelsen Schulwörterbuch ¡Apúntate! Spanisch-Deutsch/Deutsch-Spanisch 2011. Berlin: Cornelsen Verlag.

DEB. http://deb.fi.muni.cz/index.php.

DWDS. www.dwds.de.

EELex. http://www.keeletehnoloogia.ee/projects-1/lexicographers-workbench.

ELDIT. http://www.eurac.edu/eldit.

elexiko. http://www.owid.de/elexiko_/index.html; elexiko 'reference manager' (Vernetzungsmanager). http://www.ids-mannheim.de/lexik/BZVelexiko/vernetzung.html.

Emacs. http://en.wikipedia.org.wiki/Emacs.

German–Lower Sorbian Dictionary. http://www.dolnoserbski.de/dnw/index.htm.

IDM DPS. http://www.idm.fr.

iLEX. http://www.emp.dk.

Intelligent Views. http://www.i-views.de.

Johnson, Samuel (1766[6]). *A Dictionary of the English Language.* London: A. Millar (online version of the sixth edition: http://www.archive.org/stream/dictionaryofenglo2johnuoft#-page/n37/mode/2up).

Leo. http://dict.leo.org/.

Linguee. http://www.linguee.de/.

Longman. http://longmanusahome.com/dictionaries/index.php (Defining Vocabulary: http://longmanusahome.com/dictionaries/defining.php).

OWID. http://www.owid.de/.

Oxygen. http://www.oxygenxml.com/.

Referentiebestand Nederlands. RBN http://www.inl.nl/nl/lexica/referentiebestand-nederlands-(rbn).

Subversion. http://subversion.apache.org/.
Termania Portal. http://www.termania.net/.
TLex. http://tshwanedje.com.
Xmetal. http://na.justsystems.com.
XMLMind. http://www.xmlmind.com/.
XMLSpy. http://www.altova.com/xml-editor/.
yourdictionary.com. http://www.yourdictionary.com/.
(links checked on 12 June 2011)

6

Theoretical challenges in the transition from lexicographical p-works to e-tools

SVEN TARP

6.1 Introduction

Lexicography is in the midst of an important transformation process. There is little doubt that printed dictionaries will be published for a long period ahead but, at the same time, it is no secret that the electronic medium is gaining still more ground and will gradually overtake and outshine paper as the preferred platform for this secular tool which continues to be of great—and even growing—usefulness to human beings. In this transformation process, the question has been raised as to whether we need a new theory that could guide the conception and production of lexicographical e-tools or if we can use the theories already developed in the era of lexicographical printed works, henceforth referred to as 'p-works'. In order to answer this question, it is first of all necessary to determine whether a lexicographical theory exists, is possible at all, or even wanted. In fact, the very concept of theory is widely disputed within lexicographical circles (cf. Tarp 2010). In a recent publication in which he discusses the theory of lexicographical functions, Yukio Tono (2010: 2) asks: "Do we really need a 'theory'?"

After a long and fruitful discussion, Tono's final answer to his own question is affirmative, but his view is not supported by all lexicographers, especially those belonging to the Anglo-Saxon tradition. For instance, Sue Atkins and Michael Rundell (2008: 4) "do not believe that such a thing exists". Along the same lines, in a recent book on English lexicography, Henri Bejoint dedicates only half a page to the question of theory and writes:

I simply do not believe that there exists a theory of lexicography, and I very much doubt that there can be one. Those who have proposed a general theory have not been found convincing by the community, and for good reasons. A theory is a system of ideas put forward to explain phenomena that are not otherwise explainable. A science has a theory, a craft does not. All natural phenomena need a theory, but how can there be a theory of the production of artefacts? There are theories of language, there may be theories of lexicology, but there is no theory of lexicography. Lexicography is above all a craft, the craft of preparing dictionaries, as well as an art, as Landau (2001) says. It may be becoming more scientific, but it has not become a science. (Bejoint 2010: 381)

Bejoint's point of view is strongly embedded in an Anglo-Saxon tradition according to which science is related only to natural phenomena and which puts all other phenomena into the sphere of art and craft (cf. Toulmin 1990). This contrasts strongly with traditions in other parts of the world, for instance the Russian and the Germanic traditions. Hence, in Denmark you can find *cultural science* (kulturvidenskab), *art science* (kunstvidenskab), *literature science* (litteraturvidenskab), *social science* (samfundsvidenskab), *information science* (informationsvidenskab), and also *dictionary science* (ordbogsvidenskab) as defined by Tarp (2008: 4–6). Similarly, more than thirty years ago, the Russian researcher F. P. Sorokoletov defined lexicography as "the science of the classification processes of word material and its presentation in dictionaries" ["der Wissenschaft von den Verfahren der Klassifikation des Wortmaterials und dessen Präsentation in Wörterbüchern"] (Sorokoletov 1978: 79).

It is a matter of course that a craft is neither a science nor a theory, but based upon a meticulous study of the corresponding practice it is perfectly possible to form reflections and, little by little, systematize them into an organized set of ideas or statements, i.e. a theory capable of explaining, guiding, and even renovating existing practice. This was what Ščerba (1940) intended to do seven decades ago in his groundbreaking contribution to lexicography. This is what Wiegand (1987, 1998) did with his 'general theory of lexicography' and this is what has been done with the 'theory of lexicographical functions' (cf. Tarp 2008). It may be that these theories "have not been found convincing by the community", mainly the Anglo-Saxon lexicographical community, but this does not mean that they do not exist, are not possible or even much needed by those who are trying to solve the complex problems related to the present paradigm shift within lexicography.

6.2 General and specific theories

When discussing the need for a new lexicographical theory, it is necessary to bear in mind that there are various levels of theory. In this respect, a distinction should be made between *general theories*, containing general systematic statements about lexicography and *specific theories*, containing statements about its various sub-areas (cf. Tarp 2008: 9–10). At present, only two actualized and competing general theories of lexicography are known to the author of this contribution, i.e. Wiegand's theory and the function theory, although it should also be taken into consideration that:

in the Soviet period lexicography developed into an independent discipline with its own theory, own tasks and own methods for their solution. (Sorokoletov 1978: 79)

["die Lexikographie in der sowjetischen Zeit zu einer selbständigen Disziplin mit einer ihr eigenen Theorie, eigenen Aufgaben und eigenen Methoden zu deren Lösung."]

Whether these general theories will have to be renewed during the current transition from p-lexicography to e-lexicography will be discussed in the following sections. But apart from general theories, there are a considerable number of specific theories about various topics. Some of these are integrated in one of the general theories whereas others are not. It goes without saying that these theories may have to be modified in one way or another if they are integrated in a general theory subject to renovation. But apart from this, there will be specific theories dealing with topics and sub-areas of lexicography that will hardly require any changes in the present paradigm shift. In contrast, other specific theories reflect topics and sub-areas that are directly related to the new electronic platform and the corresponding new options for lexicography and therefore will have to be completely altered or even replaced by new up-to-date theories.

6.3 Human cognition and the historical dimension

According to the latest research, lexicography, in one form or another, has been a social and cultural practice for about four thousand years. During this long period, practical lexicography, i.e. lexicography as "art and craft" according to the terminology of Landau (2001) and Bejoint (2010), has developed and passed through various stages in terms of its media: lexicographical works have been carved in clay, handwritten on paper or papyrus, printed with different technologies, and, more recently, made available electronically on various platforms such as compact discs, the Internet, mobile phones, and hand-held computers. In the last resort, lexicography is a practical—and theoretical—response to needs detected in society and, as such, is strongly embedded in specific cultural, historical, and technological environments. However, at the highest level of abstraction, the needs giving rise to lexicographical products belong to the same main categories, and so do the data selected and prepared to fulfil these needs, notwithstanding the concrete type of media in which they are presented. At this level of abstraction, if a general theory of lexicography in the real sense of the word had existed four thousand years ago, there would have been no reason to change it when the practical tools of lexicography passed from clay to papyrus, and later from handwritten to printed. And neither would there be any reason to invent a new *general theory* during the present paradigm shift from p-lexicography to e-lexicography. In such an ideal world, the only thing theoretically new to be developed would be—as already mentioned—*specific theories* related to the new media, for instance specific theories about data processing, data presentation, data access, and data linking.

However, history shows that no science has ever come into the world fully-grown and fully-armed like Athena from the head of Zeus. The process of acquiring knowledge about a specific subject field is extremely complex and necessarily passes through various stages where knowledge already acquired is constantly challenged by the results of new observations, thus leading to a spiral of growing cognition through a fruitful interaction of theory and practice. In this sense, a general theory about any subject field constantly needs to be improved and sometimes even replaced with a new one (paradigm shift), as it has to adapt itself to the continuous flow of new data generated in the framework of the scientific research process. This is a general law of human cognition, and lexicographical research is no exception. However, the process is even more complex when the theoretical work is done within disciplines like lexicography and social sciences in general, where the research field is occasionally subject to qualitative transformation. Apart from finding completely new elements within such fields, researchers may also frequently come across elements that existed earlier but only in an embryonic form, for which reason they may not have noticed them, or at least paid sufficient attention to them in terms of their incorporation and place in the theoretical model or system. When the subject field passes from one qualitative stage to another, such hitherto 'hidden' elements may 'unfold' and reveal themselves to be elements that should occupy an important and central place in building the corresponding theory. This is what is happening to lexicography in its present shift from p-works to e-tools. Apart from the completely new elements which obviously exist related to the new media and technologies, there are also other elements which have existed since the very first dictionary was produced several thousand years ago. These have never really been discussed or paid sufficient attention to in the theoretical literature until now, when it has become evident that they are central and important elements which, correctly interpreted and understood, make it possible to project lexicography far beyond its traditional limits.

6.4 Lexicography and information science

What are these old elements now coming to the forefront? The answer is to be found in the completely new technological environment in which lexicography is developing today. The use of computer and information sciences, as well as the increased focus on information in present society, have made it clear that lexicography is, above all, an information discipline (cf. Tarp 2007). When an abstraction is made from the concrete and specific content of the needs that lexicographical works have aimed at meeting, what is left is their character of *information needs* in the true sense of the word. Besides, if a distinction is made between *global information needs*, i.e. the needs related to a more profound study of a specific subject field (or part of it), and *punctual information needs* related to a single and limited topic within a larger subject field, or to the solution of specific tasks or problems, then it becomes clear that lexicographical works and tools are, par excellence, *artefacts designed to be consulted* in order to meet punctual information needs.

A short panoramic overview shows that lexicographical works are not the only types of artefacts produced with a view to satisfying punctual information needs. Manuals, how-tos, user guides, telephone books, Internet-based search engines, and indexes (in textbooks and other books) are all devices totally or partially designed to be consulted in order to retrieve punctual information for one purpose or another. And the list can easily be extended. So what is the relation between lexicography and all these consultation tools? It is evident that they all have something fundamental in common, but it is also clear that they have developed from different traditions. In reality, what is gradually becoming sharper is the contours of *one big discipline embracing all types of consultation tools designed to meet punctual information needs*, a discipline which may be considered an *integrated part of information science*. This discipline should develop its own general theory as part of information science. In this respect, lexicography has a great deal to contribute to other theories dealing with punctual consultation tools and to information science in general and, in turn, it has a great deal to learn from them.

This vision of lexicography is not only shared by lexicographers working within the broad framework of the function theory (e.g. Heid 2011, Leroyer 2011, Tarp 2011, and Fuertes-Olivera and Bergenholtz 2011a), but also by information scientists such as Bothma (2011), as became clear from the very constructive confrontation of ideas at a Symposium on e-Lexicography organized at the University of Valladolid, Spain, in June 2010. By definition, the new vision of lexicography implies that the existing general theories will have to be modified and transformed accordingly. This holds true for the function theory and even more so for Wiegand's 'general theory of lexicography' which, apart from some general statements valid for all types of lexicographical works (e.g. that they are always utility products conceived to satisfy human needs), is strongly focused on the existing dictionary form and the structures found in printed dictionaries (cf. Wiegand and Fuentes Morán 2009). But, as pointed out by Rufus Gouws, in order to progress, lexicographers—and scholars from other relevant disciplines—will not only have to learn, but also to "unlearn" and get rid of some bad habits and traditions:

Looking back at the development of the theory and practice of lexicography, it is clear that for too long the practice of printed dictionaries endured without a sound theory, for too long lexicography did not establish itself as an independent discipline; for too long the pool of lexicographers was restricted to experts from a single field; for too long innovation in the lexicographic practice was impeded by its theory being based on practice, not preceding that practice; for too long lexicographic theory was exclusively directed at the production of dictionaries. Looking to the future, the planning and compilation of electronic dictionaries and the further development of a coherent and medium-unspecific theory we must unlearn a great deal of what we know, and we must learn anew so that we produce innovative reference tools, including dictionaries. (Gouws 2011: 29)

Although it will be the future confrontation of ideas that finally will decide how far the various traditions within the broader framework of information science may contribute, "unlearn", and learn from each other, it may well not be premature to claim that among lexicography's strongest contributions are the very concepts of *punctual information needs, needs satisfaction,* and *access to prepared data* from which the corresponding information may be retrieved. According to the lexicographical function theory developed over the past two decades, users' punctual information needs are intimately related not only to the type of user but also to the type of social situation or activity where the needs occur. The type of user depends on a number of criteria which, in fact, constitute an open list that may be still more detailed according to the type of situation and the type of consultation tool in question, whereas the types of relevant social situation or activity can be grouped into four fundamental types: cognitive, communicative, operational, and interpretive, each of which may be further subdivided into a number of subtypes. This complex concept of punctual information needs permits a much more precise characterization of the exact nature and content of the needs and, consequently, a much more precise characterization of the data required to satisfy these needs. And the same holds true for access to these data, at least in the case of the controlled framework of a printed consultation tool or an e-tool linked to the limited amount of data in a prepared database, i.e. without considering the possible relation to the 'unlimited' amount of data made available through connection to the Internet. In this last respect, the relation between a 'limited' database and the 'unlimited' data on the Internet, lexicography will probably have a great deal to learn from information science, although Bergenholtz and Gouws may be perfectly right when they claim that:

the applicability of the access process, as developed in lexicography, goes beyond dictionaries, illustrating the importance of a process not relevant within the field of linguistics but extremely important in the successful use of reference works. (Bergenholtz and Gouws 2010: 103)

To sum up, the new technological environment in which lexicography is developing strongly suggests that this discipline should be considered *part and parcel of a broader consultation discipline integrated into information science* through a process where lexicography is an equal and open-minded partner which has both something to contribute and something to learn. In this way, the general theory of lexicography will form a synthesis with other theories and integrate into a completely new general theory of consultation tools. This new theory, which by means of the dialectical negation of the negation, will take everything useful from previous theories, will not only be in a position to describe present lexicography and guide the conception of future consultation tools, whether lexicographical or not, but also to enlighten past lexicography and consultation practice in a wider perspective than hitherto. In this theoretical transition, the practical products of lexicography will obviously not lose their characteristic as utility tools conceived to satisfy specific types of human (information) needs. On the contrary, this character will be enhanced and lexicography may, among other things, benefit from the scientific methods of usability testing developed in the framework of information science as shown by Heid (2011).

6.5 Theory and the true advantages of e-lexicography

Although electronic dictionaries may basically meet the same types of information needs as their printed relatives, the new media—and especially the web-based tools— offer new forms of needs satisfaction, i.e. new forms of access and presentation of the selected data. In the lexicographical community there is an ongoing discussion of this question and of the true advantages of the new electronic dictionaries. Among the problems raised is the amount of data that could and should be included, which has given rise to certain disagreements among lexicographers. For instance, Wendalyn Nichols, the commissioning editor for Cambridge Dictionaries, writes that:

the true advantages of Web-based dictionaries—freedom from the space constraints of the printed book and on-demand updatability—have yet to be exploited. (Nichols 2010: 40)

It is evident that on-demand updatability is a true advantage of web-based dictionaries. But is "freedom from the space constraints" really something new and an advantage in itself? If one goes back in the history of lexicography, then there are at least two gigantic lexicographical works that seem to be free from space constraints, both produced in China. The first, the *Yongle Dadian*, was finished in 1408 in two handwritten copies and contains no less than 370 million Chinese characters and 22,937 chapters bound in 11,095 volumes covering history, philosophy, Buddhism, Taoism, drama, arts, and farming, among many other topics. The data included are structured according to a rhyming system for the characters and are also accessible through a complex system of indexes which, together with the preface, comprise sixty chapters. The second of these works is the *Gujin Tushu Jicheng*, which was printed in 1726 in about sixty copies and contains 100 million Chinese characters, 800,000 pages, and 10,000 chapters collected in 5,020 volumes. Until now, no other lexicographical work—with the possible exception of Wikipedia—has incorporated so much data as this Chinese Gargantua and Pantagruel, a fact that indicates that "freedom from the space constraints" is not something exclusively related to the new electronic media. The real innovation in this regard is that gigantic amounts of data can be stored and accessed without needing so much space as the many cubic metres required to store the Chinese works.

Robert Lew is one of the lexicographical scholars who oppose a unilateral approach to the amount of data to be included in electronic dictionaries:

On careful inspection, it appears that the notion of *dictionary space* is not specific enough as a technical term, because it is ambiguous. The suggestion that dictionary space is unrestricted is actually largely correct, but only when space is understood as the capacity to hold the total content of the dictionary—this sense of *dictionary space* could provisionally be called *storage space*. There is at least one more important sense of dictionary space which I will here call *presentation space* [...] *presentation space* refers to how much can be presented (displayed, visualized) at a given time to the dictionary user. (Lew, in press)

Lew's distinction between *storage space* and *presentation space* is highly relevant. It is perfectly understandable that he questions the idea of including the biggest possible amount of data in the individual articles and that he himself limits this to the data that can be simultaneously visualized on screen and, in the cases where it is necessary to include more data than can be displayed at once, looks for other alternatives such as "immediate cross-references (fan-outs, pop-ups, etc.) and [to] take advantage of the dynamic potential of electronic displays in other ways" (Lew, in press).

However, today it seems necessary to take further steps in order to achieve a more complete adaptation of lexicography to the new possibilities offered by the new electronic media and information science in general. But this can only be done if it is solidly based upon an advanced theory, developed around the fundamental idea that lexicographical works and tools of whatever class—just as any other type of consultation tools—are, above all, utility products conceived to meet punctual information needs that are not abstract but very concrete and intimately related to concrete and individual potential users finding themselves in concrete extra-lexico-graphical situations. This idea differs in one, and only one, fundamental aspect from the function theory as previously defined, for instance by Tarp (2008: 33-165): in its previous version, the function theory worked with *types* of needs, users, and situations, whereas the new version refers to *concrete and individual* needs, users, and situations. However, it is worth noting that this difference does not invalidate the function theory, but enriches it and places it in a better position to be used as a guide in the current transition from p-works to e-tools.

6.6 Towards the individualization of lexicographical e-tools

It is an irony of history that the function theory in its first (immature) version did not work with types, but just with users, user situations, and user needs (cf. Tarp 1995). This first version was changed and the theory improved after a highly welcome criticism by Wiegand (2001). A theory like the function theory cannot be built directly upon concrete and individual phenomena that may differ from each other in many aspects. Scientific and theoretical work presupposes an abstraction from some of the less important characteristics of the concrete and individual phenomena and the creation of concepts, categories, and types which include phenomena with some common characteristics considered essential and relevant for the research field in question. The function theory was therefore forced to re-saddle and work with *types* instead of concrete and individual phenomena.

However, no *type* of user has ever made a *type* of lexicographical consultation in order to access a *type* of data that may meet a *type* of information need occurring in a *type* of social situation. The only thing that has ever happened, and which happens every day, hour, and minute, is that an *individual user* with *individual information needs* occurring in an *individual situation* decides to make an *individual lexicographical consultation* in order to access the *concrete data* that may satisfy his or her individual needs. Although each user, user situation, user need, data, and consultation may be assigned to specific types, they themselves are not types but individual and concrete phenomena. However justified and correct a typologization may be, it is nevertheless a fact that, in the real world, the individual needs of individual users may differ from each other and that the concrete data required to meet these needs therefore may be slightly different from user to user and from user situation to user situation. This is the reason why *the individualization of user-needs satisfaction* is a question to be taken seriously at a time when computer and information sciences are gradually providing the necessary technology that may allow this gigantic and revolutionary step in the framework of renewed lexicographical theory and practice.

What does this individualization imply for lexicographical theory and for the lexicographers who conceive and plan dictionaries? First of all it is important to state that no lexicographer, however well prepared, can deal with each and every one of the infinite number of individual needs that an infinite number of individual users may have in an infinite number of situations. This is completely unthinkable and it cannot be the vision for future lexicography. Lexicographical planners—just like lexicographical theory-builders—still have to work with types of users, situations, needs, data, etc. What is needed is the gradual development of *highly sophisticated tools* that permit *both individualized access to the data* contained in a well-structured database or made available on the Internet, *and the recreation of completely new data* based upon the already existing data. Some of the required technology is already available, whereas additional technology still has to be invented. In this respect, three methods partially borrowed from information science can be used in order to achieve a more individualized satisfaction of user needs:

1. The user is, in one way or another, offered some fill-in options or questions by means of which he or she will be assisted in making a personal profile and indicating the specific type of situation or activity where information needs occur and even the specific type of need. This can be done in various steps in order to end up with a very detailed description and characterization of the

specific user, user situation, and need in question. The e-tool will then auto-matically select and filter the data required and adapt them to the individual needs according to the user profile and situation indicated.

2. Each individual user of an e-tool is given the option to design his or her own 'master article' in terms of the types of data wanted and their arrangement on the screen. The e-tool will then automatically filter the available data and present them as indicated by the user. This option requires a more active role by the user.

3. Automatic tracking of the user's behaviour during a number of consultations. In this case, the user is 'passive' while the e-tool does the calculations and creates a profile of the type of data that the user generally looks for in order to furnish the same type of data when the user once more consults the e-tool.

Both the making of user profiles (1) and the creation of a 'master article' (2) may be done at four different points: (a) when the user enters the e-tool for the first time; (b) when the user begins a specific activity where information needs may be expected; (c) when the user starts a specific consultation; and (d) when the user is already in the middle of a specific consultation. In this way, it is possible to re-saddle whenever necessary.

6.7 Short panoramic review

Based upon the above reflections and the degree to which the various lexicographical works made available on the Internet have used the new technologies, it is possible to make a preliminary classification of these works into four main categories:

1. Lexicographical works which have been either photocopied or directly copied from a text file and then placed on an electronic platform, frequently as a PDF-file.

2. Lexicographical works which have made use of the new technologies only in a very restricted way in order to provide quicker access to their data by means of links or search strings, but where the data included are still organized in traditional and static articles which are completely modelled on the corresponding articles in printed dictionaries.

3. Lexicographical e-tools that have gone beyond the traditional boundaries and not only make use of the existing technology in order to provide quicker data access, but also to adapt the dictionary articles to the various functions dis-played by the dictionary. The result is *dynamic articles with dynamic data* that correspond to the specific types of information needs which specific types of users performing specific types of lexicographically relevant activities may have in any consultation situation. These tools provide different types of interactive options where the users may define themselves and the activity for which they need information. They also frequently link to the Internet where already existing data is *reused* in order to satisfy the users' specific needs.

4. Lexicographical e-tools which permit *individualized solutions* to concrete and individual users in concrete situations, and which may also combine access to the selected data in a prepared database with browsing on the Internet in order to get dynamic solutions based upon a *recreation and re-representation of the data* made available in this way, i.e. different from the category of e-tools which link to specific web pages in order to reuse their data.

The first category of lexicographical works made available on the Internet was not unusual in the infancy of electronic media but is now becoming rarer with the exception of some old historical dictionaries which are now merely used for research purposes and not as consultation tools.

The lexicographical works belonging to the second category make up the vast majority of Internet-based dictionaries. This is probably due to the fact that many lexicographers have not paid sufficient attention to developing an independent and scientific lexicographic theory that may guide the conception and production of these important utility products which are used by millions of people every day, and instead have been guided by other theories and principles, mainly linguistic theory and the principles developed within corpus linguistics which obviously cannot provide answers to the challenges presented by the new technologies.

Until now, the third category has only comprised a few lexicographical tools, some of which include the 'Musikordbogen' (cf. Bergenholtz and Bergenholtz 2011), the 'Lexical Database for French' (cf. Verlinde 2011), and the 'Diccionario Inglés-Español de Contabilidad' (cf. Fuertes-Olivera and Niño-Amo 2011). It is the same underlying philosophy in terms of more dynamic articles and even a trend towards individualization that can be found in "the multi-layer architecture for pluri-monofunctional dictionaries" described by Spohr (2011).

The fourth category mentioned above is so far empty in the sense that no known lexicographical tool has yet been developed with characteristics that justify its inclusion in this category. Nevertheless, it is extremely relevant because it points to the future of lexicography and to the new horizons gradually being opened by the new computer and information technologies. However, it is necessary to stress that the development of the necessary technology can only happen through fruitful interdisciplinary teamwork between computer experts, on the one hand, and information specialists and lexicographers guided by an advanced theory, on the other.

6.8 Conclusion

Based upon the above reflections, it can be concluded that the truly new advantages related to the transition from lexicographical p-works to e-tools are the options offered by information and computer technologies in terms of an increasing individualization of needs satisfaction. In this light, the question of the amount of data to be included in lexicographical e-tools can be approached on a more solid basis:

1. It is necessary to distinguish between the dictionary and the database because the same database may simultaneously provide data to various dictionaries. As such, the database can and should include *the biggest possible amount of data* relevant to the dictionary or dictionaries that it supports.

2. The dictionary is created by means of an interface (and the underlying program) and should be capable of presenting *the biggest possible amount of data* relevant to the foreseen function(s).

3. The article visualized on the screen should include *the smallest possible amount of data*, i.e. exactly the amount needed to satisfy the user's needs in each consultation. If there are too few data, the user's needs cannot be satisfied. If there are too many, there is a risk that the user may be confused and that access to the data may be more difficult, slow, or even impossible (i.e. information stress and death).

The difference between this approach and that of Wendalyn Nichols (cf. Section 6.5) is that the starting point is the user's needs and not the capacity of the database and dictionary. In order to determine the exact amount of data needed in each case, it is necessary to rely on an advanced theory and, as Gouws (2011) pointed out, to "unlearn" and get rid of some bad habits and traditions, among them the belief that linguistics can provide answers to all challenges within the independent discipline of lexicography, i.e. a phenomenon described by Bergenholtz (2010) as "the linguists' occupation of lexicography" and by Fuertes-Olivera and Bergenholtz (2011a) simply as "linguistic colonialism".

Dictionaries

Musikordbogen. Edited by Inger Bergenholtz in cooperation with Richard Almind and Henning Bergenholtz. Odense: Ordbogen.com 2010. www.ordbogen.com.

El Diccionario Inglés-Español de Contabilidad. Edited by S. Nielsen, L. Mourier, H. Bergenholtz, P. A. Fuertes-Olivera, P. Gordo Gómez, M. Niño Amo, A. de los Rios Rodicio, Á. Sastre Ruano, S. Tarp, and M. Velasco Sacristán 2009. www. accountingdictionary.dk/regn/gbsp/regngbsp_index.php.

Gujin Tushu Jicheng. Volume 1–5,020. Edited by Menglei Chen and Tingxi Jiang. China 1726.

Lexical Database for French. Edited by S. Verlinde, Th. Seiva, and J. Binon. Leuven: Katholieke Universiteit Leuven 2010. http://ilt.kuleuven.be/blf.

Yongle Dadian. Volume 1–11,095. Edited by Jin Xie. China 1408.

7

Electronic lexicography for lesser-resourced languages: The South African context

D. J. PRINSLOO

7.1 Introduction

The electronic era has been met with great enthusiasm and expectations. Early publications on electronic dictionaries (EDs) were all about the potential of the new medium and the expected revolution it would bring along, e.g. antiquating the paper dictionary in a decade or two. De Schryver (2003) entitled his groundbreaking work 'Lexicographers' Dreams in the Electronic-Dictionary Age' but later expressed disappointment in respect of the pace of development of electronic dictionaries (De Schryver 2010: 585–6):

What is offered in electronic form, however, by and large mimics what used to be printed. No cognizance is taken of the true power of the digital age [...] today's dictionaries still very much look like they always have: static. To break out of the straitjacket of the paper world, many a lexicographer has touted the imminent next revolution, viz. the potential of electronic dictionaries to become dynamic. Sadly, nothing is further from the truth. [...] Apart from the addition of some trivial gimmicks to electronic dictionaries, nothing whatsoever has changed.

This view is echoed by Pastor and Alcina (2010: 308):

[...] dictionaries do not always take advantage of the full potential offered by electronic formats. Electronic dictionaries are frequently mere copies of paper dictionaries; they are texts where the same information appears in different font styles. However, these dictionaries do not offer the search possibilities of an advanced database system.

The development of most EDs occurred as existing paper dictionaries or translated lexica were transferred to computers, and an increasing number of search functions were gradually added and the data display enhanced.

This is fine, but EDs should now enter an even more advanced dimension in fulfilling more sophisticated needs of the users. Heid (2009: 1) says that EDs "could do better" and "would serve users in different situations much better if they included more relations" and that access to data should not only be based on a single lemma (headword). Rundell (2009: 9) refers to "'game changing' developments that have expanded the scope of what dictionaries can do and (in some respects) changed our view of what dictionaries are for".

The currency of dictionaries is no longer just 'words' in isolation: they now also deal with bigger language systems and syntagmatic networks (Rundell 2009: 10).

De Schryver (2010) calls for adaptive and intelligent dictionaries (aiLEX) that will be able to "study and understand [their] user[s]" and consequently to "present [themselves] to [these] user[s]". Pastor and Alcina (2010: 307) call for a "systematization of search techniques" which could generate more standardized EDs.

Lesser-resourced languages generally lack dictionaries of a high lexicographic standard and the compilation of good EDs for lesser-resourced languages is therefore of primary importance for such languages. Languages can be regarded as lesser-resourced or less-resourced on the basis of a combination of criteria such as a limited number of speakers, spoken by under-developed communities, subjected to political oppression and lacking a standardized orthography, financial resources, text and oral corpora, a dictionary culture, human language technologies (HLT) tools, paper dictionaries, etc.

It is encouraging that lesser-resourced languages enjoy some attention from scholars around the world with much focus on development through the building of language resources. Prominent examples are the two scientific meetings on computational approaches for lesser-used, lesser-standardized, and lesser-resourced languages organized by the Institute for Specialised Communication and Multilingualism at the European Academy Bozen/Bolzano. Both meetings brought together international researchers and representatives of public authorities to discuss the latest advances and needs for the computational support of lesser-used languages (see Ties 2006, Lyding 2009).

The main objective of this chapter is to provide an overview of the electronic dictionary situation in South Africa. This situation is quite representative of that of other parts of the world where lesser-resourced languages are spoken. Characteristics of EDs for lesser-resourced languages are generally the limited size of the dictionary, the small number of headwords treated, and a limited number of data types, often consisting of nothing more than word lists with one or two translation equivalents. Negligence is particularly visible in cases where lesser-resourced languages are included in lists of online dictionaries but do not contain any data. Small EDs with limited treatment of the headwords represent the lower level of electronic dictionaries. The next level is where electronic dictionaries generally resemble paper dictionaries but are enhanced by the addition of search functions which can range from fairly basic to quite sophisticated. It will be argued in this chapter that electronic dictionaries should enter a third, more advanced level of maximum utilization of electronic features. For Bantu languages, this particularly includes solving major problems in respect of lemmatization and advanced user-guidance in text production, such as the need to identify nominal and verbal stems in order to look up a word. These issues cannot be resolved in paper dictionaries.

The chapter starts with a short description of the South African context (Section 7.2). Section 7.3 briefly reviews the true electronic features in the online *Oxford English Dictionary* (*OED*) and the *Macmillan English Dictionary on CD ROM* (*MED*), two EDs that are used as a benchmark for evaluating EDs of Afrikaans and the Bantu languages, and comments on the usefulness of such international dictionaries in places where regional varieties of English are spoken. Electronic dictionaries of Afrikaans are discussed in Section 7.4. Section 7.5 focuses on EDs for the nine official Bantu languages spoken in South Africa. It is believed that the characteristics of EDs for these languages are the same as for other Bantu languages which in turn can be regarded as typical examples of lesser-resourced languages. Section 7.6 is devoted to future development of sophisticated electronic dictionaries and case examples of new imaginative ways in which the electronic dictionary can guide productive (encoding) dictionary use for text production purposes in the Bantu languages will be suggested. The chapter ends with some concluding remarks.

7.2 The South African context

South Africa has eleven official languages—Afrikaans, English, and nine Bantu languages, namely Sepedi (also called Northern Sotho or Sesotho sa Leboa), Setswana (Tswana), Sesotho (Southern Sotho), isiZulu (Zulu), isiXhosa (Xhosa), Siswati (Swazi), isiNdebele (Ndebele), Xitsonga (Tsonga), and Tshivenda (Venda). Between 1997 and 2001, the South African government established and provided funding for National Lexicographic Units (NLUs) for all of these languages. In terms of the constitution all eleven languages enjoy equal rights, but the reality is totally different. It is simply not feasible, affordable, or practical to equally treat eleven languages in any given situation, be it the translation of texts, oral communication, the rendering of services, etc. Most of the Bantu languages can be regarded as lesser-resourced languages as they are spoken by a small number of speakers and are characterized by a limited number of publications (including paper dictionaries and EDs) and in most cases have no newspapers or magazines.

Online versions of Afrikaans and Sepedi dictionaries compiled by the NLUs are now available. In addition to the NLUs, dictionaries are compiled by private entrepreneurs in most cases supported and published by publishing companies. From a commercial perspective it is not clear at this point in time what the future market for EDs will be. Publishers apparently approach the marketing of EDs in the same way as they market their paper dictionaries, i.e. they try to establish themselves in the ED market with their paper dictionaries as a basis. As is the case for paper dictionaries, economic considerations play a major role in the compilation of EDs. Publishers do not see their way clear to invest money in lesser-resourced languages where there is little potential for making a profit.

It is also difficult to define dictionary needs in the South African context. For most users they cover the entire spectrum of decoding as well as encoding needs (as can be expected from lesser-resourced languages where either no dictionary is available for the language or where a single dictionary has to fulfil the decoding as well as the encoding needs of different user groups). There is also a strong expectation that dictionaries should contribute to the development, preservation, and standardization of the languages. Given the relative low standard of EDs, however, it can be argued that they do not play any significant societal role at this stage. One clearly established need is the decoding of English texts and encoding for English text production. For economic reasons there is a strong urge for empowerment in English. Acquiring linguistic knowledge, especially in view of the complicated grammatical structure of the Bantu languages, is a growing need of primary and secondary school pupils as well as non-mother tongue (mostly Afrikaans- and English-speaking) learners of the Bantu languages.

Users also need help in terms of training in dictionary use. It has to be kept in mind that the majority of Africans do not have access to computers and lack a dictionary culture and computer skills. Atkins (1998a: 3) remarks that:

The speakers of African languages have not in their formative years had access to dictionaries of the richness and complexity of those currently available for European languages. They have not had the chance to internalize the structure and objectives of a good dictionary, monolingual, bilingual or trilingual.

Thus, in principle, the challenge for electronic lexicography in South Africa is not only to improve the dictionaries but also to improve the dictionary users. Gouws and Prinsloo (2005) summarize the ultimate goal as the urge to compile ideal dictionaries for ideal users as schematically illustrated in Figure 7.1.

7.3 Electronic dictionaries for (South African) English

The lexicographic needs of South Africans for EDs in English are to a large extent satisfied by available EDs of high standard from Europe, the UK and US (such as *MED*, the online *OED*, *Merriam-Webster Online*, and *Cambridge Dictionaries Online*). A description of the typical features of electronic dictionaries lies beyond the scope of this chapter—the interested reader is referred to De Schryver (2003) for a detailed discussion. A brief overview of typical features of EDs for English will, however, be given as a benchmark for future South African (SA) English dictionaries, as well as for the subsequent description and evaluation of electronic dictionaries for

DICTIONARIES				USERS		
►►►►	►►►►	►►►►	▼▼▼	◄◄◄	◄◄◄	◄◄◄
Bad/useless dictionary or no dictionaries available	Dictionary of relatively low lexicographic achievement	Dictionary of relatively high lexicographic achievement	▼▼▼ **Perfect dictionary** **&** **Ideal User** ▲▲▲	Relatively good dictionary using skills	Relatively poor dictionary using skills	Pre dictionary culture environment
►►►►	►►►►	►►►►	▲▲▲	◄◄◄	◄◄◄	◄◄◄

FIGURE 7.1 Towards the perfect dictionary and the ideal user (Gouws and Prinsloo, 2005: 42).

Afrikaans and the Bantu languages in Sections 7.4 and 7.5. Particular attention will be given to search functions, data display, comprehensiveness, and true electronic features.

It could be argued that the main innovations in EDs for English revolve around quicker and more sophisticated access to huge data collections, as well as enhanced presentation strategies. The online *OED*, for example, offers an impressive range of search functions and ways to find information in the dictionary. The online *OED* claims to provide "unparalleled access" to twenty-three volumes of information, to include "authoritative definitions of over 500,000 words" and to be "the most comprehensive and up-to-date reference work of its kind for any language". The online *OED* summarizes its offering as follows:

- Search the equivalent of 23 volumes of information with speed and ease
- Find a term when you know the meaning but have forgotten the word
- Find words that have come into English via a particular language
- Search for quotations from a specified year
- Search for all quotations from a particular author and/or work
- Display entries according to your needs—for the first time you can turn pronunciation, etymologies, variant spellings, and quotations on and off
- Gain unique online access to at least 1,000 new and revised words each quarter
- Compare revised entries with entries from the Second Edition to see how language has changed and how new scholarship has increased understanding of our linguistic and cultural heritage.[1]

In addition to a 'Quick Search' function, the online *OED* offers 'Advanced Search' options such as choosing the scope and search area of a search, searching for more than

---

[1] Introduction: http://o-dictionary.oed.com.innopac.up.ac.za/tour/step-1.html.

one term at once, searching for phrases, case-sensitive searches, and the utilization of wildcards and Boolean operators in searches. These search options offer exciting new options to the user. The user-friendly function relieves the user of the obligation to know the placement of hyphens and spaces in words and phrases or whether it is spelled with a capital letter or an accented letter, in order to find it in the dictionary. The proximity search function enables the user to specify and refine the search, e.g. by expressing a relationship between two items thus effectively reducing the number of hits. The exact function allows the use of wildcards '*' for an unspecified number of characters and '?' for a single character. The *Advanced search* box in Figure 7.2 is impressive and offers a variety of selections, combinations, and refinements. As far as data presentation is concerned, an individual entry may contain information on pronunciation, spelling(s), etymology, quotations, date chart, and additions.

The search options and data display are equally extensive and impressive in the *MED*. The 'Super Search' function includes the search options 'Sound Search', 'Extra Features Search', 'Advanced Search', 'Example Sentence Search', and 'Study Page Search'. Each of the categories (part of speech, grammar, region, style, frequency, and subject) offers extensive selection options. Selecting 'region', for example, allows the user to choose between American, mainly American, Australian, British, Canadian,

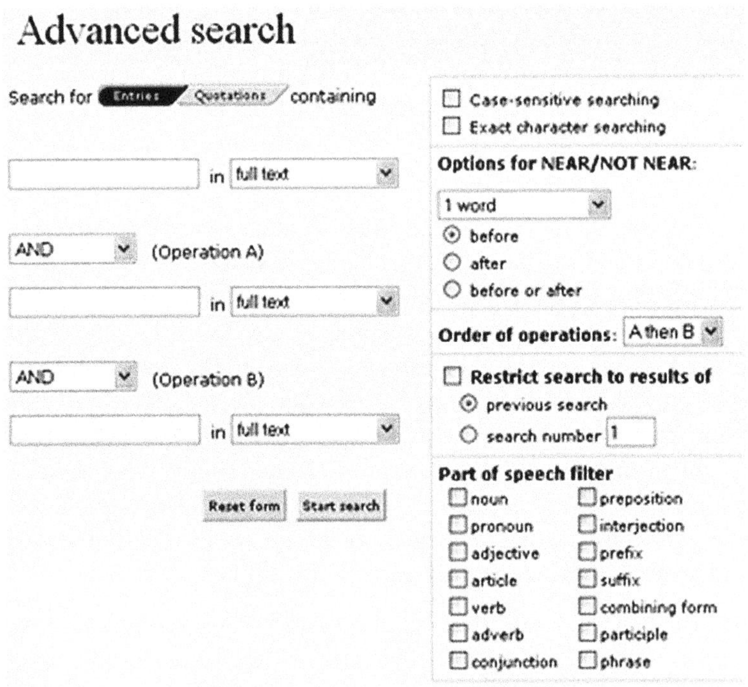

Figure 7.2 The Advanced search box in the online *OED*.

Caribbean, Indian, Irish, New Zealand, Scottish, South African, and West African English. However, it may be argued that the amount of regional information provided in international electronic dictionaries such as the *MED* is still relatively limited. What is required from a South African perspective are EDs for SA English with special attention to differences between SA and other English varieties. Silva (1997) explains that South African English developed into a variety of English by the assimilation of words and patterns from other South African languages. Wade (1997) lists a number of typical characteristics of Black South African English such as non-standard verb complementation, embedded questions, and pronoun copying (e.g. 'The parents, *they* are supposed to pay ten rand'). Dictionaries for English aimed at the South African market should reflect such borrowings and patterns.

7.4 Electronic dictionaries for Afrikaans

Afrikaans dictionaries are no match for the sophisticated tools available for English. The first Afrikaans EDs could be described as paper dictionaries on computer with relatively no difference between the paper dictionary and the electronic dictionary apart from additional search functions. Progress has now been made in respect of more advanced search functions and data display, but at this stage even the best Afrikaans online dictionaries still lack the sophistication of English online diction-aries such as the *OED* or the *MED*. A typical example is the *Pharos Afrikaans/Engels-English/Afrikaans CD-ROM Dictionary*, which is the electronic version of the Pharos Afrikaans-English / English *Pharos Afrikaans-Engels / Engels-Afrikaanse Woorde-boek*. It is claimed that the electronic version contains "all the good characteristics and more" of the printed version of 2005 as well as the correction of a number of errors and the addition of new words and expressions. It is also emphasized that "time consuming searches in the paper version can be done in a flash" in the electronic version and that it contains more than 200,000 lemmas and 120,000 phrases.[2] An advanced search option makes it possible to find articles including all of the words in the search phrase, one or more of these words or an exact match of the phrase.

The situation is more or less the same for the Afrikaans electronic dictionary *e-Hat*. It contains the complete alphabetical list and lists of abbreviations and geographical names of the fifth edition of the *Handwoordeboek van die Afrikaanse Taal (HAT)*. As for the *Pharos Afrikaans/Engels-English/Afrikaans CD-ROM Dictio-nary*, a number of errors in the paper version have been corrected and improvements in terms of the authoritative spelling rules (*Afrikaanse Woordelys en Spelreëls*, 2002) have been incorporated into the electronic version. *e-Hat* on CD-ROM is the forerunner to the sixth (paper) edition.

---

[2] www.pharos.co.za/Books/10494.

The third major ED for Afrikaans is the electronic version of the hitherto completed volumes (A-R) of the *Woordeboek van die Afrikaanse Taal* (*WAT*). In terms of its (translated) self-description, the electronic version of the *WAT* offers extensive information such as:

- Advanced search, for example, the equivalent of more than 8,300 printed pages
- The most comprehensive reflection of the Afrikaans vocabulary
- Almost 200,000 keywords (lemmas)
- The different varieties of Afrikaans
- Vocabulary from written and spoken language
- Information which has been obtained from a database of more than 20 million recordings
- A core-thesaurus of Afrikaans (*Woordkeusegids* 'guide to vocabulary selection').

The following information can be obtained with instant access: the lemma, word type, labels, and etymology. Advanced searches, such as for expressions and phrases, can also be executed.

Free electronic dictionaries bridging Afrikaans and English such as *Freedict.com* and *Freelang.net* exist, but only render very basic information limited to a translation equivalent or two. For example, a search in *Freedict.com* for Afrikaans *koop* only returns the translation equivalents *buy* and *purchase* and a search for *buy* only returns *koop*.[3] Free electronic dictionaries of Afrikaans are also characterized by a limited number of entries. For example, there is no entry for *lexicographer* in *Freedict. com* and the Freelang bidirectional Afrikaans-English dictionary consists of only 11,265 entries.[4] As illustrated in Figure 7.3, some of these entries also reflect very bad lexicography. Searching for the randomly selected Afrikaans lemma *koop* 'buy' in *Freelang.net* returns two entries: *koop* and *Goed koop kak*. *Goed koop kak* should not be displayed as a search result for *koop*. It is, however, retrieved because, as a translation equivalent for *cheap piece of crap*, the word sequence *Goed koop kak* is wrongly spelt: *Goed koop* should be one word and not start with a capital letter. *Kak* is a vulgar word and should have been labelled as such and not used in an example

Searching for: koop (2 results)

Goed koop kak	Cheap piece of crap
koop	buy, purchase

FIGURE 7.3 *Freelang.net* dictionary's treatment of *koop*.

---

[3] The terms *African to English* and *English to African* in *Freedict.com* are misleading because they bridge English with Afrikaans and not with any of the African languages.
[4] Last accessed 18 September 2011.

phrase to illustrate the meaning of *koop*. This is bad lexicography and a good example of first attempts at compiling electronic dictionaries lacking lexicographic quality.

7.5 Electronic dictionaries for the Bantu languages

The lexicography of the Bantu languages is in a developmental phase. Compiling dictionaries of high lexicographic quality for the African languages has been a vision and ongoing struggle for many decades. The statement by Gouws (1990) that African languages generally lack lexicographic quality is to a large extent still applicable two decades later.

Lexicographical activities on the various indigenous African languages [...have] resulted in a wide range of dictionaries. Unfortunately, the majority of these dictionaries are the products of limited efforts not reflecting a high standard of lexicographic achievement. (Gouws 1990: 55)

It is important to note that the electronic era dawned upon Bantu language lexicography at a time when the goal of compiling good dictionaries had not yet been attained. In most cases there were no paper dictionaries of lexicographic achievement that could be put online, and answering the call for electronic dictionaries resulted in word lists with one or more translation equivalent being uploaded to the Internet. When paper dictionaries existed, they were often representative of a major problem in dictionary compilation for lesser-resourced languages: given the paucity of lexicographic resources every new dictionary compiled is expected to fulfil the lexicographic needs of all speakers of the language and all those wishing to learn the language. This puts the lexicographer in the impossible position of compiling a single dictionary for receptive as well as for productive use by different target users. A typical example is the *Comprehensive Northern Sotho Dictionary, Northern Sotho–Afrikaans/English* (CNSD)—a single volume comprehensive paper dictionary for Sepedi. This dictionary is a monument of linguistic achievement in which headwords are entered on their stem forms and a phonetic alphabetical ordering is followed. It is generally regarded as very user-unfriendly. But even in its unrevised form, after thirty-five years, it is still the most comprehensive dictionary for Sepedi and is used by everyone for encoding and decoding purposes.

The lexicographical treatment of the Bantu languages is subject to a number of linguistic challenges related to lemmatization, orthography, and complicated grammatical systems. The Bantu languages have a common structure (Guthrie 1970) and are characterized by a number of salient features such as a nominal class system according to which nouns are sub-classified into different noun classes, a complex concordial and pronominal system, and complex word formation by means of numerous affixes to verbal and nominal stems. Identifying the headword for lookup, whether it is a nominal stem, root, or full noun (stem with prefix) has been the major problem for lexicographers and users in the compilation and use of both paper and electronic dictionaries for these languages (Prinsloo 2005). In conjunctively written languages, such as the Nguni languages isiZulu, isiNdebele, Siswati, and isiXhosa, most word forms contain verbal or nominal stems with prefixes and suffixes which are written as one orthographic word. This results in very long words, the average word length of isiZulu words in the *Pretoria isiZulu Corpus* (PZC) being 6.93 letters. Substantial linguistic knowledge of the language is required to identify the headword for look-up. Table 7.1 shows headword identification for a number of randomly selected orthographic words.

A substantial part of learners' needs is finding the meanings of words used in their prescribed books, especially isiZulu literary works such as novels, poetry, and prose. Van Wyk (1995: 87) calculates that a single verb in Zulu for example can have up to $18 \times 19 \times 6 \times 2 = 4{,}104$ combinations. For the single verb *sebenza* 'work', for example, a set of 2,525 derivations can be found in the PZC. Table 7.2 lists the sixty-five derived forms of the verb *sebenza* that occur more than fifty times in the PZC.

In order to find the meaning of *nomsebenzi* (309), *ngomsebenzi* (247), *emsebenzini* (1,438), *somsebenzi* (112), etc. the user has to identify the noun through stripping off the affixes.

A good and comprehensive ED for isiZulu should alleviate this difficulty of stem identification. In principle, catering for all 2,525 derived forms of *sebenza* in the PZC is not a problem in EDs given the almost unlimited space available and speed of information retrieval. The ED should also make it possible for the user to type in the entire form or part thereof and then be re-routed by the software to the appropriate headword(s). This is an outstanding example where a lexicographic solution to a linguistic problem (i.e. highly complex lemmatization procedures) can only be found in electronic dictionaries. Dictionary compilers should not only strive to move away

TABLE 7.1. **Orthographic word versus headword in isiZulu**

Orthographic word	Headword
Kwezinsukwana	-sukwana
Nasemfuleni	-fula
Ngamazwe	-zwe
Ngokuphindwa	-phinda
Owayelokhu	(-)lokhu
Phindela	-phinda
Ukhathazekile	-khathazeka
ukhulumela	-khulumela
Ukwenzenjani	-enza
Wokuhlabelela	-hlabelela

TABLE 7.2. **Words containing -*sebenz*- in the PZC (frequencies in brackets)**

UMSEBENZI (5582), EMSEBENZINI (1438), IMISEBENZI (996), UKUSEBENZA (548), MSEBENZI (470), LOMSEBENZI (446), NOMSEBENZI (309), USEBENZA (299), ESEBENZA (290), NGOMSEBENZI (247), UKUSEBENZISA (244), IZISEBENZI (242), SEBENZISA (219), NGOKUSEBENZISA (199), UMSEBENZL (187), NGUMSEBENZI (179), NEMISEBENZI (173), USEBENZISE (167), ABASEBENZI (167), EMISEBENZINI (153), USEBENZISA (143), ABASEBENZA (134), KOMSEBENZI (132), ASEBENZE (131), WASEBENZA (127), OSEBENZA (125), NGISEBENZA (124), SOMSEBENZI (112), NGEMISEBENZI (112), NOKUSEBENZA (108), UMSEBENZ (106), USEBENZE (101), YOMSEBENZI (100), UYASEBENZA (97), ISEBENZA (96), ASEBENZA (96), SEBENZA (94), BASEBENZA (92), SISEBENZA (90), ISEBENZISA (90), AYESEBENZA (88), KULOMSEBENZI (87), KUNGUMSEBENZI (86), ISISEBENZI (81), SISEBENZISE (74), ASEBENZISE (72), SISEBENZISA (69), LOWOMSEBENZI (68), ZOMSEBENZI (63), KOSEBENZA (63), KUSEBENZA (62), ZEMISEBENZI (58), NASEMSEBENZINI (58), WAYESEBENZA (57), NGOKUSEBENZA (56), BASEBENZE (55), YOKUSEBENZA (53), MISEBENZI (53), ISEBENZISE (53), EZISEBENZA (53), ZISEBENZISA (51), LEMISEBENZI (51), BESEBENZA (51), ZISEBENZA (50), SISEBENZE (50)

from merely adding electronic features such as search functions to a paper dictionary in electronic form, they should also (a) pursue true adaptive, interactive, and dynamic features, and (b) break new ground in lexicographic offerings in EDs in terms of information that cannot be given in paper dictionaries.

Section 7.5.1 below shows that many online dictionaries of the Bantu languages provide very little or no content. Section 7.5.2 offers a critical assessment of eleven online dictionaries for the Bantu languages. Not much progress has been made in terms of the utilization of the virtues of the electronic medium, such as the capacity and speed characteristic of electronic products, combined with enhanced query and data retrieval technology. And not much is exhibited in terms of the innovative features characteristic of online dictionaries of English, (e.g. pop-up access, bringing together of related items, new routes to the data, less dependency on alphabetical order, fuzzy spelling, incremental search, and audible pronunciation). Section 7.5.3 gives a more detailed description of isiZulu.net, i.e. an online dictionary of Zulu that offers some promising and true electronic features.

7.5.1 *Empty shells*

Internet searches for online dictionaries of the Bantu languages reveal quite a number of dictionaries that vary greatly in terms of scope, size, data types, the exhaustiveness of treatment, lemmatization strategies, and access. isiZulu.net and the Sepedi National Lexicography Unit's monolingual dictionary *Pukuntšutlhaloši ya Sesotho sa Leboa ka Inthanete* can be singled out as EDs of lexicographic achievement. They, however, are exceptions—a major shortcoming in most of the dictionaries is that they are very small and often offer not much more than translated word lists. Freelang.net indicates the sizes of their dictionaries, which can be a useful guide to the user as to whether it is worthwhile for the user to consult the dictionary. Freelang. net are at least honest in saying that "some of our dictionaries are small and you may have trouble finding some words" and that the user is advised to "check the number of words" beforehand. Thus the user can more or less judge, depending on his or her intuitive judgement of the frequency of the word, whether looking it up will be worthwhile or not.

Another negative aspect is that in many cases the Bantu languages are simply drawn into existing online dictionary networks and mathematical combinations of possible dictionaries, where the aim seems to be to collect as many languages as possible instead of compiling quality electronic dictionaries. Webster's Online Dictionary calls itself "Earth's largest dictionary with more than 1,226 modern languages and Eve!". Dicts. info offers an English to Sesotho dictionary and lists no less than fifty-five empty bilingual dictionaries with Sesotho as source language (see Figure 7.4).

These dictionaries are technically fully functional empty shells ready to be populated with lexicographic content. One can even click on the Sesotho to Afrikaans dictionary and enter the Sesotho word *hore* 'so that' in the search box: a search is performed but unsurprisingly returns a 'not found' result. Another rather senseless feature in Dicts.info is to give the same section of the alphabetical stretch for L1 look-up in L2. See, for example, Figure 7.5, where the search for the English lemma *man* also brings up the L2 word *manaka*.

A similar situation prevails in the Webster's Online Dictionary where the clickable indexes look alike for all the languages but range from virtually no words for Xitsonga to thousands for isiZulu. Underlined sub-stretches in Figure 7.6 indicate sections that contain data. The others are empty. A comparison of the lexicographical

Sesotho dictionaries	
Bilingual dictionaries	**Simple entries**
English to Sesotho dictionary	6,673
Sesotho to Afrikaans dictionary	0
Sesotho to Albanian dictionary	0
Sesotho to Arabic dictionary	0
Sesotho to Armenian dictionary	0
Sesotho to Bosnian dictionary	0

FIGURE 7.4 Extract from the list of bilingual dictionaries involving Sesotho in *Dicts.info*.[5]

---

[5] http://www.dicts.info/dictlist1.php?l=sesotho.

man ◈ man /mæn/ Pronunciation key Audiobase: en fr cs chi

English to Sesotho	Sesotho to English
man monna	**manaka, lenaka** hom

FIGURE 7.5 *Dicts.info.*[6]

treatment of Xitsonga and Setswana shows that only eight subcategories for the alphabetical stretch A contain words in the English-Tsonga dictionary but twenty categories within A contain data for the English-Tswana dictionary. In addition, each subcategory contains many more treated lemmas in the English-Tswana dictionary than in the English-Tsonga one. The total number of lemmas given for A in the English-Tsonga is ten, compared to 430 for the English-Tswana. The value of the lemmas offered in the English-Tsonga section (i.e. *adradas*, *alentisque*, and *arenillas*), with exactly the same translation in English, is also questionable because they are rare words that hardly deserve a place in such a small dictionary and the translations do not help the user to understand their meanings.

Webster's Online Dictionary does not offer Sepedi (Northern Sotho) and Sesotho (Southern Sotho) as autonomous languages but has a single category Sotho divided into two dialects: 'Sotho (Northern Dialect)' and 'Sotho (Southern Dialect)'. The status of Sepedi and Sesotho as autonomous official languages in the South African constitution is misrepresented in this way and could offend the speakers of these languages since recognition of language status is a sensitive issue in South Africa.

7.5.2 *A critical assessment of online dictionaries for the Bantu languages*

Table 7.3 summarizes the main characteristics of a number of online dictionaries for the Bantu languages in terms of their relative size, presentation of the data, presence of advanced electronic features, and degree of lexicographic achievement.

English to Tsonga Translation Browse

A B C D E F G H I J K L M N O P Q R S T U V W X Y Z
A aa ab ac a̲d ae a̲f ag ah ai aj ak a̲l am a̲n ao a̲p aq a̲r a̲s at a̲u av aw ax ay az

English to Tswana Translation Browse

A B C D E F G H I J K L M N O P Q R S T U V W X Y Z
A̲ aa a̲b a̲c a̲d a̲e a̲f a̲g a̲h a̲i aj ak a̲l a̲m a̲n ao a̲p aq a̲r a̲s a̲t a̲u a̲v a̲w ax a̲y az

FIGURE 7.6 The alphabetical stretch A in the *Webster's Online Dictionary* English-Tsonga and English-Tswana.[7]

---

[6] http://www.dicts.info/dictlist1.php?l=sesotho.
[7] http://www.websters-online-dictionary.org/browse/Tsonga and http://www.websters-online-dictionary.org/browse/Tswana.

TABLE 7.3. Online dictionaries and their main characteristics

	Dictionary	Language	Relative size	Presentation	Advanced electronic features	Lexicographic standard
1.	*Bukantswe*	Sesotho	Small (c.10,000 entries)	Indexed layout and L1 with L2 translations.	None	Low
2.	*cBold*	Tshivenda, isiNdebele, Setswana	Small	Fixed layout, L1 and L2 translations with tonal and grammatical information.	None	Low
3.	*Dicts.info*	various	Small	Basic L1 and L2 translation with same alphabetical stretch from reverse side.	Clickable pronunciation icons	Low
4.	*Freedict.com*	various	Small	Basic L1 and L2 translation.	None	Low
5.	*Freelang dictionaries*	various	Small	Basic L1 and L2 translation.	None	Low
6.	*IsiZulu for Travellers*	isiZulu	Small	L1 with L2 translations.	None	Low
7.	*isiZulu.net*	isiZulu	Big	Detailed entries.	Several	High
8.	*Pukuntšu-tlhaloši ya Sesotho sa Leboa ka Inthanete*	Sepedi	Medium (more than 20,000 entries)	Simulates a complete monolingual paper dictionary article with pronunciation and grammatical guidance as well as definitions, examples of use, etc.	Incoming and outgoing clickable cross-referencing	High Corpus-based
9.	*Sesotho sa Leboa (Northern Sotho) - English Dictionary*	Sepedi	Medium	L1 (Sepedi) with L2 (English) translations and a simulated reverse section.	Clickable pronunciation icons	Medium Corpus-based
10.	*Webster's Online Dictionary*	various		Indexed layout with clickable alphabetical sub-stretches.	None	Low
11.	*Xhosa-English Dictionary*	isiXhosa		L1 headword list with L2 translations plus additional information.	None	Low to medium

Not all Bantu languages have their own online dictionary and for many of them, the only lexicographic information available online is to be found in free dictionaries such as Freedict.com, Freelang.net, or the Webster's Online Dictionary. Dictionaries of Xitsonga and isiNdebele are available for download as .txt files from the Comparative Bantu Online Dictionary (cBold) but they are not searchable online. Most online dictionaries of the Bantu languages are of limited size (see Table 7.3) and at a low level of lexicography, in which entries typically only consist of a word and its translation. In the Webster's Online Dictionary, for example, the English word *buy* is translated by Tshivenda -*renga*. As shown in Table 7.4, the cBold Tshivenda dictionary also includes tonal and grammatical information.

The Xhosa-English Dictionary provides translation equivalents and information about lemmas. Figure 7.7 shows that a search for *umbhali*, for example, brings up the singular and plural forms as well as additional information about *bhala* 'count', the verb from which it is derived, and derivations of the verb itself, *bhalisela* 'register', etc. All these forms are clickable.

Online dictionaries of medium to high lexicographical standards are available for Sepedi and isiZulu. The Sesotho sa Leboa (Northern Sotho)-English Dictionary is

TABLE 7.4 The *cBold* Tshivenda dictionary

Lemma	Tone: H = high, L = low	Part of speech	Noun class number	Translation
funguvhu	HHH	n	5	African rook; coward
furalelo	H	n	5	refuge in time of need
furi	HH	n	5	pumpkin plant and fruit
…				
galaha	LLL	n	5	old fellow
galakuni	LLH	n	5	turkey
gali	HH	n	5	large pot; fee paid to court messenger
gamashi	HHH	n	5	grapple plant
gamba	HH	n	5	any wide-mouthed pot
…				
harani	HHL	n	9	sewing thread
hariki	HH	n	9	rake
hatsi	LH	n	14	any grass
hatsi-ha-tserekanya	LHHHLH	n	14	lots of grass

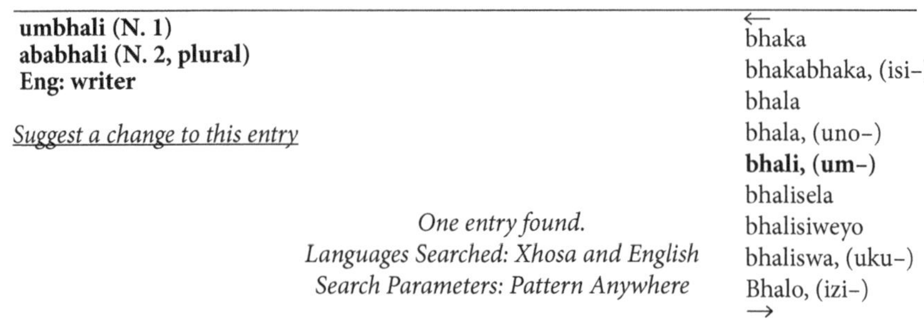

umbhali (N. 1)	←
ababhali (N. 2, plural)	bhaka
Eng: writer	bhakabhaka, (isi–)
	bhala
Suggest a change to this entry	bhala, (uno–)
	bhali, (um–)
	bhalisela
One entry found.	bhalisiweyo
Languages Searched: Xhosa and English	bhaliswa, (uku–)
Search Parameters: Pattern Anywhere	Bhalo, (izi–)
	→

FIGURE 7.7 Search results for 'umbhali' in the *Xhosa-English Dictionary*.[8]

unidirectional (from Sepedi to English) but English to Sepedi translations are simulated from the same database. In Figure 7.8, for example, the search for *bona* returned *bona* as a lemma with appropriate treatment including clickable pronunciation. The search for *see*, by contrast, returned items in which *see* occurred, but did not provide access to a specific dictionary entry for the lemma *see*. This access structure via the source language is quite acceptable as an interim stage until such time as full reversal can be offered.

The National Lexicography Unit's *Pukuntšutlhaloši ya Sesotho sa Leboa ka Inthanete* is a monolingual Sepedi dictionary that covers a substantial number of Sepedi words. It provides the same lexicographic information as available in the paper version of the dictionary but also makes good use of hyperlinks and cross-references. For example, the electronic dictionary automatically links the article of *modulasetulo* to the reference address *moetapele* 'leader', as well as to the two articles of the lemmas *bomodulasetulo* 'chairmanship' and *presitente* 'president', for which *modulasetulo* is a reference address (see Figure 7.9).

The *Sesotho sa Leboa (Northern Sotho)-English Dictionary* and the *Pukuntšutlhaloši ya Sesotho sa Leboa ka Inthanete* are based on corpora of approximately six million tokens compiled from available written texts, mostly literary works. Corpora are mainly used for the compilation of lemma lists and finding different senses as well as examples of usage. The use of corpora in the compilation of dictionaries for other Bantu languages is slowly increasing but still lacking for more than 90 per cent of the estimated 300–600 Bantu languages. The National Lexicography Units are encouraged to build and use corpora for the compilation of dictionaries in their respective languages.

---

[8] http://www.xhosadictionary.com/search.php?igama=umbhali&stype=general&lang=XE.

Result for *bona*	Result for *see*
bôna ◁ᴇ 1.see 2.look 3.find 4.get 5.they 6.them bôna kgwêdi have monthly period	**bôna** ◁ᴇ 1.see 2.look 3.find 4.get 5.they 6.them bôna kgwêdi have monthly period **bône, bônê** 1.must see 2.must look **..ga/sa/se..~** 1.not see 2.not look

FIGURE 7.8 *Sesotho sa Leboa (Northern Sotho)-English Dictionary.*[9]

7.5.3 *isiZulu.net*

isiZulu.net is probably the most sophisticated online dictionary for the Bantu languages. One of its strong points is that there is no need for stem identification before a word can be looked up. For example, isiZulu.net offers two access routes to *impilo* (i.e. *impilo* and *mpilo*), and typing either *intombi* or *ntombi* retrieves *intombi*. Plural forms of these nouns can also be directly looked up by typing their full forms, *izimpilo* and *izintombi* respectively. isiZulu.net does well in analysing complex words in terms of their morphemes and related derivations and gives semantic guidance where possible.

Consider for example the exhaustive treatment given for *emsebenzini* in Figure 7.10. The dictionary not only successfully isolates and treats the stem, it also gives the complete word as a lemma with appropriate treatment. The dictionary also does well where the learner finds it difficult to isolate the verb stem to find its meaning, and to add back the meanings of the affixes with which the verb occurs. For example, the verb *fika* 'arrive' is preceded by two prefixes in *sengifika* but can be directly looked up in isiZulu.net.

In isiZulu, capitalization is rather problematic for learners because capital letters can occur in positions other than the initial letter, as in the name of the language itself. In isiZulu.net the search words *isizulu* and *unkulunkulu* return the correct capitalization of *isiZulu* 'Zulu language' and *uNkulunkulu* 'the Lord'. isiZulu.net also offers incremental search facilities (suggesting available headwords as the user types in initial letters of the headword). So, for example, the user who wants to look up the

---

[9] http://africanlanguages.com/sdp/.

Pukuntšutlhaloši ya Sesotho sa Leboa ka Inthanete

Tlanya lentšu la Sesotho sa Leboa:

	Tšwela pele

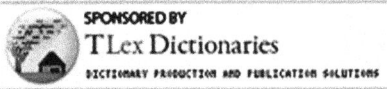

SPONSORED BY
TLex Dictionaries
DICTIONARY PRODUCTION AND PUBLICATION SOLUTIONS

Palo ya dipoelo tše di humanetšwego *modulasetulo*: **1**

modulasetulo */modulasetulô/ (leina ka botee) (1a/2a)* BAPETŠA <u>moetapele</u>
motho yo a lego maemong a boetapele mokgahlong goba lekgotleng le le itšego : *Mokhura
yoo e lego modulasetulo wa lekgotla la sekolokomiti*

> **moetapele** */moêtapele/ (leina ka botee) (1/2)* BAPETŠA <u>modulasetulo</u>
> motho yo a hlahlago batho sehlopha goba lefapha, ka maikemišetšo a go
> bona gore tshepedišo ye botse e ba gona : *Moetapele mošomo wa gagwe
> ke go bona gore ditaba tša sehlopha di sepela gabotse*
>
> **bomodulasetulo** */bomodulasetulô/ (leina ka bontši) (1a/2a)* BONA
> <u>modulasetulo</u>
>
> **presitente** */prêsitêntê/ (leina ka botee) (9/10)* BAPETŠA <u>modulasetulo</u>
> **1** moetapele wa semmušo wa naga, gantši nageng ya go se bušwe ke kgoši
> goba kgošigadi : *Mašole a Presitente Amin a be a bolaya ditlou ka
> dithunya gore a hwetše dinaka tša tšona*
> **2** moetapele wa mokgahlong wo o itšego : *Presitente ya mokgahlo wa
> rena wa polokano o kgethile khuduthamaga yeo a tla thušanago le
> yona*

FIGURE 7.9 The treatment of *modulasetulo* in *Pukuntšutlhaloši ya Sesotho sa Leboa ka Inthanete*.[10]

word *umfundisi* 'teacher' only has to type in the first three letters when *umfundisi* is offered as a clickable option.

Users are invited to contribute to isiZulu.net through dictionary forums where they can participate in general discussion, submit new entries, suggest additional translations, and report errata such as wrong translations and typing errors. The question, however, is to what extent isiZulu.net covers the isiZulu language, e.g. whether treatment is also given for words occurring with a low(er) frequency in the language. The strength/comprehensiveness of isiZulu.net can be briefly evaluated in terms of a random selection of words from three isiZulu paper dictionaries i.e. the *Oxford Bilingual School Dictionary - Zulu English*, the *Woordeboek, Afrikaans-Zoeloe, Zoeloe Afrikaans* and the comprehensive *Zulu English Dictionary*. The

---

[10] http://africanlanguages.com/psl/.

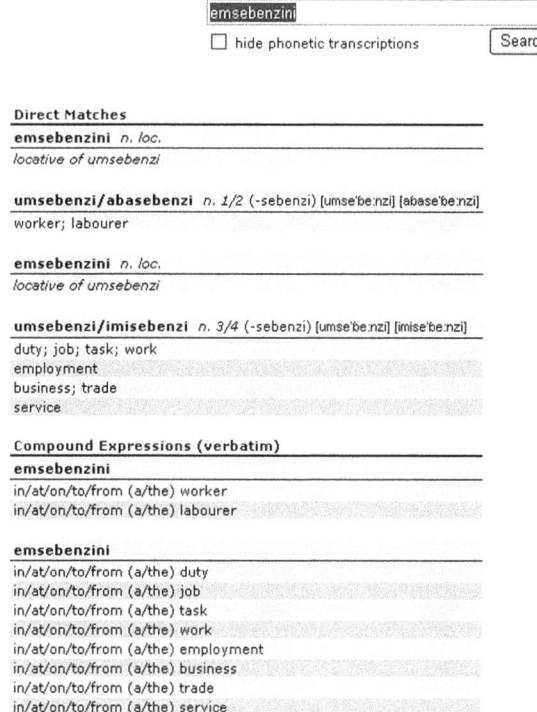

FIGURE 7.10 The treatment of *emsebenzini* in *isiZulu.net*.

presence or absence of the word in the five-million-word PZC is used as a guideline in terms of actual use in isiZulu literature. Table 7.5 shows that nine out of eleven randomly selected words in the *Oxford Bilingual School Dictionary - Zulu English* are included in isiZulu.net. The word *ukuxhumana* does not appear in isiZulu.net, but neither is it found in the PZC. The *Oxford Bilingual School Dictionary - Zulu English* is the first school dictionary published for isiZulu and provides extended/exhaustive treatment of approximately 5,000 lemmas in the Zulu to English section and 5,000 lemmas in the English to Zulu section.

Tables 7.6 and 7.7 show that a majority of the randomly selected words in the *Woordeboek, Afrikaans-Zoeloe, Zoeloe Afrikaans* and the *Zulu English Dictionary* do not appear in isiZulu.net. Neither do many of them (e.g. *exaba*, *gwica*) occur in the PZC.

From Tables 7.5 to 7.7 it is clear that isiZulu.net performs well on frequently used verbs but substantial enlargement will be required if the aim is to cover less frequently used isiZulu words as well.

TABLE 7.5. Random selection of the first lemma on every twenty-fifth page of the *Oxford Bilingual School Dictionary - Zulu English* and its inclusion or omission from *isiZulu.net* and the *PZC*

Page	Lemma	Part of speech and translation equivalent(s)	In *isiZulu. net*?	In *PZC*?
1	ababhali	*pl. n. writers, authors*	yes	yes
25	-dala	*v. cause, create, make, form*	yes	yes
50	-ethulwa	*v. + passive. be submitted, be presented , be taken off*	no	yes
75	iLembe	*n. Shaka*	yes	yes
100	isabelo	*n. portion, share, part*	yes	yes
125	izinkophe	*pl. n. eyelashes*	yes	yes
150	lokho	*demonstrative pronoun pos. that*	yes	yes
175	ngokwethuka	*temporal adverb. suddenly*	yes	yes
200	-sala	*v. remain/stay . . . be outstanding*	yes	yes
225	ukuxhumana	*n. relation(s), relationship*	no	no
250	uyisemkhulu	*n. (his/her) grandfather; (their) grandfather*	yes	yes

TABLE 7.6. Random selection of the first lemma on every twenty-fifth page of the *Woordeboek, Afrikaans-Zoeloe, Zoeloe Afrikaans* and its inclusion or omission from *isiZulu.net* and the *PZC*

Page	Lemma	Part of speech and translation equivalent(s)	In *isiZulu.net*?	In *PZC*?
241	Aba	*uitdeel, porsie of aandeel gee (distribute, give a portion or share)*	yes	yes
266	-cashacasha	*spikkels, vlekke, kolle (spots, blotches, patches)*	no	no
291	exaba	*in die moeilikheid bring (get into trouble)*	no	no
316	gwica	*lieg, jok . . . insluk, verorber (lie, swallow, devour)*	no	no
341	khanku	*grypende . . . berispende . . . wegdraffende (grasping, reproachful, running away)*	no	yes
366	-lubengu	*skerp (sharp)*	no	yes
391	-nyanga	*deskundigheid, kuns, bekwaamheid (expertise, art, capability)*	yes	yes
416	-shiyagalolunye	*nege (nine)*	yes	yes
441	-valamasango	*persoon wat die hekke saans toemaak . . . grendelhout (person who closes the gate at night, key timber)*	no	no

TABLE 7.7. **Random selection of the first lemma on every fiftieth page of the** *Zulu English Dictionary* **and its inclusion or omission from** *isiZulu.net* **and the** *PZC*

Page	Lemma	Part of speech and translation equivalent(s)	In *isiZulu.net*?	In *PZC*?
1	a	... *indefinite article*	yes	yes
50	budúkezi	*ideo*. ... of pouncing on, grabbing ...	no	no
100	umcakathiso	*n*. ... *loose grip, ineffectual act*	no	no
150	dishizela	*v*. ... *walk heavily for, be undecided for*	no	yes
200	faneka	*v. be fitting, proper, becoming*	no	no
250	-giqi	*n. hlonipha term for isigodi, valley*	no	no
300	-hehetsha	*n. anything with a rough, uneven surface (as a stone, rough hand)*	no	no
350	-hungulo	*n. species of love-charm, prob. the bulb of the rock-palm, Encephalartos caffra*	no	yes
400	kholwana	*v. trust one another, be very friendly*	no	yes
450	langaza	*v. have a longing*	no	yes
500	mf'	*Syllabic bilabial nasal preceding ejective denti-labial affricate. occurs by false analogy with usual forms found in Cl.*	no	no
550	-ngaxamatshuthweni	*n. busybody, meddler*	no	no
600	-nsizwankomo	*n. fine, strong, well-built young man*	no	no
650	-phathi	*n. one in charge; superintendent; guardian; commander*	yes	yes
700	-qhifiza	*n. large, distended tick or louse*	no	no
750	-shuwa	*n. species of climbing plant*	no	no
800	-tholonyama	*n. sodden manure of a cattle kraal*	no	no
850	-wathalala	*n. spread-out state, extended condition*	no	no
900	-Zulu	*n. member of the Zulu nation*	yes	yes

7.6 Interactive and dynamic electronic dictionaries for text production in Bantu languages

As already stated, EDs have not as yet reached their full potential and it could be argued that there is much room for improvement. One of the areas in which electronic devices could be utilized is systematic user-guidance in terms of text production, especially where a learner has to produce text and speech in a foreign language involving complicated grammatical structures. Prinsloo (2002) has pointed out that the role of the lexicographer in this regard is as a *mediator* between a complicated linguistic issue on the one hand and the dictionary user on the other (see also Tarp's, 2011, concept of dictionaries as tools).

A typical case for learners of Bantu languages is how to express *is, am, are, be, become*, etc.

(1) is ke [identifying. copulative], *ke lengwalo, ga se sephuthana it is a letter, it is not a parcel; bohodu ke sebe. theft is a sin.* o/e/le ... [descriptive. copulative], aowa, *mosadi yo o bohlale, ga a bogale! No, this woman is clever, she's not cruel!;* o/e/le na le [associative copulative]*Satsope o na le Sara. Satsope is with Sara.*

Currently, learners of Sepedi who want to use copulatives in speech or text production have to undertake intensive study of the copulatives from dictionaries and grammar books. Dictionaries typically provide basic and inadequate information. Grammar books such as Poulos and Louwrens (1994) on the other hand provide an overdose (37 pages) of grammatical information, in a desperate effort to cover all the relevant and possible copulatives (see the extract from their summary of the identifying copulative in Table 7.8).

The interactive electronic dictionary should guide the user, for example by means of decision options and pop-up boxes as guiding elements. Prinsloo *et al.* (2011: 215) argue that guidance, in terms of the encoding needs of the target users, can be seen as a decision process:

Grammar rules, semantics and communicative intentions, as well as (idiosyncratic, lexicalised) exceptions are among the parameters that influence the choice. [...] A dictionary aimed at guiding the user in lexical selection should therefore implement a type of "decision algorithm". In addition, it should flag incorrect solutions and should warn against possible wrong generalisations of (foreign) language learners.

Such an interactive dictionary could even include grammar-checking functionalities combined with guidance by means of pop-up boxes. Consider for example, in Figure 7.11, the first step in a guidance sequence offered to the user who incorrectly typed **lesogana ke bohlale* for 'the young man is clever' in Sepedi.

TABLE 7.8. **The identifying copulative (Poulos and Louwrens 1994: 320)**

The indicative series The present tense *Principal Identifying* pos. 1st and 2nd persons: *SC - CB* Classes:

CP - CB neg. 1st and 2nd persons: *ga - SC - CB* Classes: *ga - se - CB Participial* pos. 1st and 2nd person: *SC - le - CB* Classes: *CP - le - CB* neg. 1st and 2nd person: *SC - se - CB*Classes: *CP - se - CB*

The future tense Principal pos. 1st and 2nd person: *SC - tlô/tla - ba + CB* Classes: *CP - tlô/tla - ba +*

*CB*neg. 1st and 2nd person: *SC - ka - se - bê + CB SC* Classes: *CP - ka - se - bê + CB Participial* pos.

1st and 2nd person: *SC - tlô/tla - ba + CB* Classes: *CP - tlô/tla - ba + CB* neg. 1st and 2nd person:

*SC - ka - se - bê + CB*Classes: *CP - ka - se - bê + CB The past tense Principal* pos. 1st and 2nd person:

*SC - bilê + CB*Classes: *CP - bilê + CB* neg. 1st and 2nd person: *ga - se - SC - be + CB ga - se - SC2 -*

a - ba + CB ga - SC2 - a - ba + CB Classes: *ga - se - CP - bê + CB ga - se - SC2 - a - ba + CB1 ga - SC2 - a - ba - CB Participial* pos. 1st and 2nd person: *SC - bilê + CB* Classes: *CP - bilê + CB* neg. 1st

and 2nd person: *SC - sa - ba + CB*Classes: *CP - sa - ba + CB*

The potential Principal and participial 1st and 2nd person: pos. *SC - ka - ba + C*neg. *SC - ka - se - bê + CB* Classes: pos. *CP - ka - ba + CB*neg. *CP - ka - sê - bê + CB*

The subjunctive 1st and 2nd person: pos. *SC - bê + CB*neg. *SC - se - bê + CB* Classes: pos. *CP - bê +*

*CB*neg. *CP - se - bê + CB* Note also the compound negative *SC/CP - se - kê + SC2 - a - ba + CB*

The consecutive 1st and 2nd person: pos. *SC2 - a - ba + CB* neg. *SC2 - a - se - bê + CB* Classes: pos.

SC2 - a - ba + CB neg. *SC2 - a - se - bê + CB* Note also the compound negative *SC2 - a - se - ke + SC2 - a - ba + CB*

The habitual 1st and 2nd person: pos. *SC - be + CB* neg. *SC - se - be + CB - be + CB* Classes pos.

CP - be + CB neg. *CP - se - be + CB*

The infinitive pos. *go - ba + CB* neg. *go - se - bê + CB*

The imperative pos. *e - ba - ng + CB* or *ba - a - ng + CB* neg. *se - bê - ng + CB*

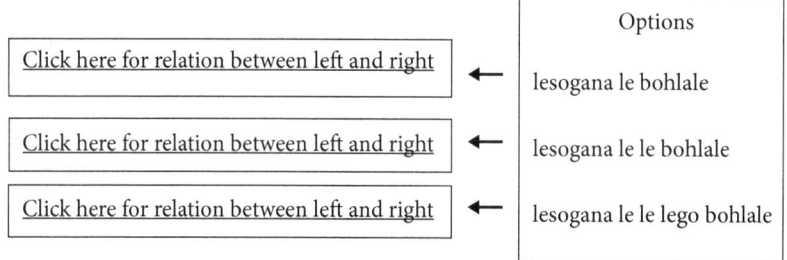

FIGURE 7.11 Pop-up box for **lesogana ke bohlale.*

TABLE 7.9. **Relations expressed by the identifying, descriptive, and associative copulatives in Sepedi**

A - Identifying copulative:
The relation is one of *identification/equality*, i.e. subject = complement
Click here for **Complete Table**

B - Descriptive copulative:
The relation is one of *description*, i.e. complement describes subject
Click here for **Complete Table**

C - Associative copulative:
The relation is one of *association*, i.e. subject is associated with complement
Click here for **Complete Table**

The three types of copulatives—identifying, descriptive, and associative—should then be hyperlinked to a pop-up box (e.g. the one shown in Table 7.9) to explain the nature of the three copulative relations. Each of the three types could then be linked to a (more) complete table giving text production guidance in terms of the different moods of the verb.

The software design for guidance in the correct compilation of copulatives will surely be challenging, but sufficient morphological, semantic, and syntactic data exist that can be utilized in the processes of disambiguation, guidance, and restrictions. It should also be a team effort by the Bantu linguist, lexicographer, and software programmer to compile such an intelligent subsection for copulatives in an advanced ED for Sepedi. Similar designs should then be attempted for text production guidance for the major part-of-speech categories in Sepedi, i.e. adjectives, linguistic verbs, and nominal phrases.

7.7 Conclusion

From the previous discussion it should be clear that exciting possibilities exist for the development of electronic dictionaries. Modern technologies enable lexicographers to enhance the quality of electronic dictionaries and to incorporate a number of true electronic features to facilitate information retrieval in ways unthinkable in the paper dictionary dimension. However, to date EDs have not fully lived up to expectations. Generally speaking one could argue that they did not supersede paper dictionaries in the imaginative ways predicted in the early 1990s. EDs to a large extent remain paper dictionaries on computer, with some enhanced features such as sophisticated search functions, pop-up boxes, and audible pronunciation. Not much is seen of dynamic, intelligent, and even adaptive EDs using the wealth of electronic features available in the modern technological age.

EDs for lesser-used languages including the Bantu languages and even Afrikaans and SA English have a long way to go before they reach a high degree of lexicographic quality. They should first match the lexicographic standard of good paper dictionaries and then be elevated to what has been referred to in this chapter as intelligent and dynamic EDs. Collaborative initiatives, such as isiZulu.net, have great potential for lesser-resourced languages. User-generated content, provided that sound quality-assurance measures are in place, could speed up the compilation of EDs for lesser-resourced languages. Likewise, the potential of linking dictionaries with corpora, and especially processed data from corpora, could be invaluable, especially for text and speech production by the target users of such dictionaries.

Global trends and changes in modern lexicography put additional pressure on the Bantu lexicographer. These include the user perspective and the emphasis on user-friendliness, a more functional approach, increased attention to dictionaries suitable for text production, and corpus-based dictionaries instead of the traditional intro-spection-based dictionaries, etc. In addition to all the influencing factors and developments in general lexicography, Bantu-language lexicography faces unique problems in terms of lexicographic traditions, lack of standardization, lemmatization, and financial challenges. Electronic features should be used in EDs for all the Bantu languages to solve problems that cannot be solved with paper dictionaries. Most of these problems are rooted in the complicated grammatical structure of the Bantu languages and relate to difficulties in respect of the stem identification of words.

Best practices have to be followed in the compilation of EDs and strenuous efforts should be made to establish a stronger dictionary culture and training in dictionary using skills. The electronic dictionary will probably eventually replace the paper dictionary, just as the computer superseded the typewriter, the jet engine the propeller, and television the radio, by replacing an older technology with a newer one. But for lesser-resourced languages the replacement of paper dictionaries by EDs will be a long, slow process.

Dictionaries

Afrikaanse Woordelys en Spelreëls: Die Taalkommissie van die Suid-Afrikaanse Akademie vir Wetenskap en Kuns (2002). Negende, verbeterde en omvattend herbewerkte uitgawe. Cape Town: Pharos Dictionaries. (14:2004)

CNSD Ziervogel, Dirk and Mokgokong, Pothinus C. M. (1975). *Comprehensive Northern Sotho Dictionary, Northern Sotho–Afrikaans/English*. Pretoria: J. L. van Schaik.

e-HAT: Handwoordeboek van die Afrikaanse Taal. Fifth Edition on CD ROM (2009). Cape Town: Pearson.

HAT Odendal, Francois F. and Rufus H. Gouws (eds.) (2005). *HAT. Verklarende handwoordeboek van die Afrikaanse taal*. Fifth Edition. Cape Town: Pearson Education South Africa.

MED Macmillan English Dictionary on CD-ROM (2007).

Oxford Bilingual School Dictionary: Zulu and English: De Schryver, Gilles-Maurice (ed.) (2010). First Edition. Cape Town: Oxford University Press Southern Africa.

Woordeboek. Afrikaans-Zoeloe, Zoeloe-Afrikaans: Dekker, A. M. and J. H. Ries (1958). Johannesburg: Afrikaanse Pers Boekhandel.

Zulu-English Dictionary: Doke, Clement. M. and J. Vilakazi Benedict (1948). Johannesburg: Witwatersrand University Press.

Websites

Bukantswe: http://bukantswe.sesotho.org/.

Cambridge Dictionaries Online: http://dictionary.cambridge.org.

cBold: http://www.cbold.ish-lyon.cnrs.fr/.

Dicts.info: http://www.dicts.info/.

Freedict.com: http://www.freedict.com/.

Freelang dictionaries: http://www.freelang.net/.

isiZulu.net. http://isizulu.net.

IsiZuluforTravellers: www.travlang.com.

Merriam-Webster Online: http://www.merriam-webster.com.

OED: http://www.oed.com.

Pharos Afrikaans/Engels-English/Afrikaans CD-ROM Dictionary. Also online: http://www.pharosonline.co.za.

Pukuntšutlhaloši ya Sesotho sa Leboa ka Inthanete: http://africanlanguages.com/psl/.

Sesotho sa Leboa (Northern Sotho) - English Dictionary: http://africanlanguages.com/sdp/.

Webster's Online Dictionary: http://www.websters-online-dictionary.org/.

WAT. Woordeboek van die Afrikaanse Taal: http://www.woordeboek.co.za.

Xhosa-English Dictionary: http://www.xhosadictionary.com.

Part II

Innovative dictionary projects

8

Data access revisited: The Interactive Language Toolbox

SERGE VERLINDE AND GEERT PEETERS

8.1 Introduction

It is generally accepted that one of the main advantages of electronic dictionaries over paper dictionaries is the speed with which information can be retrieved (e.g. Tono 2000). Most electronic dictionaries today offer a number of powerful search functions to increase look-up speed: users can make use of wildcards, search for word forms (rather than lemmas) and word combinations, conduct a full text search, query specific parts of a dictionary entry, and navigate from one entry to another via hyperlinks. These options are undoubtedly innovative technological developments, but they result from a purely technology-oriented approach to lexicography. They were developed on the assumption that, if available, dictionary users would simply use them.

Increasing attention is, however, now being paid to improving search options and data access facilities with a view to developing dictionaries that are more responsive to the needs and profile of the user (e.g. Fuertes-Olivera and Bergenholtz, 2011b, Granger and Paquot 2010a), thus paving the way for a more user-oriented lexicography. The *use* of electronic dictionaries is also increasingly being investigated, usually in comparison with paper dictionaries (e.g. Dziemianko 2010, this volume), with a view to establishing how useful a dictionary is for performing a specific task (e.g. reading a text or finding the most appropriate collocation).

As electronic dictionaries are examples of human-computer interaction (HCI), experimental techniques from HCI research could also prove useful in developing more user-friendly dictionaries. However, their *usability*, i.e. "the extent to which a product can be used by specified users to achieve specified goals with effectiveness, efficiency, and satisfaction in a specified context of use" (ISO 9241-110),[1] and *user interface design* have rarely been investigated.

The main objective of this chapter is to report on how insights from a usability study were used to customize data access and search facilities to users' needs in the *Interactive Language Toolbox (ILT)*, i.e. a new interface for the *Base lexicale du français*. Section 8.2 discusses a number of approaches to dictionary customization and lists some of the very few dictionaries that provide elements of such customization. Section 8.3 focuses on Bank's (2010) usability study, which clearly demonstrates that innovative dictionary interfaces are not always well received by their users. In Section 8.4 we describe the main characteristics of the new ILT website and propose a number of principles for the design of user-friendly dictionary interfaces, and more particularly online electronic dictionaries (henceforth *e-dictionaries*), that are based on common usability principles.

8.2 Data access and dictionary customization

Finding the appropriate information in individual entries of a paper dictionary is often quite hard for the average user (Humblé 2001). E-dictionaries offer a number of search options and facilities that are supposed to help users find the information they are looking for. By increasing the number of available lexicographical resources (e.g. thesauruses, extra examples, corpus data), however, e-dictionaries may produce an "abundance of unstructured data", leading to "information death" (Tarp 2009a: 26). It is therefore essential that the design and structure of e-dictionaries contribute to keeping lexicographic information costs, i.e. the effort required to look something up in a dictionary (*search-related cost*) and to understand and interpret the information provided (*comprehension-related cost*), at a low level (Nielsen 2008: 173–4). Ideally, e-dictionaries should also be customized to deliver targeted information at the user's own language level, in response to a specific question in a specific communicative or cognitive situation (Tarp 2008).

Customization or profiling is not a new concept in lexicography, but the number of customizable e-dictionaries is still relatively limited (cf. Granger and Paquot 2010a, Trap-Jensen 2010a: 1134). Technically, however, collecting the data required to provide at least some elements of customization is fairly simple. One method is to allow users to adapt the dictionary interface to their particular needs, for example by displaying or hiding specific elements of an individual entry (e.g. examples, collocations, etymology, pronunciation), thus limiting the amount of text displayed on the screen. This method, which Simonsen (2004: 608) referred to as *lexicographic interface customization* is in operation, for example, on the websites of the *Oxford*

---

[1] www.iso.org/iso/iso_catalogue/catalogue_tc/catalogue_detail.htm?csnumber=38009.

English Dictionary, the *Macmillan English Dictionary* and the *Danish Dictionary Online* (cf. Trap-Jensen 2010a: 1135–6).

User profile data can also be collected via an online form to be completed when users first access the website. On the basis of these details (e.g. mother tongue, language level), user-appropriate information can be provided when the dictionary is consulted. This approach has been adopted in the *Louvain English for Academic Purposes Dictionary* (*LEAD*) in which lexicographical data is customized according to the user's mother tongue and professional field (cf. Granger and Paquot 2010b, Paquot, this volume). Users could also specify whether they were beginners, inter-mediate, or advanced language users, so that the dictionary could display the most appropriate definition according to their proficiency level (Tono 2001: 216, Sánchez and Cantos 2011).

E-dictionaries can also be customized according to users' communicative or cognitive needs. In the *Danish Phraseological Dictionary* (cf. Trap-Jensen 2010a), for example, users can specify, by clicking on one of four buttons, whether (1) they are reading and would like to understand a phraseological expression, (2) they are writing and want to use a particular expression, (3) they are writing and are looking for an expression with a specific meaning, or (4) they want to know everything about an expression (see Figure 8.1).

A similar approach has been adopted in the *Base lexicale du français* (*BLF*), a lexical portal that provides access to the *Dictionnaire d'apprentissage du français langue étrangère ou seconde* (*DAFLES*) (Selva *et al.* 2003) as well as to a number of external websites that are used to complement the lexicographical data available in *DAFLES*. As shown in Figure 8.2, users first need to identify their communicative or cognitive needs by specifying whether (1) they are looking for information on a word

FIGURE 8.1 The *Danish Phraseological Dictionary*.

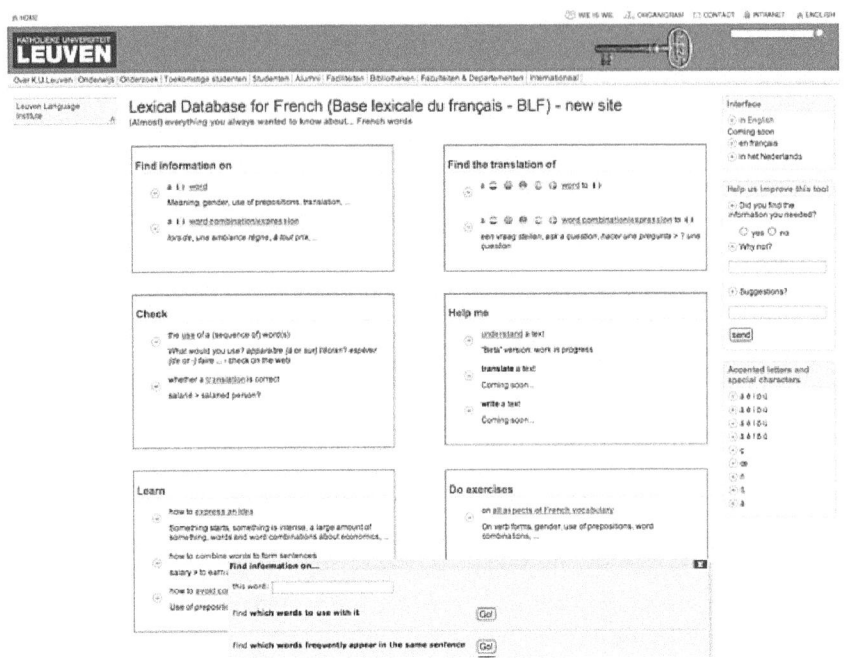

FIGURE 8.2 Homepage of the *Base lexicale du français*.

or word combination [*Find information on*]; (2) they would like to find the translation of a word or word combination [*Find the translation of*]; (3) they want to check
how to use a word or whether a translation is correct [*Check*]; (4) they would like to
get help to understand a text [*Help me*]; (5) they want to use the lexical database as a
learning tool [*Learn*]; or (6) they would like to practise by doing exercises
[*Do exercises*].

As Trap-Jensen (2010a: 1139) points out, optimal profiling of users' needs presupposes that users are "able to analyze their own needs in every look-up situation and
pick the right button". He adds, however, that "there is not much evidence to support
such rational user behaviour" and also warns that "requiring too many options and
clicks of users before they can get started may scare them away. And on the other
hand, a model with immediate look-up and only few options may lead to inaccurate
access and lack of clarity" (p. 1139).

Another approach to dictionary customization is to profile users by means of the
log files that record all requests submitted to the dictionary (De Schryver and Joffe
2004). The use of cookies (i.e. small text files stored on the user's hard drive), allows
the server to uniquely identify a returning visitor. De Schryver *et al.* (2006: 69), for
example, suggested automatically attributing a user ID to each visitor to an online
dictionary; this could be used to track user behaviour, including vocabulary

retention. Log files, however, require careful analysis. As shown by Verlinde and Binon (2010), log files should be filtered, not only because they contain a considerable number of queries made by web crawlers, but also because it seems almost impossible to distinguish between relevant intentional queries and random searches reflecting simply the user's curiosity or carelessness. For instance, there is no point in searching for the syntax of prepositions (e.g. *chez, dans, derrière*) or pronouns (*en, eux, leur*). Nevertheless, an analysis of the BLF log files (Verlinde and Binon 2010) shows that such searches were made for no less than 21.95 per cent and 13.25 per cent of prepositions and pronouns, respectively. Another striking observation is that the same information is often requested repeatedly by the same user. Such 'noise' makes the process of customization highly complex.

By far the most ambitious proposal for customization is that by De Schryver (2010), who suggested that an e-dictionary could use all available information (e.g. queries and explicit user feedback) in order to fine-tune user profiling, thus paving the way for *aiLex*, i.e. adaptive and intelligent lexicography. De Schryver argued that, to build an automatically derived dynamic user profile, "a hybrid approach seems most promising [...], initially based on expert rules that are allowed to (automatically) evolve based on observed user behaviour". It may, for example, be possible to acquire new knowledge about the user's language proficiency level on the basis of the words that are being looked up. As suggested by De Schryver (2010), "rules to implement this may take the form of: If the user mainly searches uncommon words then set the user's level to expert, together with appropriate, numerical threshold values for 'mainly' (e.g. in at least 75% of the cases) and 'uncommon' (e.g. occurs at most 20 times in a given corpus)". De Schryver's (2010) proposal also raises a number of questions and practical problems. For instance, it is not easy to determine in advance what lexicographical data should be linked to each language level. And how will the user's profile be kept up to date? What happens if the profile based on user-supplied data does not match the profile generated from the log files?

The various proposals for dictionary customization discussed in this section clearly show that lexicographers are willing to take users' needs into account when designing new electronic dictionaries. However, it may be argued that the elements of customization implemented in electronic dictionaries so far result more from the lexicographers' ideas about how users should use e-dictionaries (to the point that it might be called a 'lexicographer-oriented' lexicography) rather than from insights into the way dictionaries are actually used. If we want to keep moving towards a truly user-oriented lexicography and design user-friendly e-dictionaries, we now need to turn to the users.

8.3 Bank's (2010) usability study

Bank (2010) is, to the best of our knowledge, the first detailed usability study of e-dictionaries. The study focuses on the usability and user interface design of three e-dictionaries that offer innovative access to lexicographical data: the *Base lexicale du français*, the *Elektronisches Lernerwörterbuch Deutsch–Italienisch* (*Eldit*) and the *Online-Wortschatz-Informationsystem Deutsch* (*OWID*). The study involves three main steps: (1) a pre-test questionnaire, (2) a heuristic evaluation of the three e-dictionaries, and (3) a usability study. As a usability test can only consider a limited number of functionalities, the pre-test questionnaire aimed at identifying the most useful features and options of electronic dictionaries. Bank then evaluated these functionalities from the perspective of an expert user to identify possible violations of some of the general principles of good user-interface design as described by Dumas and Redish (1999). The usability study consisted of:

1. a think-aloud experiment in which thirty university students enrolled in an international communication or management programme were asked to carry out a number of tasks with each dictionary; and
2. a users' questionnaire which participants were requested to fill in directly after performing the different tasks.

To check whether the tasks were successfully completed and identify potential usability problems, all the actions taken by the participants were recorded by means of the Morae software, i.e. a tool for usability testing and user experience research that helps identify website and application design problems.

Bank (2010) was highly critical of the three e-dictionaries she reviewed. She argued that the *BLF*, the *Eldit*, and the *OWID* all needed to be improved with regard to search techniques, the presentation and accessibility of lexicographical information, and the interaction between the user and the dictionary.[2] In the *Base Lexicale du français,* more particularly, the following usability problems were identified:

- The large number of search and information boxes on the *BLF* homepage is confusing.
- The portal function of the *BLF* is insufficiently clear: whenever information is unavailable in the *BLF*, users are redirected to external websites. Participants in the usability study were not always sure when and why they ended up on external web pages; they also sometimes found it hard to navigate back to the dictionary itself.
- If the user makes a mistake or a wrong choice, no help is provided.
- When users explore all *BLF* options, they get distracted by too many windows opening.

---

[2] "Online-Wörterbücher sind demnach in Bezug auf ihre Usability noch verbesserungswürdig. Dies betrifft u.a. die in dieser Arbeit untersuchte Realisierung der Suchfunktionen, die Darstellung und Aufbereitung der lexikographischen Informationen und die Interaktion des Benutzers mit den Wörterbü-chern—all dies sind elementare Funktionen, die für den Nutzer eines Online-Wörterbuchs wichtig und unentbehrlich sind" (Bank 2010: 130).

In short, participants were puzzled by some of the most innovative features of the *BLF*, which seems to confirm Zaenen's conclusion that "since dictionaries are seen as a kind of Bible, a change of their format might jeopardise this status" (2002: 239).

Bank's study (2010) thus poses a dilemma to the lexicographer. Everyone seems to agree that the available, rich lexicographical data can only be fully exploited in the context of an electronic dictionary. On the other hand, it seems hard to enable the user to benefit from this wealth of data or even to make them aware of it (Trap-Jensen 2010a: 1142).

8.4 From the *BLF* to the *Interactive Language Toolbox*

As Bank's (2010) study showed that the *BLF* website did not fully meet users' expectations, we tried to design a new interface that would take into account users' comments on the *BLF*, the ergonomics of human–system interaction (cf. Bank 2010: 5–8), and current technological possibilities. This new website, the *Interactive Language Toolbox* (see Figure 8.3), is based on six key features which are discussed in more detail below.

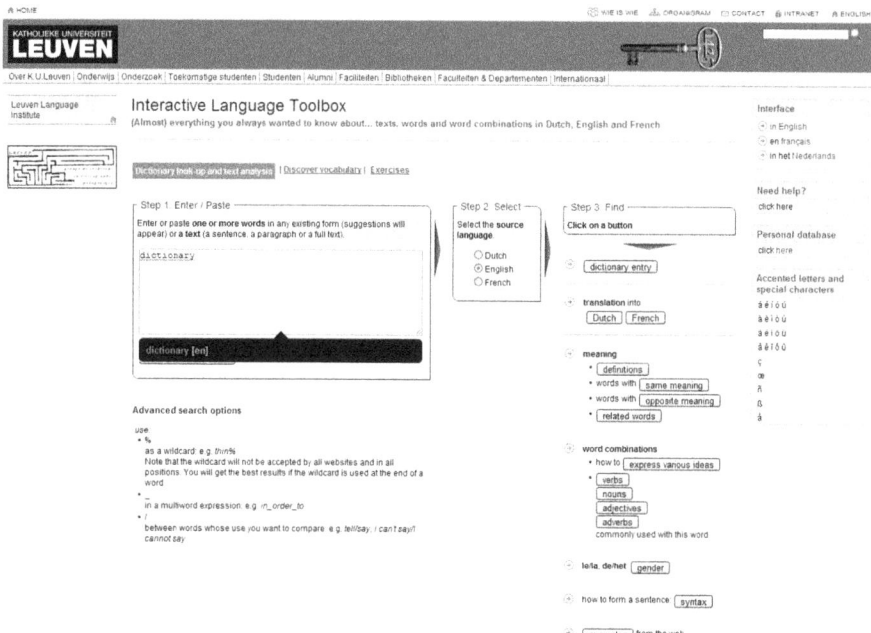

FIGURE 8.3 Homepage of the *Interactive Language Toolbox*.

8.4.1 *From word to text*

Bank's study (2010: 103) demonstrates that users prefer a single search box to multiple search boxes that correspond to different communicative or cognitive needs (e.g. check how to use a word, translate, or do exercises) which were available in the *Base lexicale du français* (see Figure 8.2). It is also important to bear in mind that the advent of electronic dictionaries has brought about major changes in users' expectations. As pointed out by De Schryver *et al.* (2006: 71):

> users increasingly assume that electronic dictionaries behave like Web search engines such as *Google*, and type in concatenations of keywords, combinations and phrases surrounded by quotes, entire sentences, and even dump full paragraphs (lifted from other sources) into the search field.

This implies that the application that processes users' input should not only be intuitive so the user has no trouble finding the search box, as is the case on the *BLF* site (Bank 2010: 50), but also sufficiently robust to handle different types of input, including input with errors (Měchura 2008). To meet this requirement, the *ILT* interface accepts any sequence of characters or words, and for any search a wildcard is available.

If the user types a word that is not recognized, the system provides a number of search suggestions, using the Levenshtein distance. This is one of the most common measures used to identify the words which are graphically nearest to a sequence of characters.[3] This convenient function can accommodate many typing and spelling errors, but it is less efficient in handling phonetically based spelling: for instance, *aldow* will not automatically be converted into *although*. However, the user's uncertainty with regard to the spelling of words can partly be resolved by providing an additional user-interface interaction method, i.e. *incremental search* or *incremental find*. As shown in Figure 8.4, as the user starts typing a word, one or more possible matches (i.e. words and word combinations starting with the letters already typed by the user) are found in the nomenclature of the dictionary and immediately presented to the user in a drop-down menu.

In their analysis of search techniques in fifteen electronic dictionaries, Pastor and Alcina (2010: 323–6) showed that, when users type two or more words into the search box, they are usually given access to a list of lexical entries whose definition or example sentences contain some or all the words included in the query. Very few electronic dictionaries provide direct access to fixed word combinations and even fewer suggest fixed word combinations when users start typing in a look-up query. One notable exception is the *Macmillan English Dictionary Online*: if a user types in the word *life*, words combinations such as *life-affirming, life assurance, life begins at*

---

[3] Such a function is available on many (dictionary) sites in the form of a list of words preceded by, for instance, *Did you mean?* The quality of the suggestions strongly depends on the measure and parameters used (e.g. cost of insertion, cost of replacement, and cost of deletion for the Levenshtein measure).

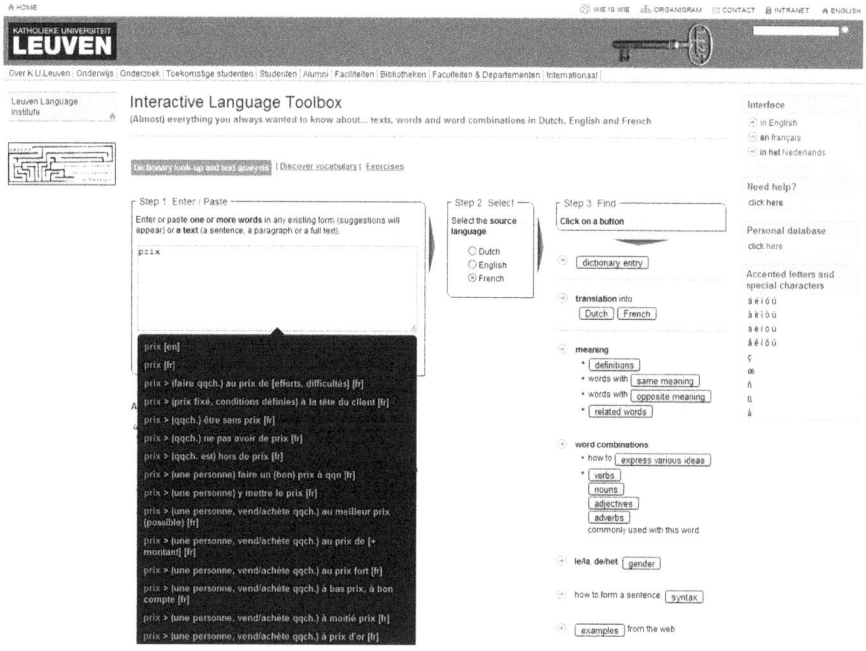

FIGURE 8.4 Incremental search in the *Interactive Language Toolbox*.

forty, *life coach*, and *life cycle* are proposed to the user. Suggestions are, however, limited to word combinations starting with the first characters being typed: the word combination *the time of your life* will not be displayed. In the *ILT*, however, the c.20,000 French word combinations in the database can be found through their constituent parts, regardless of the position of a word in the word combination: the expression *c'est une question de vie ou de mort* ('it's a question of life or death') can be found through either *vie*, *mort*, or *question*. The closest equivalent in other e-dictionaries to the search options available on the *ILT* website seems to be the bilingual Polish–English dictionary *Diki*.[4]

If a user types several words without following the search suggestions generated by the incremental search function, the *ILT* website checks whether the different words form part of a fixed word combination. For example, typing *coûts de production*, *coût production*, or *production coût* will match the word combination *les coûts de production*. If a match is found, the requested information on this word combination is provided. If not, each word is considered separately: typing *vert feuille nature* would match all words and word combinations including either *vert*, *feuille*, or *nature*. The user can indicate that a string of words is to be considered as a fixed word combination by replacing spaces by underscores (e.g. *prendre_part* 'take part').

---

[4] I would like to thank R. Lew for suggesting this website.

8.4.2 *From an "abundance of unstructured data" to restricted search functions*

In most e-dictionaries, a query is performed by clicking a *Search, Find*, or *OK* button. Generally, the query result is all the information available in the dictionary on the submitted word. Sometimes an 'advanced search' button allows the user to apply search filters and look up a word or sequence of words in particular content fields (e.g. in the definitions or example sentences) (cf. Pastor and Alcina 2010: 328). The *ILT* website works somewhat differently: its homepage offers an elaborate search menu listing the various types of information available. Such an extensive menu is typical of a web portal, i.e. a website that provides a single access point to a large number of web pages. It is also more in line with Verlinde and Binon's (2010: 1147) findings that about 90 per cent of searches in the *Base lexicale du français* were targeted dictionary look-ups (more particularly, for translation, gender information, and meaning). Log files revealed that users were rarely interested in getting access to the full lexicographical description of a particular word or word combination. In this respect, there seems to be a contradiction between what users say they expect from a dictionary, i.e. that it provides a maximum of information about a word (Bank 2010: 38), and how they actually use it.

The *ILT* search menu adapts itself to the input typed or pasted in the search box by the user (single word, more than one word, or a full sentence or text). The highest number of search options is provided when the user wants to perform a single-word search. Figure 8.3 shows that if a user types in a single word (e.g. *dictionary*) in the box under Step 1, the options available under Step 3 are: (1) go to the full lexical entry; (2) find a translation into Dutch, English, or French; (3) find a definition, a synonym, an antonym, or other types of related words; (4–6) obtain information on word combinations, gender, and syntax; (7) search web examples; (8) listen to the pronunciation; and (9) obtain frequency information (8 and 9 are not visible on Figure 8.3). As shown in Figure 8.5, as soon as the user types in a word followed by a space, the menu is automatically narrowed down to the types of information available for word combinations: definition, translation, web examples, and frequency information. Other types of information, such as semantically related words, are not shown.

If the user types in a word followed by a punctuation mark, a third menu is automatically selected and the system asks the user whether they need help in decoding, translating, or encoding a text (see Section 8.4.5).

8.4.3 *From a single dictionary to a selective dictionary aggregator*

Dictionary aggregators or metadictionaries are sites which allow the user to perform a query on a large number of lexicographical resources. The search output is typically either a list of shortcuts to relevant pages from these resources (e.g. *OneLook*) or a long page containing all the information retrieved from these resources (e.g.

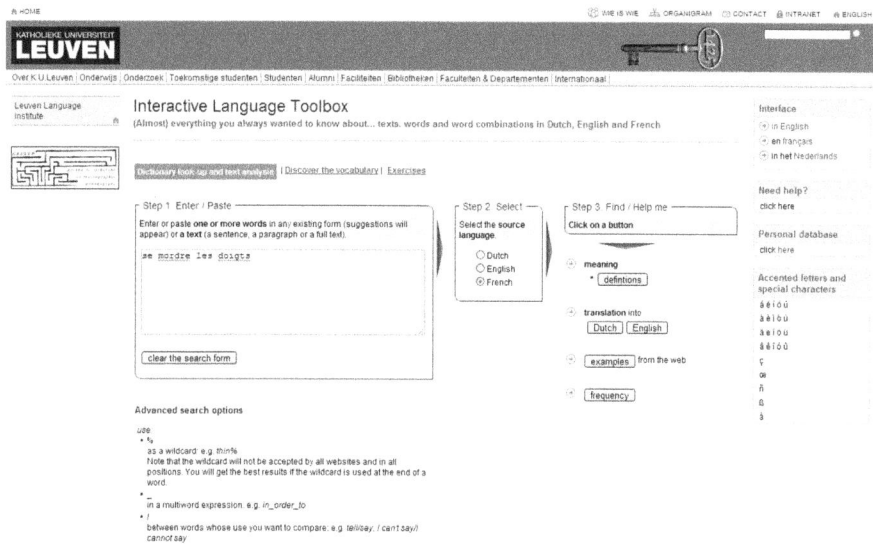

FIGURE 8.5 Search options for multiword expressions in the *ILT*.

Dictionary.com). The *ILT* adopts the *OneLook* model, by providing a page listing external links. Unlike in the *OneLook* aggregator, however, only a selected list of highly reliable dictionaries is offered on the *ILT* (see Figure 8.6).

8.4.4 *From a reference tool to a learning tool*

Atkins and Varantola (1997) conclude their extensive study of dictionary use as follows:

We believe that dictionary skills must be taught, carefully and thoroughly, if dictionary users are to extract from their dictionaries the information which lexicographers have put into them.

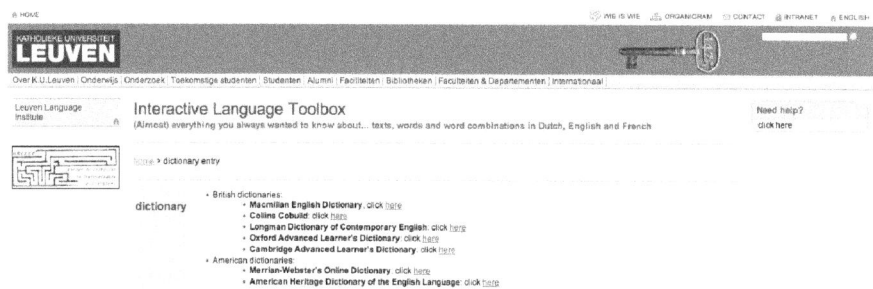

FIGURE 8.6 *ILT* shortcuts to external websites.

In the *ILT* environment, we try to meet the users' secondary needs, i.e. needs for instruction and education in dictionary usage (Tarp 2008: 57),[5] by integrating dictionary-use instruction in the interface as far as possible. Figure 8.7, for example, shows the embedded help offered for checking a translation. It also suggests different strategies for finding the translation of a word or word combination when no results were retrieved from the various sources queried by the *ILT*.

8.4.5 *From static information provider to dynamic, NLP-driven lexical tutor*

Tarp (2008: 123) argues for the development of flexible e-dictionaries as powerful search engines which give "access via active or passive searching to lexicographical data", called *leximats*, which can be consulted in different ways depending on the user's needs. The problem remains, however, that dictionaries—whether leximats or traditional dictionaries—are generally used for ad hoc searches and, after a while, most users get tired of consulting a dictionary whenever they encounter an unfamiliar word.

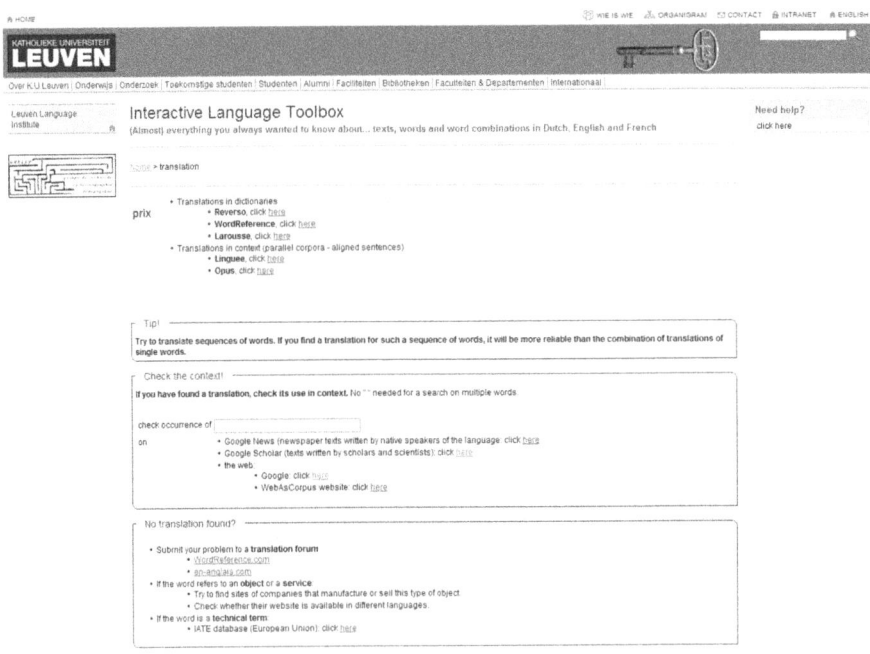

FIGURE 8.7 Embedded help in the *ILT*: checking and searching for translations.

---

[5] Tarp (2008: 56) distinguishes between primary user needs, i.e. "needs leading to a dictionary usage situation" and secondary user needs, i.e. needs "which arise when users seek assistance in a dictionary".

The *ILT* website not only accepts traditional, ad hoc searches for words and word combinations, but can also handle full sentences, paragraphs, and texts. Figure 8.8 shows that, when a text is typed in, search options are available for (1) decoding, (2) translating, (3) encoding, and (4) frequency analysis of the words.

If the user clicks on the 'understand the text' or 'translate the text' button in Figure 8.8, the application analyses the text and adds a layer of relevant lexicographical data to each word, except for a number of function words (e.g. articles, negations, and some very frequent prepositions).[6] As shown in Figure 8.9, this information is displayed in a window when the user hovers the mouse over a word in the sentence or text.

The user thus has immediate access to all relevant information to perform his or her decoding or translation task.

Verlinde *et al.* (2010a) also illustrate how grammatical feedback and information on words can be combined in the same application. Figure 8.10 shows the first of three analyses of grammatical items performed when the user clicks on the 'avoid grammar errors' button in Figure 8.8.

The *Interactive Language Toolbox* is a step towards the full integration of carefully selected resources (dictionaries and grammars) in an application that can adjust itself

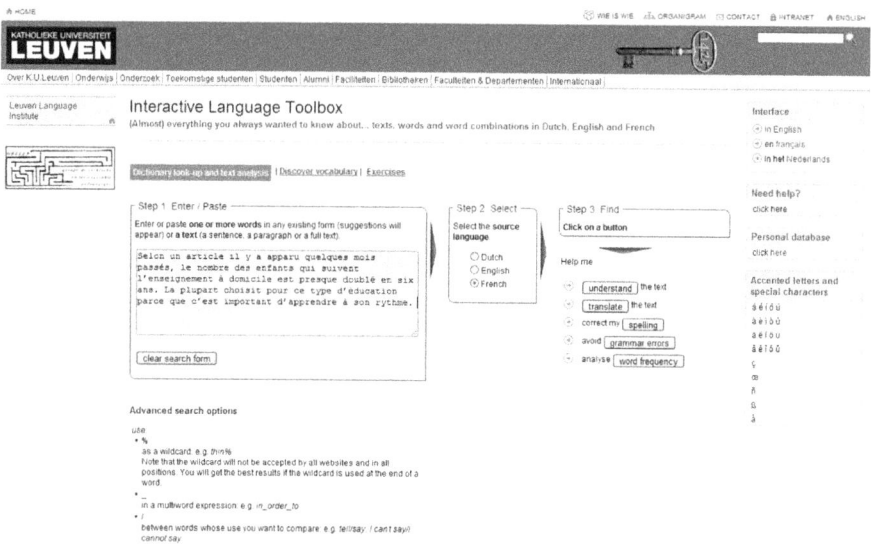

FIGURE 8.8 Search options for full text in the *ILT*.

---

[6] The text submitted is lemmatized and POS-tagged with a home-made software tool. We are currently investigating whether shallow parsing (or chunking) improves the efficiency of the tool.

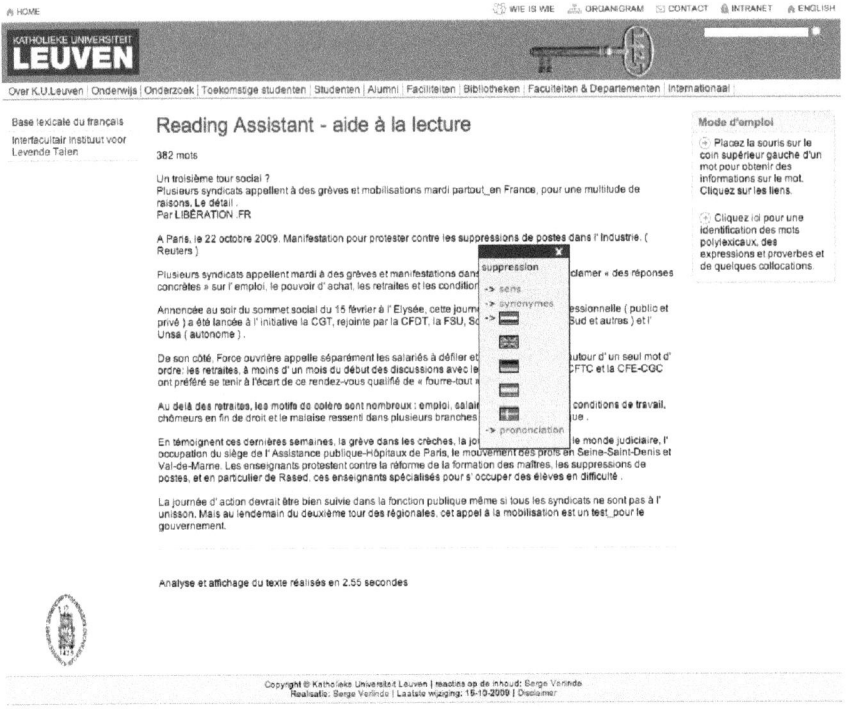

FIGURE 8.9 Reading assistant, figure taken from Verlinde *et al.* (2010a).

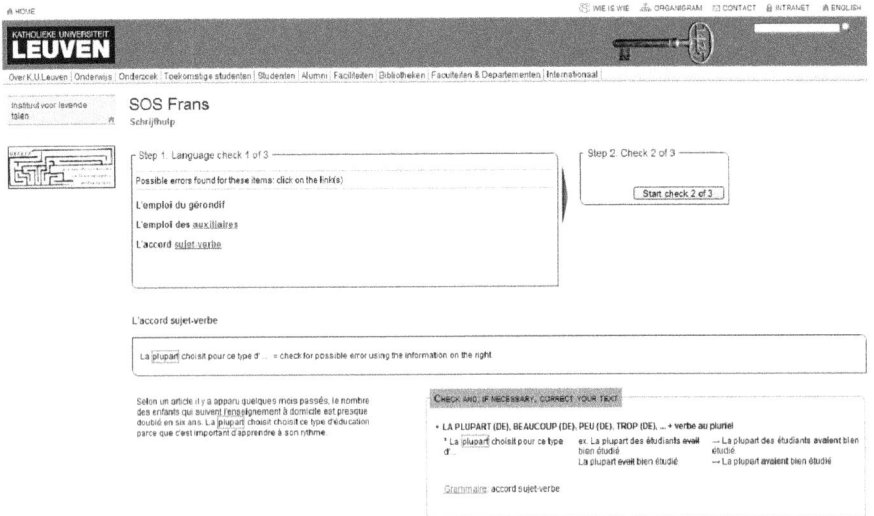

FIGURE 8.10 The grammar checker in the *ILT*.

to the user's input and needs. This approach is in sharp contrast with one offering a random collection of resources in one commercial product, as occurs, for example, in some pocket electronic dictionaries (cf. Tono 2009).

8.4.6 *In a user-friendly interface*

Bank (2010: 4) insists on the fact that usability should go hand in hand with joy-of-use.[7] Users of the *Interactive Language Toolbox* are therefore guided when they navigate through the interface. For example, a dictionary look-up involves three steps that are clearly indicated on the homepage: (1) enter or paste one or more words; (2) select the source language; and (3) find by clicking on a link (see Figure 8.3). For the same reason, the use of metalanguage is limited as this was shown to hinder the use of the *OWID* website (Bank 2010: 42). Instructions and comments are given in the language selected by the user, a procedure described by De Schryver and Joffe (2005) as 'dynamic metalanguage customization'.

A number of concerns related to ease of navigation in the *BLF* (cf. Bank 2010: 52–3, 59, 102–3) were also addressed when the new *ILT* website was devised. For example, users are notified when they are redirected to external sites and all new windows open in the same tab. A breadcrumb trail is also provided at the top of each screen to help users navigate through the different pages they visited (e.g. home > dictionary entry > corpus examples). This enables the user to return to any previous screen without needing to backtrack through several screens by using the browser's back button. In addition, all screens are standardized for ease of reading.

Thanks to these changes, the design of the *ILT* website is in line with general ergonomic principles applying to the design of dialogues between humans and information systems as established in the ISO 9241 standard (Bank 2010: 5–8) and with the general principles of good user interface design (pp. 12–13, based on Sarodnick and Brau 2006).

8.5 Conclusion

One of the main challenges for electronic dictionaries today is to find a trade-off between the huge amounts of data that are being made available to users and the effort users need to expend to find the information that is relevant to them in the dictionary. The usability study conducted by Bank (2010) demonstrates that users' expectations and habits are still insufficiently taken into account by lexicographers. The interfaces of innovative e-dictionaries such as the *BLF* seem to reflect the way in which lexicographers would like users to consult their dictionaries rather than their actual dictionary consultation practices. Bank's (2010) findings also suggest,

---

[7] Cf. http://www.joy-of-use.com.

indirectly, that greater simplicity is needed. Given the abundance of information that lexicography can provide, this objective is no small task. The *Interactive Language Toolbox* is a new attempt to achieve this objective and to implement a more user-oriented lexicography. A new usability study will, however, be necessary to confirm whether or not the best road towards this goal has been found.

Websites

BLF (*Base lexicale du français*): http://ilt.kuleuven.be/blf.

BLF (*Base lexicale du français*, log files analysis): http://ilt.kuleuven.be/blf/stats.

Danish Dictionary Online: http://ordnet.dk/ddo.

Danish Phraseological Dictionary: http://www.ordbogen.com/ (choose *Ordbogen over faste vendinger*).

Dictionary.com: http://dictionary.reference.com/.

Diki: http://www.diki.pl/.

Eldit (*Elektronisches Wörterbuch Deutsch Italienisch*): http://dev.eurac.edu:8081/MakeEldit1/Eldit.html.

ILT (*Interactive Language Toobox*): http://ilt.kuleuven.be/inlato.

LEAD (*Louvain EAP Dictionary*): http://www.uclouvain.be/en-322619.html.

MED (*Macmillan English Dictionary*) online: http://www.macmillandictionary.com/.

OED (*Oxford English Dictionary*) online: http://oxforddictionaries.com/.

OneLook: http://www.onelook.com/

OWID (*Online-Wortschatz-Informationssytem Deutsch*): http://www.owid.de/.

Software

Morae: http://www.techsmith.com/morae.asp.

9

The LEAD dictionary-cum-writing aid: An integrated dictionary and corpus tool

MAGALI PAQUOT

9.1 Introduction

English is incontestably the leading language for the dissemination of academic knowledge (Hyland and Hamp-Lyons 2002). The number of master and doctoral programmes taught in English has increased dramatically over the last decade. The careers of scholars worldwide are bound to their proficiency in a foreign language, as they need to write and publish in English to achieve international recognition in their field. Acquiring good English academic skills, and more particularly academic writing skills, is therefore essential for the large proportion of users for whom English is a non-native language. One of the resources where students and researchers can find help is the monolingual learners' dictionary. For the last fifteen years or so, monolingual learners' dictionaries have taken "more proactive steps to help learners negotiate known areas of difficulty" (Rundell 1999: 47), to the point where they now represent comprehensive writing tools.

Monolingual learners' dictionaries such as the *Longman Dictionary of Contemporary English* and the *Macmillan English Dictionary for Advanced Learners* are corpus-based and typically include productively-oriented information in areas such as syntactic behaviour, synonymy, register preferences, phraseology, and the prevention of errors (Gilquin *et al.* 2007: 325). Since space is less of an issue in electronic dictionaries, an outstanding feature of several of the latest editions of monolingual learners' dictionaries on CD-ROM is the inclusion of example banks or built-in corpus-query tools. These two components should prove advantageous for writing tasks as well as for teaching purposes.

Despite all these welcome developments, monolingual learners' dictionaries still lack one essential feature, i.e. the possibility of customizing dictionary content to users' needs. Dictionary customization has been presented for many years as one of the most promising and expected developments in lexicography (Atkins 2002, Varantola 2002, De Schryver 2003). In a recent article, Tarp (2009a: 25) pointed out that "lexicographic needs are not abstract needs, but are always related to specific types of users who find themselves in a specific type of social situation". Put differently, "users in general never need information in general" (Tarp 2009b: 46). It must be admitted, however, that only superficial elements of customization have been integrated into electronic dictionaries so far (Sobkowiak 2002), despite the fact that technological advances have put this development within the reach of dictionary producers. The focus has largely been on how to present the user with only the information needed (Trap-Jensen 2010a). The *Oxford English Dictionary Online*, for example, allows the user to configure which information categories (e.g. pronunciation, variant spellings, etymology, quotations) should be displayed on the screen. Similarly, the *Macmillan Dictionary Online* allows users to choose between two presentational modes via the buttons 'Show more' and 'Show less'. The *Base lexicale du français* innovates by allowing users to specify their needs by selecting one of six options (get information on, get the translation of, verify, help me, learn, do exercises) before querying the database (Verlinde 2010, Verlinde and Peeters, this volume). What these online dictionaries all have in common, however, is that customization is mainly implemented via the 'presentational component' (Trap-Jensen 2010a), but their 'content component', i.e. the data, is not adjusted to comply with the needs of particular user groups.

The main objectives of this chapter are to present the *Louvain English for Academic Purposes dictionary* (*LEAD*), i.e. an integrated dictionary and corpus tool intended to help non-native speakers write academic texts in English, and to show how corpus data has been used to customize it to users' needs in terms of discipline and mother tongue background. Section 9.2 discusses the role of corpus data in current pedagogical lexicography. Section 9.3 describes the main characteristics of the *Louvain English for Academic Purposes dictionary*. It describes how corpora of expert and learner writing were used to inform the writing of lexical entries in the *LEAD* and presents the main features of the corpus-query tool integrated into the dictionary. Section 9.4 focuses more particularly on the role played by corpora of general and discipline-specific academic texts in the design and compilation of the *LEAD*. Section 9.5 provides a rationale for the integration of a corpus-query tool into the dictionary environment and illustrates how it is being implemented in the *LEAD*. Section 9.6 offers concluding remarks.

9.2 Corpus data in pedagogical lexicography

Using corpora as the basis for the description of words and phrases has become widely established as state-of-the-art dictionary-making practice in pedagogical lexicography. Lexicographers have made use of corpus data to select the words they want to include in a learners' dictionary, describe their meaning and use, and illustrate their preferred environment in context (Atkins and Rundell 2008, Rundell and Kilgarriff 2011, Hanks, this volume). Monolingual learners' dictionaries are typically based on large reference corpora such as the British National Corpus (BNC), the Longman Corpus Network, or the Bank of English. These corpora consist of discourse samples from a wide range of sources such as books, newspapers, magazines, radio and TV shows, and websites, and represent different text types and genres such as fiction writing, academic writing, journalese, and conversation.

The use of genre-undistinguished reference corpora, however, has its limitations when it comes to compiling learners' dictionaries. These limitations are most severe as regards the phraseological description of words and the selection of examples to illustrate their preferred use, two lexicographical features that are essential for productive purposes. In a recent study, I analysed the phraseological treatment of verbs of evidence, i.e. verbs that are used "to discuss matters lying at the very heart of the scholarly process" (Meyer 1997: 368) and enable writers to modulate their ideas and position their work in relation to other members of the discipline (e.g. *argue, demonstrate, illustrate, imply, indicate, suggest,* and *report*), in five learners' dictionaries on CD-ROM (Paquot 2011). The results show that collocations in learners' dictionaries cover a wide range of meanings that are often characteristic of different genres and text types. Academic-like collocations are listed along with other word combinations that may not be appropriate for academic writing. In the *Macmillan English Dictionary for Advanced Learners* (2nd edition, 2007), for example, there is a collocation box for sense 2 of the verb *argue* ("to give reasons why you believe that something is right or true") that offers the following list of adverb collocates: *consistently, convincingly, forcefully, passionately, persuasively, plausibly,* and *strongly*. Non-native writers can be seriously misled by this presentation of collocations as they are not given any help to decide which collocations are most appropriate in academic writing. Put differently, the treatment of phraseology in electronic monolingual learners' dictionaries may lead non-native writers to believe that all collocations and phrases are good for all purposes (e.g. writing a research article or a short story, writing a letter to a friend or to a human resources manager).

This shortcoming holds not only for collocations but also for other features of the microstructure such as sense ordering and example sentences. The characteristics of good dictionary examples have been clearly identified by Atkins and Rundell (2008: 458): they should be (1) natural and typical, (2) informative, and (3) intelligible. However, these are not intrinsic properties, and good dictionary examples should probably vary according to the type of dictionary and the needs of its users. In the *Oxford Advanced Learner's Dictionary* (8th edition, 2010), for example, clicking on the 'Example Bank' for the verb *argue* provides access to a number of corpus examples that represent all sorts of meanings, uses, and contexts (see examples (1) to (10)).

(1) In her paper she goes on to argue that scientists do not yet know enough about the nature of the disease.
(2) Magda walked out of the room before her husband could argue back.
(3) The general argued for extending the ceasefire.
(4) The report argues convincingly that economic help should be given to these countries.
(5) They were arguing over who should have the car that day.
(6) He was too tired to argue the point.
(7) I don't want to argue with you—just do it!
(8) It could be argued that laws are made by and for men.
(9) She argued that they needed more time to finish the project.
(10) We're always arguing with each other about money.

This echoes a question that was well formulated by Williams in 2006: "Learner's dictionaries are made for learners, but who are the learners in question?" Monolingual learners' dictionaries aim to help English as a foreign language (EFL) learners write in English, but there are many types of writing, many genres and styles. In an earlier article, Williams argued for "the necessity of specialised learner's dictionaries to allow users to visualise senses in an environment close to their own working environment as the generalised senses found in dictionaries do not provide examples that will easily enable these users to instantiate their meanings in their working context" (Williams 2003). Quite understandably perhaps, and for obvious economic reasons, this request has not yet been met by learner dictionaries.

This being said, an outstanding feature of several of the latest editions of monolingual learners' dictionaries on CD-ROM is the inclusion of corpus-derived extra examples integrated into the microstructure or available via a corpus-query tool, thus answering Cobb's (2003) call for "a blend of dictionary and concordance" as "the ideal electronic resource for language learning". The fifth edition of the *Collins COBUILD Advanced Learners' English Dictionary* (2006, *COBUILD5*), for example, provides access to a Wordbank, a five-million-word representative sample of British and American English, both written and spoken, from the Bank of English Corpus. As shown in Figure 9.1, users can navigate from a lexical entry (here the entry for the lemma *challenge*) to the associated WordBank by clicking on a button on the menu bar, and get more example sentences from the corpus.

The WordBank tool also functions as a concordancer and users can not only search for single words but also phrases in the corpus. Figure 9.2 shows the output of a search for the word combination *at issue*.

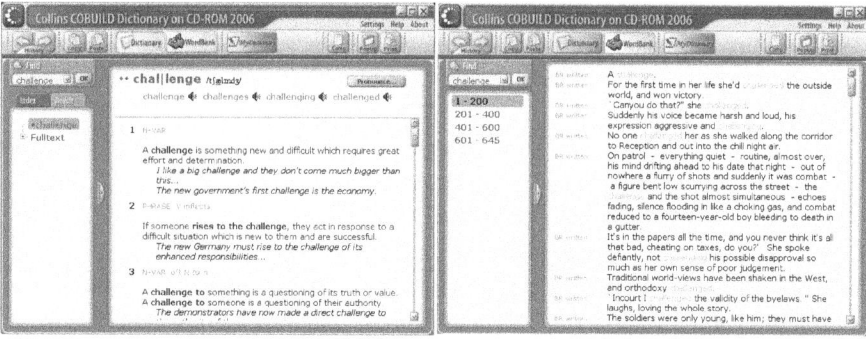

FIGURE 9.1 'Dictionary' and 'WordBank' views in *COBUILD5*.

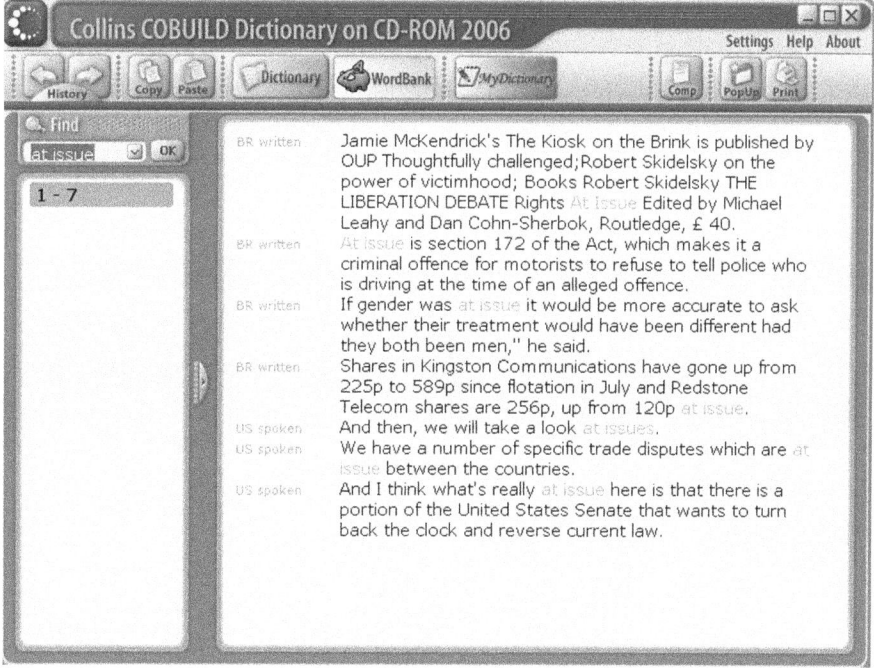

FIGURE 9.2 Searching the corpus in *COBUILD5*.

COBUILD5 certainly deserves to be praised for being the first learner dictionary that offered direct corpus access to its users.[1] The WordBank button is, however, the only access route from the dictionary to the corpus-query tool and there is no further integration of the concordance lines into the dictionary. Another problem is that, for

---

[1] In the *Collins COBUILD Advanced Dictionary* (2009), however, the WordBank tool has disappeared.

learners, the extra examples can be highly misleading as they are extracted from a raw corpus and no distinction is drawn between the different parts of speech of a given lemma. In Figure 9.1, for example, there are examples of *challenge* both as a noun and as a verb.

Extra corpus data are more fully integrated into the fifth edition of the *Longman Dictionary of Contemporary English* (*LDOCE5*, 2009). As shown in Figure 9.3, access to corpus data is offered in the microstructure of the dictionary, i.e. as part of each lexical entry. A sample of one million sentences taken from the Longman Corpus Network is used to provide additional examples (via the Example Bank frame on the menu on the right) and more collocations (via the Collocations frame on the right) for each lexical entry.

The additional examples provided for each word come from a part-of-speech tagged corpus. Querying the noun *challenge* in *LDOCE5* and clicking on 'Examples from the corpus' opens a pop-up window that gives extra examples of the noun *challenge* (but not the verb) (see Figure 9.4). Unlike in *COBUILD5*, there is no concordancer facility in *LDOCE5*: it is thus impossible to use the corpus as a stand-alone tool.

The fifth editions of the *Longman Dictionary of Contemporary English* and the *Collins COBUILD Advanced Learners' English Dictionary* illustrate two different

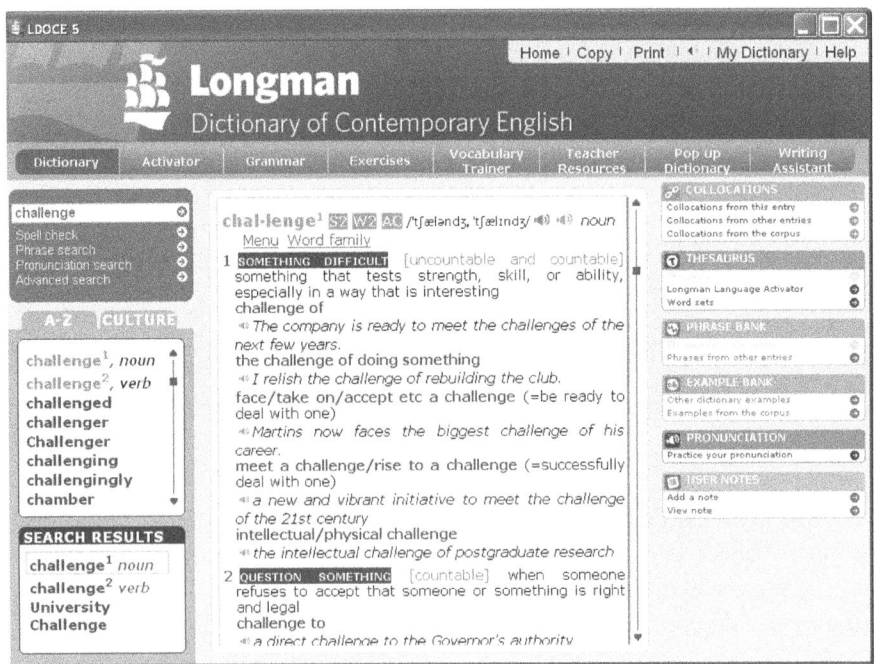

FIGURE **9.3** The *Longman Dictionary of Contemporary English* (5th edition, 2009).

FIGURE 9.4 Extra examples from the corpus in *LDOCE*5.

approaches to integrating corpus data into monolingual learners' dictionaries. As advocated by Asmussen (forthcoming), "an ideal combined dictionary-corpus product, though, should not just follow one of these two approaches, but should try to really combine them. That means that both components, dictionary and corpus, should be separately accessible and furthermore that they should be linguistically interlinked, i.e. syntactically, semantically, and that means not only by shallow string similarities". According to Asmussen, any lexicographer who wants to develop a combined dictionary–corpus product has to answer the following three questions:

1. Why would it be interesting for a dictionary user to also have access to an integrated corpus?
2. How can two linguistic resources that are as diverse as a dictionary and a corpus, and that typically address quite disparate user groups, namely linguistic laymen in the case of dictionaries and linguistic experts in the case of corpora, be combined conceptually?
3. How can corpus functionality—which differs significantly from dictionary functionality—be communicated to dictionary users? (Asmussen, forthcoming)

The author identifies five major challenges that need to be addressed when compiling a combined dictionary–corpus product:

1. The challenge of form: Non-expert users cannot be assumed to be aware of the formal difference between two types of linguistic information, i.e. search results from a dictionary and concordance lines. They "might consider a concordance as further examples on the use of a certain meaning of a word or expression, but may be confused by the fact that they are often incomplete, may illustrate a different meaning of the word or expression to the one in question, and may even show spelling mistakes or uses generally considered as substandard" (Asmussen, forthcoming).

2. The challenge of content: The contents of the dictionary and the combined corpus should be coherent (e.g. the corpus may sometimes reveal new linguistic developments that are not covered in the lexicographical descriptions provided by the dictionary). Information about the corpus should also be available (e.g. whether it consists of standard language samples compiled according to strict lexicographical design criteria, or is made up of automatically extracted texts from the Web; information about text types and date of publication).

3. The challenge of linking: Asmussen argues that the senses and constructions of lexical items in the dictionary must be linguistically linked to their occurrences in the corpus and vice versa. This requires the corpus to be morphologically, syntactically, and semantically disambiguated and tagged.

4. The challenge of reception: Users should be guided in their use of a corpus-query tool integrated into the dictionary. They should be taught that "a corpus gives info on potentially every *linguistic* question (they) might ask—if (they) know how to ask—whereas a dictionary gives answers to a subset of linguistic questions considered relevant by the editors of the dictionary" (Asmussen, forthcoming).

5. The challenge of interpretation: A key word in context (KWIC) concordance is an unfamiliar and fragmented type of data that requires the user to be able to generalize and identify structural regularities. Lexicographers need to address the question of how to present corpus results in a more intelligible way.

The *LEAD* is a combined dictionary–corpus (or dictionary-cum-corpus) product and offers two ways of using corpora: as additional example banks (Section 9.4) and via an independent corpus-query tool integrated into the dictionary (Section 9.5). The ways in which some of the challenges identified by Asmussen are addressed in the *LEAD* will also be discussed.

9.3 Major characteristics of the Louvain EAP dictionary

The *Louvain English for Academic Purposes* dictionary (*LEAD*) is a specialized dictionary which targets a specific population, i.e. non-native-speaker students and researchers who wish to write academic texts in English, and focuses on a specific set of vocabulary, viz. general academic words and phrases (Granger and Paquot 2010b). Academic vocabulary consists of "a set of options to refer to those activities that characterize academic work, organize scientific discourse and build the rhetoric of academic texts" (Paquot 2010: 28). Unlike technical vocabulary, which is often catered for in English for Specific Purposes (ESP) courses, there is a tendency to neglect general academic vocabulary in the curriculum.

The dictionary is based on the *Academic Keyword List* (*AKL*; Paquot 2010: 56–8), a new list of academic vocabulary that covers 930 non-technical words and phrases and differs widely from Coxhead's (2000) *Academic Word List* as it includes high-frequency words (e.g. *aim, argue, because, compare, explain, namely, result*) which have been shown to play an essential role in structuring academic prose. A large number of *AKL* words were found to fulfil rhetorical functions that are particularly prominent in academic discourse (e.g. give examples, express cause and effect, conclude, and express possibility and certainty). For example, *AKL* words used to describe differences include nouns such as *contrary, contrast, difference, distinction,* and *opposite*; verbs such as *contrast* and *differ*; adjectives such as *contrary, contrasting, different,* and *unlike*; adverbs such as *by comparison, by contrast, conversely,* and *on the other hand*; the conjunctions *while* and *whereas*; and prepositions such as *as against, by comparison to,* and *unlike*.

The *LEAD* is a writing and learning-aid tool. It is grounded in recent research that has shown that form-focused instruction is beneficial to vocabulary learning (Laufer and Girsai 2008) and contains rich corpus-based descriptions of academic words and phrases, with particular focus on their collocations and lexical bundles, i.e. "recurrent expressions, regardless of their idiomaticity, and regardless of their structural status" (Biber *et al.* 1999: 990). Howarth showed that collocations are an essential part of the procedural vocabulary of academic discourse and argued that learners need the lexical means that will allow them to conform to the native stylistic norms for a particular register, which "entails not only making appropriate grammatical and lexical choices but also selecting conventional collocations to an appropriate extent" (Howarth 1998: 186).

Recent studies have shown that the highly conventionalized nature of academic discourse stems largely from 'lexical extensions' of a set of academic words such as *conclusion, issue, claim,* or *argue*. These words acquire their organizational or rhetorical function in specific word sequences or lexical bundles that are essentially semantically and syntactically compositional (e.g. *as discussed below, an example of, the aim of this study is to, it has been suggested, it is important to, are more likely to, in the case of*) (e.g. Curado Fuentes 2001, Biber *et al.* 2004). To provide further help to non-native speakers, the *LEAD* also gives details about the frequency of academic words and phrases, their preferred position in the sentence, and the punctuation that usually surrounds them in academic writing. Last but not least, the dictionary

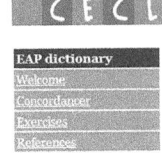  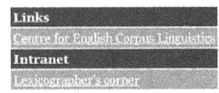

The Louvain EAP dictionary

Please select a discipline: Business

What is your mother tongue? French / French / Dutch / Other

Send

Contact : Magali Paquot & Sylviane Granger

FIGURE 9.5 The Louvain EAP dictionary's homepage.

includes about sixty exercises (fill-in-the-blank, word building, and collocation exercises) to help learners consolidate or test their knowledge of academic vocabulary.

One innovative feature of the *LEAD* is its customizability: in order to bring the dictionary closer to users' needs, the content is automatically adapted as a function of each user's discipline and mother-tongue background. The dictionary relies on a relational MySQL[2] database, the technical characteristics of which make it possible to exploit linguistic information as a 'multifunctional lexicographical database', i.e. a "modularly designed dictionary database targeting several kinds of users in many different user situations" (Pajzs 2009: 327). As shown in Figure 9.5, before using the dictionary, users select a domain (currently business, medicine, linguistics, or general English for Academic Purposes (EAP)) and specify their mother tongue (L1) background (currently French or Dutch). This stage conforms to Tarp's (2009b: 48) suggestion "to prepare a preliminary interactive phase where the lexicographic tool helps the users to identify and specify their concrete needs before being guided to the corresponding data".

The *LEAD* also makes full use of the capabilities afforded by the electronic medium in terms of multiplicity of access modes. The dictionary can be used as both a semasiological dictionary (from lexeme to meaning) and an onomasiological dictionary (from meaning/concept to lexeme), via a list of eighteen typical rhetorical or organizational functions in academic discourse. In the first mode, a user may think of a word but be unsure about how to use it (What is the exact meaning of *moreover*? What is its typical position in a sentence? Which verbs and adjectives collocate with the noun *cause*?). The second mode aims to provide help to a user who may want to express a particular function (e.g. conclude a text or contrast two arguments) but not know how to express it; or more likely, to a user who may know only one or two ways of expressing the function and would like to introduce some variation (cf. also Pecman 2008, Kübler and Pecman, this volume). One of the main advantages of

---

[2] www.mysql.com/.

this access mode is that it suggests alternatives and thereby helps users enlarge their academic repertoire. The *LEAD* is also a semi-bilingual dictionary (Laufer and Levitzky-Aviad 2006), as users who have selected a particular mother-tongue background can search lexical entries via their translations into that language.

9.4 Dictionary compilation and corpus data

The *LEAD* is fully corpus-based: we make use of corpora of both expert and learner writing to inform the lexicographical treatment of academic words and phrases. Expert corpora are used to examine how academic words are typically used by expert writers (Section 9.4.1), while learner corpora are analysed to investigate how learners differ in their use of academic vocabulary and identify their difficulties (Section 9.4.2).

9.4.1 *From expert corpora to dictionary*

Two types of corpora of expert writing were used in the compilation of the *LEAD*, i.e. a large general English for Academic Purposes corpus (the 15-million-word academic component of the British National Corpus) and three user-defined discipline-specific corpora of about one million words each in business, linguistics, and medicine. Expert corpora were not only used to provide rich lexicographical descriptions of academic words and phrases (in terms of meaning, position in the sentence, surrounding punctuation, and preferred collocations and phrases), they were also used to add frequency information to the *LEAD* (often in the form of graphs that compare the frequency of a word in different genres or the frequency of similar words in academic prose).

Special attention is also paid to meaning, especially to the meaning of connectors that are often not well differentiated in dictionaries and EFL teaching material. Figure 9.6 shows the lexical entry for the adverb phrase *on the contrary*. The

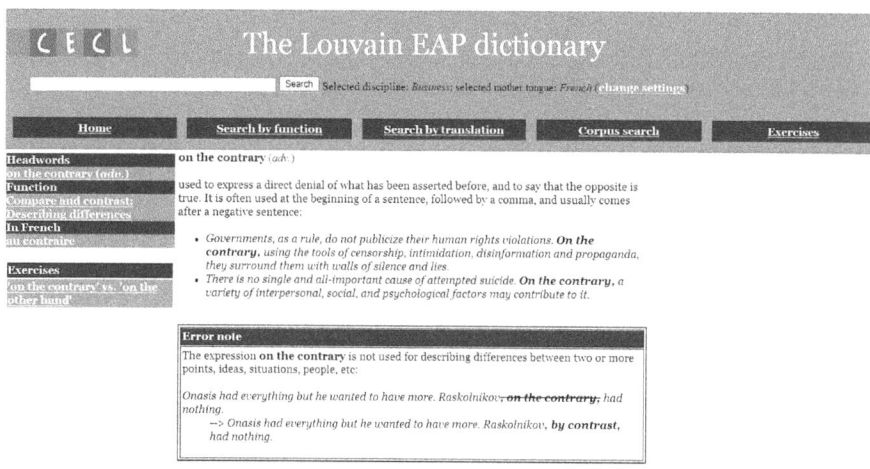

FIGURE 9.6 The entry for *on the contrary* in the *LEAD*.

definition is directly followed by information about the position of *on the contrary* in the sentence, punctuation preferences, and information about the type of sentence that usually precedes a sentence introduced by *on the contrary*. The examples given to illustrate the use of *on the contrary* are general EAP examples, i.e. they come from the academic component of the British National Corpus and are the same for all users of the dictionary.

When a lexical item has close synonyms that are more frequent in academic writing, a note is provided to highlight frequency differences. For example, there is a note in the lexical entry for *in the same way* that says that the adverb *similarly* is more frequent than *in the same way* in academic writing. As shown in Figure 9.7, the note is backed up with a chart that compares the frequencies of the two adverbs.

Corpus-based studies of academic writing have shown that "there is a shared scientific voice or 'phraseological accent'" (Gledhill 2000: 204) which leads academic writing to polarize around a number of genre-specific collocations. Collocations and lexical bundles included in the *LEAD* were carefully selected on the basis of a thorough analysis of the academic component of the British National Corpus.

---

in the same way *(adv.)*

used to show that the things or ideas you are comparing are alike:

- *Gestures are more flexible than speech and may carry very different meanings depending on the context. When a chimp stretches out an open hand, it can be asking for support during a fight or for a share of food during a meal. **In the same way**, a person raising his hand could be greeting a friend, surrendering, or answering a question in class.*

The adverb **in the same way** is often used at the beginning of a sentence, followed by a comma to modify the whole sentence.

When it is used inside the sentence, **in the same way** is normally followed by **as**:

- *Planning controls operate in rural areas **in the same way as** in urban areas.*

However, it can also be followed by **that** to introduce a clause:

- *Adverbs describe verbs **in the same way that** adjectives describe nouns.*

Note that the adverb **similarly** is much more frequent than **in the same way** in academic writing.

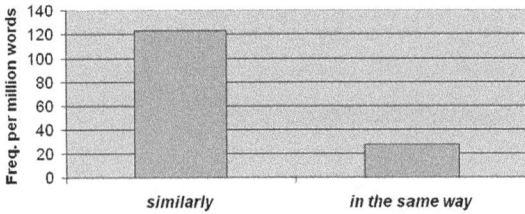

FIGURE 9.7 The entry for *in the same way* in the *LEAD*.

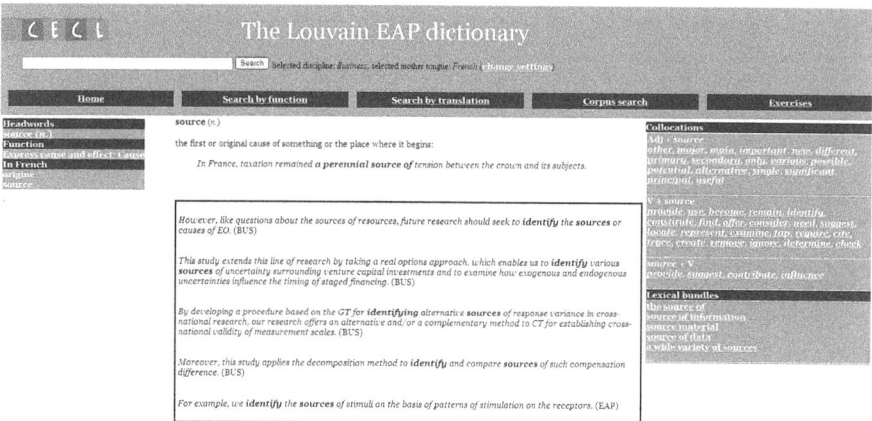

FIGURE 9.8 The entry for *source* in the *LEAD*.

They represent the core lexicographical data of the dictionary and the same academic phraseology is displayed for all users.

What differs, however, according to the user's profile is the corpus used to provide examples of collocations and lexical bundles. A major objective of the project was to make examples as useful and relevant as possible for the dictionary users, and to create a meaningful context in relation to the needs and interests of the target users. It is not very useful for a user specializing in business, for example, to get examples of collocations from medicine or linguistics or any other discipline represented in the academic component of the BNC. The dictionary was thus designed to provide discipline-specific examples of collocations and lexical bundles. As illustrated in Figure 9.8, by clicking on any collocate of the noun *source* in the right column, the user gets access to five examples of the selected word combination (here *identify* + *source*) in a box that opens up in the main frame. Examples are automatically retrieved from a corpus that represents the user's selected discipline (here business).

If the user had selected linguistics as his or her preferred discipline, by contrast, the following examples would have been displayed to illustrate the collocation *identify* + *source*:

(11) A clear grasp of the multilayered relationships among reading subskills is necessary to identify the sources of reading difficulties. (LING)

(12) Grasp of literate language has been identified as the source of the positive relation between preschool children's exposure to storybooks and successful literacy outcomes. (LING)

(13) The teacher identified the source of Camila's confusion and successfully elicited a self-correction in Lines 54–58. (LING)

Similarly, the lexical bundle *this is an example of* would be illustrated by different corpus examples according to the user's selected discipline. Examples (14) to (16) illustrate the type of corpus examples automatically retrieved for business, linguistics, and medicine.[3]

(14) This is an example of the "dual response format" introduced in commercial marketing research studies to mitigate respondents' proclivity to select the "none" option when it is included as one of the choice options. (BUS)

(15) This is an example of relatively formal, schooled talk in which speakers are discussing a set topic, adopting interactional conventions they have been taught. (LING)

(16) This is an example of targeted survival strategy. (MED)

As the corpora of business, linguistic, and medical texts available in the *LEAD* are of a relatively limited size, if five examples of a collocation or a lexical bundle are not found in the selected discipline-specific corpus, more examples are extracted from the larger academic component of the British National Corpus (see the last example in Figure 9.8).

By adopting a genre-based and discipline-specific approach to corpus data use in the *LEAD* and automatically extracting examples of frequent collocations and recurrent phrases, we overcome a number of difficulties related to form, content, and linking in the compilation of a dictionary-cum-corpus. First, the corpora were carefully designed to answer users' needs. Second, word combinations (and not just words) listed in the dictionary are linked to their occurrences in the corpus. Third, by making use of genre-based corpora, polysemy is much more limited than in large reference corpora: there are more chances that corpus examples exemplify appropriate form–meaning mappings, i.e. academic-like meanings of specific word combinations. For ease of reading (and interpretation in Asmussen's terms), corpus-derived examples are not presented as KWIC concordance lines but as full sentences (see Figure 9.8).

9.4.2 *From learner corpora to dictionary*

As Lee and Chen (2009) put it, the use of a learner corpus makes it possible to design needs-based and learner-centred applications. Two learner corpora were used to inform the compilation of the *LEAD* and investigate how learners differ in their use of academic vocabulary:

- the *International Corpus of Learner English*, a 3.6-million-word corpus of argumentative essays written by learners from sixteen different mother-tongue backgrounds (Granger *et al.* 2009);

---

[3] Three disciplines (i.e. business, linguistics, and medicine) are currently represented in the *LEAD* but the architecture makes it very easy to cover more disciplines by uploading other discipline-specific corpora.

- the *Varieties of English for Specific Purposes dAtabase* (*VESPA*), a new learner corpus, currently being developed at the Centre for English Corpus Linguistics in collaboration with several international partners. This corpus contains EFL texts from a wide range of disciplines (linguistics, business, engineering, sociology, etc.), genres (papers, reports, MA dissertations), and degrees of writer expertise in academic settings.[4]

Analysing learner corpus data and comparing them with data from expert corpora has highlighted a number of problems which non-native learners experience when writing academic texts. These include semantic and syntactic misuse, lack of register awareness, problems of frequency (what has been called 'overuse' and 'underuse' in learner corpus research), and phraseological problems (Gilquin *et al.* 2007).

The treatment of learners' errors is mainly explicit, in that the *LEAD* draws learners' attention to error-prone items and provides them with negative feedback in 'Be careful!' notes and warning boxes. Explicit feedback in the form of a metalinguistic explanation of the erroneous structure has been shown to outperform all other types of correction (Varnosfadrani and Basturkmen 2009). Heift (2004) investigated the effects of corrective feedback on learner uptake (i.e. learners' responses to corrective feedback) in computer-assisted language learning and found that participants showed the most learner uptake for feedback that provided an explanation of the error and also highlighted the error in the student input. Warning boxes in the *LEAD* thus typically provide a metalinguistic explanation of the error, followed by an indication of which form should have been used instead. The error is illustrated in authentic learner sentences and corrected. The lexical entry for *like*, for example, includes a warning against learners' attested tendency to use this preposition to introduce full clauses in academic writing instead of *as* or *in the same way* (Figure 9.9). Excerpts from learner corpora are then used to illustrate learner errors and provide correct sentences. Examples of appropriate usage of the preposition *like* are also given to help learners notice forms, and the meanings and functions these forms realize in academic discourse.

Problems of register are usually addressed via a 'Be careful!' note and a chart that compares the frequency of a lexical item in different genres (typically speech and writing). Thus, the *LEAD* provides an entry for the verb *look like* but there is a note that warns learners against its use in academic writing. This warning is reinforced by a chart that compares the frequency of the verb in speech and academic writing (Figure 9.10).

Lack of register awareness is often accompanied by overuse in learner writing. To illustrate this phenomenon and increase learners' attention to this issue, charts are sometimes used to compare academic prose, speech, and learner writing. In the lexical entry for *maybe*, for example, learners are warned against using *maybe*, as this

---

[4] http://www.uclouvain.be/en-cecl-vespa.html.

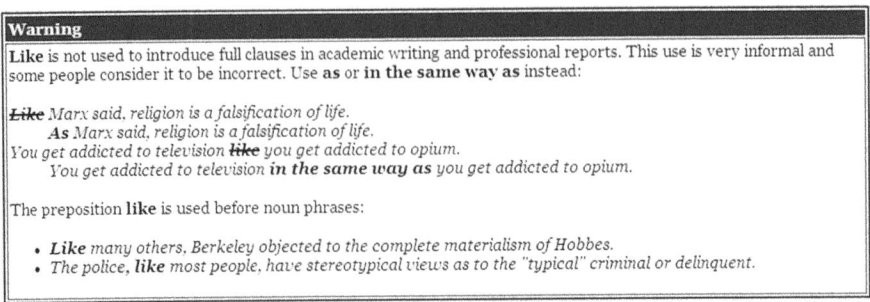

Warning

Like is not used to introduce full clauses in academic writing and professional reports. This use is very informal and some people consider it to be incorrect. Use **as** or **in the same way as** instead:

~~Like~~ *Marx said, religion is a falsification of life.*
    As *Marx said, religion is a falsification of life.*
You get addicted to television ~~like~~ you get addicted to opium.
    *You get addicted to television **in the same way as** you get addicted to opium.*

The preposition **like** is used before noun phrases:

- **Like** *many others, Berkeley objected to the complete materialism of Hobbes.*
- *The police, **like** most people, have stereotypical views as to the "typical" criminal or delinquent.*

FIGURE 9.9 Warning note under the entry for the preposition *like* in the *LEAD*.

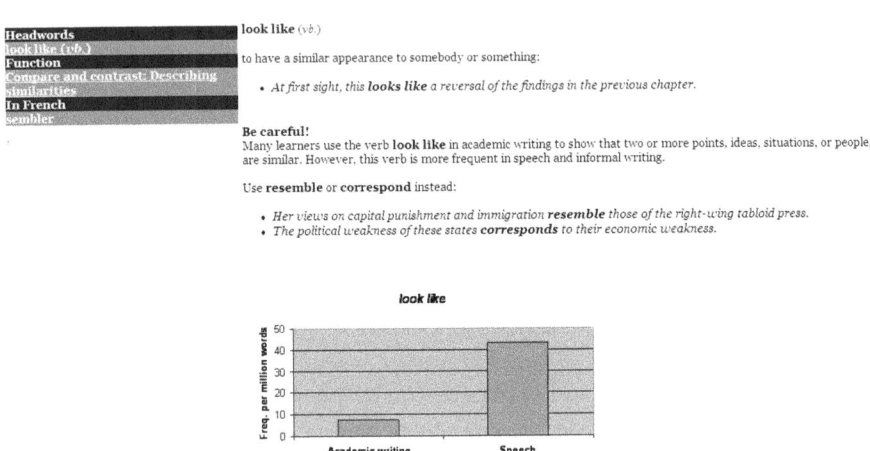

FIGURE 9.10 The entry for *look like* in the *LEAD*.

adverb is more typical of speech and less frequent in academic writing, where *perhaps* is preferred. As shown in Figure 9.11, this usage note is followed by a chart that shows that the frequency of *maybe* in learner writing is closer to its frequency in speech than in academic writing. By contrast, the frequency of *perhaps* in learner writing is lower than its frequency in both speech and academic writing.

Errors and difficulties found in the writing of a wide range of learner populations are dealt with in generic error notes that are displayed irrespective of the L1 background selected by the user. One of the purposes of L1-background identification in the *LEAD* is to give contrastive feedback on errors and problems that a specific L1 population typically encounters. In a recent article on contrastive form-focused instruction (FFI), Laufer and Girsai (2008: 696) distinguished between two types of contrastive approaches, i.e. "bilingual glosses which simply state the meaning of L2

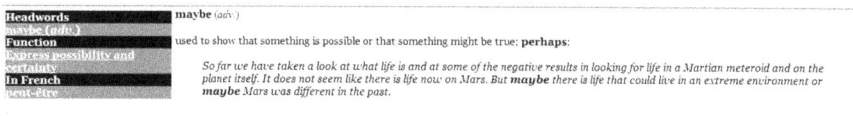

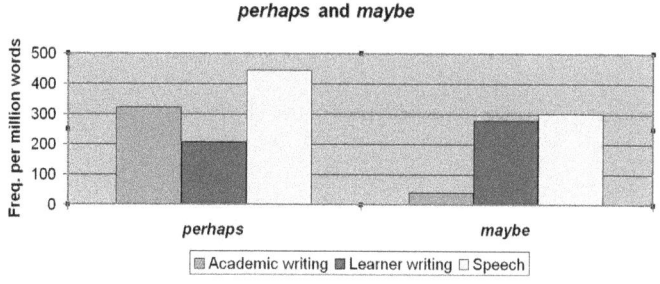

FIGURE 9.11 The entry for *maybe* in the *LEAD*.

words"[5] and "the kind of instruction which leads to learners' understanding of the similarities and differences between their L1 and L2 in terms of individual words and the overall lexical system". They illustrated this as follows:

For example, in the case of French as L2, a bilingual gloss would translate the French word 'savoir' as 'know'. Teachers using contrastive FFI, on the other hand, would point out that 'savoir' and 'know' do not overlap semantically and would provide explanation and practice of the difference between the two French translations of 'know', 'savoir' and 'connaître'. (Laufer and Girsai 2008: 696–7)

Contrastive feedback in the *LEAD* thus aims to draw learners' attention to major differences between English academic words and potential translation equivalents in the learner's L1 that often lead to errors.

An example of an error note that specifically targets the French learner population is found in the lexical entry for *according to*.[6] Figure 9.12 shows that there is a box in the main frame that comments on the difference between *according to me* and *selon moi*. It will not appear if no language background is selected as this error is limited to a small range of learner populations. However, such a note will appear if Dutch is selected as the user language, as Dutch speakers may also have a tendency to overuse *according to me* under the influence of the Dutch equivalent *volgens mij*.

---

[5] L2 is used to refer to a second or foreign language.

[6] We are currently focusing on French as an L1 background but are planning to include more L1-specific error notes in the future.

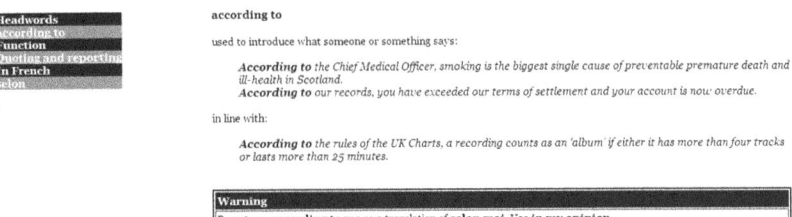

FIGURE 9.12 The entry for *according to* in the *LEAD*.

9.5 An integrated dictionary-cum-corpus-query-tool

Corpora have not only been used to inform the compilation of the *LEAD*, they are also directly accessible from the dictionary. CQPweb, an open source Web-based corpus handling tool (Hardie 2009), is integrated with the *LEAD*. CQPweb handles annotated corpora (corpora available in the *LEAD* are lemmatized and part-of-speech tagged), and offers powerful search syntax. Users can not only search for word forms or lemmas (e.g. all the word forms of the verb *contrast*) but they can also make use of regular expressions to extract word sequences (e.g. all occurrences of the noun *consequence* preceded by an adjective, or all word sequences that match the pattern *the* + NOUN + *of*). The tool also offers facilities such as sorting options and collocation analysis. Sorting concordance lines makes it possible to identify the preferred lexico-grammatical environment of a word (e.g. right-sorting concordance lines for the verb *cause* reveals that it is usually followed by a *that*-clause or by the prepositions *against* or *for*). Collocation analysis consists in the automatic extraction of all the words that appear in the vicinity of the search item or 'node' (typically in a window of up to five words to the left or right of the node). Statistical measures are then used to identify significant collocations, i.e. items that "co-occur more often than their respective frequencies and the length of text in which they appear would predict" (Jones and Sinclair 1974: 19) (for more information on statistical tests used in collocation analysis, see McEnery *et al.* 2006: 208–20).

The rationale behind the integration of a corpus tool with a dictionary is twofold. First, a dictionary user may want to get access to more examples of academic words and phrases in context, thus expanding on dictionary information through corpus consultation (Section 9.5.1). Second, a dictionary user may want to check how to use a word (most particularly a term) in a discipline-specific corpus even though it is not in the *LEAD* (which only covers general academic vocabulary; see Section 9.5.2).

The *LEAD* targets a very specific population, i.e. non-native students and researchers who need to write in academic settings. An increasing number of non-native English-speaking university students, irrespective of the discipline they are studying, have to write term papers, reports, or their MA/PhD dissertations in English. For researchers, the stakes are even higher as inappropriate language use has been shown to be a major factor in the rejection of articles submitted to international journals by non-native writers (Mungra and Weber 2010). This population can thus be described as highly motivated and familiar with learning and research strategies. These two characteristics have been shown to encourage a scientific approach to language use through concordancing (e.g. Lee and Swales 2006, Yoon 2011).

Lee and Swales (2006) reported on a corpus-based EAP course for non-native doctoral students and commented that students appreciated the value of scanning concordances lines derived from a corpus representing their own domain of research (see also Kennedy and Miceli 2001, Chambers 2010). In the *LEAD*, users can decide to look up words in the academic component of the British National Corpus or in discipline-specific corpora (business, linguistics, or medicine). When a discipline-specific corpus is selected, users can also restrict their search via the 'Restrict query' option to highly specific components of the corpus representing sub-disciplines such as respiratory and critical care medicine or applied linguistics. In the future, users will also be involved in the choice of content and allowed to upload their own 'learner-centred' corpus (Rodgers *et al.* 2011).

9.5.1 *Getting access to more examples of academic words and phrases*

The embedded corpus-query tool in the *LEAD* environment may be used to provide additional and sometimes more detailed insights into the use of academic words and phrases. Research on corpus use in the L2 writing class has shown that students usually appreciate getting access to multiple authentic examples which they regard as inspiring confidence (e.g. Yoon and Hirvela 2004, O'Sullivan and Chambers 2006). Corpora seem to be particularly useful as reference tools for problem-solving in writing (Yoon 2011). More particularly, they have been found to help learners enlarge their vocabulary, notice lexico-grammatical patterns (Rodgers *et al.* 2011) and enhance conformity to genre-based norms (Schaeffer-Lacroix 2009).

A user who specializes in medicine, for example, may want to get more examples of the preposition *in addition to* in the medical corpus. Concordance lines will provide him or her with attested examples of *in addition to* in a variety of contexts (e.g. at the beginning or in the middle of the sentence), and introducing a noun or a verb in the *-ing* form (see Figure 9.13).

Unlike dictionary consultation, scanning concordance lines may thus favour multicontextual learning (Cobb 1997). As Cobb (2003) put it:

[Learners] need to meet new words in a mix of example types, not just clear examples; they need evidence about what is *not* in a language, as well as what *is* in it; they need information about lexical phrases and collocations, not just individual words or a handful of selected phrases; and they need information about parts of words and groups of words that may extend

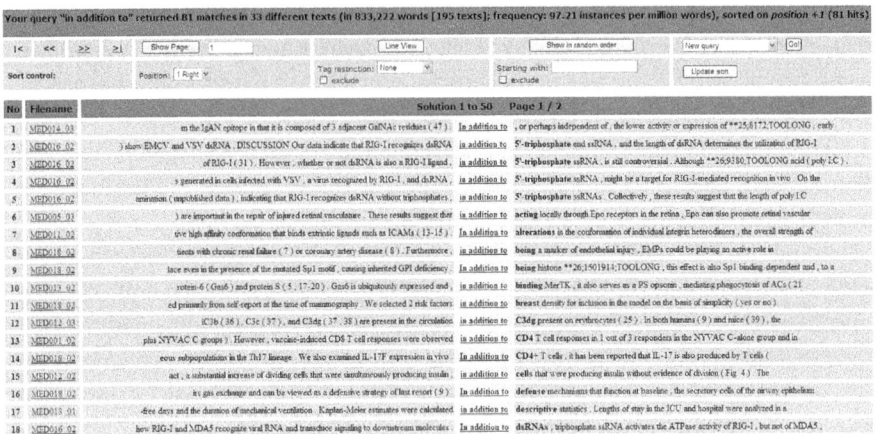

Figure 9.13 Concordance lines for *in addition to* in the medical corpus (CQPweb).

across distributed patterns, not just about continuous patterns. The concordance can provide all this, albeit in a raw form that not all learners will be able to make sense of. The dictionary provides more organized information, but at the price of leaving out important information.

The use of corpus data has also been reported to promote increased confidence and autonomy in writing, encouraging a researcher's attitude towards language learning (Lee and Swales 2006), as well as increased language awareness especially for checking existing knowledge (Yoon 2008).

9.5.2 *Checking how to use terms*

The *LEAD* is a dictionary of general academic vocabulary and does not cover discipline-specific words. However, direct access to corpora in the *LEAD* may serve to check how to use technical terms. Figure 9.14 shows the output of a corpus query for the term *surgery* in medicine. Concordance lines are alphabetically sorted on the left and provide a wealth of information on how the term *surgery* is used in medicine. Patients usually *receive* or *undergo surgery*; they can undergo *cardiac surgery, knee surgery, lung volume reduction surgery*, or *hip replacement surgery* and surgery can be *general, curative*, or *conventional*.

Users can restrict the search and make use of the CQPweb's collocation option to extract the most salient collocations of a term in a discipline-specific corpus. In Figure 9.15, for example, the collocation tool was used to extract the most frequent adjective and noun collocates of the noun *disease* in medicine.

As suggested by Rodgers *et al.* (2011: 398), users can then run individual concordances on each type of disease to identify terms and expressions which would help them to talk about that disease in English. Rodgers *et al.* (2011) investigated the use of

FIGURE 9.14 Concordance lines for *surgery* in the medical corpus (CQPweb).

Collocation controls

Collocation based on:	Word form	Statistic:	Log-likelihood
Collocation window from:	1 to the Left	Collocation window to:	1 to the Left
Freq(node, collocate) at least:	5	Freq(collocate) at least:	5
Filter results by:	specific collocate:	and/or tag: JJ (none)	Submit changed parameters Go!

There are 2,363 different words in your collocation database for "[class="(disease)_SUBST"%c]". {Your query "{disease/N}" returned 1,467 matches in 68 different texts, sorted on *position -1* (1,467 hits)} [0.035 seconds - retrieved from cache]

No.	Word	Total no. in whole corpus	Expected collocate frequency	Observed collocate frequency	In no. of texts	Log-likelihood value
1	heart	397	0.699	228	12	2388.216
2	cardiovascular	387	0.682	76	12	605.61
3	autoinflammatory	39	0.069	36	1	436.339
4	Lung	749	1.319	64	9	379.676
5	pulmonary	397	0.699	45	14	292.716
6	vascular	213	0.375	35	5	255.06
7	Autoimmune	98	0.173	29	6	249.592
8	Alzheimer	20	0.035	19	1	233.321
9	kidney	120	0.211	27	2	215.327
10	Crohn	20	0.035	16	2	183.131
11	cell	1,730	3.046	49	2	183.02
12	Castleman	12	0.021	12	1	152.339
13	artery	106	0.187	19	6	141.84
14	bowel	16	0.028	12	7	134.301
15	renal	105	0.185	14	5	95.562

FIGURE 9.15 CQPweb's collocation database for *surgery* in the medical corpus.

a corpus of articles on biotechnology in French with native English-speaking university students of biotechnology and found that students being asked to examine the use of a number of keywords selected by the teacher were able to identify specific terminology. For example, students were able to identify a number of frequent verb–noun collocations involving the French noun *récidive*, such as *prédire la récidive d'un cancer* ('to predict the recurrence of a cancer'), or *réduire de 46% la récidive* ('to reduce the recurrence by 46%'). They also identified certain frequent adjective–noun collocations of the noun *récidive*, such as *récidive tumorale* ('tumoral'), *récidive cancéreuse* ('cancerous'), and *récidive locale* ('local') (p. 399).

9.6 Conclusion

The Louvain EAP dictionary is more than just a dictionary: it is a dictionary-cum-writing-aid tool as well as a learning tool. To help non-native students and scholars write academic texts, heavy emphasis is placed on the way words are used in context (e.g. their preferred position in the sentence, the punctuation that usually surrounds them, their typical collocations, and recurrent phrases). The dictionary also includes charts to help users remember salient features (e.g. frequency differences across genres), warnings against frequent errors, and usage notes that compare learner and expert writing. Many of these features aim to enhance noticing, help learners focus on form, and facilitate the incremental learning of academic vocabulary.

Probably one of the most useful features of the *LEAD* is its context-sensitive lexicographical treatment of phraseology. The *Macmillan English Dictionary for Advanced Learners* (1st edition, 2002) innovated by providing sense-differentiated collocations. Context, however, also includes other aspects of 'collocational normality'. Almost fifteen years ago, Partington (1998: 17) wrote that "collocational normality is dependent on genre, register and style i.e. what is normal in one kind of text may be quite unusual in another". However important, this statement has still not found an echo in the latest editions of monolingual learners' dictionaries. Similarly, Moon's (2008: 333) comment that "particularly crucial is the function of phraseological information in relation to the needs and interests of the target users" has not attracted the attention it deserves.

Context-sensitivity and users' needs are two essential components of dictionary customization that are addressed by selective use of corpora in the *LEAD*. Corpora of both expert and learner writing are used in the compilation of the dictionary. The microstructure contains "dynamic data which are, so to say, unique for each search related to a specific type of user in a specific type of user situation" (Tarp 2009a: 29). Examples of collocations and lexical bundles are automatically extracted from discipline-specific corpora. Corpora of learner writing are used to inform contrastive error notes targeting specific L1 learner populations. Customization is also implemented at the mesostructure level. According to users' profiles, lexical entries are linked to relevant concordance lines in discipline-specific corpora. As the corpus-query tool is fully integrated into the *LEAD*, users also have access to these specialized corpora to search words that are not in the dictionary.

The *LEAD* offers many more features than the traditional dictionaries that students and scholars are probably used to consulting. Validation will therefore be an essential stage for obtaining feedback on whether users find these additional features useful and user-friendly. It will also be particularly interesting to check (by looking at log files for example; cf. Verlinde and Binon 2010) whether users make use of the three main components of the *LEAD* (i.e. the lexical entries proper, the corpus-query tool, and the exercises) and to what extent. One outcome of such a validation process may be that we need to provide training in the use of the *LEAD*, and more particularly in the use of its corpus-related features, as research on data-driven learning has emphasized the importance of learner training in concordancing (Yoon 2011). Training may not only take the form of classroom instruction on dictionary use but may also be provided in the form of video help files that would illustrate how to use the variety of innovative features offered in the *LEAD*.

More generally, the business model of the monolingual learners' dictionary as a "one-size-fits-all package" (Rundell 2007: 50) is probably dead, or at least seriously ill. It needs to reinvent itself to compete against all the new online dictionaries that are available free of charge. The way ahead probably lies in more customization in terms of genre, domain, and L1-background and specialized corpora definitely have a prominent role to play here.

Acknowledgements

I gratefully acknowledge the support of the Fonds de la Recherche Scientifique (FNRS), which funded this research within the framework of a project entitled "Lexicography and phraseology: onomasiological and semasiological approach to English for Academic Purposes" (FRFC 2.4501.08). I would also like to express my deep gratitude to the director of this project, Professor Sylviane Granger, for her guidance and support.

Dictionaries

Sinclair, J., A. Macaulay, and M. Seaton (2006). *Collins COBUILD Advanced Learners' English Dictionary*. HarperCollins Publishers. Fifth Edition, CD-ROM [COBUILD5].

Mayor, M. (editorial director) (2009). *Longman Dictionary of Contemporary English*. Pearson Education Limited. Fifth Edition, CD-ROM [LDOCE5].

Rundell, M. (editor in chief) (2002). *Macmillan English Dictionary for Advanced Learners*. First edition. Macmillan Education.

Rundell, M. (editor in chief) (2007). *Macmillan English Dictionary for Advanced Learners*. Second Edition, CD-ROM. Macmillan Education.

Turnbull, J., D. Lea, D. Parkinson, P. Phillips, B. Francis, S. Webb, V. Bull, and M. Ashby (2010). *Oxford Advanced Learner's Dictionary*. Eighth Edition, CD-ROM. Oxford University Press.

10

The ARTES bilingual LSP dictionary: From collocation to higher order phraseology

NATALIE KÜBLER AND MOJCA PECMAN

10.1 Introduction

The globalization process our world has undergone since the beginning of the 1980s has had an important impact on the need for language for specific purposes (LSP) lexicography, hence the numerous research projects which have flourished in this domain. LSP lexicography deals with a wide variety of fields, such as law, finance, insurance, technology, science, and commerce, but also a variety of genres, such as user manuals, research articles, technical specification, contracts, and patents to name but a few. This explains why the types of users and needs can be quite different. One particular need in monolingual LSP lexicography is terminological standardization, which aims to offer users consistent domain terminology. LSP lexicography is also useful to help users understand a specific domain, as it provides them with definitions.

The development of corpus linguistics has also greatly modified approaches to terminology, introducing the concept of fuzziness and bridging the gap to phraseology. Advances have been particularly marked in bilingual LSP lexicography, a discipline which has to address growing needs related to globalization and to the fact that English is a lingua franca for international exchanges. It is a well-known fact that more and more non-native speakers of English have to use it as a second language in science, as well as in finance, industry, and many other human activities. This does not imply that these users abandon their first language, so they have to navigate in specific subject areas between their native language and English (or, increasingly, Chinese). Not only do they need to have consistent terminology in both languages, they also need to know how to use terms in the second language, i.e. how to contextualize them. LSPs not only consist of terms, they also present a phraseology which is domain-dependent, genre-dependent, and may in some cases enter into general language usage. Therefore, bilingual LSP lexicography should deal with both terminology and phraseology. Phraseology in particular can be term-dependent or term-independent, in other words, domain-specific or domain-free. Bilingual LSP lexicography is most useful to specialized translators who first have to understand a source text, and then translate it as clearly as possible for the intended reader. Although they are normally native speakers of the target language, they may not be domain experts, which means they may not have fully mastered the terminology and (often even less so) the phraseology of the domain. As more and more translators have to translate into English as a second language, bilingual LSP lexicography is playing a crucial role in this respect. Furthermore, as growing numbers of domain experts and researchers have to write in English as a second language, making sure they use the correct phraseological equivalent in the L2 is vital to them.

This chapter tackles the question of implementing bilingual phraseology in the bilingual ARTES dictionary while taking into account many different users' needs and introducing collocations and higher-order phraseology into the dictionary by providing information on semantic preference and semantic prosody. We use the terms *phraseology* and *collocation* to refer to "arbitrary recurrent word combinations" as defined by Benson (1989: 3), thus adopting a broad vision of various co-occurrence phenomena (for further reading on collocations and other types of phraseological units, see, for instance, Granger and Paquot (2008b)). The two collocational phenomena, semantic preference and semantic prosody, are often associated as they both describe the statistically significant co-occurrence of a word with a group of other words: while semantic prosody describes the affective meaning a given node is coloured with depending on its typical collocates, semantic preference is characterized as the co-occurrence of a node with a set of words belonging to the same semantic class, i.e. partly sharing the same semantic features (Stubbs 2002). Whereas the literature on semantic prosody shows that this phenomenon has been thoroughly studied in general language (Sinclair 1991b, Louw 1993, Hunston and Thompson 2000, Sardinha 2000), the description and analysis of semantic prosody in specialized languages is quite scarce. Semantic preference, by contrast, has aroused more interest in specialized languages: inserting the collocations of a given term in a dictionary or a term base is nowadays quite common. Including semantic prosody and semantic preference information is, however, less obvious and has not been shown as a specific need. We want to argue that, according to the objectives for which an online LSP dictionary or a term base are used, phenomena such as semantic prosody and preference would provide the user with complete and necessary information.

Following on from these preliminary remarks, Section 10.2 explores the most recent tendencies in bilingual LSP lexicography as reflected by a number of ground-breaking projects. Section 10.3 is devoted to the description of the ARTES project and the online bilingual LSP dictionary that was designed within the framework of the project to respond to various users' needs when reading, writing, or translating specialized texts or genres. We particularly discuss the structure of the dictionary in relation to various target users. Special attention is paid to the overall methodology used for processing various types of phraseological data encountered in specialized texts and discourses. In Section 10.4, we evaluate the relevance of integrating information on semantic prosody and preference into the online ARTES dictionary and give examples of how to implement it. The chapter ends with some concluding remarks.

10.2 New trends in building dictionaries for LSP users

In line with the evolution of general language dictionaries, twentieth-century bilingual LSP lexicography was marked by the transition from paper to electronic dictionaries. The transfer of data from one medium to another has brought some major changes in the conception of dictionaries. Lexicographers and terminologists explored new ways of organizing data to anticipate twenty-first-century dictionary users' needs. Today, the advantages offered by electronic dictionaries are well known (cf. Fontenelle 1994, Meynard 1997, L'Homme and Meynard 1998, Cartier 2000, Maniez 2001, L'Homme *et al.* 2003, Pecman 2008): easier and quicker access to data, multiple data queries, multilingual managing solutions, unlimited storage capacities, the reusability of data, and, in general, richer information content. From the editing point of view, electronic dictionaries offer far less complicated procedures for updating resources. All these advantages have contributed to the development of improved dictionary tools in the field of LSP.

The major changes brought about by the transition from paper dictionaries to electronic ones are, first, the possibility of storing significant amounts of data and, second, of updating resources in a less complicated way. In LSP lexicography, this is all the more important as specialized languages evolve rapidly, in step with advances in knowledge, whether scientific, technological, industrial, or other. As a consequence, term banks have to provide a means for keeping up to date with the continuous creation of new terms (neologisms). Henceforward, LSP lexicography will give more emphasis to online term databanks than to dictionaries. The flexibility of the support has already resulted in a growing number of specialized online glossaries devoted to specific domains becoming available, which tends to compensate for the lack of information in multi-domain databanks.

The most specific feature of LSP electronic lexicography, in comparison to general language electronic lexicography, is the effort to provide various types of lexical information (such as definitions, synonyms, contexts, and useful notes) on an expanding and rapidly evolving terminology. Term databanks, or specialized glossaries, are rarely organized to take into account a variety of users and user situations, as in general electronic lexicography. Evidence that LSP dictionaries are overwhelmingly designed as online databases or databanks capable of storing growing amounts of data within a nevertheless complex structure scheme, and providing only one single form of access to data—through terminology—is provided by such well known sites as Termium,[1] Grand Dictionnaire Terminologique,[2] and IATE.[3]

The major changes brought about by the transition from paper dictionaries to electronic ones relate also to the presentation and access to data. LSP resources share the feature of being related to domain descriptors. Easier access gives LSP dictionary users the opportunity to retrieve information more efficiently.

More flexible ways of presenting the data have opened up two more directions in which LSP electronic lexicography can evolve. The first is related to advances in corpus linguistics techniques which allow for the creation of corpus-based LSP resources (Kübler and Volanschi 2012) in much the same way as in the domain of general language lexicography. Today, the majority of specialized lexical resources are corpus-based, and corpus linguistics offers yet another resource of great interest for lexicographers: the context (i.e. example of use taken from real evidence) and, more precisely, the possibility of investigating collocations (i.e. examples of preferential use). Thus, one of the most innovative features of modern LSP lexicography lies in investigating the place of phraseology in LSP electronic dictionaries (see Hausmann 1979, Heid 1992, Heid and Freibott 1991, Pavel 1993, Pecman 2005) and consequently the emergence of collocation dictionaries. The DicoInfo[4] project by L'Homme (1997, 2007, and this volume), the Louvain EAP dictionary (LEAD) project by Granger and Paquot (2008a, 2010b, and Paquot, this volume), the combinatory dictionary LangYeast[5] (Volanschi 2008) and the ARTES[6] scientific terminological and phraseological database (Pecman *et al.* 2010, Pecman and Kübler 2011) are all ground-breaking projects in this context.

The second direction in innovative LSP lexicography relates to the attempts to bypass classical alphabetical access to data, by offering access through the meaning. In LSP, this type of venture is all the more important as terms—in theoretical and practical approaches to terminology—are described as firmly linked to concepts. The quest for a semantic model to allow for a more ontological organization of resources stems from Wüster's (1968) onomasiological approach to terminological resources and Fillmore's later Frame Semantics (Fillmore 1976, 1977, Fillmore and Atkins 1994). With projects based on 'synsets', or synonym sets (i.e. sets of words that represent the same concept in Wordnets), or on semantic predicates (e.g. FrameNet), new LSP

---

[1] The goverment of Canada's terminology and linguistic databank.
[2] Dictionary of the *Office québécois de la langue française.*
[3] Banque terminologique multilingue de la *CEE*: http://iate.europa.eu.
[4] http://olst.ling.umontreal.ca/cgi-bin/dicoinfo/search.cgi.
[5] http://ytat2.ijm.univ-paris-diderot.fr/LangYeast.
[6] http://artes.eila.univ-paris-diderot.fr.

resources are overwhelmingly ontologically-based lexicons (see Toral *et al.* 2008, Pecman 2007).

It is important to note that the majority of these projects are designed exclusively for machine use, as in the case of the SIMPLE project, which consists of building plurilingual semantic lexicons for natural language processing (Lenci *et al.* 2003). However, a number of semantic lexicons designed for both human and machine use can be found in subject fields as diverse as soccer (Schmidt 2007, 2009), law (Venturi *et al.* 2009), and biology (Quochi *et al.* 2009). In the Kicktionary,[7] i.e. a multilingual (English, German, and French) electronic dictionary of soccer language, for example, each term is structured into a hierarchy of scenes and frames, and into a number of concept hierarchies. In addition, each word is illustrated with one or more example sentences from authentic written or spoken football language.

Some trends go even further in the quest for a semantic model to allow an ontological organization of resources: they deal with the creation of databases by using a pivot language, expected to provide access to, and consequently an inter-language transfer of, terminological data. The KYOTO project (Vossen *et al.* 2008a) is one of them: its goal is to construct a language-independent information system for a specific domain (environment/ecology) anchored in a language-independent ontology that is linked to Wordnets in several languages.

The projects adopting Wüster's approach are more clearly oriented towards human use. In the work of Wüster, the focus is on the concept, rather than on the designation, as a starting point for terminological analysis and classification (i.e. an onomasiological approach). Similarly, with special emphasis on semantic relations between terms (e.g. hyperonymy, meronymy, and synonymy), projects such as the *Analytical Dictionary of Retailing*[8] (Dancette and Réthoré 2000) or the ARTES general scientific ontology project (Pecman 2007, Pecman *et al.* 2010) go beyond a simple alphabetical classification of terminological resources.

Another original example of a semantic approach to data is the Lexical Functions approach developed by Mel'čuk *et al.* (1995, 1999) and exploited by L'Homme (1997, 2007, and this volume) in the DicoInfo project. For each term, the DicoInfo database provides the description of its argument structure (e.g. *x installs y on z*). Arguments are grouped into semantic classes (e.g. install: x{user} ~ s y{software} on z{computer}). Semantic relations shared by the terms listed in the dictionary are represented using the Lexical Functions approach, which allows the capture—using a specific formalism—of semantic relations at different levels: paradigmatic, syntagmatic, and derivational (see L'Homme 2002).

Another feature of most recent directions of research in LSP lexicography is the attempt to bridge the gap between teaching terminology and database management

---

[7] http://www.kicktionary.de.   [8] http://olst.ling.umontreal.ca/dad/.

at universities (e.g. the WebTerm[9] project from the Institute for Information Management in Cologne, Germany). This is a collection of terminology databases based on diploma theses written at the Cologne University of Applied Sciences. It offers the hierarchical organization of terminology and multiple access to bilingual (English/German) data.

Finally, in LSP lexicography some newer trends are oriented towards building dictionaries as a support for translation (Temmerman and Knops 2004) or for communication in L2 situations. Among them are the DALOS[10] project (Agnoloni *et al.* 2007) which aims to build an ontological support for multilingual legislative drafting, and the ARTES project which aims to provide ontological access to routine formulae and collocations used in scientific communication (Pecman *et al.* 2010).

At the beginning of the twenty-first century, however, the new technological possibilities offered by the electronic era are still not being fully exploited (especially the possibility of exploiting multiple approaches to LSP resources within the same project, and consequently of orienting the tools to various LSP users); moreover, other languages have yet to catch up with English. Perhaps the most significant feature of the evolution of LSP lexicography over recent decades has been that the advantages offered by the electronic medium have fostered research into the alternative structuring of language data. With such original projects as those aimed at developing corpus-based LSP collocational dictionaries or ontologically classified resources for specific domains, electronic lexicography is opening up new roads in LSP dictionary-making.

10.3 The ARTES online dictionary

After presenting the objectives and history of the ARTES project, this section will discuss the structure that was devised for the ARTES dictionary in relation to target users. We argue that ARTES is both an LSP bilingual dictionary and a terminological and phraseological database and illustrate the method used for compiling resources. Finally, the methodology used for processing various types of phraseological data is discussed.

10.3.1 *ARTES project objectives*

ARTES (Aide à la Rédaction de TExtes Scientifiques / 'Dictionary-assisted writing tool for scientific communication')[11] is an innovative project developed at the Paris Diderot University by a group of researchers working on LSP, corpus linguistics, and translation studies. Their joint research (Bordet 2009, 2011, Froeliger 2009, 2010,

---

[9] http://www.iim.fh-koeln.de/webterm/webtermsamm_e.htm.

[10] DrAfting Legislation with Ontology-based Support (DALOS).

[11] http://www.eila.univ-paris-diderot.fr/recherche/artes/index.

Humbley 2006, 2007, 2008, Kübler 2011, Kübler *et al.* 2010, Kübler and Volanschi 2012, Pecman 2005, 2008, Pecman *et al.* 2010, Volanschi and Kübler 2011) has led to the design of an online database for storing and managing structure-rich information on specialized terminology and phraseology with the possibility of multiple criteria and multiple-level queries.

The project relates to the development of a tool to help scientific drafting and translation, and has also given rise to research in a number of related areas: terminology, phraseology, translation, LSP, corpus linguistics, genre, and discourse analysis (Pecman and Kübler 2011). These studies have led to the description of the special characteristics and the invariants of scientific multi-domain discourse through the corpus-based study of scientific writing. The project thus serves as an observatory of the evolution of scientific discourses and their interactions across fields, genres, and languages. The design of an online lexical database attempts to respond to these developments, in particular with respect to scientific translation and communication.

10.3.2 *Brief history of the project*

When the ARTES project was created, in 2006, the architecture of the database was developed in a Microsoft Access database which was extensively used by researchers and students of Master's Studies at the Applied Languages department (Paris Diderot University). In 2010, the researchers working on the ARTES project seized the opportunity to bypass the limitations of an Access database by converting the database architecture into an SQL[12] online database (DB). The main stages of the transfer of technology from Access to an SQL database were achieved by November 2010. The database integrates PHP[13] source code and PostgreSQL query language, which are sufficiently flexible to handle future development and compatible with an interface for data access in the form of an LSP dictionary. Since 2011, the new ARTES database has been used for storing LSP data, and already has 10,700 English terms, 10,800 French, 1,070 German, and 550 Spanish entries. Altogether, there are 29,700 specific collocations recorded in the DB and 510 generic collocations. These data, as well as all the linguistic information recorded in relation to terms and collocations, still need to be normalized and validated.[14]

In addition, the ARTES database is a multi-domain and multilingual database. For domain categorization, the Universal Decimal Classification (UDC 2004) (a classification which provides comprehensive domain coverage) was integrated into the

---

[12] SQL (Structured Query Language) is a query language used for accessing and modifying data in relational database management systems.

[13] PHP is a server-side scripting language used to produce dynamic web pages.

[14] Our team is currently working with the IPGP (Institut de Physique du Globe de Paris) and the Speedlingua company on the GEOLAPP project, the aim of which is to standardize and validate data in earth science, provide English pronunciation for French speakers, and develop practising pronunciation units to help French speakers prepare an oral communication in earth science English.

database. Regarding language selection, although ARTES is a multi-domain database, the data are compiled from a bilingual perspective, using a pair of languages. At this stage of development, three pairs of languages have been compiled: English/French, English/German, and English/Spanish. Some encouraging tests have also been carried out for pairs of languages such as English/Japanese and English/Chinese.

Several earlier prototypes prepared the way for designing this online database, namely BasTeT designed in 2006 by Claudie Juilliard and implemented by Yamina Abdalahi, and a number of other projects carried out simultaneously e.g. Master1 DB developed in 2001 by Natalie Kübler and implemented by Raphael Juilliard, General Scientific Language Ontology developed by Pecman (2004, 2007), TerminoM1 developed in 2007 by Kübler and Pecman and encoded by Laurent Joly, and the LangYeast combinatory dictionary developed by Volanschi (2008).

One of the advantages gained from the transfer of technologies from Access DB to an online SQL DB, was the possibility of creating an application for turning the DB into an online bilingual LSP dictionary.

10.3.3 *ARTES dictionary target users*

The data disposition in the ARTES dictionary takes into account the various users and user situations targeted by the tool. The target users are:

- translators, learners and professionals
- domain experts, learners and professionals
- linguists.

The current interface has been designed to display data recorded in the database functionally, following Nielsen and Mourier (2007) and Leroyer's (2007) approach to functional lexicography according to which "development of a dictionary is determined by users' needs and made to serve communication and knowledge-oriented functions, in particular user situations" (Leroyer 2007: 110).

Learners of terminology and translation studies need to find relevant information to translate concepts and phrases which they do not necessarily understand. In contrast, learners in scientific fields need to find information that will help them understand articles and formulate their ideas in a foreign language. Thus we can distinguish two opposing situations (one which is oriented towards language comprehension and the other towards language production) and thus the necessity to make ARTES both an encoding and a decoding dictionary. The third category of users is quite different: it refers to a research setting where a linguist needs to retrieve data in order to observe the language properties. As shown in Figure 10.1, there are three major access routes to data in ARTES: through terminology ('Terminology in context' tab), through some eighty pre-identified discourse functions which offer access to transdisciplinary phraseology ('Discourse phraseology' tab), and by multiple criteria query ('Multiple query search' tab).

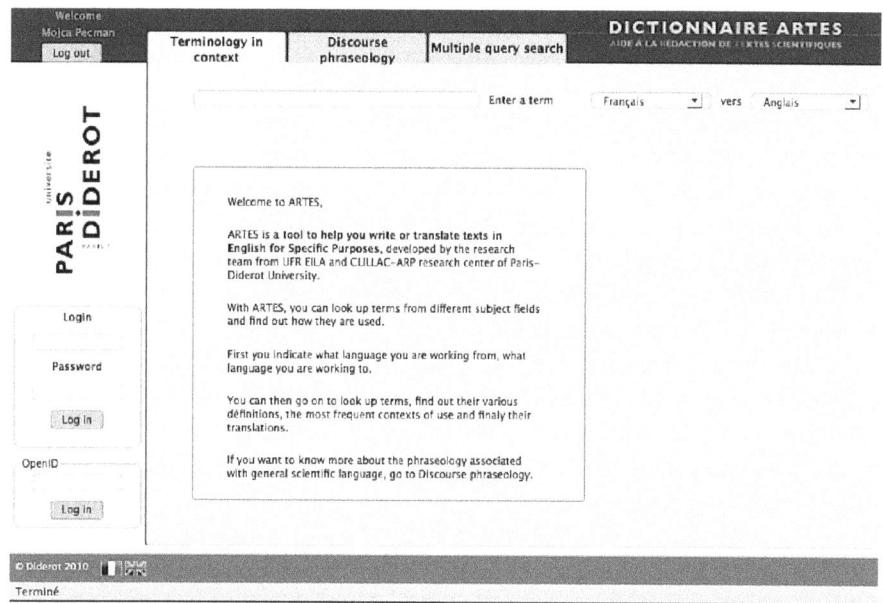

FIGURE 10.1 The ARTES dictionary interface.

The 'Terminology in context' tab allows the user to search the database for domain-dependent terms and their definitions, collocations, related terms (e.g. synonyms and hyperonyms), and equivalents in different languages. The 'Discourse phraseology' tab provides a template for navigating through phraseology which is domain-free, yet frequently used in LSP communication, and includes collocations, collocational frameworks, expressions, and other types of phraseological units (e.g. *to be described elsewhere by, in good agreement with, to provide evidence for, tremendous amount of, our conclusions focus on aspects such as, to gain considerable attention,* etc.). Access to the latter data is assured via a semantically-organized classification of all phraseological units by taking into account their general meaning and function in the LSP discourse. Those two major access points to data are targeted at learners of terminology and translation studies, and learners in the sciences. The 'Terminology in context' access is more specifically aimed at learners in translation studies in that, for example, each entry provides all the useful definitions of a specific term found in the relevant literature together with additional explanations of its meaning, and its hierarchical organization in proximity with other concepts in the same scientific field. This type of information is particularly useful for translators who need to grasp specialized knowledge quickly in order to translate an LSP text. Meanwhile, the 'Discourse phraseology' access is intended more for learners who aim to be future experts or French-speaking experts who need a tool to assist them in writing their papers or preparing a communication for a conference.

Different user situations are also taken into account within the 'Terminology in context' tab, as the data are categorized according to different settings: the term, treated from the point of view of its meaning, its usage, or its translation (Figure 10.2). In the 'Meaning' tab, various definitions and technical notes are provided, together with a list of semantically related terms such as hyperonyms, homonyms, and antonyms, which can help the users to grasp the meaning of a term. In the 'Usage' tab, the dictionary displays the most frequent collocations of a term and a list of its derivatives, which can help the users to use the term appropriately (Figure 10.3). In the 'Translation' tab, the equivalences of a term are suggested, together with the equivalences of its collocations (Figure 10.4).

The 'Discourse functions' is an example of an innovative approach to LSP lexicons in the ARTES dictionary offering dictionary users the possibility of looking for the most common formulas to express given information in a specific discourse, generally of a scientific kind (Figure 10.5). Discourse functions are categorized into some eighty semantico-discursive categories which are grouped into some ten major classes. Figure 10.5 shows the 'Organizing your discourse' class, and its sub-classes (e.g. introduce a transition, give the order of your exposition, and announce the

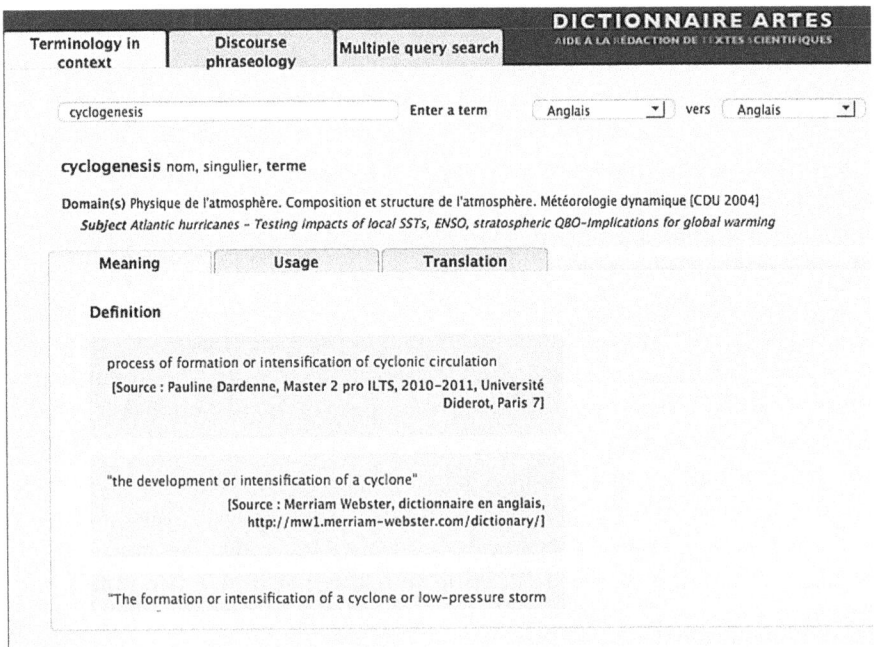

FIGURE 10.2 ARTES dictionary interface. The 'Terminology in context' tab: Meaning.

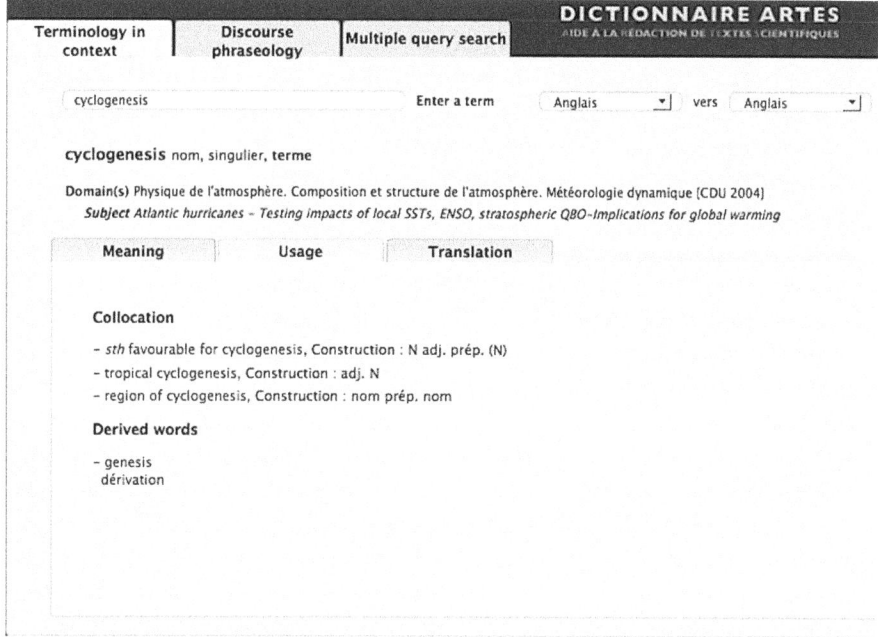

FIGURE 10.3 ARTES dictionary interface. The 'Terminology in context' tab: Usage.

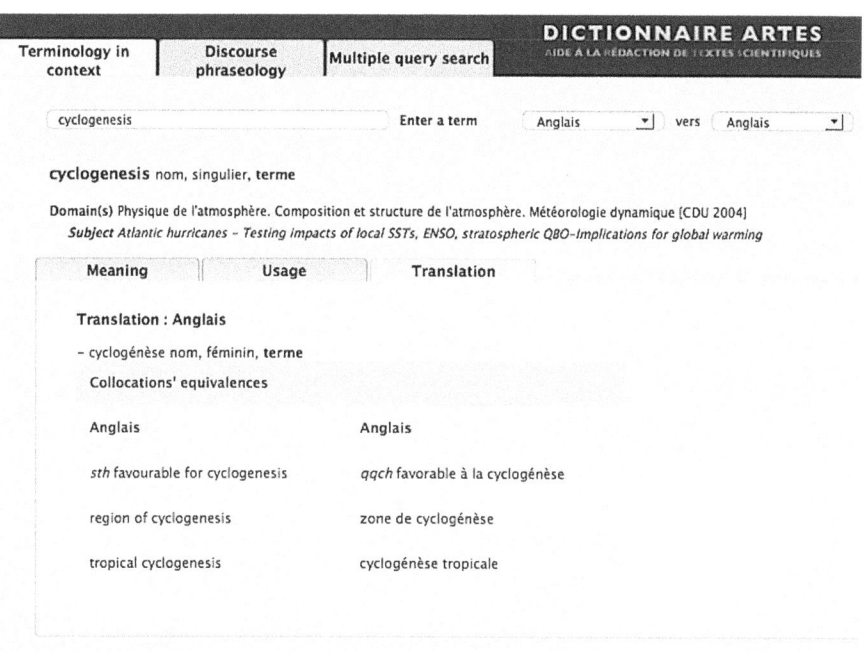

FIGURE 10.4 ARTES dictionary interface. The 'Terminology in context' tab: Translation.

subject of the current section). In the right part of the screen are displayed frequent expressions used to formulate a given discourse function.

This approach to the lexicon is based on the analysis of General Scientific Language (Pecman 2007) and lexicographical approaches to transdisciplinary phraseology (Pecman *et al.* 2010). Recently, interest has risen in this type of domain-free phraseology (Coxhead 2000, 2002, Coxhead and Hirsh 2007, Pecman 2007, 2008, Simpson-Vlach and Ellis 2010, Teufel 1998, Tutin 2007, 2008), which is being increasingly investigated in relation to the concept of *moves* (Biber *et al.* 2007, Hyland 2004)—relying on Swales's (1990) work; this approach tends to take into account the information structure of the text by dividing it into pragmatic portions, the moves, and whether they serve, for instance, the description of theoretical background, the methodologies and tools, or the results.

The 'Multiple query search' tab, targeted at linguists, allows for the retrieval of data by multiple criteria and the consequent construction of useful material for teaching or research purposes. At this stage of development, semantic prosody and preference items can also be retrieved within the 'Advanced search' function, as shown in Figure 10.6. On the left are displayed all the realizations of *to cause* (*to cause an earthquake, to cause a landslide*), which has a negative semantic prosody, the latter being illustrated on the right (*to cause [negative phenomenon]*). Our goal is to display this information also in relation to terms. Before achieving this goal, it is necessary to explore both phenomena from the lexicographical point of view by taking into account the specific functioning of semantic prosody and preference mechanisms at lexical and discourse levels.

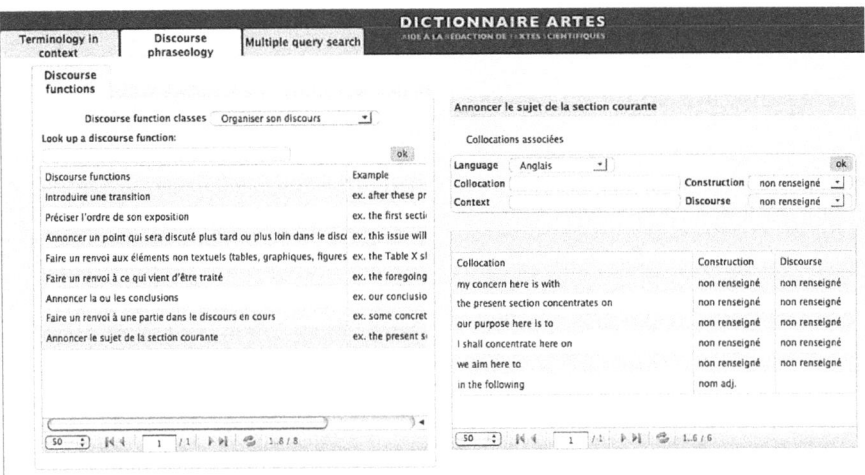

FIGURE 10.5 ARTES dictionary interface. The 'Discourse phraseology' tab: discourse functions.

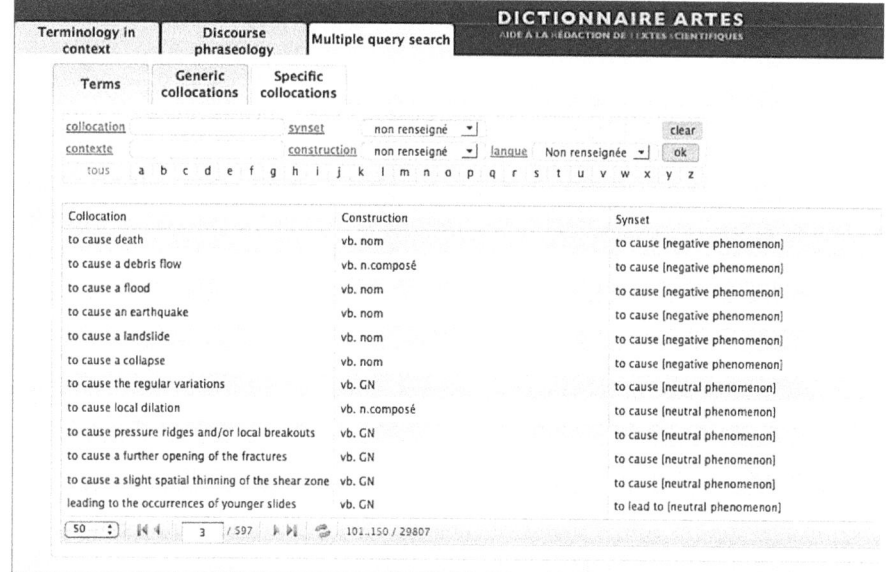

FIGURE 10.6 ARTES dictionary interface for retrieving semantic prosody and preference.

10.3.4 *ARTES: a dictionary or a database?*

ARTES is both a multilingual LSP dictionary and a terminological and phraseological database. Basically, it is a database. Nevertheless, in accordance with the project objectives, two interfaces were designed: one to create a dictionary targeting various users (as discussed above) and another to edit the data and manage the database, commonly called the 'back office'. The ARTES LSP dictionary is generated from terminological and phraseological resources built through a crowdsourcing method.[15] While access to the dictionary is free, access to the back-office interface is restricted. Only a limited quantity of language data is displayed in the dictionary—data that has undergone the various stages of normalization and validation—while the back-office interface provides access to all compiled data and necessary functionalities to control resource compilation and validation.

The ARTES database offers useful functionalities for terminology and phraseology management conducted in a university context. Like its predecessor, the Access BasTeT DB, the ARTES DB was designed to cater for teaching and learning needs

---

[15] This method consists mainly of the collection of resources by students in Master's studies at the EILA Department (intercultural studies and applied languages department). In addition there is a phase of standardization of resources by terminologists and earth science experts before the data is given public access online.

in Master's Studies in Specialised Translation and Language Engineering[16] (ILTS) at the department of Applied Languages at Paris Diderot University. The Master's Studies in ILTS offer a good balance of practical classes in current technologies of translation, lexical resource creation, applied corpus linguistics, DB management tools, and information retrieval, with more theoretical classes in translation, terminology, theoretical corpus linguistics, and discourse analysis. A combination of these courses allows students to develop skills and acquire the knowledge necessary to achieve high-quality translation of LSP texts. As part of their Master's dissertation, students have to translate a long specialized text (e.g. a scientific article) and in relation to this text, construct a comparable corpus, design a domain ontology, build terminological and phraseological resources, and contact domain experts to validate the collected data.

The ARTES database is designed to allow students to participate in the project by creating LSP resources in relation to the text they have to translate. In turn, the database offers useful functions for teachers to help them follow students' work in progress and evaluate the resources compiled by their students. Figure 10.7 shows a function allowing the retrieval of data compiled by a student according to various predesigned queries. Clicking on 'term/trad/coll' on the left menu, for example, retrieves all the terms and their equivalents, and the equivalent collocations that were found in a comparable corpus and aligned. Rapid access is also offered to the terminological record of each term.

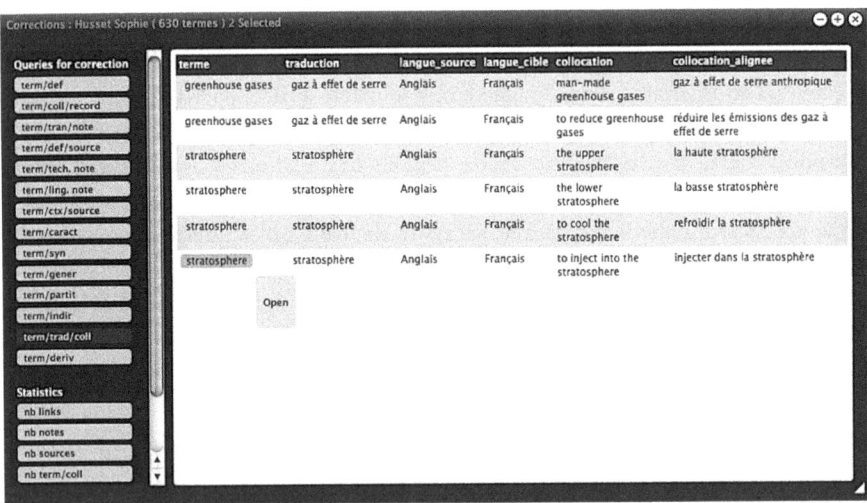

FIGURE 10.7 ARTES correction aid function.

[16] Master professionnel ILTS (Industrie de la langue et traduction spécialisée)—Master's studies in Language Engineering and Specialised Translation: http://www.eila.univ-paris-diderot.fr/formations-pro/masterpro/ilts/index.

A very important feature of the ARTES project is that the data are compiled mainly, but not exclusively, by LSP and translation learners. The overall methodology used to ensure the quality of data collected consists of three key procedures. The first is the actual method followed by learners, which is based on thorough comparable corpus analysis and an exchange with domain experts. This leads to designing the domain ontology. The acquired knowledge of the domain, combined with knowledge of terminology processing, allows the learners to select and process terms and relevant linguistic information adequately. The second procedure consists of reviewing and validating the resources by domain experts. An ongoing collaboration with experts in Earth and Planetary Sciences from the Earth Science department (STEP)[17] at Paris Diderot University and the 'Institut de Physique du Globe' de Paris (IPGP),[18] allows us to apply this procedure efficiently to a number of disciplines. Since 2011, this collaboration has been conducted within the GEOLAPP project, which was set up to establish the framework for future collaborations. The third and crucial stage in building language resources is the overall normalization, correction, and validation of resources by terminologists (also integrated into the ongoing GEOLAPP project). MA students are also invited to question the theoretical and methodological premises on which the description of language data in ARTES is based, by testing them against 'real-life' translation problems.

The crowdsourcing method may have certain drawbacks, but the overall procedure of controlling the quality of data before validating any of it will allow these disadvantages to be bypassed. Moreover, the crowdsourcing method, as devised in relation to the ARTES project, has some substantial advantages: the number of languages and domains considered can be enhanced, emerging LSP lexicons taken into account, and the focus on translational difficulties ensures that the data collected are particularly useful for LSP L2 users.

10.4 Processing phraseology within the ARTES database

As suggested above, two types of phraseological data are stored in the database: one is domain-specific and the other domain-free. Domain-specific collocations are linked to terms from which they inherit domain and language specification. Generic (i.e. domain-free) collocations, on the other hand, are linked to discourse functions, as their usage cannot be ascribed to a specific domain. The distinction between the two types of collocations is made through corpus analysis by looking at the dispersion of collocations over various LSPs. Table 10.1 shows examples of specific collocations sharing the same node, and a selection of generic collocations ascribed to various discourse functions is given in Table 10.2.

---

[17] http://step.ipgp.fr.   [18] http://www.ipgp.fr.

TABLE 10.1 **Examples of specific collocations**

Specific collocations associated with the term *greenhouse gas*	Specific collocations associated with the term *bioremediation*
major greenhouse gases	*successful bioremediation*
long-lived greenhouse gases	*suitable for bioremediation*
man-made greenhouse gases	*to enhance bioremediation*
anthropogenic greenhouse gases	*to facilitate bioremediation*
increased greenhouse gases	*to optimize bioremediation*
an increase in greenhouse gases	*to undergo bioremediation*
the impact of greenhouse gases	*to stimulate bioremediation*
to reduce greenhouse gases	*a candidate for bioremediation*

TABLE 10.2 **Examples of generic collocations**

Generic collocation	Associated discourse function
the most complete account of (sth.) is found in	Cross-referencing to an author or work
these findings are first to describe	Positive evaluation of one's results or discoveries
my concern here is with	Announcement of the subject of the current section
there is little/some/no doubt (that)	Expression of uncertainties, doubts; hedging
as previously mentioned	Cross-referencing to another section of the present discourse
in much the same manner	Expressing correlation, analogy, or similarity
by contrast	Expressing difference, contrast, or opposition
in this paper we survey the state of art in	Stating the subject of one's study

For each collocation a context is provided to illustrate it in a sentence, together with a description of its internal syntagmatic structure (e.g. *successful bioremediation*: adjective + noun, *to enhance bioremediation*: verb + noun). Like terms, collocations are not simply translated, but aligned when equivalent collocations are identified in a source and target language corpus. Generic collocations are also ascribed to the dominant type of discourse: scientific, technical, administrative, socio-economic, political, etc.

This approach to phraseology, based on the distinction between collocational structures used preferentially in the company of a specific term, and those for which it is not possible to distinguish a node-term belonging to a specific subject field, allows us to consider a whole spectrum of phraseological data in the context of LSPs, and thus provides users with a valuable resource for reading, writing, or translating specialized texts or genre. In particular, as argued above, taking domain-free phraseology into account is one of the many ambitious approaches to data offered in ARTES, providing for onomasiological access to collocations which are common to a variety of LSP discourses, as an aid to scientific drafting (Pecman 2007, 2008). Another is the organization of data around the mechanisms of semantic preference and prosody. The idea behind the ARTES dictionary is to bypass classical, alphabetical access to data by revealing multiple relations between data, of which semantic prosody and preference are particularly useful for understanding discourse and the structure of the lexicon.

10.4.1 *Defining semantic prosody and semantic preference*

Semantic prosody and semantic preference can be considered as related phenomena, semantic prosody being at the highest level of abstraction of all co-occurrence phenomena (collocation, colligation, and semantic preference). Sinclair (1996: 87) insisted that semantic prosody is on the "pragmatic side of the semantics/pragmatics continuum" and is attitudinal, while Louw (1993: 157) defined it as "a consistent aura of meaning with which a form is imbued by its collocates". He then claimed (2000) that this phenomenon can be detected by looking for a statistically significant series of collocates having a negative or positive connotation. Few authors have specifically studied semantic prosody in LSPs. Tribble (2000: 86) argued that "local prosodies" in certain genres can be established, Fuentes (2001a, 2001b) studied semantic prosody in academic and technical corpora, while Nelson (2000) focused on business English and Krausse (2011) studied how semantic prosody manifests itself in a corpus of environmental engineering texts.

Semantic preference deals with a semantic set of collocates which share part of a set of semantic features: they can be classified into a semantic class, or can be represented by a hierarchically higher lexical item, namely a hyperonym. While there is some evidence that semantic prosody can differ between what is called general language and LSPs (Hunston 2007, Louw and Chateau 2010, Kübler and Volanschi 2012), evidence that the semantic preference of a lexical item is not the same in different varieties of language is overwhelming. This is obviously linked to the difference between a word and a term in a specialized domain. The verb *run* does not co-occur with the same semantic set in general science and computer science English (Kübler and Foucou 2003), while the French verb *lancer* presents a specific semantic set in computer science French (L'Homme and Meynard 1998: 207).

Both semantic prosody and semantic preference can behave differently across languages. The English verb *commit*, described by Partington (1998), has a negative semantic prosody, as it co-occurs with nouns like *crime, murder, mistakes*, and *suicide*, all words having a negative connotation. The French equivalent *commettre* also presents a negative semantic prosody, as it also occurs with nouns having a negative connotation, such as *crime, délit, attentat terroriste, vol, erreur*, and *faute*. A more thorough analysis, however, shows differences between the French and English sets: the French noun *suicide* cannot be used with *commettre*, as an equivalent of *to commit suicide* (**commettre (un/o) suicide*), i.e. a collocation which is quite frozen (no article before the noun), and is best translated by the French synthetic verb *se suicider*. Not all typical collocates of the French *commettre* have a negative connotation: in the expression *commettre un roman / une oeuvre / une pièce de théâtre* ('a novel', 'a work', 'a play'), the nouns themselves do not have a negative connotation, but through the aura of meaning of the verb *commettre*, they take on a negative connotation, yielding a certain irony. The corresponding expression is extremely rare in English. It is very difficult for a non-native speaker to understand or even recognize semantic prosody. Taking into account such differences across languages is indispensable in designing a bilingual LSP dictionary, which aims either to help translators to understand this phenomenon, or French speakers who have to write articles in English, to be aware of the differences.

10.4.2 *On the relevance of semantic prosody for LSP users*

This section discusses the phenomenon of semantic prosody in a bilingual context and introduces the issues linked with its representation in an online LSP dictionary. Detecting semantic prosody in a specialized language by relying on intuition only is not simple. However, corpus linguistics and its tools have opened up a new approach to pinpointing semantic prosody by basing the search on statistical criteria, as Louw (1993) was the first to claim. Kübler and Volanschi (2012) have looked for examples of semantic prosody in a comparable English/French earth science corpus; they have shown that the use of the verb *to cause* presented significant differences in general and earth science English. As demonstrated by Hunston (2007), *to cause* has a negative semantic prosody, even in scientific English, when there is a negative effect on human beings, human artefacts, or animals. However, Louw and Chateau (2010) insisted that there was a certain smoothing of semantic prosodies in scientific English. Examples (1) and (2) below show a negative semantic prosody when human beings are involved (samples from a specialized corpus in earth science):

(1) *[...] in which reactivation events have **caused damage** to buildings and infra-structure [...]*

(2) *[...] the earthquake still **caused** 62 **deaths** and nearly $6 billion in **damage** [...]*

Damage and *deaths* are lexical items also used in the general language; furthermore, as in the general language, human beings (*62 deaths*) and buildings (*buildings and infrastructure*) are involved in the deaths and damage caused. These two examples must be compared with the following ones, in which *cause* does not present any negative semantic prosody and is thus smoothed:

(3)   (...) *the advanced continental breakup between eastern North America and western North Africa* **caused** *a* **transition** *from tholeiitic to alkaline basic sequences, responsible for the birth of Cape Verde* (...)

(4)   *The second modification mainly* **causes** *a* **steeper geotherm** *and, therefore,* **higher temperatures** *in the lower crust compared to the case with a (greater) constant lithosphere thickness.*

The examples above show that the English verb *to cause* has different behaviours that must be taken into account when translating into French, or when a French speaker writes in English. The analysis of the French equivalent *causer* shows that its semantic prosody is slightly different and that it is not always an equivalent for *to cause*. French *causer* has a negative semantic prosody when used with lexical items of general language, and when human beings or animals are concerned:

(5)   (...) *après chaque grand séisme, les secousses fortes du sol* **causent** *d'énormes* **dégâts** *matériels et malheureusement souvent humains* (...)

(6)   *Les éruptions du Karthala surviennent tous les 11 ans en moyenne, mais* **causent** *rarement un* **désastre** *majeur.*

On the other hand, *causer* can sometimes be used as a specialized verb having a negative connotation, as observed in example (7). Even though the verb appears in a negative context with *instabilités* and *perturbent*, it has a more neutral semantic prosody and *naissance* does not have any negative connotation:

(7)   (...) *il n'est pas impossible qu'ils déclenchent des* **instabilités** *dans le manteau et* **causent** *la* **naissance** *de points chauds, ils* **perturbent** *la rotation de la Terre et sans doute, en conséquence, le régime de la circulation atmosphérique et, qui sait, le climat.*

This use is rare, unlike in English, although there are some examples which are perceived as awkward by French native speakers and sometimes even by experts in earth sciences. In examples (8)–(10) below, we have provided a more idiomatic verb to replace *causer*, at least in general language:

(8)   *Ces modifications du régime de convergence, initiées à la suite d'un changement géodynamique, ou de la subduction de reliefs sous-marins tels que les rides asismiques de Tiburon et Barracuda (Bouysse and Westercamp, 1990) ont* **causé (provoqué)** *le* **saut du front de subduction** *vers l'Ouest.*

(9)   *Les panaches mantelliques ont par ailleurs* **causé (provoqué)** *sa* **croissance** (...)

(10)   *(...) une structure peu profonde qui serait un* **bassin causé** *(généré) par un impact.*

This can probably be perceived as an influence of English, as most international publications are in English. But this introduces an interesting issue on the relevance of including this type of information in a database. A translator must know that *to cause* is usually translated with a different verb from *causer* when there is no semantic prosody (verbs like *provoquer*, *générer*, and *engendrer*). On the other hand, a French-speaker writing a scientific paper in English should know that *provoquer, engendrer,* and *générer* can be translated by *to cause.* It is thus necessary to list the semantic set of nouns that can be direct object of *to cause*, in the case of semantic preference, and then to equally list the set of nouns having a negative connotation, in the case of semantic prosody. Then, information on the characteristics of scientific French must also be provided, so that the user can choose either to use alternative solutions to translate *to cause* into French, or to use *causer* in a neutral context, being fully aware of applying a norm that is different from the usual French general and prescriptive norm.

10.4.3 *Integrating semantic prosody into ARTES*

The difficulty we have encountered in processing semantic prosody and preference is that they are very complex mechanisms. To be able to formalize these two phenomena in the database, we need to answer the following question precisely: What data are involved in creating the semantic prosody and preference effect? If we return to our examples, or to those often referred to in studies of semantic prosody and preference, we can venture to say that semantic prosodies and preferences act at a lexical level, but actualize at a collocational, semantic, and pragmatic level. It is thus difficult to decide at which level to record these phenomena, as lexical and collocational levels are distinguished in the database.

The solution we have adopted at this stage of the ARTES database development is to consider semantic prosody and semantic preference as a possible type of intra-linguistic semantic relation between a set of collocations which share the same node and display either of those two phenomena. As a matter of fact, the collocations are simply assigned a posteriori to one or several sets which group those which reveal the same semantic preference or semantic prosody. The procedure consists first of recording collocations separately, then in creating a set, and finally in assigning collocations to a set, the final stage being illustrated in Figure 10.8. Each set is given a name, for identification purposes, which is the head-collocation (for example *to cause an earthquake*) or the association of a term and the hyperonym of all collocates (for example *to cause /negative phenomenon/*). The hyperonym encompasses all terms that can be used in a context in which human beings can be involved. This

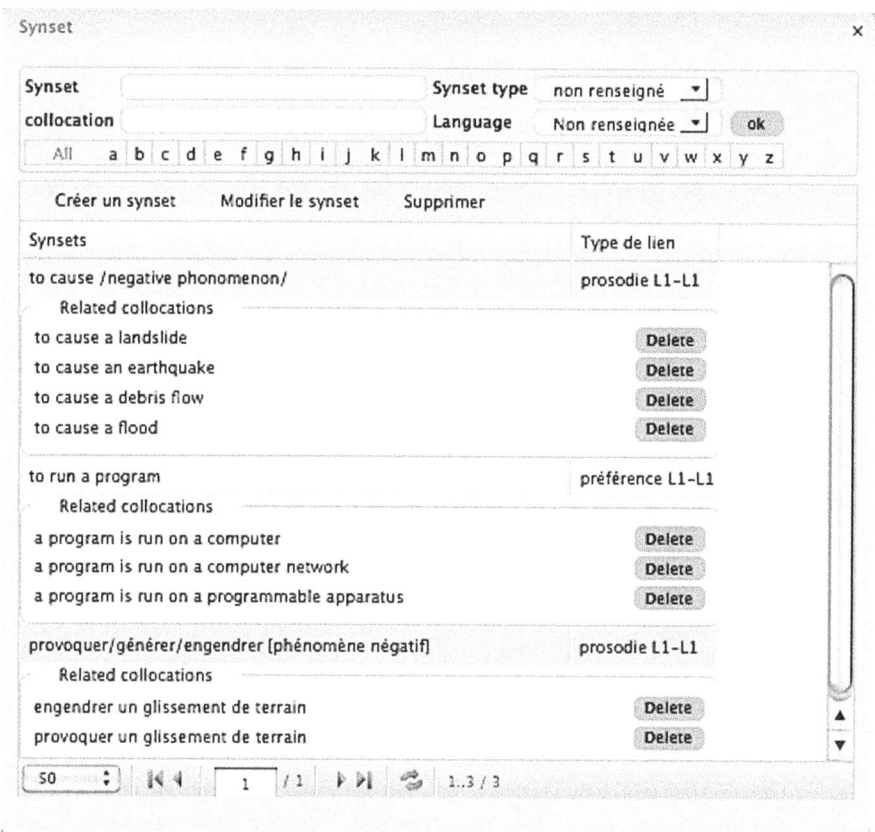

FIGURE 10.8 ARTES dictionary interface for recording semantic prosody and preference.

solution, however, is not completely satisfactory, because semantic prosody goes beyond a binary collocation.

At this stage of development, the differences between languages cannot be accounted for, as the synsets cannot be aligned, but just listed, as illustrated in Figure 10.8. Nevertheless, each collocation can be offered one or more equivalents in a target language by taking into account the specific semantic—prosodic or preferential—value of the target terms, as shown in Figure 10.9.

Our understanding of these two phenomena is still progressing and may lead to modifications in the database architecture in the near future. If we consider that semantic prosodies and semantic preferences arise from the combination of a term with a set of collocates all pertaining to a specific meaning or connotation, we can instead decide to encode semantic prosodies and preferences as a specific type of relation between terms. However, this type of relation is not similar to other typical term-term relations, such as synonymy, hyperonymy, or meronymy, which are

FIGURE 10.9 Interface for translating semantic prosody or semantic preference.

anticipated in the ARTES database. The latter relations are paradigmatic while the former are syntagmatic. Currently, ARTES is designed to encode syntagmatic relations synthetically as one whole unit (e.g. *to cause a landslide*), and not analytically as a result of a combination of two terms (e.g. *to cause* on one side, and *landslide* on the other, linked together via a semantic prosody relation). Future work is thus necessary to evaluate the advantages of each type of processing of the two phenomena for different target users of the ARTES dictionary. In parallel, future developments should improve access to, and the export of, data on semantic prosody and semantic preference.

10.5 Conclusion

In many respects, ARTES is an innovative dictionary: in the originality of the data and phenomena recorded in its database, in the disposition of the information over the online interface which takes into account a variety of user situations, and in relying on a technology that allows for future developments. Special efforts were made in the design of interfaces to anticipate various users' situations. As argued above, ARTES is a tool with a double function, as a dictionary and as a database, which was achieved by designing two distinct interfaces. The dictionary is targeted at various LSP users, translators, and domain experts, whether learners or professionals. The database is used for compiling data by students in Master's studies through a crowdsourcing method and offers useful functions for teachers for monitoring students' work in progress and validating the compiled data.

We have shown that bilingual lexicography must go beyond simple lexical description; phraseology (collocations and higher-order phraseology) must be part of a lexicographic theory. Corpus linguistics has widely influenced our perception of words. This is especially true of LSP lexicography, which deals with terms and lexical items in context. As term meanings can change depending on the field of knowledge, their phraseology also varies. The same observation can be made of more general lexical items used in LSPs. However, it is not enough to describe collocations only: phenomena such as semantic preference and semantic prosody are also part of lexicographic description. Users can take advantage of a complete description of an LSP in a bilingual perspective, when they have to write or translate in that domain.

We have also shown that the electronic medium makes it easier to incorporate such information in a dictionary, as users can navigate between different labels, in order to get the most out of the dictionary. Electronic dictionaries can also be organized at different levels, depending on and adapted to different users. However, the solutions we have adopted to introduce higher-order phraseology into the dictionary are open to improvement in line with the advances in our understanding of the phenomena and the increasing number of studies devoted to it. By offering a framework for encoding semantic prosody and semantic preference in LSP discourse, the ARTES dictionary allows the exploration of new paths in electronic lexicography. One of the next steps could be to include colligational phenomena in LSPs and in a contrastive framework between French and English.

LSP bilingual lexicography should provide users with more contextualized information. The challenge will be to make this information accessible on a simple basis, as more information generally means a more complex presentation. Linking dictionary entries to bilingual or multilingual corpora and providing users with more examples of use and more contexts to support their understanding of the definition is a possible solution. However, this will need a fine study of users' needs and of ergonomics. Another challenge for the future of bilingual electronic lexicography is expected to relate to the introduction of sound files, not only for words, but also for whole phraseological units and full sentences, providing the user with different varieties of language (such as Canadian French or Indian English). Users will be able to choose not only a specific variety for sound, but also a specific variety of phraseology. Differences in varieties can lead to linguistic and cultural misunderstanding, which can be greatly damaging for international cooperation in many industries (e.g. the automotive industry). Discovering and becoming familiar with different phraseological and phonological varieties will help improve international communication. From the theoretical point of view, the challenge lies in the description of discourse phenomena (such as indeterminacy and multi-dimensionality) in the dictionary, leading to a whole domain-based and genre-based description, accessible electronically.

11

Encoding collocations in DiCoInfo: From formal to user-friendly representations

MARIE-CLAUDE L'HOMME, BENOÎT ROBICHAUD,
AND PATRICK LEROYER

11.1 Introduction

DiCoInfo (Dictionnaire fondamental de l'informatique et de l'Internet) is an online lexical resource[1] covering terms (nouns, verbs, adjectives, and adverbs) that are related to the fields of computing and the Internet (e.g. *boot, configure, download, email, virtual*). The word list contains terms that can be found in many different texts on computing and the Internet; we avoid including very specialized units (terms that would be specific to a given programming language, for example).

DiCoInfo provides rich lexical information in various data categories and encodes it using a semi-formal system (based on Explanatory Combinatorial Lexicology, ECL; Mel'čuk *et al.* 1995). In this chapter, we explain how some of these data categories were converted to make them more accessible to users. We focus on collocations and show that their meaning can be described with natural language explanations, how actantial structures can be better reflected in these explanations, how users can browse collocations in order to find collocates that express specific meanings, and finally how they can search for translations of collocations.

Section 11.2 gives a brief description of the database, i.e. the structure of its entries and its objectives. Section 11.3 explains how collocations are encoded using lexical functions. Then, in Sections 11.4 to 11.7, we focus more specifically on the recent efforts that were made to convert the data categories that are related with collocations to make them more accessible to users. Section 11.4 shows how we created natural

---

[1] DiCoInfo can be accessed at the following address: http://olst.ling.umontreal.ca/dicoinfo/

language explanations for the meaning of collocations and how we organized long lists of collocates within entries. Section 11.5 discusses a more functional approach in which we identified specific user needs and adapted the interface of DiCoInfo to these needs. Section 11.6 describes a browsing mechanism for accessing specific collocates based on their meaning. Section 11.7 gives a brief account of how translations of collocations can now be retrieved from the database. Finally, Section 11.8 draws some conclusions and mentions some directions for future work.

11.2 DiCoInfo: a quick look at the database

DiCoInfo is an original specialized database in the sense that it differs from most terminological resources. It gives a complete picture of the lexico-semantic properties of terms while terminological resources usually focus on explaining concepts (pieces of knowledge) related to the field to which terms belong. This leads them to consider noun terms rather than verbs or adjectives and to describe a limited number of relationships (synonymy, hypernymy, meronymy, cause-effect, etc.).

The compilation process of the database started nearly a decade ago and preliminary work focused on French terms only. We recently extended the coverage of DiCoInfo to English and Spanish. The French word list contains over 1,000 entries (including 20,000 lexical relationships) and the English version currently contains approximately 800 entries (including nearly 5,000 relationships).[2] The work on Spanish started much more recently and approximately 100 entries are now online.[3] In addition, the entries in French are also much more complete than those in the other two languages.

The methodology for compiling DiCoInfo is largely corpus-based and combines automated and manual methods. A series of steps (selection of terms, collection of example sentences, and writing of entries) is carried out by lexicographers in the same order with slight variations depending on their experience (L'Homme 2008). The data is encoded in an XML structure and then converted into HTML pages for the purpose of publishing its content on the Internet.

11.2.1 *The structure of entries*

As shown in Figure 11.1, DiCoInfo first displays the following data categories after a user entered a query into the search module:[4]

---

[2] The coverage in English was boosted thanks to a project carried out in collaboration with K Dictionaries, Tel Aviv, Israel.

[3] The Spanish version is developed in collaboration with the TecnoLeTTra team of the University Jaume I (Spain), and its coverage should increase in the upcoming years.

[4] Some French entries (labelled with a status 0) are also accompanied by a definition (in which actants are formally indicated).

download ₁, vt

Status: 2

Actantial structure: download: {user ₁} ~ {application, file ₁} from {computer ₁, network} to {computer ₁}
Linguistic realizations of actants
Contexts
Lexical relations

Spanish: descargar ₁
French: télécharger ₁

Written by: MCLH
Last update: 07/06/2009

download ₁.₁, n

Status: 2

Actantial structure: a download: ~ of {application, file ₁} from {computer ₁, network} to {computer ₁} by {user ₁}
Linguistic realizations of actants
Synonym(s): downloading
Contexts
Lexical relations

Spanish: descarga ₁
French: téléchargement ₁

Written by: MCLH
Last update: 07/06/2009

FIGURE 11.1 Simplified display for *download*₁ and *download*₁.₁.

- Headword (the lemma and a number used to indicate a specific meaning).
- Grammatical information (part of speech, gender for nouns in French and Spanish, transitivity for verbs).
- Status (this number indicates how advanced the writing of the entry is: 2 is the first stage; 0 indicates that the entry is complete).
- Actantial (i.e. argumental) structure:[5] the number of actants and a first label showing the typical term(s) that can appear in that position.
- Synonyms and variants.[6]
- Equivalents in other languages (hyperlinked when the entries are available online).
- The initials of the lexicographer(s) who wrote the entry and the moment it was last updated.

Other data categories are only displayed on demand:

- Linguistic realizations of actants (Figure 11.2): forms in which actants can appear in running text (in entries labelled with a status 0, the list is complete; in others, realizations are still in the process of being added).

---

[5] Actants (or arguments) are the items that must be stated to explain the meaning of a predicative lexical unit (verbs, adjectives, and many nouns). For example, the meaning of *configure* includes two actants, namely an actant that carries out the activity and an actant that undergoes the activity. In dictionaries, actants can be indicated with different labels, such as variables (X *configures* Y), numbers (Act1 *configures* Act2), semantic roles (Agent *configures* Patient), or very general semantic classes (Someone *configures* Something).

[6] Variants are different spellings listed in the same entry (e.g. *log in, login*).

- Contexts (Figure 11.3): a sample of three sentences is displayed (these are selected among those—between fifteen and twenty—that are placed by the lexicographer in the entry).

download $_1$, vt

Status: 2

Actantial structure: download: {user $_1$} ~ {application, file $_1$} from {computer $_1$, network} to {computer $_1$}
Linguistic realizations of actants

agent
user $_1$
patient
antivirus program $_1$, applet $_1$, application , archive $_1$, compiler $_1$, copy , demo $_1$, distribution $_1$, document $_1$, driver $_1$, editor $_1$, environment $_2$, executable $_1$, file $_1$, freeware $_1$, operating system $_1$, package $_1$, patch $_1$, plug-in $_1$, program , release $_{1,2}$, shareware $_1$, software $_1$, spyware , utility $_1$, version $_1$
source
computer $_1$, Internet $_1$, network
destination
computer $_1$, system

Contexts
Lexical relations

Spanish: descargar $_1$
French: télécharger $_1$

Written by: MCLH
Last update:07/06/2009

FIGURE 11.2 Linguistic realizations of actants of *download*₁.

download $_1$, vt

Status: 2

Actantial structure: download: {user $_1$} ~ {application, file $_1$} from {computer $_1$, network} to {computer $_1$}
Linguistic realizations of actants
Contexts
   Annotated Contexts
      • *By now you should be able to locate websites on the net, download files from these websites, even set up a local front page copy of your favorite websites on your hard disk.* (Source: INTERNET)
      • *Search out the specific model number you need, download the new version and usually just double click the file to start the install. Most sites will give you instructions, too.* (Source: MAINTAINING)
      • *If the WDM drivers were previously installed, download hwclear.exe from Hauppauge's website.* (Source: GUIDE TO CAPTURING VIDEOS)
Lexical relations
   Actantial roles

Explanation - Typical term	Related term
Related Meanings	
Conversive	upload $_1$
Other Parts of Speech and Derivatives	
Noun	download $_{1,1}$
An application or a file that can be d.	downloadable $_1$
Result	download $_{1,2}$

FIGURE 11.3 Contexts and lexical relations in the entry for *download*₁.

- Lexical relations (Figure 11.3): a list of terms that are semantically related to the headword along with a short explanation of the relationship (in entries labelled with a status 0, the list is complete; in others, related terms are still in the process of being added).

The database provides a list of paradigmatic relationships (near synonymy, antonymy, other parts of speech, etc.) and syntagmatic relationships (i.e. collocations). Most paradigmatic relationships can be visualized with graphs (Robichaud 2011). A link to this graphical display is provided in the form of an icon.

11.2.2 *A multi-purpose database*

Originally, DiCoInfo was defined as a research tool. The objective of the dictionary was to assess to what extent the description of terms could lend itself to the theoretical and methodological principles of modern lexical semantics frameworks. It was designed as an environment in which researchers and students in terminology could carry out experiments on one aspect or the other of terms (semantic distinctions, actantial structure, semantic relationships, etc.). In addition, since it contained rich and semi-formal descriptions, it could also be used in natural language processing (NLP) applications.

The main framework on which our theoretical and methodological decisions were and are still based is that of Explanatory Combinatorial Lexicology (Mel'čuk *et al.* 1995). DiCoInfo adheres to Explanatory Combinatorial Lexicology principles in the following ways:

1. Each article is devoted to a specific lexical unit—a lexical item with a specific meaning—and not to a lexical item, i.e. a lexical form: for instance, *address* appears in three different articles (address$_1$ 'a physical location in a memory'; address$_2$ 'an identifier for a computer or a site'; address$_3$ 'an identifier for an email user'). In several dictionaries the three meanings of *address* would be described in the same entry.
2. Meanings are distinguished by analysing the series of interactions of a unit with other units of the field.[7]
3. The actantial structure is stated and given a central role in the description of the meaning of lexical units (here our representation model differs from the one used in Explanatory Combinatorial Lexicology in the sense that semantic roles and typical terms are listed; cf. Section 11.3).

---

[7] In DiCoInfo, only specialized meanings are considered. Hence, even if the corpus does contain occurrences of general meanings, only those related to computing or the Internet are included in the word list.

4. Much emphasis is placed on the listing of lexical relationships and the formalization of their description. In Explanatory Combinatorial Lexicology, lexical relationships are formalized using the system of lexical functions (cf. Section 11.3).

Recently, a module containing sentence annotations was included. This module is based on the methodology developed within the FrameNet project (Ruppenhofer *et al.* 2006),[8] applying Frame Semantics principles (Fillmore 1982), and aims to show how lexical units (especially verbs) interact with their participants (actants and circumstants) in running text.

Although it was originally designed as a tool for researchers, it soon became obvious that DiCoInfo could be adapted to other information needs and provide assistance in specific situations. For instance, it can help users such as students and professionals in specialized translation or technical writing. However, we were aware that the presentation of some data categories needed to be converted or adapted in order to meet the specific needs of these users. Other dictionaries along the same lines (Binon *et al.* 2000, Mel'čuk and Polguère 2007, Verlinde *et al.* 2006, Verlinde and Peeters, this volume) show that rich encodings can be converted into more user-oriented formats. In addition, the recent extension to other languages (English and Spanish) forced us to adapt our methodology to multilingual data and to allow more languages to be added in the future. These additions also made the resource much more attractive for translation purposes. In the remainder of this chapter we focus on the adaptations that were made to access and present collocations.

11.3 The modelling of collocations with lexical functions

As was mentioned above, DiCoInfo contains long lists of lexical relationships, and in noun entries the majority describes syntagmatic relationships, i.e. collocations. Our definition of *collocation* is very close to the one used in Explanatory Combinatorial Lexicology (Mel'čuk *et al.* 1995) that views it as an unpredictable combination of lexical units, i.e. a combination that cannot be produced based on the regular syntactic or semantic properties of the units involved. Collocations consist of a keyword and a collocate: the keyword is selected by the speaker (e.g. *dialog box*) and governs the selection of the collocate (e.g. *open*) to allow the expression of a given meaning (e.g. the meaning 'use' in *open a dialog box*).

The types of collocations that are taken into account in our database are those in which the keyword is a term (usually a noun). Table 11.1 shows part of the verbal collocates listed under the entry *password*. We assume that the term is freely selected, but that the selection of the collocate is imposed by the keyword. For example, verbs

---

[8] More information on our application of the FrameNet methodology to DiCoInfo is given in Pimentel *et al.* (2011).

TABLE 11.1 Verbal collocates listed under *password*

password, n.: ~ given by {user ₁} to {computer ₁, provider} to act on {account, site ₁}

The user creates a p.	*create ₁ a ~, define ₁ a ~, set a ~, chose a ~, select ₁ a ~*
The user creates a p. according to predefined parameters	*generate a ~*
The user has a p.	*have a ~*
The user causes that he has a p.	*memorize a ~, obtain a ~*
The user changes a p.	*change a ~*
The user no longer has a p.	*forget a ~, lose a ~*
The user has a p. once again	*recover a ~*
The user starts using a p.	*enter ₁ a ~, type ₁ a ~*
The user uses a p.	*use a ~*
The user uses a p. to act on the account or the site	*access ₂ ... with a ~*
The computer or the provider starts using a p.	*check a ~, ask ... for a~, prompt ... for a ~*
Someone or something uses a p. to act on the computer or the site	*protect ... with a ~*
The p. stops working	*the ~ expires*
Someone causes that a p. stops working properly	*crack ₁ a ~, guess a ~*

used to express the idea of 'use' differ according to the term selected, as shown in the examples below:

"use" Internet: *surf the ~*[9]
"use" page: *visit a ~*
"use" file: *edit a ~*
"use" mouse: *move a ~*
"use" password: *use a ~*

Similarly, verbs used to express 'create' also differ according to the keyword selected, as shown in the following examples:

---

[9] Throughout the chapter, collocations are reproduced in examples and tables as they appear in DiCoInfo. The tilde (~) replaces the keyword of collocations and is preceded by a determiner where applicable (e.g. dialog box: *open a ~*); other nouns that appear in collocations are replaced using three dots (...) without a determiner (keyboard: *enter ... on a ~*). The use of these graphical devices in DiCoInfo contributes to reducing information overload in articles, especially those that contain long lists of collocations. In addition, in all screens displaying collocational information, the keyword is always reproduced first and the use of symbols (~ and ...) allows us to distinguish clearly the linguistic components of the collocation. Hence, it appears that symbols still have a role to play for increasing the readability of certain data categories. We are aware that more intuitive methods could be devised in an electronic dictionary, but this work still needs to be done in DiCoInfo.

"create" *a password: create a ~, define a ~, set a ~*
"create" *a file: create a ~*
"create" *interface: develop an ~*
"create" *program: develop a ~, write a ~*

Since they are 'unpredictable', collocations must be listed in specialized repositories in order to provide access to this information. We also adhere to the general principle according to which collocates are listed in an entry whose headword is a term. Hence, once collocations are collected, they are classified under a specific headword along with a general explanation of their meaning. Explanations take into account three linguistic properties of collocations in accordance with Explanatory Combinatorial Lexicology.[10]

1. The syntactic relationship between the keyword and the collocate. For example, we distinguish the verbal collocates of *password*, namely *use* and *access*, based on the fact that, when combined with *use*, *password* is the first complement (direct object); but when combined with *access*, *password* is the second complement.
   use a password: verb + 1st complement
   access (e.g. a site) *with a password*: verb + 2nd complement
2. The actantial structure of the keyword. Many collocations, especially verbal and nominal collocations, convey a meaning that involves one or more actants that appear in the actantial structure of the keyword. As can be seen in the following examples, the meaning of *use a password* involves the first actant of *password*; the meaning of *access a site with a password*, involves both actants of the term.
   password, n.: ~ given by {user $_1$} to {computer $_1$, provider} to act on {account, site $_1$}
   use a password: the user uses a password
   access... with a password: the user uses a password to access an account, a site
3. The meaning of the collocate. Terms combine with collocates that convey different meanings. For example, both *use* and *access* refer to typical uses of the password; however, other collocates convey a meaning of 'creation', e.g. *create, define, set a password*.

The examples below show how the properties listed above are taken into account concretely in lexical functions:

Real$_1$(password) = use a ~
Labreal$_{12}$(password) = access ... with a ~
Caus$_1$Func$_0$(password) = create, define, set a ~

---

[10] Although an increasing number of paper dictionaries and lexical databases include collocations, few resort to lexical functions to organize them. Notable exceptions are the DiCo (Polguère 2000) and DICE (Alonso Ramos 2004). It is also worth mentioning that a specialized dictionary (the DAFA; Binon *et al.* 2000) uses a system similar to lexical functions to classify collocations.

Real$_i$ and **Labreal**$_{ij}$ represent the meaning of 'use', whereas **Caus**$_i$**Func**$_0$ represents the general meaning of 'create' (literally 'cause to exist'). **Real** is used when the keyword is first complement and **Labreal** when the keyword is second complement. Numbers appearing as indices (1, 2, n) refer to the actants that are involved in the meaning of the collocation and correspond to their position in the actantial structure.

11.4 Converting data categories to improve the readability of entries

The listing of collocates in DiCoInfo proves useful in order to identify the typical lexical units that combine with a specific term. In addition, encoding them with lexical functions allows lexicographers to organize collocates and provide a basic explanation of their meanings. While recognizing this, we are faced with two main problems as far as access to the data is concerned:

1. The complexity of lexical functions: lexical functions offer the desired expressiveness to take into account the various properties of collocations (their syntactic structure, the role of actants, their meaning). In addition, they are language-independent and can thus be used to encode collocations in different languages. However, they must be learned as such and this is not something we can ask normal users of terminological databases to do. We needed to find a more user-friendly way of presenting collocations and somehow 'hide' the formal system from users.

2. The very long lists of collocates under a given headword: some entries contain very long lists of collocates. This is the case for the French term *fichier* (English *file*) that includes about 100 collocates. We needed to find a way to allow users to find specific collocates without having to go through long lists.

In addition, since we extended our descriptions to other languages than French, a multilingual access to collocations could be provided to users. In previous versions of DiCoInfo, users would need to look at all the collocates listed in an entry in language 1, then locate the equivalent of the headword, and finally read all the collocates listed in the entry in language 2. We thought we could offer better support in that direction.

The following subsections describe the methods we devised to solve the first two problems and provide multilingual access to collocations. The process of converting and adapting some data categories of DiCoInfo started back in 2007. At the time, the objective was simply to improve the readability of entries and perhaps attract users interested in the kinds of descriptions it contained. More specific user needs were later identified, which in turn led to the development of new data presentation models and access paths (cf. Section 11.5).

11.4.1 *Natural language explanations as a substitute for lexical*
      functions and typical terms to represent actants

As mentioned in Section 11.3, lexical functions, although extremely useful to capture the complex properties of collocations, require a thorough knowledge of their structure, a kind of knowledge that users of online databases cannot be assumed to have. Hence, the first step in the conversion process of DiCoInfo was concerned with the explanations of collocations. We decided to 'translate' lexical functions into a system of natural language explanations (based on a proposal made by Polguère (2003)). However, before examining the general principles applied when defining natural language explanations per se, we must first describe our methodology for representing actants in a more user-friendly way since explanations take this into consideration.

As indicated in Section 11.2, actants of the keyword are often involved in the meaning of collocations and lexical functions refer to them with indices (**Real**$_1$, **Labreal**$_{12}$). Indices reflect the position of the actant in the actantial structure: 1 refers to the first actant of the keyword, 2 to the second one, and so forth. Although the reference to actants is necessary to explain the meaning of most collocates, a numbering system (or another abstract representation system such as variables X, Y, or Z) in the entries of DiCoInfo did not appear to be the most user-friendly way to represent actants. In fact, we were quite reluctant to use these numbers in our natural language explanations of collocations.

In DiCoInfo, actants are represented using 'typical terms' (a similar system is used in Binon *et al.* 2000), terms that are likely to realize actants in running text and that are the most representative of the kinds of units that can appear in the vicinity of the headword.[11] Below are a few examples of typical terms that were chosen for specific headwords:

click $_1$: {user $_1$} ~ on {icon $_1$} with {mouse $_1$}
debug $_1$: {programmer $_1$} ~ {program $_1$} to remove {bug $_1$}
program $_3$: {programmer $_1$} ~ {program $_1$} in {language $_1$}
store $_{1a}$: {memory, storage device $_1$} ~ {data $_1$}
store $_{1b}$: {user $_1$} ~ {data $_1$} on {memory, storage device $_1$}

The criteria for selecting typical terms are the following (more details can be found in L'Homme 2010):

- The typical actant is the one that would most naturally appear in the definition of the term. So while *user* and *programmer* are terms that can correctly refer to

---

[11] Although this is not directly relevant to the content of this contribution, it should be mentioned that actants are also expressed by means of semantic roles (Agent, Patient, Instrument, etc.) similar to those presented in Fillmore (1968). This double representation system appears in all data categories in which actants are expressed.

the first actant of the verb *edit*, the term *user* is felt to be more appropriate to describe the person who carries out this activity.

- The typical actant is the most common unit among those that occur in the vicinity of the term being described. For example, *site* is a typical actant of the verb *visit*. Other terms such as *chat room* and *page* could be used to indicate the same thing, but they are not used as often as *site* in running text.

- The typical actant is often the generic term covering a wider semantic range than the other more specific quasi-synonyms or hyponyms. This criterion explains the choice of actants such as *data*, *file*, *program*, and *hardware* as typical terms.

- Typical terms must ideally correspond to a headword in the database. This is why in some entries more than one typical term is given, since no other generic term is defined in DiCoInfo (e.g. *storage device* and *memory* in the actantial structure of *store* above).

Typical terms appear in several data categories in the entries of DiCoInfo: actantial structure, definition, and explanations of collocations that will be the focus of our discussion in the remainder of this section.

Natural language explanations are designed to 'translate' lexical functions in the sense that they aim to capture all the information encoded in a lexical function, i.e. the syntactic structure of the collocation, the meaning of the collocate, and the reference to the actantial structure of the keyword. Table 11.2 gives a few examples of the explanations provided for collocations in DiCoInfo and their corresponding lexical functions.

The correspondence between lexical functions and natural language explanations appears as follows (cf. Table 11.2):

- Syntactic structure: This is shown in the value that appears in the list of collocates (e.g. *browse the ~*). The collocate is expressed along with the keyword in the list of collocations presented to the user. In addition, a large number of

TABLE 11.2 **Natural language explanations used to translate lexical functions**

Keyword	Collocation	Lexical function	Explanation
Internet	*browse the ~*	Real_1	The user uses the I.
password	*access... with a ~*	Labreal_{12}	The user uses a p. to act on the account or on the site
password	*create, define, set a ~*	$\text{Caus}_1\text{Func}_0$	The user creates a p.
blog	*post... on a ~*	$\text{Caus}_1\text{Oper}_2$	The author places information on a b.

explanations express the syntactic relationships between the keyword and the collocate (e.g. *use the* I., *place information on a* b.).

- The actantial structure of the keyword: Actants are expressed by means of typical terms and these are stated in the explanation (e.g. in 'The user uses the I.', *user* refers to the first actant of *Internet*; in 'The user places information on a b.', *user* refers to the first actant of *blog* and *information* refers to the second actant of *blog*).
- The meaning of the collocate: This is reflected in the choice of general words that paraphrase the general and abstract meaning represented in lexical functions (e.g. **Real**$_i$ and **Labreal**$_{ij}$ are often translated into explanations containing the verb *use*; **Caus$_i$Func$_0$** is translated into explanations containing the verb *create*).

Natural language explanations are as systematic as possible. The general idea is to assign the same phrasing to a given lexical function. However, this is not always possible since the semantic class of a keyword may vary and a given phrasing may not be adequate for all instances of the same lexical function. In addition, explanations vary according to the language concerned. Hence, for the time being, we have three parallel series of explanations. Table 11.3 shows the variation admitted in the phrasing and different explanations in English, French, and Spanish.

When adding a collocation to an entry in DiCoInfo, lexicographers encode them using two different systems: lexical functions and natural language explanations. However, when clicking on the 'Lexical relations' link in the article, users access a table with the list of collocates and the natural language explanations and may completely ignore the fact that collocations are first encoded with lexical functions.

TABLE 11.3 **Variations in natural language explanations**

Keyword	Collocation	Lexical function	Explanation
hard disk	*store . . . on a ~*	**Labreal**$_{12}$	The user places the data on a h.
password	*access . . . with a ~*	**Labreal**$_{12}$	The user uses a p. to act on the account or on the site
blog	*post . . . on a ~*	**Caus$_1$Oper$_2$**	The author places information on a b.
keyboard	*enter . . . on a ~, type . . .*	**Labreal**$_{12}$	The user uses a k. to act on the data
teclado	*introducir . . . a través de un ~*	**Labreal**$_{12}$	El usuario utiliza un t. para operar con los datos
clavier	*entrer . . . au clavier, saisir . . . au clavier, taper . . .*	**Labreal**$_{12}$	L'utilisateur utilise un c. pour intervenir sur les données

11.4.2 *The ordering of collocations*

In this section, we present a first solution that was considered to solve the problem of organizing long lists of collocates in tables. This solution was later revised and another presentation method has been defined since (the new method is described in Section 11.6 and is implemented in the French version of DiCoInfo). The method presented here is still the one found in the English and Spanish versions.

Since DiCoInfo aims at providing the entire set of lexical relationships a term can have with other terms in the field (including collocates), it very soon became obvious that lists of collocates would be very difficult to manage. We reproduce below a selection of the collocates currently listed under the term *file* (and this represents only a small portion of those listed under its French equivalent *fichier*).

File: ~ created by {user $_1$} to act on {data $_1$}

backup a ~, binary ~, compress a ~, configuration ~, copy a ~ to . . . , create a ~, damage a ~, decompress a ~, delete a ~, download a ~, edit a ~, empty ~, generate a ~, HTML ~, install a ~, installation ~, load a ~, open a ~, parse a ~, PDF ~, process a ~, save a ~ to . . . , share a ~, text ~

We decided to organize collocates according to their meaning, and we did this on the basis of their lexical functions (L'Homme 2009). We first chose to separate collocates referring to 'Types of' files from the others (referring to activities, mostly verbs). These appear in two separate parts of a table in which collocates are listed. 'Types of' are grouped in the same section of the table, as shown in Figure 11.4.

Types of

That does not have a content	empty ~
That has a specific format	HTML ~
That has a specific format	binary ~
That has a specific format	PDF ~
That has a specific format	XML ~
That contains specific data	data $_1$ ~
That contains specific data	text ~
That is added to an email	attachment $_1$
That is used to carry out a specific task	cofiguration ~
That is used to carry out a specific task	installation $_2$ ~
That is used to be executed	executable $_1$
That is used to obtain help	help $_1$ ~
That contains a series of instructions	batch $_1$ ~

FIGURE 11.4 'Types of' collocates listed under *file*$_1$.

Combinations

The user creates a f.	create $_1$ a ~
The user destroys a f.	delete $_1$ a ~
The user reduces the size of a f.	compress $_1$ a ~
The user restores the original size of a f.	decompress $_1$ a ~
The user creates a f. according to predefined parameters	generate $_1$ a ~
The user places a f. on a storage device	backup $_1$ a ~
The user places a f. on a storage device	copy $_1$ a ~to ...
The user places a f. on a storage device	save $_1$ a ~to ...
The user prepares a f. to allow the f. to operate	install $_1$ a ~
The user places a f. on a computer from another computer	download a ~
The user starts using a f.	load $_{1b}$ a ~
The user starts using a f.	open $_1$ a ~
The user uses a f.	edit $_1$ a ~
The user uses a f. with other users	share $_1$ a ~
Someone or something uses a f.	pares $_1$ a ~
Someone or something uses a f.	process $_1$ a ~
Someone or something causes that a f. stops functioning properly	damage a ~

FIGURE 11.5 Ordering of the verbal collocates of *file*$_1$.

Verbal collocates are then listed according to two principles: (1) the main actant involved in the meaning of the collocation; and (2) the order in which the activities denoted by the verbs are carried out in the real world. We will illustrate these two principles with the term *file*. As can be seen in Figure 11.5, collocates that convey the meaning of 'create' are listed in the first part of the table, then followed by collocates that mean 'transform' and 'place somewhere'. Then verbs referring to typical uses carried out by the first actant are listed, followed by uses carried out by other participants.

However, this ordering principle remains a partial solution to the problem of having several collocates listed under a headword, since users are still provided with very long tables in some cases. Section 11.6.2 presents another solution to this problem.

11.5 Taking user needs into account

More recently, the adaptation of DiCoInfo to user-friendly representations has combined the resources of sophisticated linguistic encoding, a functional approach to specialized lexicography, and innovative computational programming for efficient data access and presentation. In the functional framework of lexicography (Tarp 2008, and this volume), dictionaries—and this can apply to specialized dictionaries—are considered as products designed for specific purposes, i.e. tools designed to meet information needs, and therefore solely defined according to the functions they are meant to fulfil.

The concept of 'lexicographic function' is based on the causal relation between extra- and intra-lexicographic user situations, including the following items: specific users, their specific profiles and needs, specific situations they are confronted with, and access to specific data types from which information is extracted. According to Tarp (2009c) a clear distinction must be made between two types of user situations:

- The extra-lexicographic user situation, which is a potential user situation (identifying lexicographically relevant user needs leading to consultation).
- The intra-lexicographic user situation, which is the real use situation of the dictionary.

The concept of 'dictionary assistance' establishes a link between the extra- and intra-lexicographic user situations; assistance is provided by gaining access to the requested data types from which information can subsequently be extracted. Lexicography in a functional framework also makes a distinction between cognitive and communicative user situations defined as follows:

- Cognitive user situations are determined by the need to acquire or verify knowledge. Dictionary consultation is normally of a sporadic kind (i.e. obtain a piece of information necessary to answer a specific question).
- Communicative user situations are determined by the need to obtain dictionary assistance when users are engaged in some textual activity, such as reading, writing, translating, or revising.

As far as the adaptation of DiCoInfo to user needs is concerned, two types of assistance were identified—assistance in connection with text production in L2, and assistance with translation from L2 to L1—both belonging to the category of communicative user situations:

1. In a text production situation in L2 a French user is writing an English text on computing and the Internet, and needs access to a collocate (or a group of collocates) to express a given meaning when combined with a specific term which is already present in the mind of the user: e.g. which are the collocates that can be used to express the idea of 'use' when combined with *dialog box*? The method designed for this specific need is dealt with in Section 11.6. It aims to solve the problem of having to force users to go through long lists of collocates when in most cases they are looking for a specific one.

2. In a translation situation from L2 to L1, a French user is translating an English text on computing and the Internet, and needs access to the translation of a

specific collocation, for example the French translation of *send something as an attachment* (*envoyer quelque chose en pièce jointe; transmettre quelque chose en pièce jointe*). Since DiCoInfo is trilingual, needs to access collocations in French or Spanish can also be met. The method devised for this specific need is described in Section 11.7 and seeks to exploit to their full potential the multilingual descriptions of DiCoInfo.

Finally, as we assumed no prior knowledge of Explanatory Combinatorial Lexicology from the user, the two new access paths had to be designed so as not to bother users with questions related to the linguistic properties of terms or collocates.

11.6 Browsing collocations

In order to reduce the time spent going through long lists of collocates and exploit to its full potential the expressiveness of lexical functions, a partially onomasiological access method to collocations was devised (Jousse *et al.* 2011). The method is implemented in the French version of DiCoInfo and will be adapted to English and Spanish in the future.

11.6.1 *The basic concept*

As stated above, the general objective of this new access method is to allow users to access a specific collocate (or a small number of collocates) that expresses a given meaning. Below are typical questions that might be asked and for which our method should be able to provide answers:

Question: Which French verbs express the idea of 'using' a dialog box?
Answer: *activer, afficher, ouvrir une boîte de dialogue*
(English *enable, display, open a dialog box*)
Question: Which verbs express the typical activities carried out by a virus?
Answer: *le virus s'attaque à..., infecte...., endommage...*
(English *the virus attacks..., infects..., damages...*)

Our onomasiological access to collocations is based on the general principle that some collocates can be grouped into larger semantic classes. This proposal was made by Jousse *et al.* (2008) and Jousse (2010) for general language lexical databases but can also be applied with some adaptations to specialized repositories. For instance, in DiCoInfo many different lexical functions convey the meaning of 'use' (Table 11.4). Other frequent meanings expressed by verbal collocates are 'create', 'operate', and 'place somewhere'.

Hence, lexical functions are grouped into intermediate classes according to the meaning they represent and these classes are further organized into more generic ones as shown in Tables 11.5 and 11.6, reading from bottom to top. Each (intermediate and generic) class is then assigned a label in natural language that is supposed to be indicative of the kinds of collocates it contains.

11.6.2 *Implementation*

To ease the organization and management of the classes that resulted from the previous grouping analysis, it was decided to state the lexical functions' membership to classes, as well as intermediate classes' membership to generic ones. The class system was recorded in a separate metadata file that is independent from both the dictionary entries and the program module that searches them, as shown in Figure 11.6.

TABLE 11.4 Collocations that express the meaning of 'use'

Keyword	Collocate	Lexical function	Explanation
dialog box	*open a ~*	Real$_1$	The user uses a d.
program	*quit a ~*	FinReal$_1$	The user stops using a p.
Internet	*browse the ~*	Real$_1$	The user uses the I.
keyboard	*enter . . . on a ~*	Labreal$_{12}$	The user uses a k. to act on the data
account	*access an ~*	IncepReal$_1$	The user starts using an a.
mouse	*click on . . . with a ~*	Labreal$_{12}$	The user uses a m. to act on the icon
mouse	*drag and drop . . . with a ~*	QLabreal$_{12}$	The user uses a m. to act on the icon
blog	*access a blog*	IncepReal$_3$	The user starts using a b.
file	*process a ~*	Real@	Someone or something uses a f.

TABLE 11.5 Grouping of lexical functions for the 'UTILISER / NE PAS UTILISER' generic class

Generic class	UTILISER / NE PAS UTILISER (USE / USE NOT)		
Intermediate classes	Commencer à utiliser / Apparaître (Start using / Appear)	Utiliser /Faire fonctionner (Use / Operate)	Cesser d'utiliser /de faire fonctionner (Stop using/ operating)
Possible explanations	Someone or something starts using	Someone or something uses the keyword; Someone or something uses the keyword to act on something	Someone or something stops using
Lexical functions	IncepLabreal$_{12}$, IncepReal@, IncepReal$_1$, IncepReal$_2$, IncepReal$_3$	Real$_1$, Real@, Real$_2$, Real$_3$, Labreal$_{12}$	FinReal$_1$, FinReal@, Liqu$_1$Fact$_0$

TABLE 11.6 Grouping of lexical functions for the 'FONCTIONNER / FAIRE CE QU'ON ATTEND DE' class

Generic class	FONCTIONNER / FAIRE CE QU'ON ATTEND DE (OPERATE OR DO WHAT IS EXPECTED)	
Intermediate classes	Fonctionner (Operate)	Commencer à fonctionner (Start operating)
Possible explanations	Someone or something operates; Someone or something acts on something	Someone or something starts operating
Lexical functions	Fact$_0$, Fact@	IncepFact$_0$, IncepFact@, De_nouveauIncepFact$_0$

```
<?xml version="1.0" encoding="UTF-8"?>
<HiérarchieDesClasses>
    ...
    <SuperClasse nom="Utiliser / Ne pas utiliser">
      <Classe nom="Commencer à utiliser / Apparaître">
        <Fonction nom="IncepLabreal12"/>
        <Fonction nom="IncepReal@"/>
        <Fonction nom="IncepReal1"/>
        <Fonction nom="IncepReal2"/>
        ...
      </Classe>
      <Classe nom="Utiliser / Faire fonctionner">
        <Fonction nom="Real@"/>
        <Fonction nom="Real1"/>
        <Fonction nom="Real2"/>
        <Fonction nom="Labreal2"/>
        ...
      </Classe>
      <Classe nom="Cesser d'utiliser / De faire fonctionner">
        <Fonction nom="FinReal1"/>
        <Fonction nom="FinReal2"/>
        <Fonction nom="FinLabreal12"/>
        <Fonction nom="Liqu1Fact0"/>
        ...
      </Classe>
      ...
    </SuperClasse>
    ...
</HiérarchieDesClasses>
```

FIGURE 11.6 Lexical functions' membership to classes.

The use of a separate file presents a number of advantages. First, the class system can be managed without having to edit all dictionary files to group or reorganize collocate records. Thus, the implementation, the grouping, and the labelling may be changed at will without interfering with the normal lexicographical work. Lexicographers can continue updating entries without changing their working habits or acquiring new ones. Second, the search module loads the class hierarchy as data without having to know its organization a priori, and then uses it to reorganize entry contents based on the various lexical functions that are found in the entries. Finally, knowing that users might access collocates from different class labels, this design also allows us to classify collocates in more than one intermediate class. This is the case for verbs such as *exporter* (English *to export*) that has a complex meaning: 'to move data' and 'to transform data'.

In the online French version of DiCoInfo, a new link called *Combinatoire lexicale* (English *Lexical combinations*) was added to the displayed entries. When clicking on this link, users are first presented with a list of generic classes; they can then select an intermediate class (Figure 11.7) and eventually access the specific collocates they are looking for along with the natural language explanation of its meaning (Figure 11.8). It is worth mentioning that only those classes that are relevant for a specific term are presented in entries. Hence, although there is a class 'Acquérir' (English 'Acquire'), it does not apply to *blogue* and consequently is not displayed.

11.6.3 *Testing the accessibility of the browsing module*

As mentioned above, one of the main requirements of the changes made to DiCoInfo was to adapt the data access and its presentation in order to cater more efficiently for the specific needs of intended users (i.e. *user-friendly representations* in the title of this

blogue ₁, n. m.

Status: 1

Actantial structure: un blogue : ~ créé par {auteur ₁} dans {Internet ₁} pour offrir {information ₁} à {internaute ₁}
Linguistic realizations of actants
Variant(s): blog
Synonym(s): bloc-notes, carnet Web, joueb, weblog
Contexts
Lexical relations
Combinatoire lexicale
   Créer ou supprimer
      Créer / Faire apparaître
   Posséder / Ne pas posséder
      Avoir / Être muni de
   Transformer
      Mettre ~ à jour
   Utiliser / Ne pas utiliser
      Préparer l'utilisation / Le fonctionnement
      Commencer à utiliser / Apparaître
      Utiliser / Faire fonctionner
   Mettre quelque part
      Ajouter à / Mettre dans
   Autres

FIGURE 11.7 Generic and intermediate classes of collocates appearing in the entry for French *blogue*.

Utiliser / Ne pas utiliser
  Préparer l'utilisation / Le fonctionnement

L'internaute se prépare à utiliser un b.	chercher ₁ un ~ dans Internet
L'internaute se prépare à utiliser un b.	rechercher ₁ un ~ dans Internet

Commencer à utiliser / Apparaître

L'internaute commence à utiliser un b.	aller dans un ~

Utiliser / Faire fonctionner

L'auteur utilise un b.	s'exprimer dans un ~
L'internaute utilise un b.	consulter ₁ un ~
L'internaute utilise un b.	lire un ~
L'internaute utilise un b.	visiter ₁ un ~
Nominalization of "L'internaute utilise un b. "	consultation ₁ d'un ~
Nominalization of "L'internaute utilise un b. "	lecture d'un ~
Nominalization of "L'internaute utilise un b. "	visite ₁ d'un ~
Nominalization of "L'auteur utilise un b. pour interagir avec l'internaute"	blogage ₁ avec ...
L'internaute utilise un b. pour interagir avec l'auteur	bloguer ₁ avec ...
Nominalization of "L'internaute utilise un b. pour interagir avec l'auteur"	blogage ₁ avec ...
L'internaute utilise un b. pour intervenir sur l'information	lire ... dans un ~

FIGURE 11.8 Collocates and general explanations listed under the *Utiliser/Ne pas utiliser* semantic class.

chapter). In order to assess the extent to which this was achieved, we conducted a small-scale pilot study of the usability of the new data presentation (Jousse *et al.* 2011), and for the French data only.

Ten participants were selected from among the intended core users of DiCoInfo (BA students of specialized translation and technical writing at Aarhus University, Denmark, and students in specialized translation at the University of Montreal). Prior to the test, the participants were introduced to the functionalities of DiCoInfo and to the test itself.

The test was designed as a controlled questionnaire. It contained instructions on how to perform specific search tasks and complete the surveys that followed them. The test consisted of performing four search sessions, each divided into several (between five and seven) specific search tasks: searching for syntactic information, meanings, synonyms, collocations, as well as searching for collocates expressing specific meanings.

Upon each completed search task, informants were requested to record the time spent accessing and retrieving the information and to assess the usability of DiCoInfo. As far as searching for collocates expressing specific meanings is concerned, the specific search task in search session 1 *Quels sont les verbes utilisés pour exprimer*

TABLE 11.7 **Distribution of access and retrieval time scores**

	Highest time score	Lowest time score	Average time score
SEARCH SESSION 1	7 min.	0.5 min.	2.8 min.
SEARCH SESSION 2	7 min.	0.5 min.	2.5 min.
SEARCH SESSION 3	5 min.	1 min.	2.3 min.
SEARCH SESSION 4	4 min.	0.5 min.	2.8 min.

l'idée de transformer une fenêtre, ou de la faire fonctionner et l'utiliser? (English *Find verbs that express the following meanings*: 'transform a window', 'use or operate a window') revealed that the lowest time score was 0.5 minutes, which is actually the lowest time score recorded in this session; lowest time scores in the remaining three sessions also concerned searching for collocates, cf. Table 11.7.

We also assessed whether users were satisfied with the new browsing module. The great majority of participants (85 per cent) deemed it satisfactory while 15 per cent expressed strong or moderate dissatisfaction.

Finally, we tested to what extent the new presentation could be accessed quickly and easily. Table 11.7 shows the highest, lowest, and average time scores for each of the four search sequences. The time scores are flatly distributed. There is, however, a striking gap between the highest and the lowest scores, as a few users were fourteen times slower than the quickest users.

These results are, however, indicative of a paradox: users seem to appreciate the new browsing functionalities; in addition, access and retrieval are successful for most of them provided that they are given prior instructions. However, some users fail to retrieve the information or spend much more time doing it. One possible explanation might be that they misinterpreted the instructions given prior to the test on how to perform the specific search tasks. In any case further research is needed.

11.7 Translation of collocations

The last adaptation to the online version of DiCoInfo dealt with in this chapter exploits the language-independence of lexical functions. When adding English and Spanish entries to DiCoInfo, lexicographers assign equivalence relationships at the level of headwords (e.g. *souris* ⇔ *mouse* ⇔ *ratón*) allowing users to access entries dealing with one or the other language. In addition, the interface was adapted in order to access an entry from a specific language or to all entries regardless of the language to which they belong. Users can also retrieve equivalents directly or deactivate this option (Figure 11.9).

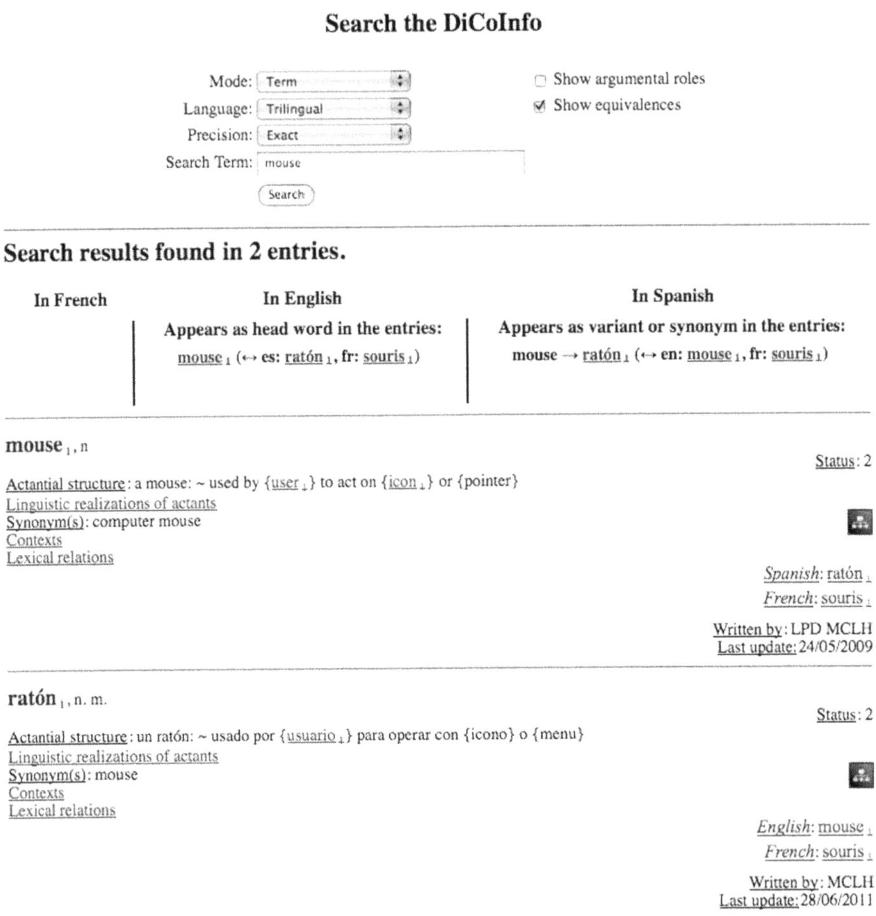

Search the DiCoInfo

Mode: [Term   ⬍]   ☐ Show argumental roles
Language: [Trilingual   ⬍]   ☑ Show equivalences
Precision: [Exact   ⬍]
Search Term: [mouse   ]

(Search)

Search results found in 2 entries.

In French	In English	In Spanish
	Appears as head word in the entries:	**Appears as variant or synonym in the entries:**
	mouse ₁ (↔ es: ratón ₁, fr: souris ₁)	mouse → ratón ₁ (↔ en: mouse ₁, fr: souris ₁)

---

mouse ₁, n   Status: 2

Actantial structure: a mouse: ~ used by {user ₁} to act on {icon ₁} or {pointer}
Linguistic realizations of actants
Synonym(s): computer mouse
Contexts
Lexical relations

Spanish: ratón ₁
French: souris ₁

Written by: LPD MCLH
Last update: 24/05/2009

---

ratón ₁, n. m.   Status: 2

Actantial structure: un ratón: ~ usado por {usuario ₁} para operar con {icono} o {menu}
Linguistic realizations of actants
Synonym(s): mouse
Contexts
Lexical relations

English: mouse ₁
French: souris ₁

Written by: MCLH
Last update: 28/06/2011

FIGURE 11.9 *Mouse and its equivalents.*

It soon appeared interesting to link equivalents not only at the level of headwords, but also to display all the potential equivalences that could be established between entries in different languages at the level of lexical relations (L'Homme *et al.* 2010).

11.7.1 *Basic concept*

The objective of the new access method was to allow users to type an expression longer than a headword and retrieve its translations in the other languages appearing in DiCoInfo. Concretely, our method is designed to provide users with the possibility of entering an English expression such as *send something as an attachment* and retrieve the information necessary to produce the equivalent French translation *envoyer quelque chose en pièce jointe*. In addition, the retrieval function should find

TABLE 11.8 **Establishing equivalence relations with lexical function encoding**

Keyword	Collocation	Lexical function	Explanation
keyboard	*enter...on a ~, type...*	$Labreal_{12}$	The user uses a k. to act on the data
teclado	*introducir...a través de un ~*	$Labreal_{12}$	El usuario utiliza un t. para operar con los datos
clavier	*entrer...au clavier, saisir...au clavier, taper...*	$Labreal_{12}$	L'utilisateur utilise un c. pour intervenir sur les données
mouse	*move a mouse*	$Real_1$	The user uses a m.
souris	*déplacer, manipuler, faire glisser une ~*	$Real_1$	L'utilisateur utilise une s.
mouse	*click on...with a ~*	$Labreal_{12}$	The user uses a m. to act on the icon
souris	*cliquer sur...avec une ~*	$Labreal_{12}$	L'utilisateur utilise une s. pour intervenir sur l'icône

more than one translation if available in the database. For instance, *move a mouse* can be translated into French with *déplacer une souris*, *manipuler une souris*, and *faire glisser une souris*; similarly *delete a file* can be translated into Spanish as *borrar*, *eliminar*, and *suprimir un archivo*. We also wanted to prevent users from having to go through the entire lists of collocates encoded under the entries of the two languages involved. Finally, the method should establish correspondences between translations of collocations without having to manually assign these translations when writing the entries.

The solution was quite simple to design since all collocations are encoded with the same lexical functions regardless of the language described, as shown in Table 11.8. The equivalence relationships can be established between collocations in different languages provided that they appear in the database.

11.7.2 *Implementation*

The general computational strategy devised to find translations of expressions is quite straightforward. First, when finding entries that fulfil a query for a collocate, the entry of the equivalent of the headword is also retrieved. Then the lexical functions chosen to encode the collocates in both languages are checked in order to validate that they are identical. The two steps of the search strategy are shown in Figures 11.10 and 11.11.

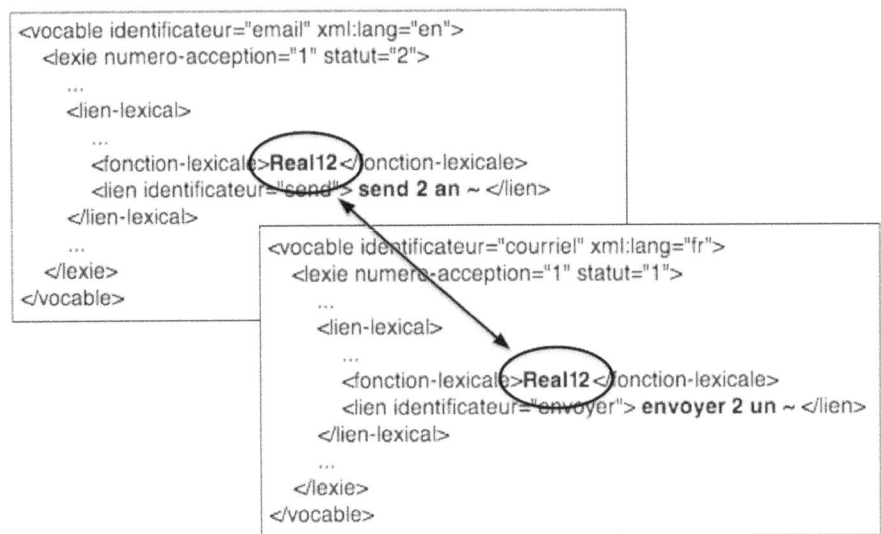

FIGURE 11.10 Finding the equivalents of collocates in the entries.

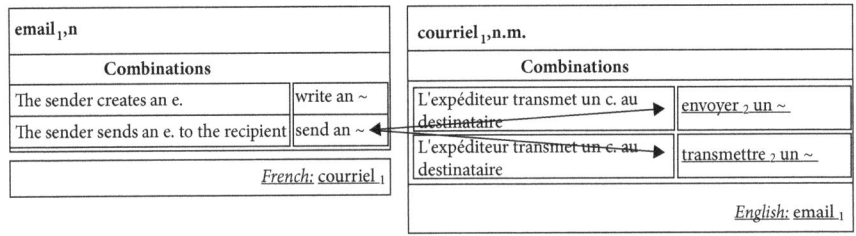

FIGURE 11.11 Linking the equivalents in the interface.

Having the means to search for equivalents of collocates, it was fairly simple to further extend the search capabilities to find complex expressions made of headwords and collocates. Instead of matching the user's query against headwords or collocates, the match direction of this search is reversed to find entries where both the headword and at least one collocate in an entry match different parts of the searched expression. This general strategy allows us to retrieve combinations that contain more than one collocation. As shown in Figure 11.12, searching for the French expression *copier un fichier sur une clé USB* (English *copy a file on a USB pen drive*) will return the two following sub-expressions: *copier₁ un ~ sur...* (from the entry *fichier₁*) and *copier₁... sur une ~* (from the entry *clé USB₁*).

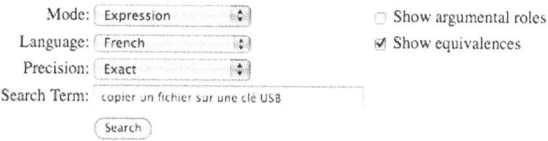

Search the DiCoInfo

Mode: [Expression ⇕]   ○ Show argumental roles
Language: [French ⇕]   ☑ Show equivalences
Precision: [Exact ⇕]
Search Term: copier un fichier sur une clé USB

(Search)

Search results found in 3 entries.

This expression is described in the following entries:

clé USB₁: *copier₁ ... sur une ~* (L'utilisateur met les données ou le logiciel sur une c.)

fichier₁: *copier₁ un ~ sur ...* (L'utilisateur met un f. sur un support de stockage)
   (↔ en: file₁: *backup₁ a ~* (The user places a f. on a storage device))
   (↔ en: file₁: *copy₁ a ~ to ...* (The user places a f. on a storage device))
   (↔ en: file₁: *save₁ a ~ to ...* (The user places a f. on a storage device))
   (↔ es: archivo₁: *copiar un ~ en ...* (El usuario pone un a. en un soporte de almacenamiento))
   (↔ es: archivo₁: *guardar₁ un ~ en ...* (El usuario pone un a. en un sorporte de almacenamiento))

fichier₁: *copier₁ un ~ dans ...* (L'utilisateur met un f. sur un support de stockage)
   (↔ en: file₁: *backup₁ a ~* (The user places a f. on a storage device))
   (↔ en: file₁: *copy₁ a ~ to ...* (The user places a f. on a storage device))
   (↔ en: file₁: *save₁ a ~ to ...* (The user places a f. on a storage device))
   (↔ es: archivo₁: *copiar un ~ en ...* (El usuario pone un a. en un soporte de almacenamiento))
   (↔ es: archivo₁: *guardar₁ un ~ en ...* (El usuario pone un a. en un sorporte de almacenamiento))

fichier₁: *copier₁ ... dans un ~* (L'utilisateur met les données dans un f.)

FIGURE 11.12 Translation for collocations found in the French expression *copier un fichier sur une clé USB*.

11.8 Conclusion

This chapter presented different kinds of adaptations made to an online specialized dictionary in order to improve the access to the data it contains and its presentation. Some of these changes (translation of collocations, browsing of collocates) were defined according to specific user needs (text production and translation); others were developed in order to hide parts of the formal linguistic system used to write the entries. We attempted to show that dictionaries that contain rich linguistic information encoded with a formal system can still become user-friendly tools.

One of the most interesting achievements of this work is that the changes did not affect the current structure of the database. They do require programming at the levels of accessing the correct data and presenting it in the interface. Otherwise, the new access and presentation methods exploit existing information without altering its richness or the way it is stored and encoded. In addition, it only slightly affects the working habits of lexicographers. The only exception to this rule is the use of natural language explanations (to translate the meaning of lexical functions) that represents an addition to the existing data categories.

Of course, more changes can be made to DiCoInfo. In line with similar endeavours (Verlinde *et al.* 2006), other adaptations can be designed in order to reduce the amount of information presented in specific displays, and simplify the metalanguage that still appears in various parts of the entries (e.g. actantial structure, linguistic realizations of actants). We have started working in this direction by adding a conversion module that will allow users to visualize typical terms in various parts of the entry (for the time being, they appear in the actantial structure and the natural language explanations). Moreover, in order to improve usability, we plan to add interactive online instructions as well as a graphical search interface. We also plan to design a more user-friendly presentation of contextual annotations in the near future. This data category remains rather technical and could certainly be improved; this could be achieved with simple methods.

We will also gather more systematic user feedback on the changes made to the database. Therefore, we will conduct comprehensive usability tests in real use situations. This will be done in connection with cognitive user situations, in which users experience knowledge gaps and need to consult DiCoInfo to solve these problems. The tests are designed in order to see to what extent students taking a course in terminology find DiCoInfo useful to perform practical exercises; in other words, they mimic normal learning situations in terminology. They focus on dictionary-using context, and satisfy the criteria of the so-called natural situation as formulated by Lew (2011b) in his description of the *naturalistic* paradigm in the field of user studies. The data gathered should give a qualitative account of the usability of DiCoInfo and help us improve both the access to its data and the presentation of the dictionary.

Finally, the lexicographical work is an ongoing process and the coverage of English and Spanish should increase in the upcoming years. One of the challenges is to implement these changes simultaneously in the three language versions.

Acknowledgements

Part of the development of DiCoInfo is supported by Canadian funding organizations (Social Sciences and Humanities Research Council, SSHRC; Fonds de recherche sur la société et la culture, FQRSC). The authors would like to thank the lexicography team of DiCoInfo and more specifically Anne-Laure Jousse, who helped develop the model for browsing collocations.

Potentials and challenges of WordNet-based pedagogical lexicography: The Transpoetika Dictionary

TOMA TASOVAC

12.1 Introduction

Dictionaries are efficient randomizers of meaning. By grouping lexemes according to their orthography, rather than their sense, standard dictionaries adhere to the abstract convention of alphabetical order, scattering words with similar or related meaning across unpredictable distances. Looking up entries—especially in electronic resources—is easy, if one knows what word one is looking for. Discovering unfamiliar words, however, is considerably more difficult.

In 1985, a group of linguists and psychologists at Princeton University began developing a reference aid that would help users search for information in traditional dictionaries conceptually rather than alphabetically (Miller 1985). As the work proceeded, the authors transformed their initial idea into a more ambitious project for a new dictionary that would overcome the limitations of sense-defying alphabetization (Miller *et al.* 1993). The result was WordNet, a comprehensive, open-sourced, machine-readable lexical database of the English language inspired by psycholinguistic theories of human lexical memory.

Today, WordNet is by far "the widest used language resource in Natural Language Processing" (Vossen, in press) and has become the cornerstone of numerous computational projects ranging from text analysis and word-sense disambiguation to question and answer (Q&A) and search-engine query expansion. Yet its innovative conceptual architecture has not been widely accepted in pedagogical lexicography or eLearning—two scholarly areas that could greatly benefit from WordNet's quest to map out human lexical knowledge.

In this chapter, I argue that WordNet can serve not only as a general lexicographic framework for building dictionaries for pedagogic purposes, but that it can, in fact, help traditional lexicographers and researchers in Natural Language Processing (NLP) bridge the disciplinary and communicative gap that, despite the booming field of eLexicography, continues to separate them. A secondary objective of this chapter is to demonstrate how WordNet's open-source licence and robust framework can be used as a basis for projects without steady academic or commercial funding, and by those dealing with lesser-taught and lesser-resourced languages, such as Serbian.

Mainstream Serbian lexicography seriously lags behind developments in eLexicography. Neither the still only half-way finished, massive *Dictionary of the Serbian Literary and Folkloric Language* (*САНУ* 1959), nor the six-volume *Dictionary of the Serbo-Croatian Literary Language* (*MC* 1967), nor its bulky, oversized one-volume counterpart (*MC* 2007), have been made available in electronic format, either on- or offline. The computational resources being developed at the University of Belgrade (Krstev *et al.* 2008, Obradović and Stanković 2008) have not been used to produce human-oriented dictionaries. And while an increasing number of scholars is working on a range of topics in Serbian as L2, lexicographic resources are still too few and mostly theoretical.[1]

The original idea for what became the Transpoetika Dictionary emerged from the evident need for digital resources to help teach and learn Serbian as a foreign or inherited language. Our initial project was to create online editions of Serbian literary works for intermediate or advanced students, but it soon became clear that such an enterprise was unthinkable without a dedicated, Internet-based lexicographic resource (Tasovac 2005).

In Section 12.2, I discuss the specifics of WordNet's complex lexical architecture. Section 12.3 explores the interfaces between WordNet and human-oriented lexicography, more particularly pedagogical and bilingual lexicography. In Section 12.4, I present the Transpoetika Dictionary, a general-purpose, WordNet-based Serbian-English pedagogical dictionary, which shows that the actual potential of relational lexical databases by far exceeds their exclusive application in language engineering and automatic text processing. My goal here is threefold: (1) to examine the peculiarities of building a WordNet-based learner's dictionary of the Serbian language; (2) to

---

[1] The specification of a Council of Europe threshold level of language proficiency for the Serbian language, for instance, was completed in 2002, but the results of this research project were never published. On the project itself, see van Ek and Trim (1991), Суботић (2004), and Vasić *et al.* (2008). For the principles of designing a minimal dictionary of Serbian as L2, see Dražić (2008); for a model of a learner's explanatory-combinatorial dictionary, see Milićević (2008); and on Serbian as L2, in general, see Дешић (2007) and Golubović and Raecke (2008).

analyse the main advantages and disadvantages of using WordNet as a model; and (3) to stress the need for refining and expanding core WordNet features in pedagogical contexts. In the concluding section, I suggest future prospects for WordNet's successful integration into pedagogical lexicography.

12.2 WordNet architecture

As a network of semantic relations between concepts that are lexically expressed in groups of cognitively equivalent synonyms, WordNet formally represents the way lexical knowledge is organized in the human mind: it is a computational approximation of our 'mental lexicon' (Singleton 1999, Aitchison 2003, Bonin 2004). More generally speaking, WordNet renders explicit what linguistics have known at least since Saussure: language is a system of negatively distinguishable, purely differential relations, in which each element is defined by its place in the system as a whole, and by the relations it maintains with other elements.

The basic unit of WordNet is a 'synset', i.e. a set of synonyms expressing one underlying concept. For example, the synset {*car, auto, automobile, machine, motor car*} consists of five lexemes, each of which corresponds to the concept of 'a motor vehicle with four wheels'. Nouns in WordNet are organized as topical hierarchies with lexical inheritance based on taxonomic relations such as hyponymy (i.e. an IS-A relationship such as a 'dog' is an 'animal') and meronymy (i.e. PART-WHOLE relationship such as a 'nose' is part of a 'face'). The WordNet synset {*car, auto, automobile, machine, motor car*}, for example, is a hyponym of the synset {*motor vehicle, automotive vehicle* (a self-propelled wheeled vehicle that does not run on rails)}. As hyponyms of *motor vehicle*, *car* and its synonyms inherit all the semantic properties of the more general term. At the same time, the car-synset is related to a series of part-meronyms such as {*car door*}, {*car mirror*}, or {*car seat*}. It is impossible for a lexical item in WordNet to stand on its own: it is always related to other items.

Adjectives and adverbs in WordNet are classified on the basis of binary oppositions (antonyms). Antonymy is a reciprocal relationship between words, not concepts: *heavy* and *weighty* may express the same concept, but each word forms its own antonym pair: *heavy/light* and *weighty/weightless*. Verbs, on the other hand, are linked through a variety of entailment relations. Troponymy is similar to hyponymy. To babble is to talk in a certain manner: hence, *babble* is a troponym of *talk*. Some verbs are related by causal entailment: it is impossible to kill somebody without that person dying, hence *kill* entails *die*, etc.

Despite the essential difference between lexicons (as linguistic objects) and ontologies (as language-independent formal representations of knowledge), WordNet is a computational lexicon with an ontological bent. Word senses in WordNet can be seen as equivalent to ontological categories, while lexical relations can be compared to ontological relations: hyperonymy, for instance, corresponds to subsumption (i.e.

an IS-A relationship) (Hirst 2004, Toral *et al.* 2008). There is a growing body of NLP research that explores precisely the interaction between lexically based ontologies and ontologically based lexicons (Huang *et al.* 2010).

WordNet's advantage over traditional dictionaries is that it treats all meanings as relational: its logical structure and explicitly defined relations make it easier for computer algorithms to process, revise, and expand lexical knowledge in various types of language-processing applications. And while it is true that traditional machine-readable dictionaries (MRD) can also contain information on lexical and semantic relations, usually only a small portion of them, if any, are explicitly encoded (Peters and Kilgarriff 2000).

The extraction of meaning from conventional dictionaries is to a considerable extent predicated upon human pragmatic knowledge. Even when some semantic relations, such as synonymy and antonymy, are explicitly expressed in a traditional dictionary, their explicitness does not necessarily guarantee consistency. If word sense S1 of lexeme L1 is marked as being synonymous with word sense S2 of lexeme L2, the bidirectional nature of synonymy would require a reverse reference point in lexeme L2. But precisely this kind of symmetry is not always enforced in traditional lexicographic sources (Müller-Spitzer 2010a).

The same can be said of *implicit* lexical-semantic relations in traditional dictionaries that can be inferred from dictionary definitions. When the *Oxford Advanced Learner's Dictionary* defines *sparrow* as "a small brown and grey bird, common in many parts of the world," it implies that *bird* is a hypernym of *sparrow*. The entry under *bird*, however, does not point back to *sparrow* or any other hyponym of *bird*.

12.3 WordNet and human-oriented lexicography

I use the term 'human-oriented' lexicography (De Schryver 2003) to distinguish the theorizing and production of dictionaries for human use from the efforts to produce machine-readable lexicons to be employed for strictly language engineering purposes. Human-oriented lexicography is no longer imaginable without computer technology (Hockey 2000, Knowles 1989, Meijs 1992). The availability of easily searchable large corpora, the study of linguistic patterns and coverage of collocational features, and the advent of the Internet as a platform for the distribution of social knowledge have already radically altered lexicographic practice. However, the mere use of computers in producing a dictionary or delivering it electronically does not automatically transform a dictionary from "a simple artefact" to a "more complex lexical architecture" (Sinclair 1991b: 193).

From the outset, WordNet was intended to be a new kind of dictionary that could make a significant contribution to human-oriented lexicography by overcoming the shortcomings of standard alphabetical procedures for organizing lexical information. These have been shown to turn many people away from dictionaries, because "finding the information [in traditional dictionaries] would interrupt their work and break their train of thought" (Miller *et al.* 1993: 1). It was compiled on the assumption that "a more effective combination of traditional lexicographic information and modern high-speed computation" could turn an electronic dictionary into something more than a "rapid page-turner" of digitized print dictionaries (p. 1). Almost two decades later, the persistent dependence on the print model continues to be a limiting factor in the field of eLexicography, resulting in what Sven Tarp has called the "lack of real visions and fantasy in the conception of electronic dictionaries, which are more or less produced as exact copies of their printed counterparts" (Tarp 2009a: 21).

By listing lexemes based on their conceptual affinity rather than on abstract, alphabetical order, WordNet belongs to a long and venerable line of onomasiological lexicons (Hartmann 2005b, Hüllen 2005). As a born-digital resource, however, WordNet manages relational complexity at a level of consistency and detail that would have been highly impractical if not altogether impossible in the pre-digital age. It is both more and less than a dictionary. It does not contain some of the features that are often expected from a human-oriented lexicographic resource (e.g. definitions of all parts of speech, not just nouns, verbs, adjectives, and adverbs; pronunciation; word stress; collocations and usage notes). On the other hand, WordNet's positioning of lexical items in a rich network of lexical and semantic relations creates new and original paths for users to access lexical material (Tasovac 2009).

Users can consult the WordNet database in the shape of a free online dictionary. The interface is rather basic, but it provides access to the full range of WordNet functionalities (see Figure 12.1). Searching for a word retrieves a list of senses, and each sense contains hyperlinks to its corresponding semantic relations. With a mouse click, it is possible to retrieve not only the direct hypernyms or hyponyms of a particular synset, but also the inherited hypernyms (chains of superordinate terms leading to one of the top basic concepts) and full hyponyms (chains of subordinate terms). The inherited hypernyms of *sparrow* are: *passerine* → *bird* → *vertebrate* → *chordate* → *animal* → *organism* → *living thing* → *whole* → *object* → *physical entity* → *entity*. Another useful function is the availability of sister terms, i.e. coordinate words that share the same hypernym: sister terms of *January*, for instance, include all the months of the year.

WordNet definitions are also featured in several online dictionary portals including Google's English Dictionary and The Free Dictionary. Additionally, the WordNet dataset is also used in the commercially available Visual Thesaurus and the open-sourced Visuwords projects, which illustrate relationships between words by means of force-directed graphs with elastic, spring-like edges and movable nodes.

The fact that WordNet is not more widely accepted in the field of human-oriented lexicography—despite its presence on the Internet in multiple incarnations—is indicative of a disciplinary and communicative gap between scholars working on language resources (LR) and NLP, on the one hand, and those involved in

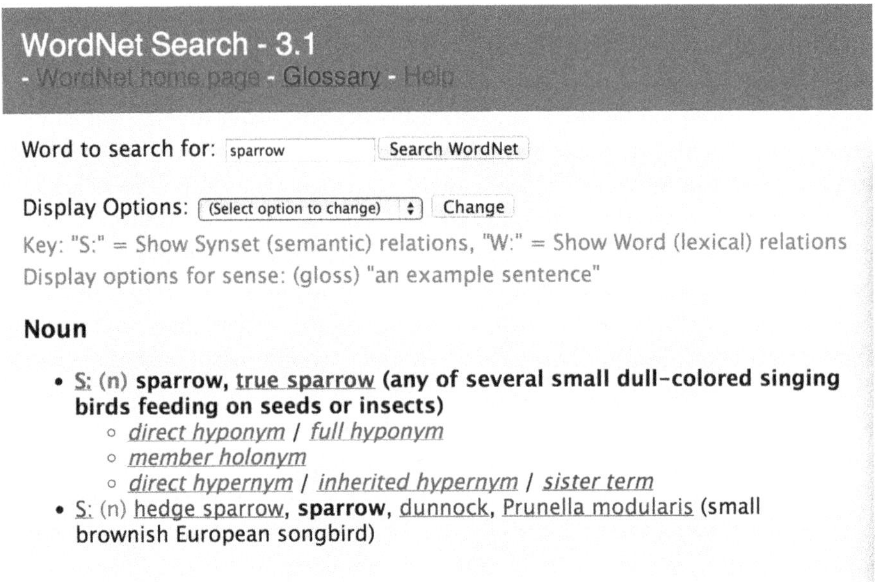

WordNet Search - 3.1

- WordNet home page - Glossary - Help

Word to search for: sparrow   [Search WordNet]

Display Options: [(Select option to change) ⬍] [Change]

Key: "S:" = Show Synset (semantic) relations, "W:" = Show Word (lexical) relations
Display options for sense: (gloss) "an example sentence"

Noun

- **S:** (n) **sparrow**, <u>true sparrow</u> **(any of several small dull-colored singing birds feeding on seeds or insects)**
  - ○ *direct hyponym* | *full hyponym*
  - ○ *member holonym*
  - ○ *direct hypernym* | *inherited hypernym* | *sister term*
- **S:** (n) <u>hedge sparrow</u>, **sparrow**, <u>dunnock</u>, <u>Prunella modularis</u> (small brownish European songbird)

FIGURE 12.1 Entry for *sparrow* in Princeton WordNet Online.

human-oriented lexicography, on the other. Yet there is little doubt that the two communities can successfully work together, as attested by the field of language for specific purposes (LSP) lexicography. Domain-specific onomasiological lexicons for both human and machine use are becoming increasingly common (see, for instance, the large-scale terminological and lexical BioLexicon (Quochi *et al.* 2009), or the ambitious, environmentally focused KYOTO project (Vossen *et al.* 2008a)).

   In pedagogical lexicography, studies have shown that providing sets of semantically related words in a dictionary entry can help language learners understand meaning and improve memorization (Geckeler 2002, Kremer *et al.* 2008). The importance of indicating lexical and semantic relations between words in learners' dictionaries has been noted in the lexicographic literature (Rundell 2008) and implemented, to a limited degree, in print dictionaries such as the *Longman Language Activator* (*LLA*) and the *Cambridge Word Routes*. The LLA, for instance, lists 1,052 concepts or 'key words' as entry points for the exploration of semantic fields associated with these words. The user searching for a word to express a particular thought is expected to look up a more general, but familiar, concept and then proceed with the help of this production-oriented dictionary. For example, if the user is looking for the correct word to express the idea of walking quietly in an attempt not to be heard by anybody, he or she will be expected to consult the key word *walk*. The entry for *walk* is divided into nineteen semantic fields, each distinguished by its own short definition. One of these semantic fields is for verbs related to the concept 'to walk quietly with light steps'. This field covers the verbs *pad, creep, tiptoe,* and *sneak*. Each of these lexemes is presented with a more detailed definition and examples of usage. The *Cambridge Word Routes* series employs a similar strategy but in a bilingual context: the dictionary offers access to thematic groups of L2 words using L1 keys, then explains these words in greater detail in the L1. In the French-English edition of the series, for instance, the user looks up the section for the verb *marcher* ('to walk'), then finds a subsection for *marcher sans se faire remarquer* ('to walk without being noticed'), and within that subsection explores entries for the English verbs *creep, crawl, prowl,* and *tiptoe* (McCarthy 1994: 333). These two dictionaries, however, cover only a limited segment of the L2 vocabulary and neither has a systematic approach to documenting semantic relations.

Computational linguists have created Wordnets[2] in languages other than English and raised a big, happy family of machine-readable lexical resources. Mutually aligned Wordnets have become indispensable resources for developing multilingual search engines and network-based classification. But these resources and their underlying principles of lexical organization have made few definitive inroads into pedagogical lexicography in general, and pedagogical bilingual lexicography in particular.

That is not to say that WordNet-like machine-readable relational databases have not had an impact on language learning as such. Selva *et al.* (1997) have used semantic relations between lexemes in their ALEXIA environment for learning French as a foreign language to enhance the selection of relevant information and to improve the efficiency of usage. ALEXIA is a computer assisted language learning (CALL) application consisting of a corpus of texts and a WordNet-inspired general dictionary. Every lexeme in the dictionary lists different semantic relations (quasi-synonymy, hypernymy, hyponymy, intersective synonymy, antonymy, etc.) and links to other lexemes.

Manning *et al.* (2001) have demonstrated how language users can benefit from a visual interface displaying a network of words and their relationship in a multimedia, hypertext system. The authors created a visual interface for a semantic network for Warlpiri, an Australian Aboriginal language, and subsequently tested the system with language learners. They concluded that the "opportunistic exploration of networks of related words seems to be able to capture and maintain attention" (Manning *et al.* 2001: 147). WordNet itself has also been employed in learning environments: for instance, as a tool to evaluate a student's command of a given language (Hu and Graesser 1998); as a component in the development of a suite of programs to help Chinese learners of English become better writers (Milton and Cheng 2010); and as a

---

[2] By convention, WordNet (capital W, capital N) is used to refer to the original, English-language lexical database. Wordnets in other languages drop the capital N.

semantic resource for improving the quality of distractors in the automatic generation of multiple-choice questions in Basque (Aldabe and Maritxalar 2010).

A Danish lexical resource (ordnet.dk) consisting of two dictionaries, one historical
and one modern, has been integrated with a reference corpus and a Wordnet to offer,
among other features, new look-up possibilities and a 'related words' function that is
"particularly useful for language production and for (advanced) language learning
purposes" (Trap-Jensen 2010b: 304). Ordnet.dk uses hierarchical data from DanNet,
the Danish-language version of WordNet, to offer a thesaurus-like function for
entries from the *Den Danske Ordbog* ('The Danish Dictionary', *DDO*) at three
different levels: more general words (hypernyms); more specific words (hyponyms);
and, finally, co-hyponyms or sister terms. As shown in Figure 12.2, an entry for
computer, for instance, contains links to *apparat* as a more general word; *terminal*,
desktop, and *personlig computer*, among others, as hyponyms; and *cd-rom-brænder*,
overheadprojektor, and *spillekonsol* as sister terms.

The Japanese WordNet, which was created by automatically translating lexemes
and definitions from English WordNet, is being manually corrected and expanded
with the goal of becoming an accessible and useful tool not only for NLP but also for

FIGURE 12.2 Entry for *computer* in the Danish lexical resource Ordnet.dk.

language education and linguistic research (Bond *et al.* 2009). The authors are increasing coverage by adding new Japanese concepts, annotating text corpora, and establishing links to other resources, such as the Suggested Upper Merged Ontology (SUMO), GoiTaikei, a Japanese lexicon, and a collection of pictures from the Open Clip Art Library (Phillips 2005) (see Figure 12.3). Furthermore, the Hindi WordNet (Chakrabarty *et al.* 2002, Sinha *et al.* 2006) is, according to its authors, already extensively used in Indian schools as a resource for language teaching and pedagogy (Bhattacharyya *et al.*, n.d.).

Despite these notable exceptions, it is surprising that more fully fledged WordNet-based bilingual resources for pedagogical purposes have not been created. As early as 1992, the WordNet authors discussed bilingual lexical matrices and vocabulary learning with online semantic networks, suggesting that "much of the structural information omitted from conventional vocabulary instruction could be provided by semantic networks like WordNet" and that "semantic networks designed along the lines of WordNet might be valuable aids in mastering the vocabulary of a foreign language" (Miller and Fellbaum 1992: 100).

The absence of WordNet-based projects in bilingual pedagogical lexicography can be explained by several factors. First, none of the Wordnets in other languages have

Figure 12.3 Entry for *seal* in Japanese WordNet.

matched the comprehensiveness of the original English WordNet. Second, many Wordnets developed for other languages are not available as free resources. And, finally, aligning complex lexical databases is inherently difficult. If monolingual mapping between words and concepts in a hierarchical system introduces a first order of complexity to a lexicographic project, cross-lingual mapping between word/ concept pairs adds a second order of complexity, which is anything but trivial.

There are two general approaches to building cross-lingual Wordnets: the so-called 'merge approach', whereby a specific-language Wordnet is built from scratch and then aligned to other Wordnets via an Inter-Lingual Index (ILI) (Vossen 1998), and the so-called 'expand approach', which starts from the English WordNet, and then maps meanings of a different language onto it (Bentivogli *et al.* 2002). In NLP contexts, WordNet architecture has been used in multilingual projects like Euro-WordNet (Vossen 1998), BalkaNet (Stamou *et al.* 2002, Tufis *et al.* 2004), and Indo-WordNet (Sinha *et al.* 2006). Cross-linguistic issues, such as representing natural gender (Ordan and Wintner 2005), dealing with lexical gaps (Bentivogli and Pianta 2000, Bentivogli *et al.* 2002, Bentivogli and Pianta 2003), or handling language-specific concepts (Крстев 2004, Krstev *et al.* 2006) are well documented and serve as a firm basis for detecting the pitfalls of basing a bilingual pedagogical resource on WordNet.

12.4 The Transpoetika Dictionary

The Transpoetika Dictionary is a collaborative, open-access bilingualized Serbian-English learners' dictionary aligned with Princeton WordNet (Tasovac 2009).[3] Aimed primarily at students of Serbian as a second or inherited language, Transpoetika is being developed at the Belgrade Centre for Digital Humanities and is part of a scalable, web-based, digital framework for editing and publishing annotated, fully-glossed study editions of literary works in Serbian. In this section, I focus on the two distinguishing characteristics of the Transpoetika Dictionary: Section 12.4.1 describes the role of WordNet as Transpoetika's semantic basis, while Section 12.4.2 illustrates how Transpoetika reaches beyond WordNet's limits by harnessing the powers of the Internet and Web 2.0.

---

[3] Technically, Transpoetika is both an online dictionary and a custom-made web-based dictionary writing system. Modelled as a tree-like structure in XML, in accordance with the Guidelines of the Text Encoding Initiative (TEI 2007), each individual piece of information is assigned an individual tag to reflect its explicit semantics (Kunze and Lemnitzer 2007, Lemnitzer *et al.* 2010). The XML model was translated into a MySQL database structure and connected to a PHP-run front-end. WordNet's lexicographer files were also translated into MySQL tables, forming the integral part of the system. Thanks to the employment of user profiles with different sets of privileges, the dictionary front-end can be used both for consulting the dictionary and for editing it. In the editing process, Web 2.0 AJAX technologies make it easy to edit a great number of functions 'in-place', i.e. directly on the web page.

12.4.1 *Transpoetika: integrating WordNet*

WordNet represents the core semantic component of the Transpoetika Dictionary: it is used for sense differentiation, definitions, and English translation equivalents based on the 'expand approach' described above. Serbian synsets are manually aligned with WordNet. If WordNet is missing an equivalent for a particular Serbian synset, a new English synset is created and added to the WordNet database. For instance, the Serbian synset {зимљив, зимогрожљив, зимогрозан, зимоморан (осетљив на хладноћу)} is aligned with a non-lexicalized English synset {sensitive to cold}. As a pedagogical dictionary, however, Transpoetika includes a wider range of features than WordNet does on its own. For example, Transpoetika encodes all parts of speech and uses morphosyntactic descriptors that fully describe grammatical phenomena in Serbian, including gender, number, verbal aspect, and reflexivity.[4]

Figure 12.4 shows that the dictionary entry for the lemma *зима* ('zima') contains three senses. For each sense, a definition is provided in Serbian followed by example sentences. Mousing over the Serbian monolingual definition displays a tooltip containing the same definition in English. The English glosses stem directly from WordNet and the Serbian glosses have been manually translated from English.

Each definition is followed by the translation equivalents in English, i.e. members of the corresponding English synset. In the default entry view, each sense shows its hypernym, while mousing over the hypernym reveals its definition. The user can click on a number of buttons ('sister terms', 'hyponyms', 'meronyms', and 'holonyms') for information about other semantic relations for each sense. Clicking on the sister terms for the first sense of *зима* (i.e. 'winter, wintertime') reveals the Serbian words *пролеће* ('proleće', 'spring'), *лето* ('leto', 'summer'), *јесен* ('jesen', 'autumn'). Moving the mouse over the label for the relations shows a tooltip explaining the nature of the semantic relation. Additionally, each sense is marked by an indicator of its semantic domain, i.e. an area of knowledge to which the given linguistic expression belongs by virtue of its meaning. The three senses of *зима* belong to three different domains: TIME PERIOD (for the sense 'the coldest season'), MEDICINE (for 'the sensation produced by low temperatures') and PHYSICS (for 'the absence of heat'). Transpoetika adopts a language-independent mapping system of the WordNet domain hierarchy (Magnini and Cavaglia 2000, Bentivogli *et al.* 2004) to automatically assign domains to Serbian synsets based on their alignment with

---

[4] Each entry in Transpoetika is also linked to the Serbian MorphoSyntax database (SMS), which contains all the forms of the lemma marked with an appropriate tag indicating its classificatory and inflectional features. The SMS database makes it possible to search for Transpoetika dictionary entries in their oblique forms, which is essential for a morphologically rich language like Serbian. The user can also retrieve all forms related to an entry and display full declensions or conjugations with a mouse click. Moving the mouse over individual word forms in the morphological view reveals the fully expanded MSD annotation.

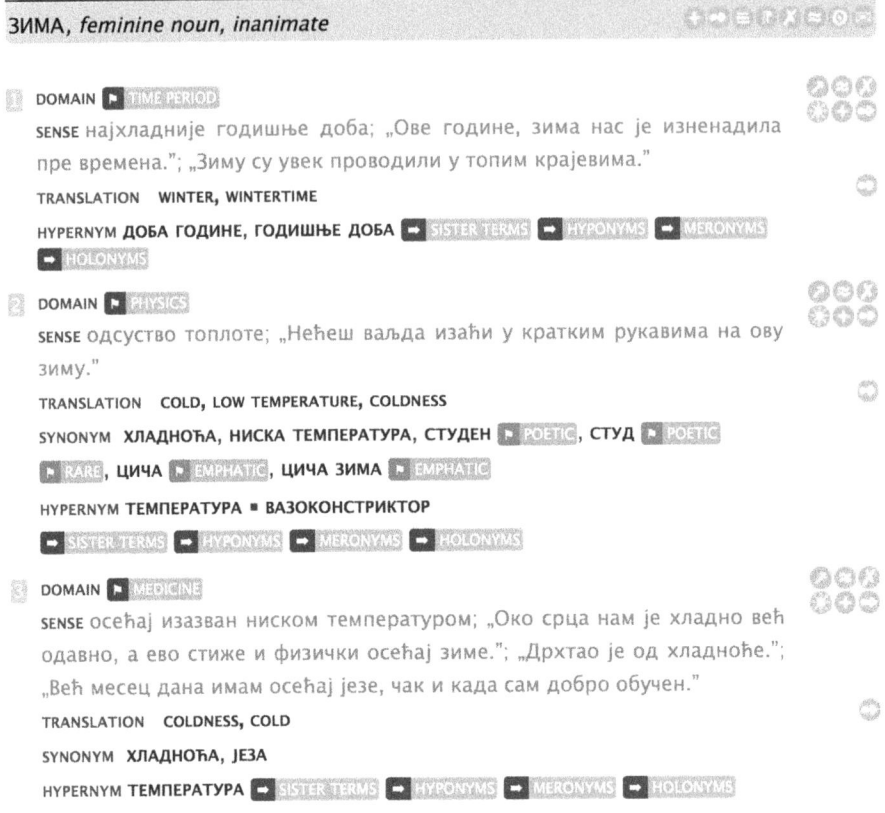

ЗИМА, *feminine noun, inanimate*

① DOMAIN ▶ TIME PERIOD

SENSE најхладније годишње доба; „Ове године, зима нас је изненадила пре времена."; „Зиму су увек проводили у топим крајевима."

TRANSLATION   WINTER, WINTERTIME

HYPERNYM ДОБА ГОДИНЕ, ГОДИШЊЕ ДОБА ➡ SISTER TERMS ➡ HYPONYMS ➡ MERONYMS ➡ HOLONYMS

② DOMAIN ▶ PHYSICS

SENSE одсуство топлоте; „Нећеш ваљда изаћи у кратким рукавима на ову зиму."

TRANSLATION   COLD, LOW TEMPERATURE, COLDNESS

SYNONYM ХЛАДНОЋА, НИСКА ТЕМПЕРАТУРА, СТУДЕН ▶ POETIC, СТУД ▶ POETIC ▶ RARE, ЦИЧА ▶ EMPHATIC, ЦИЧА ЗИМА ▶ EMPHATIC

HYPERNYM ТЕМПЕРАТУРА ∎ ВАЗОКОНСТРИКТОР ➡ SISTER TERMS ➡ HYPONYMS ➡ MERONYMS ➡ HOLONYMS

③ DOMAIN ▶ MEDICINE

SENSE осећај изазван ниском температуром; „Око срца нам је хладно већ одавно, а ево стиже и физички осећај зиме."; „Дрхтао је од хладноће."; „Већ месец дана имам осећај језе, чак и када сам добро обучен."

TRANSLATION   COLDNESS, COLD

SYNONYM ХЛАДНОЋА, ЈЕЗА

HYPERNYM ТЕМПЕРАТУРА ➡ SISTER TERMS ➡ HYPONYMS ➡ MERONYMS ➡ HOLONYMS

FIGURE 12.4 Entry for *зима* (zima) in the Transpoetika Dictionary.

English WordNet. Every synset in WordNet is augmented with at least one semantic label from the WordNet domain hierarchy: for example, {*court, tribunal, judicature*} is annotated as belonging to the category of LAW. When the Serbian synset {*суд, трибунал*} is aligned with this English synset, it automatically assumes the given domain and displays the corresponding label to the user.

Semantic domains are used as pointers to help users who are looking for a particular meaning of the word. This is particularly helpful for polysemous words. Studies have shown a tendency among users to select the first definition they encounter in polysemous entries, regardless of its precise meaning in a given context (Nesi and Haill 2002). At the same time, the domains can be used as navigation points for listing all words belonging to a given category. This is especially useful because individual domains can include synsets from across different syntactic categories and those belonging to different WordNet sub-hierarchies.

Using WordNet as a skeleton structure to construct the Serbian semantic network has both theoretical and practical consequences for the notion of lexicographic equivalence. In any bilingual dictionary, equivalence is the semantic correspondence of a lexical item in one of its senses in the source language to a particular sense of a lexical item in the target language (Atkins and Rundell 2008: 468). If two lexical items in the source language (W_{SL_1} and W_{SL_2}) are translated by the same lexical item in a target language W_{TL_1}, they are said to be synonymous in one particular sense. For example, the Serbian words *хладноħа* ('hladnoća') and *зима* ('zima') in the sense of 'the sensation produced by low temperatures' can be translated as *coldness*. In a conventional bilingual dictionary, the relationship of equivalence between W_{SL_1} ('hladnoća') and W_{TL_1} ('coldness'), as well as between W_{SL_2} ('zima') and W_{TL_1} ('coldness') has to be encoded twice: once under the heading of W_{SL_1} and once under the heading of W_{SL_2}.

The difference between the conventional bilingual model and the aligned Word-Net model is in the degree of system efficiency rather than in the fundamental understanding of how language works. The aligned WordNet model is based on the idea of conceptual equivalence between synsets rather than the direct linking of individual lexical items: lexical items W_{SL_1} ('hladnoća') and W_{SL_2} ('zima') which share the same sense belong to the same synset S_{SL_1} {*hladnoća, zima*}. If S_{SL_1} is aligned with a synset in the target language S_{TL_1} {*coldness, cold*}, i.e. if there is a conceptual equivalence established between S_{SL_1} and S_{TL_1}, any lexical item that belongs to S_{SL_1} {*hladnoća, zima*} will be considered equivalent to any lexical item that belongs to S_{TL_1} {*coldness, cold*}. Conceptual equivalence between target and source synsets is encoded once in the database, regardless of how many lexical items belong to each synset.

In spite of these advantages, the simplicity and economy of the aligned model has major drawbacks. WordNet was not designed with pragmatics or the discrimination of near-synonyms in mind. Its English synsets sometimes mix registers by clustering together words with different levels of formality {*lie, prevarication*}, domain of use {*dog, domestic dog, Canis familiaris*}, or regionally distinct orthographic variants (British *finalise* vs. US *finalize*). While it would be wrong to say that pragmatic information is completely missing from WordNet, its presence is certainly not systematic.

In some cases, WordNet groups together words of a particular register, as is the case with the noun synset {*countenance, physiognomy, phiz, visage, kisser, smiler, mug*} which WordNet defines as "the human face ('kisser' and 'smiler' and 'mug' are informal terms for 'face' and 'phiz' is British)". In this particular case, WordNet descriptively labels individual members of the synset inside the definition, which is unusual. *Countenance* and *physiognomy*, which belong to the more formal register, are not explicitly described as such; *phiz* is labelled as a Britishism but not in terms of its social register; while *kisser, smiler, and mug* are indicated as being informal, but without regional affiliation. If Serbian synsets followed the WordNet practice of ignoring the differences between conceptual and pragmatic granularity, the learners of Serbian as L2 would be denied a more complete picture of lexical entries in the dictionary.

In order to make sure that Serbian synsets are sufficiently differentiated, we have employed a flexible system of tagging or labelling individual Serbian lexemes when their contextual value diverges from other members of the same synset, even though they undoubtedly represent the same concept. Labelling is a common lexicographic technique of succinctly indicating pragmatic information (Burkhanov 2003), i.e. specifying sociocultural parameters of meaning, including relations between inter-locutors, and their social and cultural roles, attitudes, values, and beliefs (Аперсян 1988, Wierzbicka 1992, Marmaridou 2000). In the context of learners' dictionaries, it is especially important to use a labelling system to mark words which are formal or literary, informal or slang, offensive or taboo (Kirkpatrick 1985).

Labelling is all the more important because Transpoetika does not list English-language equivalents for individual lexical items, but presents instead a conceptual intersection between synsets in two languages. While an L1 student may intuitively grasp the difference between members of a synset, an L2 student needs a critical apparatus to help with the differentiation. For example, when the Serbian word *хладноћа* ('coldness') was entered into the dictionary database, it was aligned with the WordNet concept 'the absence of heat'. The Serbian definition for this synset—'*одсуство топлоте*'—is a translation of the English definition. Having established the conceptual intersection, whenever we encounter a Serbian word with the same meaning, we add it to the existing sense to form a Serbian synset for the given concept: {*зима, хладноћа, мрзлина, студен, студ, цича, цича зима*}.

The consequences of this approach are multiple: (a) any member of the given synset lists in its own entry all the other members of the synset as synonymous; (b) any member of the given synset is defined in its own entry by means of the Serbian lexical concept '*одсуство топлоте*' ('the absence of heat'); and (c) any member of the given synset is translated by all the members of the corresponding English lexical concept 'the absence of heat', i.e. {*coldness, cold, low temperature, frigidity, frigidness*}.

Corpus evidence shows that members of the above Serbian synset do not have the same contextual value. While lexical items such as *зима* and *хладноћа* are neutral and frequently encountered in this sense, *студ* ('stud' ≈ 'frigor') is found only in poetic texts. But it is rare even in this context; *мрзлина* is infrequent in standard Serbian but more common in standard Croatian; *студен* ('studen') is poetic, but would be more readily recognized by native speakers than *студ* ('stud'), etc.

To make the Serbian synset more productive for L2 users, we indicate which properties make individual words stand out from other lexical items in the synset: "*зима, хладноћа, студен* (poetic), *студ* (poetic, rare), *мрзлина* (less frequent, emphatic, Croatism), цича (emphatic), цича зима (emphatic)." Each word can be labelled with multiple tags, so that a sufficient amount of information can be provided to distinguish a particular element from others in the same synset. Labels are cross-referenced across the database, so that users can easily find other words marked by a given label. Mousing over the label itself gives the user a brief explanation of what the label stands for and a link to a more detailed metalexicographic treatment of the particular label.

By treating all entries as members of synsets, and by placing these synsets in hierarchies, Transpoetika maps linguistic meaning as a dynamic, relational system. This, in turn, makes it possible to treat a dictionary entry not only as a depository of "lexicocentric information" (Шведова 1988) about a given headword, but as a point of departure for the user's exploration of the semantic relations between words and their senses. By explicitly encoding lexical and semantic relations, Transpoetika makes it possible—even easy—for language learners to access words they do not know by starting with a familiar word and exploring its network. If, for instance, users want to make sure they know how to name all parts of the human face, it is enough for them to consult the entry лице ('lice', 'face'), which as its part meronyms lists уста ('usta', 'mouth'), око ('oko', 'eye'), нос ('nos', 'nose'), образ ('obraz', 'cheek'), etc.

To encourage the use of Transpoetika as an exploratory tool, a secondary interface—inspired by several other attempts at visualizing semantic relations (e.g. Wordnet explorer, Collins)—has been developed to display an entry as an interactive, animated graph (see Figure 12.5). The basic entry view shows the lemma at the centre, with each sense represented as a node, and each lexical item belonging to that sense as additional vertices emanating from the sense node. Dragging the mouse over the sense node displays the definition as a tooltip, while clicking the lexical item nodes creates a new graph. Currently, for simplicity's sake, each relation is displayed in a separate graph (synonyms, antonyms, hyponyms, etc.). While this may be preferable for a learner's dictionary, we may at a later stage want to explore a more complex interface where different relations are combined in the same directed graph.

12.4.2 *Transpoetika: making the most of the Internet*

Throughout the years, the Internet has proved to be a rich source of language data that can be explored for linguistic research (Kilgarriff and Grefenstette 2003, Hundt *et al.* 2007). Given the fact that the production of representative reference corpora takes considerable effort and requires significant funding, using the Web as a corpus is a particularly attractive option for smaller projects and for those dealing with the lexicographic treatment of lesser-resourced languages. It is especially useful for keeping abreast of ongoing changes and developments in language.

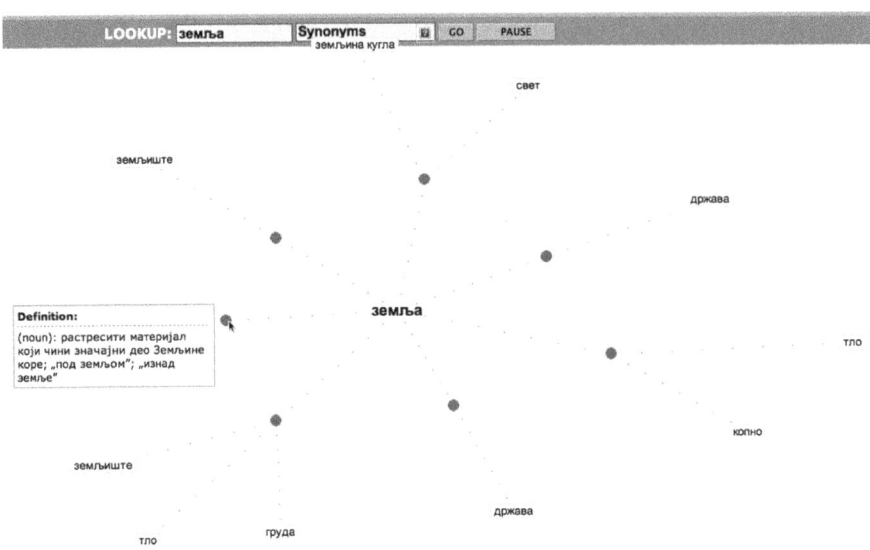

FIGURE 12.5 Synonyms of *земља* (zemlja) in the graphic interface of the Transpoetika Dictionary.

The Transpoetika dictionary, while being WordNet-aligned, is still corpus-based: all the senses are verified and examples taken (sometimes with minor modifications) from the Transpoetika corpus. A majority of the texts that form the corpus have been acquired from the Web. Our corpus is—like the dictionary itself—a moving target: at the moment it contains nearly fifty million words, and it is expanded almost daily with the addition of new texts, obtained both on- and offline.

Furthermore, Transpoetika is built on the idea that a modern electronic dictionary should be a continually-updated web-service that can not only be deployed from any web page (Tasovac 2010) but can also actively participate in the creative re-mixing of data within the network architecture of data sharing, usually referred to as Web 2.0 (O'Reilly 2007). Each entry in Transpoetika, for instance, contains a so-called 'Live Quote' link: when the dictionary user clicks on it, the system retrieves the latest examples of the entry word from Twitter (http://twitter.com)—the popular social network and microblogging platform where users post status updates and communicate with each other using short messages limited to 140 characters. The quotes are displayed directly within the entry (see Figure 12.6). The use of language on Twitter has been studied both in the context of discourse analysis (Zappavigna 2011) and foreign-language pedagogy (Antenos-Conforti 2009). Its value for lexicography is likely to continue to increase, not only as a kind of general real-time corpus, but also as a platform for discovering lexical trends and studying variations in usage, neologisms, abbreviations, etc.

LIVE QUOTES FOR "ЗЕМЉА"

Србија Данас

100.000 српске деце данас гладује. За две године #Srbija ће да званично буде и најсормашнија **земља** Европе. Сиромашнија и од Албаније.

1 minute ago Favorite Retweet Reply

НСПМ online

Новак Ђоковић: Моја **земља** је мала, још нема најбољи имиџ и ја се трудим да је промовишем на најбољи начин: Моја ... http://bit.ly/oOK8tl

3 hours ago Favorite Retweet Reply

ERP

Зашто Господ Исус није претварао **земљу** у злато и гавране у голубове? Кад је могао претворити воду у вино, без... http://fb.me/ALMRbr9j

19 hours ago Favorite Retweet Reply

Хужјо Деди

@Scarafaggi :/ Овај видео није доступан у вашој **земљи**.

23 hours ago Favorite Retweet Reply

follow this train!!

Peace on earth in Serbian Мир на **Земљи** @earthforpeace

7 Aug Favorite Retweet Reply

Ненад Димитровски

@iiwaa ја сам се недавно вратио из те **земље**, и једва чекам крај смене да јој се враатим :)

4 Aug Favorite Retweet Reply

✔ Verified Belieber

@JovanaDamn У којој **земљи** си купила парфем?Ја сам тражила тати да ми купи у Кини али тамо га нема !

2 Aug Favorite Retweet Reply

FIGURE 12.6 Live Quotes via Twitter for the entry *земља* (zemlja) in the Transpoetika Dictionary.

The Internet serves not only as a source of Transpoetika's raw linguistic data, but also as the medium for user involvement. Crowdsourcing language annotation tasks is increasingly seen as a viable option for producing cost-efficient, high-quality data in certain contexts (Snow *et al.* 2008, Callison-Burch 2009, Hsueh *et al.* 2009, Munro *et al.* 2010). Even though developing a WordNet-aligned bilingual dictionary involves complex workflows and requires a level of lexicographic expertise that does not seem easily rendered to the wisdom of the crowd, certain portions of the Transpoetika (e.g. recordings of pronunciations and filtering of illustrations) are based on user contributions and greatly enhance its textual, WordNet-based core.

Pronunciation of dictionary entries is provided by Forvo, a web-based platform for recording and listening to audio files of individual words and short phrases in more than 200 languages. The Forvo website employs a simple, Flash-based, in-browser recorder, and an application programming interface (API) that makes it possible to embed individual pronunciations as clickable sound files on other websites. Furthermore, pronunciations are linked to the pronouncer's geolocation on a Google Map to provide some indication of regional accents and stress patterns. Recorded pronunciations are dynamically retrieved from Forvo and displayed as a clickable image. If the pronunciation does not exist, the users are given the option of recording the pronunciation themselves. As each word can have more than one pronunciation, Transpoetika users are given the option to vote on the quality of pronunciations. Only the top-voted recordings are linked directly from the dictionary entry. In addition, members of the Transpoetika editorial team have editing privileges in the Serbian section of Forvo, which means that we can delete completely inappropriate or wrong pronunciations, should they appear. So far, however, only native speakers have shown interest in recording; we have removed very few pronunciations and these have generally been due to poor sound quality.

Transpoetika uses the external photo-sharing platform Flickr for displaying images related to dictionary entries. While Flickr users upload and store photographs on the Web, they can also annotate them, using freely chosen tags or keywords. This so-called social tagging system does not rely on a controlled vocabulary of any sorts, but rather on "shared and emergent social structures and behaviors, as well as related conceptual and linguistic structures of the user community" (Marlow *et al.* 2006: 31). Each tag serves as a link to other images tagged with the same keyword, and Flickr API makes it possible to retrieve images based on their tags and to display them on a different website.

The number of images on Flickr tagged in Serbian is significantly smaller than those in English. Therefore, Transpoetika uses Flickr API to search for and retrieve photos tagged with English members of a given synset. For instance, for the Serbian lexeme зима ('zima') in the sense of 'the coldest season', the user can click on a button to show images, and the system will search for images on Flickr that have been tagged with *winter* and *wintertime*. The user then sees twelve such images (see Figure 12.7). To solve the problem of incorrectly tagged illustrations and to refine retrieval results, Transpoetika users are given the option of voting on the quality and appropriateness of the image. By moving the mouse over each image, a voting interface is displayed and registered users can decide if the image in question is a good illustration of the given synset or not. Votes are accumulated and subsequently influence the display of images.

12.5 Conclusion

The Princeton WordNet project illustrates the fact that much of the knowledge necessary to understand language is not contained in lexicographic definitions

ЗИМА, *feminine noun, inanimate*

DOMAIN **TIME PERIOD**

SENSE најхладније годишње доба; „Ове године, зима нас је изненадила
пре времена."; „Зиму су увек проводили у топим крајевима."

TRANSLATION **WINTER, WINTERTIME**

HYPERNYM **ДОБА ГОДИНЕ, ГОДИШЊЕ ДОБА** **SISTER TERMS** **HYPONYMS**

MERONYMS **HOLONYMS**

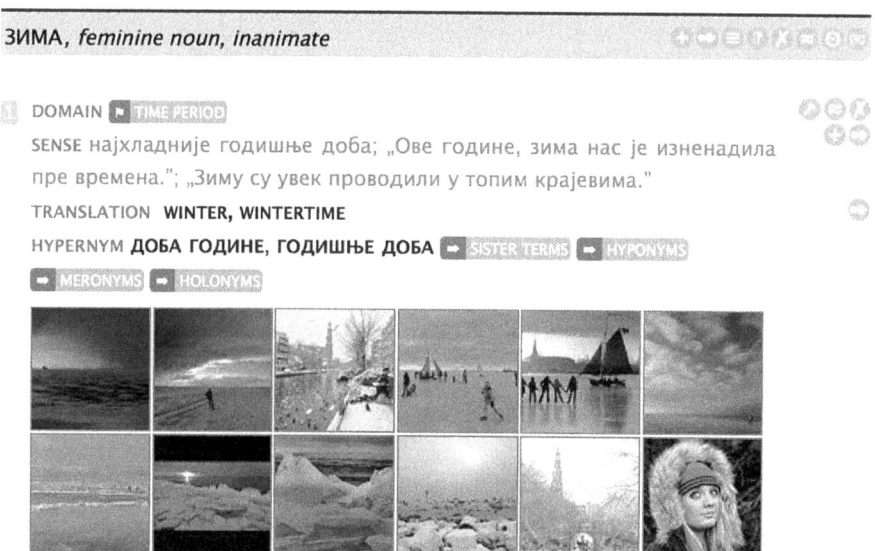

FIGURE 12.7 Illustrations via Flickr for the entry *зима* (zima) in the Transpoetika Dictionary.

alone. The Transpoetika Dictionary, on the other hand, highlights how WordNet's complex architectonic basis and rich network of semantic relations can play a vital role in the development of bilingual or bilingualized pedagogical dictionaries. At the same time, Transpoetika reveals how the limitations of a WordNet-based platform can be overcome by integrating new features and external Web services into online dictionaries.

While invaluable, it must also be noted that WordNet remains a lexicographic resource with a number of all-too-human encoding errors (lumpy synsets, questionable hierarchies, etc.). Individually, none of these errors are deal-breakers, and a careful editor can make sure that they are not reproduced in the pedagogical resource (i.e. certain synsets will have to be removed from a given WordNet hierarchy or placed in a different location). However, for WordNet to truly prosper in human-oriented lexicography as the backbone for not just bilingual, but multilingual, human-oriented projects, it would be beneficial if these inconsistencies were resolved. Because WordNet was created by scholars mainly interested in mental lexicon issues, greater involvement of lexicographers with extensive experience in compiling human-oriented dictionaries would be a welcome addition to the project.

The years ahead will undoubtedly continue to bring new challenges and push the creative boundaries of WordNet-inspired pedagogical lexicons. In the future, an expanded Transpoetika Dictionary could, for instance, feature a layered interface that helps users answer specific questions related to their particular communicative or cognitive needs rather than presenting a unified dictionary entry (Tarp 2008, Verlinde 2010, Verlinde and Binon 2009). Another issue to explore is the automatic marking of synsets that are non-lexicalized in English and are potentially 'difficult words' for foreign students. An example is the series of Serbian lexemes used to describe family relations, which are much more semantically diverse and precise than their English counterparts: *заова* ('zaova', 'husband's sister'); *девер* ('dever', 'husband's brother'), *jemрва* ('jetrva', 'wife of husband's brother'), etc. The Transpoetika search mechanism could also be improved to recognize not only oblique forms from the morphosyntactic database, but to guess misspelled words.

Phraseology is at the moment not part of the official WordNet release, but it has been suggested that idioms could be systematically added to its hierarchy as synsets of their own (Osherson and Fellbaum 2010). This approach treats components of idioms as lexical items. For instance, the phrase 'spill the beans' is interpreted as almost equal to 'reveal a secret' and the synset {*spill the beans*} can be cross-referenced with appropriate senses of *reveal* and *secret*, while another pointer mutually links idiom components *spill* and *beans* in the context of the specific idiom. The lexicographic implications of this approach in human-oriented dictionaries are significant: the user will find links to the idiom *spill the beans* from four different entries: *spill*, *beans*, *reveal*, and *secret*. Currently we are collecting Serbian phraseological units and idioms, but have not yet integrated them directly into the dictionary.

Moreover, there is no reason for pedagogical dictionaries to be limited by the traditional lexical and semantic relations already encoded in WordNet. It would be useful if some of the context-dependent, non-classical, evocative relations (Morris and Hirst 2004, Boyd-Graber *et al.* 2006), or indexes based on word associations (Zock and Schwab 2008) were added to WordNet-based resources in order to establish links between pairs like *Holland* and *tulip*, or *dog* and *bark*. Equally important is pursuing the use of derivational nests to link morphological relations across different parts of speech (see, for example, Bosch *et al.* 2008, Koeva *et al.* 2008).

WordNet-based pedagogical lexicons could benefit from integrating FrameNet—a corpus-based online lexical resource for English whose goal is to document various syntactic possibilities or valencies of word senses (Fillmore *et al.* 2003, Ruppenhofer *et al.* 2006). FrameNet describes frames or scenarios in which participants play certain roles and possibly interact with other participants or objects. For example, the Apply_heat frame covers lexical units such as *bake*, *blanch*, *boil*, *broil*, *brown*, *simmer*, and *steam*, and describes a situation involving a COOK, some FOOD, and a HEATING_INSTRUMENT.

The Cornetto project, a new complex-structured lexicon of the Dutch language, has already merged the information from the FrameNet-like Referentie Bestand Nederlands and the Dutch Wordnet, and aligned it with the English WordNet (Vossen *et al.* 2007, Horák *et al.* 2008, Vossen *et al.* 2008b). In this project, user scenarios revolve around NLP and not human-oriented lexicography. However, from a pedagogical point of view, the added value of semantic frames aligned with WordNet senses is clear: by linking lexical units such us *bake, boil,* etc. with cross-part-of-speech frame elements such as FOOD or HEATING_INSTRUMENT, the dictionary entry radically expands the user's access paths and becomes a much richer knowledge base, both semantically and syntactically.

Pedagogical lexicography has already made a quantum leap with the advent of corpus linguistics, and language learners around the world have benefited from better dictionaries, more authentic examples and observations of new linguistic patterns. But more can be done. Pedagogical lexicography can only continue to profit from rapid advances in WordNet research in computational linguistics. And Wordnets in many languages and NLP in general can equally benefit from the vast reservoirs of linguistic knowledge and unsurpassed attention to detail typical of human-oriented lexicography.

At the beginning of this chapter, I noted a gap separating human-oriented lexicography from some of the current research in NLP. Yet if we consider—in more abstract terms—the problems that these two communities address, we may come to the conclusion that this particular divide is less insurmountable than it seems at first. The goal of pedagogical lexicography is not only to describe linguistic phenomena intelligibly to its target group, but to make explicit the kind of semantic background and knowledge that an educated native speaker usually takes for granted. The same can be said of NLP efforts to extract non-trivial knowledge from free text. Of course, it would be unfair to compare learners of foreign languages to mindless automata or battery-powered sense-disambiguation robots who need computer linguists to implant dictionary chips directly into their brains. However, extracting rules and making implicit language constructs explicit is an important juncture where researchers in NLP and human-oriented L2 lexicography can find common ground for fruitful interdisciplinary collaboration. Because of its massive pedagogic potential, on the one hand, and its widespread use in NLP, on the other, WordNet can play a crucial role in forging new avenues of research.

Dictionaries

McCarthy, Michael (1994). *Cambridge Word Routes: Anglais-Français: Lexique thématique de l'anglais courant.* Cambridge; New York: Cambridge University Press.
Summers, Della (ed.) (2000). *Longman Language Activator.* Harlow: Longman.

Websites

Google's English Dictionary: http://www.google.com/dictionary.
Flickr: http://flickr.com.
Forvo: http://forvo.com.

The Free Dictionary: http://www.thefreedictionary.com.
http://ordnet.dk.
Visual Thesaurus: http://www.visualthesaurus.com.
Visuwords: http://www.visuwords.com.
WordNet: http://wordnetweb.princeton.edu/perl/webwn.

13

Wiktionary: A new rival for expert-built lexicons? Exploring the possibilities of collaborative lexicography

CHRISTIAN M. MEYER AND IRYNA GUREVYCH

13.1 Introduction

Collaborative lexicography is a fundamentally new paradigm for compiling lexicons. Previously, lexicons have been the product of a small group of expert lexicographers specializing in a particular field. In contrast, collaborative lexicography is a bottom-up approach (Carr 1997) which encourages lexicon readers to contribute to the writing of lexicon entries. The large-scale collaboration of many authors became possible with the rise of the Web 2.0 (i.e. the transition from static web pages to dynamic, user-generated content on the World Wide Web) and resulted in huge resources of very high quality (Giles 2005). These resources represent the sum of the opinions of many authors, often known as their collective intelligence or as the 'Wisdom of Crowds' phenomenon (Surowiecki 2005, Malone *et al.* 2010). The most prominent example of a collaboratively created resource is Wikipedia,[1] which has emerged as the world's largest encyclopedia.

Collaboratively constructed lexicons are continually updated by their community, and this yields a steeply increasing coverage of words and word senses. Each contributor has a certain field of expertise. This broad diversity of authors fosters the encoding of a vast amount of domain-specific knowledge. An important characteristic of collaborative lexicography is that the large number of authors has the ability to express the actual use of language in the spirit of Wittgenstein's "meaning is

---

[1] http://www.wikipedia.org/.

use" rather than the often criticized record of "how people 'ought to' use language" (Atkins and Rundell 2008: 2) in expert-built lexicons. Naturally, the entries in collaboratively constructed lexicons are repeatedly changed before a consensus is reached. Examining the complete edit history of an entry allows us to study the evolution of lexicon entries and their discussion within the community. This is not possible in expert-built lexicons, since neither the edit history nor the discussion of the lexicographers is usually publicly available.

In this chapter, we explore the possibilities of collaborative lexicography. The subject of our study is Wiktionary,[2] which is the largest available collaboratively constructed lexicon for linguistic knowledge. Previous studies have compared Wiktionary with other online lexicons (Mann 2010, Lew 2011a), but do not systematically study its collaborative construction process. Fuertes-Olivera (2009) provides a more focused qualitative study of English and Spanish entries in the English Wiktionary and compares them to expert-built lexicons. Hanks (this volume) assesses the quality and intelligibility of Wiktionary's sense descriptions. Quantitative studies have also been undertaken on the German (Meyer and Gurevych 2010a) and Russian Wiktionaries (Krizhanovsky 2010).

Our work goes beyond these research efforts by providing, in Section 13.2, a comprehensive description of Wiktionary's macro- and microstructure, its community and collaboration mechanisms, as well as its various multilingual editions. In Section 13.3, we then compare the Wiktionaries of three different languages to multiple expert-built lexicons in a qualitative and quantitative manner and study the coverage of terms, lexemes, word senses, domains, and registers. In Section 13.4, we finally investigate the question of whether collaboratively created lexicons rival expert-built ones. To conclude, we discuss the new possibilities that collaborative lexicography has opened up for a range of lexicon users and what this implies for the future development of lexicography.

13.2 Describing Wiktionary: core features

Wiktionary is a multilingual online dictionary that is created and edited by volunteers and is freely available on the Web. The name 'Wiktionary' is a portmanteau of the terms 'wiki' and 'dictionary'. A *wiki* is a web application allowing simple editing of hyperlinked web pages in a collaborative manner. Ward Cunningham set up the first system of this kind in 1995 and named it 'wiki', the Hawaiian word for 'fast' (Leuf and Cunningham 2001). Possibly the best-known example of a wiki-based resource is the online encyclopedia Wikipedia. A *dictionary* is a lexicon for human users that contains linguistic knowledge of how words are used (see Hirst 2009). Wiktionary

---

[2] http://www.wiktionary.org/.

combines these two facets. Figure 13.1 shows the article 'boat' from the English Wiktionary as an example lexicon entry.

This section first provides a short historical survey of Wiktionary. Then, we describe its multilingual aspects as well as its macro- and microstructure. We finally discuss how the Wiktionary community collaborates in order to compile the lexicon entries.

13.2.1 *Historical development*

Wiktionary was first launched for the English language on 12 December 2002 as a pure 'companion volume' to Wikipedia. It originated from a long discussion within the Wikipedia community concerning the exclusion of linguistic knowledge from its encyclopedic articles.[3] Important initiators of this development were Daniel Alston,

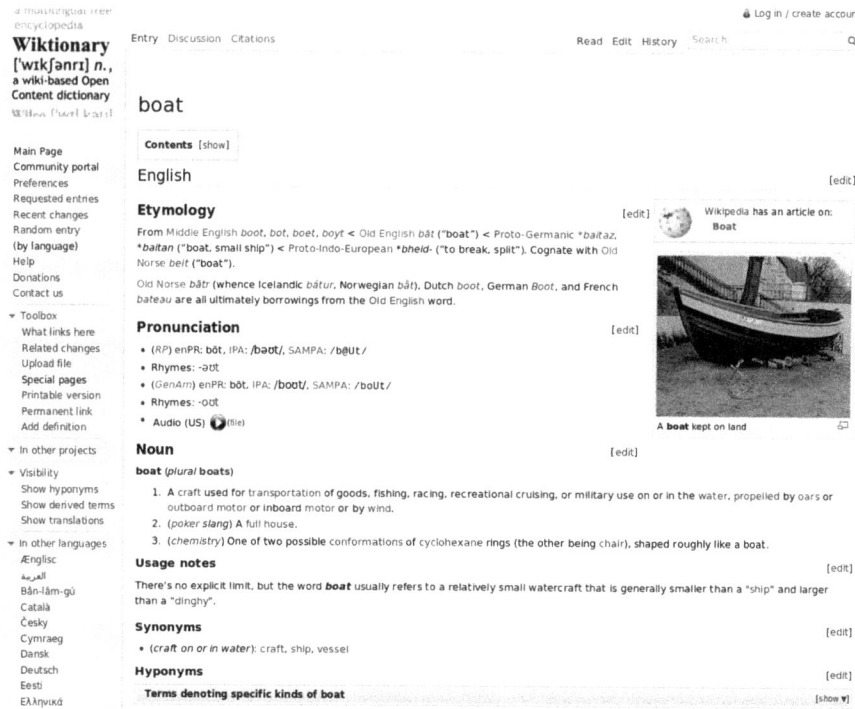

FIGURE 13.1 The English Wiktionary's entry for 'boat' (http://en.wiktionary.org/wiki/boat).

---

[3] See http://en.wikipedia.org/w/index.php?oldid=294531 and http://meta.wikimedia.org/w/index.php?oldid=403

Brion Vibber, and Tim Starling.[4] By 2004, Wiktionary had gradually turned into an independent project. Starting with the French and Polish Wiktionaries, a separate language edition had been created for all 143 active Wikipedia editions by May 2004, when Wiktionary also moved to its current URL www.wiktionary.org. Since then, Wiktionary has rapidly increased and attracted a growing number of contributors. By the end of 2006, seven Wiktionaries exceeded 100,000 articles.

The success of Wiktionary has also drawn increasing attention from both the public and academia. Descy (2006: 4) introduced Wiktionary as a "neat" platform that is "really easy to use" and "designed to be a multilingual, international dictionary". Lepore (2006: 87) raised a criticism about the large-scale import of lexicon entries from copyright-expired dictionaries such as *Webster's New International Dictionary of the English Language* and the low quality of such contributions: "'Be your own lexicographer!' might be Wiktionary's motto. [. . .] Why pay good money for a dictionary written by lexicographers when we can cobble one together ourselves?"[5] Similar issues have been discussed by Fuertes-Olivera (2009) and Hanks (this volume), who particularly criticize the low quality of some Wiktionary definitions. Notwithstanding, Wiktionary has been successfully employed in multiple natural language processing applications including information retrieval, semantic relatedness calculation, and speech synthesis (Etzioni *et al.* 2007, Müller and Gurevych 2009, Zesch *et al.* 2008b, Schlippe *et al.* 2010).

As of August 2010, there were over 170 Wiktionaries, of which 145 were active.[6] With over 1.6 million articles, the English and the French editions are by far the largest ones. Table 13.1 shows the number of articles in the largest Wiktionary editions (over 100,000 articles) as at January of each year. The column 'Recent growth' shows the average number of new articles within the last six months. Most Wiktionaries are growing, although their speed differs markedly: the largest ones are generally growing very fast. However, the Tamil Wiktionary is currently decreasing by an average of 38 articles per month, and the Greek Wiktionary was reduced by more than 10,000 articles between 2008 and 2009: this is an indicator of a consolidation process after importing data from other resources.

---

[4] See http://meta.wikimedia.org/w/index.php?oldid=3149, http://en.wikipedia.org/w/index.php?oldid=378432551, and http://meta.wikimedia.org/w/index.php?oldid=1759149.

[5] Although a large number of lexicon entries have been automatically imported to Wiktionary, these entries are not supposed to stay in their original state, but are to be revised by the community. This is why the imported entries are kept in a separate part of Wiktionary; see http://en.wiktionary.org/wiki/Wiktionary:Webster_1913.

[6] See http://stats.wikimedia.org/wiktionary/EN/TablesArticlesTotal.htm.

TABLE 13.1 **The development of the seventeen largest Wiktionary editions and their recent growth (in articles per month)**

Edition	2002	2003	2004	2005	2006	2007	2008	2009	2010	Recent growth
English	3	866	31k	51k	113k	321k	650k	1.1M	1.6M	+1,179
French	–	6	10	23k	123k	225k	698k	1.2M	1.6M	+1,697
Lithuanian	–	–	–	7	75	529	23k	108k	410k	+556
Turkish	–	–	–	707	1k	118k	185k	252k	266k	+33
Chinese	–	–	–	425	27k	113k	116k	117k	263k	+50
Russian	–	–	–	896	2k	106k	132k	189k	234k	+199
Vietnamese	–	–	–	42	605	209k	225k	228k	228k	+1
Ido	–	–	–	–	32k	104k	126k	146k	165k	+49
Polish	–	1	2	28k	37k	54k	82k	111k	147k	+115
Greek	–	4	32	87	4k	79k	121k	120k	145k	+101
Finnish	–	–	–	497	18k	44k	75k	105k	139k	+97
Hungarian	–	–	–	4k	9k	35k	45k	98k	136k	+121
Norwegian	–	–	–	39	5k	5k	6k	17k	123k	+59
Portuguese	–	–	–	1k	11k	28k	44k	53k	112k	+26
Tamil	–	–	–	27	1k	6k	7k	103k	105k	−38
German	–	2	6	4k	18k	46k	72k	88k	104k	+39
Italian	–	1	32	5k	32k	43k	66k	94k	103k	+21

13.2.2 *Wiktionary's multilingual structure and language coverage*

MULTILINGUAL STRUCTURE

Wiktionary provides two different approaches to encoding linguistic knowledge in multiple languages. First, there are independent Wiktionaries for each language—called *language editions*—that are accessible via a sub-domain denoting the respective ISO 639 language code.[7] The Russian Wiktionary can, for instance, be found at http://ru.wiktionary.org/. This language is the *native language* of a Wiktionary edition, since it is used for the graphical user interface and for describing the lexicon entries. Second, each Wiktionary edition may include lexicon entries from multiple languages. There is, for example, an article about the Russian term лодка (English 'boat') both within the English and the Russian edition (the latter is shown in Figure 13.2). The rationale behind this is to provide lexicographic descriptions in different languages: the Russian Wiktionary uses Russian to describe лодка, which

---

[7] http://www.infoterm.info/standardization/iso_639_1_2002.php.

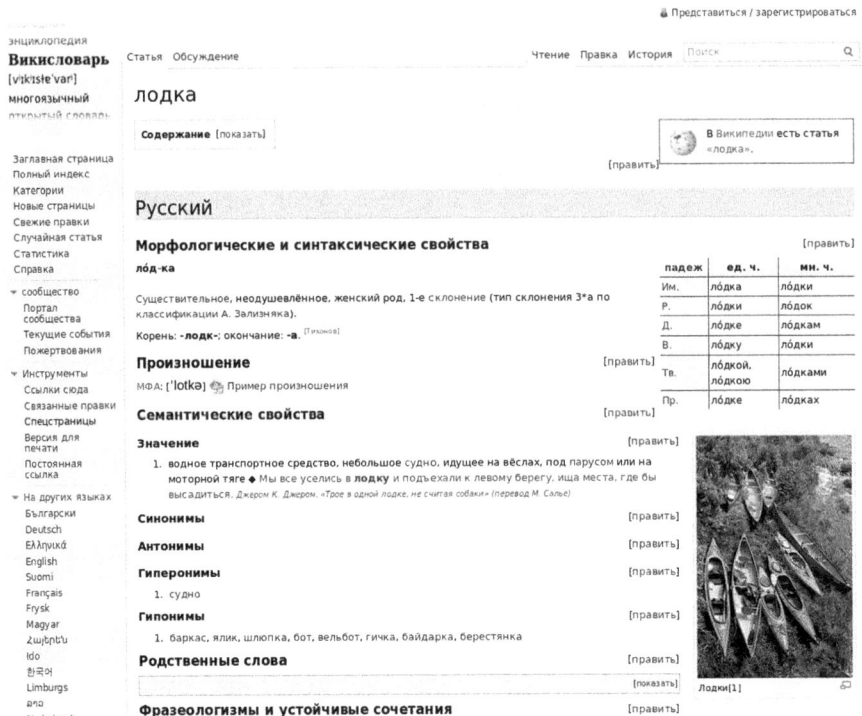

Figure 13.2 The Russian Wiktionary's entry for лодка (http://ru.wiktionary.org/wiki/Лодка).

corresponds to the practice of monolingual dictionaries. The description texts of *лодка* in the English Wiktionary are, in contrast, written in English—similar to a bilingual dictionary.[8] This makes Wiktionary useful for both native speakers and language learners. Consider for instance the definition "водное транспортное средство, небольшое судно, идущее на вёслах, под парусом или на моторной тяге" (English 'a water-based means of transport, a small vessel powered by oars, sails, or a motor') for the simple Russian term *лодка*. To understand this definition, a learner needs to have a certain level of Russian. However, if the learner is a native English speaker, he or she can easily find that *лодка* means "(nautical) boat, dinghy, gig, yawl". The language of the user interface also plays an important role here, since a menu item labelled with *Полный индекс* (English 'full index') might not be easily comprehensible for a language learner of Russian. Using

---

[8] Note that this distinction has not always been clear in previous work. Fuertes-Olivera (2009), for instance, uses the name 'Spanish Wiktionary' to refer to Spanish terms within the English-language edition. This has tended to exaggerate the claim that Wiktionary is language dominated by English, since the actual Spanish language edition that uses Spanish to define its terms was not considered in this study.

the index of his/her native language edition to browse the Russian entries is much more convenient.

COVERAGE OF LANGUAGES

We explored which languages have a separate Wiktionary edition in order to clarify whether Wiktionary covers the full variety of languages in the world or is dominated by certain countries, continents, or cultures. We grouped the Wiktionary language editions by their language family (based on Ruhlen 1987) and the main geographical region the language is spoken in.[9]

Table 13.2 shows our geographical classification of the Wiktionary language editions. We found six editions for man-made languages, namely Ido, Esperanto, Volapük, Interlingua, Interlingue, and Lojban. The English language also features a Simple Wiktionary that uses only a controlled vocabulary to describe its entries. Both constructed and simple language editions are marked as 'Other' in the table. For geographical region, we created a 'Worldwide' group covering English, Spanish, Portuguese, and French, which are spoken as a main language in several continents of the world. For the remaining languages, we grouped them by the continent where the language is mainly spoken. The group 'Near/Middle East' is an exception, as it forms the borderline between Europe, Asia, and Africa, subsuming the Arabic, Turkish, and Persian languages, as well as Hebrew.

All the main regions of the world are covered by a Wiktionary language edition. Most Wiktionaries exist for the languages spoken in Europe and Asia, while the

TABLE 13.2 **Wiktionary editions and the total of articles by region**

Region	Wiktionaries	Articles
Africa	17	86,084
Americas	8	30,012
Asia	36	1,714,125
Europe	54	2,600,675
Near/Middle East	9	511,225
Oceania	10	63,655
Worldwide	4	3,809,000
Other	7	334,210
Total	145	9,148,986

[9] We are aware that some language families are subject to discussion (e.g. for the Korean language), and that a clear allocation to certain geographical regions is very fuzzy and debatable. Nevertheless, we do not aim at a full ethnological study but at gaining insights into the type of languages for which a Wiktionary language edition exists.

Americas seem to be under-represented. This is partly due to the large share of the four worldwide languages spoken in these countries. Regarding the size of the Wiktionaries (i.e. the number of articles that are contained in the corresponding language edition), the worldwide languages contain the bulk of the articles (41%), followed by Europe (29%), and Asia (19%). Wiktionaries for the languages spoken in Africa and Oceania (including Australia) are still very small (less than 2% of the total number of articles).

Table 13.3 shows the language families covered by Wiktionary. It is not surprising that the Indo-European language families (Germanic, Romance, and Slavic) represent the largest number of both Wiktionary editions and articles, since Indo-European languages are the most widespread, including English, Spanish, French, German, Russian, etc. There are, however, many less-common languages, and we also studied under-represented and missing language families. In particular, African

TABLE 13.3 **Wiktionary editions and the total of articles by language family**

Language family	Wiktionaries	Articles
Afro-Asiatic	3	390
Austro-Asiatic	2	229,426
Austronesian	10	78,527
Baltic	2	574,000
Celtic	6	65,460
Creole	2	229
Dravidian	4	282,000
Finno-Ugric	3	346,000
Germanic	10	2,116,314
Indo-Aryan	2	38,151
Indo-Iranian	14	148,309
Inuit	3	12,319
Niger-Congo	9	54,893
Nordic	6	317,323
Romance	14	2,350,689
Semitic	5	56,847
Sino-Tibetan	3	404,000
Slavic	15	589,967
Tai	3	75,109
Turkic	8	463,923
Other	21	945,110
Total	145	9,148,986

languages from the Nilo-Saharan family (including, for example, the Masai language), the Berber family (e.g. Tarifit), and the Khoisan family are under-represented. Khoisan languages are known for their click sounds which may have impeded the creation of a corresponding Wiktionary edition due to the complicated script of the words (e.g. '!Xóõ' or '‡Hõã'). Another reason may be the lack of technical infrastructure in African countries. Besides African languages, Paleosiberian and Tungusic languages spoken in Siberia, Mongolia, and other regions of northern Asia are also missing. These languages are endangered because of their small number of speakers, which might explain the lack of Wiktionary editions. Many languages of Native American and Australian aborigines are also not yet represented in Wiktionary, probably because of the lack of written knowledge about them or technical infrastructure in cultures that live very close to nature.

Although the vast majority of encoded knowledge in Wiktionary relates to the most widespread languages, our analysis shows that Wiktionary also offers the rare chance to obtain linguistic resources for smaller languages (see also Prinsloo, this volume). Since Wiktionary is constantly growing, we expect the number of Wiktionaries for minor languages to reach a considerable size in the future. In this context, Wiktionary can become an important, easy-to-use platform for linguists who study endangered languages and want to share their research.

13.2.3 *Wiktionary's macrostructure and accessibility*

The content of Wiktionary is organized into *pages*, each of which consists of a formatted text body and a unique title describing the contents of the page. There are four main types of page:

1. *Article pages* constitute the heart of each Wiktionary edition, as they contain the actual linguistic information (see Section 13.2.4).
2. *Redirect pages* navigate the user to a certain target article. This is useful for terms with several typographic variants, such as 'you've' (Unicode character U +2019) and 'you've' (Unicode character U+0027), or varying capitalization (e.g. 'pdf and 'PDF'), that should be described on only one page.[10]
3. *Talk pages* are available for each Wiktionary page to discuss its contents, collect ideas for extension, express criticism, and ask questions (Section 13.2.5).
4. *Internal pages* describe the motivation, goals, statistics, indices, and appendices of Wiktionary as well as its guidelines for contributors (Section 13.2.5).

---

[10] In the Russian Wiktionary, redirects are often used for denoting inflected word forms or misspellings. The plural form *красные* redirects, for example, to *красный* (English 'red'). The other Wiktionary editions use separate article pages to encode inflected forms and misspellings, since they can be ambiguous. For instance, the misspelling 'lier' of 'liar' can also refer to a (rarely used) nominalization of '(to) lie' (i.e. a person or thing that is lying on a bed, for example).

In order to gain access to individual pages, Wiktionary's user interface offers four different access paths (Bergenholtz and Tarp 1995):

1. Each page can be directly accessed by typing its title. In addition to jumping quickly to the article, this also allows it to be bookmarked or linked.
2. An internal search engine can be used to find specific articles. No automatic lemmatization is performed, since inflected word forms are included as separate entries (see Section 13.2.4). The search results in a list of articles which contain the search terms.
3. Index, category, and list pages are available for browsing through Wiktionary's contents. These pages organize the lexicon entries alphabetically, or by language, domain, register, style, etc. The full alphabetical index corresponds to the organization of most printed lexicons. It is particularly useful if the spelling of a term is unclear. A currently emerging part of Wiktionary is called *Wikisaurus*, which aims to organize the article pages in an onomasiological, thesaurus-like manner using synonyms, hyponyms, hypernyms, and the like.
4. Pages are connected via hyperlinks, i.e. cross-references to other pages. This can be used to point the user to related articles with further explanation or terms that are unclear to a reader.

13.2.4 *Wiktionary's microstructure and types of linguistic knowledge*

The actual linguistic information is found on Wiktionary's article pages. The title of the article represents a certain term described in the article, for example the noun 'boat', the verb 'sleep', or the proverb 'Rome wasn't built in a day'. Article titles are case-sensitive and can distinguish diacritic variations. The terms 'cafe', 'café', and 'Café' are thus described in different articles. The text body of an article is divided into one or more lexicon entries containing a variety of linguistic information. Wiktionary has no specific target user profile (such as translators or language learners). All readers always have access to all the information available. This is usually organized in separate sections covering knowledge from all major fields of linguistics and is outlined briefly below.

It should, however, be noted that Wiktionary has no fixed structure for its entries. Rather, it allows flexible encoding schemas, which are necessary to describe culture- or language-specific information. The German language, for instance, distinguishes occupational titles of females and males (e.g. 'Mechanikerin' and 'Mechaniker'), while in English there is usually only one form ('mechanic'). Another example is the different word formation of Chinese based on radicals, which need to be encoded fundamentally differently from English entries.

LANGUAGE

As shown in Figure 13.1, each lexicon entry starts with the language of the term being described. This is necessary, as entries in multiple languages can be encoded within the same article page. There is, for example, both an English and a French entry within the article 'sensible' that need to be separated due to their different meanings. The language sections are usually ordered alphabetically. An exception is made for entries in the Wiktionary's native language, which are always the first ones. These entries are expected to be looked up most frequently and are usually the most detailed ones. Information that cannot be associated with a certain language, such as the letters of an alphabet, internationally used abbreviations (e.g. chemical symbols or the ISO language codes), or scientific names within the biological taxonomy are encoded in a separate section entitled 'Translingual'.

ETYMOLOGY

The 'Etymology' section describes the origin of a term—e.g. "from Middle English boot, bot, boet, boyt, from Old English bāt [...]" for the English 'boat'. Etymologies can help readers to understand the similarities and dissimilarities of terms, and are also useful to explore the distinction between homonymy and polysemy, which is often not clearly defined. The English term 'bass' distinguishes, for instance, two homonymous meanings originating from the Latin 'bassus' for its musical meaning and from the Proto-Indo-European '*bhors-' for its biological meaning.

PHONETIC KNOWLEDGE

Wiktionary entries often encode a term's pronunciation using the IPA (International Phonetic Alphabet) or SAMPA (Speech Assessment Methods Phonetic Alphabet) notation. Different variants can be distinguished using labels such as 'Received Pronunciation' (Standard English of England), 'General American', 'Standard German', 'Swiss German', etc. In addition to a textual representation using a phonetic alphabet, sound files may be added to help readers learn a certain pronunciation. Finally, the phonetic suffix for finding rhymes is sometimes included in a Wiktionary article. The term 'boat' is, for example, represented by the IPA string 'bəʊt' and has the rhyming suffix '-əʊt'.

MORPHOLOGICAL KNOWLEDGE

Most lexicons focus on entries for canonical word forms (e.g. the verb '(to) go'). Since Wiktionary has practically no space limitations, it can also include inflected forms (like the past tense form 'went') as separate entries. While canonical word forms are described in a fully fledged article, inflected forms usually explain the type of inflection and link to the canonical word form. In addition, Wiktionary entries often contain inflection tables explaining either the declension of a noun, adjective, etc. by noting the form for each combination of case, gender, and number (where appropriate) or the conjugation of a verb, by noting the forms for the respective combinations of person, number, gender, tense, aspect, mood, or voice. The Russian article 'лодка' in Figure 13.2 contains, for instance, an inflection table with thirteen forms.

SYNTACTIC KNOWLEDGE

Each lexicon entry is marked with a syntactic category. For single words, the part-of-speech tags 'noun', 'verb', 'adjective', etc. are used, while encoded multi-word expressions are marked as 'idiom', 'proverb', 'saying', etc. The coverage of syntactic categories is explored in detail in Section 13.3.2. Apart from the syntactic categories, basic syntactic information is often found in Wiktionary articles. Nouns are, for example, tagged as 'countable/uncountable' or as taking only the singular or only the plural form and verbs are labelled as 'transitive' or 'intransitive'. However, Wiktionary does not provide deep lexical–syntactic knowledge, such as subcategorization frames.

SEMANTIC KNOWLEDGE

The core of each Wiktionary entry is its meaning section. Following the notation of traditional lexicons, the meaning of a term is described in an enumeration of discrete word senses. A word sense is explained by a gloss, example sentences illustrating its usage, quotations, and linguistic labels. The gloss of the third word sense of the article 'boat' is, for instance, "(chemistry) One of two possible conformers of cyclohexane rings (the other being chair), shaped roughly like a boat". The prefix "chemistry" in parentheses is a *linguistic label* (Atkins and Rundell 2008), which associates word senses with a certain domain, register, style, etc. The underlined words in the gloss are hyperlinks to other Wiktionary articles. This is a useful feature for readers who have problems understanding the definition and wish to quickly look up the definition of one of these words.

The composition of glosses is known to be one of the most contentious aspects of lexicography (Johnson 1755: Preface). Wiktionary's collaborative construction process provides a fundamentally new perspective on this challenge, since readers can easily change formulations they do not understand or ask for a reformulation on the talk pages. We will analyse this further in Sections 13.2.5 and 13.3.3 below.

In addition to the hyperlinks in the glosses, there are separate sections for gathering hyperlinks to related articles. The section title denotes the type of relation between the linked terms (e.g. synonymy, hypernymy, hyponymy, antonymy, holonymy). More loosely defined relations are gathered within sections labelled 'Derived terms' and 'See also'.

CROSS-LINGUAL KNOWLEDGE

Another way of interconnecting articles is translation. Due to the multilingual nature of Wiktionary discussed in Section 13.2.2, a translation can be defined both as a link to the term within the same Wiktionary edition and to the Wiktionary edition of the target language. For the German translation 'Boot' of the term 'boat' within the English Wiktionary, there is, for instance, a link to 'Boot' in both the English and in the German Wiktionary. For each term and language, multiple translations can be encoded.

A third type of cross-language linking in Wiktionary makes use of inter-wiki links. These links are shown within the navigation pane and allow users to switch from one language edition to another without changing the term. The English article 'boat' contains, for example, inter-wiki links to the article 'boat' within the German, French, and Russian Wiktionaries (as opposed to linking the translated terms).

PICTORIAL KNOWLEDGE

A picture is worth a thousand words, as the old adage goes. Since there are usually no size restrictions in electronic lexicons, the use of drawings, photographs, etc. is becoming increasingly popular to illustrate meanings (Lew 2010a). The Wiktionary community includes pictures in the lexicon entries as an additional description of meaning (see Figure 13.1 for an example). The English Wiktionary has also set up a *picture dictionary*[11] that can be used to browse the entries graphically. This is a particularly useful feature for non-native speakers to gain a quick idea of a term's meaning. Hanks (this volume) also envisages the inclusion of other multimedia (such as sound and video) to illustrate meanings in Wiktionary.

REFERENCES

To include a new term in Wiktionary, the proposed term needs to be 'attested' (see the guidelines in Section 13.2.5 below). This attestation can be done by providing references to external sources. The article 'boat' contains, for instance, a reference to "Weisenberg, Michael (2000): The Official Dictionary of Poker. MGI/Mike Caro University. ISBN 978-1880069523." to attest the poker-related word sense of 'boat'. Besides references to published books or articles, references to publicly available online lexicons are frequently used by the Wiktionary community.

13.2.5 *Collaboration in Wiktionary*

In contrast to traditional lexicons built by individual expert lexicographers, Wiktionary is collaboratively constructed by a large community of ordinary web users. To overcome the lack of lexicographic experience in such a community, Wiktionary relies on the collective intelligence of many different authors—the 'Wisdom of Crowds' phenomenon (Surowiecki 2005). In this section, we take a closer look at this community and its workflows and habits in compiling the lexicon entries.

WIKTIONARIANS

Wiktionary contributors are called *Wiktionarians*. They can be divided into three different types:

(1) The smallest group are the ninety-eight *administrators*, who must be nominated and elected by a majority. Administrators have the right to delete pages, change user permissions, and block articles or users.

---

[11] http://en.wiktionary.org/wiki/Wiktionary:Picture_dictionary.

(2) *Registered users* are all the contributors who have created a personal account. This allows them to sign their edits with their name and make use of, for example, a watchlist to keep track of certain articles. There are currently 401,198 registered users for the English Wiktionary, 40,005 for the French edition, 36,900 for the German, and 32,692 for the Russian. In accordance with other collaboratively constructed resources, the number of edits per user follows a Zipf law. Therefore, most registered users perform only a few or perhaps not even a single article edit. When counting only users with at least ten edits, the number of actively contributing users drops to 3,958 for the English, 965 for the French, 794 for the German, and 277 for the Russian language edition.

(3) The third type of contributors is *unregistered users*. They are also called *IPs*, because of their anonymous edits that are solely distinguishable by their Internet Protocol (IP) address. It is impossible to say how many people actually contribute to the project, since an IP address can be shared by many. Unregistered users perform about 5 per cent of the article edits.

AUTOMATIC PROCESSING

In addition to human users, there are also so-called *bots*, i.e. computer programs that automatically crawl through the wiki pages and make changes according to certain patterns or rules. Currently, there are twenty-two active and seventeen inactive bots within the English Wiktionary. They have different responsibilities, which include automatic data imports, reformatting certain sections, and finding inter-wiki links to other Wiktionary language editions.

DISCUSSION CULTURE

The Wiktionary community has a lively discussion culture including both content (i.e. lexicographic) and technology (i.e. Wiki software) related concerns. As mentioned in Section 13.2.3 above, each article page has a *talk page* attached that can be used to discuss its content. It is good practice to sign a comment with one's own user name and the current date. The comments can address criticism and questions about the current state of the article or discuss possible extensions or modification of it. Figure 13.3 shows the talk page of the English Wiktionary article 'colour'. To date, the talk pages in Wiktionary have not been systematically studied. Similar works exist, however, for Wikipedia talk pages (Stegbauer 2009, Stvilia *et al.* 2008) that might serve as a good starting point.

Besides the talk pages of individual articles, Wiktionary also offers general pages for discussing its organization and development as a whole. These pages are entitled 'tea room', 'etymology scriptorium', 'beer parlour', and 'grease pit'. In general, the conversation is of an informal and colloquial style; a consensus is usually reached by voting.[12]

---

[12] http://en.wiktionary.org/wiki/Wiktionary:Votes.

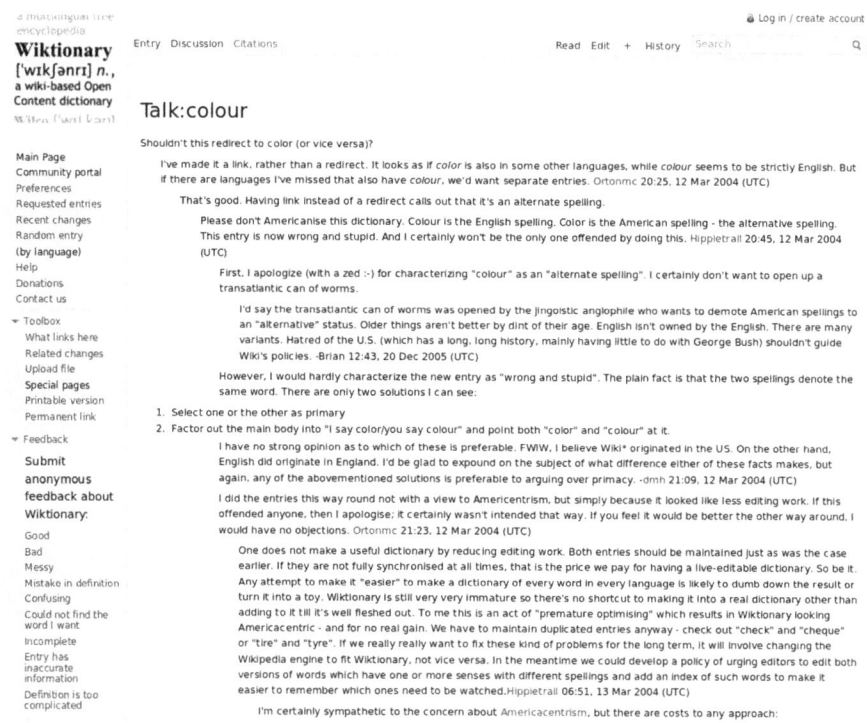

FIGURE 13.3 The talk page for the English Wiktionary entry 'colour'.

Most questions and suggestions are quickly responded to. However, there are also topics that have been under discussion for a long period or have got completely stuck.

POLICIES AND GUIDELINES

The Wiktionary community has developed a set of guidelines, mostly about the format of lexicon entries and the inclusion of new terms. Although there are slight differences in the guidelines of each language edition, they are largely similar. The main guideline for the inclusion of a new term is "if it's likely that someone would run across it and want to know what it means".[13] Each encoded term needs to be 'attested' within the language, which means "verified through (1) clearly widespread use, or (2) usage in a well-known work, or (3) usage in permanently recorded media, conveying meaning, in at least three independent instances spanning at least a year".[14] Unlike printed dictionaries, Wiktionary has practically no size restrictions. The guidelines therefore permit partial words, multi-word expressions, etc. that are often only partially considered or completely excluded from the headword list of

[13] http://en.wiktionary.org/w/index.php?oldid=13078056.
[14] http://en.wiktionary.org/w/index.php?oldid=13078056.

other lexicons. In addition, Wiktionary also encodes inflected word forms (e.g. 'went') and common misspellings (like 'aweful') as separate lexicon entries, which is not done in most other lexicons, although it provides very interesting information for language learners.

REVISION HISTORY

Every edit operation within Wiktionary is recorded and archived. In this way, a previous revision of an article can be reviewed at any time in order to inspect how the article has changed, and which users made particular changes. For each edit, the user can provide a short note describing the modifications made and their reasons. Wiktionary contributors often use the revision history to revert vandalism, i.e. changes that introduced spam or deleted important parts of an article. The revision history also allows citations of a specific version of a Wiktionary article that does not change over time. This is an important feature within the World Wide Web which is constantly changing. For lexicographers, the revision history offers the unique possibility of recording how an article develops (e.g. for exploring the semantic shift of a certain term). An example is the term 'hand-held' which in 2005, when hand-helds were usually used as personal digital assistants, was described in Wiktionary as "a computing device (e.g. organiser, Internet-enabled cell phone) that is operated while held in the hands". Today, these devices often contain portable video games, which has led the Wiktionary community to change the gloss to "a personal digital assistant or video game console that is small enough to be held in the hands". Together with the talk pages described above, Wiktionary's revision history provides us with the opportunity to study the lexicographic construction process as a whole (i.e. all decisions made on a certain entry). In a lexicographic publishing company, this information is either undocumented or private.

13.3 Analysing Wiktionary: a critical assessment

Having described Wiktionary in isolation, we now turn towards assessing its linguistic information in comparison to expert-built lexicons. Although the aim is to introduce Wiktionary in its full variety of language editions, we need to restrict our analysis to a selection of languages, due to the language skills of the authors and the limited availability of software libraries to analyse the encoded information quantitatively. As expert-built lexicons, we have chosen commonly used computational lexicons, since they allow their data to be automatically accessed in a similar way to Wiktionary. This is necessary for a fair comparison between the different types of lexicons. Traditional dictionaries are usually not intended for automatic processing and are therefore less suitable for a quantitative comparison; as Hirst (2009: 270–1) put it: "An ordinary dictionary is an example of a lexicon. However, a dictionary is intended for use by humans, and its style and format are unsuitable for computational use in a text or natural language processing system without substantial revision. [...] Nonetheless, a dictionary in a machine-readable format can serve as the basis for a computational lexicon, [...] Perhaps the best-known and most widely used computational lexicon of English is WordNet [...]."

In our study, we analysed the English Wiktionary in comparison to the Princeton WordNet 3.0 (Fellbaum 1998) and the electronic version of Roget's thesaurus (Jarmasz and Szpakowicz 2003), the German Wiktionary in comparison to GermaNet 6.0 (Kunze and Lemnitzer 2002), and OpenThesaurus (Naber 2005), as well as the Russian Wiktionary in comparison to the Russian WordNet 3.0 (Гельфейнбейн *et al.* 2003).[15] For each lexicon, we studied the coverage of terms, lexemes, word senses, domains, and registers in both a qualitative and quantitative manner.

13.3.1 *Coverage of terms*

A lexical form that consists of either a single word (e.g. 'plant'), or multiple words (e.g. 'freedom of speech') will be called a *term* throughout this chapter. Note that, according to this definition, the noun and the verb 'plant' are represented by the same term. Previously, terms (according to our definition) have also been referred to as *words* (Wilks *et al.* 1996) or *lexical items* (Atkins and Rundell 2008). The number of terms encoded in Wiktionary is equivalent to its number of article pages (i.e. 2,402,397 in the English Wiktionary, 182,688 in the German Wiktionary, and 507,100 in the Russian Wiktionary). As described in Section 13.2.2 above, each Wiktionary edition can describe terms from multiple languages, which is not true for our expert-built lexicons. Therefore, we will focus solely on the terms in the native language of the respective Wiktionary edition (English terms in the English edition, etc.). The English and the Russian WordNet contain a large number of Latin terms that are part of the biological taxonomy of organisms. These terms are excluded from our study, since they are not encoded as native terms in Wiktionary. Expert-built lexicons usually do not list inflected word forms as separate terms. Wiktionary, however, also fosters the inclusion of inflected word forms, which is particularly useful for terms with irregular inflection. For our comparison of terms, we removed all inflected word forms.[16]

Table 13.4 shows the number of comparable terms that we used. We find that the German and the Russian Wiktionaries are of similar size to the expert-built lexicons. However, the English language Wiktionary exceeds the size of the Princeton WordNet by about 1.5 times and that of the Roget's Thesaurus by more than 3.5 times. In

---

[15] We used JWKTL (Zesch *et al.* 2008a) and Wikokit (Krizhanovsky 2010) for parsing the Wiktionary data of 2 April 2011 (English edition), 6 April 2011 (German edition), and 4 April 2011 (Russian edition). For OpenThesaurus, we used a database dump from 8 September 2010.

[16] Apart from the 363 inflected word forms noted for the Russian Wiktionary, there are a large number of inflected word forms within the 103,597 redirects. Redirects are not contained in the number of native terms and are thus not included in this study.

TABLE 13.4 **The number of terms in Wiktionary and comparable resources**

English language	Wiktionary	WordNet	Roget's Thesaurus
Native terms:	352,865	148,730	59,391
– Latin terms:	160	7,080	22
– Inflected forms:	115,635	0	0
= Comparable terms:	237,070	141,650	59,369
Coverage of			
Swadesh list:	100.00%	92.68%	96.10%
Nation's BNC 1–4:	99.92%	97.75%	90.52%
West's GSL:	99.91%	97.24%	96.50%
Ogden's Basic English:	99.41%	96.94%	97.53%
Neologisms:	11.35%	0.72%	0.18%
German language	Wiktionary	GermaNet	OpenThesaurus
Native terms:	83,399	85,211	58,208
– Latin terms:	13	17	17
– Inflected forms:	34,146	0	0
= Comparable terms:	49,240	85,194	58,191
Coverage of			
Swadesh list:	97.70%	87.10%	91.71%
Guti Wortschatz 100:	98.99%	76.77%	89.90%
Guti Wortschatz 500:	99.20%	72.31%	83.47%
Neologisms:	0.37%	1.92%	0.44%
Russian language	Wiktionary	Russian WordNet	
Native terms:	133,435	130,062	
– Latin terms:	0	5,025	
– Inflected forms:	363	0	
= Comparable terms:	133,072	125,037	
Coverage of			
Swadesh list:	96.97%	84.42%	
Штейнфельдт:	97.05%	67.88%	
Neologisms:	48.52%	4.72%	

comparison to expert-built lexicons, Wiktionary is hence able to compete in terms of coverage, which makes it a valuable resource. Besides comparing the absolute sizes, we also analyse which types of terms are predominantly found in one of the lexicons by assessing the coverage of basic vocabulary and neologisms as well as the usage frequencies of the covered terms.

BASIC VOCABULARY

The basic vocabulary of a language is known to change very slowly and should always be well represented in a (general-purpose) lexicon. We compared the coverage of several word lists of basic vocabulary and report the results in Table 13.4. We used the *Swadesh* lists (Dyen *et al.* 1992) for English, German, and Russian; Ogden's (1938) *Basic English* word list, West's (1953) *General Service List (GSL)*, and Nation's (2006) *BNC 1–4* lists based on the British National Corpus for English; the *GUT1 Wortschatz*[17] 100 and 500 for German; and Штейнфельдт's (1963) list of common terms in Russian. Each Wiktionary edition covers the basic vocabulary very well. The English Wiktionary seems to be the most thorough, as it is the only lexicon that covers the full Swadesh list and over 99 per cent of the other word lists. While the expert-built lexicons of English also have a good coverage of the basic vocabulary, the problem of coverage can be more acute for German and Russian. Wiktionary can be of great help here, as it retains a high coverage of over 96 per cent.

NEOLOGISMS

Meyer and Gurevych (2010b) have noticed a high number of neologisms within the English Wiktionary. In order to quantify this observation, we compared the coverage of these newly coined terms using a list of 555 English neologisms[18] from 1997 to 2008 provided by Birmingham City University, a list of 36,220 German neologisms[19] taken from the Wortwarte project for the years 2000–2010, and 7,482 Russian neologisms[20] provided by the Russian Academy of Sciences. The results can be found in Table 13.4. Note that, due to the different size of the neologism lists and the different language characteristics (such as the extensive use of compounding in German), the numbers are not comparable across the three languages. Both the English and the Russian Wiktionary editions encode significantly more neologisms than their respective expert-built lexicons. This can be explained by the collaborative construction process of Wiktionary, which allows updating of the lexicons immediately, without being restricted to certain release cycles as is the case for expert-built lexicons. The German language lexicons cover only between 0.37 and 1.92 per cent of neologisms. GermaNet contains about 550 neologisms more than Wiktionary. Despite that, Wiktionary is a

---

[17] http://www.gut1.de/grundwortschatz/grundwortschatz_500.html.
[18] http://rdues.bcu.ac.uk/neologisms.shtml.
[19] http://www.wortwarte.de.
[20] http://dict.ruslang.ru/gram.php?act=search&orderby=word.

promising resource for neologisms, as it has the ability to encode neologisms not yet found in expert-built lexicons. We will study this in more detail in the subsequent section when measuring the overlap between the different lexicons.

13.3.2 *Coverage of lexemes*

A *lexeme* is a combination of a term and its part of speech that is used as a headword for a lexicon entry. The English Wiktionary encodes, for instance, three lexemes for the term 'bass': one for the adjective describing a sound and two for the noun distinguishing the music-related etymology from the biological organism. The latter distinction denotes homonymy—as opposed to polysemy, which is represented in Wiktionary by providing multiple word senses (described in Section 13.3.3 below).

It is surprising that the Wiktionary community distinguishes between homonymy and polysemy, since homonymy "is gradually being abandoned as an organizing principle in many types of dictionary" (Atkins and Rundell 2008: 281). The reason is that the distinction can cause confusion when looking up a term without knowing its etymology and is hence not very helpful for dictionary readers (see also Moon 1987). The layout of lexicon entries in Wiktionary has been discussed for a long time and many different ways of organizing the article pages have been proposed.[21] An early idea was to create a separate article page for each word sense. This suggestion was abandoned in 2003 because the different senses could not be easily compared. The Wiktionary community then used only a single article page per term and created separate lexicon entries whenever a term had multiple etymologies or pronunciations (e.g. two entries for the two possible pronunciations of 'read'). However, this idea was soon abandoned as it was found to be too unstable. The basic principle of describing homonymous terms in separate entries was formulated as a guideline in 2004 and is still used today. By 2006, the distinction had been questioned mostly for usability reasons. The article pages should start with the list of word senses, since they represent the most important knowledge for the lexicon users. Etymologies and pronunciations should no longer be used to distinguish different lexicon entries but merely become additional information attached to the word senses. This suggestion was, however, rejected by the community, since etymologies were seen to play a major role in distinguishing word meanings.

Table 13.5 shows the number of lexemes in each lexicon and their part-of-speech distribution. As described above, we separated out lexemes that were not directly comparable, i.e. Latin terms and inflected word forms. The English Wiktionary was again the largest lexicon. It encoded the most nouns and verbs and more than twice as many adjectives and adverbs as WordNet and Roget's Thesaurus. The

---

[21] See http://en.wiktionary.org/wiki/Wiktionary_talk:Entry_layout_explained/ and the corresponding archive pages for a full discussion on this topic.

TABLE 13.5 **The number of lexemes in Wiktionary and comparable resources**

English language	Wiktionary	WordNet	Roget's Thesaurus
Lexemes:	379,694	156,584	62,819
Comparable lexemes:	247,192	149,502	60,760
Nouns:	154,452	111,954	29,854
Verbs:	23,172	11,531	15,150
Adjectives:	58,502	21,536	12,739
Adverbs:	11,066	4,481	3,017
Other parts of speech:	13,206	0	2,037
Not comparable:	119,296	7,082	22

German language	Wiktionary	GermaNet	OpenThesaurus
Lexemes:	85,574	85,257	58,213
Comparable lexemes:	43,843	85,240	57,916
Nouns:	33,841	68,211	38,281
Verbs:	4,280	8,812	10,667
Adjectives/Adverbs:	5,722	8,217	8,968
Other parts of speech:	7,455	0	280
Not comparable:	34,276	17	17

Russian language	Wiktionary	Russian WordNet	
Lexemes:	134,994	131,251	
Comparable lexemes:	115,001	126,224	
Nouns:	64,190	97,257	
Verbs:	18,508	8,995	
Adjectives:	26,714	16,087	
Adverbs:	5,589	3,885	
Other parts of speech:	19,452	0	
Not comparable:	541	5,027	

German Wiktionary shows a different picture: it is the smallest lexicon compared to GermaNet and OpenThesaurus. Verbs seem to be particularly under-represented, as GermaNet encodes more than twice and OpenThesaurus more than three times as many verbs as the German Wiktionary. However, it also encodes a lower number of adjectives and nouns. The Russian Wiktionary contains more verbs, adjectives, and adverbs than the Russian WordNet but, in turn, contains a lower number of nouns.

TABLE 13.6 **The part-of-speech tags used in Wiktionary**

Part of speech	English Wiktionary	German Wiktionary	Russian Wiktionary
Noun	218,629	32,808	62,861
Verb	62,202	4,269	18,524
Adjective	58,872	5,015	26,717
Adverb	11,079	669	5,602
Named entity	15,635	1,062	15,063
Abbreviation	6,763	3,050	234
Phrase	3,217	1,915	930
Particle	8	36	93
Pronoun	364	132	106
Preposition	463	108	135
Numeral	376	140	63
Determiner	93	17	15
Affix	1,474	472	198
Other	519	1,610	4,453

PARTS OF SPEECH

In total, we found sixty-nine different part-of-speech tags within the three Wiktionary editions. Table 13.6 shows the number of lexemes per part-of-speech tag. Since many tags are very fine-grained, for brevity we grouped them into the fourteen general categories shown in the table. The Wiktionary community uses, for instance, three different tags for abbreviations: initialisms (pronounced letter by letter; e.g. 'CD' for 'Compact Disc'), acronyms (pronounced like a regular word, e.g. 'ROM' for 'read only memory'), and abbreviations terminated by a full stop (such as 'Apr.' for 'April'). A similar distinction is made for pronouns (e.g. demonstrative, reflexive, or possessive pronouns), particles (e.g. comparative, intensifying, and answering particles), affixes (e.g. prefixes and suffixes), and phrases. The latter are tagged as proverbs (e.g. 'love is blind'), interjections (e.g. 'good God'), idioms (e.g. 'in the same boat'), or collocations (e.g. 'strong tea'). Wiktionary encodes a high number of phrases which are particularly useful in combination with their translations into other languages, since idioms and proverbs are usually very hard to translate. This opens up very valuable opportunities for cross-lingual lexicography. The high number of named entities in the English Wiktionary is also notable. In comparison to the English WordNet, we predominantly find given names (e.g. 'Alice' or 'Nadine'), and toponyms (e.g. 'Berlin' or 'Ohio'), as well as named entities from the non-US culture (such as the Arab broadcaster 'Al Jazeera' or the Swiss canton 'Aargau'). Interestingly,

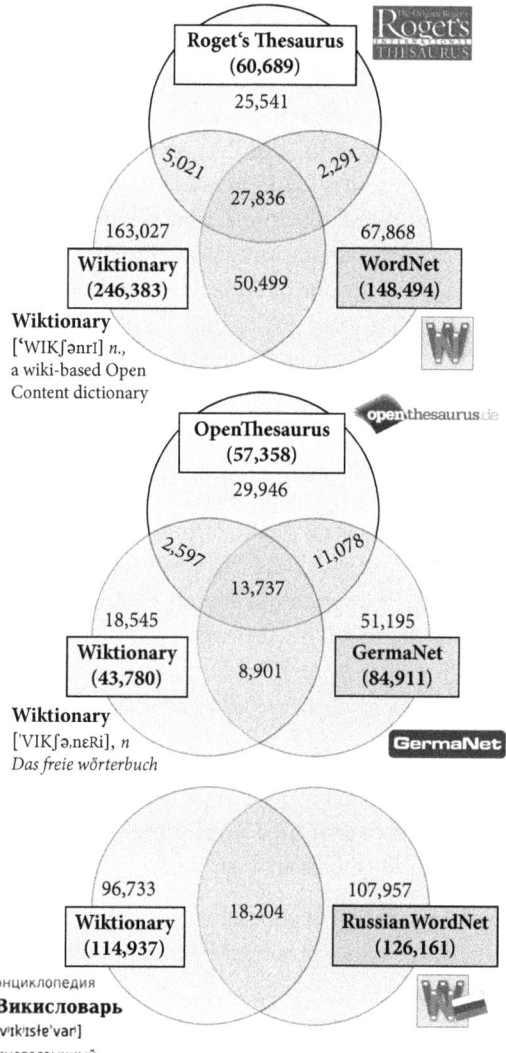

FIGURE 13.4 Overlap of lexemes between the English (top), German (middle), and Russian (bottom) lexicons.

phrasal verbs (like 'turn off') and compounds (like 'toothpaste') do not receive a special tag, but are considered as verbs, nouns, etc.

OVERLAP OF LEXEMES

To examine whether the lexicons largely overlap or contain complementary information, we aligned lexemes that shared the same term and part of speech and measured their lexical overlap. Figure 13.4 shows a Venn diagram of the number of lexemes shared by each pair of lexicons. We find that the total overlap of the lexicons is very small. For the English language, only 11 per cent of the lexemes in Wiktionary, 19 per cent of the lexemes in WordNet, and 46 per cent of the lexemes in Roget's Thesaurus are found within the respective other lexicons. The highest number of lexemes is shared by Wiktionary and WordNet, which is, however, still quite low compared to the number of lexemes found in only one of the resources.

This is a very surprising result, since one would expect two lexicons covering general language to basically encode the same list of lexemes. We therefore analysed which lexemes are encoded in only one of the lexicons and particularly found named entities (e.g. 'Grammy'), multi-word expressions (e.g. 'air sick'), and alternative spellings (e.g. 'narcist'), as well as domain-specific lexemes. Wiktionary predominantly encodes lexemes from information sciences (e.g. 'sound card'), natural sciences (e.g. 'benzyl'), and sports (e.g. 'libero'), as well as informal (e.g. 'ear candy') and archaic lexemes (e.g. 'abaculus'). In WordNet, we mainly found lexemes from the biological or medical domain (e.g. the 'napa' plant, or the 'axial muscle'), but encountered also numerous lexemes covering shades of colour (such as 'reddish-pink').

The overlap between lexemes was similarly small for the Russian lexicons, and although the number of shared lexemes was slightly higher for the German lexicons, there were still large differences in their coverage.

13.3.3 *Coverage of word senses*

In Wiktionary, the different meanings of a lexeme are enumerated in a list of *word senses*. Each word sense is described by a short gloss that is sometimes accompanied by usage examples or references to related word senses. There are, for instance, the following three word senses for the noun 'boat':

1. A craft used for transportation of goods, fishing, racing, recreational cruising, or military use on or in the water, propelled by oars or outboard motor or inboard motor or by wind.
2. (*poker slang*) A full house.
3. (*chemistry*) One of two possible conformers of cyclohexane rings (the other being 'chair'), shaped roughly like a boat.

Table 13.7 shows the number of word senses encoded in our eight lexicons. The highest number of word senses is found within the English Wiktionary, which has more than twice the number of senses as WordNet and over four times as many as Roget's thesaurus. The German lexicons are not so different, although GermaNet contains about 20,000 word senses more than the other two. However, the Russian Wiktionary encodes a much lower number of word senses than the Russian WordNet.

TABLE 13.7 **The number of word senses in Wiktionary and comparable resources**

English language	Wiktionary	WordNet	Roget's Thesaurus
Word senses:	474,128	206,978	98,464
Lexemes with 0 senses:	145	0	0
Lexemes with 1 sense:	327,274	130,207	44,317
Lexemes with 2 senses:	33,640	16,375	10,107
Lexemes with >2 senses:	18,635	10,002	8,395
Max. senses per lexeme:	59	59	18
Avg. senses per lexeme:	1.25	1.32	1.57
German language	Wiktionary	GermaNet	OpenThesaurus
Word senses:	73,500	95,715	72,897
Lexemes with 0 senses:	36,004	0	0
Lexemes with 1 sense:	36,242	77,335	49,219
Lexemes with 2 senses:	8,197	6,071	5,788
Lexemes with >2 senses:	5,131	1,851	3,206
Max. senses per lexeme:	52	26	14
Avg. senses per lexeme:	1.48	1.13	1.25
Russian language	Wiktionary	Russian WordNet	
Word senses:	80,618	182,448	
Lexemes with 0 senses:	82,261	0	
Lexemes with 1 sense:	38,060	110,387	
Lexemes with 2 senses:	8,266	11,830	
Lexemes with >2 senses:	6,407	9,034	
Max. senses per lexeme:	30	54	
Avg. senses per lexeme:	1.53	1.39	

DEGREE OF POLYSEMY

Comparing the absolute number of word senses only allows us to draw limited conclusions, since lexicographers can choose different sense granularities for their sense descriptions. A higher number of word senses hence does not necessarily imply a higher coverage of meanings per se. We therefore also compared the *degree of polysemy*, which we define as the number of word senses per lexeme. Table 13.7 shows the number of lexemes with 0, 1, 2, and more than 2 word senses as well as the maximum and the average number of word senses per lexeme in the different lexicons.

Expert-built lexicons do not contain lexemes without any word senses. This is different in Wiktionary, where users may encode entries without providing all the linguistic information at once or even as a *stub* (i.e. a skeleton of empty sections without any content-related information) that needs to be filled by other contributors over time. The low number of these lexicon entries in the English Wiktionary indicates that it is in a stable state and contains definitions for the vast majority of lexemes. This is different for the German Wiktionary, which lacks word sense definitions for 42 per cent of its lexemes and for the Russian Wiktionary, lacking definitions for as many as 60 per cent of its lexemes. Smaller Wiktionary editions obviously need more development time in order to fill their gaps.

Between 80 and 90 per cent of the lexemes in expert-built lexicons have only one word sense. In the English Wiktionary, 81 per cent of the lexemes are monosemous, which conforms to this range. The German Wiktionary, however, contains only 68 per cent monosemous lexemes and hence encodes a higher number of polysemous lexemes. A possible explanation for this discrepancy might be that the Wiktionary community is more likely to create articles for polysemous lexemes, since they can cause confusion when understanding a text and are thus felt to be more important (Meyer and Gurevych, 2010a). This also applies to the Russian Wiktionary, in which 72 per cent of the lexemes are monosemous.

The average number of encoded word senses is similar in all the lexicons, ranging between 1.14 and 1.57. The maximum number of word senses is, however, very different—ranging from eighteen word senses in Roget's Thesaurus to fifty-nine word senses in the English Wiktionary and WordNet. This can be used as an indicator for sense granularity. WordNet is known to be very fine-grained (Palmer *et al.* 2007); the English and German Wiktionary editions seem to be of similar granularity. Studying the number of word senses for a lexeme and the time when a word sense was encoded by the Wiktionary community is an important strand of lexicographic research. This is because it characterizes how the lexicon is used and what types of entries have not yet been encoded because they have not yet been looked up.

POLYSEMIC DIFFERENCE

The English Wiktionary and WordNet both have exactly one verb with fifty-nine word senses. This seems to show strong similarity. The verb is, however, '(to) break' in WordNet and '(to) go' in Wiktionary. To accommodate this issue in our analysis, we measured the *polysemic difference* between the lexicons, which we define as the difference in the number of word senses per lexeme (Meyer and Gurevych 2010b). The verb '(to) break' from the example above has thirty-four word senses in Wiktionary and hence yields a polysemic difference of $|59 - 34| = 25$.

In the English Wiktionary, 60 per cent of the lexemes shared with WordNet and 40 per cent of the lexemes shared with Roget's Thesaurus have a polysemic difference of 0 (i.e. the same number of word senses). This proportion is even higher for the German Wiktionary: 60 per cent of the lexemes are shared with GermaNet and 51 per cent of the lexemes are shared with OpenThesaurus. Over 86 per cent of the lexemes in the English Wiktionary and over 91 per cent in the German Wiktionary have a polysemic difference of less than or equal to 2, which means that the number of encoded word senses per lexeme is not dramatically different. As our example of '(to) break' shows, there are, however, also a few lexemes with a very high polysemic difference, which is again either an indicator of different sense granularities or a lack of sense coverage in one of the lexicons.

OVERLAP OF WORD SENSES

The adjective 'buggy' has two word senses both in Wiktionary and in WordNet, which yields a polysemic difference of 0 for this lexeme. However, it turns out that the two lexicons only share a single word sense "infested with bugs". Wiktionary additionally encodes "containing programming errors", while WordNet encodes "informal or slang terms for mentally irregular". In order to gain a clearer insight into the coverage of word senses, we need to align the lexicons and quantify the number of shared word senses—similar to our study concerning the overlap of lexemes reported in Section 13.3.2. While an alignment of lexemes can be achieved using simple word-matching approaches, the alignment of word senses is a very complex task that is the subject of ongoing research (Navigli and Ponzetto 2010. Niemann and Gurevych 2011).

To our knowledge, the word sense alignment by Meyer and Gurevych (2011) between the English Wiktionary and WordNet is the only work integrating Wiktionary with other lexicons. According to this word sense alignment, Wiktionary and WordNet share 56,970 word senses. For 60,707 WordNet synsets[22] there is no corresponding word sense in Wiktionary. Conversely, there are 371,329 word senses in Wiktionary that have no counterpart in WordNet. Similar to our observation regarding the overlap of lexemes in Section 13.3.2, the overlap of word senses is surprisingly small. Table 13.8 shows the number of senses per part of speech that are only found in Wiktionary or WordNet (but not vice versa) and the number of senses

TABLE 13.8 **The number of word senses only found in Wiktionary or WordNet and shared by both lexicons**

Part of speech	Wiktionary and WordNet	Only Wiktionary	Only WordNet
Nouns:	34,464	158,085	47,651
Verbs:	8,252	29,119	5,515
Adjectives/adverbs:	14,236	60,977	7,541
Other parts of speech:	0	16,778	0
Inflected word forms:	0	106,328	0

[22] Note that the alignment matches Wiktionary word senses with WordNet synsets—i.e. lists of synonymous word senses. This notion is not directly comparable to our definition of word senses.

shared by both lexicons. The word senses of inflected word forms are naturally missing from WordNet. However, both Wiktionary and WordNet encode a large number of senses that are not found in the other lexicon. The collaboratively constructed Wiktionary is hence an important resource that should be considered by lexicographers when composing the word senses of a lexicon entry. In particular, newly coined word senses such as the computer-science-related word sense of 'buggy' can be quickly included in Wiktionary due to its continual updatability.

COMPOSITION OF GLOSSES

In a qualitative study on the composition of glosses in the English Wiktionary and WordNet (Meyer and Gurevych 2010*b*), we often observed only minor differences in the wording of glosses for overlapping word senses. Wiktionary encodes, for example, "a nun in charge of a priory; an abbess or mother superior" to describe 'prioress'. This meaning is described in WordNet as "the superior of a group of nuns". The WordNet gloss is broader as it does not restrict the prioress to a female ('superior' is defined there as "the head of a religious community"). The lexeme 'tortoise' is described as "any of various land-dwelling reptiles of family *Testudinidae*, whose body is enclosed in a shell [...]. The animal can withdraw its head and four legs partially into the shell, providing some protection from predators" in Wiktionary, and as "usually herbivorous land turtles having clawed elephant-like limbs; world-wide in arid area except Australia and Antarctica" in WordNet. Although describing the same meaning, the two lexicons set a different focus: Wiktionary concentrates on the animal's anatomy and unique behaviour, while WordNet stresses its habitat and nutrition. Comparing such small differences can be very helpful in the composition of glosses, which is one of the most challenging tasks of lexicographers.

Wiktionary is often criticized for providing unspecific or too-general glosses. As Fuertes-Olivera (2009: 123) points out, the noun 'takeover' is, for instance, described as "the purchase of one company by another; a merger without the formation of a new company", which does not really differentiate between the general purchase of a company and the specialized concepts of a takeover or a merger. Other issues are spelling errors in the lexicon entries, e.g. the use of "bootle feeding" in the article 'bottle feed'. Hanks (this volume) observed many old-fashioned descriptions in Wiktionary, which stem from copying information from copyright-expired dictionaries.

Many of such errors are likely to be removed in a collaborative effort. In an experiment, Hanks (this volume) found that the Wiktionary community is very active and revises new entries within minutes. However, it is a serious problem to distinguish well-crafted entries from those that need substantial revision by the community. Although there are mechanisms to indicate a need for revision provided

---

However, this only affects the scale of senses found only in WordNet, which we will not analyse any further, but rather focus on the word senses in Wiktionary.

by the Wiki software, there is as yet no fixed review or release workflow for lexicon entries.

SENSE ORDERING

The word senses in WordNet are ordered according to the SemCor corpus frequencies (Fellbaum 1998: 41). This promotes the most frequently used word sense to the first position, which is also a common strategy in practical lexicography (Atkins and Rundell 2008: 250). However, using a corpus such as SemCor to obtain the sense frequencies might not yield very realistic data because sense-tagged corpora are usually very small and often limited to certain types of document or vocabulary (e.g. newspaper text).

Although there is no specific guideline for the sense ordering in Wiktionary, we observed that the first entry is often the most frequently used one. For the noun 'tattoo', the first word sense in Wiktionary is "an image made in the skin with ink and a needle", but "a drumbeat or bugle call that signals the military to return to their quarters" in WordNet. Intuitively, the Wiktionary word sense is the more frequently used one nowadays. The majority of the sentences in, for example, the British National Corpus refer to this meaning. Hence, the sum of subjective opinions on the usage of word senses that coins Wiktionary's sense ordering can alleviate the limitations and sparseness of sense-tagged corpora and provide a viable resource for lexicographers when ordering word senses by usage frequencies.

13.3.4 *Coverage of domains and registers*

In Section 13.2.4, we introduced the notation of *linguistic labels*, which describe the domain, register, style, time period, etc. of a word sense. We identified 714 different linguistic labels within the English Wiktionary, 238 within the German, and 125 within the Russian edition.[23] About half of the word senses, 273,960 (58%) are tagged with at least one linguistic label in the English Wiktionary. In the German and Russian Wiktionary, this percentage is lower: only 28,035 (38%) word senses in the German, and 34,937 (43%) in the Russian Wiktionary have a linguistic label.

DOMAIN LABELS

A broad and balanced coverage of domain-specific vocabulary is a common challenge when compiling a lexicon (Pantel and Lin 2002), since it largely depends on the individual expertise of the lexicographers. In Wiktionary, a large number of contributors work on the lexicon entries collaboratively and hence can develop domain-specific knowledge for practically every domain. Consequently, the majority of Wiktionary's linguistic labels denote the thematic domain in which a word sense is

---

[23] We only counted linguistic labels used at least ten times and removed labels describing grammatical properties, such as "not countable".

TABLE 13.9 The distribution of domain labels in the English, German, and Russian Wiktionaries and WordNet domains

Domain	English Wiktionary	German Wiktionary	Russian Wiktionary	WordNet domains
Biology	9.5%	13.6%	11.3%	27.8%
Chemistry	15.4%	4.8%	4.7%	5.9%
Engineering	2.3%	6.9%	9.8%	2.7%
Geology	5.9%	3.9%	5.6%	6.1%
Humanities	6.0%	11.4%	13.6%	13.7%
IT	7.6%	2.9%	2.6%	1.2%
Linguistics	2.5%	18.9%	14.5%	3.7%
Maths	6.0%	3.5%	4.0%	1.1%
Medicine	10.0%	9.5%	9.1%	8.3%
Military	1.5%	1.4%	3.8%	1.4%
Physics	6.5%	3.7%	3.9%	2.9%
Religion	2.5%	3.4%	3.4%	1.9%
Social sciences	7.6%	6.9%	7.4%	10.6%
Sports	6.6%	4.2%	2.8%	1.8%
Other	10.1%	5.0%	3.5%	10.9%

used, e.g. the label 'chemistry' of the third word sense of 'boat'. These *domain labels* are very fine-grained. In order to identify over- or under-represented domains, we manually grouped similar domain labels by their general topic. The labels 'cycling' and 'weightlifting' are, for example, combined with the category 'sports'. As a comparable resource, we use *WordNet Domains*[24] (Bentivogli *et al.* 2004), which encodes 157 different domain labels for 128,669 (62%) word senses of the English WordNet. Table 13.9 shows the distribution of domain labels in the three Wiktionary editions and WordNet Domains.

About a quarter of the domain labels in WordNet Domains are from biology, because WordNet covers the entire taxonomy of plants and animals, which is only partly encoded in Wiktionary. The Wiktionaries have a stronger focus on the other natural sciences—most prominently on chemistry (10,912 word senses) in the English Wiktionary. Other well-represented domains include information technology (IT), maths, medicine, and sports. The contributors in Wiktionary encode word senses on

---

[24] We used Version 3.2, available from http://wndomains.fbk.eu, and ignored the label 'factotum' as it does not represent a domain.

a voluntary basis, which might cause a focus on knowledge from their leisure time (such as sport) rather than from work-related topics. Clearly under-represented are the humanities and social sciences, although they are covered better within WordNet. While linguistics and engineering seem to be predominantly encoded by the German and the Russian Wiktionary communities, these domains are rarer in the English Wiktionary. The different focus of the Wiktionary language editions and WordNet Domains may help to close domain-specific coverage gaps in other lexicons in future.

REGISTER AND STYLE LABELS

In addition to domain labels, there are also a large number of linguistic labels that denote a register of language, i.e. a variety of language used in a certain manner of speech or writing. The majority of these *register labels*—about 40 per cent—comprise slang- or jargon-related word senses. This was also observed in Section 13.3.2. These labels comprise Internet jargon, argot, or young people's language. Additionally, there are register labels denoting the degree of formality or marking offensive terms. *Style labels* are similar, as they mark word senses found in a certain type of text (e.g. newspaper or literary style). In total, we counted 14,266 word senses in the English Wiktionary, 3,237 in the German Wiktionary, and 2,573 in the Russian Wiktionary that encode at least one of these register or style labels.

OTHER LABELS

A third type of linguistic label used in Wiktionary comprises *temporal qualifiers*. The word sense "A sturdy merchant sailing vessel" of 'cat' is, for example, marked as archaic. Sometimes, word senses are also associated with a particular period of time, such as the nineteenth century. Apart from that, we noticed a high number of dialect word senses marked as Scottish English, Swiss German, or Yorkshire English.

13.4 Conclusion

Collaborative lexicography is a novel paradigm for compiling dictionaries in which large communities, backed up by the phenomenon of collective intelligence, compete with expert lexicographers. In this chapter, we have studied the main principle of collaborative lexicography based on the collaboratively constructed, multilingual online lexicon Wiktionary.

First, we gave a comprehensive description of Wiktionary, including its historical development and its macro- and microstructure. We found that Wiktionary offers many different access paths to its knowledge and thus makes use of many innovative features of online dictionaries that allow users to search, cross-reference, and browse through the lexicon entries by alphabet, topic, register, or in an onomasiological way. The lexicon entries often encode a large variety of heterogeneous linguistic knowledge, including etymological, phonetic, morphological, syntactic, semantic, cross-lingual, and pictorial information. The flexible and easy-to-use Wiki software attracts a large number of contributors and enables the encoding of culture- or language-specific variations. This recipe for success has yielded over 170 language editions describing over nine million multilingual articles. In addition to the major languages (English and French), which represent the largest language editions, we also found smaller and endangered languages in Wiktionary. Finally we examined different types of contributors and how they collaborate.

In the second part of our chapter, we compared Wiktionary to multiple expert-built lexicons in three languages. We found a very high coverage of terms in the English Wiktionary and competitive coverage in the German and the Russian Wiktionaries. In particular, neologisms and the basic vocabulary of a language are well covered by Wiktionary. The lexical overlap between the different lexicons is surprisingly small, which makes Wiktionary an important resource for additional linguistic information missing from other lexicons. We found more polysemous lexemes in Wiktionary, which might be looked up more frequently than monosemous ones, because they can cause confusion when understanding a text. The creation order of the lexicon entries can help to reveal the information needs of the dictionary users. We also inspected the formation of glosses and identified important additions in them, compared to expert-built lexicons. However, we also found erroneous and unspecific glosses which are not useful for a dictionary user. Wiktionary has as yet no reviewing or releasing workflow. Quality assurance and trustworthiness are hence important determinants when working with Wiktionary (and other collaboratively constructed resources). We studied the coverage of Wiktionary's linguistic labels that are used to further describe the domains, registers, styles, etc. of its word senses. We observed a general focus on domain-specific vocabulary from natural sciences, information sciences, and leisure, while social sciences and humanities were rather under-represented.

Our analysis emphasizes many different aspects of Wiktionary that rival expert-built lexicons. We believe that its unique structure and collaboratively constructed contents are particularly useful for a wide range of dictionary users, including:

1. Laypeople who want to quickly look up the definition of an unknown term or search for a forum to ask a question on a certain usage or meaning.
2. Language learners who benefit from the densely interlinked multilingual organization, the good coverage of basic vocabulary, and the use of graphics to illustrate word senses.
3. Professional translators who can exploit the translations of proverbs, interjections, idioms, or domain-specific vocabulary which have been collaboratively contributed by a multilingual community.
4. Journalists who take advantage of Wiktionary's up-to-dateness regarding neologisms or newly coined word senses.

5. Social scientists who study how a language is used, cultural peculiarities across languages, or the collaboration of Web communities.

6. Linguists who wish to investigate semantic shifts or endangered languages.

7. Computational linguists who use Wiktionary data in natural language processing applications.

8. Lexicographers who can gain totally new insights about the users of their dictionaries. This includes questions of what it is important to include in a lexicon and what is comprehensible to the reader. In particular, the semantic knowledge of Wiktionary can be of great help for composing sense glosses (when used in addition to corpus-based methods). Since every edit is archived, Wiktionary also allows the lexicographic process to be studied as a whole, in order to examine how a lexicon develops over time and what considerations and decisions are necessary. This is a new field of lexicographic research, since no corresponding data is available from expert-built dictionary manufacturers.

In conclusion, as an exemplary product of collaborative lexicography, Wiktionary opens up a variety of interesting use cases and research opportunities. We believe that collaborative lexicography will not replace traditional lexicographic theories, but will provide a different viewpoint that can improve and contribute to the lexicography of the future. Thus, Wiktionary is a rival to expert-built lexicons—no more, no less.

Acknowledgements

This work has been supported by the Volkswagen Foundation as part of the Lichtenberg-Professorship Program under grant No. I/82806. We thank Michael Matuschek and Yevgen Chebotar for their valuable contributions to this work, and Andrew A. Krizhanovsky at the Russian Academy of Sciences Saint Petersburg for sharing the Wikokit software for parsing the Russian Wiktionary edition.

14

The electronic lexicographical treatment of sign languages: The Danish Sign Language Dictionary

JETTE H. KRISTOFFERSEN AND THOMAS TROELSGÅRD

14.1 Introduction

Sign languages use the visual modality: language is produced through gestures and perceived visually. The main structural element of a sign is the manual part, with place of articulation, handshape, orientation of hands, and movement as its major phonological features.[1] Many sign languages also include non-manual features such as facial expression, mouth movement, eye-gaze, eye-blink, and movement of the head and upper body. Sign languages are full, independent languages, with their own lexicon, morphology, and syntax, in contrast to gestures accompanying speech, or sign-supported communication, where signs—usually only representing the semantically heaviest words—accompany spoken language, following the syntactic structure of the spoken language.

Sign language is not international, although the shared visual modality entails some cross-linguistically shared features, e.g. deictic pointing, the use of spatial reference, and a number of iconic signs (i.e. signs that physically resemble what they denote). Sign languages are typically used by a minority community within a larger community with a spoken and written language, e.g. British Sign Language vs. English in the UK or American Sign Language vs. English in USA. In these situations, the sign language, being the minority language, is often influenced by the surrounding majority language, as attested by the fact that finger-spelled words are sometimes

---

[1] The term 'phonology' is used in a comparable way in sign language and spoken language linguistics. Instead of talking about the language's system of audibly perceivable elements (sounds), we here talk about the system of visually perceivable elements.

used for concepts which have no lexicalized sign, or by the existence of multi-sign expressions calqued from majority language multi-word expressions.

The manual/visual modality of sign languages puts these languages in a special position in comparison with spoken and written languages. As far as we know, no sign language has a written representation that is commonly used by native signers for everyday writing and reading. As pointed out by several researchers (e.g. Brien and Turner 1994), this entails a basic challenge for the sign language lexicographer. The absence of a written standard generates a sense of non-fixedness, and is probably one of the reasons why signed languages were not recognized as languages until the late twentieth century, and why many countries still do not give official recognition to their sign languages. The lack of standardization also creates problems for sign language lexicographers, for instance when they need to identify the basic form and word class (or word classes) of a given sign.[2]

Only in recent years have sign languages begun to be acknowledged as languages and legally recognized. For these reasons, scientific sign language research is in many ways still relatively young. This is also true for sign language lexicography, and in many respects, dictionaries of sign languages still lag considerably behind those of spoken/written languages. They often offer a small number of entries and/or very little, if any, information about sign usage. In Section 14.2, we give a brief overview of the history of sign language dictionaries and identify some of their most distinguishing characteristics. In Section 14.3, we describe the main features of electronic sign language dictionaries, focusing on areas where these dictionaries have advantages over printed dictionaries. Section 14.4 focuses on the Danish Sign Language Dictionary. We discuss the main characteristics of this dictionary and show how we have tried to accommodate the needs of different categories of users by implementing some innovative features. Finally, in Section 14.5, we explore different perspectives and look at some of the future challenges in electronic sign language lexicography.

14.2 General characteristics of sign language dictionaries

The history of sign language lexicography dates back to at least the late eighteenth century with Jean Ferrand's *Dictionnaire à L'usage des Sourds et Muets* from about 1784. This dictionary uses alphabetically ordered French words as headwords, accompanied by descriptions of the signs. Almost all sign language dictionaries compiled before the mid twentieth century can be classified as bilingual, with

---

[2] The most recent work in the area of characterizing word classes in sign languages shows that features of word classes in sign languages are unlike those in the Indo-European languages (see e.g. Schwager and Zeshan (2008) and Erlenkamp (2000)). More research on word classes in sign languages needs to be undertaken before firm generalizations and definitions are possible.

words from a written language as the source, and signs (represented by text descriptions, drawings, or photographs) as the target. An exception is dictionaries that, somewhat like phrase-books, have pairs of sign pictures and words, grouped into topically related sections (see Figure 14.1).

The first dictionary taking a sign language as its source language was the *Dictionary of American Sign Language* from 1965. In this dictionary, the headwords are signs from American Sign Language, ordered according to their phonological features, and written in a formal notation system developed by William Stokoe.

The overriding challenge in sign language lexicography is how to render signs in the absence of a written language. Several approaches to this problem have been adopted, but in recent years, the use of video recordings has predominated. This approach is obviously limited to electronic dictionaries, but it offers the possibility of showing sign production in an accurate and natural way, and it can be perceived directly by the user, requiring no particular qualifications. Video recordings, although ideal for showing sign production, usage examples, etc., have, however, the

FIGURE 14.1 From the colours section of a dictionary produced by a deaf club in Copenhagen in 1871 (Anonymous, 1871).

disadvantage of being unsuitable for representing several signs together (e.g. in search result lists), or where the sign references appear surrounded by text or within running text (e.g. in search facilities, or cross-referencing). In these situations, video recordings are both confusing and consume too much screen space to be acceptable. Furthermore, from a computational perspective, video recordings are unsuitable as lemmas in a dictionary database, as they would have to be represented by a transcription, a filename, a number, or some other sort of ID in order to be ordered or filtered.

Sign language dictionaries such as the *Einführung in die Österreichische Gebärdensprache (ÖGS) – Online* and the *K-8 Aeronautics Internet Textbook Sign Language Dictionary* use computer-generated avatars or cartoon-like animations for rendering signs, an approach which shares many of the advantages and disadvantages of video recordings. However, this approach eliminates the costs and the practical and legal problems related to working with real-life people. It also has the advantage of making it possible to rotate the avatar to view it from different perspectives. On the other hand, avatars and cartoon characters are not wholly naturalistic. As a result, the pronunciation, as is often true of generated speech, seems robotic or in other ways unnatural.

In printed sign language dictionaries, a drawing or photograph of a person producing the sign is the most common way of showing sign pronunciation. Often arrows are added to show movement; some dictionaries use a sequence of images, or multiple overlay images, for showing sign movement, change of handshape, or change of location. Still images (photographs or drawings) are also frequently used in electronic sign language dictionaries as a supplement to video clips (e.g. as clickable thumbnails in search result lists).

Textual representation of signs occurs in various forms, most commonly as glosses (i.e. translations into written language) which are used as mnemonics. These glosses are conventionally written in upper case. When used in sign language research, glosses are often not fixed translations, but chosen in a particular context. Thus, a sign can have different glosses in different contexts. Some dictionaries, however, use fixed unique glosses for the sign lemmas, sometimes referred to as ID-glosses (cf. Johnston 2010). The advantage of this approach is that the written sign representation contains only unambiguous forms, which can be used for sign identification and annotation in a sign language corpus or in other resources. Unfortunately, using ID-glosses in a sign language dictionary interface also has some disadvantages. For example, 'soul', 'mood', and 'psyche' are all valid translations of the same Danish Sign Language (*Dansk tegnsprog*, henceforth DTS) sign, and using one of the possible translations as an ID-gloss in such cases tends to lead the inexperienced dictionary user to the false conclusion that the sign only (and always) has the meaning expressed by the chosen gloss. Written text is also used in some dictionaries to describe the production of the signs, often as a supplement to a visual representation. For this purpose some dictionaries use continuous text, others have recipe-like descriptions, and yet others have more formalized, table-like descriptions (e.g. *Dictionary of British Sign Language / English*).

Yet another way of representing signs is through a formal notation system. Several such systems are in use. One of these is the Hamburg Notation System (HamNoSys) developed at the University of Hamburg (Prillwitz *et al.* 1989). In these systems, a sign is rendered as a sequence of symbols for handshape, place of articulation, movement, etc. Another family of notation systems uses an iconic approach. The SignWriting system developed by Valerie Sutton,[3] for example, consists of stylized drawings composed of standard elements denoting handshape, place of articulation, movement, etc., but, unlike HamNoSys, the elements can be placed freely in relation to each other, reflecting the actual shape of the sign.

While SignWriting is probably easier to read intuitively, its non-sequential structure poses an additional challenge for computational treatment. The system is used by sign language learners, teachers, and researchers and has been used for headword signs in a number of dictionaries published in the 1980s and later. It is, however, not in widespread use as an everyday writing and reading system. Figure 14.2 shows the DTS sign meaning 'work' written in HamNoSys and SignWriting. The sign is produced with two fists, one 'hammering' several times on the upper part of the other fist in front of the body. More examples can be found in dictionaries using the two systems (e.g. the *Fachgebärdenlexikon Gesundheit und Pflege* and the *Woordenboek Vlaamse Gebarentaal-Nederlands/Nederlands-Vlaamse Gebarentaal*).

Because of the varying suitability of different sign rendering possibilities for different purposes, many sign language dictionaries use two or more representation

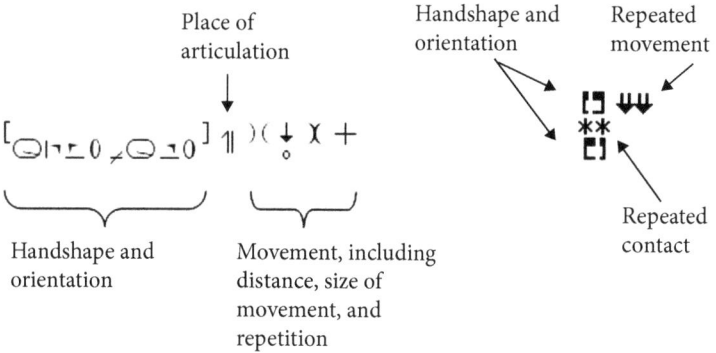

FIGURE 14.2 The DTS sign for 'work' written in HamNoSys (left) and SignWriting (right).

[3] Valerie Sutton (webmaster) (2011) *Sutton's SignWriting Site.* Available at: www.signwriting.org (last accessed 8 June 2011).

systems (e.g. video recordings for showing the sign form, and written language translations in a search result list).

14.3 Electronic sign language dictionaries

In the last two decades several electronic sign language dictionaries have been developed, the majority using written language words as search criteria, but some also offering the possibility of searching on phonological criteria (e.g. handshape and place of articulation). These dictionaries generally use video clips to illustrate the production of the signs. This section identifies a number of characteristics of electronic dictionaries that are particularly useful for sign language lexicography and illustrates them in a series of recent sign language dictionaries.

14.3.1 *Hyperlinks and multimedia*

The possibility of adding hyperlinks is a significant step forward from printed sign language dictionaries, which are sometimes difficult to navigate. Through hyperlinks the user can easily move not only between entries, user guides, appendices, and other sections of the dictionary itself, but potentially to external resources as well. Another major step forward is the possibility of presenting dictionary data not only as text and pictures, but also as multimedia, such as video clips and animations. This welcome development can be compared to the experience of an L2 learner of a spoken language with no written form who would gain access to sound recordings, instead of having phonetic transcriptions as the only language source material.

14.3.2 *Search facilities*

Searching has benefited tremendously from the development of computational lexicography. Printed dictionaries have a fixed order of entries, usually a list of headwords ordered alphabetically. Most printed sign language dictionaries follow this pattern, thus formally being bilingual with a written language as the source and adopting an onomasiological approach. Some newer dictionaries, however, use different approaches. The *Svenskt Teckenspråkslexikon*, for example, adopts an onomasiological approach but the sign language is the source language: signs from Swedish Sign Language are ordered according to handshape, with an alphabetical index of Swedish equivalents at the end of the book. By contrast, in the *Fachgebär-denlexikon Sozialarbeit/Sozialpädagogik*, signs from German Sign Language are ordered alphabetically according to their German equivalent, and a handshape index is provided at the end of the book.

   In an electronic sign language dictionary, search facilities can include several search categories, combine onomasiological and semasiological approaches, and to some extent include all the languages involved as both source and target languages, thus making it difficult to fit the dictionary into the traditional dictionary typology. In spite of these new possibilities, unidirectional text search from word to sign is still the most common search possibility in electronic sign language dictionaries, although some dictionaries offer different, or multiple, search facilities. These include topic searches in the dictionaries of Brazilian Sign Language (Dicionário Libras) and Argentine Sign Language (Manos que Hablan), where it is possible to search both on words and on topics.

Since 2000, a number of electronic sign language dictionaries that offer bidirectional search options from word to sign and from sign to word have been developed, including the online dictionaries of Swedish Sign Language, Dutch Sign Language, Flemish Sign Language, Finnish Sign Language, and New Zealand Sign Language. These new dictionaries all offer search capabilities using the sign parameters of handshape and place of articulation, and combinations of the two. Some dictionaries such as the Finnish Sign Language dictionary *Suvi Suomalaisen viittomakielen verkosanakirja* and the Swedish Sign Language dictionary *Svenskt Teckenspråkslexikon* also offer the possibility of searching on mouth gestures. In the Flemish Sign Language dictionary *Woordenboek Vlaamse Gebarentaal-Nederlands/Nederlands-Vlaamse Gebarentaal*, the type of contact between hand and place of articulation is included as a search facility. The Finnish Sign Language dictionary has movement as a search parameter and the Swedish and Flemish Sign Language dictionaries, among others, offer searches on signs that are specific to particular regions.

14.3.3 *Flexibility*

A well-known advantage of the electronic medium is the absence of space limitations, or at least their great flexibility of space, which makes it possible to present much more data than is feasible in a printed entry. This, together with features such as hyperlinks, pop-ups, tabs, sub-pages, etc., opens the way for dynamic and flexible presentations of dictionary data. Newer electronic sign language dictionaries exploit these possibilities very differently. The information given in the entries varies from simple videos of the sign and one equivalent or a gloss representing the sign, to much more elaborate entries, with information such as restrictions on use and phonological or regional variants. The Finnish Sign Language, Swedish Sign Language, and Dutch Sign Language dictionaries, for example, offer example sentences in the form of video clips and accompanying text. Written descriptions of pronunciation are provided in the Swedish Sign Language dictionary; and the German Swiss Sign Language lexicon of signs for technical terms (*Gebärden-Fachlexikon, Deutschschweizerische Gebärdensprache / Deutsch*) offers definitions in German and German Swiss Sign Language. Signs are sometimes accompanied by a special mouth gesture that is not derived from the spoken language (see Boyes Braem and Sutton-Spence 2001, Kristoffersen and Boye Niemelä 2008). In the Swedish Sign Language dictionary, these signs are marked with a T, while the Finnish Sign Language dictionary offers a written description of applicable mouth gestures, and provides an inventory of the different mouth gestures for searching facilities.

The presentation of search results is another area where different approaches have been chosen, for example in relation to what information is included in the result list (Table 14.1). Note that none of these dictionaries offers videos or animations in the result list (see the discussion in Section 14.2).

14.3.4 *Meeting diverse user needs*

The core user group of sign language dictionaries is relatively limited and diverse. It includes deaf people whose preferred language is sign language; people who use signs and/or elements of sign language in different communication forms (e.g. hard-of-hearing people), and people with acquired deafness or people with learning disabilities, such as Down syndrome, which cause communication difficulties that can be remediated through simultaneous use of signs and speech. These groups are surrounded by people with whom they interact in personal or professional contexts. Family members, friends, interpreters, teachers, and nurses are thus typically learners of sign language, or at least of signs, and constitute the largest group of potential users. Finally, sign language researchers and others with an interest in sign language are also potential dictionary users. These user groups obviously have very different needs. A deaf student is most likely to be interested in spoken/written language equivalents for a specific sign rather than in information about sign variation. By contrast, information about sign variants may be particularly useful for the hearing parents of a deaf child as this information may allow them to understand signs learned by their child in nursery or at school.

Theoretically, for each pair of languages, be they written/spoken languages or sign languages, eight types of bilingual dictionary can be created to answer different users' needs: comprehension, production, translation to L1, and translation to L2, all multiplied by two to allow for different source languages. In practice, however, bilingual dictionaries for written/spoken languages are usually combinations of some of these eight types, e.g. a unidirectional dictionary for both comprehension of and translation from the source language (cf. Svensén 2009). This is all the more true for sign language dictionaries, probably because limited financial resources usually only allow for one large-scale dictionary project for a specific language pair which should aim to satisfy the needs of all potential users. As a result, comprehensive electronic sign language dictionaries often tend to be more or less well-defined combinations of many different dictionary types. They are often bidirectional, and in some cases, include features from special-purpose dictionaries (e.g. facilities for performing topic searches or making custom glossaries). The 'vocab sheet' feature in *The Online Dictionary of New Zealand Sign Language*, for example, allows the user, typically a

TABLE 14.1 Types of information provided in the search result list in several recent sign language dictionaries

	photograph	drawing	formal notation	ID number	word class	gloss	equivalent(s)	mouth action	text description	topic
Ordbog over Dansk Tegnsprog [=Danish Sign Language]	+					+	+			
Van Dale Basiswoordenboek Nederlandse Gebarentaal [=Dutch Sign Language]						+				
Suvi Suomalaisen viittomakielen verkosanakirja [=Finnish Sign Language]	+			+			+			
Woordenboek Vlaamse Gebarentaal [=Flemish Sign Language]			+				+			
The Online Dictionary of New Zealand Sign Language [=New Zealand Sign Language]		+			+		+			
Svenskt Teckenspråkslexikon [=Swedish Sign Language]	+			+			+	+	+	+

teacher or learner of New Zealand Sign Language, to build a custom collection of signs. For each selected sign a drawing and one or more English translations are copied, and the dictionary user can rearrange and add notes before printing the custom dictionary. Because of the diversity of the user groups, it might be more practicable to consider function theory (Tarp 2008), and describe modern sign language dictionaries not by assigning them to traditional dictionary types, but rather by looking at potential user needs in different communicative situations.

14.4 The Danish Sign Language Dictionary

The Danish Sign Language Dictionary (Center for Tegnsprog 2008–2011) can best be described as a semi-bilingual dictionary. Signs/words from both DTS and Danish can be used as search criteria but the main focus is on DTS and no information is given about Danish words. The rationale has been to make a multifunctional dictionary, which at the same time is comprehensive and user friendly, and which can be of use to a wide range of users—from beginning learners of DTS to native DTS signers— rather than to create distinct DTS-Danish and/or Danish-DTS dictionaries.

14.4.1 *Search facilities*

When designing the search facilities of the DTS Dictionary, our aim was to ensure that simple as well as advanced searches could be performed through one clear and easily manageable interface. Searches in the DTS Dictionary can include criteria from five different categories: primary handshape, secondary handshape, place of articulation, text, and topic. For handshapes, the possibility of entering a primary and a secondary (different or similar) handshape is added in order to facilitate specific searches for two-handed signs. Text is entered in a text box; topic and manual criteria are chosen via pop-up windows activated by clicking a category button. The selected criteria are shown in a list on the left side of the screen. There are sixty-five searchable handshapes, divided into thirty groups with one or more members. The handshapes are selected in groups in a pop-up window. Figure 14.3 shows the handshape selection window; the '3' handshape and its subgroup are moused over for selection. After a group has been selected, the user can deselect individual handshapes by clicking them in the criteria list in order to refine the search. This enables the user to select single handshapes or custom groups of handshapes, independently of the default hand-shape grouping.

The place of articulation, i.e. the location of the sign, is chosen from a pop-up window with twenty-one location icons, representing locations on or near the body or groups of locations. As for handshapes, one or more locations can be selected, and elements can then be deselected individually. Text searches can be performed on

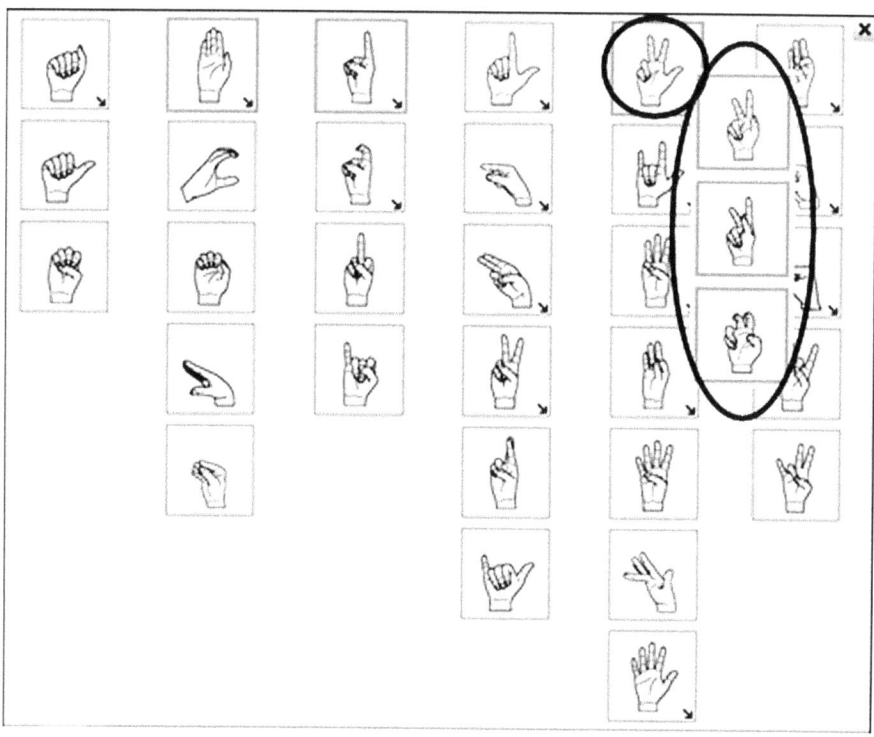

FIGURE 14.3 Window for selection of handshape in the DTS Dictionary (Center for Tegnsprog, 2008–2011).

Danish equivalents, sign glosses, and example sentences (both transcriptions and translations). This enables the user to locate signs that are not themselves lemmas in the dictionary, but appear in example sentences. Phrase search and wildcard search are possible. Topics can be chosen as search criteria from a list of seventy hierarchically ordered topics. If a superordinate topic is selected, all its daughter topics are included in the search. Criteria from multiple categories can also be combined. In this case, an 'or' condition is used inside each category, while 'and' conditions are used for category combinations. The chosen search criteria can be deselected individually, or cleared altogether by clicking a reset button.

As shown in Figure 14.4, the result list provides the following information for each hit: a unique gloss for the sign, a photograph of the sign, a meaning summary, and nought to three relevance markers. The result list is shown next to the selected search criteria in order to facilitate adjustments to the search.

In order to ensure that all possibly relevant matches are included in a search result, the search function in the DTS Dictionary is quite broad. For manual features, that means that all occurring locations and handshapes in a sign, both prominent and

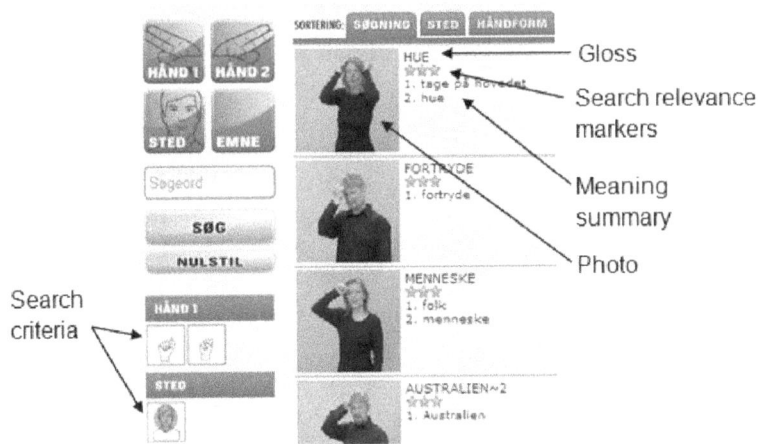

FIGURE 14.4 Search facility and result list (Center for Tegnsprog, 2008–2011).

non-prominent, are taken into account by the search function. Similarly, text matches are sought not only among the Danish equivalents, but also among glosses and translations of usage examples. For each search match a relevance score is calculated. For searches on manual features, early appearance in the sign gives a high score, late appearance a lower score. Text search matches are weighted in the following order: glosses, Danish equivalents, glosses in usage examples, words in the translations of usage examples. Thus, a matching gloss or equivalent scores higher than a match in a usage example. Based on the calculated scores, nought to three relevance markers are assigned to each match, and the matches are ordered accordingly. The presence of fewer than three markers signals to the user that the selected search criteria are met, but in a secondary position (e.g. that a search string is found not as an equivalent, but within a usage example).

In addition to the default sort order, the user can choose between two other sort orders: first by location, and second by handshape, with no regard to the original relevance score. These alternative sort orders are activated by clicking the corresponding tabs at the top of the result list. A third tab re-establishes the default, relevance-based sort order. This facility has been added because sort order is quite a complex matter in sign language lexicography. In some contexts an alphabetization of equivalents or glosses can be useful, but if the focus is on the manual expression of the sign, a sort order that reflects one of the two basic manual features (place of articulation and handshape) is more relevant. Whether place of articulation or handshape should be preferred as the primary key is still an open question. Carreiras *et al.* (2007), for example, measured reaction times for recognition of different types of Spanish Sign Language signs in different phonological surroundings, but they could not decide which of the two features (handshape and place of articulation) was more significant.

14.4.2 *Use of hyperlinks*

The DTS Dictionary makes full use of the hyperlinking facilities provided by the electronic medium. Too many links can be annoying, but considering the benefits of being able to direct the user to other entries in a dictionary, we placed very few restraints on the use of hyperlinks. For example, every lemma occurring in an example sentence is hyperlinked to its corresponding entry. One of the innovative features of the DTS Dictionary is that there are linked cross-references to synonyms, a feature that obviously presupposes a definition of synonymy, which for sign languages can be quite complex. DTS allows a great deal of variation, and therefore the question of when two similar sign forms are to be considered two different signs with the same meaning, i.e. synonyms (or lexical variants), and when are they to be considered two acceptable pronunciations of the same sign, i.e. phonological variants, needs to be considered. There are no conclusive research findings about allophonic rules, phonotactics, or free variation in DTS. In order to draw a boundary between synonyms and variants, we chose to treat signs with the same semantic content and variation in only one of the major phonological parameters as variants, while signs with two or more differences in form were treated as synonyms and placed in separate entries. Table 14.2, for example, shows how four sign forms, all meaning 'August', are treated as two lemmas (AUGUST~1 and AUGUST~2), each with a variant (~a and ~b).

Another type of cross-reference has been established to deal with synonymy between what we call long-forms and short-forms. In some sign languages there is a tendency to drop one part of a compound sign and create short-forms. For example, there are at least three DTS equivalents for 'date' (day). One is articulated at the signer's nose, one is articulated at the hand, and one is a compound of these

TABLE 14.2 **Distribution of four sign forms meaning 'August' into two synonym entries**

ID-gloss	Handshape	Orientation	Movement	Place of articulation
AUGUST~1~a	fist	fingers left up palm left down	none + twist	cheek
AUGUST~1~b	clawed hand	fingers left up palm left down	none + twist	cheek
AUGUST~2~a	fist	fingers up palm left	circular	nose
AUGUST~2~b	clawed hand	fingers up palm left	circular	nose

two forms, i.e. their long-form. None of these pronunciations can be treated as phonological variants of one or the other according to our rules, because they all differ from each other in more than one of the major parameters. As a result, the three forms each have their own entry in the dictionary. These three forms, however, are certainly more closely related than other synonyms. In order to account for this semantic relationship, special cross-references have been made between the long-form and its two short-forms, while the two short-forms are linked by a normal synonym cross-reference.

Cross-referencing is also used where partial equivalence is likely to confuse DTS learners. The Danish word *træ* ('tree', 'wood' (material)) has two DTS equivalents, one for 'tree' and one for 'wood' (and 'carpenter'). In the dictionary, special 'alert cross-references', rendered as exclamation mark icons, are given between the two signs, signalling that, although the current sign can be translated into the Danish *træ*, there is another possible DTS equivalent for this word.

Special hyperlinking facilities are also aimed at native signers of DTS for whom Danish is a second language. External links are provided for Danish equivalents which have a corresponding entry in The Danish Dictionary (Det Danske Sprog- og Litteraturselskab), i.e. a corpus-based comprehensive online dictionary of modern Danish. This, together with short specifications in parentheses added to ambiguous equivalents, should assist the user in choosing the right equivalent as well as providing the possibility of learning more about Danish words.

Figure 14.5 shows the DTS Dictionary entry for the sign HUE ('cap') with examples of three types of clickable links: an 'alert' cross-reference to a partial synonym, a gloss in the transcription of an example sentence (linked to the corresponding entry), and a Danish equivalent linked to the Danish Dictionary.

14.4.3 *Example sentences*

The DTS Dictionary entries have example sentences, rendered as videos, showing the sign used in context. About 55 per cent of the sentences are derived from video recordings of natural signing, while the remainder have been constructed by native signers. The sentences are transcribed gloss by gloss, in the same order as they appear in the video, and a translation into Danish is provided. Every occurrence of a sign lemma in the example sentences is linked to its dictionary entry. In this way we provide the user with a quick and easy way to browse entries as an alternative to the regular search facility, which otherwise might seem too complicated for some users. In addition to the example sentences provided in each particular entry, a button in the entry header opens a concordance view of all example sentences where the sign is used. This feature is particularly useful to DTS learners who want to see more sentences with the sign, or just more sign language examples, as well as to sign

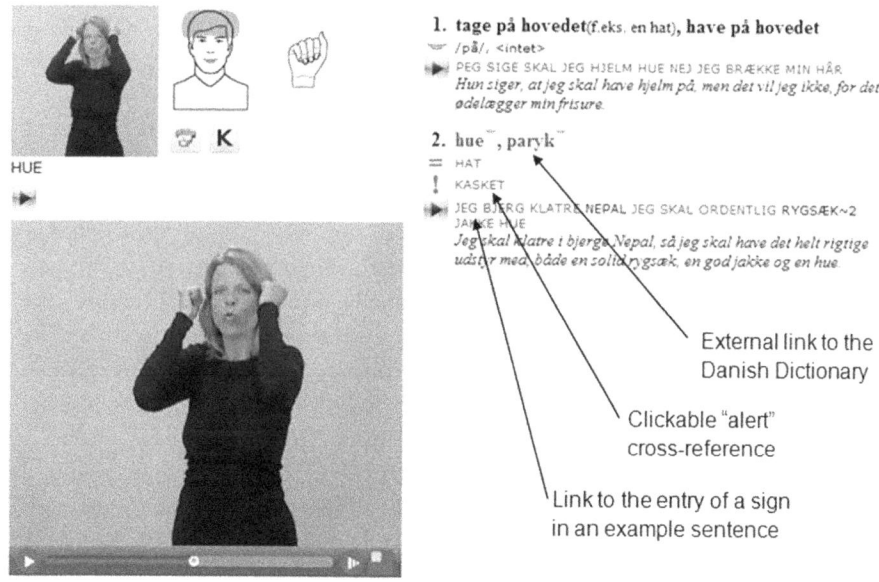

1. **tage på hovedet**(f.eks. en hat), **have på hovedet**
   ⇝ /på/, <intet>
   ▶| PEG SIGE SKAL JEG HJELM HUE NEJ JEG BRÆKKE MIN HÅR
   *Hun siger, at jeg skal have hjelm på, men det vil jeg ikke, for det
   ødelægger min frisure.*

2. **hue˜ , paryk˜**
   = HAT
   ! KASKET
   ▶| JEG BJERG KLATRE NEPAL JEG SKAL ORDENTLIG RYGSÆK~2
   JAKKE HUE
   *Jeg skal klatre i bjerge Nepal, så jeg skal have det helt rigtige
   udstyr med både en solid rygsæk, en god jakke og en hue.*

External link to the
Danish Dictionary

Clickable "alert"
cross-reference

Link to the entry of a sign
in an example sentence

HUE
▶|

Grundform af: HUE.

FIGURE 14.5 Hyperlinking facilities in the DTS Dictionary.

language researchers, who can use it as an easily accessible mini-corpus. Figure 14.6 shows the concordance view of all example sentences with the sign HUE ('cap'). By clicking one of the concordance lines (the second-lowest line was chosen in Figure 14.6), the corresponding video is shown above the concordance, accompanied by a transcription and a Danish translation.

VINTER HUSKE HANDSKE HUSKE HALSTØRKLÆDE HUSKE HUE MULIGHED
JEG BUS STIGE-AF GLEMME PRÆSENTATIONSGESTUS VARM TASKE HOLDE
-OVER-SKULDEREN
*Om vinteren skal man altid huske vanter, halstørklæde og hue, før man
står af bussen. Om sommeren er det bare at slynge tasken over skulderen.*

Sorter efter: Venstre / Højre

ØVE KASTE TO HÅNDKLÆDE T-SHIRT BADEDRAGT HUE   SVØMMEBRILLER SOMMETIDER ØREPROP
PEG SIGE SKAL JEG HJELM HUE   NEJ JEG BRÆKKE MIN HÅR
HUSKE HANDSKE HUSKE HALSTØRKLÆDE HUSKE HUE   MULIGHED JEG BUS STIGE-AF GLEMME PRÆSENTATIONSGESTUS
NEPAL JEG SKAL ORDENTLIG RYGSÆK~2 JAKKE HUE

FIGURE 14.6 Concordance view in the DTS Dictionary.

14.4.4 *Treatment of classifier constructions*

A special group of verbs in DTS (and in many other sign languages) is productively formed by combining a meaningful unit expressed by a handshape and denoting a whole entity, a limb, a hand handling something, or an instrument, and a sequence of different meaningful units denoting motion or location expressed by place of articulation and movement. The handshape units of these verbs in DTS must combine "with at least one morpheme denoting motion or the state of being located and at least one morpheme denoting relative location" (Engberg-Pedersen 1993: 254). Figure 14.7 shows the first and last segments of a polymorphemic verb that represents a person jumping downwards landing on his or her feet on a flat surface. The linguistic analysis of these verbs as classifier constructions or as polymorphemic verb constructions has been much debated in sign linguistics.[4] In this text we use the term 'classifier constructions'.

Classifier constructions are very frequent in DTS, as in many other sign languages, but so far very few sign language dictionaries have included information on signs which result from productive sign formation rules. The decision on whether to include such signs, and how to present classifier constructions in a dictionary, is not an easy one, and it has been under discussion for many years (e.g. Brien and Brennan 1994, Johnston and Schembri 1999). The surface forms of such verbs are created during conversation and can take an infinite number of forms and meanings: with a change of the orientation of the hand, the meaning of the sign shown in Figure 14.7 can change, and instead denote a person jumping and landing on their

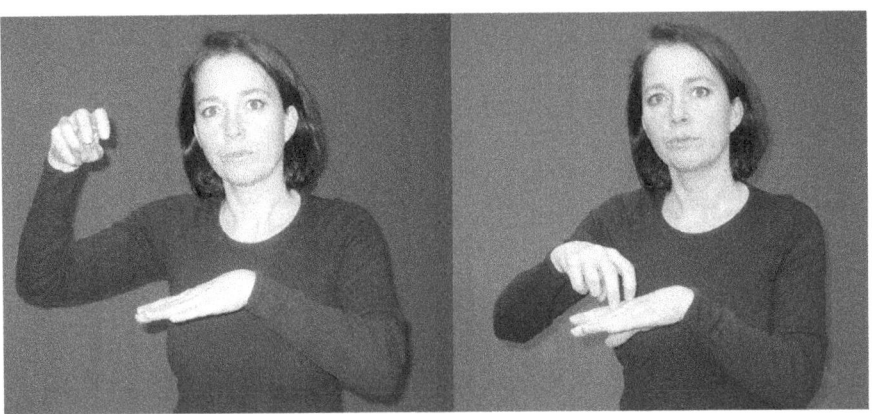

FIGURE 14.7 A polymorphemic verb in DTS.

---

[4] This problem is also an issue for lexicographers of spoken languages with polymorphemic verbs and non-concatenative structures (e.g. Semitic languages).

back or front. With a change of both movement and orientation, the sign could denote a person landing first on their head, then on their front. With a change of location, the sign could denote a person jumping from a low to a high position instead of from a high to a low position.

The way to include information on these verbs in a dictionary constitutes a real challenge.[5] As Zwitserlood argues, the dictionary could have entries for the individual units that constitute the verb constructions, "were it not for the difficulty of representing some of the morphemes, for instance a movement, without also representing a hand" (Zwitserlood 2010: 456). Nevertheless, the editorial staff of the DTS Dictionary decided it was crucial to include some information on how to produce classifier constructions. We chose to describe the forty-three most frequent meaningful handshape units in special 'classifier' entries. As it is not possible to give Danish equivalents to the handshape units in isolation, a usage note is provided. For example, the classifier entry for a fist with extended thumb (PF-1) reads: "Used to represent a person. Typically used in verbs describing how a person walks or runs in relation to another person." We also give example sentences that include one or more instances of the classifier used in verb constructions, and, finally, we provide cross-references to lexicalized forms (so called 'frozen forms') that can be analysed as derivatives of the classifier. Figure 14.8 shows the classifier entry PF-1 (the handshape denotes a person) and its three frozen forms meaning 'competition', 'go/walk together with someone', and 'catch up with someone'.

14.5 Future challenges in sign language lexicography

In the following section we focus on some of the areas where sign language lexicography could improve through increased use of the possibilities offered by the electronic medium.

14.5.1 *The corpus challenge*

Large text corpora have been accessible for several decades for many written languages. Because of the lack of a widely-used written form of sign languages, sign language corpora are built as collections of video files, combined with transcriptions or supplied with annotations. These are, to some extent, comparable to corpora of speech, which, because of the manual transcription task, are usually considerably smaller than written corpora. Another similarity between corpora of spoken languages and corpora of sign languages is the need for tools that ensure consistency in the elicited data. Samples of different types of naturally occurring sign language use

---

[5] For a discussion of the analysis of the verbs as classifier verbs, see Engberg-Pedersen (1993), and for an overview of the debate, see Schembri (2003).

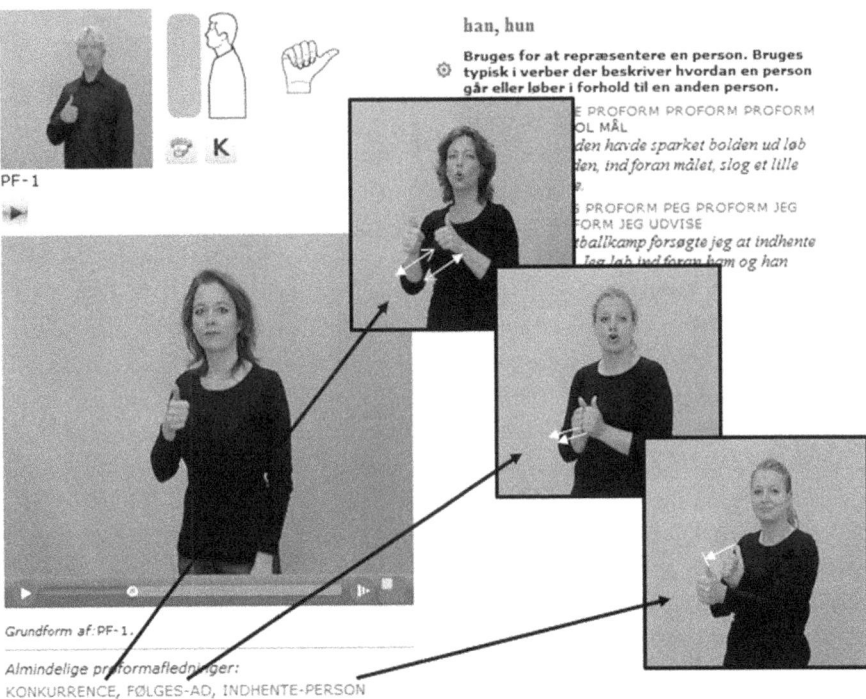

FIGURE 14.8 Classifier entry in the DTS Dictionary.

are not widely available. As a result, large-scale sign language corpora projects such as the DGS-Corpus project currently underway at the University of Hamburg,[6] are often mainly composed of clinically elicited data. Clinical elicitation involves "the use of tasks where [users] are primarily concerned with message conveyance, need to utilize their own linguistic resources to construct utterances, and are focused on achieving some non-linguistic outcome" (Ellis and Barkhuizen 2005: 23). Designing and collecting a sign language corpus thus involves a variety of time-consuming steps, e.g. the development of specific tasks (e.g. retelling of a film, description of a picture, conversation), as well as the balanced selection of informants (according to age, sex, social status, etc.), the planning and undertaking of recording sessions, and the transcription.

Although there are some similarities between spoken language and sign language corpora, there are considerable differences as well. Transcription of recordings for lexicographic use of a spoken language that has a written form basically consists of identifying (parts of) words from a known vocabulary. The basic annotation of a sign

---

[6] Information available at: www.sign-lang.uni-hamburg.de/dgs-korpus (last accessed 8 June 2011).

language recording requires not only recognition of the signs, but also unique identification of each sign in a lexical database. Consequently, the sign language corpus lexicographer often faces a dilemma: an extensive dictionary or lexical database is necessary to build a sign language corpus and transcribe video recordings, while at the same time a corpus is needed to create a dictionary of that specific sign language. Johnston (2010) suggests a solution where the corpus is first enriched with basic annotation in accordance with an existing lexical database which is then continuously expanded as new signs are found while transcribing the videos.

Another major challenge in sign language corpus production is annotation, i.e. the practice of adding linguistic information to an electronic corpus of language data (e.g. lemma, word class, sentence constituent), and more particularly the identification of tokens or signs. For text corpora, the comparable task can, at least to a certain degree, be performed with automatic tokenizers and taggers, but for sign languages—just as for spoken languages—this is far more complex. Several research projects are addressing the task of the automatic identification of clause boundaries, automatic sign recognition, etc. (e.g. Jantunen *et al.* 2010), but systems which can be applied for practical purposes are not yet available.

As more and larger sign language corpora become available, sign language lexicographers will be able to substantially improve the quality and coverage of sign language dictionaries. A task such as lemma selection will become much easier with the help of a sign frequency list, a tool that has so far not been available to sign language linguists. To date, lemma selection for sign language dictionaries has typically been based on lists of words from a spoken/written language, not necessarily applicable to the basic vocabulary of the sign language. It is obviously of great importance for sign language learners to be able to look up the signs that are actually used in the language. Another much sought-after feature for sign language learners is example sentences. Moreover, access to sign language corpora will make it possible for sign language lexicographers to browse example material with a click rather than laboriously watching hours of video recordings.

14.5.2 *Adding new types of information*

Compared to comprehensive spoken/written language dictionaries, recent sign language dictionaries still provide very limited types of information. One reason may be the short history of sign language lexicography and sign language research in general. It may be argued that a sufficiently strong base of linguistic research results to provide a dictionary with information beyond a basic description of the form and meaning of the sign vocabulary has not yet been developed. However, there has been intense scientific work in the field during the last decades, and with the appearance of sign language corpora, we now have far better means of including authentic usage

information such as morphological modifications of signs, grammatical constructions, and frequent co-occurrences in sign language dictionaries.

The semantic description of signs needs to be improved. In most existing sign
language dictionaries, the semantic descriptions are lists of equivalents in another
language, typically the dominant spoken/written language, e.g. English for American
Sign Language and British Sign Language, Danish for DTS, etc. This is, of course,
what is expected in a traditional bilingual dictionary; but in a monolingual dictionary, definitions can help the users to ensure that they have found the right word or
sign, whether the purpose is language comprehension or production (see Atkins and
Rundell 2008). Hence, an obvious enhancement of comprehensive sign language
dictionaries would be the inclusion of definitions, whether the metalanguage is a
written language or a sign language.

Another possible addition regarding semantics is the use of illustrations. The
inclusion of drawings, photographs, animations, and video clips to illustrate or
explain a specific meaning, can be very helpful for L2 learners, just as it can be in a
dictionary of a spoken/written language. The benefits are obvious for signs denoting
concrete objects, but illustrations can also be used to indicate actions, properties,
relations, etc. (Svensén 2009). As far as we know, apart from small basic dictionaries
for children or L2 learners, no existing sign language dictionary provides illustrations
for all its signs. Svensén (2009), however, argues that illustrations can be useful and
appropriate, if used with care.

14.5.3 *Sign language as metalanguage*

To the best of our knowledge the first monolingual sign language dictionary where
the sign language is also the metalanguage of the dictionary has yet to be created. In
electronic dictionaries, sign language can easily be rendered as video clips, but the
layout has to be completely rethought if sign language is to be used as the metalanguage, rather than merely replacing text with video clips in a traditional dictionary
entry. The static nature of written language makes it ideal for headers, captions,
menu items, etc., whereas a web page with many simultaneously moving video clips
would obviously be confusing, especially if the user were not familiar with the website
and its content. For this reason, websites that are mainly in sign language often turn
to written language for headers, etc., exploiting the fact that deaf children typically
learn the majority language of their region as their first written language.

14.5.4 *Exploiting the potential of information technology*

Sign language lexicography still has to explore many of the benefits offered by
information technology (IT). One obvious area for improvement is a dynamic
presentation of the dictionary data, reflecting user needs (see Tarp, this volume).
Potential users of a sign language dictionary are diverse, and it would be interesting

to facilitate adjustment of the interface to specific user needs. This could be done, for example, by giving users the possibility of expanding and collapsing different sections of an entry, or allowing them to adapt the search facilities. Another area for innovation is the development of electronic sign language dictionaries for smartphones. Some applications already exist, either as apps or as websites adapted to smartphones, e.g. the *ASL Dictionary* (English-American Sign Language), the *MobileSign* dictionary (English-British Sign Language), the *Svenskt Teckenspråkslexikon – mobilversion* (Swedish-Swedish Sign Language), and the *Dansk – Dansk tegnsprog* dictionary (Danish-DTS). These dictionaries are, however, still relatively primitive, usually offering only text and/or topic searches.

14.5.5 *Integration with other electronic language resources*

Dictionaries of spoken/written languages are currently being integrated into other electronic resources, for example by facilitating automatic word look-up in dictionaries directly from texts (e.g. the 'Pop-up Dictionary' facility in the *Longman Dictionary of Contemporary English*, fifth edition), corpus look-up from dictionary entries (see Paquot, this volume), and simultaneous word look-up in multiple dictionaries (e.g. dictionary aggregators such as dictionary.com). In the future, electronic sign language dictionaries will no doubt develop in this direction so that we will see integrated sign look-up in various electronic resources as well as in sign language dictionaries with links to other resources such as dictionaries of other sign languages, dictionaries of spoken/written languages, Wordnets, etc. To our knowledge these possibilities are still very rarely exploited in existing sign language dictionaries. One exception is the linking from Danish equivalents in the DTS Dictionary to the online version of the Danish dictionary mentioned above.

14.5.6 *Usability studies*

To the best of our knowledge, no major studies of usability have yet been carried out on sign language dictionaries. A yet-unpublished user survey conducted by the DTS Dictionary group indicates that the main user demand is for an increased number of entries, and that very few users make use of the more advanced facilities and features of the dictionary. This is in line with the results of studies of electronic dictionary use for written languages (e.g. Müller-Spitzer *et al.*, this volume). Knowing more about users' needs and their response to electronic vs. printed dictionaries of sign languages will contribute to the improvement of electronic sign language dictionaries.

14.6 Conclusion

The lack of a written form and of a means of rendering signs that provides accurate and complete information were, until recently, major impediments to creating modern comprehensive sign language dictionaries. In recent years, however, new and enhanced tools have become available to sign language lexicographers: large-scale corpora are being compiled, various methods for automatic IT-based recognition and analysis of sign language are being developed, sign language research is progressing within lexicographically relevant areas such as phonology and morphology, and the electronic medium offers new possibilities. In electronic sign language dictionaries, signs and sign language examples can be rendered as digital video recordings, thus showing the sign as it is actually produced in natural signing—a feature that printed dictionaries will always lack. Another advantage of electronic sign language dictionaries, compared to printed dictionaries, is the flexibility of the electronic medium, which enables the user to perform different kinds of searches in the dictionary, and facilitates the dynamic presentation of the dictionary data instead of a fixed sequence of fixed entries. In years to come we are likely to see the emergence of new and vastly improved electronic sign language dictionaries that benefit from these recent technical and scientific advances.

Dictionaries

Anonymous (1871). *De Dövstummes Haandalphabet samt et Udvalg af deres lettere Tegn sammenstillet, tegnet, graveret og udgivet af En Forening af Dövstumme*. København: Th. Michaelsen.

Bonnal-Vergés, Françoise (ed.) (2008). *Abbé Jean Ferrand, Dictionnaire à l'usage des sourds et des muets (ca 1784)*. Limoges: Lambert-Lucas.

Brien, David (ed.) (1992). *Dictionary of British Sign Language / English*. London: Faber & Faber.

Hedberg, Tomas (ed.) (1997). *Svenskt Teckenspråkslexikon*. Leksand: Sveriges Dövas Riksförbund.

Konrad, Rainer, Thomas Hanke, Arvid Schwarz, Siegmund Prillwitz, Susanne König, and Gabriele Langer (2003). *Fachgebärdenlexikon Sozialarbeit/Sozialpädagogik*. Hamburg: Signum Verlag.

Schermer, Gertrude M. and Corline Koolhof (eds.) (2009). *Van Dale Basiswoordenboek Nederlandse Gebarentaal*. Utrecht: Van Dale.

Stokoe, Willam.C., Dorothy C. Casterline, and Carl G. Croneberg (1965). *A Dictionary of American Sign Language on Linguistic Principles*. Washington, DC: Gallaudet College Press.

Summers, Della (2009). *Longman Dictionary of Contemporary English*. Fifth edition CD-ROM. Harlow: Pearson Longman.

References to websites

Aliabadi, Schiwa, Seda Wiederhofer, and Robert Kudej (2005). *Einführung in die Österreichische Gebärdensprache (ÖGS) – Online*. Available at http://www.oeglb.at/oegs_projekt (last accessed 8 June 2011).

Appsavers.com (2011). *ASL Dictionary.* Available at: http://www.asl-dictionary.com/asl-dictionary.html (last accessed 1 November 2011).

Boyes Braem, Penny *et al.* (eds.) (2007–2009). *Gebärden-Fachlexikon, Deutschschweizerische Gebärdensprache / Deutsch.* Available at: http://www.fachgebaerden.ch (last accessed 8 June 2011).

Center for Tegnsprog (2008–2011). *Ordbog over Dansk Tegnsprog.* Available at: http://www.tegnsprog.dk (last accessed 8 June 2011).

Center for Tegnsprog (2011). *Dansk – Dansk tegnsprog.* Available at: http://www.m.tegnsprog.dk; http://www.mobilesign.org (last accessed 1 November 2011).

Centre for Deaf Studies (2011). *MobileSign.* Available at: http://www.mobilesign.org (last accessed 1 November 2011).

Cislunar Aerospace (1997). *The K-8 Aeronautics Internet Textbook Sign Language Dictionary.* Available at http://wings.avkids.com/Book/Signing (last accessed 8 June 2011).

Det Danske Sprog- og Litteraturselskab (2009–2011). *Den Danske Ordbog.* Available at: http://ordnet.dk/ddo (last accessed 8 June 2011).

Dicionário Libras (2009). *Dicionário Libras.* Available at: http://www.dicionariolibras.com.br/website (last accessed 8 June 2011).

Institutionen för Lingvistik (2009–2011). *Svenskt Teckenspråkslexikon.* Available at: http://www.ling.su.se/teckensprakslexikon (last accessed 8 June 2011).

Institutionen för Lingvistik (2011). *Svenskt Teckenspråkslexikon – mobilversion.* Available at: http://130.237.171.78/fmi/iwp/cgi?-db=STLMOBIL&-loadframes (last accessed 1 November 2011).

Kuurojen Liitto (2003–2005). *Suvi Suomalaisen viittomakielen verkosanakirja.* Available at: http://www.viittomat.net (last accessed 8 June 2011).

Manos que Hablan (2010). *Manos que Hablan: Diccionario.* Available at: http://manosquehablan.com.ar/diccionario (last accessed 8 June 2011).

McKee, David (managing editor) (2011). *The Online Dictionary of New Zealand Sign Language.* Available at: http://nzsl.vuw.ac.nz (last accessed 28 June 2011).

Prillwitz, Siegmund (project leader) (2007). *Fachgebärdenlexikon Gesundheit und Pflege.* Available at: http://www.sign-lang.uni-hamburg.de/glex/intro/inhalt.htm (last accessed 8 June 2011).

Van Herreweeghe, Mieke *et al.* (eds.) (2004). *Woordenboek Vlaamse Gebarentaal-Nederlands/Nederlands-Vlaamse Gebarentaal.* Available at: http://gebaren.ugent.be/. (last accessed 8 June 2011).

Part III

Electronic dictionaries and their users

15

On the use(fulness) of paper and electronic dictionaries

ANNA DZIEMIANKO

15.1 Introduction

The distinction between paper and electronic dictionaries represents an aspect of the presentational, or tectonic, typology of dictionaries which focuses on the medium (Hartmann and James 1998: vi). Human-oriented electronic dictionaries (possibly with some NLP extensions), considered below, are "collections of structured electronic data that can be accessed with multiple tools, enhanced with a wide range of functionalities, and used in various environments" (De Schryver 2003: 146). Different types of electronic dictionaries can be distinguished. De Schryver (2003) reviews the classifications of electronic dictionaries developed by Martin (1992), Lehr (1996), and Nesi (2000a), but considers them inadequate to account for the increasing variety of electronic dictionaries and puts forward his own three-step typology, centred around the question "Who accesses what, where?".

The answer to the first part of the question, i.e. "*Who* accesses the dictionary?", is machines or humans. The second aspect, i.e. "*What* is accessed?", boils down to the dictionary medium, which can be non-electronic (physical) or electronic. Each medium involves hand-held devices and robust machines. Finally, the question "*Where* does one access the dictionary data?" is related to the type of storage. Considering the physical medium, the printed page, for example, is a hand-held device, while the microfiche, read with the help of non-portable equipment, is a robust machine device. With respect to the electronic medium, De Schryver (2003) draws a distinction between electronic dictionaries on stand-alone computers (e.g. hand-held dictionaries, such as pocket electronic dictionaries (PEDs) or reading pens, and robust-machine dictionaries, typically stored on CDs, DVDs, or hard disks) and those on networked computers (intranet and Internet dictionaries).

Although De Schryver (2003: 147) held that his typology was flexible enough to account for future innovations, the classification, proposed almost a decade ago, has already been extended, supplemented, and refined. Fuertes-Oliviera (2009) recognizes two types of Internet dictionaries: institutional Internet reference works and collective multiple-language Internet reference works, depending on who compiles such dictionaries for whom and whether they are available for free or not. Institutional Internet reference works are dictionaries created by an identifiable institution and may be free to use or not. Collective multiple-language reference works, such as Wiktionary, are usually free and result from collaborative effort taken by a community of users. In a recent review of online dictionaries of English, Lew (2011a) also discusses portals with hyperlinks to dictionaries (e.g. WordReference.com or Cambridge Dictionaries Online) and dictionary aggregators (e.g. TheFreeDictionary and Dictionary.com), where information drawn from several dictionaries is pasted on one website.

The potential of electronic dictionaries is widely recognized (e.g. Bergenholtz and Gouws 2007, De Schryver 2003, Harley 2000, Lew 2011a, Nesi 1999, Prinsloo 2005). De Schryver (2003: 163–87) alone mentions as many as 118 advantages of electronic dictionaries over paper dictionaries. The increasing popularity of electronic dictionaries can be put down to better readability of entries and improved retrieval systems, including hypertext, wildcards, pronunciation-based and full-text searches (Nesi 2000a: 839, Tono 2009: 40; Lew, this volume). Electronic dictionaries typically store much more than the entire content of thick paper dictionaries, offer direct access to corpus examples and citation banks, and open a number of new search routes, such as tracking down a target word via phonologically similar or lexically related words (Nesi 1999: 59). Tools for textual condensation (Wiegand 1996) like swung dashes, slashes, grammar codes, and abbreviations are less necessary, since in the electronic format space constraints are much less of an issue (except for relatively new media, such as PEDs, where not so much disc space as screen space still needs to be reckoned with). Thus, full syntactic descriptions have replaced grammar codes, and hyperlinks ensure quick access to further relevant information (Harley 2000). Figure 15.1 illustrates how the user can easily access information on semantic relations (here: synonyms of *murder*) in the *Cambridge Advanced Learners' Dictionary* (3rd edition) (*e-CALD3*).

In general, electronic dictionaries feature immediate cross-reference, typically activated by a click of the mouse, in contrast to non-immediate cross-reference in dictionaries in book form, which, unlike pop-ups and other tooltips, may lead the dictionary user to lose sight of the original article (Lew, in press). Electronic dictionaries are also very different from paper dictionaries as regards their outer and inner access structures, i.e. indicators which help dictionary users locate specific entries on the one hand, and those which guide them inside the entries to find the required information (Bergenholtz and Gouws 2007: 243). Getting to the desired entry in a

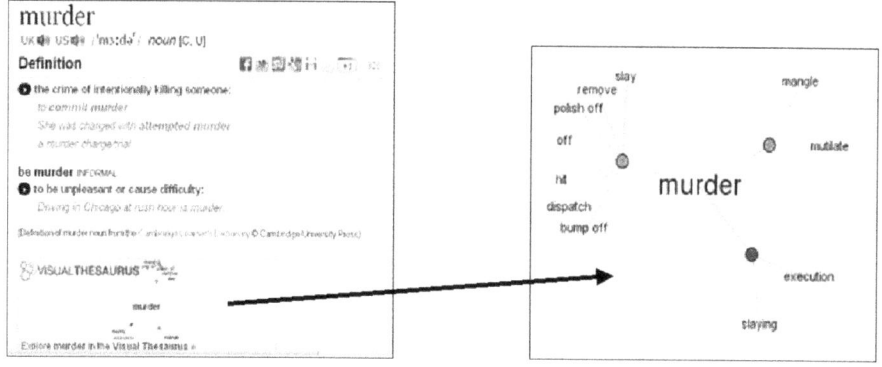

Figure 15.1 Semantic relations at *murder* in *e-CALD3*.

paper dictionary may require scanning tediously numerous running heads. By contrast, the outer access structure of electronic dictionaries is dramatically simplified. Typing in a word generally provides access to a list of relevant entries (e.g. *issue* as a noun or verb) or opens up the appropriate entry directly (e.g. *argument*). In that case, the user does not need to use the outer access structure (p. 244). Similarly, whereas paper dictionaries have only a linear, non-hierarchical microstructure, inasmuch as users cannot choose the amount of information made available to them, electronic dictionaries can offer a layered, hierarchical inner access structure. Electronic dictionaries are more flexible and dynamic: they can, for example, provide direct access to a specific definition followed by examples if the user selects a particular sense from the menu displayed at the top of the entry (Lew 2011a, Tono 2000: 855). This type of layered presentation means that the amount of information displayed at any one time is restricted: first, there is a concise overview of the senses explained in a specific entry, and once a sense is selected, the relevant information is shown either first or alone on screen. Figure 15.2 illustrates the menu in the entry for *business* in the *Macmillan English Dictionary Online* (*MEDO*).

As a result of these differences in the amount of information and access functionality between paper and electronic dictionaries, the authority of paper dictionaries may be challenged, if not jeopardized (Zaenen 2002: 239). After all, it seems that bulky paper dictionaries may be easily superseded by multifunctional electronic dictionaries. Yet, electronic dictionaries are often regarded as inferior in quality (Chen 2010: 292, 295, Nesi, this volume, Tono 2009: 48). As Béjoint (2010: 375) observed: "[e]-dictionaries do not have the appearance, the binding, the thickness, the weight, the leather of the Bible, and they do not have the respectability either: anybody can produce an electronic document and change it immediately – literally – without anybody noticing." The bird's-eye-view of the whole page in a paper dictionary, which often makes it possible for dictionary users to spot, even

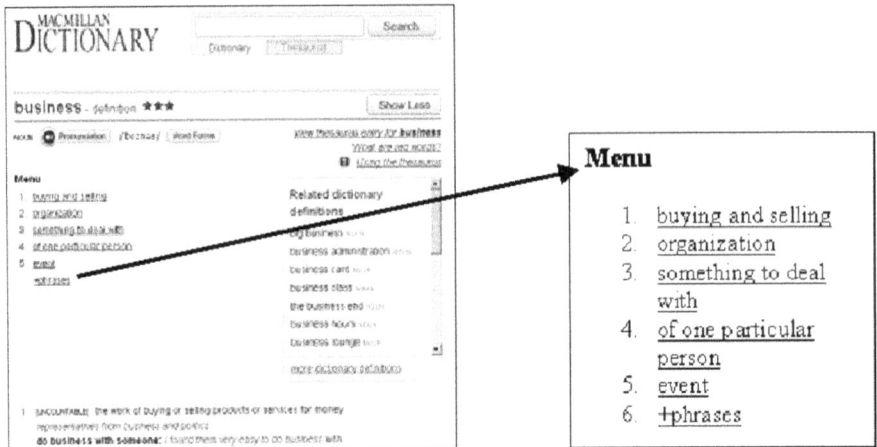

FIGURE 15.2 Menu in the entry for *business* in MEDO.

inadvertently, all sorts of additional information, including pictures and text boxes, as well as the possibility of making notes and marking information on paper, are sometimes considered the crucial advantages of dictionaries in book form (Osaki *et al.* 2003: 205). It is only natural, then, that the tradition and reliability of paper dictionaries on the one hand, and the user-friendliness and convenience of electronic dictionaries on the other, pose questions about the relative usefulness of the two dictionary formats.

The aim of this chapter is to compare the use and usefulness of paper and electronic dictionaries in the light of findings from the pertinent research published in recent years (mainly 2000–2011). Studies involving robust-machine electronic dictionaries (stand-alone or networked) as well as hand-held dictionaries such as PEDs are considered. Special attention is paid to the role of the medium in developing and altering patterns of electronic dictionary consultation as well as its effects on language reception, production, and learning.

To discuss the role of dictionary form within the confines of a chapter, studies which rely mainly on the experimental method were chosen as points of reference. Naturally, the quantitative information obtained from experiments is often supported by qualitative analyses and judgements, which typically throw light on how dictionaries are perceived by users themselves. Surveys, questionnaires, interviews, observations, and protocols are thus considered below as long as they perform an ancillary role and accompany experimentation. The selected studies are listed chronologically in the Appendix. Their main characteristics are described along four lines: task, number and types of subjects, methods of monitoring dictionary use, and testing users' familiarity with paper and electronic dictionaries.

The following section (Section 15.2) focuses on the usefulness of paper and electronic dictionaries in decoding and language production. Among other things, the effects of the medium on reading comprehension and finding contextually appropriate meaning are considered. The speed and frequency of dictionary consultation, as conditioned by dictionary format, are discussed in Sections 15.3 and 15.4, respectively. Selected changes in patterns of dictionary use and user behaviour as well as the consequences of the medium for inference and contextual guessing are also explored there. In Section 15.5, the depth of processing dictionary information on paper and on screen and its effects on language learning are discussed. An attempt is made to see whether dictionary users' involvement and retention of the information retrieved are influenced by dictionary form. Subjective opinions of both paper and electronic dictionaries are summarized in Section 15.6. Considering the wide range of the studies reviewed, comparability problems and research limitations are acknowledged in Section 15.7. Suggestions for further research, presented in Section 15.8, conclude the chapter.

15.2 Dictionary consultation for decoding and encoding purposes

One of the earliest publications concerned with language reception with the help of existing paper and electronic dictionaries was authored by Nesi (2000b). In her study, two texts had to be read and understood, one with access to the *Oxford Advanced Learner's Dictionary of Current English* (5th edition; *OALDCE5*) in book form and the other using the same dictionary on CD-ROM. Nesi (p. 111) concludes that there were no statistically significant differences in comprehension scores between the two dictionary conditions. Two versions of the same dictionary (*Collins COBUILD Advanced English Dictionary*, 6th edition (*COBUILD₆*) on paper and on the Internet) were also employed in the experiment conducted by Dziemianko (2010). In the decoding task, subjects had to explain the meaning of nine English nouns and phrases. In stark contrast to Nesi's (2000b) findings, the results suggest that the electronic dictionary was significantly more useful in this respect than the paper dictionary. More precisely, the proportion of correctly explained target items was significantly higher in the electronic-dictionary condition than in the paper-dictionary condition. It is important to note that in this study, the contrast between decoding and encoding reflects the distinction drawn by Laufer and Goldstein (2004: 405–6) between passive and active knowledge: the ability to supply the meaning of a given word form is passive knowledge (necessary for decoding), while the ability to supply the word form for a given meaning is active knowledge (necessary for encoding).

Studies which investigated the use of electronic dictionaries on hand-held devices, rather than on CD-ROMs or the Internet, have also yielded divergent conclusions. Osaki *et al.* (2003) set out to investigate the role of dictionary form (paper and PEDs) in accessing the meaning of target words underlined in a text as well as in reading comprehension. It turned out that pocket electronic dictionary consultation significantly facilitated choosing a contextually appropriate meaning and resulted in better comprehension scores than reference to the paper dictionary. The subjects using the electronic dictionary spent much less time searching for the target vocabulary items than those consulting the paper dictionary (see Section 15.3). Possibly, the time saved by using the electronic dictionary enabled the students to process the context of the passage in more depth, which, in turn, increased their accuracy in looking for contextually appropriate meanings. Quick access to the information in the electronic dictionary may also have meant less interference in the process of reading, hence the better comprehension scores (p. 210). Osaki and Nakayama (2004, cited in Koyama and Takeuchi 2007: 111) obtained broadly similar findings when they compared the role of dictionary form in text comprehension and identification of the contextually appropriate meaning of target lexical items. The results show that pocket electronic dictionaries were more useful in locating the relevant meaning, and their consultation led to better text comprehension than reference to paper dictionaries.

However, less optimistic findings follow from the studies by Koyama and Takeuchi (2007), Chen (2010), and Kobayashi (2007), who also investigated the use of electronic dictionaries available on hand-held devices. On the basis of two reading tasks, Koyama and Takeuchi (2007) conclude that reference to such electronic dictionaries contributes next to nothing to reading comprehension. Yet, as the authors themselves note, their investigations were limited, considering the small number of participants (around 30 in each task) and, consequently, poor reliability of statistical tests. In the comprehension part of the study by Chen (2010), in which choice had to be made between the suggested meaning explanations of selected infrequent words, no substantial effect of dictionary form on sense selection or vocabulary comprehension was identified. Kobayashi (2007: 659), who relied on both qualitative and quantitative methods (i.e. a questionnaire and a reading task), did not observe any statistically significant differences in reading comprehension scores between paper and pocket electronic dictionary conditions, either.

When considering meaning identification tasks, it is also worth paying attention to empirical studies which employ specifically designed consultation tools, rather than any existing paper and electronic dictionaries. In a recent study, Tono (2011) made use of the eye-tracking method to monitor the process of electronic dictionary look-up and investigate how users search for word meaning in a dictionary entry. Instead of using a real dictionary, special microstructures for the words *make* and *fast* were created based on the *Longman Dictionary of Contemporary English* (5th edition; *LDOCE5*) and *MEDO*, respectively. To investigate how guiding devices such as menus and signposts affect users' look-up processes, dictionary entries were modified to produce entries with and without these features. Tono (p. 148) observed that his subjects made almost no use of signposts, i.e. "sense indicators given at the beginning of each sense" (Lew and Tokarek 2010: 194), such as those shown in the e-*LDOCE5* entry for the adjective *fast* (i.e. MOVING QUICKLY, IN A SHORT TIME, CLOCK, COLOUR, SPORTS) (Figure 15.3).

Admittedly, more-proficient students used signposts more than less-proficient ones, who took virtually no notice of this navigation tool, presumably because they did not understand its function. The participants were sometimes misled by the oversimplified word meanings conveyed by signposts and obtained worse results in locating the relevant sense of *make* in entries with signposts than in those without them. Menus, in turn, facilitated access to the relevant sense of *fast* for less-proficient subjects, but were largely ignored by the more advanced students (Tono 2011: 136, 150).

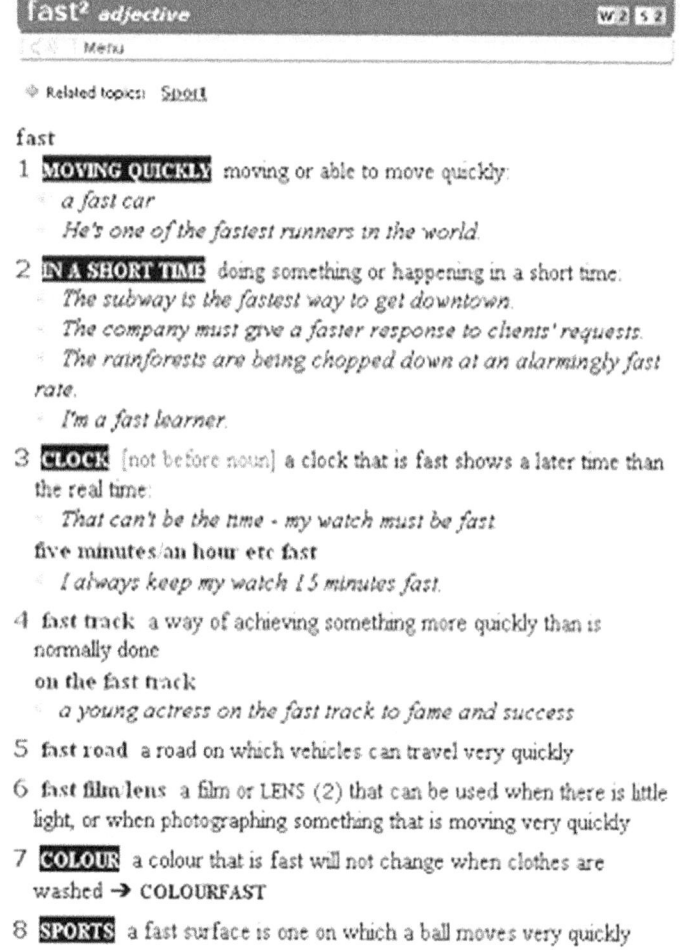

FIGURE 15.3 Signposts in the entry for *fast* in e-*LDOCE5*.

To some extent, Tono's (2011) findings concerning menus resemble the conclusions drawn by Lew and Tokarek (2010). In their study, learners were asked to complete partial English translations of Polish sentences with the help of an experimental (twenty-entry) Polish-English online dictionary, created in three different versions and assigned randomly to subjects. The versions differed in the way entries could be navigated by dictionary users to test the usefulness of entry menus as access facilitators in online bilingual dictionaries. The first version displayed complete entries with no menu. In the second version, the user was first presented with a menu of senses; once the user clicked on a specific sense, the full entry, automatically scrolled to the clicked sense, appeared. The third version was identical to the second, except that the target sense was also highlighted. It was found that, as in the study by Tono (2011), bare menus helped lower-level students to access the right sense, but were a hindrance to higher-level users. By contrast, menus with highlighting proved comparably helpful to users at both levels.

These findings, however, differ from the results of studies that focus on guiding devices in paper dictionaries. Nesi and Tan (2011), for example, compared three versions of entries for a selected list of high-frequency words in the *Macmillan English Dictionary for Advanced Learners* (2nd edition; *MEDAL2*): (1) with their original menus as available in *MEDAL2*; (2) without any guiding device; (3) in a new format where menu information was dispersed as signposts or shortcuts within the entry. They found no significant difference in the time participants took to select word senses in entries with or without guiding devices, be they menus or signposts. Menu use did not yield significantly more accurate sense selections, and there was no significant difference between the scores for menus and the scores for shortcuts. However, a significant difference between the scores for signposts and the scores for entries without any guiding device was found, which led Nesi and Tan (2011) to conclude that signposts are a more effective navigation tool than menus. This view is supported by Lew's (2010b) findings. In his experiment, students had to complete partial English translations of six English sentences with the help of English words for which paper-based dictionary entries were supplied. Half of the participants had access to unmodified *Oxford Advanced Learner's Dictionary of Current English* (7th edition; *OALDCE7*) entries featuring signposts or shortcuts. The other half worked with modified *OALDCE7* entries, in which the original shortcuts were converted into entry-initial menus. Lew (pp. 1125–6) concluded that "Shortcuts-equipped entries lead to significantly better translations, and the accuracy with which Shortcuts users identified the relevant senses was 15% higher (though not significantly so) than for those using Menus. These findings point to an advantage of Shortcuts, a distributed cues system (also known as Guidewords or Signposts), over a single entry-initial Menu."

Overall, signposts seem to be more effective than menus in facilitating sense identification in paper dictionaries (Lew 2010b, Nesi and Tan 2011), but not in electronic applications (Tono 2011). However, simple menus in entries displayed on the computer screen, either clickable or not, are typically appreciated by less-proficient subjects (Lew and Tokarek 2010, Tono 2011), but they do not prove helpful in paper-based entries (Lew 2010b, Nesi and Tan 2011). This suggests that the effectiveness of guiding devices may depend not only on their type (shortcuts vs. menus; clickable menus or not), but also on the medium in which they are used (paper, electronic) and the proficiency of dictionary users.

Compared to the number of studies that analyse dictionary use for decoding purposes, there are very few that investigate the use of electronic dictionaries for encoding purposes. Chen (2010) asked subjects to compose sentences with the low-frequency target words whose correct meaning explanations had to be identified in the comprehension task described above. The sentences produced by the subjects had to be different from any examples provided in the paper and electronic dictionaries which they consulted. If a composed sentence was semantically, grammatically, and pragmatically correct, two points were scored; if it was only semantically correct (but grammatically incorrect or pragmatically inappropriate), only one point could be gained. Framing semantically incorrect sentences or confusing the grammatical category of the target words resulted in no points. The study showed no marked effect of dictionary form on production; the scores were comparable irrespective of whether the subjects used paper or portable electronic dictionaries. Such results stand in stark contrast to those obtained by Dziemianko (2010), although, admittedly, in a different encoding task, in which subjects had to complete sentences with the right prepositions removed from collocations (e.g. *on the blink*, *wreak havoc on*, or *at gunpoint*) with the help of the paper or online versions of *COBUILD₆*. To make sure that the participants could not rely on their knowledge of English, a pre-test was run, in which the same task had to be done without access to any dictionary. The cases where the students were successful without consulting a dictionary were eliminated from further analysis. The accuracy of the subjects' responses was significantly better in electronic dictionary conditions.

15.3 Speed of dictionary consultation

Speed is seen as one of the main advantages of using electronic dictionaries, in particular those on portable devices, but also those online and on CD-ROMs (De Schryver 2003, Prinsloo 2005, Stirling 2003, Tang 1997, Tono 2000). In a study whose objective was "purely look-up speed; i.e. how quickly students could find the definition(s) of an unknown word" (Weschler and Pitts 2000), students looked up words 23 per cent faster with a portable electronic dictionary than with a paper one. Yet, look-up time was measured manually and the students were not requested to read, let alone understand, the explanations of the words checked. Weschler and Pitts (2000) concluded from the information elicited from their subjects in the accompanying questionnaire that while such a speed difference could be a decisive factor in L2 reception, almost none of the respondents could benefit from it when speaking, as consultation of portable dictionaries would still be too time-consuming to be practicable. Optimistic results concerning look-up time were also achieved in studies into portable electronic dictionary use conducted by Koyama and Takeuchi (2007: 118): portable electronic dictionaries were found to considerably reduce the time needed to read a passage in English, which was attributed to their superior search functions. Likewise, Chen (2010: 301) noted that consulting pocket electronic dictionaries was much less time-consuming than making use of paper dictionaries, and observed that it takes considerably less time to complete the same vocabulary exercise when working with PEDs than with paper dictionaries.

However, there is also research which does not confirm the advantage of hand-held electronic dictionaries with respect to consultation speed. In the reading comprehension and vocabulary exercises in the studies by Koyama and Takeuchi (2003, 2004a), the time needed to perform a vocabulary search in paper and portable electronic dictionaries was comparable. The authors put this result down to the additional work that the subjects in the electronic dictionary condition had to do, such as pushing one button after another in the case of some words or scanning the different screens to spot the necessary information, whereas in the paper dictionary all the information was usually available on the same page (Koyama and Takeushi 2004a: 36). In addition, Koyama and Takeuchi (2004a) observed that there was no difference between the two dictionary conditions in the time needed to access examples. Likewise, Shizuka (2003) found that dictionary format had no significant effect on the speed of getting to usage information in examples; the information proved to be no easier to extract from the portable electronic dictionary than from the paper one, the hierarchical nature of data display in the former notwithstanding. Such a conclusion follows from the second part of Shizuka's experiment, intended to throw light on the speed with which specific usage information was located in the numerous examples of *take, bring, have, go, keep, give, put, make, get,* and *come*. This part of the experiment aimed to test the functionality of the hierarchical information display in the portable dictionary, where examples of usage could be accessed by clicking a button next to the relevant meaning, as opposed to the one-level display in the paper dictionary, where all the information could be seen at the same time.

As regards stand-alone robust-machine electronic dictionaries, positive results on look-up time were obtained by Tono (2000), who tested the usefulness of three interfaces (i.e. traditional, parallel, and layered) against paper dictionary (control) conditions. The task consisted in identifying acceptable translation equivalents of the looked-up words, and the speed of finding the relevant information was taken to reflect look-up ease (p. 857). In the traditional interface, information was displayed as in a paper dictionary, with idioms and phrasal verbs listed at the end of the entry. In the parallel interface, information was shown in a parallel bilingual translation format: all the words as well as idioms and other multi-word expressions were accorded separate entries with translations in parallel format. In the layered interface, by contrast, the information was organized by a tab menu, where each tab offered more information than the previous one (p. 857). It turned out that access to target entries was quicker in the electronic dictionary, irrespective of the interface. However, the largest difference between the paper and electronic dictionary conditions occurred with the parallel interface. As regards the effect of the electronic dictionary interface, Tono (pp. 859–60) concluded that the parallel interface ensures much faster searches than the traditional or layered interfaces.

The superiority of stand-alone robust-machine electronic dictionaries over paper ones with respect to consultation speed was not confirmed by Nesi (2000b: 111), who, as already mentioned, investigated the usefulness of paper and CD-ROM versions of *OALDCE5* and made note of the time each subject took to complete the experiment. No significant differences in time between the two experimental conditions were observed. Yet it should be stressed that it is not the time of single look-ups that was measured, but the time needed to complete the reading task as such.

15.4 Number of look-ups

While the above conclusions concerning the relative speed of paper and electronic dictionary use are quite diverse, the results of studies into the number of look-ups are more uniform. The electronic medium was usually found to stimulate more frequent dictionary consultation, in particular when hand-held dictionaries were used (Kobayashi 2007, Koyama and Takeuchi 2003, 2007, Osaki *et al.* 2003).[1]

Most observations concerning the number of look-ups were made in studies that investigated dictionary use in reading comprehension. These studies suggest that electronic dictionaries, especially PEDs, entail very different dictionary consultation patterns. Kobayashi (2007), for example, found that the availability of pocket electronic dictionaries made the subjects almost immediately look up *any* words which were problematic and prevented them from trying to recall the words or guessing what they meant. By contrast, paper dictionaries deferred dictionary consultation: the subjects read the full text once and looked up the meaning of doubtful or unfamiliar words in dictionaries in book form only at second reading. Delayed dictionary consultation stimulated guessing and inferring the meaning of unknown words from the context. Kobayashi (p. 666) thus concluded that PEDs may not benefit all users, especially less-proficient ones, since frequent dictionary consultation means less interaction with the text. When reading a passage with the help of readily

---

[1] In the studies by Kobayashi (2007) and Koyama and Takeuchi (2003), users of pocket electronic dictionaries tended to look up more words than those who relied on paper dictionaries, but the differences did not reach statistical significance.

available electronic dictionaries, in particular PEDs, the most immediate concern of language learners is finding the translation of the words looked up rather than understanding the whole passage (see also Tang 1997: 46). As a result, such dictionary users may operate at the level of individual words, rather than discourse (see Stirling 2003).

These findings are further supported by those of Tono (2009: 58), who maintains that constant recourse to electronic dictionaries might be problematic, since learners may grow too impatient and refer to a dictionary any time they feel in doubt while reading. What they should do, in his view, is contextual guessing—they should try to form a preliminary guess on the basis of the context and only then verify it against dictionary information. Such initial assumptions are important inasmuch as they facilitate the search for the right meaning in a dictionary. Immediate recourse to a dictionary in the process of reading, encouraged by the speed and ease of electronic dictionary use, may discourage learners from making contextual guesses and, in fact, hinder effective dictionary consultation; learners may be less successful in getting to the sense appropriate for a given context.

However, Koyama and Takeuchi (2007) showed that reading comprehension remains largely unaffected by the increased frequency of dictionary consultation stimulated by the electronic medium. They also found that PEDs encourage learners to look up more words irrespective of their prior knowledge of the vocabulary. Given access to such dictionaries, learners willingly rechecked the words they thought they knew (pp. 115–16). Apparently, electronic dictionaries on hand-held devices make learners less wary of dictionary use.

It is not clear whether robust-machine (stand-alone or networked) electronic dictionaries benefit users in the same way. This might be true if the text being read is in electronic form as well. If it is on paper, decisions about using dictionaries installed on the computer or available online, but accessed through the computer, might be different, since turning attention from paper to screen is no doubt an additional effort. Admittedly, the study by Nesi (2000b), discussed above, which involved the use of paper and CD-ROM versions of one dictionary in reading a paper-based text, showed that the difference in the number of look-ups between the two experimental conditions, although still in favour of the electronic dictionary, was not statistically significant. Nonetheless, it appears that more research is needed to shed light on the effect of electronic dictionaries accessed through robust machines on look-up patterns. More attention should also be paid to task operationalization and dictionary format.

15.5 Learning

Vocabulary learning is admittedly not an immediate or typical goal of dictionary use, but rather a "by-product of dictionary consultation" (Lew and Doroszewska 2009:

240). Many studies, however, have investigated the impact of paper vs. electronic dictionaries on word retention. Empirical research most often shows that the dictionary medium (paper vs. electronic) does not have a significant bearing on learning words (Chen 2010, Kobayashi 2007, Koyama and Takeuchi 2003, Osaki *et al.* 2003, Osaki and Nakayama 2004, Xu 2010). However, Koyama and Takeuchi (2004a) found that reference to a paper dictionary resulted in much better vocabulary retention than the consultation of a PED. By way of explanation, they pointed out that accessing the right entry in paper dictionaries is typically an arduous and elaborate task, whereas in electronic dictionaries it usually boils down to inputting the spelling of the headword. Thus, the more demanding process of finding information in a dictionary in book form might pave the way for better retention (p. 42).

Koyama and Takeuchi's (2004a) results are in line with the Involvement Load Hypothesis, whereby investing greater mental effort in attaining information can pay off in better retrieval and recall than obtaining information with less intellectual effort (Laufer and Hulstijn 2001, Hulstijn and Laufer 2001). In other words, the retention of new words is contingent on the depth of processing: the deeper the processing is, the better the chances of remembering the new vocabulary are (Hulstijn and Laufer 2001: 545). Tono (2009: 64) suggested that easy access to electronic dictionaries cannot help this mechanism. In his view, lexical information can be processed more deeply and learned better if paper dictionaries are used, because such dictionaries, unlike electronic ones, make it possible for their users to mark, underline, or otherwise highlight the information that is important to them in the microstructure.

Not all studies of dictionary use, however, seem to confirm the Involvement Load Hypothesis. The results obtained by Dziemianko (2010: 262), for example, show that using an electronic dictionary can lead to better retention of both meaning and collocations. It turns out that it is not so much the effort put into the extraction of relevant information from the dictionary on paper as the saliency of an entry on the computer screen and, surprisingly, the ease of look-up that prove beneficial to learning (p. 266). The difficulty of paper dictionary use may actually put off language learners, who might be confused, if not overwhelmed and annoyed, by the wealth of information not immediately relevant to the task at hand, which they are nonetheless bound to note and wade through. However, such conclusions do not undermine the main tenet of the Involvement Load Hypothesis (Laufer and Hill 2000: 72). The question is what warrants attention. In fact, a demanding look-up process does not have to merit attention; it might rather provoke irritation and anxiety. In other words, attention does not necessarily correlate with the effort put into dictionary look-up, which is often performed quite automatically. Instead, the conspicuousness of headwords and entries on the computer screen might arrest users' attention, which, unlike in the paper dictionary, is not dispersed by other headwords crammed onto the same page (Dziemianko 2010: 265).[2]

Craik and Tulving (1975: 268) point out that the persistence of a memory trace is "a positive function of 'depth' of processing, where depth refers to greater degrees of semantic involvement". Pattern recognition and meaning extraction, however, are usually preceded by a preliminary analysis of stimuli, i.e. an "analysis of such physical or sensory features as lines, angles, brightness, pitch, and loudness" (Craik and Lockhart 1972: 673). Since human beings are concerned primarily with meaning extraction from stimuli, they tend to store products of deeper semantic and cognitive involvement, rather than those of any preliminary stages. It is therefore possible to venture a statement that, in the process of paper dictionary consultation, turning pages and wading through a large number of entries on the same page to finally track down an entry corresponds to the preliminary stages of analysis described by Craik and Lockhart (1972). These initial stages of paper dictionary look-up do not necessarily contribute to better retention or strengthening the memory trace, as they do not necessitate semantic involvement. All in all, it might be suggested that it is not *any* involvement that matters to vocabulary retention in the process of dictionary use, but *semantic* involvement. Consequently, the largely automatic stages of paper dictionary look-up which precede processing the information found in the relevant entry might not induce sufficient semantic and cognitive involvement in dictionary users to positively affect retention.

On the other hand, Shizuka (2003: 32) claimed that greater look-up frequency, typical of electronic dictionaries, especially portable ones, might benefit dictionary users. Koyama and Takeuchi's (2004a: 41) findings, however, indicate that, in reality, task-induced involvement may be more important than look-up frequency alone, which does not warrant better retention.[3] Similarly, Lew and Doroszewska (2009: 253) argued that "retention rates do not seem to be affected by the sheer amount of dictionary activity. [...] it is the quality rather than the quantity of lookups that makes a real difference: not how many, but which entry components are being consulted." In their study, subjects had to read an online text with ten difficult words highlighted. For each of the words, a dictionary entry was created with four possible types of information: English definition, Polish equivalent, animated picture, and examples of usage. The entry appeared as a menu, and the subjects could choose which information type they wished to see. In the immediate (unexpected) retention test that followed, the subjects were asked to explain the meaning of each target word

---

[2] In the electronic (online) version of *COBUILD$_6$* used in the study, the entry for the looked-up word does not appear in a sequence of entries on the computer screen, but pops-up alone.

[3] Laufer and Hill (2000: 72) came to virtually the same conclusion; in their words: "the number of times the word is looked up during a learning session bears almost no relation to its retention." It should be remembered, however, that the CALL software titled Words in Your Ear was used in the study rather than a regular dictionary in electronic form.

either in Polish or in English. Lew and Doroszewska (p. 253) found that retention rates resulting from reference to animations were surprisingly low, only about half as good as for the other look-up options, even though animations were the second most often consulted source of information (after Polish equivalents). The difference in retention scores thus did not result from the amount of dictionary activity but from the type of lexicographic data consulted. The authors suspect that the failure of their animations to stimulate better retention might, among other things, stem from the transience of the video sequences or the fact that the animations distracted the students from form–meaning associations, which are a prerequisite for successful retention (Lew and Doroszewska 2009: 253–4).

15.6 Appreciation

Search speed and ease of use rank high among the features which are most appreciated in electronic dictionaries (Kobayashi 2008, Koyama and Takeuchi 2003, Nesi 2000b, Tang 1997, Tseng 2009). Almind (2005: 39) maintains that the speed of data retrieval from electronic dictionaries, coupled with search precision, "is the reason why even internet dictionaries with sub-standard content are successful". Portability, in turn, means that any bilingual dictionary on a hand-held device can act as an "umbilical cord" linking users to their mother tongue and boosting their confidence in L2 (Stirling 2003). The ease of use and speed of electronic dictionary consultation suggest that they can lower the consultation trigger point, i.e. the moment when English as a foreign language (EFL) learners decide to refer to a dictionary for the meaning of unknown words and phrases (Shizuka 2003: 32). Aust *et al.* (1993: 70) found that readers consult hyper references much more willingly than comparable conventional (paper) references. They concluded that hyper references make learners less wary of dictionaries and help them to consult dictionaries more readily.

While such an effect has been attested for PEDs (Shizuka 2003: 27, 32), robust-machine electronic dictionaries have been found to encourage browsing in no way related to the task at hand (Nesi 2000b: 111). Such lateral browsing, previously observed by Guillot and Kenning (1994: 72–3), is no doubt facilitated by hyperlinking, whereby another dictionary entry is simply called up by double-clicking a word on the screen or hovering the mouse over a word. It is thanks to such immediate cross-references that "looking up takes a whole new meaning in electronic dictionaries: laborious page-turning and letter hunting can be replaced with a single mouse click or even hovering your mouse over the target, whereupon a small popup window can display an instant explanation" (Lew 2010c: 391). No wonder, then, that words which are in no way connected with the text being read are willingly looked up in electronic dictionaries.

Overall, it appears that electronic dictionaries in any format have gone a long way towards reducing lexicographic information costs, i.e. "the difficulty, or inconvenience, that the user of a dictionary believes or feels is associated with consulting the dictionary" (Nielsen 1999: 111), and more specifically, search-related lexicographic costs, i.e. costs connected with the look-up act (Nielsen 2008: 173). The electronic medium has relieved users of time-consuming activities such as turning pages, scanning long columns crammed with information, and deciphering phonetic transcription. Immediate cross-references, intuitive interfaces, and partial or expandable entries make electronic dictionaries even more convenient and search-cost-effective. Nonetheless, there is always the other side of the coin. Admittedly, the hierarchical display (in the form of either clickable menus, where each match is hyperlinked to a subentry, or partial entries, where the top of each match is displayed with a link to the full content of each lemma) gives a concise overview of search term matches, in contrast to the linear, much more overwhelming layout of paper dictionaries. Yet, extra search-related information costs emerge, such as additional clicking or scrolling, which might negatively affect the readiness to look up words in electronic dictionaries. That said, electronic dictionaries are no doubt much more (search-) cost-effective than those on paper.

Paper dictionaries, however, tend to be considered better learning tools than PEDs (e.g. Chen 2010). Traditional paper dictionaries are usually described as more detailed, accurate, and reliable, notwithstanding the fact that they are cumbersome to carry as well as time-consuming to consult. Surprisingly enough, the portable electronic dictionary used in Koyama and Takeuchi's (2003: 72) experiment was thought to provide insufficient information for language learning, even though the information was the same as in the paper dictionary employed in the study. Koyama and Takeuchi ascribed this assessment to the layered interface design of the PED: the small screen, a trade-off for portability, makes it possible to display only limited information and "might oblige students to push one button after another to obtain further information about the target word" (p. 73; see also Yamada 2011). PEDs are also often criticized for the limited range of meanings and paucity of examples they display (Koyama and Takeuchi 2004a, Stirling 2003). Kobayashi (2008), for example, found that pocket electronic dictionary users mainly complain about a dearth of varied examples (39%), insufficient grammatical information (32%), lack of information on usage (27%), a small screen (19%), and a relatively limited wordlist (16%). Other downsides of portable electronic dictionaries include no room for notation, high cost, and short battery life. It is possible, however, that some of these criticisms relate not so much to the medium per se as to the dictionaries consulted on portable devices, which may turn out to be less exhaustive than those loaded on robust-machine dictionaries.

Indeed, most of the criticisms levelled at PEDs do not usually apply to robust-machine dictionaries such as CD-ROM dictionaries or online dictionaries. These are typically accessed on computers with large screens that make it possible to present elaborate lexicographic information for all headwords. They are usually available for a limited fee (if not completely free), include a number of customizable or bottom-up editing features (Carr 1997: 214, Lew 2011a), and often open up the possibility of making notes, a feature traditionally associated only with the paper medium.

15.7 Comparability issues and the limitations of current research

The question of the relative usefulness of paper and electronic dictionaries does not have a simple answer. As shown in the Appendix, the studies reviewed here investigated dictionary use on the basis of many different tasks. In most cases the subjects had to carry out receptive tasks, which might give a deceptive impression of comparability. However, the tasks differed widely in design, which must have affected the results. The type of method used to evaluate comprehension ranges from true/false or open-ended text comprehension questions to vocabulary questions focusing on meaning or synonyms. Some studies require subjects to look up low-frequency words, while in others they are made to find the appropriate meaning of highly polysemous verbs. Most studies focused on single words, but others also dealt with collocations and various phraseological units. More problematically, perhaps, the results of studies that compare the use of paper and electronic dictionaries may be debatable when the paper and electronic dictionaries used do not share the same lexicographic features (e.g. coverage, layout, amount of information offered at the microstructural level, or the way in which the information is presented typographically).

The studies reviewed here covered a cross-section of the world's population (e.g. EFL students at a British university, Polish students, Japanese students). Naturally, the subjects' dictionary-using habits and skills must have been affected by their native, cultural, and linguistic backgrounds. A no less important role was played by their education and proficiency in English.[4] The wide spectrum which the participants represented in these respects must have had a bearing on the outcome of the research. In addition, the number of participants in the studies ranged from five (Tono 2011) to 781 (Weschler and Pitts 2000), and sampling procedures are typically not specified, although most subjects seemed to be university students who were accessible to the authors or their assistants. In the majority of cases, the samples were relatively small, which means that they may not have been representative. Hasty generalizations drawn on this basis may be unreliable and invalid (Tarp 2009c: 290–2). In fact, reaching conclusions about electronic dictionary usefulness is severely constrained when the types of user and usage situations are not clearly defined, lexicographic functions and data are not specific enough, and the ease or difficulty with which the data can be accessed and understood is not explained. Unfortunately, much too often such information is not divulged by researchers.

---

[4] Information on the subjects' level of English is given in the Appendix whenever it is specified in the relevant publications.

The Appendix also shows that many tools were employed to monitor dictionary consultation, including cutting-edge technology in the form of eye-tracking systems (Tono 2011; see Simonsen 2011). It remains to be seen whether this is the beginning of a new direction in which research into dictionary use will develop. It is nonetheless regrettable that so few researchers have made use of much less complicated log files, with the help of which electronic dictionary consultation can be unobtrusively studied in a natural setting, without the need to manipulate variables (De Schryver and Joffe 2004: 194). Finally, the Appendix reveals insufficient interest in the subjects' previous experience of dictionary use. Even when it was considered a possible variable, it was typically assessed on the basis of the subjects' perception of their habits and skills, rather than any objective evaluation thereof. Testing actual paper- and electronic-dictionary literacy, rather than relying on assertions, beliefs, or feelings, might give a more accurate picture.

15.8 Conclusion

To expect great uniformity across investigations into paper and electronic dictionary use would be overoptimistic, if not naive. It is only natural that different authors strive to attain their own goals and answer their research questions using the methods which they consider appropriate. Yet, a few general suggestions for further research can be formulated by way of conclusion.

First, different users approach dictionary consultation in different ways and adopt their own strategies (Tono 2011). Unlike the book format, the electronic medium makes it possible to customize dictionaries and better adjust them to the individual needs of target users. In addition, it provides new and innovative technologies to get a deeper insight into what actually happens when users look up a word in a dictionary. Log files or eye-trackers, for example, make it possible to computationally monitor all decisions made in the consultation process. These methods could also provide the information necessary to pave the way for further, or even immediate, improvements in electronic dictionary design (see De Schryver and Joffe 2004: 187).

Second, there is a need for comparative studies on the usefulness of various electronic dictionary types. Investigations into the relative usefulness of electronic dictionaries on CD-ROMs, PEDs, and online dictionaries are virtually non-existent. Some of the conclusions drawn above about the possible role of electronic dictionary formats seem speculative and should be treated as hypotheses which need to be verified by empirical studies. There is also room for more comparative research into the usefulness of paper and electronic dictionaries. It might be interesting to see whether there is indeed a positive correlation between the effort invested in (paper and electronic) dictionary search and vocabulary retention, or between the number of words looked up and reading comprehension. It is necessary, however, to distinguish the effort which is mainly cognitive or mental from the exertion which is primarily physical or mechanical. It is not at all clear whether dictionary users' cognitive involvement is different depending on whether they are faced with paper or (various types of) electronic dictionaries. Importantly, any research into the relative usefulness of paper and electronic dictionaries should be designed so that the medium, rather than just presentation issues, can be shown to be the reason for any observed differences. This might create the need for fabricated, purpose-built dictionaries, or at least dictionary entries, which would be exactly parallel not only in content, but also, as far as possible, in interface or layout. It remains to be hoped that further research into the role of dictionary form will make it possible one day to answer the seemingly simple question: Which dictionary is more useful—paper or electronic? Although this may appear a naive question to ask, the above discussion shows that formulating a straightforward and precise answer on the basis of current, highly diversified research is anything but easy, if feasible at all.

Dictionaries

[CALD₃] Walter, Elizabeth (ed.) (2008). *Cambridge Advanced Learners' Dictionary*. Third Edition. Cambridge: Cambridge University Press. http://dictionary.cambridge.org/dictionary/learner-english/.

Cambridge Dictionaries Online: http://dictionary.cambridge.org/.

[COBUILD₆] Sinclair, John M. (ed.) (2008). *Collins COBUILD Advanced English Dictionary*. Sixth Edition. Boston: Heinle Cengage Learning; Glasgow: Harper Collins Publishers. http://mycobuild.com/.

Dictionary.com: http://dictionary.reference.com/.

TheFreeDictionary: http://www.thefreedictionary.com/.

[LDOCE₅] Mayor, Michael (ed.) (2009). *Longman Dictionary of Contemporary English*. Fifth Edition. Harlow: Longman. http://www.ldoceonline.com/.

[OALDCE₅] Crowther, Jonathan (ed.) (1995). *Oxford Advanced Learner's Dictionary of Current English*. Fifth Edition. Oxford: Oxford University Press.

[OALDCE₆] Wehmeier, Sally (ed.) (2000). *Oxford Advanced Learner's Dictionary of Current English*. Sixth Edition. Oxford: Oxford University Press.

[OALDCE₇] Wehmeier, Sally (ed.) (2005). *Oxford Advanced Learner's Dictionary of Current English*. Seventh Edition. Oxford: Oxford University Press.

[MEDAL₂] Rundell, Michael (ed.) (2007). *Macmillan English Dictionary for Advanced Learners*. Second Edition. Oxford: Macmillan Education.

[MEDO] *Macmillan English Dictionary Online*: http://www.macmillandictionary.com/.

Wiktionary: http://en.wiktionary.org/.

WordReference.com: http://wordreference.com/.

Appendix A summary of the studies reviewed

Authors	Task	Subjects	Methods of monitoring dictionary use	Testing familiarity with PD and ED
Nesi (2000b)	reading texts on paper with the help of OALDCE5 in book form and on CD-ROM; true/ false comprehension questions	29 subjects, non-native speakers of English from different linguistic backgrounds	record sheets	orientation session
Tono (2000)	3 purpose-built computer-based electronic dictionary interfaces: traditional, parallel, layered; paper (control) conditions provided by Kenkyusha's College Lighthouse English–Japanese Dictionary and Shogakukan's Progressive Japanese-English Dictionary; language tasks: (a) out of context: simple look-up (single words / derivatives / idioms and compounds) (b) in context: translation and reading comprehension for a paragraph reconstruction task (c) receptive vs. productive skills [L1–L2 / L2–L1]	5 Japanese EFL students at Lancaster University	recorded with the help of Microsoft Camcorder	questionnaire
Weschler and Pitts (2000)	looking up a list of words in paper and electronic dictionaries; dictionaries used – unknown	781 first-year students at Kyoritsu Women's University and College	observation	orientation session, show-of-hands survey, questionnaire
Koyama and Takeuchi (2003)	reading a text, underlining the words looked up and answering ten comprehension and vocabulary questions; the Genius English–Japanese Dictionary (2nd edition, Taishukan) in book form and its electronic version on CASIO EX-word XD-2500; word recall and recognition after one week	42 college and high school students, 4 students in an additional study	video recording, think-aloud protocols (4 students)	questionnaire, free comments

Osaki et al. (2003)	looking up 15 target words (while reading) in the paper version of the *Genius English–Japanese Dictionary* and the electronic one on EX-word XD-R8100 from CASIO; a ten-question comprehension test; immediate and delayed vocabulary tests	167 Japanese university students divided into upper and lower proficiency levels	unknown	unknown
Shizuka (2003)	choosing Japanese synonyms for ten monosemous English nouns; completing examples for highly polysemous verbs extracted from dictionaries; *Genius English–Japanese Dictionary* on paper and its electronic version on XD-S1200 by CASIO	77 Japanese students	unknown	questionnaire
Koyama and Takeuchi (2004a)	comprehending two written texts without recourse to a dictionary and answering vocabulary questions with a paper dictionary (text 1) and an electronic dictionary (text 2); *Genius English–Japanese Dictionary* (3rd edition, Taishukan) in book form and its electronic version on CASIO EX-word XD-8100; word recall and recognition after one week	18 undergraduate university students (intermediate)	individual video recording	questionnaire, free comments
Osaki and Nakayama (2004)	reading comprehension under three conditions (paper, electronic, no dictionary), vocabulary and text comprehension as well as retention checked immediately after the reading task; paper and portable electronic dictionaries used – unknown	167 and 152 Japanese EFL students, divided into upper and lower proficiency levels	unknown	unknown
Kobayashi (2007, 2008)	*stage 1*: a questionnaire investigating dictionary using habits; *stage 2*: reading comprehension with paper and pocket electronic dictionary	*stage 1*: 279 Japanese students at three universities, 22 of them	think aloud retrospective protocols,	questionnaire, students classified as typically paper or electronic

(*continued*)

Authors	Task	Subjects	Methods of monitoring dictionary use	Testing familiarity with PD and ED
	routinely used by the subjects, six open-ended comprehension questions; two vocabulary tests to check retention, oral interviews; *stage 3*: a modified questionnaire	interviewed at *stage 2*; *stage 3*: 97 English majors	information audio-taped	dictionary users according to their responses
Koyama and Takeuchi (2007)	*study 1*: reading two texts with access to different dictionaries and circling the words looked up; *Taishukan's Genius English–Japanese Dictionary* (3rd edition) on paper and its electronic version on CASIO EX-word XD-R9000; a two-question comprehension quiz immediately afterwards; *study 2*: the same dictionaries and procedures, but a more difficult text; a six-question comprehension test after the reading task	*study 1*: 34 Japanese college students (false beginners); *study 2*: 31 undergraduate students (much more advanced in English)	observation (each subject performed the tasks individually)	orientation session, interview
Lew and Doroszewska (2009)	a purpose-built server-based online application with a vocabulary pre-test and a reading comprehension task, unexpected immediate paper-based retention and reading comprehension tests	56 Polish high school students, A2–B1 (CEFR)	log files	unknown
Chen (2010)	a vocabulary test with both receptive and productive tasks; the comprehension part— choice between three possible meaning explanations (exact, approximate, and irrelevant) of ten low-frequency words; the productive part—sentence formation with each target word; *Oxford Advanced Learner's English–Chinese*	85 advanced students, junior English majors at Putian University, Fujian	observation by the author	questionnaire

Study	Task / materials	Subjects	Data collection	Instructions
	Dictionary (6th edition), a bilingualized version of *OALDCE₆* and other bilingualized learner's dictionaries included in the portable dictionaries owned by the subjects; immediate retention test; one week later an unexpected retention test followed by a questionnaire			questionnaire
Dziemianko (2010)	explaining the meaning of nouns and phrases in the decoding task, completing the missing prepositions removed from collocations placed in sentences in the encoding task; *COBUILD₆* on paper and on the Internet; an unexpected retention test two weeks later	64 students at English at Adam Mickiewicz University in Poznań, Poland, B2–C1 (CEFR)	observation by the author	
Lew (2010b)	completing partial English translations, *OALDCE₇* entries (modified—menus, unmodified—shortcuts) on paper	90 Polish high school students A2–B1 (CEFR)	record sheets, peer observation	unknown
Lew and Tokarek (2010)	guided Polish-to-English translation under three conditions: no menu, menu, menu with highlighting; a purpose-built, Polish-English online mini-dictionary	90 Polish learners of English A2–B1 (CEFR)	observation (tasks performed individually), log files	unknown
Nesi and Tan (2011)	relevant sense identification in paper-based purpose-built entries	124 students at a university in Malaysia (Bands 2–6 in terms of Malaysian University Entrance Test scores)	a clock embedded in a purpose-built Moodle-based test to record time	briefing session
Tono (2011)	sense localization in purpose-built dictionary entries shown on the screen	8 subjects at Tokyo University of Foreign Studies; high (C1–B2) and low (A2) proficiency groups (CEFR)	eye-tracking	briefing session

16

How can we make electronic dictionaries more effective?

ROBERT LEW

16.1 Introduction

The rate at which electronic dictionaries have been replacing their printed counterparts is impressive, though not altogether unexpected, at least by some experts (Atkins 1996). As a result of the revolutionary character of the transition, designers of electronic dictionaries find themselves in a void when it comes to user studies specifically addressing this dictionary format. Naturally, it takes time to plan, conduct, analyse, and disseminate the results of empirical user studies. In a rapidly growing area such as that of e-dictionaries, user research may find itself overtaken by events. While it is certainly reassuring for designers of electronic reference works to be able to base design decisions on solid empirical evidence, holding back development until such evidence is available is often thought to be a waste of time. With such direct evidence lacking, lexicographers can instead look for design principles in user studies done on paper dictionaries: many of the material issues in dictionary design are relatively form-independent, and so findings from paper-based studies may still supply useful pointers for the design of e-dictionaries. Further relevant evidence may come from non-lexicographic studies involving human-computer interaction. Expert intuition continues to be an important source of insight, as are new feedback channels from users, including what has been termed simultaneous feedback (De Schryver and Prinsloo 2001, De Schryver and Joffe 2004) as well as the use of log files (De Schryver and Joffe 2004, Bergenholtz and Johnsen 2005; De Schryver *et al.* 2006, Bergenholtz and Johnsen 2007, Tarp 2009c, Verlinde and Binon 2010).

There is a body of studies comparing the effectiveness (and other usability aspects) of paper and electronic dictionaries—in their various mutations—and the results are summarized in Dziemianko (this volume) as well as in some other recent papers (Chen 2010, Dziemianko 2010). Without unnecessarily duplicating the discussion here, let us just observe that the picture that emerges is a somewhat confusing one, with findings from seemingly similar studies often pointing in opposite directions. Likely, this is due as much to the broader spectrum of lexicographic solutions in e-dictionaries than in paper dictionaries, as to the range of variation in the user- and task-related variables. The challenge then is to try to assess which particular e-lexicographic solutions work best (and for whom, and under what circumstances), so that future electronic dictionaries can be made more effective than their paper predecessors, and more effective than the dictionaries available today.

Caution is advised in evaluating the empirical evidence as well as users' subjective assessment of dictionaries of different types. A case in point is a study by Tan (2009), who looked at the effectiveness of sense discrimination and found electronic dictionaries to be as good as, but no better than, paper dictionaries. However, Tan probed more deeply than most previous studies and concluded that successful use of the electronic form was conditional on the users receiving sufficient focused training in using the interface, based on concrete problems they were confronted with. This is an important finding which may hold a partial clue to the disparity in the findings reported in various studies: human users find new solutions confusing before they have learnt to use them efficiently, so their performance may vary widely depending on where exactly on the learning curve they happen to be at a particular time. Tan also assessed the reliability of user declarations with regard to the efficacy of dictionaries, and found them to be out of sync with the empirical findings. Thus, the conclusion is that self-assessment is not a reliable predictor of the actual effectiveness of electronic dictionaries. This, again, is an important methodological finding, and very few studies have directly addressed such questions. Pending further results, it is probably safe to assume that the lack of reliability of self-assessment methods is not restricted to just electronic dictionaries.

16.2 What makes e-dictionaries effective?

In functional terms, the conditions for e-dictionaries being effective tools are broadly the same as those for paper dictionaries: dictionaries need to be able to answer the specific reference needs of the user, needs which typically arise in a non-lexicographic situation (cf. e.g. Tarp 2008). Dictionaries should be able to satisfy those needs within an acceptably short time and with the required degree of detail. In addition, the data have to be presented in a form that is maximally comprehensible. From this it follows that the demands on lexicographic data need not vary dramatically depending on the delivery platform of the dictionary. However, the best lexicographic description will not help the user if it fails to be located, and where e-dictionaries can make a clear difference is in the efficiency of access to lexicographic data (Verlinde and Peeters, this volume), and possibly in the use of multimedia. Therefore, we will focus here on the above two aspects, with the understanding that the notion of dictionary effectiveness extends far beyond the confines of this chapter, encompassing an enormous range of user categories (e.g. school children, language learners, content learners, teachers, translators, tourists, scholars, word game aficionados, and language purists) and uses (e.g. reading, writing, text revision, translation, word learning, and playing Scrabble). In the following section we will address issues of access to lexicographic data in the context of electronic lexicography, tracing the access process along the typical steps involved in a dictionary consultation act. Then, in Section 16.4, comments will be offered on the role of multimedia in e-dictionaries.

16.3 Effective access to lexicographic data

Metalexicographers recognize that the process of locating data in a dictionary involves a number of steps, with different skills being involved at each step. Models of the dictionary look-up process have been proposed in several publications (Scholfield 1982, Hartmann 1989, Müllich 1990, Bogaards 1993, Scholfield 1999, Hartmann 2001, Bogaards 2003). All of these models distinguish between the lemmatic or macrostructural stage (getting to the right headword) and sublemmatic or microstructural stage (locating relevant data within the entry). In this section, we shall be taking a closer look at the following issues: getting to the relevant headword when the exact spelling of the (citation) form is not known (Section 16.3.1); locating multi-word expressions (16.3.2); active assistance in entering search terms (16.3.3); the possibility of presenting the contents of the entry in an incremental fashion (16.3.4); and navigating polysemous entries (16.3.5).

16.3.1 *Headword identification*

One problematic area of dictionary consultation involves headword identification. A facet of this problem which has received some attention from metalexicographers and linguists (Scholfield 1982, Bogaards 1993, Scholfield 1999) is the need to reduce a word form encountered in the text to its base (citation) form. This operation may be problem-ridden in the user's non-native language.[1] In a paper dictionary, finding an inflected word form normally entails mentally stripping the inflection to arrive at the citation form, as a printed dictionary will not usually list regularly inflected forms as lemma signs. This may not pose much of a problem when the inflected form is alphabetically adjacent (or very close) to the citation form, so that even a user unaware of the need to extract the citation form may readily hit upon the right entry. For example, when looking up the English progressive form *involving*, one would typically arrive at the headword **involve** anyway, and in some dictionaries

---

[1] It may also occasionally be a problem in one's L1, depending on the combination of the morphological complexity of the language, the lemmatization policy adopted, and the user's level of reference skills; cf. Prinsloo, this volume.

(notably, those targeted at children and language learners) the *-ing* form may even be listed explicitly towards the top of the entry.

A well-designed electronic dictionary should be able to handle the work of reducing an inflected form to the lemma (or a menu of lemmas, if ambiguous). However, the step from the inflected form to the base form is just one step—and a relatively unproblematic one for a poorly inflected language such as English.

A more challenging aspect of lemmatic access is the dominance of the graphemic access route. The tradition-sanctioned orthographic supremacy dictates that spelling representation be the starting point of a consultation act. But this need not be the case. Dictionary users may well wish to look up items whose standard spelling they are unsure of. This may happen when they recall words from earlier encounters or when their exposure to lexical items comes from audio (including video) materials. Then again, even if the orthographic form *is* immediately available, users may not carry it over perfectly into the dictionary interface. Being able to access the right base form is thus revealed to be a central area in dictionary use, and one where the effectiveness of electronic dictionaries can probably be improved with solutions that are not necessarily very advanced technologically. For more than a decade now, Sobkowiak has argued for the implementation of phonetic access in dictionaries (e.g. Sobkowiak 1999, 2003). In a nutshell, this proposal foresees an access path that is spelling-independent, and instead uses look-up by phonetic symbols. While such access can now be found in isolated dictionaries, it has not been generally adopted. The reasons may lie in pessimism as to its real usefulness to the average user, who would need to be conversant with the particular symbol inventory and correctly distinguish between similar phonemes. This may simply be too much to ask of a casual dictionary user, especially if a second or foreign language is involved. And those few users who do have the requisite level of sophistication can probably get by with traditional access routes. In this way, the use of phonetic access would be largely restricted to users with above-average reference needs, such as teachers wishing to produce word lists with certain phonetic features. Of course, this does not in itself mean that such an access route should not be offered as an alternative, especially if it can be provided without much additional expense. Of the electronic versions of learners' dictionaries for English, the CD-ROM editions of the *Macmillan English Dictionary* stand out as offering a similar facility under the brand name of Sound-Search (for details see Sobkowiak 2003: 432–5).

Another mode of phonetic access is the direct use of the audio channel, perhaps a more promising option for the average dictionary user with moderate reference skills. Its relative success is largely due to—and contingent upon—advances in speech recognition, and here a particular problem spot lies in dealing with accented speech, as well as tuning in to the idiosyncratic accent of a particular user without being sidetracked by individual variation.

Leaving aside literal phonetic access and recognizing the orthographic supremacy in the literate world, a more modest—and more immediate—goal of electronic dictionaries should be to improve the accuracy of the standard orthographic access route by honing their ability to 'guess' the intended spelling by recognizing associations between non-identical but sufficiently close variants (i.e. fuzzy matching). In essence, this boils down to dealing effectively with misspelled words, much like the spellchecking function in word processors. However, the latter tend to be optimized for users writing in their native language, while a substantial proportion of dictionary consultation is done by non-native speakers, especially for an international language such as English, and almost invariably in learners' dictionaries. A further challenge comes from the fact that a dictionary interface does not usually have access to the textual context which a word processor usually does have, and can use as a guide in disambiguation.

A recent study (Lew and Mitton 2011) examined how well the leading English learners' dictionaries in their online versions dealt with actual misspellings by foreign learners of English. Three corpora of misspellings were tested: Polish, Finnish, and Japanese, representing three unrelated mother tongues. For each attested misspelling, the position of the intended target on the list of items suggested by the specific dictionary was noted, if it was present on the list at all. Ideally, the right word should be offered at the top of the list, but it is not realistic to expect perfect performance, given the varied nature of misspellings. Spellchecking dictionary search terms is more challenging than spellchecking a text in a word processor, as there is no textual context (i.e. co-text) here to serve as a source of additional clues. As a consequence, detecting real-word errors is impossible: for example, when a user keys in **pale** in the dictionary's search window, there is no way for the system to guess that they might have meant **pail** instead. Further, if the non-word **peil** is entered, there will be no context to help decide whether **pale** or **pail** is more likely and should be given priority on the list of suggestions.

These difficulties aside, a spellchecking system as part of an electronic dictionary should still be able to offer reasonable suggestions whenever possible. In January 2011, Lew and Mitton (2011) tested the performance of seven popular online dictionary interfaces (see Figure 16.1) on a total of 202 misspellings by looking them up in each of the dictionaries. The seven interfaces included five monolingual learners' dictionaries. Of the latter, the *Longman Dictionary of Contemporary English*[2] (two versions, *LDOCE Free* and *LDOCE Premium*) and *Merriam Webster's Advanced Learners English Dictionary*[3] (*MWALED*) performed best and were able to identify the

---

[2] Two interfaces were tested: the free-access version at http://www.ldoceonline.com/ (*LDOCE Free*) and premium version for buyers of paper copies at http://www.longmandictionariesonline.com/ (*LDOCE Premium*).

[3] http://www.learnersdictionary.com/.

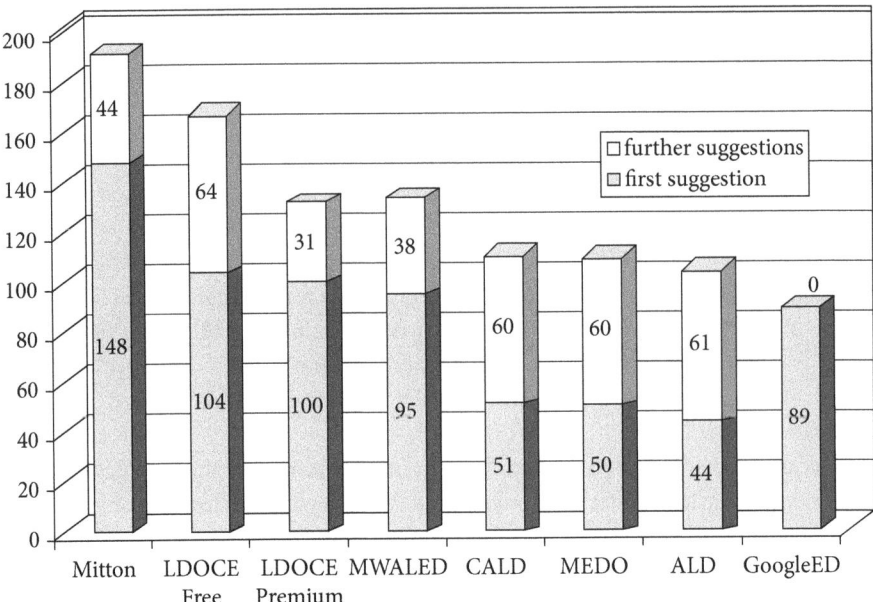

FIGURE 16.1 Success in identifying words misspelled by EFL learners in online monolingual dictionaries of English compared with Mitton's context-free spellchecker.

majority of misspelled target words, about half of them as the top suggestion in the list of alternatives returned ("first suggestion" in Figure 16.1). Somewhat unexpectedly, the Free version of *LDOCE* outperformed the Premium version. While both versions scored similarly in terms of how often they got the target headword at the top of the list of suggestions, the Free version was able to include in the list some target items which the Premium version was unable to guess at all. The other three learners' dictionaries, the *Cambridge Advanced Learner's Dictionary*[4] (CALD), the *Macmillan English Dictionary Online*[5] (MEDO), and the *Oxford Advanced Learners' Dictionary*[6] (ALD) did much worse, especially when it came to selecting the most likely suggestion. The *Google English Dictionary*[7] (GoogleED), which at the time when data were being collected appeared to be based on the content of the *New Oxford American Dictionary*, was also included, primarily to see if an interface from the world's celebrated leader in information retrieval would overtake the more traditional dictionary publishers. Quite the opposite turned out to be the case. In terms of the total proportion of target items identified, the Google dictionary

[4] http://dictionary.cambridge.org/.
[5] http://www.macmillandictionary.com/.
[6] http://www.oxfordadvancedlearnersdictionary.com/?cc=global.
[7] http://www.google.com/dictionary?langpair=en%7Cen&hl=en.

performed the worst of the lot. However, at this time the interface only offers one 'best' suggestion, which is why there are no 'further suggestions' in Figure 16.1 for this dictionary. When only the first suggestion is considered, the Google dictionary is still beaten by *LDOCE* (both versions) and *MWALED*.

There are a number of misspellings in our corpus which are understandably challenging to spellchecking systems. However, some of the dictionaries appear to be able to do a far better job of identifying headwords spelled in an unorthodox fashion than others, and the dictionaries in need of an upgrade include major and authoritative titles as well as the Google dictionary. Some of the misspellings which intuitively appear to be relatively easy to correct are nevertheless missed, with very unlikely alternatives offered instead, such as *spigot* as the top suggestion for the misspelling *spagetti* rather than the obvious *spaghetti* (*MWALED*), or *imprecisions* for *imiteision* (an attempt at the word *imitation*; *ALD*). Sometimes the 'best' suggestion is not much of an improvement on the misspelling itself, such as when *GoogleED* responds to *aidentiti* (*identity* being the target word) with *identiti*. Even the best-performing dictionaries admit defeat with items that should not be all that difficult to handle: *LDOCE Free* offers *probable* as the first suggestions for *probabli* rather than the target *probably*.

But perhaps this is as good as a context-free spellchecker can get? Are the best dictionaries doing the best job possible? To answer this question, an experimental spellchecking system designed by Roger Mitton (in its context-free version, Mitton 2009) was run on the same set of misspellings. As it turns out, Mitton's spellchecker (first from left in Figure 16.1) performed significantly better than any of the online dictionaries. In particular, it managed to offer the target item as the best suggestion in as many as 148 out of 202 cases: that is 50 per cent better than the best-performing dictionaries tested, and up to three times the rate of the less successful ones. This comparison shows rather convincingly that the spellchecking components of even the best of the dictionaries tested leave plenty of room for improvement. In fact, the success rate of Mitton's spellchecker could be improved even further by customizing the rules to reflect the misspelling errors typical of the native language of the dictionary user (Mitton and Okada 2007). This added layer of L1-sensitivity could optionally be used in those cases where the L1 of the user is known, or can reasonably be inferred from browser settings and/or IP geolocation.

16.3.2 *Accessing multi-word units*

Multi-word expressions have remained a neglected aspect of language when it comes to treatment in dictionaries (Oppentocht and Schutz 2003: 219). This is a natural consequence of the privileged status that the (orthographic) word has traditionally enjoyed in lexicography. Part of the blame for this situation lies with an attachment to the atomic view of language. But even lexicographers sympathetic to the

Sinclairian view have to contend with the fact that the orthographic word has a deeply entrenched function as the major indexical component in the organization of dictionary entries. There are many reasons why breaking with this tradition has been difficult. First, the scope and stability (fixedness) of multi-word lexical items often tend to be variable, and this creates problems if they are to be entered as pivotal units (cf. Moon 1998, Philip 2008). Second, in those cases when this is not a problem objectively speaking, dictionary users may not be sure of the exact scope or form of a multi-word unit; they may not even come to realize that their comprehension problem involves a multi-word unit (Scholfield 1999: 15). Third, even if a user does realize that a multi-word unit is involved, they are still likely to follow the ortho-graphic-word-based look-up strategy, either due to the folk-linguistic view of words as the building blocks of language, or because this is how their experience with dictionary consultation has conditioned them to operate.

Thus, raising the status of language chunks larger than the word requires, not just innovation in dictionary interfaces, but also an evolution as far as the habits and strategies of dictionary users are concerned. Advanced dictionary users tend to have a higher level of awareness of the fact that language does not portion out meaning into individual orthographic words, that larger chunks are often important, and that these chunks have a place of their own in the better dictionaries and can be looked up. Dwornik and Margol (2011) focus on the process of online dictionary consultation by advanced Polish learners of English, and report on users getting stuck on the following text fragment: "It came on the heels of a U.S. plan...". Using the free online versions of the *Longman Dictionary of Contemporary English* and the *Macmillan English Dictionary Online*, study participants tried a number of seemingly reasonable search terms, which did not, however, result in the successful identifica-tion of the phrase. The search strings attempted were the following: "come on the heels", "on the heels of", "on the heels", and finally "come on heels". Unfortunately, all of the above happen to be different from the 'canonical' form of this subentry, which in *LDOCE* is *(hard/hot/close) on the heels of something* and in *MEDO follow (hard) on the heels of something* (at the entry FOLLOW) or *(hard/hot/close) on the heels of* under HEEL,[8] and so none of those attempts succeeded in locating the expression. This finding suggests that fuzzy matching mechanisms should be employed, so that approximate matches might be recognized as well, in line with the creative variability of natural language. Apparently, this is exactly what is happening. The experimental searches described above were done in early 2010, but in the course of the preparation of this chapter the dictionaries were revisited in May 2011. At this later time, *MEDO* already supported partial matching, so that the target phrase *follow (hard) on the heels of something* (lemmatized under FOLLOW) can

---

[8] Listing the same expression differently in two different entries is another minor lexicographic sin which electronic lexicography should help eradicate.

now be accessed directly by typing into the search box the substrings "on the heels" or "on the heels of". This is a major improvement on the past versions and on the competition, and in the future this approach could be extended to handle the less mechanical types of phrase variability. However, the new functionality still needs some tweaking, as the alternative phrase form listed under HEEL remains inaccessible in this way. *LDOCE* still fails to find the expression in either its Free or Premium interface. Interestingly, the latest DVD-ROM version sold with the paper copy of *LDOCE5* does succeed in locating the complete phrase on searching for "on the heels". It is quite surprising to see the online interfaces lag behind an optical disk version in this way, as the ability to update quickly and incrementally is seen as a particular strength of online dictionaries (De Schryver 2003).

The above discussion refers to a situation in which the dictionary user encounters a text-reception problem, but realizes that they are dealing with a multi-word expression, and this is what they are actively seeking. However, in real life there must be many cases when users merely realize they are missing something, yet are oblivious to the fact that a sequence of words in the text forms a conventionalized multi-word unit. Or, if they are aware of this, they may still choose to follow the traditional word-based search strategy and only type a single word into the search box. These two scenarios might benefit from a capability of a dictionary to automatically recognize multi-word units by scanning the co-text for potential lexical units spanning several words, and suggesting these to the user (cf. also De Schryver *et al.* 2006). In order to be able to examine such a co-text, the dictionary needs to have access to the text which the user is reading. This is most readily achievable when the text itself is in the electronic format and is accessed on the same device as the dictionary. A typical example would be reading an Internet page on a laptop while consulting an online or locally-installed dictionary, or an electronic book being accessed on a dedicated e-book reading device with the help of a resident dictionary pre-loaded on the device. Such contextual sensitivity could also work, however, with printed or handwritten text, provided the device is coupled (or equipped) with a still camera and optical character recognition (OCR) technology. In this manner, a user would be able to take a snapshot of, say, a door sign in a foreign language and, via OCR, call up a co-text-sensitive dictionary entry on their mobile device.

16.3.3 *Type-ahead search*

Relevant to both headword spelling and access to multi-word units is a search interface enhancement variously known as *type-ahead search*, *search-as-you-type*, *incremental search*, *inline search*, or *instant search*. In its typical e-lexicographic application, the search box of a dictionary suggests a list of hits after typing a certain number of characters. For instance, the online version of the *Merriam-Webster's Advanced Learner's English Dictionary*, which has had the feature ever since it was launched, offers search suggestions already at the initial letter. A single-letter trigger

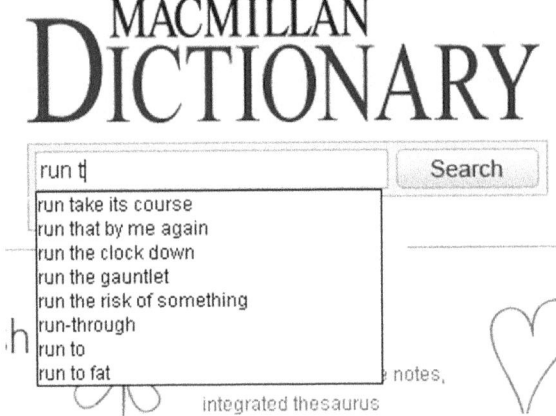

FIGURE 16.2 Type-ahead search in *Macmillan English Dictionary Online*, with a pull-down list of suggested multi-word expressions presented after typing "run t" into the search box.

is generally thought to be too intrusive and distracting, thus normally the mechanism becomes active after anything from two to five initial letters are typed.

Type-ahead search not only speeds up access to (particularly) longer words: it may partially relieve the user of having to reproduce exactly the standard spelling beyond the few initial characters. A more advanced use of the functionality is available in the *Macmillan English Dictionary Online* (see Figure 16.2). Here, a pull-down list with suggested items opens after typing the second character of the search term, and the important advantage of this particular interface is the inclusion of multi-word units already at this stage. On top of the immediate benefits of allowing the user to access complex lexical units more easily, the feature acts as a background reminder to the regular user that multi-words are valid building blocks of language (as well as search terms), and in doing so provides useful hands-on training in reference skills (cf. also Verlinde and Peeters, this volume).

16.3.4 *Step-wise outer access*

Since, in electronic dictionaries, what the user sees at any given moment need not reflect the full stored content of the underlying lexical database, the question becomes relevant as to how much of the data should be displayed, and in what progression. Hulstijn and Atkins (1998: 16) propose these three scenarios:

1. The whole entry is simultaneously available (as it is in a normal paper dictionary).
2. The information in the entry is presented in various phases. At each step, users are given two or more options to choose from, and are thus led towards the information they will finally select (whether correct or incorrect), without seeing all the rest of the information which the entry contains.

3. The computer offers preliminary customization by users of the type of information offered, and users work using their own menus.

These are thought-provoking suggestions and—over a decade later, and with electronic dictionaries having claimed much of the ground of their paper ancestors—it is interesting to reflect on how they stand up in the light of current lexicographic practice. As observed in a recent overview of online dictionaries of English (Lew 2011a), it is surprising that the paper-like option 1 is still so prevalent, even for dictionaries from well-known publishers.

As far as option 3 goes, we do see some attempts at implementing a degree of customization (cf. also De Schryver 2003, Trap-Jensen 2010a), but typically in a half-hearted fashion. For example, users may be allowed to switch phonetic transcription on and off, but are given little control over the more central entry elements. A notable counterexample would be the (subscription-based) online *Oxford English Dictionary*, where the user can select for display any combination of the following lexicographic data categories: Pronunciation, Spellings, Etymology, Quotations, Date Chart, and Additions. A problem with this particular implementation of user control is that it only works on the assumption that the users actually know which particular data fields would be helpful to them in a specific situation. While this assumption may perhaps work for the majority of users of a scholarly dictionary such as the *Oxford English Dictionary*, expecting this level of sophistication from non-academic users is unrealistic. An alternative would be to follow the lexicographic-functional approach (Tarp 2008) as implemented by Verlinde *et al.* (2010b), where the user only needs to recognize the basic type of activity or extra-lexicographic context which prompts consultation, and the best combination of lexicographic data to serve this context has already been pre-selected by the lexicographers (cf. Verlinde and Peeters, this volume). Another interesting implementation inspired by the functional approach is being developed by Granger and Paquot (2010b, c) (cf. Paquot, this volume).

As noted in Lew (2011a), there are currently few implementations of Hulstijn and Atkins's second option: step-wise access. In this connection it is important to observe that in the dynamic environment of an electronic reference work, the notion of an *entry* becomes less sharply-defined than in static paper dictionaries, as the separation of the storage and presentation layers allows for combining, in a coherent textual block, elements which need not be literally contiguous in the underlying data. Similar fuzziness encroaches on classical-structural lexicographic notions such as *microstructure*. A good illustration of this are the step-wise options open to the e-lexicographer in those cases when a search term matches more than a single lemma (e.g. homonymous items, or those characterized by syntactic class conversion, such as **trial** N → **trial** V), or else is part of a multi-word unit such as fixed phrases, idioms, or phrasal verbs. The range of solutions adopted in current online dictionaries with regard to the ways in which search results are initially presented, can roughly be clustered into the following three approaches (Lew 2011a):

1. a menu of target items is displayed in the form of a list of lemmas as well as additional multi-word items including the search item;
2. a menu of target items is displayed as in 1, but the one entry ranked as the most likely candidate is given in full right away;
3. snippets of the target entries are listed, more elaborate than in option 1, but not showing any complete entries yet.

The most common approach appears to be that under 1 above: the user is initially offered a menu of potential target items, usually arranged in a vertical list. The individual items are hyperlinked, and once the user clicks on the item of their choice, the relevant entry (or its pertinent part) is presented. This approach is illustrated in Figure 16.3 for the search string 'wine' in the free online version of the *Cambridge Advanced Learner's Dictionary*, as displayed on 30 October 2010.

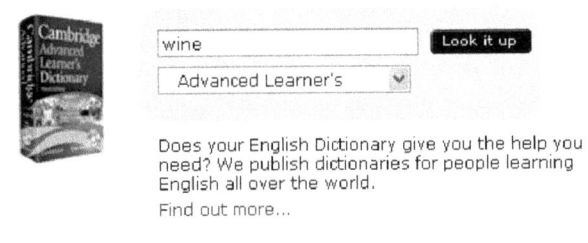

Cambridge Advanced Learner's Dictionary

wine | Look it up

Advanced Learner's

Does your English Dictionary give you the help you need? We publish dictionaries for people learning English all over the world.

Find out more...

Results for wine

wine was found in the Cambridge Advanced Learner's Dictionary at the entries listed below.

- wine *noun*
- wine *verb*
- dessert wine *noun*
- fortified wine *noun*
- ginger wine *noun*
- table wine *noun*
- wine bar *noun*
- wine rack *noun*
- a case of wine, etc.
- milk/oil/wine, etc. lake
- wine and dine sb

FIGURE 16.3 Search results screen for the search string "wine" in *Cambridge Advanced Learner's Dictionary* (30 October 2010).

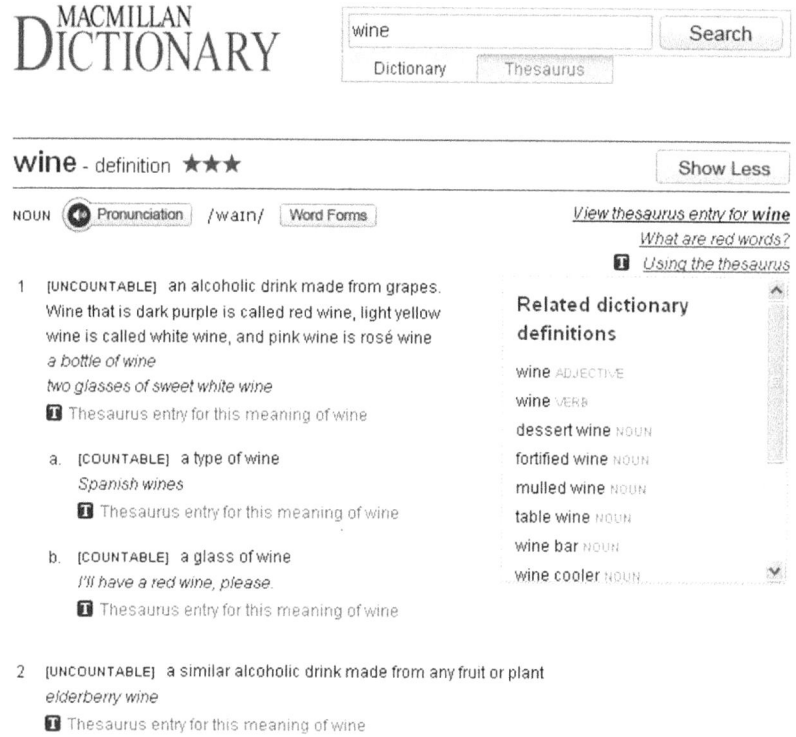

FIGURE 16.4 Search results screen for the search string 'wine' in *Macmillan English Dictionary Online* (20 May 2011).

The second approach can be illustrated using the current (May 2011) version of the *Macmillan English Dictionary Online* (Figure 16.4). Here, too, a list of items rather similar to that in *CALD* is presented in a panel on the right, with the 'Related dictionary definitions' heading on top. However, unlike in *CALD* (or, indeed, an earlier version of *MEDO*), a complete entry is presented already at this step, for the item which, according to the ranking algorithm in the dictionary, is the most likely choice (here, **wine** NOUN).

In early 2011 the interface of *CALD* was overhauled, bringing its presentation quite similar in concept to that of *MEDO* (Figure 16.4), thus properly classified as belonging with option 2.

The third approach, in turn, is implemented in the online version of *COBUILD*, myCOBUILD.com,[9] which is made available to buyers of printed copies of the *Collins COBUILD Advanced Dictionary*. This option represents something of a

---

[9] http://www.mycobuild.com/Default.aspx (login required).

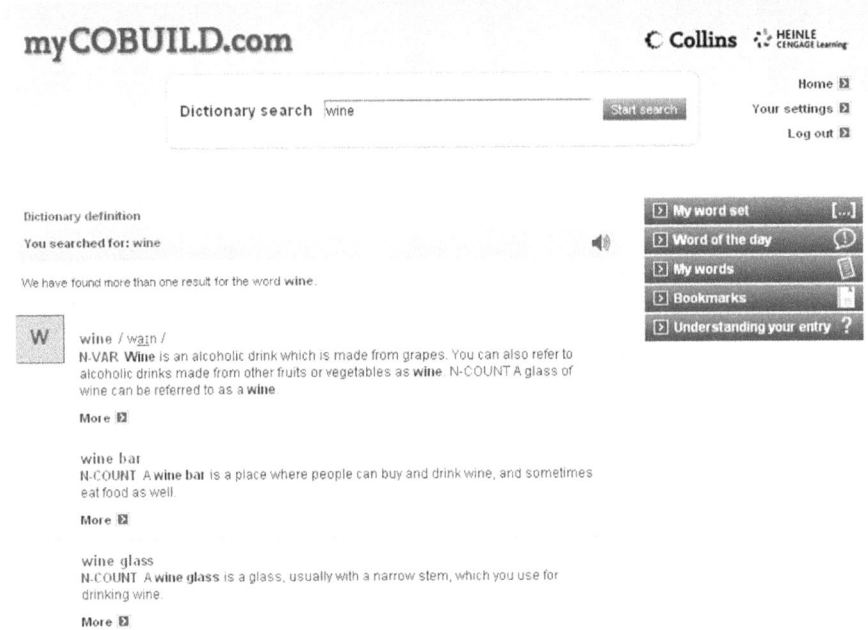

FIGURE 16.5 Search results screen for the search string 'wine' in myCOBUILD.com (available by subscription; 20 May 2011).

compromise between a bare list of lexical items and complete entries. Figure 16.5 gives the myCOBUILD.com search results screen for the same search string 'wine'. Here, the dictionary interface warns the user that multiple entries have been identified ("We have found more than one result for the word wine."), and then displays a roughly paragraph-length top section from each target entry, each followed by a '**More**' link, which then points to the complete entry.

It is hard to judge which of the three approaches illustrated is the most effective. In particular, it is risky to offer any such judgement in abstraction from the details of the extra-lexicographic situation and the needs and skill level of the user. Rather than point to one such approach, let us consider some of their benefits and potential pitfalls. An obvious advantage of the full-entry-at-once approach is that it may speed up the look-up process by relieving the user of the need to click through to the full entry, provided that the entry selected by the ranking algorithm is the one relevant to the user's search (as, in our example, **wine** NOUN). On the other hand, in cases when the presented entry happens *not* to be the right one, some users may miss this fact and still seek an answer to their query in the wrong entry. The key element here seems to be then how accurate the ranking algorithm can get in guessing the appropriate target item. The accuracy will no doubt be both item- and language-dependent, but in general we can expect this success rate to improve as artificial intelligence features in dictionaries get more sophisticated. For the moment, withholding the complete entry at stage one, and only presenting a bare list of items will probably reduce somewhat the risk of the user getting stuck in the wrong entry. On the other hand, users may dislike (and ultimately write off as unfriendly) a tool which expects them to do too much clicking, if their patience gets exhausted before they navigate through the initial menu of items to the complete lexicographic treatment.

Given these reservations, it is a little surprising that the third option, which presents a list of snippets in the initial screen, has such a modest proportion of followers. It would appear that this approach gives a better indication of the choices available than a plain list (as in approach 1), and, as a consequence, provides the user with a better basis on which to make an informed selection from the initial screen. On the downside, there is more text to process initially, and the user will still often need to take further action by clicking on one of the choices, as entry snippets may not provide sufficiently complete information. This again begs the question of whether the user will be in a position to appreciate the need to go to the full entry, which sends us back full circle to the reference skills of the user. Still, another factor that speaks in favour of the snippet-type presentation is that it is reassuringly similar to the typical output produced by Internet search engines, including Google. And, since searching the Internet is now one of the most fundamental skills of an educated human, the analogy should work for a large proportion of dictionary users, giving them the confidence of a familiar interface (see also De Schryver *et al.* 2006).

16.3.5 *Effective sublemmatic access: entry navigation*

We have known since at least Tono's (1984) study that dictionary users experience great difficulty in locating relevant senses in polysemous entries (see also Nesi 1987, Bogaards 1998, Nesi and Haill 2002, Lew 2004). All too frequently, users do not have the perseverance to examine the complete entry and will instead stop at the first sense listed, unless there is a very obvious clue that this sense is not the one they need. To help alleviate the problem, some dictionary publishers have experimented with devices designed to assist users in entry-internal navigation, mostly by placing brief cues pointing to specific senses, either at the top of the entry (as *entry menus*), or distributed across the individual senses (*signposts, guide words, shortcuts,* or *mini-definitions*). The effectiveness of entry navigation devices has been the topic of a number of studies (Tono 1992, 1997, Bogaards 1998, Tono 2001, Lew and Pajkowska 2007, Lew 2010b, Lew and Tokarek 2010, Nesi and Tan 2011, Tono 2011). The majority of these studies focused on paper dictionary entries, and their cumulative findings suggest that both menus and signposts help dictionary users get to the relevant senses faster, improve the accuracy with which these senses are identified, and provide assistance in completing the original task (which prompted dictionary consultation) with better success. In addition, two of the studies (Lew 2010b, Nesi and Tan 2011) compared different types of navigation devices, and both concurred that signpost-type cues (distributed between the respective senses) were more effective than menu-type devices (with all cues collected in a block above the entry proper). Lew (2010b) speculates that the reasons for this may be of a dual nature. The first possible factor has to do with semantic processing, and more specifically with the ability to assess the relevance of the different senses: there may be synergistic effects between the telegraphic signposting of the guiding cues and the fuller lexicographic treatment given at the sense, and these effects have a chance to exhibit themselves when the two types of data are physically contiguous and can thus be taken in at the same time. The second factor proposed is more mechanical and has to do with how accurately the user can navigate from the guiding cue to the target sense. If the cue is part of a menu at the top of the entry, then the search path from the cue to the sense is more complex (the sense may even be on a different page) and, as a consequence, more prone to error. Perhaps a combination of menus and signposts might be advantageous but this has never been investigated: printed dictionaries have never adopted this format, likely because its redundancy seems to make excessive demands on space.

While the above findings based on paper dictionaries should in broad outline also hold for electronic dictionaries, some differences are to be expected. First, users of electronic dictionaries (including those on hand-held devices) work in a familiar computing environment which is already heavily menu-driven. The salience of the menu as a concept in the information technology (IT) context could make menu-based navigation a more natural option, unlike in paper dictionaries. Second, the dynamic nature of electronic display allows one, with imaginative design, to anticipate and correct some of the problems that entry navigation exhibits in printed dictionaries.

Working along these lines, Lew and Tokarek (2010) proposed a new experimental entry menu system for online dictionaries. The starting point was a standard concept of a hyperlinked menu navigation system, wherein clicking on an item (here representing a specific dictionary sense) in the entry menu (i.e. a list of senses) would take the user to the target entry and scroll it automatically to the target sense. In addition, however, the system would highlight the target sense against a different background than the remaining senses. Such an experimental system was tested against two more conventional solutions: the menu alone and a bare entry with no access-facilitating devices. It was found that the addition of target sense highlighting resulted in a significant reduction of access time to the target sense, compared to the other two experimental conditions. In addition, error rates in the accompanying task (translation) were nearly halved in the version with target sense highlighting compared with either of the other versions, an effect which was marginally significant.

The study by Lew and Tokarek (2010) thus illustrates how a relatively simple device which takes advantage of the affordances of the electronic medium can

7 [INTRANSITIVE/TRANSITIVE] if something shows, people can see it or notice it
They managed to fix it so that the break wouldn't show.
She had chosen a colour that really showed the dirt.
and it shows (=used for saying that something is very obvious): *They used the cheapest materials they could find, and it shows.*
🅣 Thesaurus entry for this meaning of show

8 [INTRANSITIVE/TRANSITIVE] if someone shows a film or a television programme, or if it is showing, people can see it
It was the first time the film was shown on television.
Now showing at a cinema near you!
🅣 Thesaurus entry for this meaning of show

9 [TRANSITIVE] to put something such as a work of art, an animal, or a plant in an exhibition or competition
Her work was first shown at a gallery in Munich.
I've been showing my dogs for over ten years.
🅣 Thesaurus entry for this meaning of show

10 **show** or **show up** [INTRANSITIVE] INFORMAL to arrive in a place where people are expecting you
We didn't think Austin would show.
🅣 Thesaurus entry for this meaning of show

FIGURE 16.6 Partial *MEDO* entry for SHOW with sense 7 highlighted.

enhance the efficiency of entry navigation. Interestingly, in this study the menu alone was not significantly faster or more accurate than the bare entry. However, this has been the only study of sense-guiding devices using *bilingual* entries, as all the remaining studies have used monolingual entries. We might expect that the presence of the user's native language in the dictionary facilitates navigation, as scanning and skimming are naturally quicker and more successful in one's L1. This would translate into a lower functional load on extra guiding devices, which might explain the lack of benefits of a standard entry menu without target sense highlighting. That the positive effect of highlighting was noted in bilingual entries suggests that it might offer even greater benefits in monolingual entries. Currently two popular English monolingual learners' dictionaries use target sense highlighting in their online versions: *MEDO* (see Figure 16.6) and *LDOCE*.

16.4 Multimedia in dictionaries

The possibility of including multimedia in lexicographic data may seem to offer an attractive path towards enhancing the efficiency of modern dictionaries. And indeed, a pioneering study by Chun and Plass (1996) did find significant positive effects of picture annotation on vocabulary acquisition. However, video annotation did not result in a similar improvement. Chun and Plass attribute this to the transience of video material, which—unlike static pictures—may not have the stability to allow the viewer to develop a robust mental model (see also Kozma 1991).

A similar problem may affect animated graphics, as suggested by Lew and Doroszewska's (2009) findings. In their study involving an experimental online dictionary, those dictionary users who viewed animations for the target entries had significantly lower vocabulary retention rates than those who ignored the animations. The negative effect of animation was quite independent of what other lexical information participants chose to view in addition.

The use of audio recordings of headwords, on the other hand, has produced a positive effect on vocabulary retention, at least for learners of English from Hong Kong (Laufer and Hill 2000). However, this could be due to the specific reference habits of Chinese dictionary users. As the typical macrostructural organization in Chinese dictionaries is phonological (by phonetic radical; Laufer and Hill 2000: 70), phonological representation plays a practical role in dictionary consultation. As this is not the case for most other languages, it would be premature to claim that similar benefits of audio recordings would obtain for speakers with other language backgrounds.

Thus, the evidence with regard to the effectiveness of multimedia in dictionaries is rather sketchy: it involves speakers of a small subset of languages in a restricted range of situations and tasks, and is mostly restricted to general dictionaries for language learners. But multimedia may have a special role to play in specialized dictionaries, for example in a dictionary of architecture (Fernández and Faber 2011), and in some cases they are of central importance, e.g. in dictionaries of sign language (Zwitserlood 2010, Kristoffersen and Troelsgård, this volume).

Also, the primary focus of recent research seems to be on vocabulary retention seen as a long-term benefit of dictionary consultation. However, a more central role for dictionaries is to help solve immediate lexical problems as they arise, for instance during text comprehension, production, or translation. While it can be argued that comprehension is a prerequisite for acquisition, we need to be cautious not to over-extend the outcomes of acquisition studies to all dictionary uses.

What we can say at present is that the available evidence invites optimism with respect to static pictures and audio recordings, but looks less optimistic when it comes to video and animation enhancements. Here, the difficulty of matching the playback speed of the material with individual users' cognitive pace might be a large part of the problem.

16.5 Conclusion

Effective lexicographic solutions are those that are suited to the needs of a particular user in a particular situation, and it is not possible to specify all possible constellations of these factors—and the optimal lexicographic treatment they invite—within a single chapter. In fact, with respect to the nature of lexicographic data, these optimal solutions are not at all unique to the electronic format. What is more characteristic of the electronic medium is that access to data can be made more effective (i.e. successful) and efficient (quicker) in electronic dictionaries than in their paper predecessors, and this is the aspect that we have focused on. We have seen that a number of fairly straightforward improvements can be made to enhance data access in electronic dictionaries once designers liberate themselves from the constricting paper tradition, and many of these improvements require neither serious technological breakthroughs nor substantial investment.

But electronic dictionaries also form a perfect platform for non-textual media, such as sound, video, or animation. Whether and to what extent dictionaries should make use of these modalities ought to be decided on the basis of sound lexicographic principle and evidence of their effectiveness in the specific situations of use, and not by questions of fashion. There is some evidence, sketchy as it is, that not all types of media benefit dictionary users in ways that might be expected.

Dictionaries will be most effective if they are instantly and unobtrusively available during the activities in which humans engage—and ultimately aware of those activities. As more of our work, study, and play is done in an IT-enhanced environment, electronic dictionaries have a chance to blend into that environment by discreetly staying in the background and coming to the rescue when needed.

Dictionaries

Mayor, Michael (ed.) (2009). *Longman Dictionary of Contemporary English*. Fifth Edition. Harlow: Longman.

McKean, Erin (ed.) (2005). *New Oxford American Dictionary*. Second edition. Oxford: Oxford University Press.

17

Alternative e-dictionaries: Uncovering dark practices

HILARY NESI

17.1 Introduction

Most published e-dictionary research involves studies of the way e-dictionaries are used, surveys of the habits and attitudes of e-dictionary users, or accounts of the development of new experimental e-dictionaries. The e-dictionaries that are described in detail in this research tend to be the prestigious varieties emanating from university centres or established publishing houses, and although surveys suggest that less prestigious types of e-dictionaries are far more popular with the general user, they are also far less likely to be specified individually in the academic literature, or evaluated in terms of their lexicographical content. We will call these less prestigious e-dictionaries 'alternative e-dictionaries', or 'AEDs'. This chapter aims to redress the balance somewhat by considering AED resources, and in so doing will draw attention to the dangers of over-reliance on AED information.

17.2 Background

Perhaps understandably, a great deal of scholarly attention is paid to e-dictionaries that have been developed for research and educational purposes rather than for commercial gain. Such dictionaries tend to be small-scale, and are carefully designed to enable their developers to explore metalexicographical issues and concentrate on the needs of specific user groups, as advocated by Gelpi (2004) and Tarp (2009a). The *Louvain EAP Dictionary* (Granger and Paquot 2010b, and this volume), developed at the Université catholique de Louvain, for example, offers access routes not only via the lexeme or the user's first language but also via communicative function, and the *Base lexicale du français*, developed at the Katholieke Universiteit Leuven, has a task- and problem-oriented interface which allows users to begin their search by choosing from six "user-driven situations" (Verlinde 2010, Verlinde and Binon 2010, Verlinde and Peeters, this volume). Examples of other experimental e-dictionaries include *Lexin*, developed at Göteborg University to meet the needs of the immigrant community in Sweden (Hult 2008), OWID, an online portal for German developed at the Institute of German Language in Mannheim (Müller-Spitzer and Möhrs 2008), and the *Deutsch-Italienisches Fachwörterbuch der Linguistik*, a specialized linguistics dictionary developed at the University of Pisa (Flinz 2010).

In the case of experimental e-dictionaries such as these, the metalexicographers are also part of the dictionary development team, and thus have the means to record in the form of log files the transactions between the dictionary database and the user's computer. Nowadays e-dictionary developers can gather log-file data on every aspect of the consultation process, including search routes and time taken, but such details are potentially sensitive and so most published log-file studies, such as those of De Schryver and Joffe (2004), Bergenholtz and Johnsen (2007), Hult (2008), Prószéky and Kis (2002), and Verlinde (2010), continue to relate to the use of experimental or specialist e-dictionaries rather than commercial products.

The commercial e-dictionaries that receive the most metalexicographic attention are those produced by prestigious publishing houses (cf. Dziemianko, this volume). Monolingual learners' dictionaries on CD-ROM have been a major object of study by researchers not directly involved in e-dictionary development, such as Nesi (1996, 1999), Rizo-Rodriguez (2004), and Xu (2008). These dictionaries share at least some of their lexicographical content with familiar print editions, and this may make them seem more permanent and stable (Gelpi 2004: 9). They also usually include some explanatory documentation equivalent to the frontmatter in a printed dictionary. This is important for the 'lexicographical approach' to dictionary reviewing described by Nielsen (2009), which entails consideration of the interrelationship between dictionary components. Nielsen discusses the lexicographical approach to reviewing with reference to two online dictionaries, the *Oxford English Dictionary Online* (2008) and the *Merriam-Webster Online Dictionary* (2008); both are prestigious varieties with prefaces and user guides.

Alternative e-dictionaries, on the other hand, are often difficult to describe in conventional lexicographic terms. A distinguishing feature of such products is that they combine diverse resources, some of which are up-to-date dictionaries from prestigious publishing houses, some of which are local dictionaries, often of old or uncertain provenance, and some of which are not produced by lexicographers at all. AED content is available via dictionary web portals and pocket electronic dictionaries (PEDs), or it can be downloaded to a personal computer or mobile device from the Internet, a USB stick, a CD-ROM, or a memory card. It is combined and recombined for different markets, and on- and offline products with the same titles, produced by the same company, are not necessarily identical. Moreover, AED content is bewilderingly subject to change. Online dictionaries are always "under construction", as Gelpi (2004: 7) points out, and electronics firms such as Casio, Franklin, Seiko, and Sharp continually produce new PED models, each with different capabilities and features. AED companies have no interest in keeping historical records, or in referring users to earlier versions of their resources, and this makes it particularly hard for metalexicographers to keep track of the content that was available in a particular product at a particular time.

Keeping up-to-date with AED resources can also be expensive, and as commercial developers are not in the habit of offering review copies or discounts on class sets, AED studies are likely to be hampered by the cost. Shizuka (2003) and Koyama and Takeuchi (2004b, 2007) acquired pocket electronic dictionaries from the Casio computer company for use in experiments in Japan, but this kind of support from manufacturers seems to be unusual, and Chen (2010), for example, complains of lack of funding to obtain PEDs for research.

Thus, despite the prevalence of AED use, AED material receives very little scholarly attention, at least in the West. For example, the Jin Shan Ci Ba rarely features in reviews, user studies, or dictionary skills training programmes, yet it is possibly the most widely used dictionary package in the world, well known to all mainland Chinese learners of other languages. Its developers claim that it is used in more than 50,000 educational institutes, businesses, and government agencies, by more than twenty million people.

Bypassing issues of AED content, researchers have tended to concentrate instead on the advantages and disadvantages of the consultation medium. Numerous surveys have compared electronic and print dictionary use (cf. Dziemianko, this volume), particularly by Japanese learners (Weschler and Pitts 2000, Perry 2003, Bower and McMillan 2007, Kobayashi 2008) and Chinese learners (Taylor and Chan 1994, Tang 1997, Deng 2005, Chen 2010), without actually drawing attention to differences in dictionary content that exist between one AED package and another. Recently some attempts have been made to study the way learners use free bilingual dictionary portals. Tseng (2009) tested English language learners' interpretations of definitions from the Taiwanese Yahoo! portal, and Chon (2009) gathered think-aloud data on the productive use of the Korean Yahoo! and Naver portals. In both studies, however, the primary aim was to examine students' dictionary skills, and so consultation problems tended to be associated with learners' lack of dictionary strategies ("dictionary-based errors", in Chon's terms) or the unsuccessful use of these strategies (Chon's "dictionary-based problems"), rather than with the design and content of the portals themselves.

Boonmoh and Nesi (2008) conducted a questionnaire survey of attitudes to pocket electronic dictionaries at a university in Thailand, and concluded that English language lecturers often blamed PEDs for consultation problems that could just as easily arise with print dictionaries. The following are typical lecturer responses to questions about their students' PED use; some indicate bad practice or lack of skill on the part of the students rather than defects in PED content.

- *When using a pocket electronic dictionary, they just type a Thai word and pick up one English word from the list provided. They don't know how to compose a sentence by using the word.*
- *Students will look up words and use words without looking at the context.*
- *They tend to select the wrong word because of their lack of knowledge in part of speech.*
- *It is too convenient, so it is not challenging.*

Nevertheless, the lexicographic quality of AEDs is also a common cause of teachers' complaints. Tang (1997), Koren (1997), Deng (2005), Stirling (2003), and Boonmoh and Nesi (2008) all found that teachers considered electronic dictionaries to lack important elements such as grammar codes, example sentences, and collocations, although these teachers also revealed themselves to be quite ignorant of e-dictionary features (Midlane 2005, Boonmoh and Nesi 2008), and did not usually differentiate between the prestigious and less-prestigious lexicographical content of AEDs, assuming that all AED dictionaries shared the same faults.

Table 17.1 shows the distribution of dictionary ownership amongst the thirty English language lecturers who responded to Boonmoh and Nesi's questionnaire survey (2008). The older lecturers only used print dictionaries, although some of the younger lecturers sometimes referred to online dictionaries and prestigious monolingual dictionaries on CD-ROM (mostly those published by Longman, COBUILD, and Macmillan).

TABLE 17.1. **Thai English language lecturers' ownership of dictionaries**

Monolingual dictionaries in book form	29
Monolingual dictionaries on CD-ROM	22
Bilingual dictionaries online	11
Bilingual dictionaries in book form	10
Monolingual dictionaries online	9
Pocket electronic dictionaries	4

Most lecturers rejected the idea of PEDs, and expressed little faith in their lexicographical content. Typically, PEDs were characterized as inaccurate and lacking in usage examples:

- *It doesn't give the correct meaning and doesn't tell students clearly how to use the word in different contexts.*
- *It always gives the wrong usage.*
- *limited vocabulary and doesn't provide sentence examples, too expensive.*

- *it is not as detailed as a dictionary in book form.*
- *A PED does not provide usage, examples. And as a consequence, students are likely to make mistakes.*

The only lecturer who preferred the PED format used it in combination with other sources:

- *I will use it only when I cannot think of English vocabulary. However, I will have to check how that word is used from a monolingual either in book form or on CD-ROM.*

All these respondents were apparently ignorant of the fact that the most popular PED model at their university contained the *Oxford Advanced Learner's Dictionary*. The majority (18 out of 30) admitted that they had no idea what dictionaries PEDs were likely to contain.

Those who are not teachers seem on the whole to be less worried about the accuracy and detail of dictionary entries. As Kilgarriff (2005b) pointed out, "a dictionary is a dictionary is a dictionary, good or bad". Studies of students' attitudes towards e-dictionary use suggest that they like AED bilingual dictionaries, and tend to value them for their advanced technology and accessibility rather than for their lexicographic content. The 1,211 Thai student respondents in Boonmoh and Nesi's (2008) survey, for example, had been recommended by their teachers to buy a *Longman Active Study Dictionary* (*LASD*) package, complete with CD-ROM, but although 82 per cent claimed to own a monolingual print dictionary (probably *LASD*), only 28 per cent claimed to own a monolingual dictionary on CD-ROM, suggesting that many had not even bothered to open the CD-ROM envelope inside their *LASD* copies. AEDs were used far more frequently. Nesi (2010: 214–16) found that students who were given copies of a Macmillan learners' dictionary on CD-ROM rated its quality more highly than the AEDs they normally consulted, acknowledging that it had "better explanations" and "more information". However, most of these students quickly reverted to AED use (in the form of PEDs and/or software on their home computers), because they liked the many additional features AEDs offered, for example ready-made wordlists, language tests, games, and personal organizer functions. They also found it easier to understand bilingual dictionary information, whether on CD-ROM, the computer hard drive, or in a more portable format; PEDs were particularly convenient for use in class or when travelling. In Nielsen's (2009) terms, AEDs had lower "lexicographic information costs" and required less effort to consult. The distinction between "usability" and "usefulness" (Laufer and Kimmel 1997: 362) is relevant here. Laufer and Kimmel define "dictionary usability" as "the willingness on the part of the consumer to use the dictionary in question, and his/her satisfaction from it", while "dictionary usefulness" is "the extent to which a dictionary is helpful in providing the necessary information to its user". AEDs have high usability ratings, despite the doubts expressed regarding their usefulness.

Some surveys report teachers' suspicions that e-dictionary consultation is too fast and too easy for deep learning to take place (Taylor and Chan 1994, Sharpe 1995, Zhang 2004, Stirling 2003, Boonmoh and Nesi 2008). In experimental studies where subjects have consulted identical lexicographical content on a computer screen or in print, however, task performance has either not differed significantly (Nesi 2000b, Koyama and Takeuchi 2004b, 2007) or has been significantly better for e-dictionary users (Shizuka 2003, Dziemianko 2010) (cf. Dziemianko, this volume). Thus, although the restricted size of PED screens doubtless impedes consultation of longer entries, and there is certainly scope for further investigation into the pedagogical effects of e-learning, the evidence so far suggests that teachers' reported dislike of e-dictionaries is largely due to the low quality of some AED resources, and their ignorance of better-quality AED resources, rather than the electronic medium itself.

Gelpi (2004) offers some guidelines for the evaluation of online bilingual dictionaries, presenting a list of quality indicators, including the need for a "real and public author", and explicit indications of when and how often the source is updated. AEDs often fail to meet both of these criteria, and in the next part of this chapter I will demonstrate how, with some notable exceptions, the world's most popular e-dictionaries are unreliable sources of linguistic information.

17.3 Alternative electronic dictionary content

In order to critique AEDs, this section will examine their various components, their lexicographical content, and the potential of new collaborative procedures to influence AED content development.

17.3.1 *AED components*

Alongside local dictionaries and non-lexicographical resources, AEDs typically contain some monolingual, bilingual, and/or bilingualized dictionaries licensed from highly regarded international publishing houses. For example, the PEDs used in Nesi and Boonmoh's (2009) study contained the monolingual *Concise American Heritage Dictionary*, the *Oxford Advanced Learner's Dictionary*, and the *Longman Dictionary of American English*, and Chen (2010) reports that her students' PEDs were installed with bilingualized learner's dictionaries from Longman, Oxford, and COBUILD. Lingoes, a popular Chinese dictionary portal, offers access to the *Merriam Webster's Collegiate* and the *American Heritage Dictionary*, together with all the major monolingual English advanced learners' dictionaries: the *Cambridge Advanced Learner's Dictionary* (*CALD*), the *Collins COBUILD English Dictionary* (*COBUILD*), the *Longman Dictionary of Contemporary English* (*LDOCE*), the *Macmillan English Dictionary* (*MED*), and the *Oxford Advanced Learner's Dictionary* (*OALD*). The Babylon website offers dictionaries published by Oxford, Duden, Larousse, and

Merriam Webster, and the Jin Shan Ci Ba CD-ROM and Internet download contains the *American Heritage Chinese-English Dictionary* and a bilingualized version of the *Oxford Advanced Learner's Dictionary*, as well as many other dictionaries and thesauruses of more varying quality.

Licences from famous brands are useful for AED developers because they add prestige to the dictionary package as a whole. Some AEDs such as Jin Shan Ci Ba offer free web access to unlicensed dictionary material, but require users to purchase the package containing licensed dictionaries such as the *Oxford Advanced Learner's Dictionary*. This practice is comparable to that of many publishers who offer a simple web interface in order to boost sales of their dictionaries in print or on CD-ROM. On the AED sites, however, specific information about their prestigious dictionaries is sometimes left deliberately vague, perhaps through ignorance on the part of the site developers, perhaps to allow for last-minute alterations to AED content, or perhaps to imply more extensive prestige content than is actually the case. On some portal sites various publications from Oxford University Press are referred to by the blanket term "Oxford Dictionary" or "Oxford English Dictionary", for example. This is the case with the popular e-dictionary portal Babylon, as is evident in the extract in Figure 17.1, from an online synchronous conversation between myself and 'Michelle', a Babylon representative.

You are now chatting with "Michelle"

Michelle: Hey

Hilary: Can you give me full details of Oxford Dictionary mentioned as part of the Lifetime License package? Is it available by monthly subscription?

Michelle: nope

Hilary: So you don't know anything about the Oxford Dictionary?

Michelle: the monthly version is a light version paid for every month

Michelle: Yes i do

Michelle: the full version of Babylon is for lifetime use

Michelle: with the Oxford

Hilary: But what about the Oxford Dictionary? What is its full title?

Michelle: Oxford dictionary is the most professional English dictionary we work with. It adds an extensive content in English, technical terms, example of a usage of the work you are searching for in a sentence, and a professional thesaurus.

Hilary: Is it published by Oxford University Press?

Michelle: yes, it's the same famous old Oxford dictionary book published by Oxford, all its content goes into your Babylon.

FIGURE 17.1 A conversation with a Babylon representative.

I had expressed interest in subscribing to Babylon's 'Lifetime License' package, an upgrade from a cheaper monthly subscription package.

When pressed, Michelle did provide two Oxford titles, but still failed to provide explicit information about the updating process, one of Gelpi's quality indicators (2004) (see Figure 17.2).

Hilary: Ther are many (possibly hundreds) of dictionaries published by Oxford University

Press. Which one is it?

Michelle: The Concise Oxford Dictionary

Michelle: The Concise Oxford Thesaurus

Hilary: That's helpful, thanks. Publication date? Or edition?

Michelle: it's updated all the time.

FIGURE 17.2 Further conversation with a Babylon representative.

It is perhaps not surprising that information about Oxford products is so vague, given that, according to their website, syndicated material from the Oxford Reference Online can be selected and tailored according to a company's wishes, with all kinds of modifications to its "functionality, content and design".

However, although arrangements with prestige publishing houses such as Oxford must help to sell AED products, in fact the dictionaries from these publishers may not be the ones that are usually consulted. The default dictionary offered in dictionary portals and PEDs is often a local one, and unless the settings are changed, or the search word is not in the local dictionary database, the entries for this local dictionary are the ones that automatically appear. Thus although the various versions of the Jin Shan Ci Ba ('Kingsoft Powerword') contain international resources, the default setting seems to be the Jian Ming Ying Han Ci Dian, a somewhat unreliable, undated, general Chinese-English dictionary. The Wikipedia entry for the dictionary package advises users to bypass this default and "pick good dictionaries" instead, although it also acknowledges that it "is not clear how to do this". Nesi and Boonmoh (2009) found that the prestigious monolingual dictionaries in Thai students' PEDs were never consulted, as local English-Thai and Thai-English dictionaries were offered as the default choice.

17.3.2 *AED quality*

E-dictionaries are particularly popular in East Asia, and for some East Asian languages there are no bilingualized dictionaries, and the only available bilingual dictionaries are locally produced without the benefit of corpus resources. Some of these dictionaries are simply basic translation tools, with little or no information about grammar and usage. Chon (2009), for example, notes the lack of grammar information on the Korean Naver website. Some of the dictionaries also contain serious mistranslations. For example, Nesi and Boonmoh (2009) found PEDs listing *bulb* as a verb, supposedly equivalent to the archaic Thai form /ngok hua/ ('to appear') and Boonmoh *et al.* (2005) found PEDs translating the Thai noun /bot/ ('chapter' or 'unit') as "a foot; a stanza of verse; the words of a song or a play" (see also Hanks, this volume, on bad definitions). Moreover, some local dictionaries are digitalized versions of older print dictionaries, and errors seem to have crept in during the digitization process. The misprints in Thai PEDs reported by Boonmoh *et al.* (2005), for example "hehind" for *behind*, and "lear" for *learning*, would appear to be scanning errors.

The poor quality of many local dictionaries is exacerbated by the AED tendency to aggregate large numbers of dictionaries compiled at different times and for different purposes, offering a 'jump' facility between sources. The current Jin Shan Ci Ba download offers "more than 140 practical dictionaries", and "98 Academic and Professional Directions" [sic] which appear to be thesauruses of various kinds, for example for "Soil Science", "Ship Engineering", and "Railway Science". Thus when the dictionary package is used productively, typing in just a few letters can lead, via the jump facility, to a display of archaic, technical, or misprinted word forms each of which may originate in just one source.

This problem is compounded by the tendency for local dictionary compilers to over-extend lexical derivation rules, adding affixes wherever they might potentially occur. For example, Boonmoh *et al.* (2005) found the following words beginning with *suppo-* in the PED CyberDict 3 Advance: *support, supportable, supporter, supportive,* and *supposable. Supportable* has very low frequency in the British National Corpus (BNC), and there are no recorded instances of *supposable* in the BNC. Similarly, Nesi (2010) found the sample of headwords in Figure 17.3 offered in a Jin Shan Ci Ba download.

Words marked * in Figure 17.3 do not appear in the 56-million-word Collins COBUILD Wordbank, and *board* is the only collocate of *examination* to be counted amongst the 100 most statistically significant.

Some AEDs also include figurative expressions that are no longer current, perhaps originating in out-of-date sources or added to enlarge the advertised lemma stock. The Jin Shan Ci Ba translation *nigger brown* has now been removed, but the Korean Naver site and the Japanese and Korean versions of Yahoo! online all include the biblical expression *not worth a jew's eye*, apparently originally listed in *Brewer's Dictionary of Phrase and Fable* (undated). Similar entries with the potential to offend can be found in many AEDs, often without any kind of taboo warning. Other rather quaint but less offensive expressions listed in AEDs include *not worth a leek, thick as mutton,* and *thick as herrings*. It could be argued that such entries might one day be useful to those who use AEDs for receptive purposes, but AEDs are also very widely employed as writing aids, and the *nigger brown* translation caused an outcry when it was used in 2007 by a Chinese furniture company exporting goods to the West. This incident features in the Wikipedia entry for PowerWord[1] (see also Balemans 2007 and many other online blogs citing the CNN news report 'Chinese translation error blamed for slur on sofa label').

exam
examen*
EXAMETNET*
examinable*
examinant*
examinate*
examination
examination board
examination class
examination finding
examination in chief
examination of scheme
examination of auditor
examination of budget
examinationism*
examinationist*
exanination procedure
examinator*
examinatorial*

FIGURE 17.3 A sample of headwords from Jin Shan Ci Ba.

AED headword lists are vastly increased by aggregating large numbers of dictionaries, and by including rare multi-word expressions and potentially acceptable but actually unattested derived forms. This may benefit an AED by raising its status, especially in the eyes of more unsophisticated dictionary users who may be impressed by the sheer size of the package, and by the fact that there are translations for almost all the words they will ever encounter receptively. All commercial publishers emphasize the extent of their dictionary's coverage in order to attract customers, and Nielsen (2009: 27) points out that reviewers tend to evaluate dictionaries in terms of the size of their lemma stock, placing too much emphasis on linguistic categories rather than significant lexicographical features. The lack of restrictive labels and usage information in the entries provided by local and specialist AED dictionaries is a problem for writers and for language learners, however, especially as many AEDs seem to be intended as learning tools, given their facilities for word-list creation and vocabulary testing.

The unreliability of AEDs stems partly from their reliance on poor-quality dictionaries, but also partly from their use of unedited non-lexicographical data. Many

---

[1] http://en.wikipedia.org/wiki/PowerWord (last accessed 29 April 2011).

AEDs supplement their dictionary resources with examples taken from online encyclopedias and media websites, as is the case with Lingoes and the Korean Doosan Dong-A Prime on the Daum portal. Some, like the online Jin Shan Ci Ba, offer web examples as a free resource while reserving their more prestigious dictionaries for paying customers to download. Some AEDs also make use of automatic translators. Lingoes, for example, draws on the Jukuu search engine for sentence translation in Chinese, English, and Japanese, and the Jin Shan Ci Ba works with the machine translation device Jinshan Kuaiyi.

The results of these approaches are often disastrous. Mair (2007) blames a combination of the Jin Shan Ce Ba and the Jinshan Kuaiyi for the production of "absurdly crude English mistranslations in bizarrely inappropriate contexts" in China, and the same seems to be true for the *Doosan Dong-a Prime* English dictionary, online on the Daum South Korean web portal. On this site lexicographical content similar to that provided in the *Doosan Dong-a Prime* print dictionaries is supplemented with bar charts showing quantitative collocation information based on web data, and illustrative examples taken from online sources. The amount of additional illustrative material on the website may give Korean English language learners the impression that the compilers are concerned with contextual appropriacy, but in fact the illustrations are unedited and highly misleading. Examples (1) to (3) provide contexts for 'dark coffee' (available at the time of writing by typing 'dark coffee' in the search box on the homepage at http://engdic.daum.net/). These sentences appear to be automatically generated translations of Korean postings to USENET, the Internet discussion system.

(1) What did Francis arrive the cup before the dark coffee?
(2) It should change the dark coffee and arrive it through its monolith.
(3) She'd rather kick furiously than call with George's dark coffee.

17.3.3 *Collaborative approaches to AED content development*

Collaborative or "bottom-up" lexicographical methods (Carr 1997) have the potential to correct mistranslations and absurd examples, and generally improve online AED resources, although quality control remains an issue (Docherty 2000, De Schryver 2003). The bottom-up approach has been facilitated by the invention of Wiki software, which became available in the early 2000s as an open source tool (Nesi 2009). The Wiktionary, which describes itself as a "wiki-based Open Content dictionary", appeared in 2002, and the Wiktionary system now covers more than 400 languages (cf. Meyer and Gurevych, this volume). Although many apparent neologisms and local slang expressions are recorded, Wiktionary contributors rarely seem to have taken the trouble to provide source details or usage information, and some entries over-extend the English lexical derivation rules in order to include derived forms which are only potentially acceptable, such as *examinable, supportable,* and *supposable,* all listed without restrictive labels.

Many other AEDs are now starting to invite user contributions through wikis, or via postings on blogs or fora. For example, the German bab.la, a dictionary and language learning portal which claims about 30,568 unique visitors per day, operates on a wiki-style model, allowing users to contribute content and give feedback. Similarly, CC-CEDICT invites contributions to a wiki and encourages users to submit new entries to its 'editor' website. These contributions are then used to inform the development of the MDBG, a Chinese-English online dictionary which claims 400,000 unique visitors per month.

The Leo Dictionary, on the other hand, hosts fora in order to discuss difficult translations and questions concerning the dictionary. The collaborative nature of Leo is critiqued in Wikipedia (3 March 2011), where it is argued that the absence of an editorial hand results in "duplication and a lack of additional lexical information such as gender, inflected and irregular forms, plurals, and other contextual indicators". Nevertheless the Leo fora are very active and quick to identify problems with the dictionary content, as demonstrated in the exchange in Figure 17.4, where participants JTB and CM2DD discuss (bilingually) the use of the word *unthink,* translated as *umdenken* in Leo's English-German dictionary. *Unthink* is a typical potentially acceptable derivation for which there are translations in a number of AEDs, for example ET House, Doosan Dong-a Prime, Wikipedia, and the Yahoo! sites for Japan, Korea, and Hong Kong.

MDBG and Leo are not typical AEDs because they originated in research projects and still seem to be motivated at least in part by academic rather than commercial interests. MDBG is powered by CC-CEDICT, an offshoot of Jim Breen's EDICT Japanese dictionary project now managed by the Electronic Dictionary Research and Development Group at Monash University. It is funded by donations as well as advertising revenue. Leo started life as a research project at the Technische Universität München and is now operated commercially by a company formed by members of the original research team. Some of the other more commercially-minded AEDs seem to manage collaborative input less successfully, perhaps because they do not want to encourage criticism of the content on offer, or because their users are less disposed to critique their perceived authority.

I searched for *unthink* in the free online version of the Jin Shan Ci Ba, which has no official dictionary content but refers users to its own blog and forum contributions, and to various local web sources such as the China Daily. In the online version of the Jin Shan Ci Ba the entry for *unthink* offers a translation into everyday Chinese, with no accompanying warning about the rarity of the English word (the Chinese translation roughly means 'don't want to'). However, the entry also contains a footnote signalling that the translation does not come from an authoritative source, and it offers users the opportunity to edit and amend the entry information.

Betrifft   Beispiel für "to unthink" - "umdenken"
      Kommentar   Hallo!

      Bei der Suche bin ich auf "to unthink" gestoßen, einmal übersetzt mit "aus dem Gedächtnis
      verbannen" und einmal mit "umdenken". Ich habe das noch nie gehört und mein Sprachgefühl
      meutert (was an sich nichts zu bedeuten hat) und wollte fragen, ob das wirklich das "wir müssen in
      dieser Sache umdenken" meint oder ein anderes "umdenken" und ob mir vielleicht jemand ein
      Kontextbeispiel geben könnte.

      Vielen Dank & viele Grüße.

      JTB

      Autor: JTB   02 Mar 11 09:41

      Kommentar   I don't think "unthink" and "umdenken" match at all. You need something more like "rethink" or
      "change our way of thinking", depending on the context.

      unthink
      Forget; remove from thought; cancel out or reverse by a mental effort.
      New SOED

1   Autor   C M 2 D D   (238324)   02 Mar 11 10:03

      Kommentar   Thank you!

      So my feeling that it sounded weird didn't betray me. Should I open a "Falscher Eintrag?" thread
      and may I cite your source for that?

2   Autor   jtb   02 Mar 11 10:08

      Kommentar   The Macquarie Dictionary does give a definition "to reverse or retract by thinking, as in changing
      one's mind" and I've found examples where it seems to be used kind of that way:

      "The ambition was to "unthink" and revive the intellectual tradition of holistic theorizing about large
      historical processes that was started by Marx and Weber" (Encyclopedia of Nationalism:
      Fundamental Themes.)

      Or here:

      In addition to rethinking, which is "normal," I believe we need to "unthink " nineteenth-century
      social science, because many of its presumptions - which, in my view, are misleading and
      constrictive - still have far too strong a hold on our mentalities http://books.google.de/books?
      id=H8wnle1KwMUC&pg=PA1&dq=%22to+unthink%22...

      Looks as if it may be used to mean "reverse our way of thinking about sth" - seems to be transitive,
      perhaps. A scholarly use which people would probably understand if they read, but it isn't
      commonly known in non-scholarly English AFAIK.

      Maybe someone with the big OED can see if it's marked as rare or anything?

3   Autor   C M 2 D D   (238324)   02 Mar 11 10:14

FIGURE 17.4 A discussion on the *Leo* site about the use of *unthink*.

Unfortunately, there is no real evidence that amendments to such entries actually take place. Contributions to the Jin Shan Ci Ba blogs and fora seem to consist almost entirely of didactic material. Contributors assume the role of authoritative teachers, and present advice to users on how to translate a Chinese word or phrase into English, or an English expression into Chinese. Subsequent messages then tend to thank the contributor and practise the vocabulary information that has been imparted. The posting in Figure 17.5 is typical.

今天的几个句子是有关预订的 1. I'll see if there are any flights.

我来看看有没有班机。 2. I don't want a night flight. 我不要夜航班机。

3. When am I supposed to check in?

我应该在什时候飘办理续 呢   ?

FIGURE 17.5 *A Jin Shan Ci Ba blog posting.*

The contributor presents some language data with what appear to be his or her own translations, as no source is provided. The follow-on postings do not develop any discussion about the appropriacy of the translations in various contexts, but instead reproduce the English sentences, presumably as a means of memorizing them. In the process, two mistakes are introduced—one respondent writes "I don't want a right fight" instead of "I don't want a night flight"—but this is not corrected. My helpful Chinese informants suggested that those who registered to contribute to the Jin Shan Ci Ba sites might have the right to delete any critical comments relating to their postings. My informants were not eager to correct any of the mistakes themselves, because they thought that this might result in the withdrawal of their own posting rights. Thus these and many other errors remain, and are incorporated into the reference material on the site.

Like many AEDs, the Jin Shan Ci Ba seems keen to record idioms and new words, but of course postings on these topics are particularly problematic, because figurative language does not easily translate, and the new words are often nonce formations created for humorous effect in a specific media context. These additions to the dictionary seem to be treated with the same seriousness as the most essential vocabulary, although they are of little communicative use. Thus numerous unattested expressions are presented as English idioms in the Jin Shan Ci Ba fora, such as "Many girls want to marry into the purple" (where "purple" is intended to imply wealth). I also found definitions for English words that had no currency, or a very restricted one, for example: "The husbeen is the insignificant other, the husband that has given up all sense of individuality and independence to keep his wife happy."

17.4 Conclusion

As has been noted, the digital content of AEDs is difficult to pin down, and it is scarcely surprising that they are rarely described in either the didactic or the metalexicographic literature. However, we should take note of the fact that AEDs are increasingly the reference sources of choice for language learners around the world. Rather than ignoring them, we should be discussing them, drawing attention to their defects, and also analysing their appeal. The more dictionary users learn to critique lexicographical content, the more likely it is that they will turn to electronic sources which provide accurate advice about lexical meaning and use. Published reviews of AEDs will help this to happen, as will classroom intervention and dictionary skills materials which direct users to the best AED components, even if these are packaged together with multiple lower-quality dictionaries. Producers of high-quality dictionaries may still be able to maintain a competitive edge, especially if they continue to develop those peripheral e-dictionary facilities such as audio and video files, word-list creation tools, language tests, and language games, all popular with users and unique to the electronic medium.

Perhaps in time user contributions will help AEDs to improve, but it seems clear that although collaboratively produced encyclopedias can be made worthy of comparison with eminent published brands, good modern dictionaries cannot be created without corpus-derived insights into grammar and usage, and collaboratively produced dictionaries will always require additional lexicographical input in order to be really useful reference tools.

Acknowledgments

I wish to thank Yeon-Kyung Bae, Liang Liao, and Wang Liyuan for their invaluable help with the translation and interpretation of Chinese and Korean e-dictionary material.

Dictionaries

Summers, Della (ed.) (2004). *Longman Active Study Dictionary*. Harlow: Pearson Education.

Alternative e-dictionary references

bab.la language portal: http://bab.la/.
Babylon online: http://dictionary.babylon.com/.
CC-CEDICT Wiki: http://cc-cedict.org/wiki/.
Doosan Dong-a Prime on the *Daum* portal: http://engdic.daum.net/.
ET-House Korean-English Dictionary: http://www.et-house.com/.
Jin Shan Ci Ba (Kingsoft Powerword) online portal: http://www.iciba.com/.
Jin Shan Ci Ba (Kingsoft Powerword) download site: http://ciba.hp009.com/.
Jin Shan Ci Ba (Kingsoft Powerword) discussion forum: http://bbs.hp009.com/.
Leo Dictionary: http://www.leo.org/.
Lingoes: http://www.lingoes.cn/zh/dictionary/index.html.
MDBG free online Chinese-English dictionary: www.mdbg.net.

Naver dictionary portal: http://dic.naver.com/.
Wiktionary (English language version): http://en.wiktionary.org/wiki/Wiktionary:Main_Page.
Yahoo! Hong Kong: http://hk.dictionary.yahoo.com/.
Yahoo! Japan: http://dic.yahoo.co.jp/.
Yahoo! Korea: http://kr.dic.yahoo.com.

18

Meeting the needs of translators in the age of e-lexicography: Exploring the possibilities

LYNNE BOWKER

18.1 Introduction

Translators have long been users of lexicographic resources. However, depending on the design and content of such resources, these have been more or less successful in meeting the needs of the translation community. In fact, as pointed out by Roberts (1992: 49), translators are well known for having a rather vociferous love-hate relationship with dictionaries.

Many dictionary design and content issues are legitimately determined by the profile of the intended user group. In the case of translators, this profile can be a complicated one because translators have both decoding and encoding needs, and the texts that they work with operate in a range of situations and communicative settings. However, in the past, a number of aspects of dictionary design and content were primarily restricted by factors that are less present in the age of e-lexicography. For instance, limitations on space that were necessarily imposed on printed volumes no longer apply in the case of electronic resources. Meanwhile, new research methods in lexicography, such as corpus-based approaches (e.g. Sinclair 1991b, Ooi 1998, Bowker and Pearson 2002), have made it possible to improve and augment the content of electronic dictionaries.

E-lexicography can mean a number of different things, such as using technology to make dictionaries, publishing dictionaries in electronic form, or integrating lexical resources into high-tech applications. The focus of this chapter will be on exploring how electronic lexicographic resources can address the needs of translators. Following an introduction and discussion of some of the different types of lexicographic needs of translators, this chapter will explore some possibilities as to how such resources may be enhanced with regard to both content and presentation, in order to make them more useful for translators in the future.

18.2 Translators as users of lexicographic resources

According to Josselin-Leray and Roberts (2005), dictionary producers have traditionally taken users for granted, making little effort to find out what they want. In recent decades, this has begun to change, and the concept of user needs has begun to be more actively explored in the literature (e.g. Atkins 1998b, Chen 2011, Hartmann 2001, Humbley 2002). Indeed, as noted by Lew (2011c: 1), "most experts now agree that dictionaries should be compiled with the users' needs foremost in mind", with the result that "interest in this strand of research is on the rise". The essential idea that dictionaries should be designed with a particular set of users in mind and for their particular needs has been refined to include the specific type of *situation* where these users may have precise lexicographically-relevant needs requiring dictionary consultation (Bergenholtz and Tarp 2010: 29–30).

This development is highly relevant in the case of translators because this user group has significantly different needs in different situations (e.g. Meyer 1988, Mackintosh 1998, Varantola 1998) and, according to Durán-Muñoz (2010: 55–6), the needs of translators with regard to lexical resources have for too long been ignored. Translation is a complex process involving both decoding or comprehension (i.e. a need to understand the source text that is being translated), and encoding or communication (i.e. a need to produce an accurate and natural-sounding text in the target language). Moreover, each of these is composed of several possible phases and sub-phases. From the point of view of dictionary design, things are further complicated by the fact that some translators work into their native language, while others translate out of their mother tongue and into a foreign language. In addition, while an experienced translator may have a high degree of comfort with the subject matter being translated, a translation student is often a learner of both the subject matter and of the specialized language used to discuss it. In each of these different situations, a translator with a given profile may have specific types of needs that can be met by consulting dictionary data.

The major steps of translation have been well documented in the literature (e.g. Newmark 1988, Bell 2000, Robinson 2003). However, for those not intimately familiar with the translation process, it may help to provide a brief and general outline of the principal tasks undertaken by a translator. For instance, translators need to have an understanding of the subject matter that is covered in the text which they are translating. Given that the vast majority of translation deals with specialized fields of knowledge, and since translators may not have received any formal training in these fields, they frequently prepare themselves by doing some background reading about the subject before they begin the task of translation proper. Next, the translators must read and understand the specific source text that is to be translated. Here, they may need to refer to monolingual definitions or explanations of specific concepts discussed in the text. During the transfer phase, a bilingual lexicographic resource proposing equivalent terms may be useful. In cases where multiple possible equivalents may exist, definitional or explanatory information might help to enable meaning differentiation and the selection of the most suitable equivalent. Frequency data may also prove to be an additional aid for helping translators to make such a decision. Moving on to the production phase, translators have the task of producing an accurate, idiomatic, and stylistically-appropriate *text* in the target language. Accordingly, they may need access to grammatical and syntactic information, and details about collocations and phraseological data, as well as stylistic and pragmatic information, in the target language.

With so many different communicative situations in play, it is clearly challenging to produce a single lexicographical resource that contains a broad enough range of data types to satisfy all translation-related needs. For many years, the majority of electronic dictionaries took the form of machine-readable editions of printed dictionaries (i.e. with the same information and organization) and the querying systems used to consult them remained relatively primitive (Pastor and Alcina 2010: 308). More recently, however, lexicographers have begun talking more earnestly to dictionary users and adjusting both the content and presentation of lexicographic resources to meet these users' needs (Humbley 2002: 95, Bergenholtz and Tarp 2010: 32).

Without denying that there remains room for improvement, lexicographers working in the electronic era are certainly taking steps towards creating resources that are more useful for translators. The following sections will look at a few possibilities— some of which are beginning to be implemented and others which are still on the horizon—with regard to e-lexicography and translation in particular. The information will be divided into two main categories. The first will focus mainly on the content of translation-oriented dictionaries, and the second primarily on the way in which this content is presented, though in some cases, there is overlap between the two (e.g. word clouds).

18.3 Content-related issues in translation dictionaries

Translators working in the twenty-first century are under enormous pressure to work quickly (Bowker 2004: 970, Charron 2005). Deadlines and turnaround times seem to be growing ever shorter, and for many translators, an ideal resource would be one that allowed them to do 'one-stop shopping' when looking for information to help them with their task. As pointed out by Campoy Cubillo (2002: 225), a translator in a working environment would benefit from having as much information as possible packed into a single resource because, in many cases, the resource on hand becomes *the* source of information. Newmark (1988: 174), too, alludes to this challenge when he comments:

Multilingual dictionaries give few collocations and are therefore useful only as initial clues to a further source; bilingual dictionaries are indispensable but they normally require checking in at least two TL [target language] monolingual dictionaries and sometimes in SL [source language] monolingual dictionaries.

The following sections consider some of the types of content that are useful for translators, and that can now be more easily incorporated into lexical resources in this age of e-lexicography, particularly with the advent of corpus-based approaches.

18.3.1 *Combination of general and specialized content*

One type of improvement that might benefit translators would be a resource that combines both general and specialized linguistic knowledge. Most of the translation that takes place is in specialized fields of knowledge (e.g. medical translation, legal translation, technical translation), and accordingly, translators regularly make use of specialized terminographic resources such as term banks (e.g. *Termium, Inter-Active Terminology for Europe* (IATE), *Grand dictionaire terminologique*). Nevertheless, it is generally acknowledged (e.g. Nielsen 2010: 70) that, even in specialized translation, specialized terms make up only about 20 per cent of a text. Therefore, a terminographic resource, with its focus on terms and terminological equivalence, can only provide help to translate a small portion of a text. For assistance with general language issues, a translator must turn to a dictionary.

Evidence of translators' desire to have access to both general and specialized knowledge can be seen in the resources that they create for themselves. Although the literature on terminology and specialized lexicography outlines strict principles for including only specialized terms in terminographic resources (e.g. Dubuc 2002: 33), the goal of a translator is to produce an acceptable translation within a short timeframe. As such, any information that will help them to meet this goal—whether it pertains to general or specialized language—could be useful. Therefore, translators creating their own resources tend to record a mixture of general and specialized language information (Bowker 2011: 222–3). For example, a lexical resource created by a translator in the field of Human Rights might include entries for specialized terms, such as *non-discrimination* and *equal opportunity*. However, it may also contain entries for items that do not meet the strict criteria required to be considered as terms, but which may nonetheless appear frequently in texts in this field, and which the translator may wish to keep track of, such as *between men and women*. This is particularly true when the tool used to create and manage the translator's personal lexical resource can be integrated with other tools (e.g. word processors, term extractors, corpus tools) because this can allow translators to take advantage of time-saving features such as one-click insertion, as well as to be consistent in the translation of a lexical string, which will in turn improve the performance of other tools that they may use for other aspects of the translation task (e.g. translation memory systems).

Similarly, translators are often interested in learning more about the general language words that collocate with specialized terms. For example, in scientific discourse, it is useful for translators to know that the specialized term *hypothesis* can collocate with the verbs *advance, formulate,* or *put forward* because this type of information can help them to produce more idiomatic texts. Pecman *et al.* (2010) and Kübler and Pecman (this volume) describe a project based at Universtité Paris-Diderot–Paris 7, which seeks to capture and encode such collocations in a terminological database of scientific language known as the Dictionnaire ARTES (Aide à la Rédaction de TExtes Scientifiques).

Traditionally, however, producers of commercial resources have tended to implement a rather strict separation between the general lexicographic and the more specialized terminological information. Yet if the value and usefulness of a resource depends on its capacity to support the translation process as a whole, it could be beneficial to create one that contains information about both general language words and specialized terms.

In another example, this one a project based at the Université de Montréal and focusing on word meanings, Pimentel *et al.* (2011) report on a comparative study in which the definitions of a variety of lexical items were compared in both a general lexical resource (FrameNet) and a specialized lexical resource (DiCoInfo). Using examples such as *attach, chat, execute, forward, insert,* and *load*, the researchers set out to investigate the possibility of enriching general lexical resources by adding meanings that are associated with a specialized domain. For a given lexical item, the general language definition from FrameNet was compared against a definition from the specialized field of computing taken from the DiCoInfo (cf. L'Homme *et al.*, this volume). The researchers observe that, in the case of verbs at least, the different definitions provided by the two resources were helpful in differentiating the meanings of the lexical items, and they conclude that it would be useful to add specialized meanings to the contents of general lexical resources to provide a richer resource.

Meanwhile, Campoy Cubillo (2002: 225) reports on an experience where students who were required to translate a specialized source text also needed a significant amount of information about general language words in order to understand the text. Therefore, they preferred to search in general language dictionaries, but they felt frustrated when some specialized terms could not be found in such resources. This type of experience would seem to further support the notion that there is a need for a translation resource that addresses both general and either specialized or semi-technical language.

In fact, some 'hybrid' resources that combine general and specialized lexicographic information are already beginning to appear. For instance, according to the website of the *Macmillan English Dictionary* (*MED*), a major survey conducted among nearly 2,000 users of the first edition of the *MED* (2002) revealed that a growing number of users need and expect their dictionary to explain the specialist terms they encounter on a regular basis. As a result, when compiling the second edition of the *MED* (2007), the lexicographers

made the dictionary more useful for professional and academic users by adding hundreds of specialist terms. These come from a range of subject-fields, especially business and finance, science, information technology, medicine, and the arts. People studying to be doctors or nurses, for example, can now look up terms like *ventricle, lymphocyte, carcinoma*, and *synovial fluid*. Similar technical vocabulary is now included for many other fields as well.[1]

Even though translators are not specifically named, they are indeed a user group who could benefit from such hybrid content. In fact, Josselin-Leray and Roberts (2005) report on another survey which had as one of its objectives the goal of determining the degree to which users consider it important to include specialized terms in general dictionaries. One group of users surveyed included language professionals (e.g. translators, editors), for which there were 251 respondents. In answer to the question of whether they would purchase a dictionary that did not contain any specialized terminology, the majority of these respondents answered no.

Of course, it may not be practical or even necessary to include *all* general language words in such a hybrid resource aimed at translators. To decide which words might usefully be included, lexicographers could take advantage of corpus-based approaches to assist with the selection of headwords. Using corpus-based frequency data, lexicographers could identify those general language words that are used and recur most often in a specialized domain to create a dictionary that incorporates general words alongside specialized terms in accordance with their frequency of use by a given professional community. This type of hybrid dictionary, which combines specialized terms with relevant and frequently-used general language words, would be of great value to many translators because it could bring them closer to the ideal of a sort of 'one-stop shop'. Resources such as *MED* and ARTES, as mentioned above, represent a first step in this direction.

18.3.2 *Addition of frequency and terminometric data*

Corpus-based frequency data could also be used to serve the needs of translators in a more direct fashion. As reported by Kilgarriff (1997), some monolingual learner's dictionaries, such as the *Longman Dictionary of Contemporary English* (*LDOCE*), already provide a broad indication of how common a word is within the general language. For example, in *LDOCE*, if the entry for *ability* is marked S2 W1, this means

---

[1] http://www.macmillandictionaries.com/features/how-dictionaries-are-written/med/.

it is in the most common 2,000 items used in spoken English and the most common 1,000 items used in written English. It could be interesting to adapt and refine this strategy for translation resources; in cases where multiple target language equivalents are presented for a given lexical item, it would be useful if information about the relative frequency of each option were included, or if the list of options could at least be presented in order of frequency. In an online lexical resource, it could even be interesting to consider whether a sort of 'word cloud' could be generated to give a rough idea of frequency. A word cloud is a visual representation for text data. Readers may be familiar with the concept of a tag cloud, which is typically used to depict keyword metadata (tags) on websites, or to visualize free form text. 'Tags' are usually single words, normally listed alphabetically, and the importance of each tag is shown with font size and colour. This format is useful for quickly perceiving the most prominent terms and for locating a term alphabetically to determine its relative prominence. When used as website navigation aids, the terms are hyperlinked to items associated with the tag; in an online lexical resource, the terms in a word cloud could be hyperlinked back to the dictionary entry, to the corpus, or to other pertinent information about the term. Although translators do not rely on frequency alone when selecting the most appropriate translation, this type of data can certainly contribute to helping them to make such decisions (Bertels *et al.* 2009: 203).

Research in the developing field of terminometrics (e.g. Quirion 2003, Quirion and Lanthier 2006), which uses corpus-based methods to measure the degree to which competing terms take hold and become implanted in a given specialized language, could contribute also to this aspect of e-lexicography.[2] For example, Quirion and Lanthier (2006: 109–10) describe a study in which a French-Canadian corpus of texts produced by Quebec institutions involved in the field of retirement and pension plans contained four different terms that refer to the concept of pension plan: *plan de retraite, régime de pension, régime de rente*, and *régime de retraite*. Using the terminometric tool Barçah, the corpus was analysed to reveal the number of occurrences of each of the competing terms: *régime de retraite* (8,092), *régime de pension* (61), *plan de retraite* (33), and *régime de rente* (2). From this information, it can be determined that Quebec institutions involved in the field of retirement and pension plans used the term *régime de retraite* 99 times out of 100 to designate the notion "plan set up to provide a retirement pension to its participants". The term *régime de retraite* therefore has an implantation coefficient of 0.99; the three other expressions used in the corpus have a cumulative implantation coefficient of 0.01.

---

[2] Terminometrics could perhaps be likened to a scientific version of Googlefight (http://www.google-fight.com/), which is a website that allows users to compare the number of search results returned by the search engine Google for two given queries.

18.3.3 *Explicit inclusion of information on relations*

Because translators deal with text rather than with lexical items in isolation, and because they must gain an understanding of the specialized subject field in question, as well as its associated discourse, it is useful for them to understand various types of relations—both lexical and conceptual—that they encounter. Traditionally, such information has not been represented in a very explicit fashion in dictionaries, though a recent survey of 402 translation professionals conducted by Durán-Muñoz (2010: 63) indicates that translators think it would be desirable for information on relations to be included in terminological resources. WordNet is a general language resource for English that has sought to explicitly represent such relations, and similar resources have since been developed for other languages also (e.g. DanNet for Danish, GermaNet for German). Now, some more specialized dictionaries are adopting a similar approach to mapping out the language and semantic relations found in specialized subject fields. For example, the DiCoInfo is seeking to systematically include in each entry, descriptions of paradigmatic relations, such as antonymy (e.g. *install, uninstall*); (quasi-)synonymy (e.g. *start, boot*), hyponymy (e.g. *word processor, application*), or meronymy (*string, character*), as well as syntagmatic relationships, such as collocations (e.g. *Internet; browse, surf*) (cf. L'Homme *et al.*, this volume).

18.3.4 *Inclusion of more usage information*

One of the areas where translators have been most critical of existing lexical resources, both general and specialized, has been in relation to usage information (Pearson 1998: 71, Humbley 2002: 96, Bergenholtz and Tarp 2010: 33). For many years, the focus of lexicographic resources was on defining meanings, but relatively little information was provided about how to properly use the associated terms in text.[3] Consequently, the entries were likely to contain only a very limited amount of information pertaining to phraseological preferences, collocational restrictions, usage notes, or even grammar. However, translators have advocated that this type of information, which would show users how to employ the term correctly, should be included (e.g. Durán-Muñoz 2010: 63). This is important because, as pointed out by Bowker and Pearson (2002: 26):

Although the specialized vocabulary of an LSP [language for special purposes] is often its most striking feature, it is important to note that LSP is not simply LGP [language for general purposes] with a few terms thrown in. An LSP may also have special ways of combining terms or of arranging information that differ from LGP.

---

[3] An exception would be the case of monolingual learners' dictionaries, which were early adopters of the corpus-based approach to lexicography (Bowker, 2010: 162–5).

As was the case with frequency data, corpora can be a rich source of usage information. Because combinations of words are much less frequent than the individual words, a large corpus of authentic texts can supply the data necessary to see the phraseology of a language clearly and accurately. By consulting a corpus, lexicographers can access many authentic instances of a given lexical item and select examples that are representative of how the lexical item is actually used (i.e. those that show typical grammatical patterns, selectional restrictions, collocates, and context) (Fox 1987: 137, Landau 2001: 209). While this type of information may seem obvious, it is often so only in hindsight. According to Fox (1987: 146): "once a collocate is given, it is so obvious that no one can imagine not guessing it correctly. Yet, when people are asked to give the collocates of words, they frequently do not do well." If this is the case for general language, imagine how much greater the challenge becomes for translators who may not be formally trained experts in the specialized fields in which they are translating. A corpus can provide striking evidence showing the extent to which language users rely on pre-assembled chunks of language to encode a wide variety of concepts. Lists of collocations with which a headword most frequently combines can be valuable additions to translation dictionaries (Bertels *et al.* 2009: 211–13). For instance, ARTES provides the following list of collocations for the term *ice sheet*: *beneath the ice sheet, migration of the ice sheet, retreat of the ice sheet, to be overridden by the ice sheet, ice sheet flows, ice sheet melts, ice sheet slides, ice sheet spreads*. This list of frequent collocational patterns in which a term appears can be of great assistance to translators who need to communicate using the appropriate phraseology of the scientific discourse. Moreover, similar to the generation of word clouds discussed above, it could be even more helpful to generate collocate clouds in online lexical resources as these can give users a quick visual appreciation of which words are most typically found in the company of the search term, and an indication of the relative frequency of each.

Likewise, information about style—that is, words or meanings that are used mainly by particular groups of people, or in particular contexts—is very helpful for translators. As observed by Wright (1993: 70):

Documents must speak 'the language' of the target audience and should resemble other texts produced within that particular language community and subject domain. [. . .] These considerations frequently require that the translator move beyond *merely correct* strategies in terms of lexical and grammatical content in order to account for *stylistically appropriate* solutions.

While lexicographers have long marked words for extralinguistic features of this type, access to corpora allows them to give more reliable accounts of information concerning regional varieties, register, genre, etc., and this should be incorporated into dictionaries aimed at translators.

Pragmatic strategies are the ways in which people use language to achieve a goal (e.g. criticizing, persuading, and encouraging). Just as people choose a goal, they must also choose the appropriate language that will help them to achieve this goal. This aspect of language use is very important, but it is also easy to miss because the patterns only become apparent when many examples are gathered together, which is made possible using a corpus-based approach. Because different types of specialized languages may use different pragmatic strategies, translation dictionaries could usefully provide translators with information about the ways in which speakers of a given language use that language to communicate. However, as pointed out by Nielsen (2010: 78–80), including information about stylistics, pragmatics, or even syntax within dictionary entries themselves may not be easy or indeed may not be the best strategy since it may overload an entry (e.g. by appearing alongside morphological data, explanatory data, equivalents, collocations, phrases, examples, synonyms, and cross-references), and may therefore be overlooked. For that reason, a different format could prove to be more effective for presenting information about syntactic structures, textual conventions, genres, and registers. For example, the *Base lexicale du français*, developed at the Katholieke Universiteit Leuven, employs a portal format to allow users to access information about expressing ideas or combining words, but without inserting all this information directly into the dictionary entry (Verlinde 2010, Verlinde and Peeters, this volume). Hyperlinks are also used to connect related information.

18.3.5 *Cautions about inappropriate usage*

While translators frequently ask for additional usage information to be included in lexicographic resources, they may also benefit from counsel regarding inappropriate usage. As noted by Nielsen (2010: 74), for example, translators may encounter problems with those structures that cannot be transferred from the source to the target language, a problem that is especially tricky for those working towards a foreign language. Similarly, trainee translators, or translators who are tackling a relatively unfamiliar subject field and its associated specialized language, are other groups who may also benefit from explicit advice about what not to say.

A source that could be useful in helping lexicographers to provide some of this type of information could be learner corpora (Granger 1998, Landau 2001: 293, Granger *et al.* 2002). The standard type of corpus consulted by lexicographers (e.g. the British National Corpus, the Bank of English), contains texts that were written by native speakers. As such, they are useful for revealing the conventional and repetitive nature of most linguistic behaviour, as well as understanding the fundamental importance of context and co-text in the way we use and understand words. In contrast, a learner corpus comprises texts that were produced by foreign-language learners, and it allows lexicographers to identify phenomena such as common linguistic problems faced by language learners or typical errors committed by non-native speakers (e.g. adding -*s* to *information* to try to make it plural, or using the preposition *about* after the verb *discuss*). A corrective note can be added to the relevant dictionary entry to warn learners about such common mistakes and to provide alternative strategies, and indeed this has already been implemented in some monolingual learners' dictionaries, such as the *Macmillan English Dictionary for Advanced Learners* (2007), and it is currently being implemented in the specialized *LEAD* dictionary, i.e. a dictionary-cum-writing-aid for English for Academic Purposes (cf. Granger and Paquot 2010c, Paquot, this volume). As was the case with standard corpora, learner corpora allow lexicographers to move beyond their own intuition about problems that learners may have and to consult authentic evidence based on texts actually produced by such learners.

Translation dictionaries could also take greater advantage of different types of learner corpora, for example, corpora produced by trainee translators (e.g. Bowker 2003), by translators working into a non-native language, or by translators working in an unfamiliar subject field. These needs have traditionally received less attention in translation dictionaries, but in more recent times specialized lexicographers have begun to recognize the importance of addressing the encoding needs of translators who must learn how to *use* a specialized language. Adopting a corpus-based approach could help with this. As noted above, in addition to being characterized by specialized terms, a specialized language has its own syntax and idiomatic structures which may differ from those used in general language. So, it is useful, for example, that the *Danish–English Accounting Dictionary* indicates that the English equivalent for *resultatoppstilling* should not take an indefinite article nor appear in the plural form, and that the verb *fakturere* is most commonly translated using a passive construction. While texts produced by subject specialists who are native speakers can provide evidence of the characteristics and conventions of the specialized language, different types of learner corpora consisting of texts produced by semi-experts or experts working in a foreign language could be used to provide data that shows exactly which aspects of the text production task these different groups are having difficulty with. To this end, specialized lexicographers may find it beneficial to consider teaming up with terminology and translation researchers who could help to compile such corpora.

18.3.6 *Increased integration of multimedia content*

A crucial issue when developing specialized lexicographic resources is to determine how specialized concepts can best be represented in order to provide users with an adequate understanding of their meaning as well as sufficient knowledge of their location within the general knowledge structure of a scientific or technical domain. Various formats can contribute to creating a well-rounded conceptual representation. However, most dictionaries favour linguistic descriptions over graphical ones. Nevertheless, as advocated by Faber *et al.* (2007) and supported by Pastor and Alcina (2010: 312), the description of a specialized entity can sometimes be most effectively presented by a combination of the two, which can contribute to a better understanding of complex and dynamic concepts.

While some large-scale translation-oriented lexical resources do include graphics, such as the *Grand dictionnaire terminologique* (e.g. see the entries for *paperclip* or for the musical instrument *triangle*), these appear on only a small proportion of term records in the collection. As noted by Durán-Muñoz (2010: 63) in her survey of 402 translation professionals, the inclusion of a greater number of pertinent graphics, illustrations, video clips, or animations in dictionaries aimed at translators would be welcomed by this user community. Projects such as PuertoTerm, based at the Universidad de Granada, are making significant headway in this regard (León Araúz *et al.* 2009). The records in the PuertoTerm term base in the field of coastal engineering contain a substantial number of multimedia elements to enhance the more conventional textual descriptions.

18.4 Presentation-related issues in translation dictionaries

In addition to containing new types of content, contemporary electronic dictionaries also have the potential to allow information to be displayed and accessed in new or different ways. For example, some search programs may actually highlight or draw attention to the specific information that a user is seeking within an entry, thus reducing the chances that it will be overlooked in an electronic dictionary, as compared to a printed dictionary. In the following sections, some presentation-related issues of particular interest to translators will be discussed.

18.4.1 *Capturing the intermediary steps of lexicographic research*

Traditionally, lexicographic resources have acted as a source of distilled knowledge. Skilled lexicographers carefully sift through vast reams of information, winnowing it down to useful and manageable chunks that are included in dictionaries. There is certainly great value in this: many users are seeking a snapshot of the prototypical meaning, use, and description of a given word or concept, and a well-crafted dictionary entry can typically meet these needs. Such users value not only the fact that they are directed to the most essential information pertaining to a word or concept, but also the fact that, in most cases, accessing it is neither time-consuming nor labour-intensive. The lexicographer has done the hard work so that the user does not have to.

Translators, likewise, both value and appreciate having access to distilled lexical knowledge. However, as noted above, there is not one single profile of translator, nor one sole translation situation. For many translators, the challenges arise when they need to find solutions to problems that are not prototypical in nature: new concepts that do not have an established term, creative coinages, semantic extensions, lexical gaps, culture-bound concepts, etc. In such cases, the distilled knowledge that meets the needs of prototypical users may not be sufficient for meeting the needs of translators. Moreover, translators may sometimes not even know what it is that they need; they are seeking inspiration, associations, similar examples, parallel situations that can be adapted, etc. It is often a case of "I don't know what I'm looking for, but I'll recognize it when I see it".

Some online dictionary sites have discussion forums where users can ask such questions. For example, LookWAYup is an online resource that combines a multilingual dictionary, thesaurus, translation, and other handy tools. It also features a LookWAYup Dictionaries Forum, which has a sub-forum called 'Translation and Terminology Help'. Here, translators can seek assistance, bounce ideas around, and pick the brains of others who may have been faced with a similar lexical challenge.

Another useful option could be for the translators to have access to the original corpora, so that they can browse on-the-fly, and generate collocations and frequency counts. This allows translators to see terms in a range of contexts, rather than in just a single context. This is important because although one particular context could prove helpful for dealing with a given translation problem, a different context may be more useful when tackling another one. As Lauriston (1997: 180) notes: "for translators [...] the quantity of information provided is often more important than the quality. They are usually able to separate the wheat from the chaff and even turn the chaff into palatable solutions to a particular communication problem." A number of different lexicographic projects are now linking dictionaries to the corpora on which they are based and giving users the option to search these corpora directly. One such project is ordnet.dk, an online dictionary site that brings together two Danish-language dictionaries as well as a Danish general language corpus (Trap-Jensen 2010b). The *LEAD* dictionary does the same but for specialized language, giving users access to discipline-specific corpora via a 'Corpus search' icon. *LEAD* users can search the corpora using an open source web-based corpus analysis system to see terms from the dictionary in a wider variety of contexts, or to search for terms that do not have an entry in the dictionary (cf. Paquot, this volume).

At other times, it may be useful for the translators to have access to something in between the raw source corpora and the finalized and distilled dictionary entry. In order to arrive at that entry, lexicographers have gone through a number of intermediary steps, where they learn about the various characteristics of the words and concepts being described, such as their grammatical and collocational behaviours, the different relationships that hold between words and their underlying concepts, and the characteristics that are necessary and sufficient for distinguishing one concept in an intensional definition. As lexicographers go through this learning process, they record information in different formats. For example, the characteristics for several related concepts may be laid out systematically in comparative tables, while relations between the concepts may be mapped out graphically in the form of a concept tree using directional arrows. A tool such as the Sketch Engine (Kilgarriff *et al.* 2004, Kilgarriff and Kosem, this volume) can be used to create a word sketch, which is a one-page corpus-based summary of a word's grammatical and collocational behaviour. It also generates a thesaurus and 'sketch differences', which specify similarities and differences between near-synonyms. Humbley (2002: 103) points out that translators, too, need to gain a deeper understanding of the concepts they are translating, and having access to a word sketch or to some other form of the output of the intermediary steps undertaken by the lexicographers during their own learning process may be instructive for the translators or other dictionary users. An example of this approach can be seen in the Ecosistema project based at the Universidad de Granada, which provides a conceptual representation of the specialized domain of the Environment in the form of a visual thesaurus of specialized concepts organized in a constellation of interrelated dynamic knowledge frames. This visual thesaurus has been integrated with the PuertoTerm term base to form the EcoLexicon (León Araúz *et al.* 2011).

18.4.2 *Greater standardization in design of search techniques in electronic dictionaries*

Pastor and Alcina (2010: 310) observe that the majority of electronic dictionaries have a different interface and different means of executing searches. In addition, similar types of searches may be referred to using a different nomenclature depending on the dictionary (e.g. anagram search vs. crossword search, Boolean search vs. combination search), while different dictionaries may use the same term to refer to different types of searches (e.g. a context search may simply show the context included in the dictionary entry, or it may take the user to a concordance in a complementary corpus). This can lead to confusion and means that users must devote considerable time to learning how to use each individual dictionary.

Without discounting the desire of individual companies to set their products apart from their competitors, it would nonetheless be appreciated by translators if a greater degree of high-level harmonization could be achieved. Pastor and Alcina (2010: 345) propose a classification of search techniques for translators that could be a useful starting point in this regard. Their typology contains suggestions for five types of query (exact word, partial word, approximate word, anagram search, combination search), and three types of filter (part of speech, thematic area, language). It also lists the types of resources and fields that may be searched, as well as the intended outcome of the various searches.

18.4.3 *Allowing customization of resources*

As noted above, there is not one single profile that applies to all translators or translation situations, which means that even among translators, different dictionary users will have different needs or be seeking different types of information. Even the same translator will have differing needs from one job to the next, depending on the source text to be translated. While translators have expressed an interest in 'one-stop shopping', it is also important to realize that too much information can be overwhelming or even confusing, and it can be time-consuming to sort through it. For instance, dictionary aggregators such as Dictionary.com allow users to retrieve entries from multiple online dictionaries with a single search, but it is still up to the user to sift through the results, which are not necessarily presented in a useful order. It is therefore important to present information in a way that makes it easy to access and to digest.

One interesting possibility could be to allow users to define a profile that would determine the nature of the information presented to them, or to allow them to select particular categories of information for display. For example, Bergenholtz and Tarp (2010: 34-6) describe a scenario where a subject expert, a semi-expert, and a layperson would have different needs when consulting a dictionary in the field of biotechnology. Different entries for a given term (e.g. RNA) can be prepared for these different users. In this example, Bergenholtz and Tarp note that, for the layperson, the information has been chosen in such a way that it focuses on molecular biological functions. Semi-experts are not necessarily given more detailed encyclopedic information, but the description is of a more technical nature and it uses a terminology which presupposes a certain basic knowledge of the field. With printed dictionaries, the easiest way to address these different user groups would be to develop two different dictionaries, whereas "in an electronic dictionary the user could switch between the two versions, defining himself either as a layman or a semi-expert", or even using trial-and-error methods to find the level that is most suited to a given situation (Bergenholtz and Tarp 2010: 36).

In the case of translators, it could be useful to present detailed definitions to users who are tackling a new subject field, or to present advice regarding inappropriate usage to those translating towards a foreign language, or to use a more pedagogical layout for trainee translators, etc. More or less information can be presented as necessary, depending on the needs specified by the user. Once user profiles have been defined, it may even be possible to think of adapting the approach used by recommender systems (e.g. similar to the systems used by Amazon.com) for filtering information in dictionaries. Typically, a recommender system compares a user profile to some reference characteristics, and seeks to predict the rating or preference that a user would give to an item they had not yet considered (Vellino and Zeber 2007).

18.4.4 *Creating integrated collections of resources*

Customization will become increasingly important as the development of integrated collections of resources takes hold. Translators have long been aware of the diversity of their needs. In Section 18.2 above, it was noted that with so many different communicative situations in play, it is clearly challenging to produce a single lexicographical resource that contains a broad enough range of data types to satisfy all translation-related needs. In the past, when resources were paper-based, translators relied heavily on dictionaries because it was simply too impractical and time-consuming to conduct their own extensive research. However, as electronic resources and associated tools began to occupy a greater place and to facilitate access to information, translators began looking elsewhere for solutions when existing dictionaries did not meet their needs. Indeed, some translators began to question whether there was any point in consulting such resources when they could conduct their own linguistic research on the fly using authentic and up-to-date sources.[4] Electronic corpora—including the Web-as-corpus—offered translators the possibility to do their own terminological research, finding a greater number of current usage examples, gleaning information about frequencies, consulting graphics or multimedia, etc. The explosion of interest in corpus-based resources in the translation industry can be seen in the number of articles appearing in the professional and academic literature, as well as in the content of workshops and conferences aimed at translators. Translators have embraced corpus-based research, and have become very adept at ferreting out solutions to their translation problems. For instance, translators often use Web search engines such as Google to manually search in bilingual websites containing parallel texts, particularly those produced by government and international organizations (e.g. Canadian government, European Union organizations), where the assumption is that if something is published on the Web by a government or international organization, its quality is likely to be high. This search procedure is fairly involved, and Désilets *et al.* (2010: 1) conservatively estimate that it requires in the order of two minutes to retrieve a single pair of aligned sentences. Given that generic search tools and techniques do not always meet the specific needs of translators, more customized options are now being developed. One such tool is WeBiText (Désilets *et al.* 2010), which is an online parallel concordancer that allows translators to search in large, high-quality multilingual websites in order to find solutions to translation problems.

While tools such as WeBiText offer translators an option for conducting their own corpus-based research, it must be said that translators are not, in principle, against consulting lexicographic resources. They respect the fact that lexicographers and

---

[4] Note that the earliest electronic dictionaries were often simply a machine-readable version of the printed dictionary and did not take full advantage of the possibilities offered by the electronic medium.

terminologists have conducted very detailed and thorough investigations—something they themselves do not always have time to do—but they are also mindful that specialized subject fields and the language used to describe these fields are constantly expanding and changing, so no conventional lexicographic resource can provide exhaustive, up-to-date coverage. Therefore, unless lexicographic resources can be adapted to the needs of translators, they run the risk of falling by the wayside.

A number of producers of lexicographic resources are beginning to recognize this, and there is a noticeable trend towards offering hybrid resources, where a dictionary is one part of a larger, integrated collection of language resources. For example, the Linguee tool combines an editorial dictionary with a search engine that allows users to search through hundreds of millions of bilingual texts for words and expressions. The Linguee search results are divided into two sections. On the left-hand side are the results from an edited bilingual dictionary, while on the right-hand side, aligned sentences from other sources provide users with contextualized examples of how the search expression has been translated in other texts.

This combining of different types of resources not only meets a wider range of needs, it also goes some way towards addressing the translator's desire for a 'one-stop shop' where they can find all the information they require. This hybridization strategy is being adopted by other resource developers as well. For instance, the *Base lexicale du français* is mainly based on the *Dictionnaire d'apprentissage du français langue étrangère ou seconde* (*DAFLES*), but it employs a hyperlinked portal format to allow users to also access information about different aspects of translation, grammar, and writing. A similar approach is taken by the ordnet.dk website, which brings together data from a historical dictionary, a modern dictionary, a reference corpus, and a wordnet with cross-resource look-up possibilities across all components. Likewise, the Termium Plus site allows users to access not only the Termium term bank, but also resources offering grammatical and writing assistance, while the *LEAD* is designed as an integrated tool where the actual dictionary part is linked up to other language resources and learning tools.

While the increasing availability of online resources and tools led many translators to bypass conventional dictionaries, the integrated model is likely to meet with success as it addresses the dual requirements of enabling translators to access a variety of types of information in a convenient and centralized format. As noted by Hutchins (1998), translators have already shown their appreciation for various types of translator's workstations or translator's toolboxes (e.g. LinguisTech), which provide an integrated platform for accessing various translation tools (e.g. term extractors, translation memory systems, terminology management systems). Ensuring ease of access and restricting the potential for information overload by allowing for customizability will be important factors for the success of this similar approach to lexicographic resource development.

18.5 Conclusion

The aim of this chapter was to consider the lexicographic needs of translators and to explore how these might be met in the age of e-lexicography. Without making claims to be exhaustive, we have considered a variety of possibilities covering both content-related and presentation-related aspects.

Durán-Muñoz (2010: 55–6) suggests that one reason why current lexicographic resources seem to fall short of meeting the needs of translators is because lexicographers have not consulted widely with translation experts. This is echoed by Nielsen (2010: 72), who notes that if lexicographers give more consideration to the advances in translation studies in future, they may be able to make improved dictionaries that help translators to produce high-quality translations. The question may be asked as to whether it is financially viable for companies to make dictionaries aimed exclusively at the translation market. However, as the volume of information produced in our society continues to grow, and as we continue to embrace globalization, the need for translation will not diminish.[5] Moreover, if we consider the trend towards creating multi-purpose, customizable tools described in Section 18.4.4 above, then it becomes more economically feasible to think of producing a resource that can be customized and filtered to better meet translators' needs.

Meanwhile, Humbley (2002: 103–4) notes that in this electronic age, lexicographers have an exciting world of tools and techniques at their disposal, but cautions that these bring with them a new set of expectations on the part of users. The key, in Humbley's opinion, is for lexicographers to listen to users.

It is our belief that the channels of communication are beginning to open up more widely, and we hope that this chapter can contribute in some small way to the ongoing dialogue between lexicographers and translators. Working together, they have the potential to create resources that will be greater than the sum of their parts.

Dictionaries and other lexical resources

ARTES: https://artes.eila.univ-paris-diderot.fr/.
Base lexicale du français: http://ilt.kuleuven.be/blf/.
Danish-English Accounting Dictionary / Regnskabsordbogen. Engelsk-Dansk: http://www.ord-bogen.com/ordboger/regn/index.php?dict=1007.
DiCoInfo: http://olst.ling.umontreal.ca/cgi-bin/dicoinfo/.
EcoLexicon: http://ecolexicon.ugr.es/visual/index_en.html.

---

[5] In the United States alone, the federal Bureau of Labor Statistics reports that the number of people employed in the translation industry rose by 40 per cent between 2000 and 2004, and forecasts that this will increase by a further 20 per cent by the year 2014. The Bureau goes on to note that the number of people actually employed in this industry is probably significantly higher because many work part-time (Fried 2006).

FrameNet: https://framenet.icsi.berkeley.edu/fndrupal/.
Grand Dictionnaire Terminologique: http://www.granddictionnaire.com.
Interactive Terminology for Europe (IATE): http://iate.europa.eu.
Linguee: http://www.linguee.com/.
LinguisTech: http://www.linguistech.ca.
Longman Dictionary of Contemporary English (LDOCE): http://www.ldoceonline.com/.
LookWAYup: http://lookwayup.com/free/forum.htm.
Louvain EAP Dictionary (LEAD): http://www.uclouvain.be/en-322619.html.
ordnet.dk: http://ordnet.dk.
PuertoTerm: http://ecolexicon.ugr.es/visual/index_en.html.
Sketch Engine: http://trac.sketchengine.co.uk.
Termium Plus: http://www.termiumplus.gc.ca.
WeBiText: http://www.webitext.com/bin/webitext.cgi.
WordNet: http://wordnet.princeton.edu/.

On the usability of free Internet dictionaries for teaching and learning Business English

PEDRO A. FUERTES-OLIVERA

19.1 Introduction

Proponents of the function theory of lexicography (or the theory of lexicographical functions) claim that there is a need for a theory of lexicography, i.e. a system of ideas put forward to explain the making of dictionaries, as well as their characteristics, usefulness, history, and future developments in a systematic and reflective way (Bergenholtz and Tarp 2003, 2004; see Tarp 2008 for a review; and Tono 2010 for critical comments on function theory). One of the main principles of function theory is that lexicography can no longer be categorized as a subset of disciplines within applied linguistics, but rather that it should be seen as part of an information science discipline that offers a theoretical and practical response to information needs detected in society, and as such it is strongly embedded in specific cultural, historical, and technological environments (Tarp 2011, and this volume). It also maintains that the needs giving rise to information tools—be they dictionaries, glossaries, or knowledge databases—belong to the same categories at the highest level of abstraction, as are the data selected to solve these needs irrespective of the specific medium in which the data are presented (Bergenholtz 2011, Gouws 2011, Tarp 2011, and this volume).

Within this functional approach to lexicography, research on e-lexicography, i.e. the lexicographic sub-discipline that is mainly concerned with the development, planning, compilation, and publication of electronic lexicographic reference tools, focuses on aspects that are common to all reference tools, both printed and electronic, such as the extra-lexicographical social situation analysed in Section 19.2, as well as on specific issues related to the new media and to elements that have been rediscovered and judged necessary and central in the corresponding theory building (e.g. data presentation and data access) (Tarp 2011, and this volume, Verlinde and Peeters, this volume).

Below is a list of some of the issues that are currently debated in the field of e-lexicography (Fuertes-Olivera and Bergenholtz 2011b):

- The use of databanks from which different types of dictionaries, and even different dictionaries of the same type, can be extracted.
- Means of coping with the mistake of including much more data than needed, referring to the traditional view espoused by linguistic-oriented lexicographers, who defend the aggregation of as much data as possible in a dictionary article, regardless of whether or not this is useful for the potential user (Tarp 2009b).
- The broadening of lexicographical theory to the development, planning, compilation, and publication of other reference sources, which are also focused on the users of these sources, the data presented in them, the structures to accommodate the data and, of utmost importance, access to the data in order to achieve an optimal retrieval of information. Verlinde (2011), for example, presents the *Base lexicale du français* as a web-based system that has task-oriented access to lexicographic information by allowing users to identify their use situation(s) and need(s).
- The explanation of a paradigm shift, which is placing lexicography within the realm of information science, taking into consideration the fact that dictionary users are also Internet users who upload and download all types of data. Heid (2011), for example, claims that if electronic dictionaries are to be understood as (software) tools, they should also be designed according to the principles applicable to software tools. One such principle is *usability*, a concept developed within information science with the aim of assessing the effectiveness and efficiency of the tool when used in a particular situation and for a particular task (see Section 19.3).

A theory of e-lexicography cannot, therefore, be built directly upon concrete and individual phenomena, but from an abstraction with which we can work by referring to potential users, potential user situations, potential user needs, and potential types of data that may satisfy these potential needs. Within this general framework, however, each user, user situation, user need, item of data, and consultation is an individual act and, therefore, the individualization of user-needs satisfaction is a question to be taken seriously. Of particular relevance here is the fact that electronic dictionaries, especially Internet dictionaries, allow lexicographers to provide the necessary mechanisms for dictionary customization, i.e. the individualization of dictionary contents, in order to assist specific types of users who find themselves in specific types of use situations and require specific types of data (Paquot, this volume, Tarp 2011, and this volume, Verlinde 2011, Verlinde and Peeters, this volume).

There have been several attempts at drawing up electronic dictionary typologies (e.g. De Schryver 2003, Fuertes-Olivera 2009, Lew 2011a, Tarp 2011). These have identified the Internet dictionary as a type of electronic information tool that contains a collection of structured data that can be accessed with multiple Internet tools with or without paying a subscription fee, is enhanced with a wide range of functions, can be used in various environments, and is linked to both external and internal information sources. The main objective of this chapter is to examine free Internet dictionaries (Fuertes-Olivera 2009, Lannoy 2010a) and reflect on their usability in an English for Specific Purposes (ESP) context, i.e. the teaching and learning of Business English.

The range of Internet dictionaries that can be accessed freely is very broad and subject to constant changes. As the free versus paid category is almost impossible to delimit—for example, there are syndicated services, promotional campaigns, ad-supported dictionaries, and bonuses for buyers of paper editions, etc. (Lew 2011a)—'free Internet dictionary' refers in this chapter to web-based lexicographic information systems that were accessed online and for free at the time of writing this chapter.

Lannoy (2010a) showed that free Internet dictionaries are very popular with users, who welcome the possibilities of multiple access routes, external hyperlinks, and incorporation of extra data (e.g. sounds and videos). Dictionaries are also essential tools for autonomous language learning, and therefore ideal candidates for investigating new questions on the teaching and learning process in the digital era (Mackey and Ho 2008). Free online dictionaries are analysed with a view to discovering whether or not they are suitable for satisfying the information requirements users might have in several use situations, most particularly in a cognitive and/or communicative Business English use situation. Section 19.2 first presents the extra-lexicographical social situation, i.e. the teaching and learning of Business English, and its lexicographical implications. A major objective of this chapter is to investigate the role of the medium, i.e. the Internet, in the teaching and learning of Business English. Section 19.3 thus elaborates on a number of characteristics of free Internet dictionaries that might make them usable in this specific extra-lexicographical social situation and consequently candidates for overcoming restrictions such as the paucity of teaching resources and the necessity for constant retraining in today's world in which knowledge is being created at a brisk pace, which makes it necessary for both instructors and learners of Business English to constantly upgrade their business knowledge. Section 19.4 offers a comparison between printed and free Internet dictionaries for Spanish users of Business English. In Section 19.5, I illustrate how free Internet dictionaries can be used for teaching and learning Business English in the Spanish university context, thus increasing the dictionary culture of instructors and students of Business English. I also show how it is possible to overcome some of the defects that have been signalled in free Internet dictionaries (Fuertes-Olivera 2009) and have led to suspicion among teachers (Nesi, this volume). In Section 19.6 some general conclusions are drawn.

19.2 Business English and lexicography

The function theory of lexicography shifts the focus from actual dictionary users and dictionary use situations to potential users and the social situations in which they participate. This requires an investigation of extra-lexicographical social situations in order to evaluate their possible lexicographical influence (Tarp 2008, and this volume).

Extra-lexicographical situations are usually examined deductively, i.e. researchers hypothesize on the conditions under which a potential user can gain assistance from dictionary consultation (Fuertes-Olivera and Tarp 2011). For example, an analysis of the teaching and learning environment associated with Business English can shed light on why and how dictionaries can help users learn the language of business as well as business concepts. In particular, I will elaborate on three characteristics of Business English that have lexicographical implications: (a) the hybrid nature of Business/Economics English; (b) the classification of learners of Business English as semi-experts; and (c) the necessity of enhancing the dictionary culture of potential users of Business English dictionaries (Andersen and Fuertes-Olivera 2009, Fuertes-Olivera and Arribas-Baño 2008).

Business English is usually presented as a hybrid that mixes specific and general content and is concerned with the teaching and learning of the strategic communication system in the business domain, in "which participants, adopting/adapting business conventions and procedures, make selective use of lexico-grammatical resources of English as well as visual and audio semiotic resources to achieve their communicative goals via the writing modality, speaking modality, and/or multi-modality" (Zhang 2007: 406).

Teachers of Business English face challenges related to the focus of the course. In general, such courses aim to equip students with disciplinary knowledge, professional practice, and discursive competence by preparing integrated approaches to the teaching of Business English that focus on business knowledge (equipping students with disciplinary cultures and preparing them for membership of their target discourse community), business practice (making students familiar with the procedures, conventions, systems of politeness, strategies, and tactics for addressing various goals in the professional community), and business discourse (raising student awareness of the use of English in contextualized business communication and offering learners "strategies that can be associated with effective communication in business, regardless of whether the speaker/writer is a native or non-native speaker" (Nickerson 2005: 369)).

As the teaching and learning environment of Business English consists of an array of communicative-oriented (i.e. reading, writing, and translating) and cognitive-oriented (i.e. acquiring knowledge on business concepts) use situations, Business

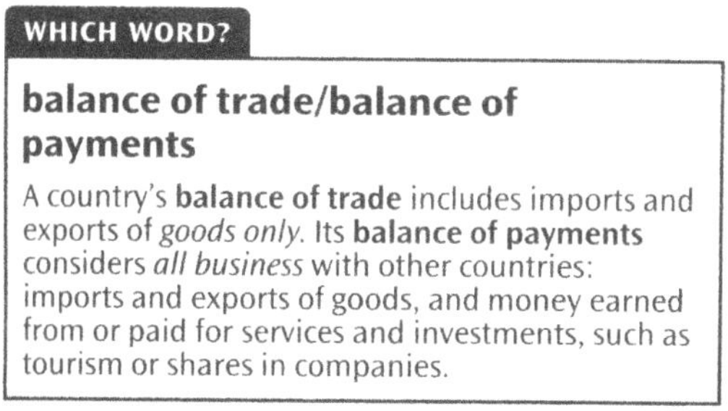

balance of trade/balance of payments

A country's **balance of trade** includes imports and exports of *goods only*. Its **balance of payments** considers *all business* with other countries: imports and exports of goods, and money earned from or paid for services and investments, such as tourism or shares in companies.

FIGURE 19.1 Word Box in the *New Oxford Business English Dictionary.*

English dictionaries have to cater for both needs by offering encyclopedic and linguistic data. In general, research on these dictionaries has found that they cover general words and specialized business terms and that they are all-inclusive dictionaries, i.e. they cater for both communicative and cognitive use situations (Fuertes-Olivera and Arribas-Baño 2008, Walker 2009). For example, in the *New Oxford Business English Dictionary for Learners of English*, users have access to grammar data, pronunciation, geographical labels, short definitions, collocations, examples, and, in some entries, several boxes with knowledge data that differentiate competing business concepts, such as **balance of trade/balance of payments** (Figure 19.1).

Second, the nature of Business English influences users' needs and the best lexicographical way for assisting potential users. Research on Business English dictionaries has concluded that most users are typically semi-experts, i.e. students of Business/Economics degrees enrolled on Business English courses, whose degree of expertise in the subject field and in English ranges from medium to advanced, depending on personal circumstances and the speed at which they acquire fluency in Business English and the characteristics of the trade they are most familiar with (Andersen and Fuertes-Olivera 2009, Fuertes-Olivera and Arribas-Baño 2008). These potential users typically consult dictionaries and use them as a source of learning or studying business/economics concepts (i.e. they are in a knowledge-oriented or cognitive-use situation) and in order to facilitate an existing or planned act of communication (i.e. they are in a communicative-oriented use situation).

At an abstract level these users' needs are similar to those of upper-intermediate to advanced English learners (Tarp 2008), but different in that Business English learners also need knowledge of the subject field and its discourse properties (Andersen and Fuertes-Olivera 2009, Fuertes-Olivera and Arribas-Baño 2008). In lexicography, knowledge of the subject field is related to the distinction between multi-field, single-field, and sub-field specialized dictionaries (Nielsen 1990). Single-field dictionaries (e.g. the *New Oxford Business English Dictionary for Learners of English*) cover the terms of an entire subject field, whereas sub-field and multi-field specialized dictionaries contain word lists that cover part of the domain (e.g. the *English*

Accounting Dictionary), or two or more domains (e.g. the *Dictionary of Business and Law English–Macedonian, Macedonian–English*). This distinction is very important and determines whether or not the dictionary should have a maximized word list (Nielsen 1990), as well as the amount of information included in the entries, the functional orientation, and the process of updating the dictionary (Andersen and Fuertes-Olivera 2009).

Business/economics is a very broad subject field that can be broken down into around forty different sub-fields, such as accounting, marketing, etc. My opinion, therefore, is that learners of Business English will gain more assistance by consulting sub-field business dictionaries, i.e. those that cover each of the forty or so sub-domains into which business and economics is broken down, than by using a single-field Business English dictionary, such as the *New Oxford Business English Dictionary for Learners of English*.

My view is based on the idea that the concept of *frequency*, a notion taken from corpus linguistics, is not as important for compiling specialized dictionaries as it is for compiling general learners' dictionaries. Terms that are infrequent and yet really necessary for users are not usually retrieved from either language for specific purposes (LSP) word lists (e.g. Nelson 2000, Curado Fuentes 2001) or from general specialized corpora such as those used for selecting the wordlist of single-field business dictionaries, e.g. the *New Oxford Business English Dictionary for Learners of English*.

Instead, the extra-lexicographical situation associated with specialized lexicography requires the exploration of new methods, one of which is based on the concept of *relevance*, a notion that connects the making of specialized dictionaries with the function theory of lexicography (see Tarp, this volume). Within the tenets of function theory, the concept of relevance has led us to consider, first, whether the lexicographic methods and procedures that are currently used in general lexicography are also adequate for working with specialized dictionaries, and second, which lexicographic data are really necessary in specialized dictionaries and which method(s) can be used for compiling and revising them in a brief span of time, a must for specialized lexicography (Fuertes-Olivera and Nielsen 2011). For instance, the application of the principle of relevance for lemma selection in the *Diccionario Español de Contabilidad*, a sub-field accounting dictionary we are currently compiling at the University of Valladolid, resulted in a wordlist of around 6,000 terms which were chosen from existing accounting dictionaries, a three-million word in-house accounting corpus, and intensive reading of very basic accounting texts. The word list was selected by a team of three experts in accounting and economics and one lexicographer who devoted around 500 hours to the process (around 20 hours a week for 25 weeks).

Existing dictionaries allowed the lemma selection team to choose around 3,000 terms, mainly those that are very traditional and typical in the field, particularly those that are loaded with cultural connotations and are usually included in dictionaries as one-word or two-word terms. For instance, the terms *amortización* and *depreciación* (English 'amortization'), and *deterioro* (English 'impairment') are frequent and specific terms that also need the inclusion of usage and contrastive notes as they changed their traditional meanings after Spain's entry into the European Union.

The keyness method[1] could not be used for extracting specialized terms (there are no Spanish general corpora such as the British National Corpus with which such a comparison could be established). What the team did was to select a list of frequent words in our in-house corpus and use it for carrying out Google searches of frequent terms, each of which was restricted by adding the symbol "+" and relevant keyword(s). For instance, searching *metodo + contabilidad + coste* (English 'principle' + 'accounting' + 'cost') in Google retrieved terms concerned with cost accounting, most of which can be defined as *translated cognates*, i.e. Spanish accounting terms that are the result of word-by-word translations from English. This method is explained in terms of the workings of the literal translation hypothesis (Fuertes-Olivera, submitted), i.e. the assumption that translators of Spanish specialized texts are primed to offer word-by-word renderings of English terms, either without any syntactic modification (e.g. *resultados consolidados* from English 'consolidated results') or with some adaptation to Spanish rules, e.g. an *of-* phrase instead of the English genitive, as in *método de conferencia* (English 'conference method') (Fuertes-Olivera 2011, Fuertes-Olivera and Bermúdez Bausela 2011). This method is especially productive for selecting multi-word English borrowings, loans, and calques that crop up in Spanish accounting texts, perhaps a remainder of the status of English as the lingua franca of accounting. With this method we selected around 1,000 new terms, most of which are two- or three-word Spanish literal translations of original English terms: *consideraciones de prudencia* (English 'consideration of prudence'), *inventario en consignación* (English 'consignment inventory'), etc.

Finally, the lemma selection team selected around 2,000 new terms by intensive reading of basic accounting texts such as *Plan General Contable, Normas Internacionales de Contabilidad* (English 'International Accounting Standards'), *Normas Internacionales de Información Financiera* (English 'International Financial Reporting Standards'), and European accounting directives and regulations. We consider intensive reading a more suitable method than inverted frequency for searching for very idiosyncratic, domain-specific, and infrequent terms, many of which cannot be extracted by any electronic means. For instance six- and seven-word terms[2] such as *fecha de transición a las NIIFs* (English 'date of transition to IFRSs'), *estado de resultados del ingreso marginal* (English 'contribution income statement'), and *re-*

---

[1] 'Keyness' is used in corpus linguistics to extract salient terms from a corpus. The method compares word frequencies in the corpus under study and in a reference corpus.

[2] There are around 500 six- and seven-word terms in *El Diccionario Español de Contabilidad*.

sultado antes de intereses, impuestos y amortizaciones (EBITDA) (English 'Earnings before Interest, Tax, Depreciation, and Amortization (EBITDA)), were extracted from the definition sections included in the Spanish translations of the International Accounting Standards, the International Financial Reporting Standards, and the *Plan General Contable*, respectively. In sum, the practical application of the principle of relevance is the production of a sub-field accounting dictionary that aims to assist semi-experts in communication-oriented situations. This dictionary contains a maximized word list of around 7,500 lemmas, which can easily be updated. We consider this to be more suitable than a single-field Business English dictionary of around 200,000 lemmas, which might take a long time to produce and cannot be easily updated on a regular basis (Fuertes-Olivera and Nielsen 2012).

Dictionary use for teaching and learning has been subject to scrutiny recently, and this may lead to enhancement of the dictionary culture of users. Lew and Galas (2008) comment on two complementary approaches aimed at narrowing the gap between the sophistication of dictionary structure and the lack of reference skills possessed by the average dictionary user, a gap to which lexicographers have not traditionally paid much attention. The first approach aims to make users more skilful in using dictionaries. Lew and Galas add that, in spite of the various calls to include training in dictionary use in school and academic curricula (Atkins and Varantola 1998), no large-scale teaching of dictionary skills has ensued, and current research into the effectiveness of training in dictionary use lacks convincing results.

A recent exception is provided by Lew and Galas (2008), who showed that a dictionary-skills training programme may be effective for language learners, although its effectiveness is not evenly distributed among the different dictionary skills that might be taught. For example, they reported huge improvements in performance for dictionary skills such as the ability to differentiate between countable and uncountable nouns, but less noticeable and modest results for dictionary skills such as alphabetical ordering.

The second approach is concerned with adjusting dictionaries to the technical possibilities of the medium. For example, Internet dictionaries are appropriate for integrating data, users, and access in a more focused way, e.g. by favouring customization and the production of mono-functional dictionaries with which users will retrieve neither more nor less than the data they need (Bergenholtz 2011, Paquot, this volume, Spohr 2011, Tarp 2009b). The *English Accounting Dictionary* illustrates the way ahead for adjusting dictionaries to the technical possibilities of the Internet (cf. Figure 19.2).[3] It is updated regularly, has an elegant and pleasant layout, is provided with interactivity facilities (for example, users can e-mail editors and discuss lexicographical problems), uses a familiar and reassuring virtual environment (e.g. it

---

[3] The *English Accounting Dictionary* is accessed on the homepage Ordbogen.com, an Internet site from which users can access more than twenty Internet dictionaries by paying a subscription fee.

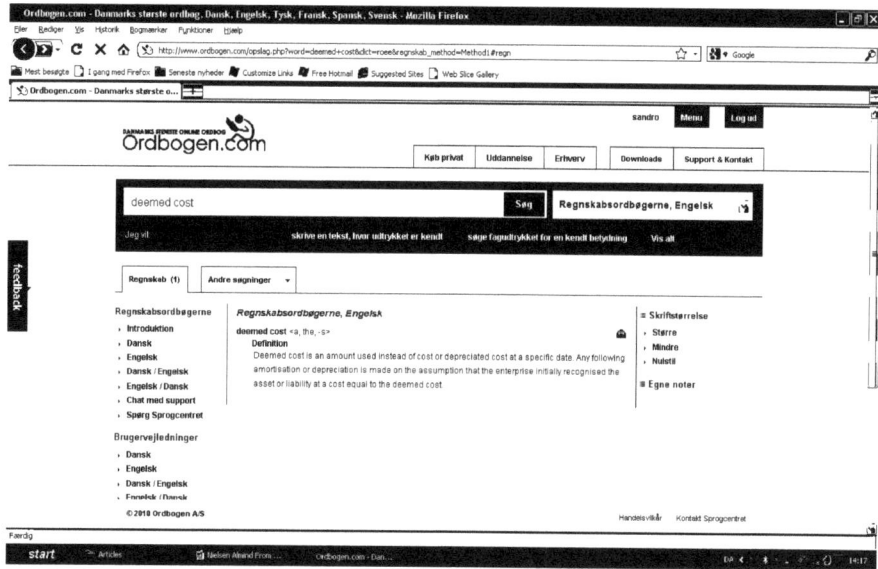

FIGURE 19.2 Ordbogen.com homepage.

employs user-friendly colours and fonts, and divides the page into a static part for header, footer, and navigational menu, as well as a dynamic part), displays the results logically (using, for instance, superscripts to differentiate homonyms and Arabic numbers to disambiguate polysemous terms), and is equipped with smart search engines that offer different search options (Nielsen and Almind 2011).

The *English Accounting Dictionary* also has dynamic articles with dynamic data corresponding to the specific types of information needs which specific types of users performing specific types of lexicographically relevant activities may have in any consultation situation (Paquot, this volume, Tarp 2011, Verlinde and Peeters, this volume). Users reading an accounting text can, for example, consult the *English Accounting Dictionary* and specify their needs by selection the option 'help to understand an accounting term' (i.e. they are having a reception problem), thereby obtaining the result shown in Figure 19.3.

The definition explains the meaning of an important US accounting term and the usage note informs users of a change in the substantive accounting rules and refers to a term that has replaced the lemma in connection with business combinations. Users who want extra information may select the search option 'show everything', and the result will be the entire article, including the synonyms and antonyms, as shown in Figure 19.4.

Synonyms and antonyms representing varieties of accounting English (labelled 'IAS/IFRS'—International Accounting Standards/International Financial Reporting

pooling-of-interests method US

   Definition

   The pooling-of-interests method is an accounting method applied in the US until 2001 in connection with business combinations. Under this method, all assets and liabilities in the acquired company were recognized at carrying value at the time of combination rather than at fair value and no goodwill was recorded. The acquiring company would issue common stock in exchange for the voting stock of the acquiree.

   Usage note

   The pooling-of-interests method has been replaced by the purchase method of accounting.

FIGURE 19.3 Definition and usage note in the article **pooling-of-interests method** in the *English Accounting Dictionary.*

   Synonyms
   merger accounting method UK
   merger method UK
   uniting-of-interests method IAS/IFRS

   Antonyms
   acquisition method UK
   pruchase method IAS/IFRS, US

FIGURE 19.4 Synonyms and antonyms in the article **pooling-of-interests method** in the *English Accounting Dictionary.*

Standards, UK and US) may help those users who are more or less familiar with these terms from American, British, or IAS/IFRS English. The synonyms and antonyms function as cross-references (or dictionary-internal hyperlinks) and can be clicked so that users can quickly and easily access other data in the dictionary (for instance, the article **purchase method**). In addition, these synonyms and antonyms help users to place the terms in relation to each other, indicate geographically-based usage restrictions, and help those users who produce, copy-edit, and translate financial reporting texts.

   It goes without saying that most, if not all, free Internet dictionaries are not constructed in order to solve the specific needs a specific user has in a specific use situation. However, my contention is that they can be used to overcome restrictions (such as limited teaching resources), and for constant retraining in a specialized field, especially if potential users are aware of their usability.

19.3 On the usability of free Internet dictionaries for teaching and learning Business English

Mackey and Ho (2008: 388) pointed out that the term *web usability* is grounded in research focused on human-computer interaction and user-centred design, and added that usability is defined as "the degree to which people (users) can perform a set of required tasks". They enumerated a list of elements (e.g. the effectiveness of a given product, its efficiency, and user satisfaction with it) which indicate that usability is the measure of how easily a thing, typically a software application or a piece of hardware, can be used. Usability, therefore, is generally defined in terms of the needs of the users of the information system. The fact that dictionaries are tools, at least for proponents of the function theory of lexicography, has led researchers such as Heid (2011) to claim that Internet dictionaries share numerous characteristics with information systems, both search engines and database access tools. These characteristics include needs-driven access, means of consultation (search and browsing), or access to particularized information (Bothma 2011, Heid 2011, Verlinde and Peeters, this volume). Consequently, there have been attempts at assessing the usability of Internet dictionaries via subjective and objective methods (Heid 2011). Objective methods focus on content, file size, access structure, response time, screen size, display, and user control (Heid 2011, Mackey and Ho 2008).

Some of these factors—typically, response time, screen size, and display—are dependent on technical considerations (for example, the availability of broadband connections). On the other hand, content, access structure, file size, and user control may be examined to assess the potential usability of free Internet dictionaries in the extra-lexicographical situation associated with teaching and learning Business English. For example, they can be examined by performing usability tests in a usability laboratory. This research is "often seen as a sub-domain of areas such as man–machine interaction (MMI), human-computer interaction (HCI), or user-centred design (UCD)" (Heid 2011: 293).

In addition, and this is my contention in this chapter, the usability of Internet dictionaries can be examined by evaluating whether or not these dictionaries are equipped with Internet gadgets that connect them with information science (Bothma 2011). Hence, I propose a list of features which I use to argue that usability also refers to having the potential of being usable in one or several use situations (for example the teaching and learning of Business English), as such features facilitate the human-computer interaction which benefits potential users in communication- and cognition-oriented use situations.

Lannoy (2010a) has referred to the popularity of free Internet dictionaries among users, and has concluded that there is room for many new players in the field of e-lexicography. Nesi (this volume) also mentions the necessity for further research on e-dictionaries (e.g. free Internet dictionaries) in order to bring their characteristics into the spotlight and thus eliminate many of the defects that have made online dictionaries the object of suspicion among teachers. Nesi comments that most published e-dictionary research is concerned with prestigious dictionaries (those that emanate from university centres or established publishing houses), and adds that less prestigious dictionaries (she calls them "alternative dictionaries" or "AEDs") also merit study of the way they are used as well as surveys of the habits and attitudes of e-dictionary users. Following suit, I propose to examine some of the features of free Internet dictionaries with the aim of assessing their degree of usability for over-coming material shortcuts and favouring learning autonomy in the Business English pedagogical context described in Section 19.2.

My list of features is:

1. A free Internet dictionary is more than a container of the lexicon of a language. It is a tool equipped with (some of) the technological possibilities the Internet offers. This means that a free Internet dictionary can incorporate search options that link a dictionary entry with (an) Internet text(s) and/or files in which users can access the data they need. For example, the functionality 'source' in the *Diccionario Inglés-Español de Contabilidad* will help students and instructors of Business English by linking certain dictionary articles to Internet texts (for instance, to the EU homepage or the International Financial Reporting Standards (IFRS) homepage) in which official bodies communicate possible modifications, adaptations, or corrections, etc., which represent essential data in cognitive use situations where users such as those just mentioned consult dictionaries to acquire knowledge of something. Similarly, in BusinessDictionary.com users can access data lexicographers recommend but have not prepared (e.g. videos that deal with business topics, such as 'career coaching', 'economy', 'investing', 'legal', 'marketing', 'personal finance', 'real estate', 'sales', 'web', 'business tips', and 'others'. These videos can help users in both communicative and cognitive use situations, as they are suitable for acquiring knowledge in terms of both reception and production (for example, they can be used to show the characteristics of a business presentation)).

2. Accessing videos, images, tables, graphs, etc., from a dictionary illustrates that free Internet dictionaries are also integrated into a 'language portal' in which users have access to an array of useful data. For example, in the Interactive Language Toolbox (ILT), a free single-access website offering various online resources designed for learners of French, Dutch, and English (Verlinde this volume), users can access Dave Volek's Business English course with free MP3 lessons and online activities, simulations, online listening, and information on more Business English courses. Consequently, the ILT does not work as a stand-alone product. Rather, it provides links to teaching materials, which

makes it an example of a 'language portal', in six different user-driven situations (Verlinde and Peeters, this volume).

3. Integration in a language portal indicates that free Internet dictionaries favour interconnectivity among users. In addition to the e-mail facility which allows users to contact editors through e-mail, some free Internet dictionaries allow users to build a kind of 'teaching/learning social network' (e.g. with Twitter), where users can instantly receive updated information. For example, in Your-Dictionary.com, the Twitter facility allows users to obtain updates via SMS texting, thus taking part in social networks (e.g. those dealing with 'words of the day', 'spellings', and 'grammar'), using the *RSS feed* file for obtaining the latest information, and connecting with web-based teaching resources (e.g. online glossaries) with which users of Business English can access data that is useful in both cognitive and communicative use situations.

4. Free Internet dictionaries also offer updated data, a must when we are dealing with specialized subjects. Potential users find it of the utmost importance that these e-tools include information indicating when the data was included, corrected, or updated, and so on. An example is the functions 'recent changes' and 'view history' in Wikipedia and Wiktionary. For example, on 23 April 2011, the revision history of **accountancy** in Wikipedia records the number of previous versions, as well as the revision history statistics and the main differences between them. It is interesting to observe that this term has had more than 2,736 revisions, which highlights the popularity of these e-tools and their frequent use by the logophile community (Santana and Wood 2009).

5. Free Internet dictionaries are also appropriate for overcoming the frequently discussed issue of the type of dictionary that is most suitable for students of Business English. Empirical studies on dictionary use have found discrepancies between the type of dictionary students really use and the type they say they would like to use. On the one hand, students report that they use bilingual dictionaries much more frequently than monolingual ones, regardless of the language level and the specific task. On the other hand, they report more satisfaction with the information found in monolingual learners' dictionaries, saying that their entries provide more detailed and precise information (Atkins and Varantola 1998, Cowie 1999). Although these findings seem contradictory, they are easily understandable if we assume that most Business English students lack lexicographical training and, therefore, take it for granted that they access route to unknown lexical items is more familiar in a bilingual dictionary than in a monolingual one, and that equivalents are more meaningful than definitions.

From a pedagogical perspective, however, the practice of relying on bilingual dictionaries should be regarded with a certain amount of caution, as it suffers from several weaknesses in the teaching and learning environment reported here. Dissatisfaction with current bilingual dictionaries is based on three main claims. First, the bilingual dictionary encourages the study of L2 via L1. Second, it is influential in promoting the illusion of isomorphism between languages through inter-linguistic lexical equivalents. Third, many specialized bilingual dictionaries do not offer adequate ways of eliminating meaning ambiguity and, moreover, they cannot be used in certain cognitive and communicative use situations (see Fuertes-Olivera and Arribas-Baño 2008 for a review). Free Internet dictionaries may help users overcome these drawbacks by allowing them to retrieve definitions and equivalents, as well as images, examples, and other useful data from the same homepage. For example, the search engine in Dictionary. com allows users to search in six tabs—'Dictionary', 'Thesaurus', 'Encyclopedia', 'Quotes', 'Flashcards', and 'Translator'—which are placed in the horizontal menu and retrieve different data. **Management** in the search engine retrieves the following: six English definitions (general and specialized), examples, collocations, pronunciation, etymology, related words, etc., under the tab 'Dictionary'; forty-eight definitions as well as graphs, synonyms, antonyms, etc., under the tab 'Thesaurus'; five long descriptions of the concept, and cross-references to related concepts under the tab 'Encyclopedia'; and equivalents in several languages under the tab 'Translator'. Recent proposals in the framework of function theory defend the construction of monolingual dictionaries (Bergenholtz 2011), an option that runs contrary to the wealth of information that is displayed in this dictionary aggregator. Its usability, therefore, might be restricted to students and instructors with dictionary culture, an idea that will be discussed in more detail in Section 19.5.

6. Free Internet dictionaries also incorporate gadgets that facilitate their use in several use situations. For example, Ultralingua.net offers vocabulary support for independent online reading (LeLoup and Ponterio 2005). It gives students interactive vocabulary help by turning every word into a link that opens a pop-up dictionary entry for that word. For instance, a Business English student reading *The Economist* can insert the URL for a magazine article and choose several options, e.g. 'English definitions', 'English to Spanish', etc., for the pop-up dictionary selection (Figure 19.5).

Ultralingua.net displays a copy of the article from *The Economist* (see Figure 19.6). All the words are now hypertext links and clicking on a word will open a pop-up window with vocabulary support in several forms: an English definition, a translation equivalent in several languages (French, Spanish, German, Italian, and Portuguese), videos, related articles, etc. For example, by clicking on **Eurozone debt crisis,** users can access a definition from Wikipedia, translation equivalents, four related articles, grammar data, and a video lasting more than seven minutes, explaining why the Eurozone has a debt crisis.

To sum up, this list of features shows that web-based systems, such as free Internet dictionaries, can be used for teaching and learning Business English. This may help to

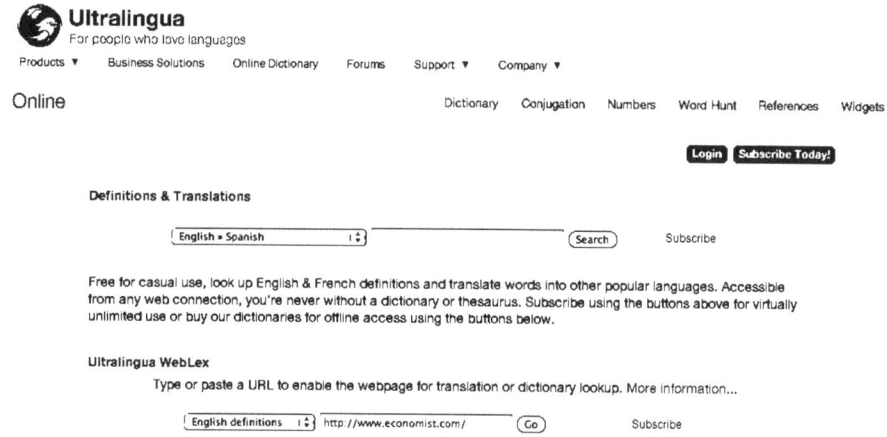

FIGURE 19.5 Ultralingua.net.

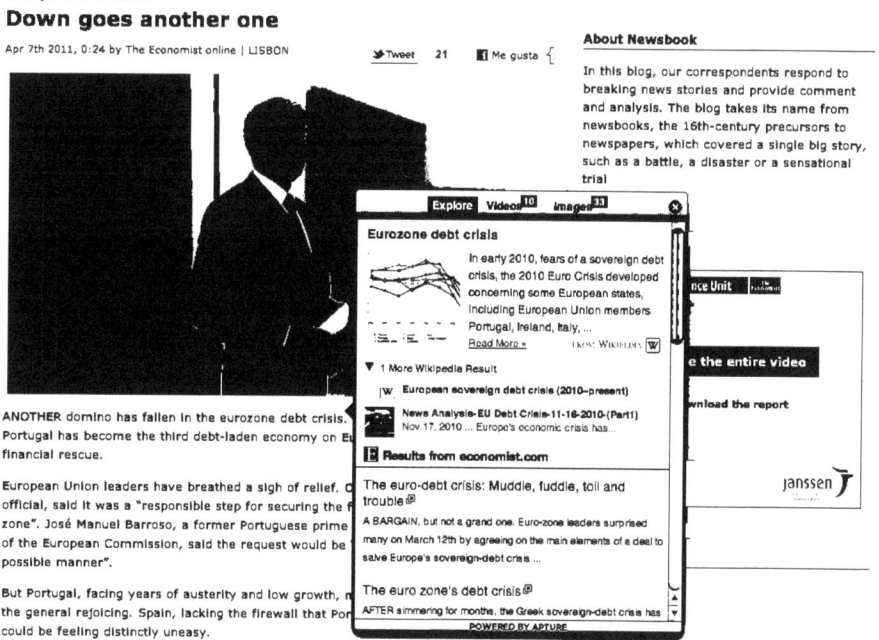

FIGURE 19.6 Screenshot for **eurozone debt crisis** taken from Ultralingua.net.

allay teachers' suspicions about their usability in a teaching and learning environment, an idea that can be reinforced by increasing the dictionary culture of their potential users. This could be done for instance, by making a comparison between printed Business English and free Internet dictionaries (as proposed in Section 19.4), as well as by listing some of the possible weaknesses of free Internet dictionaries in a specific extra-lexicographical environment and possible ways of overcoming them (see Section 19.5).

19.4 Printed and free Internet dictionaries for Spanish users of Business English in communicative use situations: a comparison

Tarp (2008: 45-50) enumerated several relevant communicative situations in which potential dictionary users may find themselves, and which are connected with the production, reception, and translation of texts. Hence, communication-oriented dictionaries should include data on the meanings of the words, and their pragmatic and stylistic properties, as well as their semantic relations and grammatical constraints. For the sake of simplicity, the analysis summarized in Table 19.1 will be restricted to the functions of production and reception of English business texts by learners.

From a methodological point of view, learners of Business English are identified as intermediate to advanced semi-experts who need dictionary data to read, write, and speak English in their work. Business English coursebooks and dictionaries are usually prepared in the same way for every potential user, irrespective of his or her local background, native language, and/or teaching tradition. In general, when these users need dictionary help for production and/or reception, they expect to retrieve short definitions written as full sentences using natural controlled language, polysemous and homonymous words, synonyms and antonyms, grammar data, collocations, examples, usage notes, pragmatic labels, and cross-references.

The analysis summarized in Table 19.1 shows the overall results for six reference tools, namely, three printed business dictionaries (the *New Oxford Business English Dictionary for Learners of English (OBED)*, the *Longman Business English Dictionary*, and Peter Collin's (2001) *Dictionary of Business*), two free Internet business dictionaries (BusinessDictionary.com and Glossarist), and one free dictionary aggregator (YourDictionary.com). These dictionaries were selected on the basis of their popularity. A random Google search of "Business Dictionary" retrieved them in the top positions, sometimes in connection with the bibliographical recommendations posted on the Internet by Business English instructors.

The comparison does not focus on the specifics of a single dictionary article, but on the analysis of five words (*asset, bank, payment, honour,* and *valuable*). A positive sign (+) is shown in Table 19.1 when the information category is found in at least one

TABLE 19.1. Information in the articles for *asset, bank, payment, honour,* and *valuable*

	OBED	Longman Business	Peter Collin Business	BusinessDictionary.com	Glossarist	YourDictionary.com
Pronunciation	+	+	+	+	−	+
Word class	+	+	+	−	−	+
Countability	+	+	−	−	−	+
Verb complementation	+	+	−	−	−	+
Verb preposition(s)	+	+	−	−	−	+
Usually singular	NA	NA	NA	NA	NA	NA
Irregular plural	NA	NA	NA	NA	NA	NA
Plural noun	+	+	+	+	+	+
Singular noun	+	+	+	+	+	+
American/English spelling	+	+	+	−	−	+
Synonym/antonym	+	−	−	−	−	+
Polysemy	+	+	+	+	−	+
Homonymy	+	+	+	+	−	+
Usage or pragmatic label	+	+	−	+	+	+
Semantically related words	+	+	−	+	+	+
Idioms	+	+	−	+	+	+
Style labels	NA	NA	NA	NA	NA	NA
Collocation	+	+	+	+	+	+
Example sentences	+	+	+	+	+	+
Definition as full sentence	Not always	+	+	+	+	Not always
Cross-references	+	+	Indirectly	+	+	+

+ = The information category is included in the dictionary at least in one of the words studied.
− = The information category is not included in the dictionary for any of the words studied.
NA = The information category is not applicable.

of the entries. The selection of three nouns (*asset, bank,* and *payment*), one verb (*honour*), and one adjective (*valuable*) is based on current research which has identified that around 90 per cent of the lemmata in Business English dictionaries consist of these three word classes, and that in the same dictionaries nouns are usually three to four times more frequent than verbs and adjectives (Andersen and Fuertes-Olivera 2009: 223, Fuertes-Olivera and Arribas-Baño 2008: 16-17).

From a pedagogical point of view, the analysis summarized in Table 19.1 shows two main results. First, free Internet dictionaries offer similar information categories to those of printed Business English dictionaries, perhaps because some of them, especially those included in dictionary aggregators, are printed dictionaries that have been uploaded to the Internet. Consequently, they can be used in teaching and learning environments with the same level of confidence as that traditionally afforded to the use of printed dictionaries in the area of teaching and learning a second language (Bogaards and Laufer 2004). Second, there are differences among the free Internet dictionaries used in the analysis. For instance, the free Internet dictionaries uploaded in dictionary aggregators such as YourDictionary.com retrieve much more data than needed. The next section focuses on these differences by elaborating on their possible pedagogical applications in a Spanish university context.

19.5 Pedagogical applications of free Internet dictionaries for teaching and learning Business English in Spanish universities

Spanish university students do not have a sound dictionary culture, as they are not usually taught what to look for and how to access data in dictionaries (Fuertes-Olivera and Arribas-Baño 2008). Free Internet dictionaries can help instructors of Business English overcome the drawbacks associated with a deficient dictionary culture by illustrating their usability during teaching hours, e.g. by illustrating the features presented in Section 19.3 and the lexicographic data they offer, which is similar to the data contained in printed Business English dictionaries. Instructors can also increase students' dictionary culture by commenting on some of the main weaknesses of free Internet dictionaries and possible ways to overcome them (Nesi, this volume).

The first weakness relates to the fact that a search in free Internet dictionaries retrieves so much data that they can easily lead to information suffocation, i.e. the user retrieves several dictionary articles and has to identify which one, if any, is likely to assist them in their particular use situation. This is especially true for dictionary aggregators. For example, a search for **asset** in YourDictionary.com retrieves entries from: *Webster's New World Collegiate; The American Heritage Dictionary of the English Language; Roget's II The New Thesaurus; Acronyms, Initialisms & Abbreviations Dictionary; Webster's New World Finance and Investment Dictionary; Wall*

Street Words: An A to Z Guide to Investment Terms for Today's Investors; *Webster's New World Law Dictionary*; and *Webster's New World Dictionary of Quotations*.

This can be overcome by giving users a handout with comments on three key aspects of free Internet dictionaries, as shown in Boxes 1, 2, and 3. The combined use of a specific business dictionary (Box 3) and a general dictionary (Box 2) offers more focused data than the exclusive use of either a printed Business English dictionary (Box 1) or Internet dictionary aggregators. With the data retrieved from the general dictionary *Encarta MSN* and the business dictionary BusinessDictionary.com, users can increase their disciplinary knowledge, professional practice, and discursive competence. For example, they can understand the gist of the concept, as the definitions indicate that there are tangible and intangible assets, that assets are listed on a firm's balance sheet, that there are different types of assets (e.g. physical, intellectual, and enforceable claim, etc.), that assets can be bought and sold, and that they can be human or non-human. In the definition given in the *New Oxford Business English Dictionary for Learners of English*, the conceptual (i.e. encyclopedic) data are less precise and partly misleading, as the concept **asset** can also be applied to humans (for example, **human asset management**).

The data retrieved in the *Encarta MSN* and BusinessOnline.com illustrate the characterization of **asset** as a semi-term, that is, a term that has different meanings in different fields (e.g. in general English, accounting English, and legal English). It has been shown that semi-terms always pose difficulties in LSP situations, perhaps because they can refer to very different concepts (Alcaraz Varó 2000). Commenting on these aspects will teach students how to handle them, for example, by indicating that their conceptual domain is very specific in accounting and less specific in general English. This information is also missing from the *New Oxford Business English*

BOX 1: **Asset In The** *New Oxford Business English Dictionary For Learners Of English*

* asset /ˈæset/ *noun* [C, usually pl.]

    SEE ALSO: capital asset, chargeable ~, charge on ~, circulating ~, current ~, financial ~, fixed ~, etc

    a thing of value that a person or a company owns, such as money or property or the right to receive payment of a debt: *The group has total assets of € 1.2 billion.* ◊ *The vehicle is recorded as an asset in the company accounts.* ◊ *Foreign companies were prevented from buying local media assets* (= media businesses). ◊ *(figurative) Our staff are our most valuable asset.* → LIABILITY.

    ⊕ *to have/hold/own/possess assets • to acquire/buy/dispose of/increase/reduce/sell assets • to record/show sth as an asset • to freeze/release/unfreeze assets.*

BOX 2: **Asset in *Encarta MSN***

a. Dictionary

asset	asset (image of a loudspeaker) + asset
asset acquisition	as-set [á sèt]
asset-backed security	noun (*plural* as-sets) Definition
asset-based lending	1. somebody or something useful: somebody or something that is useful and contributes to the success of something
	• *Good health is a great asset.*
asset conversion loan	2. Valuable thing: a property to which a value can be assigned
asset coverage	plural noun assets
asset demand	Definition:
asset financing	1. owned items: the property that is owned by a person or organization
asset for asset swap	2. LAW seizable property: the property of a person that can be taken by law for the settlement of debts or that forms part of a dead person's state.
asset play	3. ACCOUNTING balance sheet items: the items on a balance sheet that constitute the total value of an organization
asset pricing model	[Mid-16ᵗʰ century. Via Anglo-Norman *assetz* "sufficient goods" (to settle an estate) < Latin *ad satis* "sufficiency"]
asset protection trust	
asset-stripping asset swap	

b. Thesaurus

asset (n)

Synonyms: advantage, strength, benefit, plus, plus point, positive feature, quality, skill, talent, ability, qualification, power, endowment, boon, blessing, resource

Antonym: drawback

Synonyms: possession, property, resource, holding

c. Translation

English – Spanish

FINANCIAL activo MASCULINE

She's an asset to the company es un gran valor para la compañía

English – French

['æset] FINANCE actif MASCULINE; FIGURATIVE atout MASCULINE

English – German

['æset] trade and industry

Vermögenswert

figuratively : Nutzen Vorteil

he's a real asset to the team er ist wirklich ein Gewinn für die Mannschaft

English – Italian
FINANCE attivo MASCULINE
FIGURATIVE: THING vantaggio MASCULINE
PERSON elemento MASCULINE prezioso
Spanish – English
No translation result for "asset"
French – English
No translation result for "asset"
German – English
No translation result for "asset"
Italian – English
No translation result for "asset"

BOX 3: **Asset in *BusinessDictionary.com***

Definition:

Something valuable that an entity owns, benefits from, or has use of, in generating income. In accounting, an asset is something an entity has acquired or purchased, and which has money value (its cost, book value, market value, or residual value). An asset can be (1) something physical, such as cash, machinery, inventory, land and building, (2) an enforceable claim against others, such as accounts receivable, (3) right, such as copyright, patent, trademark, or (4) an assumption, such as goodwill. Assets shown on their owner's balance sheet are usually classified according to the ease with which they can be converted into cash. See also intangible assets and tangible assets.

Questions related to "*asset*"

1. "Assets under management" / "Investments as principal"
2. Fixed and Total Asset ratios
3. How to calculate the foreign exchange gain/loss on the foreign monetary assets?
4. I want all the accounting related terms
5. debt ratio .45, current 1.25. Liabilities $875, sales $5,780. profit 9.5%, ROE18.5% What is the firm's net fixed assets?

Interested in learning more about "*asset*"? Click here
Business Tips
How to Win a Standards Battle
The keys to winning a standardization battle are the ownership of assets; specifically, the installed base, the intellectual property rights, superior ability to innovate, first-mover advantages, supe . . . Read more

More Tips				
(1) Things to Consider When Forming a Partnership				
asset is ..... in the subjects	Mentioned in these definitions	Mentioned in these terms	Nearby Terms *assessment bond*	Popular 'Accounting & Auditing' Terms
Accounting & Auditing	*clear title levy*	*asset rationalization*	*assessment insurance*	
Banking, Commerce, Credit, & Finance	*corporate logo*	*asset financing*	*assessment of tax*	*accounting*
Investing	*historical cost*	*total asset turnover*	*assessment ratio*	*payment terms*
...an essential investing term.	*asset turnover ratio*	*short term asset*	*assessor*	*accounting concepts financial management*
...#80 on our list of the most popular terms	*tangible common equity*	*asset availability*	*asset*	*marginal benefit*
	financial capital	*asset impairment accounting*	*asset acquisition strategy*	*letter of credit (L/C) asset*
	physical deterioration	*asset-led marketing*	*asset allocation*	*revenue*
	inflation accounting	*asset approach*	*asset allocation fund*	*pro forma invoice*
	chief knowledge officer (CKO)	*intellectual asset*	*asset approach*	*fixed cost*
		average current assets	*asset availability*	

Related Videos:

1. Accounting Income Summary Account
2. Accounting Classic Balance Sheet
3. Account GAAP Guidance

Dictionary for Learners of English, which includes only a very general definition without subject field labels.

As discussed above, free Internet dictionaries allow users to retrieve external data, e.g. videos, as well as to contact editors and take part in social networks. For example, BusinessDictionary.com provides users with videos, questions related to the term, equivalents in several languages, links to external Internet texts, information on how to form a collocation (a word partnership), and a 'dialogue box' which they can use to ask questions.

The second weakness is concerned with the editorial and authorship policy of free Internet dictionaries. Lim and Kwon (2010) indicated that some American universities do not allow their students to quote from free Internet dictionaries and encyclopedias when they submit assignments. Research has spotted some important flaws in collective free multi-language dictionaries, such as Wiktionary (Fuertes-Olivera 2009, Hanks, this volume). A possible solution to this weakness is to explain to potential users what authoritative sources are and what they mean from a lexicographical point of view. For example, YourDictionary.com and Wikipedia include the source and date of the data retrieved as well as the subject labels and updates, which helps users to assess their reliability.

Finally, the most important weakness of free Internet dictionaries may be the philosophy according to which they are usually constructed, which runs contrary to recent lexicographical practices aiming to offer monofunctional or individualized access (see Section 19.2 above). This means that free Internet dictionaries do not favour quick and easy access to needs-adapted data. This flaw can be partially circumvented by training potential users with regard to the main characteristics of communication-oriented and cognition-oriented business dictionaries (Andersen and Fuertes-Olivera 2009), and by offering them training on the type of information they can obtain to satisfy their primary (i.e. function-related) and secondary (i.e. use-related) user needs. For example, information on the meaning of a term is a primary need and information on the orthography of a term a secondary need when reading a Business English text (Tarp 2008: 56–8).

The information categories recorded in Table 19.1 can initially be used for training users of Business English about the information they contain and its appropriateness for the reception and production of Business English texts. Subsequently, users can be provided with details of specific aspects by retrieving a dictionary article (such as **asset**) and commenting on the kind of data they can obtain in each tag (with illustrations such as those recorded in Boxes 1 to 3, above). For instance, if someone consults the data retrieved for **asset** when there is a reception problem, we can inform them that the definitions usually indicate the meaning of the term, whereas the indication of part of speech and plural form relates to how the term is used in a text (e.g. only in the plural).

Similarly, we can point out that if users have a reception problem concerning word combinations or idioms, etc., they can consult the word combinations by means of the hyperlinks on the left side of *Encarta MSN*, which are offered as lemmata for each of the many word combinations which may generate such problems. This solution is user-friendly in terms of providing quick and easy access to the place where the needs of the foreign learner, in terms of reception problems relating to English word combinations, may be satisfied. For example, the hyperlink of, say, **asset coverage**, goes directly to the article where a short explanation of the word combination is provided. As an added bonus, the articles are well structured, in that the dictionary article is drawn up according to the principle of search fields, has a friendly layout, and the use of meaning discriminators in several formats (typically, numbers and superordinates), together with synonyms and antonyms, helps users to place the term in its conceptual realm, facilitating its use in language production.

Briefly, then, I feel that a combination of the two dictionaries illustrated in Boxes 2 and 3 has more advantages than drawbacks, particularly when compared to the articles in printed business dictionaries such as the *New Oxford Business English Dictionary for Learners of English*. My conclusion, then, on the usability of free Internet dictionaries is that they can be reliable teaching and learning tools and that their usability is highly related to the type of dictionary culture of the potential users, which will increase as long as such tools are accessed critically. For example, the theoretical and practical framework advocated here may be a starting point in our quest for using free Internet materials in the multifaceted situations where instructors and students of Business English perform their daily activities.

19.6 Conclusion

This chapter has adopted a functional, user-oriented approach to lexicography. The user-based orientation has led lexicographers to regard lexicography as an independent science with three basic angles or dimensions: *access*, *users*, and *data*. The analysis of free Internet dictionaries carried out in this chapter has discussed these three angles and has found that free Internet dictionaries are not constructed for solving the specific needs a specific user has in a specific use situation, nor are they at the forefront of e-lexicography. Although these drawbacks cannot be forgotten, I have made a case for considering these Internet dictionaries useful for teaching and learning Business English.

This position can be defended on two grounds. First, free Internet dictionaries are web-based systems whose usability in teaching/learning environments will increase as websites improve and potential users upgrade their dictionary culture. This might involve an explanation of the access routes and possibilities of such dictionaries, with comments on the data that can be retrieved and its transposition to an extra-lexicographical situation. Second, free Internet dictionaries can be helpful as supporting reference tools. For example, if lexicographers are constructing an English accounting dictionary to help users in a cognitive use situation (i.e. when users need to gain knowledge about accounting), they can hyperlink this dictionary to web-based systems such as BusinessDictionary.com, and thus provide access to texts such as 'Small Business Accounting Practices' (retrieved on 3 October 2011) which explain the existence of different accounting practices, depending on the size of the company. This text is very useful for knowing which accounting documents must be prepared by small and medium-size enterprises.

Furthermore, following recent holistic pragmatic approaches to ESP (e.g. Chan 2009), the usability of web-based systems such as free Internet dictionaries may also be connected to the explanation of lexicographical data and their usability for over-coming possible weaknesses in extra-lexicographical social situations such as teaching and learning Business English in the Spanish university context. These have been discussed in this chapter, in which several general assumptions about the characteristics of free Internet dictionaries, together with a comparison of printed and Internet reference tools, have been made. The results lead me to conclude that these dictionaries can help teachers and learners of Business English and are, therefore, appropriate tools for satisfying users' needs in such a situation.

Dictionaries

1 Paper dictionaries

Collin, Peter (2001). *Dictionary of Business.* Third Edition. Peter Collin Publishing.
Murgoski, Zoze (2008). *Dictionary of Business and Law English–Macedonian, Macedonian–English.* Skopje: Avtor.
Parkinson, D. (assisted by J. Noble) (2005). *New Oxford Business English Dictionary for Learners of English* (OBED 2005). Oxford: Oxford University Press.
Summers, D. (2007). *Longman Business English Dictionary.* New Edition. Harlow: Longman.
Valverde, A. (ed.) (1995). *Tesauro ISOC de Economía.* Madrid: CESIC.

2 Online dictionaries

Base lexicale du français: http://ilt.kuleuven.be/blf/ (last accessed 15 April 2011).
BusinessDictionary.com: http://www.businessdictionary.com/ (last accessed 15 April 2011).
Dictionary.com: http://dictionary.reference.com/ (last accessed 15 April 2011).
Encarta MSN: http://encarta.msn.com/encnet/features/dictionary/dictionaryhome.aspx (last accessed 15 April 2011).
Glossarist: http://www.glossarist.com/gsearch.asp (last accessed 15 April 2011).
Interactive Language Toolbox: http://www.kuleuven.be/english/ (last accessed 4 October 2011).

Nielsen, Sandro, Lise Mourier, and Henning Bergenholtz (2010). *English Accounting Dictionary*. http://www.ordbogen.com (last accessed 15 April 2011).

Nielsen, Sandro, Lise Mourier, Henning Bergenholtz, Pedro A. Fuertes-Olivera, Pablo Gordo Gómez, Marta Niño Amo, Ángel de los Rios Rodicio, Ángeles Sastre Ruano, Sven Tarp, and Marisol Velasco Sacristán (2009). *El Diccionario Inglés–Español de Contabilidad*. http://www.accountingdictionary.dk/regn/gbsp/regngbsp_index.php (last accessed 15 April 2011).

YourDictionary.com: http://www.yourdictionary.com/ (last accessed 15 April 2011).

Ultralingua.net: http://www.ultralingua.com/onlinedictionary/index.html (last accessed 15 April 2011).

Wikipedia: http://en.wikipedia.org/wiki/Main_Page (last accessed 15 April 2011).

Wiktionary: http://en.wiktionary.org/wiki/Wiktionary:Main_Page (last accessed 15 April 2011).

Online dictionary use: Key findings from an empirical research project

CAROLIN MÜLLER-SPITZER, ALEXANDER KOPLENIG,
AND ANTJE TÖPEL

I have been in rooms with data, and listened very carefully.
They never said a word.

Milford Wolpoff

20.1 Introduction

Until now, there has been very little research into the use of online dictionaries. In contrast, the market for online dictionaries is increasing both for academic lexicography and for commercial lexicography, while sales figures for printed reference works are in continual decline. This has led to a demand for reliable empirical information on how online dictionaries are actually being used and how they could be made more user-friendly. In this context, the need for the scientific development of a user-adaptive interface on the basis of general lexicographical resources is the subject of much discussion among internationally renowned experts from various disciplines, such as academic lexicography (cf. Verlinde and Binon 2010, Trap-Jensen 2010a, Müller-Spitzer 2008), commercial lexicography (cf. Rundell 2009), and meta-lexicography (cf. Tarp 2009a, Anderson and Nielsen 2009: 360, Wiegand 1998: 259).

Many researchers have called for a more intensive focus on empirical research to establish a better understanding of specific user needs (see Atkins and Varantola 1997, Hartmann 2000, Hulstijn and Atkins 1998: 16), because research on electronic dictionary use is "still in its infancy" (Nesi 2000a: 845). Loucky reached a similar conclusion for online dictionaries in relation to the current state of knowledge on the dictionary usage of Japanese teachers of English, because "even less available are any studies of online web dictionary use" (2005: 390). This situation has not changed significantly in more recent years and "the dictionary users and their actions are to some extent still unknown, especially in Internet lexicography" (Simonsen 2011: 77). Even the latest special issue of the *International Journal of Lexicography* "Studies in Dictionary Use: Recent Developments" only contains one study focusing solely on electronic dictionaries (Tono 2011), although several studies of varying length have been published in the last twenty years.

The project 'User-adaptive access and cross-references in elexiko (BZVelexiko)'[1] aims to make a substantial contribution to closing this research gap. BZVelexiko is an externally funded joint research project at the Institute for German Language (IDS) in Mannheim. For a period of three years, a group of researchers from a variety of academic backgrounds (lexicography, linguistics, and social sciences) have undertaken several extensive studies on the use of online dictionaries, using established methods of empirical social research. The main objective of this chapter is to report on the key findings of two online surveys launched in 2010. The aim of these studies was to clarify general questions of online dictionary use (e.g. which electronic devices are used to access online dictionaries) and to identify different needs for online dictionaries.

The chapter is structured as follows. Section 20.2 reviews a number of empirical studies that have examined the use of electronic dictionaries. Section 20.3 describes the general design of the two online surveys and the methodology used to analyse the data, and provides detailed information about the participants. Section 20.4 discusses the major findings of the two surveys. The chapter ends with some concluding remarks in Section 20.5.

20.2 Research on electronic dictionary use

The majority of studies of the use of electronic dictionaries focus on multilingual, mainly bilingual, dictionaries (e.g. Leffa 1993, Corris *et al.* 2000, Selva and Verlinde 2002, De Schryver and Joffe 2004, De Schryver *et al.* 2006, Laufer and Levitzky-Aviad 2006, Chen 2011, Simonsen 2011). Further studies aim at comparing bilingual dictionaries with monolingual ones (e.g. Aust *et al.* 1993, Hill and Laufer 2003, Petrylaitė *et al.* 2008, Lew and Doroszewska 2009). This is due to the fact that most of the studies were concerned with the effectiveness of dictionary usage for vocabulary acquisition and text comprehension (e.g. Leffa 1993, Laufer and Hill 2000, Laufer 2000, Lew and Doroszewska 2009, Chen 2010, Dziemianko 2010). The majority of them confirmed that looking up different types of lexical information can enhance vocabulary retention rates. To our knowledge, the only usage studies that focus solely

---

[1] www.using-dictionaries.info.

on monolingual electronic dictionaries are Bergenholtz and Johnsen (2005), Haß (2005), and Tono (2011).

In addition to the comparison of bilingual and monolingual dictionaries, many research projects have contrasted electronic dictionaries with printed ones (e.g. Leffa 1993, Aust *et al.* 1993, Laufer 2000, Nesi 2000b, Corris *et al.* 2000, Tono 2000, Winkler 2001, Boonmoh and Nesi 2008, Petrylaitė *et al.* 2008, Dziemanko 2010, Chen 2010). The most important results of those studies are that, compared to printed diction-aries, electronic dictionaries are used more often and provide faster access to the required information. Many studies have also emphasized the positive attitude of respondents towards electronic dictionaries, resulting in a higher level of satisfaction by dictionary users (see Dziemianko, this volume).

Most existing empirical research into electronic dictionary use deals with docu-menting and analysing user behaviour through the analysis of log files. In some cases, the results are used to improve the electronic dictionary, for example by adding entries for lemmas that are frequently searched for, but were not originally included in the dictionary (De Schryver and Joffe 2004: 191).

There are only a few studies that have specifically evaluated the use of online dictionaries (e.g. Selva and Verlinde 2002, De Schryver and Joffe 2004, Bergenholtz and Johnsen 2005, Haß 2005, De Schryver *et al.* 2006, Petrylaitė *et al.* 2008, Bank 2010). This is due to the fact that online dictionaries are only one type of electronic dictionary. It is worth mentioning that scientists in the Asian region frequently conduct empirical studies into the use of pocket electronic dictionaries (e.g. Boon-moh and Nesi 2008, Tono 2009, Chen 2010), because this type of dictionary is especially popular in Japan and neighbouring countries.

Regarding the type of data collection, Simonsen (2009, 2011) and Tono (2011) conducted eye-tracking studies to observe dictionary usage behaviour. The studies by Haß (2005), Sánchez Ramos (2005), Boonmoh and Nesi (2008), and Petrylaitė *et al.* (2008) used a survey design. Several other studies used additional (direct) observa-tional methods (e.g. Aust *et al.* 1993, Tono 2000, Dziemanko 2010). However, data collection in empirical research on electronic dictionary use is dominated by the analysis of log files. Over a long period of time, digital traces of the dictionary users' consultation behaviour (e.g. number of searches, search terms) are collected and stored in log files, and then analysed statistically (e.g. De Schryver and Joffe 2004, Bergenholtz and Johnsen 2005, De Schryver *et al.* 2006, Verlinde and Binon 2010). The great advantage of collecting log files is that it is unobtrusive. In general, an unobtrusive method can be understood as a method of data collection without the knowledge of the participant, whereas obtrusive measurement means that the researcher has "to intrude in the research context" (Trochim 2006). Interviews and laboratory tests are also social interactions between the respondents and the researcher, and so respondents try to present themselves in a favourable light; this is called 'social desirability bias' (Diekmann 2002: 382–6). Furthermore, filling in a questionnaire or taking part in a laboratory test can be exhausting or boring, which can also lead to biased results.

It is impossible to answer important lexicographical questions with log file analyses alone.[2] For example, Hartmann (1989: 103) hypothesizes that "[d]ifferent user groups have different needs", therefore,"[t]he design of any dictionary cannot be considered realistic unless it takes into account the likely needs of various users in various situations" (p. 104). Of course, log files do not contain individual information about the dictionary user, such as his or her academic background, age, usage experience, and language skills. It is reasonable to assume that these factors influence the dictionary usage process (cf. Lew 2011b). From a methodological point of view, the current state of knowledge of electronic dictionary usage is more limited than that of printed dictionary usage (e.g. Ripfel and Wiegand 1988, Tono 1998), and this in turn reduces the usability of the findings.

As mentioned above, analysing log files can show which headwords are the most frequently searched for, and which types of information are most frequently accessed. However, this knowledge is not sufficient to design a user-adapted access, because much of the necessary information on relevant key variables is missing (for example, what are the most important characteristics that determine the quality and usefulness of an online dictionary). It is also important to know whether different user groups (e.g. linguists or translators) have different preferences for such characteristics, or whether, in a given usage situation (e.g. text production or text reception), a special type of data presentation or alternative ways of presenting word entries in an online dictionary is preferred by the users and why. Again, it is important to know whether different user groups (e.g. native speakers vs. L2 speakers) have different preferences regarding the types and ways of presenting data in online dictionaries.

Since very little data relating to these questions is available,[3] user demands and preferences have not so far been taken into consideration in the design and development of an electronic dictionary or the presentation of information. Verlinde and Binon (2010) argued that it would be better to combine different types of data, in order to make dictionaries more user-friendly, or to construct an adaptive user interface:

[I]t will almost be impossible to conceive smart adaptive interfaces for dictionaries, unless more detailed data combining tracking data and other information as age or language level for instance, would eventually infirm this conclusion. (Verlinde and Binon 2010: 1150)

---

[2] In addition, many countries (e.g. Germany) have very strict laws governing data privacy. For example, collecting individual data (e.g. the IP address, the URLs of the referring web page or of outward links followed from the current page) without the user's agreement can be a legal issue. Thus, it is not possible to identify individual search patterns.

[3] One exception is Haß's (2005) study. In her study, she asked the respondents to rate the language of the user interface of the online dictionary elexiko. Furthermore, Simonsen (2009) investigated what types of information presentation were preferred by the respondents.

20.3 Research background

Within the framework of the BZVelexiko project, we conducted two online surveys in 2010. The design of these surveys is described in Section 20.3.1; Section 20.3.2 provides some details about the participants, while Section 20.3.3 provides information about the basic structure used to analyse the data.

20.3.1 *Survey design*

The first study investigated general questions about the use of online dictionaries, such as the activities during which online dictionaries are typically used, the occasions for using online dictionaries, the social situations in which online dictionaries are consulted (see Tarp 2009a: 19), and different user demands. The survey was made available in German and in English because of the intended international target group. It was designed using the online survey software UNIPARK as a web-based survey that took approximately 20 to 25 minutes to complete. It consisted of six core elements: an introduction (language selection, general survey conditions), a set of questions on Internet usage (e.g. frequency, duration, self-assessment), a set of questions on the use of printed dictionaries (e.g. types of dictionary used), a set of questions on the use of online dictionaries (e.g. types of dictionary used, devices used, activities, usage occasions, user demands), a set of questions on demographics (e.g. sex, age, occupation), and a conclusion (thanks, prize draw details).

In order to design a survey that was easy for everybody to understand, great emphasis was placed on the implementation of several examples and illustrative transitional paragraphs. For example, all the basic terms were explained fully (e.g. "by online dictionary, we mean a dictionary that can be accessed via the internet as opposed to other electronic dictionaries, such as CD-ROM-based dictionaries or dictionaries which can be used on a pocket PC"). The survey was activated from 9 February 2010 to 14 March 2010.

Drawing on the results of the first study, the second one examined more closely whether the respondents had differentiated views on individual aspects of the criteria rated in the first study. For example, "reliability of content" was the criterion that the majority of participants in the first study rated as the most important criterion of a good online dictionary. In the second study, we tried to determine precisely what the respondents meant by "reliability of content". The purpose of the second survey was mainly to collect empirical data about the respondents' evaluation of different visual representations (views) of the same content. It consisted of seven core elements: an introduction (language selection, general survey conditions), a set of questions on the criteria rated as most important for a good online dictionary in the first study, a set of questions on the criteria rated on average as unimportant for a good online dictionary in the first study, a set of questions on different search functions of online dictionaries, a set of questions on different visual representations (views) of the same content, a set of questions on demographics (e.g. sex, age, occupation), and a conclusion (thanks, prize draw details).

Using the same methodology as the first study, the second study was designed as an online survey that took approximately 20 to 30 minutes to complete and was conducted both in German and in English. All other general conditions, such as the construction of the survey and its distribution, were also in accordance with the first study. The survey was activated from 11 August 2010 to 16 September 2010.

Both surveys were distributed through multiple channels such as 'Forschung erleben' ('experience research'), which is an online platform for the distribution of empirical surveys run and maintained by the chairs of social psychology at the University of Mannheim and visited by students of various disciplines, mailing lists (including the Linguist List (a list for students of linguistics and linguists all over the world hosted by the Eastern Michigan University), the Euralex List (a list from the European Association of Lexicography), and U-Forum (a German mailing list for professional translators), and various disseminators (e.g. lecturers at educational institutions)).

20.3.2 *Participants*

A total of 684 participants completed the first survey and 390 the second survey. For a better understanding of possible user requirements, participants were asked about their academic and professional background. Data on demographic characteristics was also collected. Tables 20.1 and 20.2 summarize the results.

20.3.3 *Methodology used to analyse the data*

Each of the following subsections is divided into four parts: (1) an introduction section framing the research questions, (2) a method section explaining the exact procedures,

TABLE 20.1. **Demographics—academic and professional background**

	First survey (N = 684)		Second survey (N = 390)	
	Yes	No	Yes	No
Linguist	54.82%	45.18%	46.39%	53.61%
Translator	41.96%	58.04%	37.89%	62.11%
Student of linguistics	41.08%	58.92%	37.89%	62.11%
English/German teacher (with English/German as mother tongue)	11.55%	88.45%	11.37%	88.63%
EFL/DAF teacher	16.52%	83.48%	10.82%	89.18%
English/German learner	13.89%	86.11%	9.04%	90.96%

TABLE 20.2. Demographics—personal background

	First survey (N = 684)	Second survey (N = 390)
Language version of the questionnaire	• English: 46.35% • German: 53.65%	• English: 47.69% • German: 52.31%
Sex	• Female: 63.29% • Male: 36.71%	• Female: 60.52% • Male: 39.48%
Age	• Mean: 37.97 • SD: 14.29	• Mean: 39.81 • SD: 14.70
Command of English/German	• Mother tongue: 64.33% • Very good: 27.78% • Good: 6.14% • Fair: 1.46% • Poor: 0.29% • None: 0.00%	• Mother tongue: 69.77% • Very good: 24.81% • Good: 3.62% • Fair: 1.81% • Poor: 0.00% • None: 0.00%

(3) a result section presenting and illustrating the results, and (4) a discussion section interpreting the results in relation to the research question. The results sections include statistical details about how the results are calculated in order to make them comprehensible. All statistical coefficients are included in the footnotes. The results are summarized concisely and interpreted without statistical terminology in the discussion section in a way that is easier to understand. We decided to present our findings according to the so-called IMRAD structure (abbreviation for introduction, method, results, and discussion; see Day 1989), which is the usual norm for the structure of a scientific paper in the empirical social sciences and the natural sciences. The writing style is somewhat different from writing in the humanities, but it is both accurate and comprehensible and—by summarizing the research process—it systematically informs the reader about the most important details. Therefore, the reader is able to reproduce and criticize the reported findings.

To determine whether there are any group differences, we used some of the demographic data in each subsection, For example, the analysis of the individual ratings of the criteria of a good online dictionary (Section 20.4.3) was combined with demographic data in order to analyse whether different user groups have different needs. Thus, a remark like "there are significant differences between linguists and non-linguists" means that the differences in the proportions of respondents who answered 'yes' or 'no' to the question of their linguistic background (see Tables 20.1 and 20.2) is unlikely to have arisen by chance. The data analysis was carried out using STATA 11, except for the two-step cluster analysis (Section 20.4.3), which was performed with SPSS 16.

20.4 Key findings

In this section, we present the key findings of our empirical studies. By focusing on some of the most important results, several issues of practical relevance for electronic lexicography are presented. First, we analyse which electronic devices are used to access online dictionaries (Section 20.4.1). Second, we investigate which way of presenting word entries in online dictionaries with a detailed microstructure is best suited to users' needs (Section 20.4.2). Third, we describe how users rate different characteristics of online dictionaries (Section 20.4.3). And lastly, we examine how users form evaluative judgements about innovative features of online dictionaries (Section 20.4.4).

20.4.1 *Research Question 1: devices used to access online dictionaries*

Unlike traditional printed dictionaries, electronic dictionaries can be accessed on different devices, such as notebooks, personal computers, mobile phones, smartphones, and personal digital assistants (PDAs). From the user's point view, this device independence allows maximum flexibility and efficiency. When designing an online dictionary, however, a practical problem arises, since the electronic dictionary has to be capable of adapting to different screen sizes. The rationale for this requirement is clear: the information must be readable both on a small screen (e.g. on a mobile phone), and on a big one (e.g. a PC). Because the implementation of this function can be costly, it is first necessary to enquire as to which devices are most frequently employed with electronic dictionaries.

This information, in turn, can be used to decide if it is worthwhile creating an entry structure that is capable of adapting to different screen layouts, or which screen size should be given priority in design decisions. Furthermore, in relation to the design of a user-adaptive interface, it is interesting to know if there are any differences in the use of devices between different user groups. For example, is it reasonable to assume that younger users tend to consult online dictionaries on more devices than older users, since the former group is more familiar with new technologies and devices?

To summarize, the research questions relating to this issue were: first, which devices are used to access online dictionaries; second, which of these devices is used most often to access online dictionaries; third, whether there are any differences in the use of devices for different consultation purposes (private vs. professional); and last, if there are any differences in the use of devices between different user groups.

METHOD

Among other questions, respondents in the first survey who indicated that they had already used an online dictionary were asked the following two questions:

- On which device/s have you used online dictionaries?
- Which device do you use most often to access online dictionaries?

TABLE 20.3. Distribution of devices used to access online dictionaries

Device	Frequency	Percent of cases
Notebook/Netbook	499	75.59
Desktop computer	613	91.63
Mobile phone, smartphone	72	10.76
PDA	23	3.44
Other	7	1.05
Total	1214	181.46

Both questions had the following response options: (1) notebook/netbook, (2) desktop computer, (3) mobile phone, smartphone, (4) PDA, or (5) other.[4] The first question was designed as a multiple response question ("Please tick all the devices on which you have already used online dictionaries"). The second question only had a single response list ("Please tick only the device which you use most often to access online dictionaries").

To test if the consultation purpose is relevant in this context, respondents were asked if they used online dictionaries for private or professional purposes, by selecting one of the following response options: private only, mainly private, both private and professional, mainly professional, professional only.

RESULTS

Descriptive results   A detailed distribution of respondents' answers to the first question ("On which device/s have you used online dictionaries") is shown in Table 20.3. The majority of the respondents (86.25%) indicated that they had only used an online dictionary on a desktop computer (91.63%) or on a notebook/netbook (75.59%). Only a minority of the respondents (13.75%) selected (at least) one of the other response alternatives.

In total, 99.85% of the respondents indicated that they had already used online dictionaries on a notebook/netbook and/or on a desktop computer. Only one respondent claimed that she had only used an online dictionary on a mobile phone/smartphone and on another device ("iPod") so far.

The distribution of responses to the second question ("Which device do you use most often to access online dictionaries?") was quite similar (Table 20.4). The vast majority (98.95%) of respondents most frequently use an online dictionary on a desktop computer (56.50%) or on a notebook/netbook (42.45%). In what follows, only the first question will be further analysed, since only a small minority (1.05%) of the respondents indicated that they most frequently used online dictionaries on devices other than a notebook/netbook or a desktop computer.

---

[4] All the respondents who choose this option were asked to specify their choice in a text box.

TABLE 20.4. **Distribution of devices most often used to access online dictionaries**

Device	Frequency	Percent (%)
Notebook/Netbook	284	42.45
Desktop computer	378	56.50
Mobile phone, smartphone	4	0.60
PDA	2	0.30
Other	1	0.15
Total	669	100

TABLE 20.5. **Distribution of device usage as a function of language version**

	Language version			
Device usage (%)	German	English	Total	X^2 / p-value[a]
Notebook/Netbook	80.91	69.17	74.59	12.090/ 0.003
Desktop computer	90.29	92.78	91.63	1.340 / 1.000
Mobile phone, smartphone	5.50	15.28	10.76	16.547 / 0.000
PDA	0.97	5.56	3.44	10.528 / 0.006
Other	0.65	1.39	1.05	0.883 / 0.100
Total	184.67	178.86	181.45	

[a] p values (last column) are Bonferroni adjusted.

Subgroup analyses   There were no significant distributional differences between linguists and non-linguists,[5] or between translators and non-translators.[6] However, there were highly significant differences regarding the language version of the survey chosen by the respondents.[7] It is worth noting that respondents in the English language version selected devices other than a notebook/netbook or a desktop computer, such as mobile phones/smartphones or PDAs, significantly more often than respondents to the German language version (see Table 20.5).[8] To analyse this relationship further, we generated a binary variable, named SMALL SCREEN, indicating whether a respondent selected at least one device other than a notebook/netbook or a desktop computer. Some 13.75% of the respondents clicked at least one of the other three alternative devices indicating that they had already used an online dictionary on a small-screen device, while the rest (86.25%) only selected notebook/netbook and/or desktop computer. Some 19.72% of the respondents in the English

[5] $X^2(12) = 11.47$, p = 0.49.   [6] $X^2(12) = 17.94$, p = 0.12.   [7] $X^2(12) = 44.87$, p < 0.00.
[8] Mobile phones/smartphones: $X^2(1) = 16.55$, p < 0.01; PDAs ($X^2(1) = 10.53$, p < 0.01.

TABLE 20.6. **Distribution of small-screen device usage as a function of purpose of use**

		Purpose (%)			
		Private	Both	Professional	Total
Small screen	No	92.86	81.15	92.31	86.25
	Yes	7.14	18.85	7.69	13.75

language version had already used an online dictionary on a small-screen device, compared to 6.80% of the respondents in the German language version.[9]

Further statistical analysis revealed that the age of the respondent was not a significant predictor of the SMALL SCREEN variable. This indicates that younger respondents did not use small-screen devices significantly more often than older respondents.[10]

To examine the influence of the consultation purpose in this context, we generated a nominal variable with three categories: the first category covered respondents who use online dictionaries mainly or exclusively for PRIVATE purposes, the second category those who use them for both PRIVATE and PROFESSIONAL purposes, and the last category for respondents who use them mainly or exclusively for PROFESSIONAL purposes. Table 20.6 reveals an interesting pattern: respondents who use online dictionaries for both private *and* professional purposes had already used an online dictionary on a small-screen device more often (18.85%) than respondents who used online dictionaries (mainly or only) for private purposes (7.14%), and those who used them only for professional purposes (7.69%). This effect was highly significant.[11]

DISCUSSION

On the one hand, the results clearly demonstrate that the respondents to our first study mainly tended to use online dictionaries on big-screen devices (e.g. desktop computers). Only a small proportion had already used online dictionaries on devices with a smaller screen (e.g. a mobile phone). Subgroup analyses showed that neither the academic or professional background, nor the age of the respondent were significant predictors of the device-usage pattern. Respondents to the English language version of the questionnaire were substantially more likely to indicate that they

[9] $X^2(1) = 23.42$, p < 0.00.

[10] We fitted a binary logistic regression model to predict the probability of belonging to one of the two categories of the SMALL SCREEN variable, using age of the respondent as an explanatory variable. To reduce the effects of outliers, the age variable was log-transformed. A binary logistic regression (N = 661; Nagelkerke R^2 = 0.00; $X^2(1)$ = 0.90, p = 0.34) indicated that the age of a respondent was not a significant predictor of the SMALL SCREEN variable (β = −0.29; p = 0.35). Seven respondents had not indicated their year of birth, and so were excluded from this analysis.

[11] $X^2(2) = 17.74$, p < 0.00.

had already used an online dictionary on a small-screen device than respondents to the German language version. A similar relationship was found regarding the purpose of consultation. Nevertheless, the great majority of respondents had only ever used them on notebook/netbook and/or desktop computers.

However, we do not conclude from these results that the development of an online dictionary that is capable of adapting to different screen sizes is pointless. At least three objections could be raised to this conclusion. First, it is reasonable to assume that screen-size adaptable online dictionaries will become more important in the near future, since the market for small-screen devices (smartphones, tablets, ebook readers) is constantly expanding. Second, although our sample of respondents is quite large, it is somewhat biased towards Europe (especially Germany) and the US (Section 20.3.3). This could lead to an underestimation of the percentage of online dictionary users who have already used online dictionaries on a small-screen device, as a result of the fact mentioned in the 'Introduction' that pocket electronic dictionaries are especially popular in Japan and other Asian countries (see Nesi, this volume). Third, more empirical research is needed, because our study left out certain important issues: if people really do start to use online dictionaries on small-screen devices more often in the future, it will be important to know if there are any differences in the dictionary consultation process. For instance, is it possible that small-screen devices (e.g. smartphones) are used more often during oral text production? If this is so, the dictionary should be designed accordingly.

To summarize, it seems to be appropriate to optimize the screen design to big-screen devices without losing sight of the smaller ones. However, further insights into this topic would be valuable for practical lexicography.

20.4.2 *Research Question 2: presenting word entries*

Nowadays, the design of most online dictionaries is notably different from that of printed dictionaries. Instead of arranging the dictionary entries unidimensionally using compressions and common abbreviations typical of conventional printed dictionaries, alternative ways of presenting word entries can be used in online dictionaries (see Lew, this volume). Hence, when designing an online dictionary, it is necessary to decide which format is best suited for the intended target user group. In this section, we provide empirical data to evaluate this question, again using a survey design, since this problem is difficult to answer using log file analyses alone and requires a high number of participants to have a sound empirical basis.

METHOD

In one set of questions, the respondents to our second study were asked to rate different basic alternative ways of presenting word entries in an online dictionary and to decide which they preferred. To do this, we selected four prototypical ways of presenting word entries for scientific dictionaries with a detailed microstructure that is divided into different screens or different parts of a screen. We chose this type of dictionary because, on the one hand, these dictionaries are especially affected by the

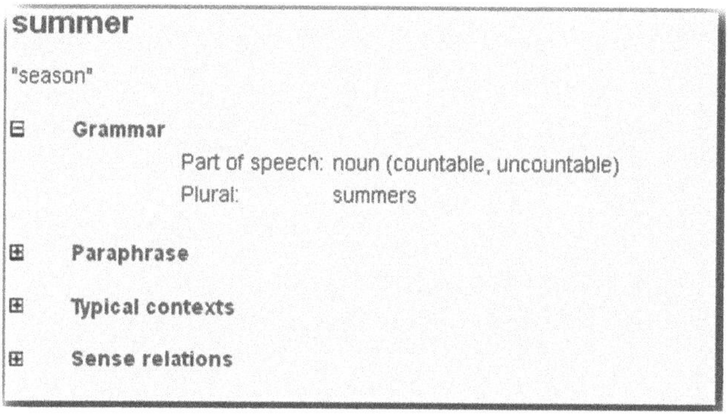

FIGURE 20.1 Explorer view.

question of how to present their word entries, and, on the other hand, there are no studies of their layout. All the alternatives included in the survey used the same word entry ('summer') covering (as far as possible) identical content. All the alternatives except the last were implemented using JAVA script.[12] Thus, the participants could interactively navigate their way through the content of the word entry.

The first alternative is an adaption of the well-known Microsoft Windows EXPLORER VIEW (Figure 20.1). In this layout, the word entry is structured as a tree. The user can change the information displayed by expanding (with a click on the plus sign) or collapsing (with a click on the minus sign) different parts of the nodes. Two examples of online dictionaries that use this kind of layout are the Danish dictionary Den danske Ordbog[13] and the Algemeen Nederlands Woordenboek,[14] an online dictionary of contemporary Dutch.

The second layout is structured as a table, with different modules of information. The Digital Dictionary of the German Language in the 20th Century (DWDS)[15] uses a screen layout that allows the user to select between multiple panels (although in the DWDS, the content of the different panels are not parts of a word entry as in our example, but include additional information on an entry, such as corpus samples etc.). This view is called the PANEL VIEW (Figure 20.2).

The third alternative way of presenting word entries is the so-called TAB VIEW (Figure 20.3), which allows selective switching between different components ('tabs') of the word entry. This layout structure is used in elexiko,[16] a monolingual German dictionary, and ELDIT,[17] an electronic learners' dictionary for German and Italian.

---

[12] We thank our colleague Peter Meyer for preparing the relevant scripts.
[13] http://ordnet.dk/ddo.   [14] http://anw.inl.nl/.   [15] http://www.dwds.de.
[16] http://www.elexiko.de.   [17] http://www.eurac.edu/eldit.

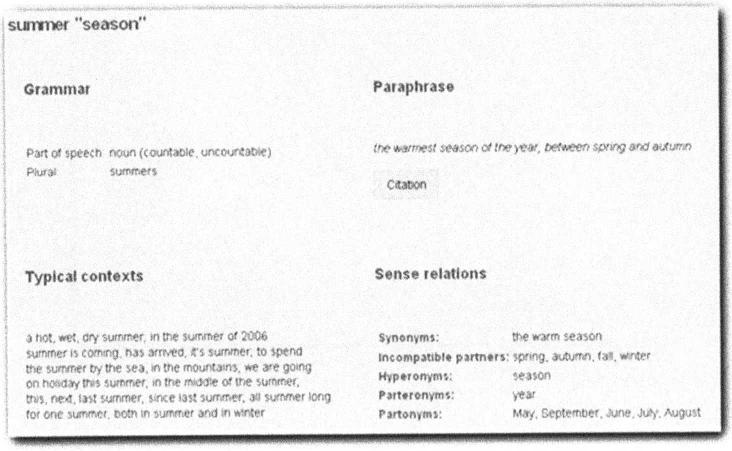

FIGURE 20.2 Panel view.

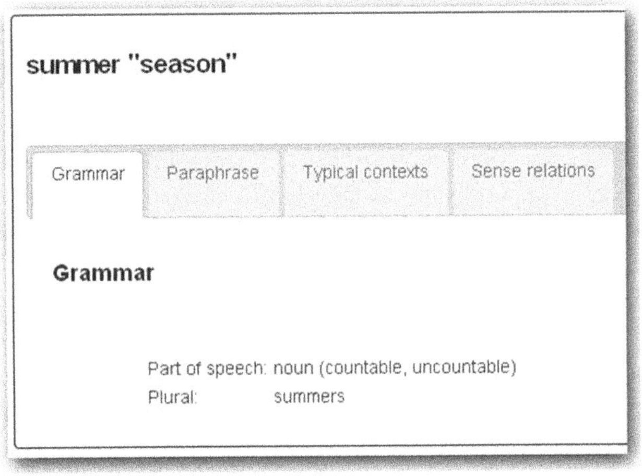

FIGURE 20.3 Tab view.

The final alternative we implemented was a PRINT-oriented version of the entry (Figure 20.4), since there are still some online dictionaries which closely resemble their printed counterparts (e.g. the French online dictionary TLFi[18]).

The procedure was as follows. First, every respondent was shown the four alternative views one after another. The alternatives were randomly selected to avoid any order effects. After the respondents had had the opportunity to have a look and try out each alternative, they were asked to use 7-point Likert scales to rate all four types

---

[18] http://atilf.atilf.fr/.

summer, noun (countable, uncountable): *the warmest season of the year, between spring and autumn*; a hot, wet, dry summer; in the summer of 2006; the summer is coming, has arrived; it's summer; to spend the summer by the sea, in the mountains; we are going on holiday this summer; in the middle of the summer; this, next, last summer; since last summer; all summer long; for one summer; both in summer and in winter; **Syn.**: the warm season; **Incomp.**: autumn, fall, spring, winter; **Hyper.**: season; **Parter.**: year; **Parto.**: May, September, June, July, August

FIGURE 20.4 Print view.

TABLE 20.7. **Means and standard deviations of the ratings and percentage ranked first for each view tested**

Alternative	Mean-rating[a]	SD	Ranked first (%)
Tab view	5.43	1.39	42.82
Panel view	5.15	1.46	32.82
Explorer view	4.93	1.44	17.69
Print view	3.36	1.55	6.67

[a] All means were significantly different from each other as indicated by separate *t*-tests ($ps < .05$).

of presentation with respect to the following characteristics: Quality (1 = not good, 7 = very good); Arrangement (1 = not well arranged, 7 = very well arranged); Comprehensibility (1 = not comprehensible, 7 = very comprehensible). The participants were then asked to rank the four options according to their overall preference, from best to worst. When the respondents had finished the ranking task, they were shown the view they had rated best and asked what they particularly liked about it in an open-ended question.

To identify potential user group differences, we used similar background variables to those in the last section: academic and professional background and the language version of the survey.

RESULTS

Descriptive results   All the ratings of all four alternatives were averaged to form a reliable rating scale with higher values indicating greater preferences.[19] Table 20.7 summarizes the average ratings and first rank percentages for each alternative way of presenting word entries.

---

[19] To test for reliability we used Cronbach's alpha. All the coefficients were above .89, indicating that the scales have a strong internal consistency. However, we only compared the percentage of first rank preferences, since it does not seem meaningful to compute means and standard deviations of a ranking of four items.

TABLE 20.8. Percentage of first ranks as a function of language version

| First rank | Language version | | % |
	German	English	Total
Tab view	38.24	47.85	42.82
Panel view	36.76	28.49	32.82
Explorer view	18.14	17.20	17.69
Print view	6.86	6.45	6.67

TABLE 20.9. Percentage of first ranks as a function of professional background

| First rank | Professional background | | % |
	Non-translator	Translator	Total
Tab view	47.74	34.69	42.82
Panel view	30.04	37.41	32.82
Explorer view	16.05	20.41	17.69
Print view	6.17	7.48	6.67

The TAB VIEW was both rated best and chosen as the best view most often. Although the PANEL VIEW and the EXPLORER VIEW received somewhat lower scores, but still high ratings, they were chosen less often as the favourite view. The PRINT VIEW was rated worst, as well as chosen least often as the best view.

Subgroup analyses   To analyse potential group differences, we conducted several X^2 difference tests. Neither language version (Table 20.8)[20] nor academic background[21] were significant predictors of preference for a screen format. However, there was a significant relationship between professional background and preferred view (Table 20.9):[22] non-translators strongly preferred the TAB VIEW—roughly one out of two non-translators preferred this way of presenting word entries. Most translators preferred the PANEL VIEW (37.41%), although almost as many respondents in this group chose the TAB VIEW (34.69%).

Analysis of the open-ended responses   To explain the reasons for preferring one particular type of presentation, we manually inspected the answers to the open-ended question ("This is the view you rated best. What do you particularly like about it?"). This yielded a number of categories. Table 20.10 presents the categories we selected and provides examples of typical answers for each one.

---

[20] $X^2(3) = 4.20$, p = 0.24.   [21] $X^2(3) = 3.08$, p = 0.38.   [22] $X^2(3) = 6.38$, p < 0.10.

TABLE 20.10. **Coding scheme used to categorize the open-ended question**

Category	Examples
Clarity	• easy to read • clearly separated • uncluttered
No need to click	• no clicking involved • no need to click on anything • all information can be accessed without clicking through the links.
No need to scroll	• doesn't force the user to scroll • no need to scroll
No information overload	• simple • not too much information at once • concise
Navigation	• easy to navigate • easy to use • comprehensible
Look and feel	• stylish • visually appealing • large buttons
Efficiency	• functional • intuitive • consistent
Adaptability/Selectivity	• it is possible to select only the information required • adaptability of dictionary contents • I can choose
Essential information	• information unnecessary for me is not shown • without sacrificing information to brevity • hierarchical
Familiarity	• like the one I am used to • similar to other applications • consistent with web browser formatting
Quickness	• quick, open view • presents all the data quickly • does not take up traffic if used on a mobile phone
Others Don't know / no answer	

TABLE 20.11. **Reason for preference (percentages) as a function of chosen alternative of presentation**

Category [a]	Preferred alternative of presentation (%)				Total	X^2/p-value[b]
	TAB	PANEL	EXPLORER	PRINT		
Clarity	**63.64**	**55.12**	**56.06**	28.00	57.18	11.76/0.10
No need to click	5.45	**76.38**	16.67	16.00	31.59	179.64/0.00
Navigation	**36.12**	**29.13**	**25.76**	16.00	30.81	5.92/1.00
Adaptability/Selectivity	**32.12**	3.94	**56.06**	8.00	25.33	71.68/0.00
No information overload	24.24	8.66	16.70	**28.00**	18.54	13.30/0.05
Essential information	12.73	12.60	22.73	4.00	13.84	6.74/0.97
Efficiency	10.30	11.02	9.09	12.00	10.44	0.24/1.00
Look and feel	12.73	4.72	7.58	16.00	9.40	6.94/0.89
Familiarity	12.12	0.79	1.52	**40.00**	8.36	49.28/0.00
Quickness	5.45	6.30	7.58	12.00	6.53	1.67/1.00
Others	3.03	3.15	0.00	0.00	2.35	2.88/1.00
No need to scroll	1.82	0.79	0.00	0.00	1.04	2.00/1.00
Total [c]	220.00	212.60	222.73	180.00	215.40	

[a] The three most frequently mentioned categories for each alternative are indicated in bold.
[b] p values are Bonferroni adjusted.
[c] Some values sum to over 100 as multiple answers are allowed.

In Table 20.11, the frequency distributions of the categories for each alternative are displayed. The three most frequently mentioned categories for each alternative are highlighted. All the alternatives are preferred for being clear, and 'Clarity' is the most mentioned criterion overall (57.18%), especially by respondents who favour the TAB VIEW (63.64%). Compared to the PANEL VIEW (3.94%) and the PRINT VIEW (8.00%), both the TAB VIEW (32.12%) and the EXPLORER VIEW (56.06%) stand out for being adaptable to the preferences of the user. This difference is highly significant.[23] A user interface that is easy to navigate also seems to be an important factor in the decision, especially for respondents who chose the TAB VIEW (36.12%), the PANEL VIEW (29.13%), and the EXPLORER VIEW (25.76%). Compared to the three other ways of presenting word entries, the PANEL VIEW (76.38%) is preferred because it allows the user to access all information without clicking.[24] Unsurprisingly, the PRINT VIEW is mostly chosen for being familiar (40.00%). The contrast to the other three alternatives is highly significant.[25]

DISCUSSION

Our analyses show that most of our respondents tended to prefer the TAB VIEW. Potential group differences in this context only seem to play a minor role. Further analyses (not reported here) reveal that neither age nor command of German (in the German

---

[23] $X^2(3) = 71.68$, $p < 0.00$.   [24] $X^2(3) = 179.64$, $p < 0.00$.   [25] $X^2(3) = 49.28$, $p < 0.00$.

language version) / command of English (in the English language version) affected the outcome. In almost every subgroup, the TAB VIEW received the most first-preference votes. The analyses of the open-ended responses show that the respondents like this way of presenting word entries because it is clear, easy to navigate, and adaptable.

One may object that this could be a social desirability bias. It is commonly known that respondents tend to present themselves in a favourable light (Diekmann 2002: 382–6). Since our project is closely related to elexiko, and this online dictionary uses the tab structure, respondents might have claimed to prefer the TAB VIEW, because they assumed that we would be impressed by this decision. However, this objection does not hold: as mentioned above, there is no significant relationship between the language version of the survey and the preference distribution (Table 20.8). Due to the fact that elexiko is a German monolingual online dictionary, it is rather unlikely that respondents in the English language version from all over the world would prefer the TAB VIEW as a result of a social desirability effect. Additionally, we know from our third survey (German language version only) that elexiko is only known by 21.46% of German-speaking respondents.

20.4.3 *Research Question 3: demands on online dictionaries*

As mentioned in the 'Introduction', one of the aims of the first two studies was to obtain reliable data on online dictionaries in general.[26] Thus, the priority was not to receive data to deduce practical possibilities for improving one particular online dictionary. However, we believe that this information can be used to decide on more general questions that have to be answered when designing a user-friendly online dictionary. For example, in recent years it has become increasingly common that the content on information websites is contributed to by the Internet community in a collaborative manner (Wikipedia is, of course, the prime example; see Meyer and Gurevych, this volume). As a consequence, it is essential to assess the degree of importance that online dictionary users attach to the accuracy and authorship of the dictionary content. Other relevant questions are whether it is preferable to use financial and human resources to extend the corpus and improve its accessibility for the user community, or to focus on keeping the dictionary entries up to date and quick (meaning that there is hardly any delay when the pages are loaded), or whether it is more user-friendly to provide a fast or a customizable user interface. Different user groups may of course have different answers to all these questions. Therefore, providing reliable empirical data that can be used to explore how users rate different aspects of online dictionaries is an important issue for practical lexicography, because it can be used as the basis of various decisions that have to be made in this context.

---

[26] A summary of the results presented in Section 20.4.3 and 20.4.4 can also be found in Müller-Spitzer *et al.* (2011) and in Koplenig (2011).

Regarding differences between user groups, one of our hypotheses was that, compared to non-linguists, linguists would have a stronger preference for the entries to be linked to the relevant corpus, because this documents the empirical basis of the given information. Another hypothesis was that we expected translators to rate, on average, a user interface that is adaptable as more important than non-translators for an online dictionary, since professional translators rely heavily on dictionaries in their daily work. An adaptable user interface could enhance their individual productivity.

METHOD

Among other questions, respondents in the first survey were asked to rate ten items on the use of an online dictionary on 5-point Likert scales (1 = not important at all, 5 = very important):

- Adaptability: the user interface is customizable.
- Clarity: the general structure of the website enables you to easily find the information you need.
- Links to other dictionaries: the entries also contain links to other dictionaries.
- Links to the corpus: the entries also contain links to the relevant collection of texts (corpus).
- (Long-term) accessibility: you can be certain of accessing the different entries by using the previous URL (i.e. web address) for future references.
- Multimedia content: the online dictionary also contains multimedia files, e.g. visual and audio media.
- Reliability of content: you can rely on the accuracy and authorship of the content.
- Speed: there is hardly any delay when the pages are loaded.
- Suggestions for further browsing: the entries contain links to other entries you might find interesting.
- Up-to-date content: possible mistakes are corrected on a regular basis; new word entries and linguistic developments are regularly published online.

After this, the participants were asked to create a personal ranking according to importance. The most important criterion was placed highest, whereas the least important criterion was placed in the last position (Figure 20.5).[27]

RESULTS

Correlation analysis Analysis of (Spearman's rank) correlation revealed a significant association between importance and ranking.[28] This means that the importance measured on the Likert scale and the ranking of the criteria had a similar outcome.

---

[27] Methodologically speaking, we implemented two indicators to measure individual importance, because using multiple indicators increases the validity of the test. Furthermore, we thought that it was likely that many respondents would rate most aspects as important, so when the respondents are asked to create a personal ranking, they were forced to discriminate between the different aspects.

[28] $r = 0.39$ [0.20; 0.56]; $p < 0.01$.

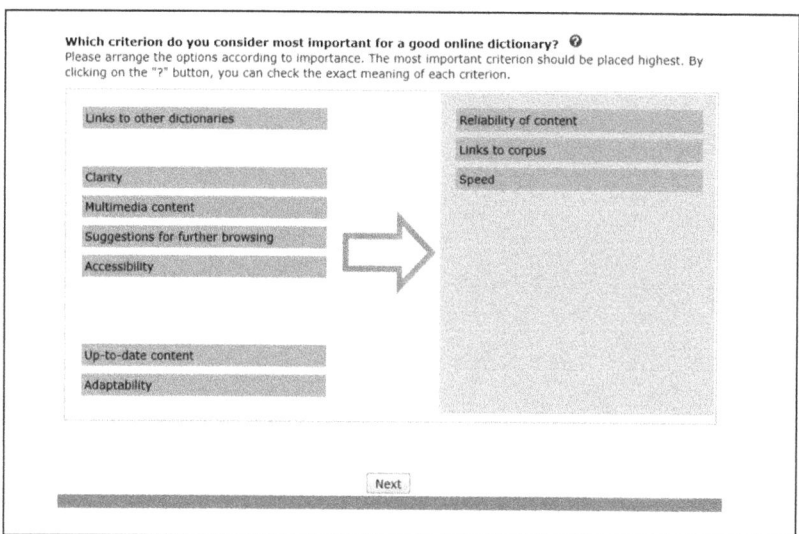

FIGURE 20.5 The ranking task (screenshot).

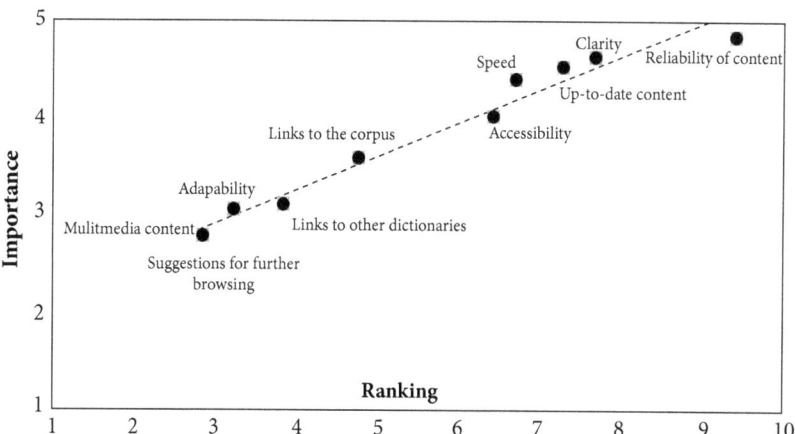

FIGURE 20.6 Correlations between mean rankings and mean importance in the use of an online dictionary.

These results indicate that the individual ranking can be used as a reliable indicator of users' demands (Figure 20.6).

Descriptive results   The analysis of the ratings reveals that one aspect stands out above all others: 71.35% of the respondents chose 'Reliability of content' as the most important aspect of a good online dictionary. In addition to this, other classical

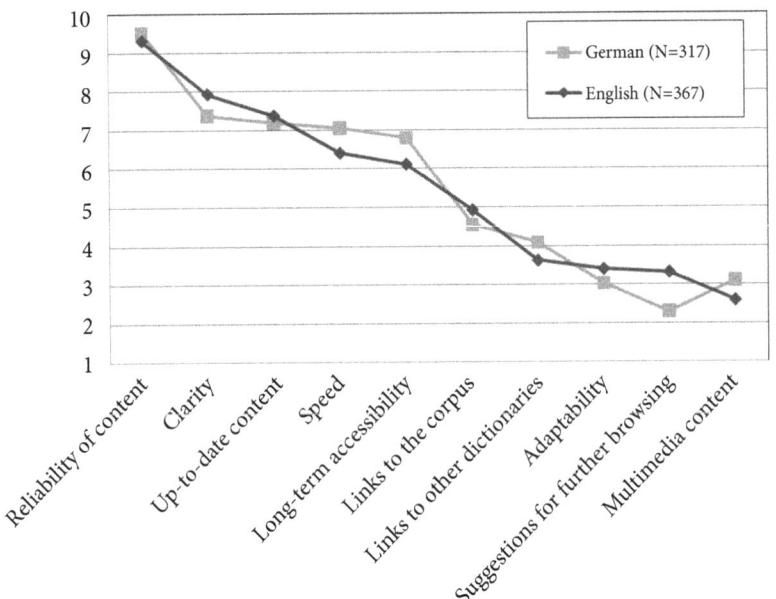

FIGURE 20.7 Mean rankings as a function of language version.

criteria of reference books (e.g. 'Up-to-date content' and 'Clarity') were both ranked and rated highest, whereas the unique characteristics of online dictionaries (e.g. 'Multimedia content', 'Adaptability') were rated and ranked as less important (see Section 20.4.4.).

Subgroup analyses   Another objective of the study was to assess whether the size of this difference depended on further variables, especially the participants' background and the language version of the online survey they used. Surprisingly, there were no noteworthy rating differences—on average—between the different groups, as a visual representation clearly demonstrates (see Figures 20.7, 20.8, and 20.9).[29]

Statistical analyses of variance (not reported here) reveal that some of the differences in average ratings across subgroups were significant. However, this was mainly due to the high number of participants.[30]

---

[29] These figures show the means of rankings as a function of language version (Figure 20.7), of professional background (Figure 20.8), and of academic background (Figure 20.9). The means are shown on 10-point scales with higher values indicating higher levels of importance for the use of an online dictionary.

[30] In fact the F-Value $(1, 682)$ ranged from 0.20 to 59.11 with 8.08 on average, yielding highly significant differences $(p < 0.00)$ in only eight out of thirty cases.

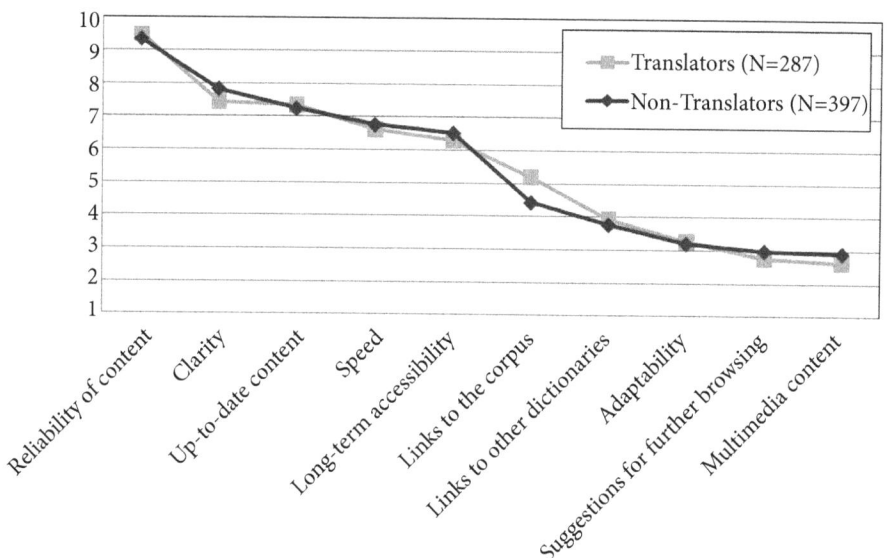

FIGURE 20.8 Mean rankings as a function of professional background.

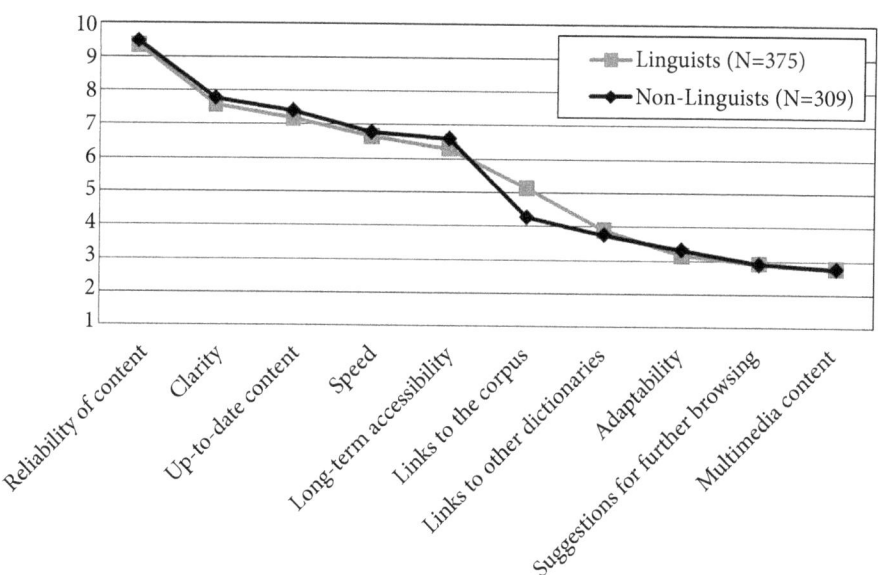

FIGURE 20.9 Means rankings as a function of academic background.

TABLE 20.12. **Means and standard deviations of average rankings in the cluster analysis**

	Cluster 1 (N = 206)		Cluster 2 (N = 478)	
	M	SD	M	SD
Criterion				
Reliability of content	9.09	1.79	9.54	0.91
Clarity	6.96	1.98	7.97	1.35
Up-to-date content	6.89	2.28	7.45	1.50
Speed	5.52	2.56	7.21	1.47
Long-term accessibility	5.43	2.47	6.86	1.86
Links to the corpus	7.01	1.93	3.77	1.60
Links to other dictionaries	4.72	2.11	3.46	1.47
Adaptability	3.59	2.04	3.08	1.73
Suggestions for further browsing	3.35	2.19	2.64	1.55
Multimedia content	2.43	1.75	3.02	1.89

Another way of framing these findings is to state that the relative ranking orders represented by the shapes of the curves were the same in each figure.[31]

It is important to mention that there were no noteworthy rating differences when we compared the different age groups. For example, the average ranking of respondents younger than twenty was hardly different from that of respondents over fifty.

Cluster analysis   In order to interpret these results better, we conducted a cluster analysis to see how users might group together in terms of their individual rankings. Clusters were formed on the basis of a two-step cluster analysis.[32] A two-cluster solution was identified. The parameters of (means, standard deviations, and N) of each cluster are presented in Table 20.12.

Analyses of variance, with the cluster as independent variable and the respective criterion as the response variable, yielded highly significant differences (p < 0.00) for every criterion (10 out of 10 cases).[33] Most strikingly, preceded only by 'Reliability of content', respondents in Cluster 1 rated the criterion 'Links to the corpus' on average as the second most important aspect of a good online dictionary (M = 7.01, SD = 1.93), whereas this criterion only played a minor role for respondents in Cluster 2 (M = 3.77,

---

[31] The only exception occurred in Figure 20.7, where there was a small difference between the two criteria rated on average as least and second least important (suggestions for further browsing and multimedia content).

[32] We used the log-likelihood distance measure. The total number of clusters was not restricted, but was chosen automatically by Schwarz's Bayesian Criterion (BIC).

[33] F (1, 682) ranging from 11.22 to 520.30 (93.08 on average); ps < 0.00.

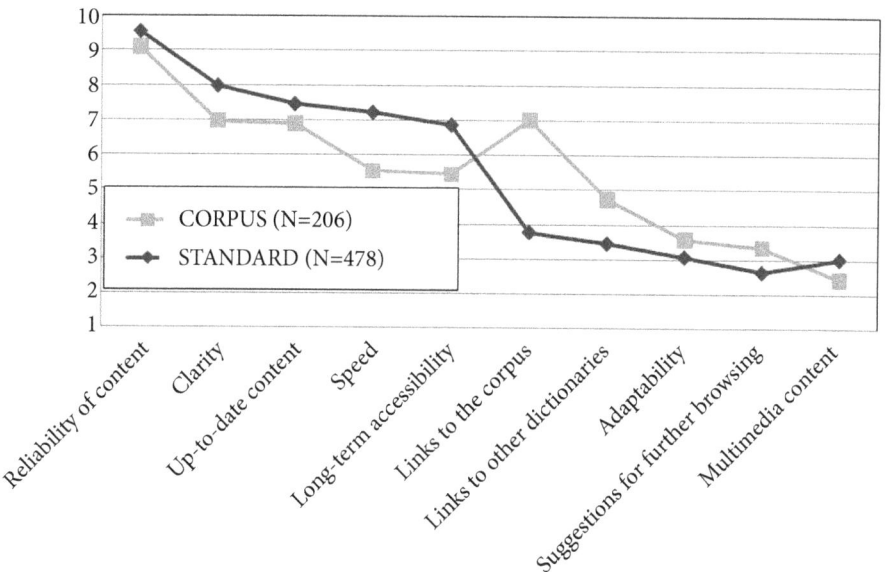

F<small>IGURE</small> 20.10 Mean rankings as a function of the cluster analysis.

T<small>ABLE</small> 20.13. **Results of the binary logistic regression model[a]**

Variable	Coefficient	Std. error	p-Value	Odds-Ratio
Language version	0.447	0.174	0.010	1.563
Professional background	0.454	0.173	0.009	1.575
Academic background	0.603	0.176	0.001	1.827
Constant	−1.654	0.178	0.000	

[a] N = 684; Nagelkerke R^2 = 0.064; $X^2(3)$ = 31.67, p < 0.00. All coefficients are significant at the 0.01 level.

SD = 1.60) (see Figure 20.10).[34] Cluster 1 (N = 206) is termed C<small>ORPUS</small> C<small>LUSTER</small> whereas Cluster 2 (N = 478) is named S<small>TANDARD</small> C<small>LUSTER</small> below.

Regression analysis   To test our hypothesis that different users groups have different demands, we fitted a binary logistic regression model to predict the probability of belonging to one of the two clusters (as an indicator for sharing similar individual needs when using an online dictionary). The cluster variable was used as the binary response, and academic background, professional background, and the language version chosen by the respondent as explanatory variables. The results of the logistic regression model are presented in Table 20.13.

[34] $F(1, 682)$ = 520.30, p < 0.00.

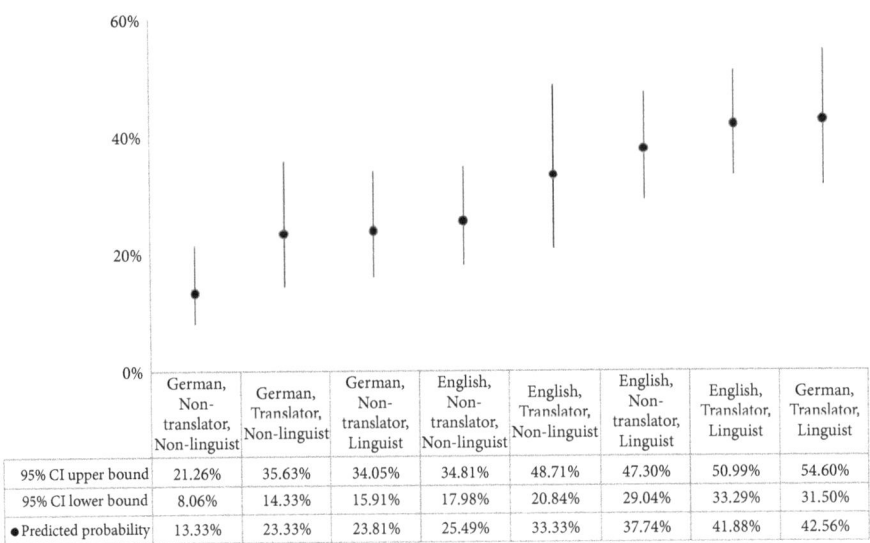

	German, Non-translator, Non-linguist	German, Translator, Non-linguist	German, Non-translator, Linguist	English, Non-translator, Non-linguist	English, Translator, Non-linguist	English, Non-translator, Linguist	English, Translator, Linguist	German, Translator, Linguist
95% CI upper bound	21.26%	35.63%	34.05%	34.81%	48.71%	47.30%	50.99%	54.60%
95% CI lower bound	8.06%	14.33%	15.91%	17.98%	20.84%	29.04%	33.29%	31.50%
● Predicted probability	13.33%	23.33%	23.81%	25.49%	33.33%	37.74%	41.88%	42.56%

FIGURE 20.11 Predicted probabilities of belonging to the 'corpus cluster' as a function of language version, professional background, and academic background.

To visualize these results, we extended our model, allowing for interaction between the explanatory variables.[35] Figure 20.11 shows the results of this model. For example, the model predicts (as indicated by the black circle) that the probability of belonging to the CORPUS CLUSTER for participants using the English language version who work as translators and who have a linguistic academic background is 41.88% (95% confidence interval (as indicated by the solid line): 33.29–50.99%). This compares to a likelihood of only 13.33% for subjects using the German language version who do not work as translators and who do not have a linguistic background (95% confidence interval: 8.06–21.26%).

DISCUSSION

As mentioned above, we expected many respondents to rate most aspects as important. This assumption turned out to be wrong, as the correlation between the ratings and the individual ranking revealed. This seems to indicate that users have a clear conception of a good online dictionary. Of course, it is not surprising that 'Reliability of content' is ranked highly. However, its dominance is worth mentioning. Instead of classifying it as a variable, it should be considered as a constant of a good online dictionary, since it hardly varies between the different respondents.

The analysis of the individual ratings and rankings shows that the classical criteria of reference books (e.g. 'Reliability of content', 'Clarity') were both ranked and rated

---

[35] N = 684; Nagelkerke R^2 = 0.07; X^2(3) = 35.49, p < 0.00.

highest, whereas the unique characteristics of online dictionaries (e.g. 'Multimedia content', 'Adaptability') were rated and ranked as less important. These results conflict with the general lexicographical need both for the development of a user-adaptive interface and the incorporation of multimedia elements to make online dictionaries more user-friendly and innovative (e.g. De Schryver 2003, Müller-Spitzer 2008, Verlinde and Binon 2010 present evidence challenging this view). This raises the question of whether the design of an adaptive interface really makes online dictionaries more user-friendly, or whether this is just a lexicographers' dream (De Schryver 2003). Nevertheless, we believe that our results do not mean that the development of innovative features of online dictionaries is of negligible importance. As we show in the next section, users tend to appreciate good ideas, such as a user-adaptive interface, but they are not used to online dictionaries incorporating such features. As a result, they have no basis on which to judge the usefulness of those features.

Regarding the subgroup analyses, the findings reported here suggest that our initial hypothesis that different subgroups have different demands was too simple. Both a visual inspection of the data in Figures 20.7, 20.8, and 20.9 and statistical analyses of variance revealed that knowledge of the participant's background allows hardly any conclusions to be drawn about the participant's ranking of features of online dictionaries. By conducting a cluster analysis and using a binary logistic regression model, we have shown that the probability of belonging to one of the two clusters (as an indicator for sharing similar individual demands regarding the use of an online dictionary) depends on academic and professional background and on the language version chosen. For example, more than 40% of respondents who work as translators and who have a linguistic academic background belong to the CORPUS CLUSTER. In this group, the link to the empirical basis of the information is rated as very important. Respondents who do not work as translators, and who do not have a linguistic background, only have a probability of roughly 13% in the German language version and roughly 25% in the English language version of belonging to this cluster. One could speculate that there have to be other (background) variables that account for this variation. This leaves room for further studies focusing on the nature of this relationship.

20.4.4 *Research Question 4: the evaluation of innovative features of online dictionaries*

In the last section we showed that, compared to more conventional criteria (e.g. 'Reliability of content', 'Clarity', 'Up-to-date content'), users found the unique features of online dictionaries (e.g. 'Multimedia content', 'Adaptability') not to be particularly important. On the one hand, this hardly comes as a surprise, given the fact that an online dictionary that is highly innovative but unreliable is not very useful, while the opposite—reliable but conventional—only slightly changes the practical value of the reference tool.

On the other hand, we assume that an additional explanation for this result is the fact that respondents are not used to online dictionaries incorporating multimedia and adaptability. Thus, respondents currently have no basis on which to judge their potential usefulness. This line of reasoning predicts a learning effect. That is, when users are fully informed about possible multimedia and adaptable features, they may come to judge these characteristics to be more useful than do users who have not experienced such facilities. To test this assumption, we incorporated an experimental element into our second survey.

METHOD

The participants in our survey were presented, both visually and linguistically, with several possible multimedia applications and various features of an adaptable online dictionary in a set of statements (S1). Each feature was explained in detail and/or supplemented by a picture illustrating its potential function (Figure 20.12). The participants were then asked to rate each feature with respect to three different characteristics regarding the use of an online dictionary (importance/benefit/helpfulness).

In a second set (S2), participants were asked to indicate how much they agreed with the following two statements:

The application of multimedia and adaptable features...

- ...makes working with an online dictionary much easier.
- ...in online dictionaries is just a gadget.

To induce a learning effect, we randomized the order of the two sets: participants in the learning-effect condition (L) were first presented with the examples in S1. After that, they were asked to indicate their opinion in S2. Participants in the non-learning-effect condition (N) had to answer S2 followed by S1. Thus, to judge the potential usefulness of adaptability and multimedia, the participants in the learning-effect condition could use the information presented in S1, whereas the participants in the non-learning-effect condition could not rely on this kind of information. If our assumption is correct, participants in the learning-effect condition L will judge adaptability and multimedia to be more useful than participants in the non-learning-effect condition N.

RESULTS

The dependent variables were measured as described above (S2). Both ratings were made on 7-point Likert scales (1 = strongly disagree, 7 = strongly agree). The answers to these two items were averaged and oriented in the same direction to form a reliable scale of adaptability and multimedia benefit judgements ($\alpha = 0.75$), with higher values indicating more perceived benefit.

Multimedia

Collocation graphs: An online dictionary can represent collocations, i. e. frequently occurring word combinations, in a visual form.
The picture below shows an example of this.

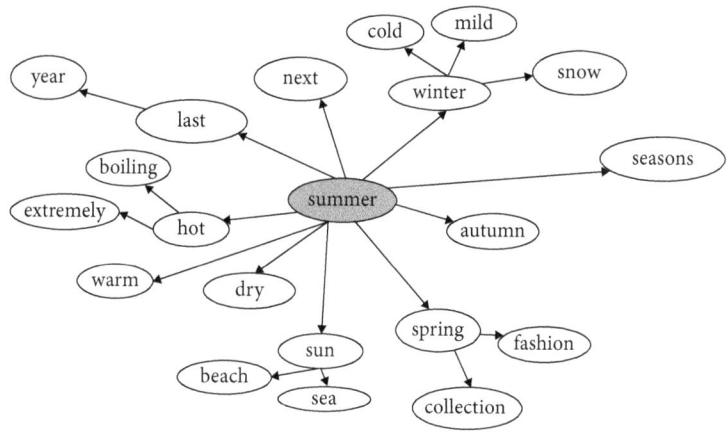

Please rate this feature with respect to the following characteristics regarding the use of an online dictionary.

Please use a scale from 1 to 7, where 1 represents 'Not important / beneficial / helpful at all' and 7 represents 'Very important / beneficial / helpful'. Of course, you may select any number between 1 and 7.

	1	2	3	4	5	6	7	
not important at all	○	○	○	○	○	○	○	very important
not beneficial at all	○	○	○	○	○	○	○	very beneficial
not helpful at all	○	○	○	○	○	○	○	very helpful

FIGURE 20.12 Example of a multimedia application presented in the survey (screenshot).

Analysis of variance   An ANOVA yielded a significant effect of learning condition.[36] As hypothesized, the results showed that participants in L judged adaptability and multimedia to be more useful (M = 5.02, SD = 1.30, N = 175) than participants in N (M = 4.50, SD = 1.54, N = 206; cf. Figure 20.13).

[36] $F_{(1, 379)} = 12.27$, $p < 0.00$; $R^2 = 0.03$.

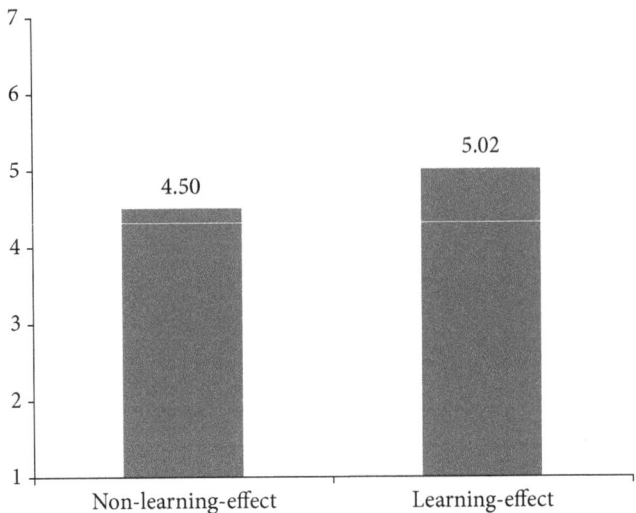

FɪɢᴜʀE **20.13** Mean adaptability and multimedia benefit judgements as a function of the learning-effect condition.

Subgroup analyses   In order to interpret these results better, we conducted a three-way ᴀɴᴏᴠᴀ with learning condition, background, and language version as independent factors. The statistical analysis revealed significant main effects for condition, background, and language version. In addition, a significant three-way interaction between experimental condition, background, and language version was found.[37] Post hoc comparisons using the Tukey ʜꜱᴅ test indicated that in the German language version, the mean difference between the L and N conditions was significant for the non-linguists but not for the linguists, whereas the difference between the two conditions was highly significant for the linguists and insignificant for the non-linguists in the English language version (Table 20.14).

DISCUSSION

As predicted, the results revealed a learning effect. Participants in the learning-effect condition, that is, respondents who were first presented with examples of possible innovative features of online dictionaries, judged adaptability and multimedia to be more useful than participants who did not have this information. However, a closer inspection (Table 20.14) showed that this difference was mediated by linguistic background and language version: while there was a significant learning effect in

---

[37] Main effects: condition: $F_{(1, 373)} = 9.11$, $p < 0.01$, background: $F_{(1, 373)} = 4.36$, $p < 0.05$), language version: $F_{(1, 373)} = 6.76$, $p < 0.01$. Interaction between experimental condition, background, and language version: $F_{(3, 371)} = 3.78$, $p < 0.05$.

TABLE 20.14. **Means of adaptability and multimedia benefit judgements as a function of condition, background, and language version**[a]

German language version

	Background	
	Linguistic	Non-linguistic
Condition		
Non-learning-effect	5.02 (1.47)	**4.45** (1.66)
Learning-effect	5.02 (1.18)	**5.09** (1.35)

German language version

	Background	
	Linguistic	Non-linguistic
Condition		
Non-learning-effect	**4.23** (1.47)	4.12 (1.63)
Learning-effect	**5.15** (1.26)	4.45 (1.50)

[a] Significant differences in bold (p <0 .05). Standard deviations in parentheses.

the German version for non-linguists only, there was a highly significant learning effect in the English version, but only for linguists.

The overall effect turned out to be modest in size, but highly significant. Furthermore, it should be noted here that we implemented only a weak manipulation of the learning effect. Due to the nature of our survey design, we simply presented several features of multimedia and adaptability. One could argue that if the participants had had the opportunity to actually use these features, the observed learning effect would have been even more pronounced.

20.5 Conclusion

In our surveys, we focused on general questions of online dictionary use. To summarize, our results indicate that the participants in our surveys tended to use online dictionaries mostly on big screens (e.g. notebooks or desktop computers). Devices with smaller screens (e.g. smartphones) were less often used for online dictionary consultation. Furthermore, the classical properties of reference books (such as reliability of content or clarity) were rated as most important for a good online dictionary whereas new innovative and media-specific features (such as a user-adaptive access) were rated as less important. We believe that this is partly due to the fact that users are currently unfamiliar with online dictionaries effectively incorporating innovative features. Our results show that respondents who were first presented with examples of actual innovative features of online dictionaries judged innovative features to be more useful than respondents who had not been exposed to this kind of presentation. Thus, when implementing innovative features in online dictionaries, it is important to ensure that users are informed about the way in which they could benefit from these features. This area of digital lexicography still has considerable potential for development.

We also evaluated different ways of presenting word entries. Our analyses show that the so-called TAB VIEW was preferred over the other alternatives. Our respondents liked this view for being clear, easy to navigate, and adaptable. We can safely draw the conclusion that these characteristics are critical factors to be considered when designing an online dictionary.

The fact that we found no link between the age of the respondent on the one hand and either the device usage pattern or individual preferences on the other hand came as somewhat of a surprise. We expected younger respondents who have grown up with digital technologies ("digital natives", as Rundell, this volume, calls them) to have different needs from older users. This leaves room for further studies focusing on this rather puzzling result.

All in all, our studies supplement existing work on any one special dictionary or concrete usage situation. We have conducted three studies of that type in our project. Two survey studies focused on monolingual online dictionaries such as elexiko, while one eye-tracking study assessed the usability of the lexicographic internet portal OWID.[38] As a next step, we plan to develop and evaluate strategies and options to inform potential online dictionary users about the benefits of innovative features, for example, a user-adaptive interface.

Undoubtedly, the collection of data using surveys plays an essential role in many areas of empirical research, e.g. economics, education, marketing, political science, (social) psychology, and sociology. This is due to the fact that whenever a research project focuses on the analysis or the evaluation of individual properties (e.g. opinions, attitudes, behaviour, preferences, and socio-demographic factors), conducting a survey is obviously an efficient strategy. However, Bergenholtz and Johnsen (2005) argue as follows regarding the usefulness of survey methods for empirical research into dictionary usage:

In such questionnaire surveys, the same methods are employed as in other forms of market analysis: a number of standard questions or behavior, e.g. of a selected sample concerning a certain product or behavior [...] However, the answers from the informants do not necessarily reflect a real genuine user situation. It cannot be ruled out that the problems, behavior, etc. described by the informants differ from their real problems. The questions asked have to do with future activities, as in "Under which headword would you look for the following

---

[38] OWID (Online Vocabulary Information System of German) (Müller-Spitzer 2010b; Engelberg and Müller-Spitzer, in press) is hosted at the Institute for German Language (IDS), and contains elexiko and other online dictionaries (http://www.owid.de).

collocations?", or with past activities "Which types of information do you look for most often?". There is no guarantee that the answers correspond to why and how the informants really have used or will use dictionaries. Such surveys are quite problematic because they presuppose that the informants remember exactly how they have used dictionaries in the past and that they are able to predict how they will do it in the future. (Bergenholtz and Johnsen 2005: 119–20)

In this contribution, we hope that we have shown that this argument does not prove that survey methods cannot be applied in a fruitful way to empirical research into dictionary usage. Bergenholtz and Johnsen (2005) only outline some problems resulting from unsound empirical approaches. Analysing log files is a smart way to receive unobtrusive data about real dictionary consultations. However, other methods, such as surveys or usability tests, are equally justified. For research into the use of online dictionaries, this strategy can only be beneficial. Picking up Nesi's (2000a: 845) comment again: at the moment, research on empirical research use may be "still in its infancy", but—on the basis of thorough empirical scrutiny combining different methodological approaches—it is maturing steadily.

Bibliography

Abel, Andrea (2006). Elektronische Wörterbücher: Neue Wege und Tendenzen. In F. San Vincente (ed.), *Lessicografia bilingue e Traduzione: metodi, strumenti e approcci attuali*, 35–56. Milano: Polimetrica Publisher.

——(2010). Towards a systematic classification framework for dictionaries and CALL. In S. Granger and M. Paquot (eds), *eLexicography in the 21st century: New challenges, new applications*, 3–11. Louvain-la-Neuve: Presses universitaires de Louvain.

Abel, Andrea, and Vanessa Weber (2000). ELDIT – A prototype of an innovative dictionary. In U. Heid, S. Evert, E. Lehmann, and C. Rohrer (eds), *Proceedings of the Ninth EURALEX International Congress*. 807–818. Stuttgart: Institut für Maschinelle Sprachverarbeitung, Universität Stuttgart.

Agnoloni, Tomaso, Lorenzo Bacci, Enrico Francesconi, Pier-Luigi Spinosa, Daniela Tiscornia, Simonetta Montemagni, and Giulia Venturi (2007). Building an ontological support for multilingual legislative drafting. In *Proceedings of the International Conference on Legal Knowledge and Information Systems (JURIX 2007)*, 12–15 December, 2007, Leiden, the Netherlands, 9–18.

Aitchison, Jean (2003). *Words in the Mind: An Introduction to the Mental Lexicon*. Malden, MA: Blackwell Publishing.

Alcaraz Varó, Enrique (2000). *El Inglés Profesional y Académico*. Madrid: Alianza.

Aldabe, Iztiar, and Montse Maritxalar (2010). Automatic distractor generation for domain specific texts. *Lecture Notes in Computer Science* 6233: 27–38.

Alexa, Melina, Bernd Kreissig, Martina Liepert, Klaus Reichenberger, Lothar Rostek, Karin Rautmann, Werner Scholze-Stubenrecht, and Sabine Stoye (2002). The Duden ontology: An integrated representation of lexical and ontological information. In K. Simov, N. Guarino, and W. Peters (eds), *Proceedings of the Ontologies and Lexical Knowledge Bases Workshop (OntoLex02)*, 3rd International Language Resources and Evaluation Conference, LREC2002, 27 May 2002, Las Palmas, Canary Islands, Spain, 1–8. Available from www.bultreebank.org/OntoLex02Proceedings.html.

Almind, Richard (2005). Designing internet dictionaries. *Hermes* 34: 37–54.

Alonso Ramos, Margarita (2004). Elaboración del Diccionario de colocaciones en español y sus aplicaciones. In P. Bataner and J. de Cesaris (eds), *De Lexicographia. Actas del I Simposio internacional de Lexicografía*, 149–162. Barcelona: IULA-Edicions Petició.

Andersen, Birger Enevold, and Pedro A. Fuertes-Olivera (2009). The application of function theory to the classification of English monolingual business dictionaries. *Lexicographica* 25: 213–240.

Andersen, Birger Enevold, and Sandro Nielsen (2009). Ten key issues in lexicography for the future. In H. Bergenholtz, S. Nielsen, and S. Tarp (eds), *Lexicography at a Crossroads: Dictionaries and Encyclopedias Today, Lexicographical Tools Tomorrow*, 355–365. Bern, Berlin, Brussels, Frankfurt am Main, New York, Oxford, Wien: Peter Lang.

Antenos-Conforti, Enza (2009). Microblogging on Twitter: Social networking in intermediate Italian classes. In L. Lomicka and G. Lord (eds), *The Next Generation: Social Networking and Online Collaboration in Foreign Language Learning*, 59–90. San Marcos, TX: Computer Assisted Language Instruction Consortium (CALICO).

Asmussen, Jörg (forthcoming). Combined products: Dictionary and corpus. In R. H. Gouws, U. Heid, W. Schweickard, and H. E. Wiegand (eds), *Dictionaries. An International Encyclopedia of Lexicography*. Volume 5.4 (suppl.). Berlin and New York: Walter de Gruyter.

Atkins, Beryl T. Sue (1996). Bilingual dictionaries: Past, present and future. In M. Gellerstam, J. Järborg, S.-G. Malmgren, K. Norén, L. Rogström, and C. R. Papmehl (eds), *EURALEX'96 Proceedings*, 515–546. Göteborg: Department of Swedish, Göteborg University.

——(1998a). Some discussion points arising from Afrilex-Salex '98. Unpublished course evaluation document, University of Pretoria.

——(ed.) (1998b). *Using Dictionaries: Studies of Dictionary Use by Language Learners and Translators*. Tübingen: Max Niemeyer.

——(2002). Bilingual dictionaries: Past, present and future. In M.-H. Corréard (ed.), *Lexicography and Natural Language Processing. A Festschrift in Honour of B. T. S. Atkins*, 1–29. United Kingdom: EURALEX.

Atkins, Beryl T. Sue, and Valérie Grundy (2006). Lexicographic profiling: An aid to consistency in dictionary entry design. In E. Corino, C. Marello, and C. Onesti. (eds), *Proceedings of 12th EURALEX International Congress*, 1097–1108. Alessandria: Edizioni Dell'Orso.

Atkins, Beryl T. Sue, Adam Kilgarriff, and Michael Rundell (2010). Database of ANalysed Texts of English (DANTE): The NEID database project. In A. Dykstra and T. Schoonheim (eds), *Proceedings of the XIV EURALEX International Congress*, 549–556. Afûk, Ljouwert: Fryske Akademy.

Atkins, Beryl T. Sue, and Beth Levin (1991). Admitting impediments. In U. Zernik (ed.), *Lexical Acquisition: Using On-Line Resources to Build a Lexicon*, 233–262. Hillsdale, NJ: Lawrence Erlbaum Associates.

Atkins, Beryl T. Sue, and Michael Rundell (2008). *The Oxford Guide to Practical Lexicography*. Oxford: Oxford University Press.

Atkins, Beryl T. Sue, and Krista Varantola (1997). Monitoring dictionary use. *International Journal of Lexicography* 10(1): 1–45.

——(1998). Monitoring dictionary use. In Beryl T. Sue Atkins (ed.), *Using Dictionaries. Studies of Dictionary Use by Language Learners and Translators*, 83–122. Tübingen: Niemeyer.

Aust, Ronald, Mary Jane Kelley, and Warren B. Roby (1993). The use of hyper-reference and conventional dictionaries. *Educational Technology Research and Development* 41: 63–73.

Balemans, Percy (2007). Chinese translation error blamed for slur on sofa label. Available from http://pbtranslations.wordpress.com/2007/04/20/chinese-translation-error-blamed-for-slur-on-sofa-label/ (last accessed 29 April 2011).

Bank, Christina (2010). *Die Usability von Online-Wörterbüchern und elektronischen Sprachportalen*. Unpublished Master's thesis, Universität Hildesheim.

Bartels, Hauke (2010). The German–Lower Sorbian Online Dictionary. In A. Dykstra and T. Schoonheim (eds), *Proceedings of the XIV EURALEX International Congress*, 1450–1462. Afûk, Ljouwert: Fryske Akademy.

Bejoint, Henri (2010). *The Lexicography of English*. Oxford: Oxford University Press.

Bell, Roger (2000). *Translation and Translating: Theory and Practice.* London and New York: Longman.

Benson, Morton (1989). The structure of the collocational dictionary. *International Journal of Lexicography* 2(1): 1–14.

Bentivogli, Luisa, Pamela Forner, Bernardo Magnini, and Emanuele Pianta (2004). Revising the Wordnet domains hierarchy: Semantics, coverage and balancing. In Association for Computational Linguistics (ed.), *Proceedings of the Workshop on Multilingual Linguistic Resources,* 101–108. Geneva.

Bentivogli, Luisa, and Emanuele Pianta (2000). Coping with lexical gaps when building aligned multilingual Wordnets. *Proceedings of LREC-2000, Second International Conference on Language Resources and Evaluation,* 993–997.

——(2003). Beyond lexical units: Enriching Wordnets with phrasets. *Research Note Sessions of the 10th Conference of the European Chapter of the Association for Computational Linguistics (EACL'03),* 67–70.

Bentivogli, Luisa, Emanuele Pianta, and Christian Girardi (2002). MutiWordNet: Developing an aligned multilingual database. *1st International Global WordNet Conference, January 21–25, 2002: Proceedings.* Mysore: Central Institute of Indian Languages.

Bergenholtz, Henning (2003). Two opposing theories: On H. E. Wiegand's recent discovery of lexicographic functions. *Hermes* 31: 171–196.

——(2004). The concept of dictionary usage. *Nordic Journal of English Studies* 3: 23–36.

——(2005). Electronic dictionaries: Old and new lexicographic solutions. *Hermes* 34: 7–9.

Bergenholtz, Henning (2010). *Discurso de Investidura como Doctor Honoris Cause de D. Henning Bergenholtz. La Presentación y el Acceso a los Datos Adaptados a las Necesidades de los Usuarios.* Valladolid: Universidad de Valladolid.

——(2011). Access to and presentation of needs-adapted data in monofunctional Internet dictionaries. In P. A. Fuertes-Olivera and H. Bergenholtz (eds), *e-Lexicography. The Internet, Digital Initiatives and Lexicography,* 30–53. London and New York: Continuum.

Bergenholtz, Henning, and Inger Bergenholtz (2011). A dictionary is a tool, a good dictionary is a monofunctional tool. In P. A. Fuertes-Olivera and H. Bergenholtz (eds), *e-Lexicography: The Internet, Digital Initiatives and Lexicography,* 187–207. London and New York: Continuum.

Bergenholtz, Henning, and Rufus Gouws (2007). The access process in dictionaries for fixed expressions. *Lexicographica. International Annual for Lexicography* 23: 237–260.

——(2010). A new perspective on the access process. *Hermes* 44: 103–127.

Bergenholtz, Henning, and Mia Johnsen (2005). Log files as a tool for improving Internet dictionaries. *Hermes* 34: 117–141.

Bergenholtz, Henning, and Mia Johnsen (2007). Log files can and should be prepared for a functionalistic approach. *Lexikos* 17: 1–20.

Bergenholtz, Henning, Sandro Nielsen, and Sven Tarp (2009). Introduction. In H. Bergenholtz, S. Nielsen, and S. Tarp (eds), *Lexicography at a Crossroads. Dictionaries and Encyclopedias Today, Lexicographical Tools Tomorrow,* 7–16. Bern: Peter Lang.

Bergenholtz, Henning, and Sven Tarp (eds) (1995). *Manual of Specialised Lexicography: The Preparation of Specialised Dictionaries,* Benjamins Translation Library 12. Amsterdam: John Benjamins Publishing.

——(2010). LSP lexicography or terminography? The lexicographer's point of view. In P. A. Fuertes-Olivera (ed.), *Specialised Dictionaries for Learners*, 27–37. Berlin and New York: Walter de Gruyter.

——(2002). Die moderne lexikographische Funktionslehre. Diskussionsbeitrag zu neuen und alten Paradigmen, die Wörterbücher als Gebrauchsgegenstände verstehen. *Lexicographica* 18: 253–263.

Bertels, Ann, Cédrick Fairon, Jörg Tiedemann, and Serge Verlinde (2009). Corpus parallèles et corpus ciblés au secours du dictionnaire de traduction. *Cahiers de lexicologie* 94: 199–219.

Bhattacharyya, Pushpak, Prabhakar Pande. Laxmi Kashyap and Salil Joshi (n.d.). *Netting among Words*. Available at http://dep.iitb.ac.in/wordnet/wordnet.html (last accessed 8 September 2010).

Biber, Douglas, Ulla Connor, and Thomas A. Upton (2007). *Discourse on the Move*. Amsterdam and Philadelphia: Benjamins.

Biber Douglas, Susan Conrad, and Viviana Cortes (2004). If you look at . . . : Lexical bundles in university teaching and textbooks. *Applied Linguistics* 25(3): 371–405.

Biber Douglas, Stig Johansson, Geoffrey Leech, Susan Conrad, and Edward Finegan (1999). *Longman Grammar of Spoken and Written English*. Harlow: Longman.

Bick, Eckhard (2009). DeepDict—A graphical corpus-based dictionary of word relations. *Proceedings of NODALIDA 2009. NEALT Proceedings Series Vol. 4*, 268–271. Tartu: Tartu University Library.

Binon, Jean, Serge Verlinde, Jan Van Dyck, and Ann Bertels (2000). *Dictionnaire d'apprentissage du français des affaires. Dictionnaire de compréhension et de production de la langue des affaires*. Paris: Didier.

Bogaards, Paul (1993). Models of dictionary use. *Toegepaste Taalwetenschap in Artikelen* 47/48: 17–28.

——(1998). Scanning long entries in learner's dictionaries. In T. Fontenelle, P. Hiligsmann, A. Michiels, A. Moulin, and S. Theissen (eds), *EURALEX '98 Actes/Proceedings*, 555–563. Liege: Université de Liège, Départements d'anglais et de néerlandais.

——(2003). Uses and users of dictionaries. In P. van Sterkenburg (ed.), *A Practical Guide to Lexicography, Terminology and Lexicography Research and Practice 6*, 26–33. Amsterdam and Philadephia: John Benjamins.

Bogaards, Paul, and Batia Laufer (eds) (2004). *Vocabulary in Second Language*. Amsterdam and Philadelphia: John Benjamins.

Bond, Francis, Hitoshi Isahara, Sanae Fujita, and Kiyotaka Uchimoto (2009). Enhancing the Japanese WordNet. *Proceedings of the 7th Workshop on Asian Language Resources*, 6–7 August 2009, Suntec, Singapore. 1–8.

Bonin, Patrick (ed.) (2004). *Mental Lexicon: Some Words to Talk About Words*. Hauppauge, NY: Nova Science Publishers.

Boonmoh, Atipat, and Hilary Nesi (2008). A survey of dictionary use by Thai university staff and students, with special reference to pocket electronic dictionaries. *Horizontes de Lingüística Aplicada* 6(2): 79–90.

Boonmoh, Atipat, Wareesiri Singhasiri, and Jonathan Hull (2005). Problems using electronic dictionaries to translate Thai written essays into English. *rEFLections* 8: 8–18. Available at http://arts.kmutt.ac.th/sola/rEFL/REFL8.pdf.

Bordet, Geneviève (2009). A comparative study of PhD abstracts written in English by native and non-native speakers across different disciplines. *Proceedings from Corpus Linguistics*. Liverpool, 20–23 July 2009. Available from ucrel.lancs.ac.uk/publications/cl2009/162_Full-Paper.doc.

——(2011). Etude discursive des résumés de thèse dans une perspective d'analyse de genre. Unpublished PhD thesis, CLILLAC-ARP, Université Paris 7-Paris Diderot.

Bosch, Sonja, Christiane Fellbaum, and Karel Pala (2008). Enhancing WordNets with morphological relations: A case study from Czech, English and Zulu. *Global WordNet Conference*, 74–90.

Bothma, Theo J. D. (2011). Filtering and adapting data and information in an online environment in response to user needs. In P. A. Fuertes-Olivera and H. Bergenholtz (eds), *e-Lexicography: The Internet, Digital Initiatives and Lexicography*, 71–102. London and New York: Continuum.

Bowdle, Brian, and Dedre Gentner (2005). The career of metaphor. *Psychological Review* 112(1): 193–216.

Bower, Jack, and Brian McMillan (2007). Learner's use and views of portable electronic dictionaries. In K. Bradford-Watts (ed.), *JALT 2006 Conference Proceedings*, 697–708. Tokyo: JALT.

Bowker, Lynne (2003). Corpus-based applications for translator training: Exploring the possibilities. In S. Granger, J. Lerot, and S. Petch-Tyson (eds), *Corpus based Approaches to Contrastive Linguistics and Translation Studies*, 169–183. Amsterdam and New York: Rodopi.

——(2004). What does it take to be a translator in Canada in the 21st Century? Exploring a database of job advertisements. *Meta* 49(4): 960–972.

——(2010). The contribution of corpus linguistics to the development of specialised dictionaries for learners. In P. Fuertes Olivera (ed.), *Specialised Dictionaries for Learners*, 155–168. Tübingen: Max Niemeyer Verlag.

——(2011). Off the record and on the fly: Examining the impact of corpora on terminographic practice in the context of translation. In A. Kruger, K. Wallmach, and J. Munday (eds), *Corpus-based Translation Studies: Research and Applications*, 211–236. London and New York: Continuum.

Bowker, Lynne, and Jennifer Pearson (2002). *Working with Specialized Language: A Practical Guide to Using Corpora*. London and New York: Routledge.

Boyd-Graber, Jordan, Christiane Fellbaum, Daniel Osherson, and Robert Schapire (2006). Adding dense, weighted connections to WordNet. *Proceedings of the Third International WordNet Conference*, Masaryk University Brno, 29–36.

Boyes Braem, Penny, and Rachel Sutton-Spence (eds) (2001). *The Hands are the Head of the Mouth: The Mouth as Articulator in Sign Languages*. Hamburg: Signum Verlag.

Brien, David, and Mary Brennan (1994). Sign language dictionaries: Issues and developments. In H. F. Bos and G. M. Schermer (eds), *Sign Language Research 1994: Proceedings of the Fourth European Congress on Sign Language Research, Munich, September 1–3, 1994*, 313–338. Hamburg: Signum Verlag.

Brien, David, and Graham Turner (1994). Lemmas, dilemmas and lexicographical aniso-morphism: Presenting meanings in the first BSL–English dictionary. In I. Ahlgren,

B. Bergman, and M. Brennan (eds), *Perspectives on Sign Language Usage: Papers from the Fifth International Symposium on Sign Language Research*, vol. 2, 391–407. Durham: International Sign Linguistics Association (ISLA).

Burkhanov, Igor (2003). Pragmatic specifications: Usage indications, labels, examples; dictionaries of style, dictionaries of collocations. In P. van Sterkenburg (ed.), *A Practical Guide to Lexicography*, 102–111. Amsterdam and Philadelphia: John Benjamins.

Callison-Burch, C. (2009). Fast, cheap, and creative: Evaluating translation quality using Amazon's mechanical Turk. *Proceedings of the 2009 Conference on Empirical Methods in Natural Language Processing*, 286–295. Singapore: Association for Computational Linguistics.

Campoy Cubillo, Mari Carmen (2002). Dictionary use and dictionary needs of ESP students: An experimental approach. *International Journal of Lexicography* 15(3): 206–228.

Carr, Michael (1997). Internet dictionaries and lexicography. *International Journal of Lexicography* 10(3): 209–230.

Carreiras, Manuel, Eva Gutiérrez-Sigut, Silvia Baquero, and David Corina (2007). Lexical processing in Spanish Sign Language (LSE). *Journal of Memory and Language* 58: 100–122.

Cartier, Emmanuel (2000). Eléments pour une modélisation des dictionnaires électroniques. In Thomas Szende (ed.), *Dictionnaires bilingues: méthodes et contenus*, 135–152. Paris: Honoré Champion.

Chakrabarty, Dipak Kumar, Debasri Narayan, Prabhakar Pande, and Pushpak Bhattacharyya (2002). An experience in building the Indo WordNet – a WordNet for Hindi. *Proceedings of the First International Conference on Global WordNet*, Mysore, India.

Chambers, Angela (2010). L'apprentissage de l'écriture en langue seconde à l'aide d'un corpus spécialisé. *Revue française de linguistique appliquée* 15: 9–20.

Chan, Clarice S. C. (2009). Forging a link between research and pedagogy: A holistic framework for evaluating business English materials. *English for Specific Purposes* 28: 125–136.

Charron, Marc (2005). Plus vite, encore plus vite: la traduction à l'heure de la mondialisation. *Translation Studies in the New Millennium: An International Journal of Translation and Interpreting* 3: 15–27.

Chen, Yuzhen (2010). Dictionary use and EFL learning: A contrastive study of pocket electronic dictionaries and paper dictionaries. *International Journal of Lexicography* 23(3): 275–306.

——(2011). Studies on bilingualized dictionaries: The user perspective. *International Journal of Lexicography* 24(2): 161–197.

Chon, Y. V. (2009). The electronic dictionary for writing: A solution or a problem? *International Journal of Lexicography* 22(1): 23–54.

Christ, Oliver (1995). *The IMS Corpus Workbench Technical Manual: Technical Report*. Institut für maschinelle Sprachverarbeitung, Universität Stuttgart.

Chun, Dorothy M., and Jan L. Plass (1996). Effects of multimedia annotations on vocabulary acquisition. *Modern Language Journal* 80(2): 183–198.

Church, Kenneth Ward, and Patrick Hanks (1989). Word association norms, mutual information, and lexicography. In *Proceedings of the 27th Annual Meeting of the Association for Computational Linguistics, 26–29 June 1989*, 76–83. University of British Columbia. Revised version published 1990 in *Computational Linguistics* 16(1): 22–29. Reprinted in Fontenelle (ed.) (2008) *Practical Lexicography: A Reader*, 285–295. Oxford: Oxford University Press; and Hanks (ed.) (2008) *Lexicology: Critical Concepts in Linguistics*, vol. VI, 150–167. London and New York: Routledge.

Clear, Jeremy (1987). Computing. In John McHardy Sinclair (ed.) *Looking Up: An Account of the COBUILD Project in Lexical Computing*, 41–61. London: Collins ELT.

Cobb, Tom (1997). Is there any measurable learning from hands on concordancing? *System* 25(3): 301–315.

——(2003). Do corpus-based electronic dictionaries replace concordancers? In B. Morrison, G. Green, and G. Motteram (eds). *Directions in CALL: Experience, Experiments, Evaluation*, 179–206. Hong Kong: Polytechnic University.

Collins, Christopher. Wordnet Explorer: Applying Visualization Principles to Lexical Semantics. Available at http://faculty.uoit.ca/collins/research/wordnet-explorer.pdf (last accessed 15 September 2010).

Convery, Cathal, Pádraig Ó Mianáin, Muiris Ó Raghallaigh, Beryl T. Sue Atkins, Adam Kilgarriff, and Michael Rundell (2010). Database of ANalysed Texts of English (DANTE): The NEID database project. In Anne Dykstra and Tanneke Schoonheim (eds), *Proceedings of the XIV EURALEX International Conference*, 293–295. Leeuwarden: Fryske Akademy.

Corris, Miriam, Christopher Manning, Susan Poetsch, and Jane Simpson (2000). Bilingual dictionaries for Australian languages: User studies on the place of paper and electronic dictionaries. In U. Heid, S. Evert, E. Lehmann, and C. Rohrer (eds), *Proceedings of the IX EURALEX International Congress*, 169–181. Stuttgart.

Cowie, Anthony P. (1999). *English Dictionaries for Foreign Learners: A History*. Oxford: Clarendon Press.

Coxhead, Averil (2000). A new Academic Word List. *TESOL Quarterly* 34(2): 213–238.

——(2002). The Academic Word List: A corpus-based word list for academic purposes. In B. Kettemann and Georg Marko (eds), *Teaching and Learning by Doing Corpus Analysis. Proceedings of the Fourth International Conference on Teaching and Language Corpora, Graz 19–24 July 2000*, 73–89. Amsterdam: Rodopi.

Coxhead, Averil, and David Hirsh (2007). A pilot science-specific word list. *Revue française de linguistique appliquée. Le lexique de la langue scientifique* 12(2): 65–78.

Craik, Fergus I. M., and Robert S. Lockhart (1972). Levels of processing: A framework for memory research. *Journal of Verbal Learning and Verbal Behavior* 11: 671–684.

Craik, Fergus I. M., and Endel Tulving (1975). Depth of processing and the retention of words in episodic memory. *Journal of Experimental Psychology: General* 104(3): 268–294.

Culy, Chris, and Verena Lyding (2010). Visualizations for exploratory corpus and text analysis. In *Proceedings of the 2nd International Conference on Corpus Linguistics (CILC-10)*, 257–268. Spain: A Coruña.

Curado Fuentes, Alejandro (2001). Lexical behaviour in academic and technical corpora: Implications for ESP development. *Language Learning and Technology* 5(3): 106–129.

Dancette, Jeanne, and Christophe Réthoré (2000). *Dictionnaire analytique de la distribution / Analytical Dictionary of Retailing*. Montréal: Les Presses de l'Université de Montréal.

Davies, Mark (2009). The 385+ million word Corpus of Contemporary American English (1990–2008+): Design, architecture, and linguistic insights. *International Journal of Corpus Linguistics* 14(2): 159–190.

Day, Robert A. (1989). The origins of the scientific paper: The IMRAD Format: The sameness of a manuscript's organization provides reliability. *American Medical Writers Association Journal* 4(2): 16–18. Available at www.amwa.org/default/publications/journal/scanned/vo4.2.pdf (last accessed 17 October 2011).

De Schryver, Gilles-Maurice (2003). Lexicographer's dreams in the electronic-dictionary age. *International Journal of Lexicography* 16(2): 143–199.

——(2010). State-of-the-art software to support intelligent lexicography. In R. Zhu (ed.), *Chinese Lexicographic Research 2*, 584–599. S.l.: Chinese Social Sciences. Available at www.hcxf.cn/read.asp?id=570.

——(2011). Why opting for a dedicated, professional, off-the-shelf dictionary writing system matters. In K. Akasu and S. Uchida (eds), *ASIALEX 2011 Proceedings. Lexicography: Theoretical and Practical Perspectives. Papers Submitted to the Seventh ASIALEX Biennial International Conference,Kyoto Terrsa, Kyoto, Japan, August 22–24, 2011*, 647–656. Kyoto: Asian Association for Lexicography.

——(in print). The concept of simultaneous feedback. In R. H. Gouws, U. Heid, W. Schweickhard, and H. Ernst Wiegand (eds), *Dictionaries. An International Encyclopedia of Lexicography. Supplementary Volume: Recent Developments with Special Focus on Computational Lexicography*. Berlin and New York: de Gruyter.

De Schryver, Gilles-Maurice, and David Joffe (2004). On how electronic dictionaries are really used. In G. Williams and S. Vessier (eds), *Proceedings of the Eleventh EURALEX International Congress, Lorient, France, July 6–10, 2004*, 187–196. Lorient: Faculté des Lettres et des Sciences Humaines, Université de Bretagne Sud.

——(2005). Dynamic metalanguage customisation with the dictionary application Tshwane-Lex. In F. Kiefer, G. Kiss, and J. Pajzs (eds), *Papers in Computational Lexicography*, COMPLEX 2005, 190–199. Budapest: Linguistics Institute, Hungarian Academy of Sciences.

——(2006). The users and uses of TshwaneLex One. In G.-M. de Schryver (ed.), *DWS 2006: Proceedings of the Fourth International Workshop on Dictionary Writing Systems*, 41–46. Pretoria: (SF)^2 Press.

De Schryver, Gilles-Maurice, David Joffe, Pitta Joffe, and Sarah Hillewaert (2006). Do dictionary users really look up frequent words? On the overestimation of the value of corpus-based lexicography. *Lexikos* 16: 67–83. Available at http://tshwanedje.com/publications/KDP.pdf.

De Schryver, Gilles-Maurice, and D. J. Prinsloo (2001). Fuzzy SF: Towards the ultimate customised dictionary. *Studies in Lexicography* 11(1): 97–111.

——(2011). Do dictionaries define on the level of their target users? A case study for three Dutch dictionaries. *International Journal of Lexicography* 24(1): 5–28.

Deng, Yanping (2005). A survey of college students' skills and strategies of dictionary use in English learning. *CELEA Journal* 28(4): 73–77.

Descy, Don E. (2006). The wiki: True web democracy. *TechTrends* 50(1): 4–5.

Désilets, Alain, Benoît Farley, Marta Stojanovic, and Frances Urdininea (2010). Using WeBi-Text to search multilingual web sites. *Proceedings of the Association of Machine Translation in the Americas (AMTA) conference*, 31 October–4 November 2010, Denver, CO. Available at http://nparc.cisti-icist.nrc-cnrc.gc.ca/npsi/ctrl?action=rtdoc&an=16959071 (last accessed 2 February 2012).

Diekmann, Andreas (2002). *Empirische Sozialforschung: Grundlagen, Methoden, Anwendungen* (8th edition). Reinbek: Rowohlt Taschenbuch Verlag.

Docherty, Vincent (2000). Dictionaries on the Internet: An overview. In U. Heid, S. Evert, E. Lehmann, and C. Rohrer (eds), *Proceedings of the Ninth EURALEX International Congress*, 67–74. Stuttgart: Universitat Stuttgart.

Dražić, Jasmina (2008). Principles for the design of the monolingual minimal dictionary of Serbian as a foreign language. In B. Golubović and J. Raecke (eds), *Bosnisch. Kroatisch. Serbisch. B.K.S. als Fremdsprachen an den Universitäten der Welt*, 43–50. München: Verlag Otto Sagner.

Dubuc, Robert (2002). *Manuel Pratique de Terminologie* (4th edition). Brossard, Québec: Linguatech.

Dumas, Joseph S., and Janice C. Redish (1999). *A Practical Guide to Usability Testing*. Norwood: Ablex Publishing Corporation.

Durán-Muñoz, Isabel (2010). Specialised lexicographical resources: A survey of translators' needs. In S. Granger and M. Paquot (eds), *eLexicography in the 21st Century: New Challenges, New Applications. Proceedings of eLEX2009*, 55–66. Louvain-la-Neuve: Presses universitaires de Louvain.

Dutton, Marsha (2011). Embracing the digital siren: Collaborative lexicography in the twenty-first century. In Michael Adams and Anne Curzan (eds), *Contours of English and English Language Studies*, 237–248. Ann Arbor: University of Michigan Press.

Dwornik, Katarzyna, and Kacper Margol (2011). Monolingual and Bilingual Online Dictionaries in the Comprehension of Written English Text by Polish Advanced Learners: A Think-Aloud Study. Unpublished BA thesis, Wydział Humanistyczny, Collegium Balticum, Szczecin.

Dyen, Isidore, Joseph B. Kruskal, and Paul Black (1992). *An Indoeuropean Classification: A Lexicostatistical Experiment*. Transactions of the American Philosophical Society 82. Philadelphia, PA: American Philosophical Society.

Dziemianko, Anna (2010). Paper or electronic? The role of dictionary form in language reception, production and the retention of meaning and collocations. *International Journal of Lexicography* 23(3): 257–273.

Ellis, Rod, and Gary Barkhuizen (2005). *Analysing Learner Language*. Oxford: Oxford University Press.

Engberg-Pedersen, Elisabeth (1993). *Space in Danish Sign Language: The Semantics and Morphosyntax of the Use of Space in a Visual Language*. Hamburg: Signum Verlag.

Engelberg, Stefan, and Carolin Müller-Spitzer (in press). Dictionary portals. In Rufus H. Gouws, Ulrich Heid, Wolfgang Schweickhard, and Herbert Ernst Wiegand (eds), *Dictionaries. An International Encyclopedia of Lexicography. Supplementary volume: Recent Developments with Special Focus on Computational Lexicography*. Berlin and New York: De Gruyter.

Erlenkamp, Sonja (2000). *Syntaktische Kategorien und lexikalische Klassen. Typologische Aspekte der Deutschen Gebärdensprache*. München: Lincom Europa.

Etzioni, Oren, Kobi Reiter, Stephen Soderland, and Marcus Sammer (2007). Lexical translation with application to image search on the web. In *Proceedings of Machine Translation Summit XI*, Copenhagen, Denmark.

Evert, Stefan, and Brigitte Krenn (2001). Methods for the qualitative evaluation of lexical association measures. *Proceedings of the 39th Annual Meeting of the Association for Computational* Linguistics, 188–195. Toulouse: ACL.

Faber, Pamela, Pilar León Araúz, Juan Antonio PrietoVelasco, and Arianne Reimerink (2007). Linking images and words: The description of specialized concepts. *International Journal of Lexicography* 20(1): 39–65.

Fellbaum, Christiane (ed.) (1998). *WordNet: An Electronic Lexical Database (Language, Speech, and Communication)*. Cambridge, MA: MIT Press.

Fernández, Trinidad, and Pamela Faber (2011). The representation of multidimensionality in a bilingualized English–Spanish thesaurus for learners in architecture and building construction. *International Journal of Lexicography* 24(2): 198–225.

Ferraresi, Adriano, Eros Zanchetta, Marco Baroni, and Silvia Bernardini (2008). Introducing and evaluating ukWaC, a very large web-derived corpus of English. In Stefan Evert, Adam Kilgarriff, and Serge Sharoff (eds), *Proceedings of the 4th Web as Corpus Workshop (WAC-4) – Can we beat Google?*, 47–54. Marrakech, 1 June 2008.

Fillmore, Charles J. (1968). The case for case. In E. Bach and R. T. Harms (eds), *Universals in Linguistic Theory*, 1–88. New York: Holt, Rinehart, and Winston.

——(1975). An alternative to checklist theories of meaning. In *Papers from the First Annual Meeting of the Berkeley Linguistics Society*, 121–131. Berkeley, California.

——(1976). Frame semantics and the nature of language. *Annals of the New York Academy of Sciences* 280: 20–32.

——(1977). The need for a frame semantics in linguistics. In Hans Karlgren (ed.), *Statistical Methods in Linguistics* 12, 5–29. Stockholm: Skriptor.

——(1982). Frame semantics. In The Linguistic Society of Korea (ed.), *Linguistics in the Morning Calm*, 111–137. Seoul: Hanshin Publishing Co.

——(2006). Frame semantics. In Keith Brown (ed.), *Encyclopedia of Language and Linguistics* (2nd edition), 613–620. Oxford: Elsevier.

Fillmore, Charles J., and Beryl T. Sue Atkins (1992). Towards a frame-based lexicon: The semantics of *risk* and its neighbors. In A. Lehrer and E. Feder Kittay (eds), *Frames, Fields, and Contrasts: New Essays in Semantic and Lexical Organization*, 75–102. Hillsdale, NJ: Lawrence Erlbaum Associates.

——(1994). Starting where the dictionaries stop: The challenge for computational lexicography. In Beryl T. Sue Atkins and A. Zampolli (eds), *Computational Approaches to the Lexicon*, 349–393. Oxford: Oxford University Press.

Fillmore, Charles J., Christopher Johnson, and Miriam R. L. Petruck (2003). Background to Framenet. *International Journal of Lexicography* 16(3): 235–250.

Firth, J. R. (1950). Personality and language in society. *Sociological Review* 42: 37–52. Reprinted in J. R. Firth (1957) *Papers in Linguistics 1934–1951*, 177–189. Oxford: Oxford University Press.

——(1957a). Modes of meaning. In J. R. Firth (ed.), *Papers in Linguistics 1934–1951*, 190–215. Oxford: Oxford University Press.

——(1957b). A synopsis of linguistic theory 1930–1955. In J. R. Firth, W. Haas, and M. A. K. Halliday (eds), *Studies in Linguistic Analysis*, 1–32. Oxford: Philological Society. Reprinted in F. R. Palmer (ed.) (1968), *Selected Papers of J. R. Firth*. London: Longman.

Flinz, Carolina (2010). DIL: A German–Italian online specialized dictionary of linguistics. In S. Granger and M. Paquot (eds), *eLexicography in the 21st Century: New Challenges, New Applications. Proceedings of eLEX2009*, 67–76. Louvain: Presses universitaires de Louvain.

Fontenelle, Thierry (1994). Towards the construction of a collocational database for translation students. *Meta* 39(1): 47–56.

——(ed.) (2008). *Practical Lexicography: A Reader*. Oxford: Oxford University Press.

Fox, Gwyneth (1987). The case for examples. In John Sinclair (ed.), *Looking Up: An Account of the COBUILD Project in Lexical Computing*, 137–149. London: Collins.

Fried, Joseph P. (2006). Speaking in (many) tongues can be profitable. *New York Times*, 30 April 2006. Available at www.nytimes.com/2006/04/30/nyregion/30homefront.html? ex=1304049600&en=5ced97b426f03864&ei=5090&partner=rssuserland&emc=rss.

Froeliger, Nicolas (2009). Mettre en cycle les savoirs, l'enseignement de la traduction à l'Université Paris Diderot. In M. Ballard (ed.), *Traductologie et enseignement de la traduction à l'université*, 235–248. Artois: Artois Presses Université.

——(2010). Le facteur local comme levier d'une traductologie pragmatique. *Meta* 55(4): 642–660.

Fuentes, Alejandro Curado (2001a). Lexical behavior in academic and technical corpora: Implications for ESP development. *Language Learning and Technology* 5(3): 106–129.

——(2001b). Lexical acquisition in ESP via corpus tools: Two case studies. *Scripta Manent: ICT in Teaching Languages for Specific Purposes* Volume 3/1. Available at www.sdutsj.edus.si/ScriptaManent/2007_1/Contents3-1.html (last accessed 18 November 2011).

Fuertes-Olivera, Pedro A. (2009). The function theory of lexicography and electronic dictionaries: Wiktionary as a prototype of collective free multiple-language internet dictionary. In H. Bergenholtz, S. Nielsen, and S. Tarp (eds), *Lexicography at a Crossroads: Dictionaries and Encyclopedias Today, Lexicographical Tools Tomorrow*. Linguistic Insights: Studies in Language and Communication 90, 99–134. Bern: Peter Lang.

——(2011). Equivalent selection in specialized e-Lexicography: A case study with Spanish accounting terms. *Lexikos* 21: 95–119.

——(submitted). Translator studies and the literal translation hypothesis. *Meta*.

Fuertes-Olivera, Pedro A., and Ascensión Arribas-Baño (2008). *Pedagogical Specialised Lexicography. The Representation of Meaning in Business and Spanish Business Dictionaries*. Amsterdam and Philadelphia: John Benjamins.

Fuertes-Olivera, Pedro A., and Henning Bergenholtz (2011a). Introduction: The construction of Internet dictionaries. In P. A. Fuertes-Olivera and H. Bergenholtz (eds), *e-Lexicography: The Internet, Digital Initiatives and Lexicography*, 1–16. London and New York: Continuum.

——(eds) (2011b). *E- Lexicography. The Internet, Digital Initiatives and Lexicography*. London and New York: Continuum.

Fuertes-Olivera, Pedro A., and Montserrat Bermúdez Bausela (2011). La hipótesis de la traducción literal en el discurso especializado. In A. Olivares Pardo, A. Sopeña Balordi, F. Navaroo Domínguez, and M. Tricás Preckler (eds), *Discurso y mente: de los textos especializados a los traducidos*, 99–112. Granada: Comares.

Fuertes-Olivera, Pedro A., and Sandro Nielsen (2011). The dynamics of terms in accounting: What the construction of the *accounting dictionaries* reveals about metaphorical terms in culture-bound subject fields. In R. Temmerman and M. Van Campenhoudt (eds), *The*

Dynamics of Terms in Specialized Communication. An Interdisciplinary Perspective. Special Issue of *Terminology. International Journal of Applied Issues in Specialized Communication* 17(1): 157–180.

——(2012). Online dictionaries for assisting translators of LSP texts: The *Accounting Dictionaries. International Journal of Lexicography* 25. Doi: 10.1093/ijl/ecr034.

Fuertes-Olivera, Pedro A., and Marta Niño-Amo (2011). Internet dictionaries for communicative and cognitive functions: El diccionario Inglés–Español de contabilidad. In P. A. Fuertes-Olivera and H. Bergenholtz (eds), *e-Lexicography: The Internet, Digital Initiatives and Lexicography*, 168–186. London and New York: Continuum.

Fuertes-Olivera, Pedro A., and Sven Tarp (2011). Lexicography for the third millennium: Cognitive-oriented specialised dictionaries for learners. *Ibérica* 21(1): 141–162.

Gamper, Johann, and Judith Knapp (2000). Towards an adaptive learners' dictionary. In P. Brusilovsky, O. Stock, and C. Strappavara (eds), *Proceedings of International Conference on Adaptive Hypermedia and Adaptive Web-Based Systems (AH2000)*, 311–314. Berlin and New York: Springer.

——(2002). Adaptation in a vocabulary acquisition system. *KI – Zeitschrift Künstliche Intelligenz* 3(2): 27–30.

Geckeler, Horst (2002). Anfänge und Ausbau des Wortfeldgedankens. In D. A. Cruse, M. J. Hundsnurscher, and P. R. Lutzeier (eds), *Lexikologie. Ein internationales Handbuch zur Natur und Struktur von Wörtern und Wortschätzen*, 713–728. Berlin and New York: de Gruyter.

Gelpi, Cristina (2004). Reliability of online dictionaries. In H. Gottlieb and J. E. Mogensen (eds), *Dictionary Visions, Research and Practice*, 3–12. Amsterdam: John Benjamins.

Gibbs, Raymond W., Jr. (ed.) (2008). *The Cambridge Handbook of Metaphor and Thought.* Cambridge: Cambridge University Press.

Giles, Jim (2005). Internet encyclopaedias go head to head. *Nature* 438: 900–901.

Gilquin, Gaëtanelle, Sylviane Granger, and Magali Paquot (2007). Learner corpora: The missing link in EAP pedagogy. In P. Thompson (ed.), *Corpus-based EAP Pedagogy*. Special issue of the *Journal of English for Academic Purposes* 6(4): 319–335.

Giora, Rachel (2003). *On Our Mind: Salience, Context, and Figurative Language.* Oxford: Oxford University Press.

Gledhill C. (2000). *Collocations in Science Writing.* Language in Performance 22. Tuebingen: Gunter Narr Verlag.

Glucksberg, Sam (2001). *Understanding Figurative Language.* Oxford: Oxford University Press.

Golubović, Biljana, and Jochen Raecke (eds) (2008). *Bosnisch. Kroatisch. Serbisch. B.K.S. als Fremdsprachen an den Universitäten der Welt.* München: Verlag Otto Sagner.

Gouws, Rufus H. (1990). Information categories in dictionaries with special reference to Southern Africa. In R. R. K. Hartmann (ed.), *Lexicography in Africa*, 52–65. Exeter: University of Exeter Press.

——(2006). Die zweisprachige Lexikographie Afrikaans-Deutsch. Eine metalexikographische Herausforderung. In A. Dimova, V. Jesenšek, and P. Petkov (eds), *Zweisprachige Lexikographie und Deutsch als Fremdsprache. Drittes Internationales Kolloquium zur Lexikographie und Wörterbuchforschung.* Konstantin Preslavski-Universität Schumen, 23–24 Oktober

2005 (= Germanistische Linguistik 184–185), 49–58. Hildesheim, Zürich, New York: Georg Olms.

——(2011). Learning, unlearning and innovation in the planning of electronic dictionaries. In P. A. Fuertes-Olivera and H. Bergenholtz (eds), *e-Lexicography: The Internet, Digital Initiatives and Lexicography*, 17–29. London and New York: Continuum.

Gouws, Rufus H., and D. J. Prinsloo (2005). *Principles and Practices of South African Lexicography*. Stellenbosch: African Sun Media.

Granger, Sylviane (ed.) (1998). *Learner English on Computer*. London and New York: Addison Wesley Longman.

Granger, Sylviane, Estelle Dagneaux, Fanny Meunier, and Magali Paquot (2009). *The International Corpus of Learner English. Handbook and CD-ROM. Version 2*. Louvain-la-Neuve: Presses universitaires de Louvain. Available at www.i6doc.com.

Granger, Sylviane, Joseph Hung, and Stephanie Petch-Tyson (eds) (2002). *Computer Learner Corpora, Second Language Acquisition and Foreign Language Teaching*. Amsterdam and Philadelphia: John Benjamins.

Granger, Sylviane, and Magali Paquot (2008a). From dictionary to phrasebook? In E. Bernal and J. DeCesaris (eds), *Proceedings of the XIII EURALEX International Congress*, Barcelona, Spain, 15–19 July 2008, 1345–1355.

——(2008b). Disentangling the phraseological web. In S. Granger and F. Meunier (eds), *Phraseology: An Interdisciplinary Perspective*, 27–49. Amsterdam and Philadelphia: Benjamins.

——(eds) (2010a). *eLexicography in the 21st Century. New Challenges, New Applications. Proceedings of eLex 2009, Louvain-la-Neuve, 22–24 October 2009*. Louvain-la-Neuve: Presses universitaires de Louvain.

——(2010b). Customising a general EAP dictionary to meet learner needs. In S. Granger and M. Paquot (eds), *eLexicography in the 21st Century: New Challenges, New Applications. Proceedings of eLex 2009, Louvain-la-Neuve, 22–24 October 2009*, 87–96. Louvain-la-Neuve: Presses universitaires de Louvain.

——(2010c). The Louvain EAP dictionary (LEAD). In A. Dykstra and T. Schoonheim (eds), *Proceedings of the XIV EURALEX International Congress*, Leeuwarden, 6–10 July 2010, 321–326. Ljouwert: Afûk.

Grefenstette, Gregory (1998). The future of linguistics and lexicographers: Will there be lexicographers in the year 3000? In Thierry Fontenelle, Philippe Hiligsmann, Archibald Michiels, André Moulin, and Siegfried Theissen (eds), *Proceedings of the Eighth EURALEX Congress*, 25–41. Liege: University of Liege. Reprinted in Thierry Fontenelle (ed.) (2008) *Practical Lexicography: A Reader*, 307–323. Oxford: Oxford University Press.

Guillot, Marie-Noelle, and Marie-Madeleine Kenning (1994). Electronic monolingual dictionaries as language learning aids: A case study. *Computers in Education* 23(1/2): 63–73.

Guthrie, Malcolm (1970). *Comparative Bantu Vol. III. An Introduction to the Comparative Linguistics and Prehistory of the Bantu Languages*. Farnborough: Gregg Press.

Hahn, Marion, Annette Klosa, Carolin Müller-Spitzer, Ulrich Schnörch, and Petra Storjohann (2008). elexiko – das elektronische, lexikografisch–lexikologische korpusbasierte Wortschatzinformationssystem. Zur Neukonzeption, Erweiterung und Revision einzelner

Angabebereiche. In A. Klosa (ed), *Lexikografische Portale im Internet. (= OPAL Sonderheft 1/2008)*, 57–85. Mannheim: Institut für Deutsche Sprache.

Hanks, Patrick (1990). Evidence and intuition in lexicography. In J. Tomaszczyk and B. Lewandowska-Tomaszczyk (eds), *Meaning and Lexicography*, 31–41. Amsterdam and Philadelphia: Benjamins.

——(1994). Linguistic norms and pragmatic explanations, or why lexicographers need prototype theory and vice versa. In F. Kiefer, G. Kiss, and J. Pajzs (eds), *Papers in Computational Lexicography: Complex '94*, 89–113. Research Institute for Linguistics, Hungarian Academy of Sciences. Reprinted in Hanks (ed.) (2008), *Lexicology: Critical Concepts in Linguistics*, volume V, 233–255. London and New York: Routledge.

——(2008). Mapping meaning onto use: a Pattern Dictionary of English verbs. Paper presented to the American Association for Corpus Linguistics, 15 March 2008, Utah.

——(2009). The impact of corpora on dictionaries. In P. Baker (ed.), *Contemporary Corpus Linguistics*, 214–236. London: Continuum.

——(2010). Terminology, phraseology, and lexicography. In A. Dykstra and T. Schoonheim (eds), *EURALEX Proceedings*, 1299–1308. Leeuwarden: Frisian Institute.

Hanks, Patrick, and Rachel Giora (eds) (2011). *Metaphor and Figurative Language: Critical Concepts.* 6 volumes. Oxford: Routledge.

Hanks, Patrick, and James Pustejovsky (2005). A Pattern dictionary for natural language processing. *Revue française de linguistique appliquée* 10(2): 63–82.

Hardie, Andrew (2009). CQPweb – combining power, flexibility and usability in a corpus analysis tool. Paper presented at the 30th ICAME conference, Lancaster, 27–31 May 2009. Available at www.lancs.ac.uk/staff/hardiea/cqpweb-paper.pdf.

Harley, Andrew (2000). Cambridge dictionaries online. In U. Heid, S. Evert, E. Lehmann, and C. Rohrer (eds), *Proceedings of the Ninth EURALEX International Congress, EURALEX 2000, Stuttgart, Germany, August 8–12, 2000*, 85–88. Stuttgart: Institut für Maschinelle Sprachverarbeitung, Universität Stuttgart.

Hartmann, Reinhard R. K. (1989). Sociology of the dictionary user: Hypotheses and empirical studies. In F. J. Hausmann, O. Reichmann, H. E. Wiegand, and L. Zgusta (eds), *Wörterbücher/Dictionaries/Dictionnaires. An International Encyclopedia of Lexicography*, Vol. 1, *Handbücher zur Sprach- und Kommunikationswissenschaft*, 102–111. Berlin and New York: Walter de Gruyter.

——(2000). European dictionary culture. The Exeter case study of dictionary use among university students, against the wider context of the reports and recommendations of the thematic network project in the area of languages (1996–1999). In U. Heid, S. Evert, E. Lehmann, and C. Rohrer (eds), *Proceedings of the IX EURALEX International Congress*, 385–391. Stuttgart.

——(2001). *Teaching and Researching Lexicography.* Harlow: Pearson Education.

——(2005a). Pure or hybrid? The development of mixed dictionary genres. *Facta Universitatis* 3(2): 193–208.

——(2005b). Onomasiological dictionaries in 20th-century Europe. *Lexicographica* 21: 216–219.

Hartmann, Reinhard R. K., and Gregory James (1998). *Dictionary of Lexicography.* London and New York: Routledge.

Haß, Ulrike (2005). Nutzungsbedingungen in der Hypertextlexikografie. Über eine empirische Untersuchung. In D. Steffens (ed.), *Wortschatzeinheiten: Aspekte ihrer (Be)schreibung. Dieter Herberg zum 65. Geburtstag, amades—Arbeitspapiere und Materialien zur deutschen Sprache*, 29–41. Mannheim: Institut für Deutsche Sprache.

Hausmann, Franz Joseph (1979). Un dictionnaire des collocations est-il possible? *Travaux de linguistique et de littérature* 17(1): 187–195.

Heid, Ulrich (1992). Décrire les collocations: deux approches lexicographiques et leur application dans un outil informatisé. *Terminologie et traduction* 2(3): 523–548.

——(2009). Aspects of lexical description for electronic dictionaries. In S. Granger and M. Paquot (eds), *eLexicography in the 21st Century: New Challenges, New Applications*. Conference abstracts of eLex2009, 22–24 October 2009, Louvain-la-Neuve: Centre for English Corpus Linguistics, Université catholique de Louvain, 1–3.

——(2011). Electronic dictionaries as tools: Towards an assessment of usability. In P. A. Fuertes-Olivera and H. Bergenholtz (eds), *e-Lexicography: The Internet, Digital Initiatives and Lexicography*, 287–304. London and New York: Continuum.

Heid, Ulrich, and Gerhard Freibott (1991). Collocations dans une base de données terminologiques et lexicales *Meta* 36(1): 77–91.

Heift, Trude (2004). Corrective feedback and learner uptake in CALL. *ReCALL* 16(2): 416–431.

Hill, Monica, and Batia Laufer (2003). Type of task, time-on-task and electronic dictionaries in incidental vocabulary acquisition. *IRAL-International Review of Applied Linguistics in Language Teaching* 41: 87–106.

Hirst, Graeme (2004). Ontology and the lexicon. In S. Staab and R. Studer (eds), *Handbook on Ontologies*, International Handbooks on Information Sciences, 209–230. Berlin and Heidelberg: Springer.

——(2009). Ontology and the lexicon. In Steffen Staab and Rudi Studer (eds), *Handbook on Ontologies*, International Handbooks on Information Sciences (2nd edition), 269–292. Berlin and Heidelberg: Springer.

Hockey, Susan (2000). Dictionaries and lexical databases. In S. Hockey (ed.), *Electronic Texts in the Humanities: Principles and Practice*, 146–171. Oxford and New York: Oxford University Press.

Hoey, Michael (2005). *Lexical Priming: A New Theory of Words and Language*. Oxford: Routledge.

Horák, Aleš, and Adam Rambousek (2007). Dictionary management system for DEB development platform. In B. Sharp and M. Zock (eds), *Proceedings of the 4th International Workshop on Natural Language Processing and Cognitive Science*, 129–138. Funchal: INSTICC Press.

Horák, Aleš, Piek Vossen, and Adam Rambousek (2008). The development of a complex-structured lexicon based on WordNet. In *Proceedings of the Fourth Global WordNet Conference*, 200–208. Szeged: University of Szeged.

Howarth, Peter (1998). The phraseology of learners' academic writing. In A. P. Cowie (ed.), *Phraseology: Theory, Analysis and Applications*, 161–186. Oxford: Oxford University Press.

Hsueh, Pei-Yun, Prem Melville, and Vikas Sindhwani (2009). Data quality from crowdsourcing: A study of annotation selection criteria, *Proceedings of the NAACL HLT 2009 Workshop on Active Learning for Natural Language Processing*, 27–35.

Hu, X., and A. Graesser (1998). Using WordNet and latent semantic analysis to evaluate the conversational contributions of learners in tutorial dialogue, *Proceedings of ICCE*, 337–341.

Huang, Chu-ren, Nicoletta Calzolari, Aldo Gangemi, Alessandro Lenci, Alessandro Oltramari, and Laurent Prevot (eds) (2010). *Ontology and the Lexicon: A Natural Language Processing Perspective*. Cambridge: Cambridge University Press.

Hüllen, Werner (2005). Onomasiologische Wörterbücher europäischer Sprachen in Geschichte und Gegenwart: Einführung, *Lexicographica* 21: 211–213.

Hulstijn, Jan H., and Beryl T. Sue Atkins (1998). Empirical research on dictionary use in foreign-language learning: Survey and discussion. In Beryl T. Sue Atkins (ed.), *Using Dictionaries. Studies of Dictionary Use by Language Learners and Translators, Lexicographica Series Maior 88*, 7–19. Tübingen: Niemeyer.

Hulstijn, Jan H., and Batia Laufer (2001). Some empirical evidence for the involvement load hypothesis in vocabulary acquisition. *Language Learning* 51: 539–558.

Hult, Ann-Kristin (2008). Från ord till handling. En studie i ordboksanvändning på nätet. In Á. Svavarsdóttir, G. Kvaran, G. Ingólfsson, and J. Hilmar Jónsson (eds), *Nordiska studier i lexikografi. Rapport från 9. Konference om leksikografi i Norden*, 243–257. Akureyri, Iceland: NFL.

Humblé, Philippe (2001). *Dictionaries and Language Learners*. Frankfurt am Main: Haag und Herchen.

Humbley, John (2002). Nouveaux dictionnaires, nouveaux rapports avec les utilisateurs. *Meta* 47(1): 95–104.

——(2006). Metaphor and secondary term formation. *Cahiers du CIEL 2000–2003: La métaphore: du discours général aux discours spécialisés*, 199–212. Paris: Université Paris 7.

——(2007). Horses for courses. A quoi sert la terminologie pour les traducteurs? Journée Traduction plein champ, UFR EILA 10 février 2007, in *La tribune internationale des langues vivantes*, 76–80.

——(2008). Les dictionnaires de néologismes, leur évolution depuis 1945: une perspective européenne. In J.-F. Sablayrolles (ed.), *Néologie et terminologie dans les dictionnaires*, 37–60. Collection Lexica, Mots et Dictionnaires. Paris: Honoré Champion.

Hundt, Marianne, Nadja Nesselhauf, and Carolin Biewer (eds) (2007). *Corpus Linguistics and the Web*. Amsterdam and New York: Rodopi.

Hunston, Susan (2007). Semantic prosody revisited. *International Journal of Corpus Linguistics* 12(2): 249–268.

Hunston, Susan, and Geoff Thompson (2000). *Evaluation in Text*. Oxford: Oxford University Press.

Hutchins, John (1998). The origins of the translator's workstation. *Machine Translation* 13(4): 287–307.

Hyland, Ken (2004). *Disciplinary Discourses: Social Interactions in Academic Writing*. Ann Arbor, MI: University of Michigan Press.

Hyland, Ken, and Liz Hamp-Lyons (2002). EAP: Issues and directions. *Journal of English for Academic Purposes* 1: 1–12.

Ide, Nancy, and Yorick Wilks (2006). Making sense about sense. In E. Agirre and P. Edmonds (eds), *Word Sense Disambiguation: Algorithms and Applications*, 47–73. New York: Springer.

Jantunen, Tommi, Markus Koskela, Jorma Laaksonen, and Päivi Raino (2010). Towards automated visualization and analysis of signed language motion: Method and linguistic issues. *Proceedings of the 5th International Conference on Speech Prosody, Chicago, Illinois, USA, 2010.* Available at http://speechprosody2010.illinois.edu/papers/100006.pdf (last accessed 8 June 2011).

Jarmasz, Mario, and Stan Szpakowicz (2003). Roget's thesaurus and semantic similarity. In *Proceedings of the International Conference on Recent Advances in Natural Language Processing*, 212–219. Borovets, Bulgaria.

Joffe, David, and Gilles-Maurice De Schryver (2004a). TshwaneLex—A state-of-the-art dictionary compilation program. In Geoffrey Williams and Sandra Vessier (eds), *Proceedings of the 11th EURALEX International Congress*, 99–104. Lorient, France: Université de Bretagne Sud.

——(2004b). TshwaneLex—Professional off-the-shelf lexicography software. In *Third International Workshop on Dictionary Writing Systems*, 17–20. Brno: Faculty of Informatics, Masaryk University.

Johnson, Samuel (1755). *A Dictionary of the English Language.* London: W. Strahan.

Johnston, Trevor (2010). From archive to corpus: Transcription and annotation in the creation of signed language corpora. *International Journal of Corpus Linguistics* 15(1): 106–131.

Johnston, Trevor, and Adam Schembri (1999). On defining lexeme in a sign language. *Sign Language and Linguistics* 2: 115–185.

Jones, S., and J. M. Sinclair (1974). English lexical collocations. *Cahiers de Lexicologie* 24: 15–61.

Josselin-Leray, Amélie, and Roda P. Roberts (2005). In search of terms: An empirical approach to lexicography. *Meta* 50(4). Available at http://id.erudit.org/iderudit/019920ar.

Jousse, Anne-Laure (2010). Modèle de structuration des relations lexicales fondé sur le formalisme des fonctions lexicales. Unpublished PhD dissertation, Département de linguistique et de traduction, Université de Montréal and UFR de linguistique, Université Paris Diderot – Paris 7.

Jousse, Anne-Laure, Marie-Claude L'Homme, Patrick Leroyer, and Benoît Robichaud (2011). Organizing collocates in a dictionary of computing and the Internet according to user needs. In I. Bogulavsky and L. Wanner (eds), *Proceedings of the Fifth Meaning–Text Theory Conference (MTT 2011)*, 134–144. Barcelona: Universitat Pompeu Fabra.

Jousse, Anne-Laure, Alain Polguère, and Ophélie Tremblay (2008). Du dictionnaire au site lexical pour l'enseignement/apprentissage du vocabulaire. In F. Grossmann and S. Plane (eds), *Lexique et production verbale. Vers une meilleure intégration des apprentissages lexicaux*, coll. «Éducation et didactiques», 141–157. Villeneuve d'Ascq: Presses Universitaires du Septentrion.

Kehoe, Andrew, and Antoinette Renouf (2002). WebCorp: Applying the web to linguistics and linguistics to the web. *Proceedings of the World Wide Web Conference*, Honolulu, Hawaii. Available at http://www2002.org/CDROM/poster/67/.

Kennedy, Claire, and Tiziana Miceli (2001). An evaluation of intermediate students' approaches to corpus investigation. *Language Learning and Technology* 5(3): 77–90.

Kilgarriff, Adam (1997). Putting frequencies in the dictionary. *International Journal of Lexicography* 10(2): 135–155.

Kilgarriff, Adam (2005a). Language is never ever, ever, ever random. *Corpus Linguistics and Linguistic Theory* 1(2): 263–275.

—— (2005b). If dictionaries are free, who will buy them? *Kernerman Dictionary News*. Number 13, June 2005. Available at http://kdictionaries.com/kdn/kdn1307.html.

—— (2006). Word from the Chair. In G.-M. De Schryver (ed.), *DWS 2006: Proceedings of the Fourth International Workshop on Dictionary Writing Systems*, 7. Pretoria: (SF)² Press.

—— (2009). *How to monetise a web presence (and hoover a moose)*. A report on the e-lexicography conference at Louvain-la-Neuve, Belgium, 22–24 October 2009. Available at www.uclouvain. be/en-307398.html.

Kilgarriff, Adam, and Gregory Grefenstette (2003). Introduction to the special issue on Web as corpus. *Computational Linguistics* 29(3): 333–348.

Kilgarriff, Adam, Miloš Husák, Katy McAdam, Michael Rundell, and Pavel Rychlý (2008). GDEX: Automatically finding good dictionary examples in a corpus. In E. Bernal and J. DeCesaris (eds), *Proceedings of the XIII EURALEX International Congress*, 425–431. Barcelona: Universitat Pompeu Fabra.

Kilgarriff, Adam, Vojtech Kovar, Simon Krek, Irena Srdanović, and Carole Tiberius (2010a). A quantitative evaluation of word sketches. In A. Dykstra and T. Schoonheim (eds), *Proceedings of the 14th EURALEX International Congress*, 372–379. Leeuwarden, the Netherlands: Fryske Akademy.

Kilgarriff, Adam, Vojtěch Kovár, and Pavel Rychlý (2010b). TickBox Lexicography. In S. Granger and M. Paquot (eds), *eLexicography in the 21st Century: New Challenges, New Applications*, 411–418. Louvain-la-Neuve: Presses universitaires de Louvain.

Kilgarriff, Adam, and Michael Rundell (2002). Lexical profiling software and its lexicographic applications—a case study. In A. Braasch and C. Povlsen (eds), *Proceedings of the Tenth EURALEX Congress*, 807–818. Copenhagen: University of Copenhagen.

Kilgarriff, Adam, and Pavel Rychlý (2008). Finding the words which are most X. In E. Bernal and J. DeCesaris (eds), *Proceedings of the XIII EURALEX International Congress*, 433–436. Barcelona: Universitat Pompeu Fabra.

Kilgarriff, Adam, Pavel Rychlý, Pavel Smrz, and David Tugwell (2004). The Sketch Engine. In G. Williams and S. Vessier (eds), *Proceedings of the 11th EURALEX International Congress*, 105–116. Lorient, France: Université de Bretagne Sud.

Kirkpatrick, Betty (1985). A lexicographical dilemma: Monolingual dictionaries for the native speaker and for the learner. In R. Ilson (ed.), *Dictionaries, Lexicography, and Language Learning*, 7–13. Oxford and New York: Pergamon Press in association with the British Council.

Klein, Wolfgang, and Alexander Geyken (2010). Das digitale Wörterbuch der Deutschen Sprache (DWDS). *Lexicographica* 26: 79–96.

Knowles, Francis E (1989). Computers and dictionaries. In F. J. Hausmann, O. Reichmann, and H. E. Wiegand (eds), *Wörterbücher: ein internationales Handbuch zur Lexikographie*, 1645–1672. Berlin and New York: W. de Gruyter.

Kobayashi, Chiho (2007). Comparing electronic and printed dictionaries: Their effects on lexical processing strategy use, word retention and reading comprehension. In K. Bradford-Watts (ed.), *JALT 2006 Conference Proceedings*, 657–671. Tokyo: JALT.

——(2008). The use of pocket electronic and printed dictionaries: A mixed-method study. In K. Bradford Watts, T. Muller, and M. Swanson (eds), *JALT 2007 Conference Proceedings*, 769–783. Tokyo: JALT.

Koeva, Svetla, Cvetana Krstev, and Duško Vitas (2008). Morpho-semantic relations in Word-Net—A case study for two Slavic languages, *Global WordNet Conference*, 239–253.

Komuro, Yuri, Yuko Shitara-Matsuo, Yasutake Ishii, Satoru Uchida, Akihiko Kawamura, and Takashi Kanazashi (2006). An analysis of the Oxford Advanced Learner's Dictionary of Current English, Seventh Edition, with special reference to the CD-ROM. *Lexicon* 36: 55–146.

Koplenig, Alexander (2011). Understanding how users evaluate innovative features of online dictionaries: An experimental approach. In I. Kosem and K. Kosem (eds), *Proceedings of eLEX2011*. Trojina: Institute for Applied Slovene Studies, 147–150. Available at www.trojina.si/elex2011/Vsebine/proceedings/eLex2011-18.pdf (last accessed 28 November 2011).

Koren, Shira (1997). Quality versus convenience: Comparison of modern dictionaries from the researcher's, teacher's and learner's points of view. *TESL-EJ* 2(3). Available from http://tesl-ej.org/ej07/a2.html.

Kosem, Iztok (2010). Designing a model for a corpus-driven dictionary of academic English. Unpublished PhD thesis, Aston University, Birmingham.

Kosem, Iztok, Miloš Husák, and Diana McCarthy (2011). GDEX for Slovene. In Iztok Kosem and Karmen Kosem (eds), *Electronic Lexicography in the 21st Century: New Applications for New Users*, 151–159. Ljubljana: Trojina.

Koyama, Toshiko, and Osamu Takeuchi (2003). Printed dictionaries vs. electronic dictionaries: A pilot study on how Japanese EFL learners differ in using dictionaries. *Language Education and Technology* 40: 61–79.

——(2004a). Comparing electronic and printed dictionaries: How the difference affected EFL learning. *JACET Bulletin* 38: 33–46.

——(2004b). How look-up frequency affects EFL learning: An empirical study on the use of handheld electronic dictionaries. In W. Meng Chan, K. Nyet Chin, P. Martin-Lau, and T. Suthiwan (eds), *Proceedings of CLaSIC 2004*, 1018–1024. Singapore: National University of Singapore.

——(2007). Does look-up frequency help reading comprehension of EFL learners? Two empirical studies of electronic dictionaries. *CALICO Journal* 25(1): 110–125.

Kozma, Robert B. (1991). Learning with media. *Review of Educational Research* 61: 179–211.

Krausse, Susanna (2011). Semantic preference and semantic prosody in the specialist language class. In N. Kübler (ed.), *Language, Corpora, and Resources: From Theory to Practice*, 155–164. Bern: Peter Lang.

Krek, Simon (2010). Termania—free on-line dictionary portal. In A. Dykstra and T. Schoonheim (eds), *Proceedings of the XIV EURALEX International Congress*, 928–930. Afûk, Ljouwert: Fryske Akademy.

Kremer, Gerhard, Andrea Abel, and Marco Baroni (2008). Cognitively salient relations for multilingual lexicography. *Proceedings of the Workshop on Cognitive Aspects of the Lexicon (COGALEX2008)*, Manchester, August 2008, 94–101.

Kristoffersen, Jette H., and Janne Boye Niemelä (2008). How to describe mouth patterns in the Danish Sign Language Dictionary. In R. Müller de Quadros (ed.), *Sign Languages: Spinning and Unraveling the Past, Present and Future. TISLR9, Forty-five Papers and Three Posters from the 9th Theoretical Issues in Sign Language Research Conference. Florianopolis, Brazil, December 2006*, 230–238. Petropolis: Editora Arara Azul.

Krizhanovsky, Andrew A. (2010). The comparison of Wiktionary thesauri transformed into the machine-readable format. ARXIV eprint *arXiv:1006.5040v1* [cs.IR].

Krstev, Cvetana, Ivan Obradović, and Duško Vitas (2006). Developing Balkan specific concepts within BalkaNet – A multilingual database of semantic networks. *5th International Conference on Formal Approaches to South Slavic and Balkan Languages, FASSBL 2006*, 94–98.

Krstev, Cvetana, Duško Vitas, and Gordana Pavlović-Lažetić (2008). Resources and methods in morphosyntactic processing of Serbo-Croatian. In G. Zybatow (ed.), *Formal Description of Slavic Languages: The Fifth Conference, Leipzig 2003*, 3–17. Frankfurt am Main and New York: Peter Lang.

Kruyt, Truus (2003). Multifunctional linguistic databases: Their multiple uses. In P. van Sterkenburg (ed.), *A Practical Guide to Lexicography*, 194–203. Amsterdam: John Benjamins Publishing Company.

Kübler, Natalie (2011). Working with different corpora in translation teaching. In A. Frankenberg-Garcia, L. Flowerdew, and G. Aston (eds), *New Trends in Corpora and Language Learning*, 62–80. London: Continuum.

Kübler, Natalie, Geneviève Bordet, and Mojca Pecman (2010). La linguistique de corpus entretient-elle d'étroites relations avec la traduction pragmatique? In M. Van Campenhoud, T. Lino, and R. Costa (eds), *Passeurs de mots, passeurs d'espoir: lexicologie, terminologie et traduction face au défi de la diversité*, 579–592. Paris: AUF.

Kübler, Natalie, and Pierre-Yves Foucou (2003). Teaching English verbs with bilingual corpora: Examples in the computer science area. In S. Granger and S. Petch-Tyson (eds), *Contrastive Linguistics and Translation Studies*, 185–206. Amsterdam: Rodopi.

Kübler, Natalie, and Alexandra Volanschi (2012). Semantic prosody and specialised translation, or how a lexico-grammatical theory of language can help with specialised translation. In A. Boulton, S. Carter-Thomas, and E. Rowley-Jolivet (eds), *Corpus-informed Research and Learning in ESP: Issues and Applications*, 105–135. Amsterdam and Philadelphia: John Benjamins.

Kunze, Claudia, and Lothar Lemnitzer (2002). GermaNet – representation, visualization, application. In *Proceedings of the Third International Conference on Language Resources and Evaluation Vol. 5*, 1485–1491, Las Palmas, Spain.

——(2007). *Computerlexikographie: Eine Einführung*. Tübingen: Gunter Narr Verlag.

Kuzmina, Vera, and Anna Rylova (2010). ABBY Lingvo electronic dictionary platform and Lingvo Content dictionary writing system. In S. Granger and M. Paquot (eds), *eLexicography in the 21st Century: New Challenges, New Applications*, 419–423. Louvain-la-Neuve: Presses universitaires de Louvain.

L'Homme, Marie-Claude (1997). Méthode d'accès informatisé aux combinaisons lexicales en langue technique. *Meta* 42(1): 15–23.

——(2002). Fonctions lexicales pour représenter les relations sémantiques entre termes. *Traitement Automatique des Langues* 43(1): 19–41.

——(2007). De la lexicographie formelle pour la terminologie: projets terminographiques de l'Observatoire de linguistique Sens-Texte. In *Actes du colloque BDL-CA* (Bases de données lexicales: construction et applications), 23 avril 2007, OLST, Université de Montréal, 29–40.

——(2008). Le DiCoInfo. Méthodologie pour une nouvelle génération de dictionnaires spécialisés. *Traduire* 217: 78–103.

——(2009). A methodology for describing collocations in a specialized dictionary. In S. Nielsen and S. Tarp (eds), *Lexicography in the 21st Century. In Honour of Henning Bergenholtz*, 237–256. Amsterdam and Philadelphia: John Benjamins.

——(2010). Designing terminological dictionaries for learners based on lexical semantics: The representation of actants. In P. Fuertes-Olivera (ed.), *Specialised Dictionaries for Learners*, 141–153. Berlin and New York: De Gruyter.

L'Homme, Marie-Claude, Ulrich Heid, and Juan C. Sager (2003). Terminology during the last decade (1994–2004). *Terminology* 9(2): 151–161.

L'Homme, Marie-Claude, and Patrick Leroyer (2009). Combining the semantics of collocations with situation-driven search paths in specialized dictionaries. *Terminology* 15(2): 258–283.

L'Homme, Marie-Claude, Patrick Leroyer, and Benoît Robichaud (2010). Advanced encoding for multilingual access in a terminological database – A matter of balance. In Ú. Breathnnach and F. De Barra Cusack (eds), *Presenting Terminology and Knowledge Engineering Resources Online: Models and Challenges, Terminology and Knowledge Engineering Conference 2010*, 12–13 August, 33–54. Dublin: Fiontar, Dublin City University.

L'Homme, Marie-Claude, and Isabelle Meynard (1998). Le point d'accès aux combinaisons lexicales spécialisées: présentation de deux modèles informatiques. *TTR: traduction, terminologie, rédaction* 11(1): 199–227.

Lakoff, George, and Mark Johnson (1980). *Metaphors We Live By*. Chicago: Chicago University Press.

Landau, Sidney (2001). *Dictionaries: The Art and Craft of Lexicography* (2nd edition). Cambridge: Cambridge University Press.

Langemets, Margit, Andres Loopmann, and Ülle Viks (2010). Dictionary management system for bilingual dictionaries. In S. Granger and M. Paquot (eds), *eLexicography in the 21st Century: New Challenges, New Applications*, 425–429. Louvain-la-Neuve: Presses universitaires de Louvain.

Lannoy, Vincent (2010a). Free online dictionaries: why and how? In S. Granger and M. Paquot (eds), *eLexicography in the 21st Century: New Challenges, New Applications. Proceedings of ELEX2009*, 173–181. Louvain-la-Neuve: Presses universitaires de Louvain.

——(2010b). The IDM free online platform for dictionary publishers. In A. Dykstra and T. Schoonheim (eds), *Proceedings of the XIV EURALEX International Congress*, 389–401. Afûk, Ljouwert: Fryske Akademy.

Laufer, Batia (2000). Electronic dictionaries and incidental vocabulary acquisition: Does technology make a difference? In U. Heid, S. Evert, E. Lehmann, and C. Rohrer (eds), *Proceedings of the IX EURALEX International Congress*, 849–854. Stuttgart.

Laufer, Batia, and Nancy Girsai (2008). Form-focused instruction in second language vocabulary learning: A case for contrastive analysis and translation. *Applied Linguistics* 29(4): 694–716.

Laufer, Batia, and Zahava Goldstein (2004). Testing vocabulary knowledge: Size, strength and computer adaptiveness. *Language Learning* 54: 399–436.

Laufer, Batia, and Monica Hill (2000). What lexical information do L2 learners select in a CALL dictionary and how does it affect word retention? *Language Learning and Technology* 3(2): 58–76.

Laufer, Batia, and Jan H. Hulstijn (2001). Incidental vocabulary acquisition in a second language: The construct of task-induced involvement. *Applied Linguistics* 22: 1–26.

Laufer, Batia, and Michal Kimmel (1997). Bilingualised dictionaries: How learners really use them. *System* 25(3): 361–369.

Laufer, Batia, and Tamar Levitzky-Aviad (2006). Examining the effectiveness of 'bilingual dictionary plus' – a dictionary for production in a foreign language. *International Journal of Lexicography* 19(2): 135–155.

Lauriston, Andy (1997). Terminology and the Computer. In Robert Dubuc (ed.), *Terminology: A Practical Approach*, 179–192. Brossard, Quebec: Linguatech.

Lea, Diana (2008). Making a thesaurus for learners of English. In E. Bernal and J. DeCesaris (eds), *Proceedings of the 13th EURALEX International Congress*, 543–50. Barcelona: Universitat Pompeu Fabra.

Lee, David, and John Swales (2006). A corpus-based EAP course for NNS doctoral students: Moving from available specialized corpora to self-compiled corpora. *English for Specific Purposes* 25(1): 56–75.

Lee, David Y. W., and Sylvia Xiao Chen (2009). Making a bigger deal of the smaller words: Function words and other key items in research writing by Chinese learners. *Journal of Second Language Writing* 18: 281–296.

Leech, Geoffrey (1992). 100 million words of English: The British National Corpus. *Language Research* 28(1): 1–13.

Leffa, Vilson J. (1993). Using an electronic dictionary to understand foreign language texts. *Trabalhos em Linguistica Aplicada* 21: 19–29.

Lehr, Andrea (1996). Zur neuen Lexicographica-Rubrik 'Electronic dictionaries'. *Lexicographica. International Annual for Lexicography* 12: 310–317.

LeLoup, Jean W., and Robert Ponterio (2005). Vocabulary support for independent online reading. *Language Learning & Technology* 9(2): 3–7. Available at http://llt.msu.edu/vol9-num2/pdf/net.pdf (last accessed 8 May 2011).

Lemnitzer, Lothar, Laurent Romary, and Andreas Witt (2010). Representing human and machine dictionaries in markup languages (SGML, XML). Available at http://arxiv.org/pdf/0912.2881.

Lenci, Alessandro, Nicoletta Calzolari, and Antonio Zampolli (2003). SIMPLE: Plurilingual semantic lexicons for natural language processing. In A. Zampolli, N. Calzolari, and L. Cignoni (eds), Computational Linguistics in Pisa – Linguistica Computazionale a Pisa. *Linguistica Computazionale*, Special Issue, XVI–XVII. Pisa-Roma, IEPI. Tomo I, 323–352.

León Araúz, Pilar, Arianne Reimerink, and Pamela Faber (2009). PUERTOTERM & MAR-COCOSTA: A Frame-based knowledge base for the environmental domain. *Journal of Multicultural Communication* 1: 47–70.

——(2011). Environmental knowledge in EcoLexicon. In K. Jassem, P. Fuglewicz, M. Piasecki, and A. Przepiórkowski (eds), *Proceedings of the Computational Linguistics Applications Conference*, 9–16. Jachranka, Poland: Polskie Towarzystwo Informatyczne. Available at www.proceedings2011.cla-conf.org/pliks/34.pdf.

Lepore, Jill (2006). Noah's Mark: Webster and the original dictionary wars. *The New Yorker* LXXXII (36): 78–87. New York: Condé Nast Publications.

Leroyer, Patrick (2007). Bringing corporate dictionary design into accord with corporate image. From words to messages and back again. In H. Gottlieb and J. E. Mogensen (eds), *Dictionary Vision, Research and Practice: Selected Papers from the 12th International Symposium on Lexicography*, 109–117. Amsterdam and Philadelphia: John Benjamins.

—— (2011). Change of paradigm: From linguistics to information science and from dictionaries to lexicographic information tools. In P. A. Fuertes-Olivera and H. Bergenholtz (eds), *e-Lexicography: The Internet, Digital Initiatives and Lexicography*, 121–140. London and New York: Continuum.

Leuf, Bo, and Ward Cunningham (2001). *The Wiki Way: Quick Collaboration on the Web.* Boston, MA: Addison-Wesley.

Levin, Beth (1993). *English Verb Classes and Alternations: A Preliminary Investigation.* Chicago: University of Chicago Press.

Lew, Robert (2004). *Which Dictionary for Whom? Receptive Use of Bilingual, Monolingual and Semi-Bilingual Dictionaries by Polish Learners of English.* Poznań: Motivex.

—— (2010a). Multimodal lexicography: The representation of meaning in electronic dictionaries. *Lexikos* 20: 290–306.

—— (2010b). Users take shortcuts: Navigating dictionary entries. In Anne Dykstra and Tanneke Schoonheim (eds), *Proceedings of the XIV EURALEX International Congress*, 1121–1132. Ljouwert: Afûk.

—— (2010c). New ways of indicating meaning in electronic dictionaries: Hope or hype? In Yihua Zhang (ed.), *Learner's Lexicography and Second Language Teaching*, 387–404. Shanghai: Shanghai Foreign Language Education Press.

—— (2011a). Online dictionaries of English. In P. A. Fuertes-Olivera and H. Bergenholtz (eds), *e-Lexicography. The Internet, Digital Initiatives and Lexicography*, 230–250. London and New York: Continuum.

—— (2011b). User studies: Opportunities and limitations. In K. Akasu and S. Uchida (eds), *Lexicography: Theoretical and Practical Perspectives*. Asialex2011. Proceedings of the Seventh Asialex Conference, 7–16. Tokyo: Asian Association for Lexicography.

—— (ed.) (2011c). Studies in dictionary use: Recent developments. *International Journal of Lexicography* 24(1): 1–4.

—— (in press). Space restrictions in paper and electronic dictionaries and their implications for the design of production dictionaries. In P. Bański and B. Wójtowicz (eds), *Issues in Modern Lexicography*. München: Lincom Europa.

Lew, Robert, and Joanna Doroszewska (2009). Electronic dictionary entries with animated pictures: Lookup preferences and word retention. *International Journal of Lexicography* 22(3): 239–257.

Lew, Robert, and Katarzyna Galas (2008). Can dictionary skills be taught? The effectiveness of lexicographic training for primary-school-level Polish learners of English. In E. Bernal and J. DeCesaris (eds), *Proceedings of the XIII EURALEX International Congress*, 1273–1385. Barcelona: Universitat Pompeu Fabra.

Lew, Robert, and Roger Mitton (2011). Not the word I wanted? How online English learners' dictionaries deal with misspelled words. In I. Kosem and K. Kosem (eds), *Electronic*

Lexicography in the 21st Century: New Applications for New Users. Proceedings of eLex 2011,
Bled, 10–12 November 2011, 165–175. Ljubljana: Trojina, Institute for Applied Slovene Studies.

Lew, Robert, and Julita Pajkowska (2007). The effect of signposts on access speed and lookup
task success in long and short entries. *Horizontes de Lingüística Aplicada* 6(2): 235–252.

Lew, Robert, and Patryk Tokarek (2010). Entry menus in bilingual electronic dictionaries. In
S. Granger and M. Paquot (eds), *eLexicography in the 21st Century: New Challenges, New
Applications, Proceedings of eLEX2009,* 193–202. Louvain-la-Neuve: Presses universitaires de
Louvain.

Lim, Sook, and Nahyun Kwon (2010). Gender differences in information behavior concerning
Wikipedia, an unorthodox information source. *Library & Information Science Research* 32:
212–220.

Logan, Harry (1991). Electronic lexicography. *Computers and the Humanities* 25: 351–361.

Loucky, John Paul (2005). Combining the benefits of electronic and online dictionaries with
CALL web sites to produce effective and enjoyable vocabulary and language learning
lessons. *Computer Assisted Language Learning* 18: 389–416.

Louw, Bill (1993). Irony in the text or insincerity in the writer? The diagnostic potential of
semantic prosodies. In M. Baker, G. Francis, and E. Tognini-Bonelli (eds), *Text and
Technology: In Honour of John Sinclair,* 157–176. Amsterdam and Philadelphia: John
Benjamins.

——(2000). Contextual prosodic theory: Bringing semantic prosodies to life. In C. Heffer,
H. Sauntson, and G. Fox (eds), *Words in Context: A Tribute to John Sinclair on his
Retirement,* 48–94. Birmingham: University of Birmingham.

Louw, Bill, and Carmela Chateau (2010). Semantic prosody for the 21st century: Are prosodies
smoothed in academic context? A contextual prosodic theoretical perspective. In S. Bolasco,
I. Chiari, and L. Giuliano (eds), *Statistical Analysis of Textual Data: Proceedings of the Tenth
JADT Conference,* 755–764. Available at http://lexicometrica.univ-paris3.fr/jadt/jadt2010/
tocJADT2010.htm (last accessed 7 May 2011).

Lyding, Verena (ed.) (2009). *LULCL II 2008 – Proceedings of the Second Colloquium on Lesser
Used Languages and Computer Linguistics.* Bozen-Bolzano, 13–14 November 2008. EURAC
book 54, Bozen-Bolzano: EURAC research.

Mackey, Thomas P., and Jinwon Ho (2008). Exploring the relationships between web usability
and students' perceived learning in web-based multimedia (WBMM) tutorials. *Computers
and Education* 50: 386–409.

Mackintosh, Kristen (1998). An empirical study of dictionary use in L2–L1 translation. In Beryl
T. Sue Atkins (ed.), *Using Dictionaries: Studies of Dictionary Use by Language Learners and
Translators,* 123–149. Tübingen: Max Niemeyer.

Magnini, Bernardo, and Gabriela Cavaglia (2000). Integrating subject field codes into Word-
Net. *Proceedings of LREC-2000, Second International Conference on Language Resources and
Evaluation,* 1413–1418.

Mair, Victor (2007). The etiology and elaboration of a flagrant mistranslation. *Language Log.*
Available at http://itre.cis.upenn.edu/~myl/languagelog/archives/005195.html (last accessed
29 April 2011).

Malone, Thomas W., Robert Laubacher, and Chrysanthos Dellarocas (2010). Harnessing
crowds: Mapping the genome of collective intelligence. *MIT Sloan SchoolWorking Paper*
n°4732-09.

Mangeot, Mathieu (2006). Dictionary building with the Jibiki platform. In E. Corino, C. Marello, and C. Onesti (eds), *Proceedings of XII EURALEX International Congress*, 185–188. Alessandria: Edizioni dell'Orso.

Maniez, François (2001). Extraction d'une phraséologie bilingue en langue de spécialité: corpus parallèles et corpus comparables. *Meta* 46(3): 552–563.

Mann, Michael (2010). Internet-Wörterbücher am Ende der 'Nullerjahre': Der Stand der Dinge. Eine vergleichende Untersuchung beliebter Angebote hinsichtlich formaler Kriterien. In Ulrich Heid, Stefan Schierholz, Wolfgang Schweickard, Herbert Ernst Wiegand, Rufus H. Gouws, and Werner Wolski (eds), *Lexicographica 26*, 19–46. Berlin and New York: de Gruyter.

Manning, Christopher D., Kevin Jansz, and Nitin Indurkhya (2001). Kirrkirr: Software for browsing and visual exploration of a structured Warlpiri dictionary. *Literary and Linguistic Computing* 16(2): 135–151.

Manning, Christopher D., and Hinrich Schütze (1999). *Foundations of Statistical Natural Language Processing*. Cambridge, MA: MIT Press.

Marlow, Cameron, Mor Naaman, Danah Boyd, and Marc Davis (2006). HT06, tagging paper, taxonomy, Flickr, academic article, to read. *Proceedings of the Seventeenth Conference on Hypertext and Hypermedia*, 31–40.

Marmaridou, Sophia (2000). *Pragmatic Meaning and Cognition*. Amsterdam and Philadelphia: John Benjamins Publishing.

Martin, Willy (1992). On the organization of semantic data in passive bilingual dictionaries. In M. Alvar Ezquerra (ed.), *EURALEX '90 Proceedings / Actas del IV Congreso Internacional / IV International Congress*, 193–201. Barcelona: Biblograf.

——(2000). On the making of bilingual dictionaries. In G. Hirschfelder, D. Schell, and A. Schrutka-Rechtenstamm (eds), *Kulturen, Sprachen, Übergänge*, 225–237. Cologne: Böhlau.

Martin, Willy, and Hennie van der Vliet (2003). Design and production of terminological dictionaries. In P. van Sterkenburg (ed.), *A Practical Guide to Lexicography*, 333–349. Amsterdam: John Benjamins Publishing Company.

McEnery, Tony, Richard Xiao, and Yukio Tono (2006). *Corpus-based Language Studies: An Advanced Resource Book*. New York: Routledge.

Měchura, Michal B. (2008). Giving them what they want: Search strategies for electronic dictionaries. In E. Bernal and J. DeCesaris (eds), *Proceedings of the XIII EURALEX Internal Congress (Barcelona, 15–19 July 2008)*. Barcelona: Institut Universitari de Lingüistica aplicada, Universitat Pompeu Fabra. Available at http://prettydata.eu/mbm/EuralexBarcelona2008.pdf.

Meijs, Willem (1992). Computers and dictionaries. In C. Butler (ed.), *Computers and Written Texts*, 141–65. Oxford and Cambridge, MA: Blackwell.

Mel'čuk, Igor, Nadia Arbatchewsky-Jumarie, Lida Iordanskaja, Suzanne Mantha, and Alain Polguère (1999). *Dictionnaire Explicatif et Combinatoire du Français Contemporain: Recherches Lexico-sémantiques IV*. Montréal: Les Presses de l'Université de Montréal.

Mel'čuk, Igor, André Clas, and Alain Polguère (1995). *Introduction à la lexicologie explicative et combinatoire*. Louvain-la-Neuve: Duculot / Aupelf—UREF.

Mel'čuk, Igor, and Alain Polguère (2007). *Lexique actif du français. L'apprentissage du voca-bulaire fondé sur 20 000 dérivations sémantiques et collocations du français.* Bruxelles: De Boeck.

Meyer, Christian M., and Iryna Gurevych (2010a). Worth its weight in gold or yet another resource – A comparative study of Wiktionary, OpenThesaurus and GermaNet. In Alexander Gelbukh (ed.), *Computational Linguistics and Intelligent Text Processing: 11th International Conference* (Lecture Notes in Computer Science 6008), 38–49. Berlin and Heidelberg: Springer.

——(2010b). How web communities analyze human language: Word senses in Wiktionary. In *Proceedings of the Second Web Science Conference*, Raleigh, NC, USA.

——(2011). What psycholinguists know about chemistry: Aligning Wiktionary and WordNet for increased domain coverage. In *Proceedings of the 5th International Joint Conference on Natural Language Processing*, 883–892, Chiang Mai, Thailand.

Meyer, Ingrid (1988). The general bilingual dictionary as a working tool in Thème. *Meta* 33(3): 368–376.

Meyer, Paul Georg (1997). *Coming to Know: Studies in the Lexical Semantics and Pragmatics of Academic English*. Tübingen: Gunter Narr Verlag Tübingen.

Meynard, Isabelle (1997). Approche hypertextuelle via HTML pour un outil de consignation bilingue des combinaisons lexicales spécialisées. *Actes du Congrès international de terminologie*, San Sebastian (Spain), 12–14 novembre 1997, San Sebastian, IVAP/UZEI, 675–689.

Midlane, Vivian (2005). Students' Use of Portable Electronic Dictionaries in the EFL/ESL Classroom: A Survey of Teacher Attitudes. Unpublished MEd dissertation, Faculty of Education, University of Manchester.

Milićević, Jasmina (2008). Towards an explanatory-combinatorial dictionary for BCS learners. In B. Golubović and J. Raecke (eds), *Bosnisch. Kroatisch. Serbisch. B.K.S. als Fremdsprachen an den Universitäten der Welt*, 155–168. München: Verlag Otto Sagner.

Miller, George A. (1985). Wordnet: A dictionary browser. *Information in Data. Proceedings of the First Conference of the UW Centre for the New Oxford Dictionary*, 25–28. Waterloo, Canada: University of Waterloo.

Miller, George A., Richard Beckwith, Christiane Fellbaum, Derek Gross, and Katherine J. Miller (1993). *Introduction to WordNet: An Online Lexical Database*. ftp://ftp.cogsci.princeton.edu/pub/wordnet/5papers.ps (last accessed 1 December 2008).

Miller, George A., and Christiane Fellbaum (1992). WordNet and the organization of lexical memory. In M. Swartz and M. Yazdani (eds), *Intelligent Tutoring Systems for Foreign Language Learning: The Bridge to International Communication*, 89–101. Ljubljana: Springer-Verlag.

Milton, John, and Vivying S. Y. Cheng (2010). A toolkit to assist L2 learners become independent writers. *NAACL HLT2010 Workshop on Computational Linguistics and Writing*, 33–41.

Mitton, Roger (2009). Ordering the suggestions of a spellchecker without using context. *Natural Language Engineering* 15: 173–192.

Mitton, Roger and Takeshi Okada (2007). The adaptation of an English spellchecker for Japanese writers. *Symposium on Second Language Writing*. Nagoya, Japan.

Mongwe, Mkomati John (2006). The Role of South African National Lexicography Units in the Planning and Compilation of Multifunctional Bilingual Dictionaries. Unpublished Master thesis, Stellenbosch University. Available ay http://scholar.sun.ac.za/bitstream/handle/ 10019.1/2177/MongweM.pdf?sequence=1.

Moon, Rosamund (1987). The analysis of meaning. In John M. Sinclair (ed.), *Looking Up: An Account of the COBUILD Project in Lexical Computing*, 86–103. London: Collins.

——(1998). *Fixed Expressions and Idioms in English*. Oxford: Clarendon Press.

——(2008). Dictionaries and collocation. In S. Granger and F. Meunier (eds), *Phraseology: An Interdisciplinary Perspective*, 313–336. Amsterdam: Benjamins.

Morris, Jane, and Graeme Hirst (2004). Non-classical lexical semantic relations. *Proceedings of the HLT-NAACL Workshop on Computational Lexical Semantics*, 46–51.

Müller, Christof, and Iryna Gurevych (2009). Using Wikipedia and Wiktionary in domain-specific information retrieval. In C. Peters, D. Giampiccol, N. Ferro, V. Petras, J. Gonzalo, A. Penas, T. Deselaers, T. Mandl, G. Jones, and M. Kurimo (eds), *Evaluating Systems for Multilingual and Multimodal Information Access: Proceedings of the 9th Workshop of the Cross-Language Evaluation Forum* (Lecture Notes in Computer Science 5706), 219–226. Berlin and Heidelberg: Springer.

Müller-Spitzer, Carolin (2008). Research on dictionary use and the development of user-adapted views. In A. Storrer, A. Geyken, A. Siebert, and K.-M. Würzner (eds), *Text Resources and Lexical Knowledge. Selected Papers from the 9th Conference on Natural Language Processing KONVENS 2008*, 223–238. Berlin: de Gruyter.

——(2010a). The consistency of sense-related items in dictionaries: Current status, proposals for modelling and applications in lexicographic practice. In P. Storjohann (ed.), *Lexical–Semantic Relations: Theoretical and Practical Perspectives*, 145–162. Amsterdam and Philadelphia: John Benjamins Publishing Company.

——(2010b). OWID—A dictionary net for corpus-based lexicography of contemporary German. In A. Dykstra and T. Schoonheim (eds), *Proceedings of the XIV EURALEX International Congress*, 445–452. Leeuwarden/Ljouwert: Fryske Akademy.

——(2011). Der Einsatz einer maßgeschneiderten, feingranularen XML-Modellierung im lexikografischen Prozess. In A. Klosa (ed.), *elexiko. Erfahrungsberichte aus der lexikographischen Praxis eines Internetwörterbuchs*, 173–191. Tübingen: Narr.

Müller-Spitzer, Carolin, Alexander Koplenig, and Antje Töpel (2011). What makes a good online dictionary? Empirical insights from an interdisciplinary research project. In I. Kosem and K. Kosem (eds), *Proceedings of eLEX2011*. Trojina: Institute for Applied Slovene Studies, 203–208. Available at www.trojina.si/elex2011/Vsebine/proceedings/eLex2011-27.pdf (last accessed 28 November 2011).

Müller-Spitzer, Carolin, and Christine Möhrs (2008). First ideas of user-adapted views of lexicographic data exemplified on OWID and elexiko. In M. Zock and C.-R. Huang (eds), *COGALEX 2008: Proceedings of the Workshop on Cognitive Aspects on the Lexicon*, Manchester, August 2008, 39–46. Stroudsburg, PA: Association for Computational Linguistics.

Müllich, Harald (1990). *Die Definition Ist Blöd! Herübersetzen mit Dem Einsprachigen Wörterbuch. Das Französische und Englishe Lernerwörterbuch in der Hand der Deutschen Schüler*. Tübingen: Niemeyer.

Mungra, Philippa, and Pauline Webber (2010). Peer review process in medical research publications. Language and content comments. *English for Specific Purposes* 29(1): 43–53.

Munro, Robert, Steven Bethard, Victor Kuperman, Vicky Tzuyin Lai, Robin Melnick, Christopher Potts, Tyler Schnoebelen, and Harry Tily (2010). Crowdsourcing and language studies: The new generation of linguistic data. *Proceedings of the NAACL HLT 2010 Workshop on Creating Speech and Language Data with Amazon's Mechanical Turk*, 122–130.

Naber, Daniel (2005). OpenThesaurus: ein offenes deutsches Wortnetz. In Bernhard Fisseni, Hans Ch. Schmitz, Bernhard Schröder, and Petra Wagner (eds), *Sprachtechnologie, mobile Kommunikation und linguistische Ressourcen: Beiträge zur GLDV-Tagung*, 422–433. Frankfurt: Peter Lang.

Nation, I. S. P. (2006). How large a vocabulary is needed for reading and listening? *The Canadian Modern Language Review / La revue canadienne des langues vivantes* 63(1): 59–82.

Navigli, Roberto, and Simone Paolo Ponzetto (2010). BabelNet: Building a very large multilingual semantic network. In *Proceedings of the 48th Annual Meeting of the Association for Computational Linguistics*, 216–225, Uppsala, Sweden.

Nelson, Mike (2000). A Corpus-Based Study of Business English and Business English Teaching Materials. Unpublished PhD thesis, University of Manchester. Available at http://users.utu.fi/micnel/thesis.html (last accessed 4 October 2011).

Nesi, Hilary (1987). Do dictionaries help students write? In T. Bloor and J. Norrish (eds), *Written Language, Vol. 2, British Studies in Applied Linguistics*, 85–97. London: CILT.

—— (1996). For future reference? A review of current electronic learners' dictionaries. *System* 24(4): 537–557.

—— (1999). A user's guide to electronic dictionaries for language learners. *International Journal of Lexicography* 12(1): 55–66.

—— (2000a). Electronic dictionaries in second language vocabulary comprehension and acquisition: The state of the art. In U. Heid, S. Evert, E. Lehmann, and C. Rohrer (eds), *Proceedings of the Ninth EURALEX International Congress, EURALEX 2000*, 839–847. Stuttgart: Universität Stuttgart.

—— (2000b). On screen or in print? Students' use of a learner's dictionary on CD-ROM and in book form. In P. Howarth and R. Herington (eds), *EAP Learning Technologies*, 106–114. Leeds: Leeds University Press.

—— (2009). Dictionaries in electronic form. In A. P. Cowie (ed.), *The Oxford History of English Lexicography*, 458–478. Oxford: Oxford University Press.

—— (2010). The Virtual Vocabulary Notebook: The electronic dictionary as vocabulary learning tool. In G. Blue (ed.), *Developing Academic Literacy*, 213–226. Oxford: Peter Lang.

Nesi, Hilary, and Atipat Boonmoh (2009). A close look at the use of pocket electronic dictionaries for receptive and productive purposes. In T. Fizpatrick and A. Barfield (eds), *Lexical Processing in Second Language Learners*, 67–81. Clevedon: Multilingual Matters.

Nesi, Hilary, and Richard Haill (2002). A study of dictionary use by international students at a British university. *International Journal of Lexicography*, 15(4): 277–305.

Nesi, Hilary, and Kim Hua Tan (2011). The effect of menus and signposting on the speed and accuracy of sense selection. *International Journal of Lexicography* 24(1): 79–96.

Newmark, Peter (1988). *A Textbook of Translation*. New York: Prentice Hall.

Nichols, Wendalyn (2010). I've heard so much about you: Introducing the native-speaker lexicographer to the learner's dictionary. In I. J. Kernerman and P. Bogaards (eds), *English Learners' Dictionaries at the DSNA 2009*, 29–44. Jerusalem: Kdictionaries.

Nickerson, Catherine (2005). Editorial: English as a *lingua franca* in international business contexts. *English for Specific Purposes* 24: 367–380.

Nielsen, Sandro (1990). Contrastive description of dictionaries covering LSP communication. *Fachsprache/International Journal of LSP* 3/4: 129–136.

——(1999). Mediostructures in bilingual LSP dictionaries. *Lexicographica. International Annual for Lexicography* 15: 90–113.

——(2008). The effect of lexicographical information costs on dictionary making and use. *Lexikos* 18: 170–189.

——(2009). Reviewing printed and electronic dicitonaries: Atheoretical and practical framework. In S. Nielsen and S. Tarp (eds), *Lexicography in the 21st Century*, 23–41. Amsterdam and Philadelphia: John Benjamins.

——(2010). Specialised translation dictionaries for learners. In P. A. Fuertes-Olivera (ed.), *Specialised Dictionaries for Learners*, 69–82. Berlin and New York: Walter de Gruyter.

Nielsen, Sandro, and Richard Almind (2011). From data to dictionary. In P. A. Fuertes-Olivera and H. Bergenholtz (eds), *e-Lexicography. The Internet, Digital Initiatives and Lexicography*, 141–167. London and New York: Continuum.

Nielsen, Sandro, and Lise Mourier (2007). Design of a function-based internet accounting dictionary. In H. Gottlieb and J. E. Mogensen (eds), *Dictionary Vision, Research and Practice: Selected Papers from the 12th International Symposium on Lexicography*, 119–135. Amsterdam and Philadelphia: John Benjamins.

Niemann, Elisabeth, and Iryna Gurevych (2011). The people's web meets linguistic knowledge: Automatic sense alignment of Wikipedia and WordNet. In J. Bos and S. Pulman (eds), *Proceedings of the Ninth International Conference on Computational Semantics*, 205–216, Oxford.

Niestadt, Jan (2009). De ANW-artikeleditor: software als strategie. In E. Beijk, L. Colman, M. Göbel, F. Heyvaert, T. Schoonheim, R. Tempelaars, and V. Waszink (eds), *Fons Verborum. Feestbundel voor prof. dr. A. M. F. J. (Fons) Moerdijk, aangeboden door vrienden en collega's bij zijn afscheid van het Instituut voor Nederlandse Lexicologie*, 215–222. Leiden and Amsterdam: Instituut voor Nederlandse Lexicologie and Gopher BV.

O'Reilly, Tim (2007). What is Web 2.0: Design patterns and business models for the next generation of software. *Communications & Strategies* 1: 17–27.

O'Sullivan, Íde, and Angela Chambers (2006). Learners' writing skills in French: Corpus consultation and learner evaluation. *Journal of Second Language Writing*, 15(1): 49–68.

Obradović, Ivan, and Ranka Stanković (2008). Software tools for Serbian lexical resources. *Infotheca* IX(1/2): 43a–57a.

Ogden, Charles K. (1938). *Basic English: A General Introduction with Rules and Grammar* (7th edition). London: Kegan Paul, Trench, Trubner & Co.

Ooi, Vincent (1998). *Computer Corpus Lexicography*. Edinburgh: Edinburgh University Press.

Oppentocht, Lineke, and Rik Schutz (2003). Developments in electronic dictionary design. In P. van Sterkenburg (ed.), *A Practical Guide to Lexicography, Terminology and Lexicography Research and Practice 6*, 215–227. Amsterdam: John Benjamins.

Ordan, Noam, and Shuly Wintner (2005). Representing natural gender in multilingual databases. *International Journal of Lexicography*, 18(3): 357–370.

Osaki, Satsuki, and N. Nakayama (2004). Denshijisyo vs. insatujisyo: Yuyosei to jikkousei no chigainituiteno kosatu [Electronic dictionary vs. paper dictionary: A comparison of the two dictionary studies]. *Bulletin of Tokyo Denki University, Arts and Sciences* 2: 77–83.

Osaki, Satsuki, Natsue Ochiai, Tatsuo Iso, and Kazumi Aizawa (2003). Electronic dictionary vs. printed dictionary: Accessing the appropriate meaning, reading comprehension and retention. In M. Murata, S. Yamada, and Y. Tono (eds), *Proceedings of ASIALEX '03 Tokyo*, 205–212. Tokyo: Asialex.

Osherson, Anne, and Christiane Fellbaum (2010). The representation of idioms in WordNet, *5th Global WordNet Conference*. Available at http://www.globalwordnet-iitb2010.in/proceedings.php.

Pajzs, Julia (2009). On the possibility of creating multifunctional lexicographical databases. In H. Bergenholtz, S. Nielsen, and S. Tarp (eds), *Lexicography at a Crossroads: Dictionaries and Encyclopedias Today, Lexicographical Tools Tomorrow*, 327–354. Bern: Peter Lang.

Palmer, Martha, Hoa Trang Dang, and Christiane Fellbaum (2007). Making fine-grained and coarse-grained sense distinctions, both manually and automatically. *Natural Language Engineering* 13(2): 137–163.

Pantel, Patrick, and Dekang Lin (2002). Discovering word senses from text. In *Proceedings of the Eighth ACM SIGKDD International Conference on Knowledge Discovery and Data Mining*, 613–619, Edmonton, AB, Canada.

Paquot, Magali (2010). *Academic Vocabulary in Learner Writing: From Extraction to Analysis*. London and New York: Continuum.

——(2011). Towards a genre-based approach to the lexicographical treatment of phraseology in electronic monolingual learners' dictionaries. Paper presented at eLexicography, 10–12 November, Bled, Slovenia. Available at http://videolectures.net/elex2011_paquot_treatment/.

Partington, Alan (1998). *Patterns and Meanings: Using Corpora for English Language Research and Teaching*. Amsterdam and Philadelphia: John Benjamins.

Pastor Verónica, and Amparo Alcina (2010). Search techniques in electronic dictionaries: A classification for translators. *International Journal of Lexicography* 23(3): 307–354.

Pavel, Sylvia (1993). La phraséologie en langue de spécialité. Méthodologie de consignation dans les vocabulaires terminologiques. *Terminologies nouvelles* 10: 23–35.

Pearson, Jennifer (1996). The expression of definitions in specialised texts: A corpus-based analysis. In M. Gellerstam, J. Järborg, S.-G. Malmgren, K. Norén, L. Rogström, and C. Röjder Papmehl (eds), *EURALEX'96 Proceedings*, 817–824. Gothenburg: Gothenburg University.

——(1998). *Terms in Context*. Amsterdam: John Benjamins Publishing Company.

Pecman, Mojca (2004). Phraséologie contrastive anglais–français: analyse et traitement en vue de l'aide à la rédaction scientifique. Unpublished PhD thesis, Université de Nice-Sophia Antipolis.

——(2005). Les apports possibles de la phraséologie à la didactique des langues étrangères. *Apprentissage des Langues et Systèmes d'Information et de Communication (ALSIC)* 8(1): 109–122.

——(2007). Approche onomasiologique de la langue scientifique générale. *Revue française de linguistique appliquée* 12(2): 79–96.

——(2008). Compilation, formalisation and presentation of bilingual phraseology: Problems and possible solutions. In F. Meunier and S. Granger (eds), *Phraseology in Foreign Language Learning and Teaching*, 203–222. Amsterdam and Philadelphia: Benjamins.

Pecman, Mojca, Claudie Juilliard, Natalie Kübler, and Alexandra Volanschi (2010). Processing collocations in a terminological database based on a cross-disciplinary study of scientific texts. In S. Granger and M. Paquot (eds), *eLexicography in the 21st Century: New Challenges, New Applications. Proceedings of ELEX2009*, 249–262. Louvain-la-Neuve: Presses universitaires de Louvain.

Pecman, Mojca, and Natalie Kübler (2011). ARTES: An online lexical database for research and teaching in specialized translation and communication. *Proceedings from International Workshop on Lexical Resources (WoLeR) 2011* at ESSLLI, 1–5 August 2011, Ljubljana, Slovenia, 87–93.

Penta, Darrell J. (2011). The Wiki-fication of the dictionary: Defining lexicography in the digital age. Paper presented at 'Unstable platforms: the promise and peril of transition', 7th Media in Transition Conference, Massachusetts Institute of Technology, Cambridge, MA, 13–15 May, 2011. Available at http://web.mit.edu/comm-forum/mit7/papers/Penta_Wikification_of_Dictionary%20(Draft).pdf.

Perry, Brian (2003). The use of pocket electronic dictionaries (PEDs) by Japanese university students. *Otaru University of Commerce Review of Liberal Arts* 105: 165–176.

Peters, Wim, and Adam Kilgarriff (2000). Discovering semantic regularity in lexical resources. *International Journal of Lexicography* 13(4): 287–312.

Petrylaitė, Regina, Diana Vaškelienė, and Tatjana Vėžytė (2008). Changing skills of dictionary use. *Studies about Languages* 12: 77–82.

Philip, Gill (2008). Reassessing the canon: 'Fixed' phrases in general reference corpora. In S. Granger and F. Meunier (eds), *Phraseology. An Interdisciplinary Perspective*, 95–108. Amsterdam and Philadephia: John Benjamins Publishing Company.

Phillips, Jonathan (2005). *Introduction to the Open Clip Art Library*. Available at http://rejon.org/media/writings/ocalintro/ocal_intro_phillips.html (last accessed 18 March 2011).

Pimentel, Jeanine, Marie-Claude L'Homme, and Marie-Ève Laneville (2011). General and specialized lexical resources: A study on the potential of combining efforts to enrich formal lexicons. *International Journal of Lexicography*, Advance Access published 5 September 2011. Available at http://ijl.oxfordjournals.org/content/early/2011/09/05/ijl.ecr025.full.pdf+html.

Polguère, Alain (2000). Towards a theoretically-motivated general public dictionary of semantic derivations and collocations for French. In U. Heid, S. Evert, E. Lehmann, and C. Rohrer (eds), *Proceedings of the 9th EURALEX International Congress*, 517–527. Stuttgart: University of Stuttgart.

——(2003). Collocations et fonctions lexicales: pour un modèle d'apprentissage. In F. Grossmann and A. Tutin (eds), *Les Collocations. Analyse et traitement*, 117–133. Amsterdam: De Werelt.

Poulos, George, and Louis J. Louwrens (1994). *A Linguistic Analysis of Northern Sotho*. Pretoria: Via Afrika.

Prillwitz, Siegmund, Regina Leven, Heiko Zienert, Thomas Hanke, and Jan Henning (1989). *HamNoSys. Version 2.0; Hamburg Notation System for Sign Language: An Introductory Guide*. Hamburg: Signum Verlag.

Prinsloo, D. J. (2002). The lemmatization of copulatives in Northern Sotho. *Lexikos* 12: 21–43.

—— (2005). Electronic dictionaries viewed from South Africa. *Hermes* 34: 11–35.

Prinsloo, D. J., Ulrich Heid, Theo J. D. Bothma, and Gertrud Faasz (2011). Interactive, dynamic electronic dictionaries for text production. In I. Kosem and K. Kosem (eds), *Proceedings eLEX 2011: eLexicography in the 21st Century: New Applications for New Users*. Bled, Slovenia, 10–12 November 2011, 215–220.

Prószéky, Gábor, and Balazs Kis (2002). Development of a context-sensitive electronic dictionary. In A. Braasch and C. Povlsen (eds), *Proceedings of the Tenth EURALEX International Congress, EURALEX 2002* Volume I, 281–290. Copenhagen: Center for Sprogteknologi.

Pustejovsky, James (1995). *The Generative Lexicon*. Cambridge, MA: MIT Press.

Pustejovsky, James, Patrick Hanks, and Anna Rumshisky (2004). Automated induction of sense in context. In *Proceedings of ACL-COLING*, 924–931. Geneva, Switzerland.

Putnam, Hilary (1975a). Is semantics possible? In *Mind, Language, and Reality: Philosophical Papers*, 139–152. Cambridge: Cambridge University Press.

—— (1975b). The meaning of 'meaning'. In *Mind, Language, and Reality: Philosophical Papers*, 215–271. Cambridge: Cambridge University Press.

Quirion, Jean (2003). Methodology for the design of a standard research protocol for measuring terminology usage. *Terminology* 9(1): 29–49.

Quirion, Jean, and Jacynthe Lanthier (2006). Intrinsic qualities favouring term implantation: Verifying the axioms. In L. Bowker (ed.), *Lexicography, Terminology and Translation: Text-based Studies in Honour of Ingrid Meyer*, 107–118. Ottawa: University of Ottawa Press.

Quochi, Valeria, Riccardo Del Gratta, Eva Sassolini, Roberto Bartolini, Monica Monachini, and Nicoletta Calzolari (2009). A standard lexical-terminological resource for the bio domain. In Z. Vetulani and H. Uszkoreit (eds), *Human Language Technology. Challenges of the Information Society*, 325–335. Berlin: Springer.

Rangelova, Albena, and Jan Králík (2007). Wider framework of the research plan creation of a lexical database of the Czech language of the beginning of the 21st century. In J. Levická and R. Garabík (eds), *Proceedings of the Computer Treatment of Slavic and East European Languages 2007*, 209–217. Bratislava: Tribun.

Renouf, Antoinette (1987). Corpus development. In John Sinclair (ed.), *Looking Up: An Account of the COBUILD Project in Lexical Computing*, 1–40. London: Collins.

Ridings, Daniel (2003). Lexicographic workbench: A case history. In P. van Sterkenburg (ed.), *A Practical Guide to Lexicography*, 204–214. Amsterdam: John Benjamins Publishing Company.

Ripfel, Martha, and Herbert Ernst Wiegand (1988). Wörterbuchbenutzungsforschung. Ein kritischer Bericht. In Herbert Ernst Wiegand (ed.), *Studien zur neuhochdeutschen Lexikographie VI*, Vol. 2, 491–502. Hildesheim: Georg Olms Verlag.

Rizo-Rodriguez, Alfonso (2004). Current lexicographical tools in EFL: Monolingual resources for the advanced learner. *Language Teaching* 37(1): 29–46.

Roberts, Roda P. (1992). Translation pedagogy: Strategies for improving dictionary use. *TTR: traduction, terminologie, redaction* 5(1): 49–76.

Robichaud, Benoît (2011). A graph visualization tool for terminology discovery and assessment. In I. Boguslavsky and L. Wanner (eds), *Proceedings of the Fifth Meaning-Text Theory Conference (MTT 2011)*, 242–252. Barcelona: Universitat Pompeu Fabra.

Robinson, Doug (2003). *An Introduction to the Theory and Practice of Translation*. London: Routledge.

Rodgers, Ornaith, Angela Chambers, and Florence Le Baron-Earle (2011). Corpora in the LSP classroom: A learner-centred corpus of French for biotechnologists. *International Journal of Corpus Linguistics* 16(3): 391–411.

Rohrdantz, Christian, Steffen Koch, Charles Jochim, Gerhard Heyer, Gerik Scheuermann, Thomas Ertl, Hinrich Schütze, and Daniel A. Keim (2010). Visuelle Textanalyse. *Informatik-Spektrum* 33(6): 601–611.

Ruhlen, Merritt (1987). *A Guide to the World's Languages. Vol. 1: Classification*. Stanford, CA: Stanford University Press.

Rundell, Michael (1999). Dictionary use in production. *International Journal of Lexicography* 12 (1): 35–53.

——(2007). The dictionary of the future. In S. Granger (ed.), *Optimizing the Role of Language in Technology-Enhanced Learning*. Proceedings of the expert workshop organized in Louvain-la-Neuve (Belgium), 4–5 October 2007, 49–51. Available at http://dial.academielouvain. be/handle/boreal:75590.

——(2008). Recent trends in English pedagogical lexicography. In T. Fontenelle (ed.), *Practical Lexicography: A Reader*, 221–243. Oxford and New York: Oxford University Press.

——(2009). The road to automated lexicography: First banish the drudgery then the drudges? In S. Granger and M. Paquot (eds), *eLex2009: eLexicography in the 21st Century: New Challenges, New Applications*. Conference Abstracts of eLex2009, 22–24 October 2009. Louvain-la-Neuve: Centre for English Corpus Linguistics, Université catholique de Louvain, 9–10.

Rundell, Michael, and Adam Kilgarriff (2011). Automating the creation of dictionaries: Where will it all end? In F. Meunier, S. De Cock, G. Gilquin, and M. Paquot (eds), *A Taste for Corpora. In honour of Sylviane Granger*, 257–281. Amsterdam: Benjamins.

Ruppenhofer, Josef, Michael Ellsworth, Miriam R. L. Petruck, Christopher R. Johnson, and Jan Scheffczyk (2006). *Framenet II: Extended Theory and Practice*. Berkeley, CA: FrameNet. Available at http://framenet.icsi.berkeley.edu/ (last accessed 12 November 2011).

Rychly, Pavel (2008). A lexicographer-friendly association score. In P. Sojka and A. Horák (eds), *Proceedings of Second Workshop on Recent Advances in Slavonic Natural Languages Processing, RASLAN 2008*, 6–9. Brno: Masaryk University.

Rychly, Pavel, and Adam Kilgarriff (2007). An efficient algorithm for building a distributional thesaurus (and other Sketch Engine developments). In *Proceedings of the 45th Annual Meeting of the Association for Computational Linguistics*, 41–44. Prague, Czech Republic.

Rylova, Anna (2010). Electronic dictionary and dictionary writing system: How this duo works for dictionary user's needs (ABBY Lingvo and ABBY Lingvo Content case). In A. Dykstra and T. Schoonheim (eds), *Proceedings of the XIV EURALEX International Congress*, 1105–1111. Afûk, Ljouwert: Fryske Akademy.

Sánchez, Aquilino, and Pascual Cantos (2011). e-Dictionaries in the information age: The Lexical Constellation Model (LCM) and the definitional construct. In P. A. Fuertes-Olivera and H. Bergenholtz (eds), *e-Lexicography: The Internet, Digital Initiatives and Lexicography*, 251–274. London and New York: Continuum.

Sánchez Ramos, Maria del Mar (2005). Research on dictionary use by trainee translators. *Translation Journal* 9(2). Available at http://vls.proz.com/translation-articles/articles/227/1/ Research-on-Dictionary-Use-by-Trainee-Translators (last accessed 2 February 2012).

Santana, Adele, and Donna, J. Wood (2009). Transparency and social responsibility issues for Wikipedia. *Ethics in Information Technology* 11: 133–144.

Sardinha, Tony Berber (2000). Semantic prosodies in English and Portuguese: A contrastive study. *Cuadernos de Filologia Inglesa* 9(1): 93–110.

Sarodnick, Florian, and Henning Brau (2006). *Methoden der Usability Evaluation. Wissenschaftliche Grundlagen und praktische Anwendungen.* Bern: Verlag Hans Huber.

Sčerba, Lev V. (1940). Towards a general theory of lexicography. *International Journal of Lexicography* 8(4), 1995: 314–350.

Schaeffer-Lacroix, Eva. (2009). Corpus numériques et production écrite en langue étrangère : Une recherche avec des apprenants d'allemand. Unpublished PhD thesis. Paris: Sorbonne Nouvelle Paris 3. Available at http://tel.archivesouvertes.fr/docs/00/43/90/95/PDF/Eva_ Schaeffer-Lacroix_these_tome_1_CNU_V0.pdf (last accessed 13 June 10).

Schembri, Adam (2003). Rethinking 'classifiers' in signed languages. In K. Emmorey (ed.), *Perspectives on Classifier Constructions in Sign Languages*, 3–34. Mahwah, NJ: Lawrence Erlbaum Associates.

Schlippe, Tim; Sebastian Ochs, and Tanja Schultz (2010). Wiktionary as a source for automatic pronunciation extraction. In *Proceedings of the 11th Annual Conference of the International Speech Communication Association*, 2290–2293, Makuhari, Japan.

Schmidt, Thomas (2007). The Kicktionary: A multilingual resource of the language of football. In G. Rehm, A. Witt, and L. Lemnitzer (eds), *Data Structures for Linguistic Resources and Applications*, 189–196. Tübingen: Gunter Narr.

——(2009). The Kicktionary—A multilingual lexical resource of football language. In H. C. Boas (ed.), *Multilingual Framenets in Computational Lexicography*, 101–134. New York: de Gruyter.

Scholfield, Phil (1982). Using the English dictionary for comprehension. *TESOL Quarterly* 16 (2): 185–194.

——(1999). Dictionary use in reception. *International Journal of Lexicography* 12(1): 13–34.

Schwager, Waldemar, and Ulrike Zeshan (2008). Word classes in sign languages: Criteria and classifications. *Studies in Language* 32(3): 509–545.

Scott, Mike (1997). PC analysis of key words—and key key words. *System* 25(3): 1–13.

Scott, Mike, and Christopher Tribble (2006). *Textual Patterns: Keyword and Corpus Analysis in Language Education.* Amsterdam: Benjamins.

Selva, Thierry, Fabrice Issac, Thierry Chanier, and Christophe Fouqueré (1997). *Lexical Comprehension and Production in Alexia System.* Available at http://edutice.archives-ou-vertes.fr/edutice-00180329/ (last accessed 5 May 2010).

Selva, Thierry, and Serge Verlinde (2002). L'utilisation d'un dictionnaire électronique: une étude de cas. In A. Braasch and C. Povlsen (eds), *Proceedings of the X EURALEX International Conference*, 773–783. Copenhagen: Center for Sprogteknologi.

Selva, Thierry, Serge Verlinde, and Jean Binon (2003). Vers une deuxième génération de dictionnaires électroniques. *Traitement automatique des langues* 44(2): 177–197.

Sharpe, Peter (1995). Electronic dictionaries with particular reference to the design of an electronic bilingual dictionary for English-speaking learners of Japanese. *International Journal of Lexicography* 8(1): 39–54.

Shizuka, Tetsuhito (2003). Efficiency of information retrieval from the electronic and the printed versions of a bilingual dictionary. *Language Education and Technology* 40: 15–33.

Silva, Penny M. (1997). South African English: Oppressor or liberator? In *The Major Varieties of English*, Papers from MAVEN 97, Vaxjo, 20–22 November 1997. Available at www.ru.ac.za/media/rhodesuniversity/content/documents/dsae/articles/Silva_article.pdf.

Simonsen, Henrik Køhler (2004). Nine key principles on corporate LSP intranet lexicography. In G. Williams and S. Vessier (eds), *Proceedings of the Eleventh EURALEX International Congress*, Vol. II: 603–613. Lorient: Université de Bretagne Sud. Available at www.euralex.org/publications/.

——(2009). *Vertical or Horizontal? That is the Question: An Eye-Track Study of Data Presentation in Internet Dictionaries*. Copenhagen: Copenhagen Business School. Available at www.cbs.dk/forskning/konferencer/eye_to_it (last accessed 17 October 2011).

——(2011). User consultation behaviour in Internet dictionaries: An eye-tracking study. *Hermes* 46: 75–101.

Simpson-Vlach, Rita, and Nick C. Ellis (2010). An Academic Formulas List: new methods in phraseology research. *Applied Linguistics* 31(4): 487–512.

Sinclair, John (1966). Beginning the study of lexis. In C. E. Bazell, J. C. Catford, M. A. K. Halliday, and R. H. Robins (eds), *In Memory of J. R. Firth*, 410–430. London: Longman. Reprinted in P. Hanks (ed.) (2008), *Lexicology: Critical Concepts in Linguistics*, vol. 4, 16–34. London and New York: Routledge.

——(1984). Naturalness in language. In J. Aarts and W. J. Meijs (eds), *Corpus Linguistics: Recent Developments in the Use of Computer Corpora in English Language Research*, 203–210. Amsterdam: Rodopi.

——(1987). The nature of the evidence. In J. Sinclair (ed.), *Looking Up. An Account of the COBUILD Project in Lexical Computing*, 150–159. London and Glasgow: Collins Publishers.

——(1991a). The automatic analysis of corpora. In Jan Svartvik (ed.), *Directions in Corpus Linguistics: Proceedings of the Nobel Symposium*, 379–397. The Hague: Mouton de Gruyter.

——(1991b). *Corpus, Concordance, Collocation*. Oxford: Oxford University Press.

——(1996). The search for units of meaning. *Textus* IX: 75–106.

——(2004). *Trust the Text*. London: Routledge.

——(2010). Defining the definiendum. In G.-M. De Schryver (ed.), *A Way with Words: Recent Advances in Lexical Theory and Analysis*, 37–47. Kampala and Ghent: Menha Publishers.

Singleton, David (1999). *Exploring the Second Language Mental Lexicon*. Cambridge and New York: Cambridge University Press.

Sinha, Manish, Mahesh Reddy, and Pushpak Bhattacharyya (2006). An approach towards construction and application of multilingual Indo-WordNet. *Proceedings from the 3rd Global Wordnet Conference (GWC 06), Jeju Island, Korea*.

Snow, Rion, Brendan O'Connor, Daniel Jurafsky, and Andrew Ng (2008). Cheap and fast – but is it good? Evaluating non-expert annotations for natural language tasks. *Proceedings of the Conference on Empirical Methods in Natural Language Processing*, 254–263.

Sobkowiak, Włodzimierz (1999). *Pronunciation in EFL Machine-Readable Dictionaries*. Poznań: Motivex.

——(2002). What can be but is not (and why) in learners' MRDs. *Teaching English with Technology*, 2(3). Available at www.iatefl.org.pl/call/j_article9.htm.

——(2003). Pronunciation in *Macmillan English Dictionary for Advanced Learners* on CD-ROM. *International Journal of Lexicography* 16(4): 423–441.

Sorokoletov, Fedor Pavlovich (1978). Traditionen der sowjetrussischen Lexikographie. In W. Wolski (ed.) (1982), *Aspekte der sowjetrussischen Lexikcographie. Übersetzungen, Abstracts, bibliographische Angaben*, 63–88. Tübingen: Niemeyer.

Spohr, Dennis (2011). A multi-layer architecture for 'pluri-monofunctional' dictionaries. In P. A. Fuertes-Olivera and H. Bergenholtz (eds), *e-Lexicography – The Internet, Digital Initiatives and Lexicography*, 103–120. London and New York: Continuum.

Stamou, S, Kemal Oflazer, Karel Pala, Dimitris Christoudoulakis, Dan Cristea, Dan Tufis, Svetla Koeva, George Totkov, Dominique Dutoit, and Maria Grigoriadou (2002). BALKANET: A multilingual semantic network for the Balkan languages. *Proceedings of the International Wordnet Conference*, Mysore, India, 21–25.

Stefanowitsch, Anatol, and Stefan Th. Gries (eds) (2006). *Corpus-based Approaches to Metaphor and Metonymy*. Berlin: Mouton de Gruyter.

Stegbauer, Christian (2009). *Wikipedia: Das Rätsel der Kooperation*. Wiesbaden: VS Verlag für Sozialwissenschaften.

Stirling, Johanna (2003). The portable electronic dictionary: Faithful friend or faceless foe? Available at www.elgweb.net/ped-article.html (last accessed 20 April 2011).

Stubbs, Michael (2002). Two quantitative methods of studying phraseology in English. *International Journal of Corpus Linguistics* 7(2): 215–244.

Stvilia, Besiki, Michael B. Twidale, Linda C. Smith, and Les Gasser (2008). Information quality work organization in Wikipedia. *Journal of the American Society for Information Science and Technology* 59(6): 983–1001.

Summers, Della (1993). Longman/Lancaster English language corpus – criteria and design. *International Journal of Lexicography* 6(3): 181–208.

Surowiecki, James (2005). *The Wisdom of Crowds*. New York: Anchor Books.

Svensén, Bo (2009). *A Handbook of Lexicography. The Theory and Practice of Dictionary-Making*. Cambridge: Cambridge University Press.

Swales, John M. (1990). *Genre Analysis: English in Academic and Research Settings*. Cambridge: Cambridge University Press.

Tan, Kim Hua (2009). How effective is the electronic dictionary in sense discrimination? *Lexikos* 19: 262–274.

Tang, Gloria M. (1997). Pocket electronic dictionaries for second language learning: Help or hindrance? *TESL Canada Journal* 15(1): 39–57.

Tarp, Sven (1995). Wörterbuchfunktionen: Utopische und realistische Vorschläge für die bilinguale Lexikographie. In H. E. Wiegand (ed.), *Studien zur zweisprachigen Lexikographie mit Deutsch II*, 17–51. Hildesheim and New York: Olms.

——(2007). Lexicography in the information age. *Lexikos* 17: 170–179.

——(2008). *Lexicography in the Borderland between Knowledge and Non-knowledge. General Lexicographical Theory with Particular Focus on Learner's Lexicography*. Tübingen: Max Niemeyer Verlag.

——(2009a). Beyond lexicography: New visions and challenges in the information age. In H. Bergenholtz, S. Nielsen, and S. Tarp (eds), *Lexicography at a Crossroads: Dictionaries and Encyclopedias Today, Lexicographical Tools Tomorrow*, 17–32. Bern: Peter Lang.

——(2009b). Reflections on data access in lexicographic works. In S. Nielsen and S. Tarp (eds), *Lexicography in the 21st Century: In Honour of Henning Bergenholtz*, 43–62. Amsterdam and Philadelphia: Benjamins.

——(2009c). Reflections on lexicographical user research. *Lexikos* 19: 275–296.

——(2010). Reflections on the academic status of lexicography. *Lexikos* 20: 450–465.

——(2011). Lexicographical and other e-tools for consultation purposes: Towards the individualization of needs satisfaction. In P. A. Fuertes-Olivera and H. Bergenholtz (eds), *e-Lexicography. The Internet, Digital Initiatives and Lexicography*, 54–70. London and New York: Continuum.

Tasovac, Toma (2005). Transpoetika Project: Digital technologies and distributed learning in foreign language study. *Pregled Nacionalnog centra za digitalizaciju* 6: 53–57.

——(2009). More or less than a dictionary? Wordnet as a model for Serbian L2 lexicography. *Infotheca: Journal of Informatics and Librarianship* 10(1/2): 13a–22a.

——(2010). Reimagining the dictionary, or why lexicography needs digital humanities. *Digital Humanities* 2010. Available at http://dh2010.cch.kcl.ac.uk/academic-programme/abstracts/papers/html/ab-883.html.

Taylor, Andrew, and Adelaide Chan (1994). Pocket electronic dictionaries and their use. In W. Martin, W. Meijs, M. Moerland, E. ten Pas, P. van Sterkenburg, and P. Vossen (eds), *Proceedings of the 6th EURALEX International Congress*, 598–665. Amsterdam: EURALEX.

TEI Consortium (eds) (2007). *TEI P5: Guidelines for Electronic Text Encoding and Interchange*. Available at www.tei-c.org/release/doc/tei-p5-doc/en/html/ (last accessed 10 May 2011).

Temmerman, Rita, and Uus Knops (2004). *The Translation of Domain Specific Languages and Multilingual Terminology Management*. Linguistica Antverpiensia New Series 3. Antwerp: Hogeschool Antwerpen.

Teufel, Simone (1998). Meta-discourse markers and problem-structuring in scientific articles. In M. Stede, L. Wanner, and E. Hovy (eds), *ACL 1998 Workshop: Discourse Structure and Discourse Markers*, 43–49. Montreal.

Thompson, Liz (2005). Pasadena: A brand new system for the OED. *OED News*, December 2005, 2.

Tiberius, Carole, and Adam Kilgarriff (2009). The Sketch Engine for Dutch with the ANW corpus. In E. Beijk, L. Colman, M. Göbel, F. Heyvaert, T. Schoonheim, R. Tempelaars, and V. Waszink (eds), *Fons Verborum, Feestbundel voor Fons Moerdijk*, 237–255. Leiden: Instituut voor Nederlandse Lexicologie.

Ties, Isabella (ed.) (2006). *LULCL 2005—Proceedings of the Lesser Used Languages and Computer Linguistics Conference*, Bozen-Bolzano, 27–28 October 2005. Bozen-Bolzano: EURAC Research.

Tittel, Sabine (2010). Dynamic access to a static dictionary: A lexicographical 'cathedral' lives to see the twenty-first century—the *Dictionnaire étymologique de l'ancien français*. In S. Granger and M. Paquot (eds), *eLexicography in the 21st Century: New Challenges, New Applications*, 295–301. Louvain-la-Neuve: Presses universitaires de Louvain.

Tono, Yukio (1984). On the Dictionary User's Reference Skills. BEd thesis, Tokyo Gakugei University, Tokyo.

—— (1992). The effect of menus on EFL learners' look-up processes. *Lexikos* 2: 230–253.

—— (1997). Guide Word or Signpost? An experimental study on the effect of meaning access indexes in EFL learners' dictionaries. *English Studies* 28: 55–77.

—— (1998). Interacting with the users: Research findings in EFL dictionary user studies. In T. McArthur and I. Kernerman (eds), *Lexicography in Asia: Selected Papers from the Dictionaries in Asia Conference, Hong Kong University of Science and Technology*, 97–118. Jerusalem: Password Publishers Ltd.

—— (2000). On the effects of different types of electronic dictionary interfaces on L2 learners' reference behaviour in productive/receptive tasks. In U. Heid, S. Evert, E. Lehmann, and C. Rohrer (eds), *Proceedings of the Ninth EURALEX International Congress, EURALEX 2000, Stuttgart, Germany, August 8–12, 2000*, Vol. II, 855–861. Stuttgart: Institut für Maschinelle Sprachverarbeitung, Universität Stuttgart.

—— (2001). *Research on Dictionary Use in the Context of Foreign Language Learning: Focus on Reading Comprehension* (Lexicographica Series Maior 106). Tübingen: Max Niemeyer Verlag.

—— (2009). Pocket electronic dictionaries in Japan: User perspectives. In H. Bergenholtz, S. Nielsen, and S. Tarp (eds), *Lexicography at a Crossroads. Dictionaries and Encyclopedias Today, Lexicographical Tools Tomorrow*, 33–67. Bern: Peter Lang.

—— (2010). A critical review of the theory of lexicographical functions. *Lexicon* 40: 1–26.

—— (2011). Application of eye-tracking in EFL learners' dictionary look-up process research. *International Journal of Lexicography* 24(1): 124–153.

Toral, Antonio, Valeria Quochi, Riccardo Del Gratta, Monica Monachini, Claudia Soria, and Nicoletta Calzolari (2008). Lexically-based ontologies and ontologically based lexicons. In *Proceedings of the 10th Congress of Italian Association for Artificial Intelligence*, Cagliari, Italy, 49–59.

Toulmin, Stephen (1990). *Cosmopolis: The Hidden Agenda of Modernity*. Chicago: University of Chicago Press.

Trap-Jensen, Lars (2010a). One, two, many: Customization and user profiles in Internet dictionaries. In A. Dykstra and T. Schoonheim (eds), *Proceedings of the XIV EURALEX International Congress*, 1133–1143. Afûk, Ljouwert: Fryske Akademy. Available at http://dsl. dk/medarbejdere/medarbejdere-publikationer-m-m/ltj/ELX2010_Trap-Jensen.pdf.

—— (2010b). Access to multiple lexical resources at a stroke: Integrating dictionary, corpus and Wordnet data. In S. Granger and M. Paquot (eds), *eLexicography in the 21st Century: New Challenges, New Applications. Proceedings of eLEX2009*, 303–312. Louvain-la-Neuve: Presses universitaires de Louvain.

Tribble, Chris (2000). Genres, keywords, teaching: Towards a pedagogic account of the language of project proposals. In L. Burnard and T. McEnery (eds), *Rethinking Language Pedagogy from a Corpus Perspective: Papers from the Third International Conference on Teaching and Language Corpora*, 74–90. Bern and New York: Peter Lang.

Trochim, William (2006). Design. *Research Methods Knowledge Base*. Available at www. socialresearchmethods.net/kb/design.php (last accessed 14 September 2011).

Tseng, Fan-ping (2009). EFL students' *Yahoo!* Online bilingual dictionary use behavior. *English Language Teaching* 2(3): 98–108. Available at www.ccsenet.org/journal/index.php/elt/article/viewFile/3221/3290.

Tufis, Dan, Dan Cristea, and Sofia Stamou (2004). BalkaNet: Aims, methods, results and perspectives. A general overview. *Science and Technology* 7(1/2): 9–43.

Tutin, Agnès (2007). Modélisation linguistique et annotation des collocations: application au lexique transdisciplinaire des écrits scientifiques. In S. Koeva, D. Maurel, and M. Silberztein (eds), *Formaliser les langues avec l'ordinateur*, 189–215. Besançon: Presses universitaires de Franche-Comté.

——(2008). L'apport des corpus annotés pour l'élaboration semi-automatique d'une base de collocations de la langue scientifique générale. In F. Maniez, P. Dury, N. Arlin, and C. Rougemont (eds), *Corpus et dictionnaires de langues de spécialité*, 45–65. Grenoble: Presses Universitaires de Grenoble.

UDC Consortium (2004). *Classification Décimale Universelle*. Liège: Editions du CEFAL.

Urdang, Laurence (1966). The systems design and devices used to process The Random House Dictionary of the English Language. *Computers and the Humanities* 1(2): 31–33.

van der Vliet, Hennie (2007). The Referentiebestand Nederlands as a multi-purpose lexical database. *International Journal of Lexicography* 20(3): 239–257.

van Ek, Jan Ate, and John Leslie Melville Trim (1991). *Threshold Level 1990*. Strasbourg: Council of Europe Press.

Van Wyk, Egidius B. (1995). Linguistic assumptions and lexicographical traditions in the African languages. *Lexikos* 5: 82–96.

Varantola, Krista (1998). Translators and their use of dictionaries. In Beryl T. Sue Atkins (ed.), *Using Dictionaries: Studies of Dictionary Use by Language Learners and Translators*, 179–192. Tübingen: Max Niemeyer.

——(2002). Use and usability of dictionaries: Common sense and context sensibility. In M.-H. Corréard (ed.), *Lexicography and Natural Language Processing: A Festchrift in Honour of B. T. S. Atkins*, 30–44. United Kingdom: EURALEX.

Varnosfadrani, Azizollah Dabaghi, and Helen Basturkmen (2009). The effectiveness of implicit and explicit error correction on learners' performance. *System* 37: 82–98.

Vasić, Vera, Vladislava Ružić, and Ljiljana Subotić (2008). Serbian language threshold level: Concept and design. In B. Golubović and J. Raecke (eds), *Bosnisch. Kroatisch. Serbisch. B.K. S. als Fremdsprachen an den Universitäten der Welt*, 195–202. München: Verlag Otto Sagner.

Vellino, André, and David Zeber (2007). A hybrid, multi-dimensional recommender for journal articles in a scientific digital library. In *WI-IATW '07: Proceedings of the 2007 IEEE/WIC/ACM International Conferences on Web Intelligence and Intelligent Agent Technology*, 111–114. Available at http://cuvier.cisti.nrc.ca/~vellino/documents/WPRS2007-vellino-zeber.pdf.

Venturi, Giulia, Alessandro Lenci, Simonetta Montemagni, Eva Maria Vecchi, Maria Teresa Sagri, Daniela Tiscornia, and Tomaso Agnoloni (2009). Towards a FrameNet resource for the legal domain. In N. Casellas, E. Francesconi, R. Hoekstra, and S. Montemagni (eds), *Proceedings from the 3rd Workshop on Legal Ontologies and Artificial Intelligence Techniques* joint with *2nd Workshop on Semantic Processing of Legal Text (LOAIT 2009)*, IDT Series, 8 June 2009 Barcelona, Spain, 67–76.

Verlinde, Serge (2010). The Base lexicale du français: A multi-purpose lexicographic tool. In S. Granger and M. Paquot (eds), *eLexicography in the 21st Century: New Challenges, New Applications. Proceedings of ELEX2009*, 335–342. Louvain-la-Neuve: Presses universitaires de Louvain.

——(2011). Modelling interactive reading, translation and writing assistants. In P. A. Fuertes-Olivera and H. Bergenholtz (eds), *e-Lexicography: The Internet, Digital Initiatives and Lexicography*, 275–286. London and New York: Continuum.

Verlinde, Serge, and Jean Binon (2009). Pedagogical lexicography revisited. In H. Bergenholtz, S. Nielsen, and S. Tarp (eds), *Lexicography at a Crossroads: Dictionaries and Encyclopedias Today, Lexicographical Tools Tomorrow*, 69–90. Bern: Peter Lang.

——(2010). Monitoring dictionary use in the electronic age. In A. Dykstra and T. Schoonheim (eds), *Proceedings of the XIV EURALEX International Congress*, 1144–1151. Ljouwert: Fryske Akademy.

Verlinde, Serge, Hans Paulussen, An Slootmaekers, and Lieve De Wachter (2010a). La conception de didacticiels intégrés d'aide à la lecture, à la traduction et à la rédaction. *Revue française de linguistique appliquée* 15(2): 53–65. Available at www.cairn.info/revue-francaise-de-linguistique-appliquee-2010-2-page-53.htm.

Verlinde, Serge, Patrick Leroyer, and Jean Binon (2010b). Search and you will find. From stand-alone lexicographic tools to user driven task and problem-oriented multifunctional leximats. *International Journal of Lexicography* 23(1): 1–17.

Verlinde, Serge, Thierry Selva, and Jean Binon (2006). The Base Lexicale du Français (BLF): A multifunctional online database for learners of French. In E. Corino, C. Marello, and C. Onesti (eds), *Proceedings of the 12th EURALEX International Congress*, Turin, 6–9 September, 471–483. Alessandria: Edizioni dell'Orso.

Volanschi, Alexandra (2008). Étude et modélisation des phénomènes collocationnels: Implémentation dans un système d'aide à la rédaction en anglais scientifique. Unpublished PhD thesis, Université Paris Diderot.

Volanschi, Alexandra, and Natalie Kübler (2011). The impact of metaphorical framing on term creation in biology. *Terminology* 17(2): 198–223.

Vossen, Piek (ed.) (1998). *EuroWordNet: A Multilingual Database with Lexical Semantic Networks*. Dordrecht, the Netherlands, and Boston: Kluwer Academic.

——(in press). WordNet: Principles, developments and applications. In R. H. Gouws, U. Heid, W. Schweickard, and H. E. Wiegand (eds), *Handbook of Linguistics and Communications (HSK), volume Dictionaries, an International Encyclopedia of Lexicography, Supplementary Volume: Recent Developments with Special Focus on Computational Lexicography*. Berlin: Mouton de Gruyter.

Vossen, Piek, Eneko Agirre, Nicoletta Calzolari, Christiane Fellbaum, Shu-Kai Hsieh, Chu-Chen Huang, Hitoshi Isahara, Kyoko Kanzaki, Andrea Marchetti, Monica Monachini, Federico Neri, Remo Raffaelli, German Rigau, and Maurizio Tesconi (2008a). KYOTO: A system for mining, structuring, and distributing knowledge across languages and cultures. In European Language Resources Association (ELRA) (eds), *Proceedings of LREC 2008*, Marrakech, Morocco, 28–30 May 2008, 1462–1469.

Vossen, Piek, Katja Hofmann, Maarten de Rijke, Erik Tjong Kim Sang, and Koen Deschacht (2007). The Cornetto database: Architecture and user-scenarios. *Proceedings of 7th Dutch–Belgian Information Retrieval Workshop DIR2007*, 89–96. University of Leuven.

Vossen, Piek, Isa Maks, Roxane Segers, Hennie van der Vilet, and Hetty van Zutphen (2008b). The Cornetto Database: Architecture and alignment issues of combining lexical unites, synsets and an ontology. *Fourth Global WordNet Conference*, 485–505.

Wade, Rodrik (1997). Arguments for Black South African English as a distinct 'new' English. Paper presented at the 4th International Conference on World Englishes, December 1997, Singapore.

Walker, Crayton (2009). The treatment of collocation by learners' dictionaries, collocational dictionaries and dictionaries of business English. *International Journal of Lexicography* 22 (3): 281–299.

Wallraff, Barbara (2009). The uncertain future of dictionaries. *The Atlantic*, 12 January 2009. Available at http://barbarawallraff.theatlantic.com/archives/2009/01/the_uncertain_future_of_dictio.php.

Weschler, Robert, and Chris Pitts (2000). An experiment using electronic dictionaries with EFL students. *The Internet TESL Journal* 6. Available at www.iteslj.org/ Articles/Weschler-ElectroDict.html.

West, Michael (1953). *A General Service List of English Words: With Semantic Frequencies and a Supplementary Word-list for the Writing of Popular Science and Technology*. London: Longman, Green & Co.

Wiegand, Herbert Ernst (1987). Zur handlungstheoretischen Grundlegung der Wörterbenutzungsforschung. *Lexicographica. International Annual for Lexicography* 3: 178–227.

—— (1996). Textual condensation in printed dictionaries: A theoretical draft. *Lexikos* 6: 133–158.

—— (1998). *Wörterbuchforschung. Untersuchungen zur Wörterbuchbenutzung, zur Theorie, Geschichte, Kritik und Automatisierung der Lexikographie.1. Teilband*. Berlin and New York: de Gruyter.

—— (2001). Was eigentlich sind Wörterbuchfunktionen? Kritische Anmerkungen zur neueren und neuesten Wörterbuchforschung. *Lexicographica. International Annual for Lexicography* 17: 217–248.

Wiegand, Herbert Ernst, and Ma Teresa Fuentes Morán (2009). *Estructuras Lexicográficas. Aspectos Centrales de una Teoría de la Forma del Diccionario*. Granada: Tragacanto.

Wierzbicka, Anna (1992). *Semantics, Culture and Cognition: Universal Human Concepts in Culture-Specific Configurations*. New York: Oxford University Press.

Wilks, Yorick A., Brian M. Slator, and Louise M. Guthrie (1996). *Electric Words: Dictionaries, Computers, and Meanings* (ACL-MIT Press series in natural-language processing). Cambridge, MA: MIT Press.

Williams, Geoffrey (2003). From meaning to words and back: Corpus linguistics and specialised lexicography. *ASp* 39/40. Available at http://asp.revues.org/1320.

—— (2006). Advanced ESP and the learner's dictionary: Tools for the non-language specialist. *EURALEX 2006 Proceedings*. Available at www.euralex.org/elx_proceedings/Euralex2006/.

Winkler, Birgit (2001). Students working with an English learners' dictionary on CD-ROM. In *ELT Perspectives on Information Technology & Multimedia: Selected Papers from the ITMELT 2001 Conference* (Hong Kong, 1–2 June 2001). Hong Kong, English Language

Centre, Hong Kong Polytechnic University, 227–254. Available at www.eric.ed.gov/PDFS/ ED459601.pdf (last accessed 17 October 2011).

Wright, Sue Ellen (1993). The inappropriateness of the merely correct: Stylistic considerations in scientific and technical translation. In S. E. Wright and L. D. Wright Jr. (eds), *Scientific and Technical Translation*, 69–86. Amsterdam: John Benjamins.

Wüster, Eugen (1968). *The Machine Tool. An Interlingual Dictionary of Basic Concepts Comprising an Alphabetical Dictionary and a Classified Vocabulary with Definitions and Illustrations*. English–French Master Volume. London: Technical Press.

Xu, Hai (2008). Exemplification policy in English learners' dictionaries. *International Journal of Lexicography* 21(4): 395–417.

Xu, Xiaohui (2010). Study on the effect of dictionary use on second language incidental vocabulary acquisition: An empirical study of college English vocabulary learning strategy. *Journal of Language Teaching and Research* 1(4): 519–523.

Yamada, Shigeru (2011). The challenges of the shift from print to electronic dictionaries. In K. Akasu and S. Uchida (eds), *ASIALEX2011 Proceedings Lexicography: Theoretical and Practical Perspectives*, 566–575. Kyoto: Asian Association for Lexicography.

Yoon, Choongil (2011). Concordancing in L2 writing class: An overview of research and issues. *Journal of English for Academic Purposes* 10: 130–139.

Yoon, Hyunsook. (2008). More than a linguistic reference: The influence of corpus technology on L2 academic writing. *Language Learning & Technology* 12(2): 31–49. Available at http://llt. msu.edu/vol12num2/yoon.pdf (last accessed 15 March 2009).

Yoon, Hyunsook, and Alan Hirvela (2004). ESL student attitudes toward corpus use in L2. *Journal of Second Language Writing* 13(4): 257–283.

Zaenen, Annie (2002). Musings about the impossible electronic dictionary. In Marie-Hélène Corréard (ed.), *Lexicography and Natural Language Processing: A Festschrift in Honour of B. T. S. Atkins*, 230–244. Stuttgart: EURALEX.

Zampolli, A. (1987). Perspectives for an Italian multifunctional lexical database. In A. Zampolli, A. Cappelli, L. Cignoni, and C. Peters (eds), *Studies in Honour of Roberto Busa S.J. Linguistica Computazionale*, IV–V, 301–341. Pisa: Giardini Editori e Stampatori.

Zappavigna, Michele (2011). Ambient affiliation: A linguistic perspective on Twitter. *New Media & Society* 13(5): 788–806.

Zesch, Torsten, Christof Müller, and Iryna Gurevych (2008a). Extracting lexical semantic knowledge from Wikipedia and Wiktionary. In N. Calzolari, K. Choukri, B. Maegaard, J. Mariani, J. Odjik, S. Piperidis, and D. Tapias (eds), *Proceedings of the 6th International Conference on Language Resources and Evaluation*, 1646–1652, Marrakech, Morocco.

——(2008b). Using Wiktionary for computing semantic relatedness. In *Proceedings of the Twenty-Third AAAI Conference on Artificial Intelligence*, 861–867, Chicago, IL, USA.

Zhang, Ping (2004). Is the electronic dictionary your faithful friend? *CELEA Journal* 27(2): 23–28.

Zhang, Zuocheng (2007). Towards an integrated approach to teaching business English: A Chinese experience. *English for Specific Purposes* 26: 399–410.

Zimmermann, Harald H. (1984). Multifunctional dictionaries. In Antonio Zampolli and Amadeo Cappelli (eds), *The Possibilities and Limits of the Computer in Producing and Publishing Dictionaries. Linguistica Computationale III*, 279–288. Pisa: Giardini Editori e Stampatori.

Zock, Michael, and Didier Schwab (2008). Lexical access based on underspecified input. *Proceedings of the Workshop on Cognitive Aspects of the Lexicon*, 9–17.

Zwitserlood, Inge (2010). Sign language lexicography in the early 21st century and a recently published dictionary of sign language of the Netherlands. *International Journal of Lexicography* 23(4): 443–476.

Аперсян, Ю. Д. (1988). Прагматическая информация для толкового словаря. In Арутюнова, Нина Давидовна (ed.), *Прагмамика и проблемы интенсиональности (Сб. науч. тр.)*, Москва: Институт языкознания АН СССР. [Aspersian, Iu. D. (1988) Pragmatic information in dictionaries. In Nina Davidovna Arutiunova (ed.), *Pragmatics and issues of intentionality (collection of essays)*. Moscow: Linguistics Institute of the USSR Academy of Sciences.]

Гельфейнбейн, Илья Г., Артем В. Гончарук, Влад П. Лехельт, Антон А. Липатов, and Виктор В. Шило (2003). Автоматический перевод семантической сети WordNet на русский язык. *Труды Международного семинара Диалог по компьютерной лингвистике и её приложениям*, Протвино, Россия. [Gelfenbeyn, Ilya, Artem Goncharuk, Vladislav Lehelt, Anton Lipatov, and Victor Shilo (2003). Automatic translation of WordNet's semantic network into Russian. In *Proceedings of the International Dialog Conference*. Protvino, Russia.]

Дешић, Милорад (ed.) (2007). *Српски као страни језик у теорији и пракси: зборник радова*. Београд: Министарство просвете и спорта Републике Србије; Филолошки факултет, Центар за српски као страни језик. [Dešić, Milorad (ed.) (2007). *Serbian as a foreign language in theory and practice: A collection of essays*. Belgrade: Ministry of Education and Sport; Philological Faculty of the University of Belgrade, Center for Serbian as a Foreign Language.]

Крстев, Цветана (2004). Специфични концепти Балкана у семантичкој мрежи Wordnet. In Суботић, Љиљана et al. (ed.), *Сусрети култура*, 275–85. Нови Сад: Универзитет у Новом Саду, Филозофски факултет. [Krstev, Cvetana (2004). Balkan-specific concepts in the semantic network of Wordnet. In Subotić, Ljiljana et al. (ed.), *Cultural encounters*, 275–85. Novi Sad: University of Novi Sad, Philosophical Faculty.]

MC (1967). *Речник српскохрватскога књижевног језика*. Нови Сад: Матица српска. [MS (1967). *Dictionary of the Serbo-Croatian literary language*. Novi Sad: Matica srpska.]

——(2007). *Речник српскога језика*. Нови Сад: Матица српска. [MS (2007). *Dictionary of the Serbian language*. Novi Sad: Matica srpska.]

САНУ (1959) *Речник српскохрватског књижевног и народног језика*. Београд: Институт за српскохрватски језик. [SANU (1959). *Dictionary of the Serbo-Croatian literary and folkloric language*. Belgrade: Institute for Serbo-Croatian Language.]

Суботић, Љиљана (2004). Праг знања и речник (историјат проблема), *Научни састанак слависта у Вукове дане: Граматички опис српског језика*, 33(1): 167–177. [Subotić, Ljiljana (2004). Threshold knowledge and the dictionary, *Meeting of Slavists: Grammatical description of the Serbian language*, 33(1): 167–177.]

Шведова, Наталья (1988). Парадоксы словарной сатьи. In Караулов, Юрий Николаевич (ed.), *Национальная специфика языка и ее отражение в нормативном словаре. Сборник статьей*, 6–11. Москва: Наука. [Shvedova, Natalia (1988). Paradoxes of the dictionary entry. In Iurii Nikolaevich Karaulov (ed.), *National specifics of language and its reflection in the normative dictionary. Collection of papers*, 6–11. Moscow: Nauka.]

Штейнфельдт, Э. (1963). *Частотный словарь современного русского литературного языка*. Москва: Прогресс. [Steinfeldt, E. (1963). *Frequency dictionary for the Modern Russian literary language*. Moscow: Progress.]

Author Index

Subject Index